AUSTRALIA
The Law Book Company Ltd.
Sydney : Melbourne : Brisbane

CANADA AND U.S.A.
The Carswell Company Ltd.
Agincourt, Ontario

INDIA
N. M. Tripathi Private Ltd.
Bombay
and
Eastern Law House Private Ltd.
Calcutta
M.P.P. House
Bangalore

ISRAEL
Steimatzky's Agency Ltd.
Jerusalem : Tel Aviv : Haifa

MALAYSIA : SINGAPORE : BRUNEI
Malayan Law Journal (Pte.) Ltd.
Singapore

NEW ZEALAND
Sweet & Maxwell (N.Z.) Ltd.
Auckland

PAKISTAN
Pakistan Law House
Karachi

Trade Union Law

By

RICHARD KIDNER,
M.A., B.C.L.

Lecturer in Law, University College of Wales
Aberystwyth

LONDON
STEVENS & SONS
1979

Published in 1979 by
Stevens & Sons Limited of
11, New Fetter Lane, London
Computerset by
MFK Graphic Systems (Typesetting) Ltd., Saffron Walden
Printed in Great Britain by
Page Bros.(Norwich) Ltd.

ISBN 0 420 45450 0

PREFACE

Labour law has undergone a number of changes in recent years, and although many of these have occurred in the field of individual employment, trade union law has also been substantially affected. This is so, not only because the existing law has been amended, but also because the greater role given to trade unions today has added a new dimension to collective labour law altogether, so that this book must deal with topics which have not hitherto been discussed in books on the subject.

I have tried to deal with all those topics customarily found in books on the subject, but have also added sections on the rights of union members against their employers and on statutory assistance for collective bargaining. The former is necessary because although in strict legal analysis they are rights of the individual employee, they are also seen as fundamental in protecting the interests of trade unions. The latter section is the more important of the two innovations and is likely to increase in scope considerably during the next few years, especially as the problems over recognition, redundancy procedures and the right to information come to be resolved.

Some topics have however had to be omitted, even though closely related to the activities of trade unions. In particular it is felt that Health and Safety at Work and Employers' Liability are subjects which could not be adequately dealt with here and which have specialist books of their own. Workers' democracy has been excluded, at least for the time being, partly through the belief that it is difficult to separate it from company law where it can be dealt with in its proper context, but also because the proposals are not sufficiently certain of enactment to justify exposition at the moment.

Although this is intended to be a book for lawyers I am conscious that others may also wish to use it and in presenting the subject I have attempted to make the text as readable as possible but without avoiding any of the difficulties inherent in the subject. I have also tried to provide in the footnotes sufficient references to provide the practitioner with ready access to the sources.

The modern law is an amalgam of present political and past historical forces. Although the study of the history of any particular topic may be a useful tool to its understanding, it was thought better to achieve in the body of the text a clear statement of the modern law, unencumbered by the complexities of its history, and accordingly a brief historical survey has been added as a separate chapter. Furthermore, while this is a book on law and not on industrial relations the political and social context cannot be ignored. Thus it was felt that the primary need was for a coherent statement of the modern law put into the context of the activities of trade unions. Unfortunately trade union law is not and never has been a coherent subject in its own right, but is rather a mixture of statute law, contract, tort, trusts and commercial law, and one of the tasks of the labour lawyer is to apply these concepts in a rational manner to the problems concerning trade unions and industrial relations.

Of recent developments which it has not been possible to deal with in the text, the most important is the attempt to interpret the phrase "in contemplation or furtherance of a trade dispute" so as to exclude secondary activity. This is a matter of fundamental importance as the phrase in effect defines the ambit of the right to strike, and no doubt it will be considered by the House of Lords and perhaps also by Parliament in the near future.

My thanks are due to a number of my colleagues for reading various parts of the manuscript, and especially to Mr. Bill Hines for being a sympathetic and efficient librarian. I also owe a debt to the Certification Officer and his staff, and to Mr. Ben Hooberman, for their help. However my principal debt of gratitude is to Mrs. Christine Davies who willingly performed the laborious task of decyphering and typing the manuscript. The text was completed in September 1978 but a few minor corrections have been made since that date.

Richard Kidner

January, 1979.

CONTENTS

PART FOUR: STATUTORY ASSISTANCE FOR COLLECTIVE BARGAINING

TABLE OF CASES

TABLE OF STATUTES

TABLE OF STATUTORY INSTRUMENTS

TABLE OF DECISIONS OF THE NATIONAL INSURANCE COMMISSIONER

TABLE OF AWARDS OF THE CENTRAL ARBITRATION COMMITTEE

TABLE OF DECISIONS OF THE REGISTRAR OF FRIENDLY SOCIETIES AND HIS SUCCESSORS

TABLE OF ACAS REPORTS ON THE RECOGNITION OF TRADE UNIONS UNDER SECTION 12 OF THE E.P.A. 1975

ABBREVIATIONS

Statutes

E.P.A. 1975	Employment Protection Act 1975.
E.P.C.A. 1978	Employment Protection (Consolidation) Act 1978.
T.U.A.E.A. 1964	Trade Union (Amalgamations, Etc.) Act 1964.
T.U.L.R.A. 1974	Trade Union and Labour Relations Act 1974.
T.U.L.R. (Amdt.) 1976	Trade Union and Labour Relations (Amendment) Act 1976.
W.C.A. 1959	Wages Councils Act 1959.

Institutions

ACAS	Advisory Conciliation and Arbitration Service.
C.A.C.	Central Arbitration Committee.
C.I.R.	Commission on Industrial Relations.
E.A.T.	Employment Appeal Tribunal.
N.I.R.C.	National Industrial Relations Court.
N.I.L.T.	National Insurance Local Tribunal.
I.T.	Industrial Tribunal.
S.B.A.T.	Supplementary Benefits Appeal Tribunal.

Names of trade unions

Note: in abbreviating the names of unions the practice has been adopted of placing full stops between the initials only in cases where those initials are commonly spelled out; where the initials form an acronym, no full stops are included.

ACTAT	Association of Cinematograph, Television and Allied Technicians.
A.E.S.D.	Association of Engineering and Shipbuilding Draughtsmen.
A.E.U.	Amalgamated Engineering Union.
APEX	Association of Professional Executive Clerical and Computer Staff.
A.P.T.	Association of Polytechnic Teachers.
ASLEF	Associated Society of Locomotive Engineers and Firemen.
A.S.R.S.	Amalgamated Society of Railway Servants.
ASSET	Association of Supervisory Staffs, Executives and Technicians.
A.S.T.M.S.	Association of Scientific Technical and Managerial Staffs.
A.U.E.W.	Amalgamated Union of Engineering Workers.

BISAKTA	British Iron, Steel and Kindred Trades Association.
C.P.S.A.	Civil and Public Services Association.
E.E.S.A.	Electrical and Engineering Staff Association.
E.E.T.P.U.	Electrical Electronic Telecommunications and Plumbing Union.
E.M.A.	Engineers' and Managers' Association.
E.P.E.A.	Electrical Power Engineers Association.
E.S.U.	Electricity Supply Union.
E.T.U.	Electrical Trades Union.
I.O.J.	Institute of Journalists.
I.T.F.	International Transport Workers Federation.
NACODS	National Association of Colliery Overmen, Deputies and Shotfirers.
NALGO	National and Local Government Officers Association.
N.A.L.H.M.	National Association of Licensed House Managers.
N.A.S.D.S.	National Amalgamated Stevedores and Dockers Society.
NATSOPA	National Society of Operative Printers, Graphical and Media Personnel.
N.G.A.	National Graphical Association.
NUBE	National Union of Bank Employees.
N.U.D.A.G.M.W.	National Union of Domestic Appliance and General Metal Workers.
NUFLAT	National Union of Footwear, Leather and Allied Trades.
N.U.G.M.W.	National Union of General and Municipal Workers.
NUGSAT	National Union of Gold, Silver and Allied Trades.
N.U.J.	National Union of Journalists.
N.U.M.	National Union of Mineworkers.
N.U.P.B.P.W.	National Union of Printing, Bookbinding and Paper Workers.
NUPE	National Union of Public Employees.
N.U.R.	National Union of Railwaymen.
N.U.S.	National Union of Seamen.
N.U.T.	National Union of Teachers.
N.U.T.G.W.	National Union of Tailors and Garment Workers.
N.U.V.B.	National Union of Vehicle Builders.
P.O.E.U.	Post Office Engineering Union.
P.T.U.	Plumbing Trade Union.
SAGA	Staff Association General Accident.
SOGAT	Society of Graphical and Allied Trades.
T.G.W.U.	Transport and General Workers Union.
T.S.A.	Telecommunications Staff Association.
T.S.S.A.	Transport Salaried Staffs Association.
TUC	Trade Union Congress.

UCATT	Union of Construction, Allied Trades and Technicians.
UKAPE	United Kingdom Association of Professional Engineers.
U.P.W.	Union of Post Office Workers.
U.R.T.U.	United Road Transport Union.
U.S.D.A.W.	Union of Shop, Distributive and Allied Workers.

CHAPTER 1

INTRODUCTION

THE extent to which the law affects industrial relations is changing. It is in the nature of the subject that there must be a balance between the controls over employment that are determined by collective bargaining and those that are determined by Statute, and until a few years ago it could be said that collective bargaining was almost the only determinant of the terms of employment and that the law abstained, except perhaps in matters of safety, from setting even minimum standards. Despite the inherent instability of the collective bargaining process it has been said to be one of the great achievements of British society that it has nevertheless resulted in relative industrial peace and security during most of this century.

This is equally true of the other aspect of collective labour law, that is the law relating to the structure of trade associations and the law which limits the range of permissible activity both by unions and employers in industrial action. Again few countries have as little law on this subject as Britain, but there is no evidence that this leads to any greater instability.[1]

It may be thought that recent changes have fundamentally altered this structure but it is suggested that this is not so. The fact remains that despite the greater degree of intervention in industrial matters by the law today, it nevertheless pursues the connected policies of abstention from controls over industrial action and support for collective bargaining. While some of the recent legislation has, in line with the requirements of European legislation, been setting minimum standards in some areas, much of it has been aimed at enlarging the scope of bargaining and helping the parties to set up procedures for negotiation.

Thus while legislation provides a few substantive rights (and more procedural ones), it is still true that the sanctions used in industrial relations are social and economic rather than legal. To this extent therefore the law is abstentionist. But this does not mean to say that there is little or no law, for the subject is rapidly expanding, and, given the political scrutiny to which labour law is subjected, that expansion is likely to continue. A number of people believe that the law can play a greater role in industrial relations, for on the one hand there are those who see the law as providing minimum terms of employment over a wider area, and on the other hand there are those who believe the law can provide closer control of the permissible range of indus-

---

[1] See generally Kahn-Freund, *Labour Law: Old Traditions and New Developments* (1968); Kahn-Freund, "Labour Law" in Ginsberg, *Law and Opinion in England in the 20th Century* (1959); Kahn-Freund, *Labour and the Law* (2nd ed.); Wedderburn, *The Worker and the Law* (1971), Chap. 1.

trial sanctions. However, the traditional and still widely held view is that the law should have as little to do with industrial relations as possible for it can only be a disruptive influence. Organisational strength and not legal right is seen as the best way to promote the interests of employees and preserve industrial peace. This argument should, however, apply equally to trade unions and employers and it may be that now that unions are beginning to achieve greater statutory rights to protect their interests it will be less easy to argue that the law has no place in industrial relations.

Too much, however, should not be claimed for the law. It is unlikely that the law, at least for the foreseeable future, could provide the central structure for a system of industrial relations and indeed it is unlikely that anybody would want it to do so. The law can only operate on the fringe of the dynamic system of bargaining which is maintained by social and economic power rather than by legal rights. Indeed the law has little to do with the central core of industrial relations, but rather operates as a guarantee against abuse of the system, whether by employer, union, employee or member. Whether these limits on the proper activities of the parties have been put in the right place is a matter of debate but that does not alter the fact that the law does not in general seek to regulate the central terms of the various relationships.

While it is likely that this principle will be maintained, it is equally likely that inroads will continue to be made upon it, so that the relationships between employer and employee, between employer and union and between union and member will become more closely controlled by the law.

Historical Introduction[2]

To a considerable extent the structure of present trade union law can only be explained as the result of an historical process. It is unlikely that anyone would consciously devise a code of law similar to that which exists today, for more often than not it consists of a patchwork of statute and common law which has been created as a reaction to specific problems. Thus the common law has often reacted to inhibit increased trade union activity, and Parliament has often replied with legislation designed to subdue excessive zeal on the part of the common law. The basis of this conflict still exists today, for the judges and the politicians are often to be found working from different assumptions; the judges adopting the principle of freedom of the individual and some politicians preferring collective security and the protection of status.

In addition, attitudes of trade unions towards the law are sometimes influenced by legal barbarisms of the past so that some cases and principles become enshrined in a dogma that outlives rationality. But their wariness may well be justified, for the law and its application by the judges has seldom in the past been successful in protecting the aspirations of trade unionists. Whether it does so today is more a matter of politics than history, but perhaps trade union law is destined never to satisfy both parties to the argument at the same time.

The Ordinance of Labourers 1349: 1349–1562

The preamble to the Ordinance of Labourers of 1349 recites that "because a great Part of the People, and especially of Workmen and Servants, late died of

---

[2] For legal histories see Hedges and Winterbottom, *The Legal History of Trade Unionism* (1930); D. N. Pritt, *Employers, Workers and Trade Unions* (1970); Lewis, "The historical development of labour law" (1976) 14 B.J.I.R. 1. For histories of trade unionism see S. & B. Webb, *History of Trade Unionism* (1920); Pelling, *A History of British Trade Unionism* (1967); Clegg, Fox and Thompson, *A history of British trade unions since 1889* (1964). Also of interest are the histories of individual unions such as Bagwell, *The Railwaymen* (1963).

the Pestilence, many seeing the Necessity of Masters, and great Scarcity of Servants, will not serve unless they may receive excessive Wages...." The reaction of the government was to pass a statute of great severity which contained three main points. First, any person under 60 who was covered by the Ordinance[3] could be required to work, secondly the wages were to be those applicable in 1346, and thirdly it became a crime to leave a job before the expiry of the contract.

The original Ordinance does not appear to have been as successful as had been hoped but the Statute of Labourers 1351[4] considerably extended and strengthened the system which was further developed by later statutes. By 1389 fixed wages were abandoned and the power was given to the Justices to establish appropriate rates having regard to "the Dearth of Victuals"[5] and it was also stated that "Victuallers ... shall have reasonable Gains, according to the Discretion and Limitation of the said Justices."

The effect of the Ordinance of Labourers and subsequent legislation was to deny freedom of contract on the part of the worker and to institute a system of directed labour and controlled prices. In such an atmosphere combination of workers was irrelevant.

The Statute of Artificers 1562: 1562–1799

The Statute of Artificers[6] "digested and reduced" the previous legislation and stated that the statute should banish idleness, advance husbandry and yield to the hired person both in time of scarcity and in the time of plenty a convenient proportion of wages. To this end it continued the policy of the Ordinance of Labourers of permitting the justices to fix wage rates; of compulsory labour for certain workers between the ages of 12 and 60; and of punishing those who leave their service in breach of contract. There were also provisions covering the movement of workers out of a town or parish without permission and controlling the hours of work. In addition the statute established compulsory apprenticeship of seven years and included a provision making it an offence to refuse to become an apprentice.

In time policies which had been introduced as a method of keeping down wages were no longer needed by the employers and the system of wage regulation gradually lapsed, although on occasions attempts were made by workers to call upon the justices to fix a rate in order to keep wages up, and these often depended on statutes related to particular trades. The fact that the justices were not under any duty to fix a rate but had discretion whether or not to do so[7] meant that the wage fixing system was of little use to workers.

Until the eighteenth century, although combinations of workmen had been forbidden,[8] prosecutions do not appear to have been laid, perhaps because the combinations were mainly directed to inducing the justices to fix a rate, and were thus conspiracies to enforce the law. A system of statutory wage fixing had as its obvious corollary the prohibition of conspiracies to raise wages but

---

[3] The scope was extended by the Statute of Labourers 1351 to cover some skilled trades and all other "Workmen, Artificers, Labourers and Servants."

[4] The preamble states that "the Servants having no regard to the said Ordinance, but to their Ease and singular Covatise do withdraw themselves...."

[5] 13 Ric. 2, c. 8.

[6] Also known as the Statute of Apprentices.

[7] *R.* v. *Justices of Kent* (1811) 14 East 395; 104 E.R. 653.

[8] Initially as regards particular trades but later generally: Bill of Conspiracies of Victuallers and Craftsmen 1548. The statute covered not only conspiracies by workmen but also price fixing by "victuallers."

by the early part of the eighteenth century the control of the terms of employment was becoming less effective[9] and rights of status gradually became rights of contract. Towards the end of the century the exploitation by the employers of the freedom of contract left workmen unprotected unless they acted in combination, and hence the need for trade unions arose.

The reply was prosecutions for conspiracy. Thus in *R.* v. *Journeymen Tailors of Cambridge*[10] several tailors[11] were found guilty of a conspiracy to raise wages. There is some doubt whether such a conspiracy was by itself criminal at common law or whether the criminality lay in the conspiracy to break a wage fixing statute,[12] but in later years it was assumed that the common law was itself sufficient.

The Combination Acts 1799 and 1800: 1799–1824

During the latter part of the eighteenth century a number of statutes were passed restricting combinations in particular industries. Economic theory had turned in favour of freedom of contract and freedom of property and both government control and combinations by workmen were regarded as an interference with such rights. The fact that capital was inherently powerful and the individual workman weak did not lead parliament to protect combinations although they were the only method whereby the workmen could effectively bargain with the masters, but rather the demands of the masters to be free to use their capital as they wished were acceded to. Thus, when in 1799 Parliament was asked to deal with a strike of millwrights by suppressing combinations in the engineering industry, the government proposed instead a Bill of general application.[13] The resulting Combinations Act 1799 was rushed through Parliament in great haste and was superseded in the following year by a slightly amended version, the Combinations Act 1800.

In effect the Act rendered all combinations illegal for it made it an offence to make any agreement for the purpose of improving conditions of employment or to call or attend a meeting for such a purpose. In addition it became an offence to attempt to persuade another person not to work or to refuse to work alongside another worker. Many of these provisions had existed in earlier statutes but one of the more important changes brought about by the Act was that the case could now be heard before two justices[14] rather than at Assize, thus providing a more immediate and effective procedure for the masters.[15] The penalty was a maximum of three months imprisonment.

It is now generally thought that the Combination Acts did not represent any great change in industrial relations policy, for little became illegal that was not so before, and both the common law and the Combination Acts relating to particular industries remained applicable. Nor it seems was the Act particu-

---

[9] The statute was partially repealed in 1813 and completely repealed in 1875.

[10] (1821) 8 Mod. 10; 88 E.R. 9.

[11] The tailors were amongst the first to form trade unions; this was so because by the early eighteenth century they had become life long wage earners: S. & B. Webb, *History of Trade Unionism* (1920), p. 31. Note also the very early case before the Star Chamber in 1477 concerning tailors in Exeter who intimidated and drove out a person who refused to join the guild. *Mayor of Excestre* v. *Stoden* Select Cases in the Star Chamber, 16 Selden Society 1. Noted (1934) 12 Can.B.R. 23.

[12] Hedges and Winterbottom, *Legal history of trade unionism* (1930), Chap. 2.

[13] Amulrie, *Industrial Arbitration in Great Britain* (1929), p. 5.

[14] The Combination Act 1799 had provided that one magistrate was sufficient.

[15] Bagwell, *Industrial Relations in Nineteenth Century Britain* (1974), p. 10.

larly effective for its application was haphazard.[16] Nevertheless, the effect of the Act was to expose workmen who combined to considerable risks and there were a number of prosecutions[17] of which perhaps the most famous was the prosecution of compositors at *The Times* in 1810. The Act did not, however, significantly delay the advance of trade unionism despite the clandestine way it had to be carried on. But as the men could not bargain lawfully the Act may have been responsible for the increasing violence in industrial disputes which was exemplified by the outbreaks of Luddism during the second decade of the century.

The Act also applied to combinations of employers and prohibited agreements to reduce wages, alter hours of work or increase the quantity of work, but this provision did little to protect workmen and although several prosecutions were brought no case was known of a master having been punished for belonging to a combination.[18]

As a recompense for the prohibition of combinations the Act provided for a system of compulsory arbitration in disputes. It was provided that the dispute could be submitted to arbitrators appointed by each side, but that if no decision were forthcoming within three days the parties could require the arbitrators to submit the case to a justice of the peace whose decision was final. It seems, however, that these provisions were not put into force.[19]

Combination Laws Repeal Act 1824: 1824–1825

The Combination Laws Repeal Act 1824 reached the statute book with few people realising its true significance. The fact that it existed at all was principally due to the efforts of Francis Place, J. R. McCullock and Joseph Hume, the last of whom chaired, and manipulated to a successful conclusion, the select committee on Artisans and Machinery which produced six reports in the early part of 1824. The motives of the proponents of the statute were not to increase the power of the trade unions but were based on a completely *laissez-faire* philosophy which would permit both masters and workmen to combine, and which would prohibit all interference in or regulation of the relations between the employers and the employed. Francis Place stated under examination by the committee that the combination laws were "a bond of union to the men," and that, with their repeal, combinations, as they then existed, would cease.[20] He was to be proved wrong.

The committee did not produce a reasoned report, but rather presented to Parliament a series of eleven resolutions on combinations[21] upon which the bill was based.[22] The resolutions pointed out that the law had been ineffective in preventing combinations, that masters frequently combined and had not been punished, and that the combination laws had engendered mutual distrust between masters and workmen and should be repealed.

---

[16] Musson, *British Trade Unions, 1800–1875* (1972).

[17] See S. & B. Webb, *History of Trade Unionism* (1920), p. 78 *et seq.* But it was never entirely certain whether prosecutions were brought under this or some other Act, or under the common law.

[18] Sixth report of the Select Committee on Artisans and Machinery, 1824.

[19] S. & B. Webb, *History of Trade Unionism* (1920), p. 71. Note also the Cotton Arbitration Act 1800 which although operative was not successful in helping the cotton workers.

[20] First Report of the Committee on Artisans and Machinery, p. 45.

[21] There were also a few resolutions on artisans. The question of export of machinery was thought to need further investigation, but little serious attention had been paid to it by the committee.

[22] The sixth report was presented on May 21, 1824 and by June 21, of the same year the Bill had been enacted.

The Act itself began by repealing 35 statutes on combinations, beginning with one of 1305,[23] and including most of the Combinations Act 1800.[24] But prosecutions had not only been based on statute, but also on conspiracy at common law, so section 2 declared that combination was not to be a criminal offence at common law. The Act did, however, make it an offence to use violence, threats or intimidation either against a fellow worker, to force him to leave his job, or to prevent him being employed; or against a master in order to interfere with the management of the business.

The Combination Act 1825: 1825–1871

Following the Act of 1824 workmen took advantage of their new freedoms[25] but a number of cases of violence occurred. Accordingly in 1825 the Select Committee on the Combination Laws recommended new legislation as a compromise between the demands of the masters to return to the old law and the aspirations of the workers to use their new freedom. One of its purposes was to confine the objects of association "to those objects alone which are essential to the protection of both the workman and the master, and may be secured without impairing the freedom of either, or endangering the public tranquility." In other words the activities of trade unionists were to be limited strictly to negotiations over wages, and other action, particularly the refusal to work with non-union men was to be illegal.

The Combination Act 1825 repealed the Act of 1824 but re-enacted much of its contents. Thus the earlier statutes prohibiting combinations were repealed but the common law doctrine of conspiracy was allowed to be revived. However, the Act did exempt from the rigours of the common law those combinations whose sole function was determination of wages or hours of work.[26] In addition the 1825 Act adopted the provisions of the 1824 Act concerning intimidation of workmen and masters, but strengthened them considerably. Thus the requirement that the intimidation must be malicious or wilful was dropped and, in addition to violence or intimidation, it was stated that molestation and obstruction were also criminal. These provisions proved to be potent weapons in the hands of the judges.

Thus, while the 1825 Act had adopted the liberal basis of its predecessor, it had so limited the freedom of workmen as to render the right to combine nugatory. But the most serious defect was in resurrecting the common law doctrine of conspiracy and leaving the regulation of union activity to the discretion of the judiciary who were able to take advantage of the uncertain meaning of intimidation, molestation and obstruction.

One of the most difficult questions was the extent to which trade unionists could prosecute a strike, and it became clear that although a combination to raise wages was in itself lawful it was very difficult to pursue such a combination lawfully. Thus in *R.* v. *Rowlands*[27] Erle J. pointed out that a conspiracy to injure another by unlawful means was a criminal offence, and this included any threats in order to persuade a person to join the strike, and also included molestation and obstruction of the employer. This was widely defined so as to encompass "creating alarm in the minds of [the employers] and so to force their assent to any alteration in the mode of carrying on their business."[28]

---

[23] 33 Edw. 1, St. 1. An Ordinance concerning conspirators.
[24] Sections 18–22 dealing with arbitration were not repealed.
[25] For example see Aspinall, *The Early English Trade Unions* (1949), p. xxix.
[26] Combination Act 1825, s. 4.
[27] (1851) 5 Cox C.C. 436. See also *R.* v. *Duffield* (1851) 5 Cox C.C. 404.
[28] *Ibid.* at 462.

It was also held to be an offence to conspire to induce workmen to leave their employer in breach of their contracts. In *R.* v. *Druitt*[29] Bramwell B. re-enforced the view that a conspiracy to injure the employer by "compulsion and restraint" was a criminal offence both at common law and under the statute. A similar point was made in *Walsby* v. *Anley*[30] in relation to a threat to strike in an attempt to secure the discharge of non unionists.[31] The court recognised the freedom of individuals to refuse to work with others, but held that a conspiracy to do so was an offence at common law that was not saved by the Act of 1825.

It can, however, be said that the 1825 Act represented a considerable theoretical advance, for it recognised the existence of collective bargaining and gave a limited right of combination to the workers, even if effective action in pursuit of those objectives was rendered illegal by the application of the common law. Thus the action of the judges and the rigours of the master and servant law inhibited the full development of trade unions.

Molestation of Workmen Act 1859

Some relief from the wide range of potential liability was secured by the passing of the Molestation of Workmen Act 1859 which was intended to reverse the effect of dicta in *R.* v. *Rowlands*. The statute re-iterated the fact that a combination to raise wages was lawful and added that it was not an offence to endeavour "peaceably and in a reasonable manner, and without threat or intimidation, direct or indirect, to persuade others to cease or abstain from work," if the object was a change in wages or hours. However, in *R.* v. *Druitt*[33] it became clear that this statute was in practice of little assistance. In that case the defendants were charged with conspiracy for organising a picket amongst tailors who were on strike and Bramwell B. pointed out that "if picketing could be done in a way which incited no reasonable alarm, or did not coerce or annoy those who were the subjects of it, it would be no offence in law," but that if it was "calculated to have a deterring effect on the minds of ordinary persons, by exposing them to have their motions watched, and to encounter black looks, that would not be permitted by the law of the land."[34] Peaceful picketing was thus severely circumscribed.

The Tolpuddle martyrs

It was during the period under consideration that there took place the famous prosecution of six agricultural labourers from the village of Tolpuddle in Dorset.[35] As the 1825 Act had made the fact of combination lawful a complicated series of statutes relating to unlawful oaths was used instead to curb trade societies. The case produces no point of legal significance but is

[29] (1867) 10 Cox C.C. 592 at 601.

[30] (1861) 3 El. & El. 516; 121 E.R. 536.

[31] The employer had been attempting to enforce "the document," *i.e.* an undertaking by an employee not to join a union. He had persuaded two men to sign the document and the remainder threatened a strike unless they were dismissed.

[32] (1851) 5 Cox C.C. 436.

[33] (1867) 10 Cox C.C. 592.

[34] *Ibid.* at 601, 602.

[35] They were George and James Loveless, James Brine, Thomas and John Stanfield and James Hammett. James Hammett was not at the vital meeting but his brother John had been. At the time of the arrest John was about to become a father, but whether this induced James to remain silent is not known; but it is likely that he was also a member of the society.

nevertheless of considerable interest.[36] It was alleged that the defendants had administered to one Edward Legg an unlawful oath as part of the initiation ceremonies of a trade union on December 9, 1833. In February 1834 the presiding magistrate, James Frampton, had a number of circulars distributed warning against the giving of unlawful oaths, and on February 24, the men were arrested.

The charge turned upon three statutes: The Unlawful Oaths Act 1797, The Unlawful Societies Act 1799 and The Seditious Meetings Act 1817. These provisions, as used in the case, were mutually dependent and interlocking, for it appears that the charge was based upon the fact that it was unlawful by virtue of the Act of 1799 as confirmed in the Act of 1817 to administer an oath "not required or authorised by Law." These statutes made the individual guilty of unlawful combination and the Act of 1797 made it an offence to administer an oath not to reveal the existence of an unlawful combination. Thus the charge was in effect one of administering an oath not to reveal the existence of a society which administers oaths. The Act of 1797 was not aimed at trade unions but at naval mutinies and its use in this case, while technically permissible, reveals the lengths to which some were prepared to go to suppress combinations. The defendants were sentenced to transportation for seven years, but such was the public outcry that all were eventually pardoned, but it took the last of them almost five and a half years to return.

Trade Union status: civil proceedings

One of the problems that arose during this period was that as a trade union amounted to a combination in restraint of trade at common law it suffered from a number of legal disabilities. Further difficulties arose from the fact that a union was an unincorporated association.

As to the first problem, in *Hilton* v. *Eckersley*[37] an employer's association had agreed to employ labour at certain rates and each member had promised to pay £500 if he failed to abide by this undertaking. The court held that the association was in restraint of trade and the amount promised by way of penalty could not be recovered. In other words the decision meant that the rules of a combination could not be enforced.

Some unions had attempted to avoid some consequences of this by registering as friendly societies under the Friendly Societies Act 1855, but in *Hornby* v. *Close*[38] it was held that as one of a union's purposes was the support of members on strike, the association was in restraint of trade and could not therefore take the benefit of the provisions of the Act concerning defaulting officials.[39] This particular defect was put right by the Trades Union Funds Protection Act 1869 which was limited to allowing the prosecution of such officials, but the union remained in restraint of trade and its rules were still unenforceable.

The difficulty concerning unincorporated associations was common to all such societies and concerned the association's property. As the property was held by all the members jointly, the common law view was that a person who

---

[36] See generally Marlow, *The Tolpuddle Martyrs* (1971), and Loveless, *The Victims of Whiggery* (1837), reprinted in *British Labour Struggles: Contemporary Pamphlets 1827–1850* (1972).

[37] (1855) 6 El. and Bl. 46; 119 E.R. 781.

[38] (1867) L.R. 2 Q.B. 153.

[39] s. 24 of the Friendly Societies Act 1855 permitted the prosecution of an official who withheld funds from the society. The union alleged that Close had withheld £24 18s. 5½d. A similar attempt failed later in *Farrer* v. *Close* (1869) L.R. 4 Q.B. 602.

took some of the society's property could not be convicted of stealing it as in law it belonged to him as well as the other members. This defect was cured by the Larcency and Embezzlement Act 1868 so that such a person could be dealt with as if he were not a co-owner.[40]

Trade Union Act 1871: 1871–1971

Thus by 1871[41] the increasing stability of trade union organisation had meant that the civil status of a union was now a significant issue, and the gradual extension of trade unionism had meant that reform was needed to alter the very narrow interpretation of statutes which exempted union members from the criminal law, and also to deal with the wide ambit of the crime of conspiracy. Hence the significance of the Trade Union Act 1871[42] which was to form the basis of trade union law for a century.

Trade Union Act 1871: Criminal provisions

Section 2 of the Act stated that the purposes of a trade union should not be regarded as being in restraint of trade so as to expose a member to prosecution for criminal conspiracy, thus attempting to carry out the intention that membership of a trade union and taking part in its activities should no longer be regarded as criminal.

Criminal Law Amendment Act 1871

This Act repealed the Combination Act 1825 and the Molestation of Workmen Act 1859 and substituted for them similar but more liberal provisions. Thus while the offences of intimidation, molestation and obstruction were retained, these concepts were now defined in such a way as to reverse earlier interpretations. From 1871 threats meant in effect threats of violence, and molestation and obstruction covered only persistently following another, hiding a person's tools or watching and besetting, and in particular it was stated that mere interference with trade should not amount to molestation and obstruction. By this means it was hoped to establish that the act of striking was not of itself a criminal offence.

Such a view, however, left out of account the ingenuity of the judiciary. In *R.* v. *Bunn*[43] some gas stokers had gone on strike to protest against the dismissal of a fellow worker and were convicted of conspiracy; despite the terms of the Criminal Law Amendment Act 1871, Brett J. held that this statute had not affected the crime of conspiracy at common law, which could consist of an agreement to act improperly by molesting the employer; molestation was taken to exist "if anything was done with an improper intent which . . . was an unjustifiable annoyance and interference with the masters in the conduct of their business, and which in any business would be such annoyance and interference as would be likely to have a deterring effect upon masters of ordinary nerve."[44]

---

[40] For an example see *R.* v. *Blackburn* (1868), 11 Cox C.C. 157, where a retiring secretary had failed to account for the balance of union money.

[41] A useful summary of the state of the law before the Trade Union Act 1871 is contained in the memorandum by Sir William Erle printed in the 11th Report of the Trade Union Commissioners 1869.

[42] The statute followed the eleventh Report of the Trade Union Commissioners, 1869, and relied particularly on the third dissent signed by the Earl of Lichfield, Thos. Hughes and Frederic Harrison.

[43] (1872) 12 Cox C.C. 316.

[44] *Ibid.* at 349.

By this means not only was the Criminal Law Amendment Act 1871 subverted but so was section 2 of the Trade Union Act 1871 which had attempted to establish that a strike was not a criminal conspiracy. Although in strict theory a strike was still not of itself a conspiracy it would almost always amount to a conspiracy to molest or obstruct the employer.

Conspiracy and Protection of Property Act 1875

Once again a change in labour law conformed to the pattern which was to become increasingly frequent during the next century, in that a reactionary judicial decision was soon followed by legislation. The Conspiracy and Protection of Property Act 1875 repealed the Criminal Law Amendment Act 1871, recast some of its provisions and reversed *R.* v. *Bunn.*[45]

First the statute made it clear that a person could not be convicted of conspiracy if he was acting in furtherance of a trade dispute and if the act would not have been a crime had it been done by a person acting alone. In effect this provision at long last removed the doctrine of criminal conspiracy from trade dispute cases, and reaffirmed the view taken in 1871 that striking was not a criminal offence.

Secondly, the statute recasts the crimes of molestation and obstruction into five heads of liability covering such matters as watching and besetting, intimidation and persistently following.[46] Although this provision is still in force it is now moribund.

Thirdly, the statute began the process of defining permissible picketing for it established that mere attendance at a place for the purpose of peacefully communicating information should not amount to the crime of watching and besetting within the statute. The principle of exempting attendance for that purpose from the criminal law still represents the basis of the more sophisticated modern provision.[47] Following 1875 attempts were made to establish that peaceful picketing was of itself a crime at common law. This proposition was put forward by Lindley L.J. in *Lyons* v. *Wilkins*[48] and is a concept which still bedevils the law.[49] Despite the probability that another case[50] had rendered the idea harmless, it was thought necessary to reverse *Lyons* v. *Wilkins*[51] by statute in 1906,[52] thus once again repeating the familiar pattern.

Since 1875, except for the issue of picketing, the criminal law has played little part in the control of trade unions, but the civil law was found to possess a potent armoury with which the struggle could be continued.

Trade Union Act 1871: the civil provisions

The unlawful nature of trade associations due to the doctrine of restraint of trade was a matter of considerable concern and the primary function of the Trade Union Act 1871 was to provide such organisations with legitimate status before the civil law. The Act, therefore, first provided unions with power to enforce certain kinds of contracts and to hold property, and secondly, it provided for voluntary registration.

---

[45] (1872) 12 Cox C.C. 316.

[46] Conspiracy and Protection of Property Act 1875 s. 7.

[47] T.U.L.R.A. 1974, s. 15.

[48] [1896] Ch. 811.

[49] *Hubbard* v. *Pitt* [1975] I.C.R. 77 and 308.

[50] *Ward Lock* v. *Operative Printers' Assistants Society* (1906) 22 T.L.R. 327.

[51] [1896] 1 Ch. 811.

[52] Trade Disputes Act 1906, s. 2; but this was only true if there was a trade dispute.

As to the first point, section 3 of the Act declared that the purposes of a trade union were not to be regarded as being in restraint of trade so as to invalidate any contract or trust, but the Act went on to limit the kinds of contracts that could be enforced. Section 4 in effect prevented a court from directly enforcing any agreement between trade unions or certain contracts between members within a trade union; but nevertheless after 1871 the rule book became partially enforceable.[53] The reason for refusing to enforce all the provisions of the contract of membership was partly the fear that to do so would allow an action to be brought by a union for an injunction to order its members to go on strike,[54] and partly the desire of unions to be self regulating bodies free from interference by the courts in their domestic affairs. In fact the interpretation of section 4 by the courts was such that they were able to exercise a considerable degree of control over internal affairs, particularly in disciplinary matters.[55]

Secondly, the 1871 Act established a system of voluntary registration with the Registrar of Friendly Societies and listed a number of matters, mainly of an administrative nature, that must be provided for in the rules. Registered unions were granted some privileges, again of a technical nature, such as the ability of trustees to sue in their own names in matters "touching and concerning" the property of the union. A number of further technical matters were dealt with by the Trade Union Amendment Act 1876, including the provision of a statutory power to amalgamate.[56]

By 1880, therefore, trade unions had been relieved of much of the criminal liability and had been given sufficient civil status to encourage permanent and stable institutions. But within the next quarter century the judges were once more to become active and inventive in their use of the common law.

Civil liability before 1906

(a) *Inducing breach of contract.* This tort had been established in *Lumley* v. *Gye*[57] in 1853 and was applied to a situation involving trade unions in *Temperton* v. *Russell*[58] in 1893. The essence of the tort was the interference by A with a contract between B and C causing a breach of that contract.

(b) *Allen* v. *Flood.*[59] The tort of inducing breach of contract at least involved an unlawful act in the sense that the act of A brought about a breach of contract between B and C, but in *Allen* v. *Flood* an attempt was made, fortunately unsuccessfully, to make A liable even though there had been no breach of contract between B and C, but on the grounds only that either B or C had suffered injury. In other words certain members of the House of Lords wished to establish that A could be liable to B on the grounds that he intentionally did an act calculated to injure B. In the case the plaintiffs, Flood and Taylor, were working as shipwrights on the *Sam Weller* in a dry dock at Millwall for the Glengall Iron Company. The defendant, who was an official of

---

[53] For an exhaustive discussion of the effect of s. 4 see Citrine, *Trade Union Law* (3rd ed.) pp. 106–140.

[54] *Russell* v. *Amalgamated Society of Carpenters* [1912] A.C. 421 at 441.

[55] *Yorkshire Miners Assoc.* v. *Howden* [1905] A.C. 256; *Amalgamated Society of Carpenters and Joiners* v. *Braithwaite* [1922] 2 A.C. 440; *Bonsor* v. *Musicians Union* [1956] A.C. 104.

[56] Amalgamations were further dealt with by the Trade Union (Amalgamation) Act 1917 and by the Trade Union (Amalgamations, etc.) Act 1964.

[57] (1853) 2 E. & B. 216; 118 E.R. 749.

[58] [1893] 1 Q.B. 715.

[59] [1898] A.C.1.

the Independent Society of Boiler Makers and Iron and Steel Ship Builders, was asked by the boilermakers on the site to demand the dismissal of the plaintiffs who were known to have previously done some iron work which should have been done by boilermakers. When Allen said that the men would "leave off work" this did not involve a threat of an unlawful act as the men could lawfully leave, and be dismissed, without notice.

In an attempt to secure a decision for the plaintiffs Lord Halsbury resurrected the obsolete procedure of having the case re-argued and asking the judges to advise the House,[60] but to no avail for although there was a majority of judges in favour of liability, a majority in the House was against it.[61] Had the case gone the other way trade unionists taking industrial action would have been exposed to civil liability.

(c) *Conspiracy*. Unfortunately it was not long before what could not be achieved in *Allen* v. *Flood*[62] was achieved by the tort of conspiracy in *Quinn* v. *Leathem.*[63] On this occasion Lord Halsbury, who selected the membership of the House, found more support for his views and the House established that where two or more combine without justification to injure another they will be liable in tort. In other words what *Allen* v. *Flood*[64] decided was not a tort for one person to do was now a tort if done by two people.

A further significant facet of the law was the fact that although it had been decided in *Mogul Steamship Co.* v. *McGregor Gow*[65] that commercial self interest could justify a conspiracy, the self interest of workers could not, and it was not finally until 1942 that the same privilege was extended to unions and employees.[66]

(d) *Taff Vale Railway Co.* v. *A.S.R.S.*[67] The issues have so far been discussed on the basis of the liability of the individuals engaging in the action, but the crucial question before 1906 was the extent to which the union itself could be made liable.

The *Taff Vale* case[68] arose out of a strike initially brought about by the attempt by the company to move a signalman called Ewington from a box at Abercynon to one at Treherbert, but beneath this was the unsatisfactory state of industrial relations on the Taff Vale Railway. On the day the strike ended Farwell J. granted an interlocutory injunction against the union in its own name to prevent the watching and besetting of Cardiff Railway Station.[69] It had been thought that although actions could be maintained against individual union officials,[70] an action could not be maintained against a union because it

---

[60] See Paterson, "Judges a Political Elite?" (1974) 1 Brit.J. Law and Society 118; Heuston, *Lives of the Lord Chancellors*, 1885–1940 (1964), p. 119 *et seq*; Griffith, *The Politics of the Judiciary* (1977), p. 58.

[61] The judges were 6–2 for liability and the House 6–3 against.

[62] [1898] A.C.1.

[63] [1901] A.C. 495.

[64] [1898] A.C.1.

[65] [1892] A.C. 25.

[66] *Crofter Hand Woven Harris Tweed Co.* v. *Veitch* [1942] A.C. 435. But see also *Reynolds* v. *Shipping Federation* [1924] 1 Ch. 28 and *Sorrell* v. *Smith* [1925] A.C. 700.

[67] [1901] A.C. 426.

[68] For the full story of this case see Bagwell, *The Railwaymen* (1963), Chap. 8, to which I am much indebted.

[69] The strikers had amongst other things been "turning round" blacklegs supplied by Collison's National Free Labour Association.

[70] Injunctions had in fact been taken out against two such organisers, Bell and Holmes.

was an unincorporated association.[71] The House of Lords held, however, that the Trade Union Act 1871 had given the union sufficient powers to make it a quasi-corporate body and thus able to be sued in its own name. It was, therefore, now established that union funds were accessible to those injured by strike action.

Although the case is now part of the folklore of trade unionism, at the time it was decided there was considerable division amongst the unions about the best way to respond, and some unions preferred to accept the principle of liability and responsibility except in cases where members of the union had acted without authority. Eventually the more militant unions won the day at the TUC which accepted the policy of complete immunity and this became embodied in the Trade Disputes Act 1906.[72]

In the event the Taff Vale Company received damages of £23,000, and Ammon Beasley, the general manager who had instituted the action received a gratuity of £1,000 from the Company, and £1,000 and a silver candelabra from an "Employers Testimonial Committee." But the lasting effect was that the case brought about stronger links between the trade unions and the nascent Labour Party.

Trade Disputes Act 1906

Following the election of 1906 in which a Liberal government was returned with a substantial majority and in which 29 Labour candidates were successful, Parliament passed the Trade Disputes Act 1906 to repair much of the damage inflicted by the judiciary in the previous decade. It is the substance of this statute which forms the basis of the protection of trade unions today.

First, the Act relieved unions, as such, from liability in tort altogether, thus reversing the effect of the *Taff Vale*[73] case.[74] Secondly, as to the liability of individual members and officials the Act relieved them of liability for conspiracy and inducing breach of contract if the action was taken in contemplation or furtherance of a trade dispute.[75] Finally a limited immunity from prosecution was given to peaceful picketing.[76]

Although the phrase "in contemplation or furtherance of a trade dispute" had been used since the Conspiracy and Protection of Property Act 1875, the phrase was here defined for the first time. The significance of the phrase lies in the fact that as it is the necessary condition for exemption from civil liability it describes the ambit of legitimate strike activity, and it is the acceptance of the need for such protection that is the most important contribution of the 1906 Act.

Trade Union Act 1913: political funds

In *Amalgamated Society of Railway Servants* v. *Osborne*[77] the House of Lords held that a union could not levy money for political purposes. The case was brought by W. V. Osborne, Secretary of the Walthamstow branch of the union, apparently because he objected to the fund being made available to the

[71] Although Lord Lindley thought a representative action could have been maintained [1901] A.C. 426 p. 443.

[72] Lovell, *British Trade Unions, 1875–1933* (1977), Chap. 3.

[73] [1901] A.C. 426.

[74] The immunity is now more limited: T.U.L.R.A. 1974, s. 14.

[75] See now T.U.L.R.A. 1974, s. 13.

[76] See now T.U.L.R.A. 1974, s. 15.

[77] [1910] A.C. 87. See Bagwell, *The Railwaymen* (1963), Chap. 9.

Labour Party and not because he wished to prevent all support for parliamentary representation. Although the political levy had earlier been held to be lawful,[78] the House of Lords declared it to be *ultra vires* as the payments were not for a purpose within the definition of a trade union in the Trade Union Act 1871.[79] In other words the House regarded the objects as outlined in the statutory definition as analogous to those in the memorandum of association of a company and accordingly any other purpose was *ultra vires*.

Once again Parliament was called upon to reverse the effect of a judicial decision, and by the Trade Union Act 1913 a union was empowered to apply its funds to any lawful object or purposes so long as it was authorised to do so by its rules. As to the political levy the Act laid down complicated and clumsily drafted provisions to control payments for political purposes and to ensure that such payments come only from the political fund and not the general fund. In addition, protection was provided for the member who did not contribute to the political fund. The sections of the Act relating to the political fund are still in force.

Trade Disputes and Trade Unions Acts 1927 and 1946

The period following the First World War and until 1960 was characterised by the abstention of the judiciary from changes in the law relating to trade unions.[80] But if creativity was not to be the function of the judges, Parliament amply fulfilled that role when it passed the Trade Disputes and Trade Union Act 1927, following the general strike of 1926.[81]

The Act, which in the event had little effect except in relation to political funds, provided that a strike was to be illegal if it had any object other than the furtherance of a trade dispute or if it was a sympathy strike by workers in a different industry, or if it was of such a nature as to coerce the government by the infliction of hardship upon the community. Incitement of such a strike became a criminal offence. Secondly, the closed shop was prohibited in the case of employees of a local or public authority and civil servants were not allowed to join any trade union except one which catered only for Crown employees. Thirdly, picketing which involved large numbers or was otherwise likely to cause apprehension of injury was made a criminal offence, and it was also stated that the offence of intimidation included the case where a person apprehended injury not to his person or property but to his business, so that almost all picketing became illegal.

Finally, and perhaps most seriously of all, the rules concerning the political fund were changed. The Trade Union Act 1913 had enacted that where a political levy was properly established each member was obliged to contribute unless he specifically contracted out. The 1927 Act, however, reversed that presumption so that a person who wished to contribute now had to contract in to the levy. The consequence was dramatic, for in 1927 76 per cent of members of unions with political funds had paid the levy, but in 1928 this fell to 58 per cent.[82] It was not surprising, therefore, that one of the first acts of the

---

[78] *Steele* v. *South Wales Miners Federation* [1909] 1 K.B. 361.

[79] As amended by the Trade Union Act Amendment Act 1876, s. 16.

[80] Most notable was the decision of the House of Lords in *Crofter Hand Woven Harris Tweed* v. *Veitch* [1942] A.C. 435. Note also *White* v. *Kuzyck* [1951] A.C. 585.

[81] On the issue of the legality or otherwise of the general strike see the unsatisfactory judgment of Astbury J. in *National Sailors' and Firemen's Union* v. *Reed* [1926] Ch. 536, and Goodhart, "The legality of the general strike in England" (1927) 36 Yale L.J. 464.

[82] Reports of the Chief Registrar of Friendly Societies for the relevant years.

Labour Government on its return to power after the Second World War was the peremptory repeal of the 1927 statute by the Trade Disputes and Trade Unions Act 1946.

Wage Regulation: Trade Boards Act 1909

During the nineteenth century a number of statutes had been passed dealing with the regulation of conditions of employment, especially in such industries as mining and transport, but not since the eighteenth century had the law involved itself in the regulation of wages. However, it had become apparent that in some industries the lack of union organisation and the absence of collective bargaining procedures produced appallingly low wages, and so by the Trade Boards Act 1909 there was instituted what later came to be called the wages council. This was initially applied to such industries as paper box making, lace finishing and chain making, but was later extended. The wages councils did not, however, derogate from the principles of "collective *laissez-faire*" as it was always intended that they should only exist so long as collective bargaining was unable to produce adequate minimum levels and should be abolished as soon as union organisation became effective. There are, however, still over 40 wages councils still in existence.

More in accord with the usual policy of the law were attempts to provide machinery for arbitration and conciliation under the Conciliation Act 1896 and the Industrial Courts Act 1919. The essential features of the powers provided in these statutes still exist today in the services provided by the Advisory Conciliation and Arbitration Service and by the Central Arbitration Committee. The principal point was that the government saw that in the public interest it had an obligation to provide ways of resolving disputes, but that this was best done by voluntary means rather than by compulsory arbitration.

Conditions of Employment and National Arbitration Order 1940

Just as emergency measures had been taken during the First World War to limit strikes and regulate wages,[83] so in the Second World War the Conditions of Employment and National Arbitration Order 1940[84] prohibited strikes and introduced compulsory arbitration. The conclusion has, however, been drawn from experience under this Order that the criminal prosecution of strikers is ineffective;[85] this view is based on lessons learned from the attempt to prosecute 1,000 miners who went on strike at Betteshanger Colliery, Kent, in December 1941 in breach of the Order. The men were fined £1 each and three of the union officials were sent to prison, but when it was realised that the only people who could call off the strike were in prison steps were taken to have them released and after 11 days the strike was called off; only nine men paid their fines.[86]

The arbitration side of the order was more effective, and parts of it became the Industrial Disputes Order 1951[87] when the 1940 order was revoked. This

---

[83] See for example the Munitions of War Act 1915 as amended by the Munitions of War (Amendment) Act 1916 and by the Munitions of War Act 1917. See also the Wages (Temporary Regulation) Act 1918.

[84] S.R. & O. No. 1305.

[85] Donovan Commission 1968, Cmnd. 3623 para. 486.

[86] *Ibid.* app. 6: a statement by Sir Harold Emmerson.

[87] 1951 S.I. No. 1376.

order was in turn revoked in 1958 but the paragraphs dealing with the extension of terms and conditions became part of the Terms and Conditions of Employment Act 1959.[88] This, together with the Fair Wages Resolution passed by the House of Commons in 1946, produced a form of wage regulation which now, especially in times of pay restraint, is of considerable importance. But again it is wrong to regard this form of compulsory arbitration as detracting to any great extent from the general principles of unhindered collective bargaining, for the effect of the provisions is to extend a collective agreement reached between a union and an employer to other similar areas of employment.

Trade Disputes Act 1965

By the 1960s judicial creativity was again apparent, especially in the field of control of the internal disciplinary decisions of trade unions.[89] But of more concern to trade unions was the potential extension of liability that followed the decision of the House of Lords in *Rookes* v. *Barnard*[90] in 1964. The facts were remarkably similar to *Allen* v. *Flood*[91] for the defendants had told the employer that there would be a strike unless Rookes, who was not a member of the union, was dismissed. The essential difference, however, was that whereas in *Allen* v. *Flood*[92] the threat was to do a lawful act, the threat in *Rookes* v. *Barnard*[93] was to do an act which was a breach of contract.[94] The legal point was whether the existing but ancient tort of intimidation could be revived and extended to cover a threat of a breach of contract as well as threats of bodily violence. The House of Lords held that it could and thus made it a tort in some cases to threaten to go on strike.

Once again Parliament was called upon to reverse a judicial decision and the Trade Disputes Act 1965 extended the protection of the Trade Disputes Act 1906 to such cases.[95]

Proposals for reform: 1965–70

In 1965 the Royal Commission on Trade Unions and Employers Associations was set up under the chairmanship of Lord Donovan, and the report was published in 1968.[96] The then Labour government put forward its proposals (including some that went further in controlling unofficial strikes than had been recommended) in a White Paper entitled "In place of strife"[97] but withdrew in the face of opposition from the unions. Although further proposals were made, the general election of 1970 returned the Conservative government to office and the way was open for the introduction of the Industrial Relations Act.

[88] See now E.P.A. 1975 Sched. 11. See generally Hepple, "Compulsory Arbitration in Great Britain" in Loewenberg *et al.*, *Compulsory Arbitration,* 1976.

[89] *e.g. Bonsor* v. *Musicians Union* [1956] A.C. 104.

[90] [1964] A.C. 1129; see also *Stratford* v. *Lindley* [1965] A.C. 269.

[91] [1898]A.C. 1.

[92] *Ibid.*

[93] [1964] A.C. 1129.

[94] At least by all the defendants except one, who was not employed by the employer.

[95] See now T.U.L.R.A. 1974, s. 13.

[96] Cmnd. 3623.

[97] Cmnd. 3688.

Industrial Relations Act 1971: 1971–1974

The Industrial Relations Act 1971[98] was the greatest revolution in legal thinking about trade union law since the Trade Union Act 1871, a century earlier. It was based on legalistic concepts, some of which were borrowed from the United States, and attempted to impose a duty on the unions to be responsible for the acts of their members. But more importantly it tried to bring to an end the era of abstention by the law from industrial relations, and this view was rejected totally by the unions and largely by the employers. The fact that it failed was perhaps due more to dogma than rationality, for the government insisted upon discriminatory provisions which were impractical and the unions rejected the entire Act because it was interventionist. The Act may have failed but it cannot be forgotten, partly because much of what it contained is still the law and partly because the lessons that are drawn from its failure are bound to affect the future of labour law.

The closed shop

One of the more controversial aspects of the Act was its attempt to control the incidence of the closed shop, but in the event it appears that the Act had very little effect on the numbers of workers covered by closed shop agreements. The Act provided that a pre-entry closed shop (that is where a person must be a member before he is employed) was to be void,[99] but certain post-entry closed shops were permitted[1] in areas where organisation was difficult[2] or a closed shop was necessary to protect employees against exploitation.[3] Furthermore, a variety of the post-entry closed shop, called the agency shop, was permitted after inquiry by the Commission on Industrial Relations and a ballot. But whatever might have been the legal status of closed shop agreements (if such formal documents ever existed) the practice of the closed shop went on.

The rights of union members

Of less emotive appeal but perhaps of greater significance were the sections dealing with the rights of members within the union and the extent to which the internal affairs of the union could be controlled by the courts. Section 65 of the Act established a number of rights, of which only one, the right to resign from a union, has re-appeared in later legislation.[4] Thus, there was a right not to be excluded or expelled by way of arbitrary or unreasonable discrimination;[5] the right to be a candidate to hold office;[6] the right to attend meetings and vote;[7] the right not to be subjected to unreasonable disciplinary action;

[98] For a retrospective discussion see Weekes, Mellish, Dickens & Lloyd, *Industrial Relations and the Limits of Law* (1975); Kahn-Freund, "The Industrial Relations Act—some retrospective reflections" (1974) 3 I.L.J. 186.

[99] s. 7.

[1] s. 17.

[2] For example the National Union of Seamen gained such a closed shop.

[3] For example actors and musicians.

[4] T.U.L.R.A. 1974, s. 7 as amended.

[5] This involved difficult issues regarding the Bridlington agreement: see *Phillips* v. *NALGO* [1973] I.R.L.R. 19; *Remington* v. *NUPE* [1973] I.R.L.R. 273; Kidner, "The Individual and the collective interest in trade union law" (1975) 4 I.L.J. 90.

[6] *Carling* v. *N.U.G.M.W.* [1973] I.C.R. 267; Kidner, "The Right to be a Candidate for Union Office" (1973) 2 I.L.J. 65.

[7] See the Goad Saga: *Goad* v. *A.U.E.W.* No. 1 [1972] I.C.R. 429; *ibid.* No. 2 [1973] I.C.R. 42; *ibid.* No. 3 [1973] I.C.R. 108; *Eckman* v. *Midland Bank* [1973] I.C.R. 71.

the right not to be penalised for refusing to engage in an unlawful act;[8] and the right to the benefit of the rules of natural justice at a disciplinary hearing.[9]

These provisions foundered on two grounds: first the unions claim to be voluntary organisations which should be left free to regulate their own affairs and secondly it was claimed that a legal process was unsuitable for setting a balance between the interests of the individual and the collective interests of the union. When the Act was repealed an amendment was made to the Trade Union and Labour Relations Act 1974 by the Conservative opposition to protect the individual in a similar way,[10] but it was eventually repealed by the Amendment Act of 1976.[11] But the ideological tussle on the extent to which individuals should be protected within unions will no doubt continue, and is likely to increase in importance as the corporatist trend of trade unions becomes more apparent.

Industrial action

Although the 1971 Act substantially re-enacted the immunities from the law of tort which had been introduced by the Trade Disputes Act 1906, it nevertheless exposed unions to a very similar kind of liability by sections 96–98 which dealt with new wrongs created by the Act and called "unfair industrial practices." These sections created liability for some kinds of sympathetic action and for secondary activities (that is aiming not at the party in dispute but at an extraneous party). But by far the most significant section was section 96 which in effect provided that an unregistered union should be liable for inducing breach of contract[12] and thus for most cases of strike action.

As this section only applied to unregistered unions and as the government had hoped that by inducement or threat all unions would become registered and therefore subject to some degree of control, the unions had the opportunity they needed to fight the Act. By virtue of section 96 when a strike had occurred it was not difficult for an employer to obtain an order from the National Industrial Relations Court prohibiting a breach of the section[13]; but it was not so easy to enforce it. Thus in *Churchman* v. *Joint Shop Stewards Committee of the Workers of the Port of London*[14] the N.I.R.C. had committed three shop stewards to prison for contempt of court in refusing to obey an order of the court under section 96 of the Act. The stewards refused to explain their action and it looked as though serious confrontation was inevitable, until the Official Solicitor[15] appeared and appealed to the Court of Appeal on behalf of the men who were then released.

In another case the A.U.E.W. had refused to obey an order of the N.I.R.C. and were initially fined £75,000 for the contempt.[16] Such cases and the depth

---

[8] *Hill* v. *A.U.E.W.* (1973) 8 I.T.R. 4141. This provision was known as "the scabs' charter."

[9] This was a statutory version of the rules of natural justice.

[10] T.U.L.R.A. 1974, s. 5.

[11] Trade Union and Labour Relations (Amendment) Act 1976.

[12] On ss. 96–98 see Lewis, "The Solar Plexus" in Carby-Hall, *Studies in Labour Law* (1976).

[13] On the rise of the labour injunction see Anderman and Davies, "Injunction Procedure in Labour Disputes" (1973) 3 I.L.J. 113, (1974) 4 I.L.J. 30.

[14] [1972] I.C.R. 222.

[15] The Official Solicitor has authority in all cases of committal for contempt by a direction of the Lord Chancellor of May 29, 1963.

[16] *Con-Mech* v. *A.U.E.W.* [1973] I.C.R. 620; *Con-Mech* v. *A.U.E.W. No. 2* [1974] I.C.R. 332; *ibid.* No. 3 [1974] I.C.R. 464. Lewis, "Con-Mech: Showdown for the N.I.R.C." (1974) 3 I.L.J. 201.

of resistance shown by some unions showed how the framers of the act had miscalculated. Whether the Act would have survived if sections 96–98 had been omitted is impossible to tell, but it would have had a better chance.

One of the major problems that arose out of these sections was the question of the legal responsibility of a union for the acts of its officials and members. In the celebrated case of *Heatons Transport* v. *T.G.W.U.*[17] the House of Lords held the defendant union liable for contempt for the acts of its shop stewards on the grounds that by implication the rule book authorised the shop stewards to take industrial action and the union had not done enough to withdraw that authority. This decision put unions in a very difficult position for they either had to defy the court or deny their members[18] and once again it exposed union funds to actions by those who suffered damage from a strike. The dangers were well illustrated by *General Aviation Services* v. *T.G.W.U.*[19] where the union was sued for nearly £2,000,000 for interfering with a contract between the plaintiffs and the British Airports Authority for the provision of ground handling services. Fortunately the court was able to distinguish the *Heaton's* case[20] and the union was held not liable.[21]

Emergency procedures

The Industrial Relations Act introduced two new procedures, partly based on American practice, to deal with emergencies: first the court could order a "cooling off period" and secondly, it could order a ballot of all the union members. These provisions were totally ineffective.

As to the cooling off period, section 138 provided that the court could order that no strike should be called during the specified period if the strike would be gravely injurious to the national economy or create a risk of disorder or endanger lives, and so long as the delay would be conducive to a settlement. In the only case where an order of this kind was made[22] there was little negotiation during the cooling off period which only served to delay industrial action rather than prevent it.

The other procedure available to the government in an emergency was to request the N.I.R.C. to order a ballot of the members to ascertain whether the membership in fact supported the executive in its call for industrial action. Again this procedure was only used once[23] and that was during the rail strike of 1972 following the unsuccessful cooling off period. In the ballot the members voted overwhelmingly in favour of the executive's position, and it is difficult to see how anything else could have been expected since no doubt many members felt that their loyalty to the union was being impugned.

The use of the new emergency procedure in the railway dispute clearly failed in its objective and the provisions were not used again during the life of the Act.

---

[17] [1972] I.C.R. 285. See Hepple, "Union Responsibility for Shop Stewards" (1972) 1 I.L.J. 197.

[18] In fact the T.G.W.U. issued all shop stewards with cards defining their authority, which excluded the calling of industrial action.

[19] [1975] I.C.R. 276.

[20] [1972] I.C.R. 285.

[21] See also *Howett* v. *T.G.W.U.* [1973] I.C.R. 1; *Hanseatic* v. *I.T.F.* [1974] I.C.R. 112.

[22] *Sec. of State for Employment* v. *ASLEF* [1972] I.C.R. 7.

[23] *Sec. of State for Employment* v. *ASLEF (No. 2)* [1972] I.C.R. 19.

Collective bargaining

One of the most important innovations of the 1971 Act was the introduction of compulsory bargaining procedures.[24] Thus it was possible to have an issue referred to the Commission on Industrial Relations either because no procedure agreement existed (or such an agreement was defective)[25] or for the establishment of a sole bargaining agency.[26] While the large unions had no need of such machinery because they could achieve their ends by industrial strength, the Act did significantly increase the area of employment in which collective bargaining took place for, for the first time, a union which had little industrial muscle could demand that the employer negotiate to grant recognition.

One of the difficult issues that arose out of the Act was the relationship between the collective provisions and the rights of the individual to engage in trade union activities and not to be discriminated against for doing so.[27] The difficulty arose after the House of Lords held that discrimination against a person's union was a discrimination against the man himself and therefore actionable.[28] This meant that a union that had failed to gain collective rights under sections 37–45 of the Act could achieve similar results by using the individual procedure of section 5.[29]

While the format of the legislation has altered considerably, the effect of the collective rights given to trade unions is not very different and the legal right of a union to demand recognition has been continued.[30] The procedures and the remedies are today less legalistic, and to that extent may be less adequate for it is now difficult to enforce a recommendation for recognition against an obdurate employer.

Trade Union and Labour Relations Act 1974: 1974-date

The experiment of the Industrial Relations Act 1971 cannot simply be dismissed as a failure for the Act contained much of value, notably the unfair dismissals provisions, and introduced new concepts which have been subsequently developed, particularly the right to recognition and the right of union members not to be discriminated against by their employers.

Although section 1 of the 1974 Act simply states "The Industrial Relations Act 1971 is hereby repealed," such a statement gives a wholly misleading impression for not only does Schedule 1 to the Act contain 22 pages of provisions re-enacted from the 1971 Act, but also it would be wrong to suggest that the law could return to the simple abstentionist policy that prevailed before 1970. The fact is that labour law is becoming very much more complicated and interventionist in nature.

The 1974 Act engaged in the dogmatic rejection of much that had gone before (including such technical issues as rejecting incorporation of trade

---

[24] The introduction of the rule that a collective agreement was deemed to be legally binding (s. 34) was of no consequence whatever as almost all parties exempted their agreements from the rule.

[25] I.R.A. 1971 s. 37.

[26] I.R.A. 1971 s. 45.

[27] Kidner, "The Individual and the Collective Interest in Trade Union Law" (1976) 5 I.L.J. 90.

[28] *Post Office* v. *U.P.W.* [1974] I.C.R. 378.

[29] The issue is presented in *Howle* v. *G.E.C. Power Engineering* [1973] I.R.L.R. 339; *E.S.U.* v. *C.E.G.B.* [1972] I.C.R. 418; *C.E.G.B.* v. *Coleman* [1973] I.C.R. 230; *Rees* v. *N.C.B.* [1973] I.R.L.R. 450.

[30] E.P.A. 1975 s. 11.

unions and reviving the trade union functions of the Registrar of Friendly Societies),[31] but the principal effect of the Act is to restore the immunity from legal action for strikers and expand, by enlarging the definition of trade dispute, the area in which such activity is legitimate.

Employment Protection Act 1975

While much concerned with the individual rights of employees, the Employment Protection Act 1975 considerably enhanced the collective rights of trade unions and exemplified the new interventionist approach. In particular the Act placed on a statutory basis the Advisory Conciliation and Arbitration Service and the Central Arbitration Committee, and established a procedure for the acquisition of recognition by trade unions. In addition unions were accorded a number of negotiating privileges, such as the right to information and the right to be consulted over redundancies, and individual trade unionists given further protection against discrimination. The statute acted as a kind of statutory collective bargain enabling many unions to bring conditions of employment up to the minimum standard.

Trade Union and Labour Relations (Amendment) Act 1976

When the 1974 Act was passed the debate centred on two highly contentious issues. The first was the closed shop and the second the rights of a member against his union. As the result of the then government's very small working majority the Conservative opposition were able to make a number of changes in the Bill: the object of the 1976 Act was to repeal these amendments.

The principal issue concerning the closed shop was the effect it would have on the freedom of the press and a new section was inserted to deal with that issue on the basis of a code of practice. As to membership rights, section 5 of the 1974 Act which provided rights for the union member against arbitrary or unreasonable discrimination was repealed, as was section 6 which provided that a union's rule book must include rules on certain subjects. Finally the immunity from the law of tort contained in section 13 of the 1974 Act was completely restored.

The last decade has thus seen considerable changes in trade union law, but while the law has generally become more sophisticated, two issues remain unresolved between the principal protaginists. The first is the degree of immunity from legal action that should be allowed to a trade union and the second is the degree of protection that should be afforded to a member within his union. These topics have been argued over for most of this century and will no doubt continue to be controversial.

---

[31] The functions are now performed by the Certification Officer (who keeps not a register but a list).

Part One

THE INTERNAL STRUCTURE OF A UNION

CHAPTER 2

THE LEGAL DEFINITION AND STATUS OF A UNION

THE DEFINITION OF "TRADE UNION"

THE real importance of trade unions lies in their social, economic and industrial power, but they are nevertheless legal entities subject to the law and as such are given a number of legal duties and privileges. Accordingly, a statutory definition of trade unions is necessary and this is done by reference both to its membership and to its purposes.

Thus a trade union is defined[1] as, an "organisation (whether permanent or temporary) which ... consists wholly or mainly of workers of one or more descriptions and is an organisation whose principal purposes include the regulation of relations between workers of that description or those descriptions and employers or employers' associations."[2]

It should be noted that in addition to this definition, further distinctions are taken between a listed and an un-listed union, and between one that is "independent" and one that is not. However, neither registration nor independence is necessary to gain trade union status and no legal act of creation is required; and indeed many informal organisations may in fact be trade unions (or employers' associations) without realising it. But that does not mean that the status is unimportant, nor that the definition does not give rise to difficulty, and a number of points need to be made on it.

"Workers"

The association must consist wholly or mainly of "workers," a word which is defined at length by section 30 of the 1974 Act.[3] The definition covers an individual who either works, normally works or seeks to work under either a contract of employment, or any other contract by which he agrees to perform personally any service for another,[4] and also includes government servants. Exceptions are made for those in the armed forces or the police service.

It should be noted that "worker" is wider than "employee" since it includes the self-employed. Thus in *Broadbent* v. *Crisp*[5] the applicant was a pools

---

[1] T.U.L.R.A. 1974, s. 28 (1): the definition applies for the purposes of that and a number of other Acts, *e.g.* Trade Union Act 1913, Wages Councils Act 1959, Employment Protection Act 1975 and Road Haulage Wages Act 1938, but note that for the purposes of the Social Security Act 1975 a trade union means "an association of employed earners" (Sched. 20).

[2] The remainder of s. 28 (1) includes federal unions and federations of unions within the definition. For example in *Camellia Tanker Ltd.* v. *International Transport Workers Federation* [1976] I.C.R. 274 the I.T.F. was held to be a trade union.

[3] For the purposes of the meaning of "trade dispute" only, the definition of worker is extended by s. 29 (6) of the 1974 Act to include any worker, whether the person he is in dispute with is his own employer or not.

[4] Except where the work is done for a professional client.

[5] [1974] I.C.R. 248 (N.I.R.C.).

collector, and the court held that although he was not an employee he was a worker, on the grounds that he was under the control of the defendant and under a *personal* obligation to perform his contract. On the other hand in *Writers Guild* v. *BBC*[6] the court held that authors were not "workers," since their contracts contained no *personal* obligation to do work. The court found that even in the case of commissioned work there was no obligation to complete the script, and decided that the transactions were contracts of sale. It is therefore clear that the obligation to "perform personally" is of fundamental importance in distinguishing between employment contracts and commercial contracts.

One problem is the extent of the exclusion from the meaning of "worker" of those who are not employed under a contract of employment but who do work or provide a service for a person who is a "professional client."[7] It is suggested that although many groups lay claim to "professional" status the phrase should be interpreted very narrowly. The statute itself[8] excludes from the professional exemption those who provide general medical, dental or opthalmic services under the National Health Service Act 1977, so that such people are still "workers."

"Organisation"

The association must be an "organisation whether permanent or temporary." This phrase leaves vague the degree of stability an association must possess before it can be a trade union, and it is suggested that it must possess some degree of formality.[9] It would not include a casual grouping, although it may cover an "ad hoc" association limited to a specific and temporary purpose if there is a degree of formality in its institution. Thus in *Frost* v. *Clarke & Smith*[10] it was held that a joint works committee representing *all* the workers could not be an "organisation" because it had no name and no rules, but on the other hand in *Midland Cold Storage* v. *Turner*[11] Donaldson J. held that a committee of shop stewards from various unions was an "organisation," since it at least had a name and a fairly basic structure in so far as it had a chairman and a secretary. There seems to be no reason to suggest that there need be a written constitution, although that might be more usual if the necessary degree of formality is taking place. What is clear is that it is not the likely life span of the association that matters, but the degree to which the association is based on conscious decisions about its structure.

The principal purposes

The principal purposes of the organisation must *include* the regulation of relations between workers and employers. As the reading of any rule book will readily indicate, trade unions have a large number of expressed objects, ranging from the provision of provident society benefits to the abolition of capitalism.[12] The Act does not, however, state that *the* principal purpose must

---

[6] [1974] I.C.R. 234 (N.I.R.C.).

[7] In *Carter* v. *The Law Society* [1973] I.C.R. 113, (N.I.R.C.) the Law Society was held not to be an organisation of workers within the definition in the Industrial Relations Act 1971. But an organisation of *employed* solicitors would be a trade union.

[8] s. 30 (2) of the 1974 Act as amended by the National Health Service Act 1977.

[9] *Weeks* v. *National Amalgamated Stevedores & Dockers Union* (1940) 67 Ll.L.Rep. 282.

[10] [1973] I.R.L.R. 216 (N.I.R.C.).

[11] [1972] I.C.R. 230 (N.I.R.C.).

[12] See for example rule 3 of the National Union of Mineworkers.

be the regulation of relations with employers, but only that that must be one of the principal purposes.

This aspect of the definition was used to prevent an organisation being regarded as a trade union[13] in two cases involving the Midland Cold Storage Co.[14] The issue arose out of the activities of the Joint Shop Stewards' Committee of the Workers of the Port of London and the question arose whether action could be taken against the committee on the grounds that it was an "organisation of workers" within the Industrial Relations Act 1971, or only against the members individually. Both Donaldson J. in the National Industrial Relations Court and Megarry J. in the Chancery Division took the view that the committee was immune. In *Midland Cold Storage* v. *Turner*[15] it was said that the committee was an "organisation," and that it consisted of "workers," (for the shop stewards were members), but that its objects did not include the necessary "principal purposes." Donaldson J. said[16] that:

> "its most apparent activity seems to consist of recommending the taking or abandonment of industrial action.... Thereafter it does not seem to enter into negotiations with the employers but leaves this task to the established union machinery.... No body whose principal objects included [the regulation of relations between workers and employers] could fail at least to seek recognition from employers."[17]

It may be that such a severe test is necessary in order to exclude not only organisations with limited objectives but also those organisations that have only an advisory function, for it may be that "regulation" requires that the organisation must wish to affect relations between the employer and the workforce.

The Definition of "Employers' Association"

Section 28 (2) of the Trade Union and Labour Relations Act 1974 also defines an employers' association. The terms used are similar to those in the definition of trade union, for the association must be an organisation which "consists wholly or mainly of employers or individual proprietors ... and is an organisation whose principal purposes include the regulation of relations between employers ... and workers or trade unions."[18] Section 30 of the Act defines an "employer" as a person "for whom one or more workers work, or have worked, or normally work or seek to work,"[19] and an "individual proprietor" is one who is the owner of an undertaking.

The problem of applying the definition arose in the interesting case of *Greig* v. *Insole*[20] where two cricketing authorities, the International Cricket Conference (I.C.C.) and the Test and County Cricket Board (T.C.C.B.) claimed immunity from legal action[21] on the grounds that they were unincorporated

---

[13] And thus prevent it being sued under the Industrial Relations Act 1971. The situation would now be different.

[14] *Midland Cold Storage* v. *Turner* [1972] I.C.R. 230 (N.I.R.C.); *Midland Cold Storage* v. *Steer* [1972] Ch. 630.

[15] *Ibid.*

[16] [1972] I.C.R. 230 at 248.

[17] A similar point was made by Megarry J. in *Midland Cold Storage* v. *Steer* [1972] Ch. 630.

[18] The remainder of the subsection again deals with federal or federated organisations of employers.

[19] This definition was inserted in T.U.L.R.A. 1974, s. 30 by the Employment Protection Act 1975 Sched. 16, Pt. III.

[20] [1978] 1 W.L.R. 302 at 356–362.

[21] Under T.U.L.R.A. 1974, s. 14 (1).

employers' associations. As to the I.C.C. it was held that on the proper interpretation of the rules the members of the organisation were not the governing bodies of cricket in the relevant countries, but rather the countries themselves,[22] and as the countries were not employers so the association was not an "employers' association."

As to the T.C.C.B. the difficulty was that the rules appeared to make the organisation responsible not to its constituent members as a whole but rather to a third body, the Cricket Council. Slade J. stated that:

> "if an organisation is to fall within the statutory definition, it must be *responsible to the members who have associated themselves for such purposes.* If, under the terms of its constitution, it were made responsible for the exercise of its functions not to its members but to other persons, this would in my judgment be quite inconsistent with its being an 'employers' association'." This was so because if their purpose in associating was to regulate industrial relations they would have been expected to have kept control of their affairs.

The Legal Status of Trade Associations

Trade Unions

In legal theory[23] a trade union[24] is an unincorporated association, although in fact it obtains most of the benefits and bears most of the burdens of incorporation. This situation exists because while the Industrial Relations Act 1971 (following the advice of the Donovan Commission)[25] conferred corporate status on trade unions, the Trade Union and Labour Relations Act 1974 reverted to the unincorporated status, but retained many of the advantages of incorporation. In legal theory therefore, the trade union, being an unincorporated association, does not exist as a separate entity from its members. It is rather an association of individuals bound together by contract with the rule book providing the terms of the contract.[26]

It used to be said that the members of a union are also bound together by the fact that they share property interests in the union funds and that certain rights might flow from this. It is suggested, however, that this is no longer so as the beneficial interest in the assets is vested in the union itself,[27] and therefore any property interest of the members in the assets must derive from the contract of association, that is from the rule book.

It has, however, been argued that the effect of statutory intervention, and especially the provision of a system for registration, has in the past conferred on trade unions a quasi-corporate status, thus giving them a legal status different from social and other clubs with which they have in reality little in common. In *Taff Vale Rly.* v. *Amalgamated Society of Railway Servants*[28] the House of Lords permitted a trade union to be sued in its own name, but in doing so did not (with the exception of Lord Brampton) see itself as conferring on the union any new juristic status by way of quasi-corporate personality.

---

[22] A somewhat strict interpretation, but made so because to decide otherwise would have provided immunity from action: [1978] 1 W.L.R. 302 at 359.

[23] For a socio-legal view of associations see Selznick, *Law Society and Industrial Justice (1969).*

[24] Except a special register body, for which see below.

[25] Royal Commission on Trade Unions and Employers' Associations, Cmnd. 3623 para. 785.

[26] For a discussion of the role of the rule book as the constitution of the union see Chap. 3.

[27] T.U.L.R.A. 1974 s. 2 (1) (*a*). On this question generally, see Chafee, "The internal affairs of associations not for profit" (1930) 43 Harv.L.R. 993.

[28] [1901] A.C. 426.

However, in *Bonsor* v. *Musician's Union*[29] some members of the House of Lords, in deciding that a member of a registered union could sue for damages, went further, but the overall result on the question of the precise juridical nature of the union was inconclusive. Thus Lord Morton supported the view[30] that "a registered trade union is recognised by the law as a body distinct from the individuals who from time to time compose it," and Lord Parker called it "an entity, a body, a near corporation." But Lords MacDermott and Somervell would not have given it any special status.[31]

It seems likely that the matter has now been put beyond doubt by section 2 (1) of the 1974 Act which states that a trade union shall not be *or be treated as if* it were a body corporate. But even so difficulties could arise in some areas, for example, in relation to legacies given to a trade union, for it might be asked whether a union can be the recipient of a gift otherwise than as an unincorporated association. If it can only be treated as an unincorporated association it may in certain circumstances fall foul of the rule against inalienability, thus rendering the gift void.[32] It would be difficult to argue that as unions now have so many of the trappings of corporate status they should be regarded as quasi-corporate legal entities separate from their members, for Parliament has provided unions with special powers and liabilities and these should be regarded as the exclusive limit of their capacity, and therefore unions must in legal theory remain unincorporated legal associations. However, one can only regard it as unfortunate that corporate status was ever abandoned at all.

In accordance with the policy of non-corporate status for trade unions section 2 (2) of the Trade Union and Labour Relations Act 1974 renders void any registration under the Companies Act 1948, and section 2 (3) does the same in relation to registration under the Friendly Societies Act 1974 or under the Industrial and Provident Societies Act 1965.

However, section 2 also confers on trade unions many of the benefits of incorporation:

(1) *Contracts*

It is declared that a trade union shall be capable of making contracts in its own name.

(2) *Property*

All property belonging to the trade union shall be vested in trustees in trust for the union. For some years unincorporated associations have created great difficulties for the law of trusts[33] due to the fact that their membership often fluctuates. Such problems are avoided for trade unions by saying that the

---

[29] [1956] A.C. 104. The case turned on the argument, which originated in *Kelly* v. *NATSOPA* (1915) 31 T.L.R. 632, that although an injunction could be issued damages could not be awarded since, assuming a trade union to be merely a collection of individuals, the union officials who were in breach of the rules were as much the plaintiff's agents as agents of other members, and that the plaintiff should not be able to seek damages against himself. *Kelly's* case was overruled on this point by *Bonsor*.

[30] Put forward by Uthwatt J. in *N.U.G.M.W.* v. *Gillian* [1946] K.B. 81.

[31] Lord Keith thought that a union whilst being a statutory entity was at the same time an unincorporated association.

[32] *Re Amos* [1891] 3 Ch. 159; *Leahy* v. *Att.-Gen. for N.S.W.* [1959] A.C. 457, but see also *Re Lipinski* [1977] 1 All E.R. 33 which could validate such a gift.

[33] The difficulties revolve around such abstruse topics as the rule against perpetuities and s. 53 (1) (*c*) of the Law of Property Act 1925.

trustees hold the property not on trust for the members but on trust for the *union*. If this is so, in whom or in what is the beneficial interest vested? At common law the union, not being a body corporate has no separate existence, but one has to say that it has a statutory existence for the purpose of holding the beneficial interest in the assets, and that beneficial interest can only be dealt with according to the terms of the rule book.[34]

(3) *Suing and being sued*

A union is capable of suing or being sued in its own name. In addition the section declares that proceedings may be brought against a trade union for a criminal offence and that any judgment is enforceable against the property of the union as if it were a body corporate. This subsection is procedural, and it should be noted that as a matter of substantive law trade unions enjoy considerable but not complete[35] immunity from civil and criminal action.

It is also provided[36] that a trade union may carry on insurance business without the authorisation of the Secretary of State if that business is limited to the provision of provident benefits or strike benefits.

Immunity from actions in tort

While trade unions may be sued in their own name in respect of a wide variety of civil actions, they enjoy considerable immunity from actions in tort. This general immunity belongs to the union itself and does not apply to the individual who commits the tortious act, for the immunity is seen as a desire to protect union funds rather than as a desire to render certain acts lawful. But the law does provide protection for individuals against liability for particular torts likely to be committed in the course of strike action.[37]

In relation to the general immunity of a union, section 14 of the Trade Union and Labour Relations Act 1974 states that "no action in tort shall lie in respect of any act alleged to have been done by or on behalf of a trade union," either against the union in its own name or by way of a representative action.[38] It is clear from *Vacher* v. *London Society of Compositors*[39] that this immunity is not confined to trade dispute cases but is general in its application, for in that case the House of Lords refused to entertain an action for libel against a trade union.[40] The effect of the immunity is not to render potential torts lawful, but rather to accept that the act is illegal, and prevent if from being actionable; but the immunity cannot be extended to joint tortfeasors, so that, for example, in *Eglantine Inn* v. *Smith*[41] a printer who had printed a defamatory handbill for a trade union was successfully sued.

[34] See *Cotter* v. *N.U.S.* [1929] 2 Ch. 103 for comments on an analogous provision in the Trade Union Act, s. 8 (now repealed).

[35] See T.U.L.R.A. 1974, s. 14.

[36] Insurance Companies Act 1974, s. 2 (1) (*e*); Companies Act 1967, s. 60 (*e*). But a union may not insure money to be paid on the death of a child under the age of 10: Industrial Assurance and Friendly Societies Act 1948, s. 6.

[37] T.U.L.R.A. 1974, s. 13. See Chap. 12.

[38] The section also applies to unincorporated employers' associations; and also to special register bodies and incorporated employers' associations in so far as the act is done in connection with the regulation of relations between employers and workers.

[39] [1913] A.C. 107.

[40] Lord MacNaughten said "If I had not had the pleasure of listening to a most ingenious argument on the part of the appellants, I should not have thought the question arguable either here or anywhere else in the world." [1913] A.C. 107 at 117.

[41] [1948] N.I. 29. See also *London Motor Cab Proprietors* v. *Twentieth Century Press* (1917) 34 T.L.R. 68 per Younger J.

Until recently there was considerable controversy over the question whether a union was exposed to an action for an injunction or a declaration to prevent future action, but the 1974 Act now includes within the immunity acts "alleged to be threatened or to be intended to be done," thus putting the matter beyond doubt.[42]

But one question that does remain is what is to be included within the phrase "action in tort" so as to qualify for the immunity. The issue arose in *Gouriet* v. *Union of Post Office Workers*[43] where the plaintiff wanted action to be taken against the defendants for threatening to disrupt postal communications between Britain and South Africa. He first applied to the Attorney-General for his consent to act as plaintiff in a relator action for an injunction against the union on the ground that it was committing offences under the Post Office Act 1953, and when this consent was refused he began actions before the courts in order to persuade the court to review the Attorney-General's action and also to allow him to bring an action himself against the union. The House of Lords held that the courts had no power to review the discretionary power of the Attorney-General to refuse his consent and that the plaintiff could not himself seek an injunction or a declaration to enforce *public* rights, but could only do so (subject to the immunity in section 14 (1)), if the action of the defendant would affect his private rights, and therefore as the plaintiff had only sued as a member of the general public rather than a private individual who had suffered damage, the action failed.

As to the immunity from action in tort it is clear that where the case is brought to protect public rights the action is not an "action in tort,"[44] (but the consent of the Attorney-General is necessary). The difficulty arises on the question whether the courts could be prevented by section 14 (1) from issuing an injunction to prevent a criminal act where the act threatened is both criminal and an interference with a private right (in which case the consent of the Attorney-General is not necessary).[45] In the House of Lords only Lord Edmund Davies considered the point[46] and he said that if the Post Office Act 1969 had given the plaintiff a private right to the facilities of the Post Office (which it did not), an action to enforce such a right would be an action in tort just as much as that brought in *Ashby* v. *White*[47] for interference with the right to vote.

The position, therefore, appears to be that a union may be exposed to private prosecution for acts actually committed; so far as threatened breaches of the criminal law are concerned a person who is suing as a member of the public may do so only with the leave of the Attorney-General; but if the invasion of the private rights can be classified as a tort it is suggested that the action is prevented by the immunity conferred by section 14 (1) and the plaintiff must rely upon his rights as a member of the public and so seek the consent of the Attorney-General.

---

[42] The cases in favour of the immunity applying were *Ware and De Freville Ltd.* v. *Motor Trade Association* [1921] 3 K.B. 40, *per* Scrutton and Atkin L.JJ. and *Torquay Hotels Ltd.* v. *Cousins* [1969] 2 Ch. 106. On the other side were *Boulting* v. *ACTAT* [1963] 2 Q.B. 643 and *Bowles* v. *Lindley* [1965] 1 Lloyds Rep. 207.

[43] [1977] Q.B. 729 (C.A.); [1978] A.C. 435 (H.L.). See (1978) 41 M.L.R. 64–67 (R.C. Simpson).

[44] [1977] Q.B. 729 at 737 *per* Lord Denning M.R.

[45] *Springhead Spinning Co.* v. *Riley* (1868) L.R. 6 Eq. 551; *Gouriet* v. *U.P.W.* [1978] A.C. 435 at 506.

[46] [1978] A.C. 435 at 517.

[47] (1703) 2 Ld. Raym. 938; 92 E.R. 126.

Exceptions to the immunity

Despite the general wording of section 14 (1) of the 1974 Act, section 14 (2) does expose unions to actions in tort in two cases so long as the act is not done in contemplation or furtherance of a trade dispute.[48] First a union may be liable in negligence, nuisance or for breach of any other duty where the act results in personal injury. Thus employees of trade unions who drive vehicles can render the union liable if due to their negligence there is an accident causing personal injury.

The second limitation is, however, more difficult to construe, for that exposes a union to an action for any breach of duty imposed upon it "in connection with the ownership, occupation, possession, control or use of property (whether real or personal . . .)." Clearly, therefore, it is possible to sue a union in nuisance or occupiers liability, for these are duties imposed in connection with the control of property. But difficulties may arise for example in relation to property damage caused by the negligent acts of the union's officers or employees. The subsection is limited to cases where the duty is imposed on the union itself in connection with the control and use of property so that the question becomes whether the union owes a direct duty to the owner of the thing injured. Thus, if, for example, an employee of the union negligently drives the union's car causing property damage it could be argued that if traditional tests of vicarious liability are adopted then the duty is imposed on the driver and not on the union; but if the "master's tort" theory is adopted it could be argued that the union owes the duty directly.[49] If the latter view prevailed (and it has not so far in the law of tort) then the union could be made liable by virtue of section 14 (2) (*b*) of the 1974 Act so long as it could be said that the duty arises in connection with the use of property.

Again, although the section does not clearly say so it must be presumed that the duty is imposed in connection with the use of property *belonging to the union.* The point can be illustrated by asking whether a trade union can be sued for trespass on the land of another by one of its employees. It could be argued that there is a breach of duty in connection with the ownership of property but only if "property" can be said to include the plaintiff's property and is not limited to the unions property. The implication must, however, surely be that the union's property is intended.[50]

A further problem concerns the meaning of "in connection with" property. It had been suggested that under previous legislation an action for libel might have been maintained against a union, on the ground that such an action would "touch and concern" property of the union within the Trade Disputes Act 1906, s. 4 (2). This argument was, however, rejected in *Shinwell* v. *National Seamen's and Firemen's Union*[51] and impliedly by *Langden-Smith* v. *Griffiths*,[52] and it is suggested that it is even less likely to succeed under the new wording since the duty not to be defamatory is not imposed "in connec-

---

[48] "Trade dispute" is defined by T.U.L.R.A. 1974 s. 29 (1). See Chap. 11.

[49] See generally Winfield & Jolowicz, *Tort* (10th ed.), pp. 540–543.

[50] The legislation which this section replaces (Trade Union Act 1871, s. 9 as applied by Trade Disputes Act 1906, s. 4 (2)) was limited to the union's property.

[51] [1913] 2 S.L.T. 83, but see *Linaker* v. *Pilcher* (1900) 17 T.L.R. 256, where the union newspaper (which was registered in the name of the trustees and not the union) defamed someone. The trustees were liable and could be indemnified out of union funds.

[52] [1951] 1 K.B. 295. See also *Drennan* v. *Beechey* [1935] N.I. 74.

tion with" the use of the paper on which the libel is written.[53]

In conclusion, the question inevitably arises whether provisions of such potential complexity and breadth are necessary. The Donovan Commission[54] said that having tried to envisage the position of trade unions if their immunity were confined to torts committed in contemplation or furtherance of a trade dispute they were not convinced that they would be seriously prejudiced, and therefore recommended such a limitation. Certainly it is not a privilege enjoyed by any other organisation and while it is essential to maintain the exemption in cases involving trade dispute,[55] one wonders why a union should also be protected in relation to its ordinary activities. The need to protect the union funds may be significant, but is there any real suggestion that trade unions would be in jeopardy of bankruptcy if they were exposed to non-trade dispute liability?

Restraint of trade

At common law a trade union was regarded as being in restraint of trade[56] and thus the contract contained in the rule book was unenforceable. That impediment was partially relieved by the Trade Union Act 1871, and is now totally relieved by the Trade Union and Labour Relations Act 1974 s. 2 (5).

First the section states that the purposes of a trade union shall not be unlawful only by reason of being in restraint of trade so as to (a) make any member of the union liable to criminal proceedings for conspiracy, or (b) to make any agreement (including the rule book), or trust void or voidable.[57]

Secondly, no *rule* of a trade union shall be regarded as being in restraint of trade so as to render it unenforceable. It is thought that this second principle is necessary in order to nullify the effect of *Edwards* v. *Society of Graphical and Allied Trades*,[58] where Sachs L.J. thought a rule which permitted capricious and despotic action was not proper to the purposes of the union and thus would be void as being in restraint of trade.[59] It has, however, been suggested by Slade J. in *Greig* v. *Insole*[60] that the phrase "restraint of trade" in this section should be narrowly construed in view of the degree of immunity given to trade unions, and that, therefore, it may not be sufficient to prevent a rule

---

[53] The view of Darling J. in *Richards* v. *Bartram* (1908) 25 T.L.R. 180 that such an action is possible is wrong in the light of the view of the House of Lords decision in *Vacher* v. *London Society of Compositors* [1913] A.C. 107 that s. 4 of the Trade Disputes Act was not confined to trade dispute cases. *Vacher* was itself a libel case and although the point arising from the phrase "touching or concerning" was not argued, the House thought that s. 4 (2) could not assist the plaintiffs.

[54] Cmnd. 3623 (1968) paras. 902–911.

[55] Although one may wonder if it is necessary to protect them from liability for personal injury caused in furtherance of a trade dispute, at least if the rules of responsibility for the acts of members and officials are clarified so as to make a union liable only for the acts of its employees and not for its members.

[56] *Rigby* v. *Connol* (1880) 14 Ch. D. 482; *Russell* v. *Amalgamated Society of Carpenters and Joiners* [1912] A.C. 421. See Kahn-Freund, "The illegality of a trade union" (1944) 7 M.L.R. 192.

[57] The same rule applies to a special register body, but only in so far as its purposes relate to the regulation of relations between employers and workers.

[58] [1971] Ch. 365. For, the "right to work" principle enunciated in this case see Chap. 5.

[59] The attempt by T.U.L.R.A. 1974, s. 5 (5) to preserve the effect of this case in certain circumstances was nullified by the repeal of that subsection by the Trade Union and Labour Relations Amendment Act 1976.

[60] [1978] 1 W.L.R. 302 at 363.

being void as being against public policy. However, no final view was expressed on the point.

Employers' associations

An employers' association may be either incorporated or unincorporated. If it is unincorporated it obtains the same quasi-corporate benefits in relation to contracts, property and suability as a trade union.[61] In addition section 3 (4) of the 1974 Act states that the provision of the Companies Acts[62] that associations of over twenty members formed for certain purposes must be incorporated shall not apply to an employers' association.

In relation to the restraint of trade rule section 5 makes a distinction between the two types of association. An unincorporated association is completely protected both so far as its purposes and its rules are concerned, but if the association is a body corporate it is protected only in so far as the rule or the purposes relate to the regulation of relations between employers and workers or trade unions.

Special register bodies

The special register was set up by the Industrial Relations Act 1971, s. 84, to cater for those organisations which, while active in the industrial relations field, did not necessarily have as their principal objects the regulation of relations between employers and employees. Those bodies included the British Medical Association, the Royal College of Nursing and the United Commercial Travellers Association. Such organisations must already have been incorporated either under the Companies Act or by charter or letters patent.

"Special register body" is defined by section 30 of the 1974 Act as one which was on the special register on September 15, 1974. It should be noted that not all such organisations are necessarily within the definition of trade union, but those that are may retain their corporate status as well as the benefits of being a trade union. The list of special register bodies is closed.

Listing of Trade Unions

One of the functions of the Certification Officer,[63] who took over the functions of the Registrar of Friendly Societies in relation to trade unions, is to maintain a list of trade unions and employers' associations in accordance with section 8 of the Trade Unions and Labour Relations Act 1974. Listing is voluntary and the Certification Officer is obliged to enter the name if he is satisfied that the association is within the definition of trade union or employers' association as the case may be, so long as the form prescribed by section 8 (4) has been complied with and the association has sent the requisite documents. These are a copy of the rules,[64] a list of the officers, the address of head office and the union's name. The only other qualification is that registration may be refused under section 8 (5) if the proposed name is the same as

---

[61] T.U.L.R.A. 1974, s. 3.

[62] Companies Act 1948, s. 434.

[63] The title is not a happy one. The function was exercised by the Registrar of Friendly Societies until 1971, and then by the Registrar of Trade Unions until 1974, when he briefly became the Registrar of Friendly Societies again until the arrival of the Certification Officer in 1975.

[64] A copy of the rule book of each listed union is kept by the Certification Officer and may be inspected by anyone for a reasonable charge, which in 1978 was 50p.

that of an organisation already on the list,[65] or so nearly resembling it as to be likely to deceive the public. The Certification Officer may by virtue of section 8 (6) remove a name from the list if it appears to him that an organisation is not a trade union or employers' association after giving due notice to the association concerned. In addition he must remove a name if he is requested to do so by the organisation concerned or he is satisfied that the association has ceased to exist. An appeal against refusal to register, or against removal from the register may be made to the Employment Appeal Tribunal.

The advantages of being a trade union in general apply whether the union is on the list or not. Thus section 9 of the Trade Union and Labour Relations Act 1974 specifically states that any reference[66] in any statute to a registered[67] trade union shall apply to any union within the meaning of the 1974 Act whether listed or not.[68] However, despite the desire to render the difference between listed and unlisted unions as insignificant as possible, some important points of distinction remain. First only listed unions are entitled to tax relief on income and chargeable gains applied for the purpose of provident benefits.[69] Secondly, as will be seen, only listed trade unions may apply for a certificate of independence, which confers very considerable advantages over a non-independent union.[70] Since the advantages of registration far outweigh the disadvantages, the large majority of trade unions are on the list. Thus on December 31, 1977 the number of listed unions was 485[71] of which about 200 were affiliated to the TUC. The number of unlisted unions is not known, but 47 such associations made annual returns to the Certification Officer, and in his report for 1977 he stated that he knew of some 70 such unions.

In relation, however, to employers' associations, as there is no incentive to register,[72] there can be much less certainty about the numbers. On December 31, 1977, there were 196 associations on the list, and 245 unlisted associations had made returns for the previous year.

"Independent" Trade Unions

The law accords to "independent" trade unions a number of advantages which are of considerable significance. In particular the most important[73] are that

[65] See *R.* v. *Registrar of Friendly Societies* (1872) 7 L.R.Q.B. 741.

[66] Except in the Income and Corporation Taxes Act 1970 for which see below. T.U.L.R.A. 1974, s. 9 (3).

[67] That is registered as a trade union or as an employers' association under the Trade Union Acts 1871 to 1964 or under the Industrial Relations Act 1971. The provision also covers organisations of workers or employers under the Industrial Relations Act 1971.

[68] For example the reference in the Libraries Offences Act 1898, s. 3 which permits summary conviction for misbehaviour in a reading room belonging to a registered trade union.

[69] See the Income and Corporation Taxes Act 1970, s. 338 as applied to listed trade unions by the Finance Act 1974, s. 28. See further Chap. 6.

[70] The other advantages are that entry on the list is evidence that the organisation is in fact a trade union or an employers' association: (T.U.L.R.A. 1974, s. 8 (9) as amended by E.P.A. 1975 Sched. 16.) T.U.L.R.A. 1974, s. 4 permits the discharge of a trustee and the appointment of a new trustee by a written document rather than by deed, for the purposes of the Trustee Act 1925, ss. 39 and 40.

[71] Report of the Certification Officer for 1977.

[72] Only the minor items noted in n. 70 apply to employers' associations, and even then the point concerning trustees only applies to listed unincorporated employers' associations.

[73] The other advantages are: the right to be consulted over redundancies (E.P.A. 1975, s. 99); the right of an individual to join the union (E.P.C.A. 1978, s. 23); to take part in trade union activities (E.P.C.A. 1978, s. 23), and to take time off for trade union duties (E.P.C.A. 1978, s. 27) or activities (E.P.C.A. 1978, s. 28); the right to present a claim for extension of terms and conditions (E.P.A. 1975 Sched. 11).

only an independent union may enter into a union membership agreement,[74] start in motion the machinery for recognition of the union by the employer,[75] or be entitled to information for the purposes of collective bargaining.[76] The reason for distinguishing between independent and other unions over these matters was the fear, which was largely justified by experience under the Industrial Relations Act, that employers may prevent recruitment and organisation by "real" or "bona fide" unions by entering into special arrangements with unions which they can influence. In particular when the Industrial Relations Act 1971 was in force an employer might recognise a staff association which had a close relationship with that employer, making it difficult for any other union to gain a bargaining position in the firm.[77] The purpose of the distinction is thus to promote genuine trade unionism and to prevent "cosy" relationships between employers and unions stultifying the aspirations of "real" trade unions.

While the Certification Officer has said that the phrase "bona fide trade union" is an "unhelpfully vague concept in the context of the statutory definition,"[78] it nevertheless conveys to a number of people the general purpose of the provision. In particular the unions affiliated to the TUC hoped that certificates of independence would be largely confined to themselves, but this has proved not to be the case,[79] principally because there is no requirement that an independent union must be "effective" and while some non-affiliated unions are thought not to be effective they may still be independent. The principal area of contention concerns staff associations, which have been described as "organisations usually of white collar workers, not affiliated to the TUC where membership is confined to the employees of a single employer....[80] The Certification Officer has noted a wide variety amongst these associations, but whilst a number have been given certificates of independence, such bodies in fact account for nearly all the refusals. Whereas an organisation cannot be ruled out simply because it is a staff association, the fact that it is a single company association and has been set up with the assistance of the employer clearly imposes a burden on the organisation to establish its independence.

The decision as to whether the trade union is independent is made by the Certification Officer by virtue of the powers contained in the Employment Protection Act 1975, s. 8, which also lays down the procedures connected with granting the certificate. In particular an application may only be made by a listed trade union and the Certification Officer may make such inquiries as he thinks fit and shall take into account any relevant information submitted to

---

[74] T.U.L.R.A. 1974, s. 30 (1). Any union may enter into a closed shop agreement but only in the case of a "union membership agreement" with an independent union will an employer be protected from an action for unfair dismissal by a person who has been dismissed for non membership of the closed shop union. E.P.C.A. 1978, s. 58 (3).

[75] *i.e.* apply to the Advisory Conciliation and Arbitration Service under the Employment Protection Act 1975, s. 11.

[76] E.P.A. 1975 s. 17.

[77] For example the National Union of Bank Employees had various difficulties of this kind: see *NUBE* v. *Anglia Building Soc.* [1973] I.C.R. 597; *NUBE* v. *Coventry Economic Building Soc.* [1973] I.R.L.R. 30; *NUBE* v. *Barclays Bank Int'l.* [1973] I.C.R. 167 (N.I.R.C.).

[78] Report of the Certification Officer 1976, p. 12.

[79] Between Feb. 1, 1976 and April 10, 1978, certificates were issued to 280 trade unions, of which 157 were affiliated to the T.U.C. or constituents of affiliated unions (32 applications were refused and 4 were withdrawn). H.C. Debs. vol. 949 *col. 71* (May 2, 1978).

[80] Report of the Certification Officer 1976, p. 12.

him by any person. It is thus open to a rival union to oppose the grant of a certificate[81] and indeed a number of T.U.C. affiliated unions have opposed grants to staff associations. Such objectors, however, have no right to appeal against the grant of a certificate which they have opposed,[82] although the union which is the subject of the application does have the right to appeal to the Employment Appeal Tribunal if the certificate is refused. The grant or refusal of the certificate is conclusive evidence of the status of the union, and indeed if any question arises in any proceedings about the status of a union which has never applied for a certificate, the tribunal may refer the matter to the Certification Officer for a decision.[83]

The meaning of "independent"

An independent trade union is defined by the Trade Union and Labour Relations Act 1974, s. 30, as a trade union which:

"(a) is not under the domination or control of an employer or a group of employers or of one or more employers' associations; and

(b) is not liable to interference by an employer or any such group or association (arising out of the provision of financial or material support or by any other means whatsoever) tending towards such control."[84]

In relation to the first limb (whether the union is under the domination or control of employer), the Employment Appeal Tribunal in *Association of H.S.D. Employees* v. *Certification Officer*[85] has said that it may require both a subjective and an objective approach, and that certain criteria adopted by the Certification Officer were appropriate to this test. However, in relation to the second limb the Court said that it involves a forward look and perhaps a degree of speculation which requires an essentially subjective approach in which the criteria adopted under the first limb may not always be appropriate. Whereas the first limb may be a relatively easy test to apply, the second is rather more difficult, but it is also the one on which all refusals of certificates have been based. While it is clear that in such a speculative venture as trying to test for "tendency to control" each case must to a large extent rest on its own special facts, the criteria approved for use in the first limb,[86] may also be a guide as to what one is looking for under the second limb.

The criteria adopted by the Certification Officer are set out in his report for 1976 and repeated in a slightly different form in *Blue Circle Staff Association* v. *Certification Officer.*[87] These are:

(1) *History*

Where an association has only been founded recently with the help of the

[81] It is now the regular practice of the Certification Officer to hold discussions with objecting unions after detailed investigations are complete. In addition if an applicant union comments on the objections, these comments are passed to the objecting union which may make further representations. Report of the Certification Officer for 1977.

[82] *G.M.W.U.* v. *Certification Officer* [1977] I.C.R. 183.

[83] E.P.A. 1975, s. 8 (12). There were two such cases in 1977.

[84] The test is to be applied strictly and the burden is on the applicant union: *Association of H.S.D. Employees* v. *Certification Officer* [1978] I.C.R. 21 *per* Kilner Brown J.

[85] [1978] I.C.R. 21.

[86] *Blue Circle Staff Assoc.* v. *Certification Officer* [1977] I.C.R. 224.

[87] [1977] I.C.R. 224; the order and titles adopted in the report of the Certification Officer will be used here.

employer this may be an argument against independence unless cogent evidence can be presented of a rapid change in character. Thus in *Blue Circle Staff Association* v. *Certification Officer*[88] it was thought relevant that the association had been formed only six years earlier with complete employer control, and although the rules had been changed the degree of effective control had not. On the other hand in *Association of H.S.D. (Hatfield) Employees* v. *Certification Officer,*[89] although the association started with the active encouragement of the employer, special facts (in this case nationalisation) had permitted it to mature to independence more rapidly than might have been expected.

(2) *Membership base*
It is thought that a single company union is more vulnerable to employer interference than a broadly based union and that therefore it is less likely to be independent. Such a view is of course of greatest significance to staff associations,[90] but it should be remembered that it is not a bar to the granting of a certificate, for a number of single company unions have successfully proved their independence.

(3) *Organisation and structure*
The point here relates to the extent that members can play a full part in union affairs and also the extent of involvement of the employer. For example in *Blue Circle*[91] only employees of three or more years standing were eligible for election as area committee representatives, and the employer could insist on the withdrawal of the credentials of a union representative on the Joint Central Council. In addition the employer always nominated the chairman of the council.

(4) *Finance*
A union which receives a direct subsidy from an employer would not be eligible for a certificate, and the Certification Officer has said that a union with weak finances and inadequate reserves is more vulnerable to employer interference. However, it must be noted that there is no requirement that a union be "effective" as well as independent and a low bank balance cannot of itself be grounds for refusing a certificate, unless it can be shown that this would open up the possibility of interference by the employer. In *Squibb U.K. Staff Association* v. *Certification Officer*[92] Forbes J. at first instance said:

> "it might have been expected that one of the more important criteria in deciding independence would be effectiveness in representing the interest of its members. An independent trade union might well be thought to be one which was capable of standing on its own feet in the sense that it was not only independent of the employer but able, if need be, to adopt as uncompromising an attitude towards an employer as might be necessary in any given circumstances. If that were so then its ability to dispose of sufficient funds to support its members in, for instance, the taking of

---

[88] [1977] I.C.R. 224.
[89] [1978] I.C.R. 21.
[90] Of the 17 certificates refused in 1976, 14 related to staff associations: but of those that applied just over half were granted certificates.
[91] [1977] I.C.R. 224.
[92] [1978] I.C.R. 115 (E.A.T.); *The Times*, October 11, 1978 (C.A.).

industrial action or in litigation of one kind or another might well be decisive."

The importance of this principle is, however, limited by the view taken by the Court of Appeal in the same case that the possibility of interference by the employer is sufficient grounds for denying a certificate; although "possibility of interference" and "effectiveness" are different principles.

(5) *Employer provided facilities*

Although it is of course good industrial relations practice to provide facilities for trade unions, too great a reliance on such provision may require justification. The question is not one of finance but rather of whether the union could cope if the facilities were withdrawn.[93]

(6) *Collective bargaining record*

A "robust attitude in negotiation" is regarded as an item on the credit side. There are, however, dangers, for as the court said in the *Blue Circle Case*[94] "we deplore any suggestion that a record of bad relations is an index of freedom from domination or control." In addition of course there is the danger of turning such a factor into a test of effectiveness.

In returning to the statutory definition it should be noted that those criteria while decisive under the first limb need to be used with care in relation to the second limb because of the speculative nature of the test to be applied. One further point about the second limb is the meaning of the phrase "liable to interference tending towards control." In *Squibb U.K. Staff Association* v. *Certification Officer*[95] it had been argued that this meant whether interference was likely and would be effective if it took place, but the Court of Appeal preferred the simpler and more straightforward meaning of "exposed to, vulnerable to or at risk of interference". Thus it is only necessary to establish the possibility of interference rather than the likelihood of interference.

[93] This issue was raised successfully in *Squibb U.K. Staff Association* v. *Certification Officer*, *The Times*, October 11, 1978.

[94] [1977] I.C.R. 224.

[95] *The Times*, October 11, 1978.

CHAPTER 3

THE RULE BOOK

THE legal basis for the constitution of a trade union, and the extent to which the courts will intervene in internal trade union affairs to enforce that constitution, remains a matter of considerable controversy.[1] The problem of unincorporated associations was first brought to prominence by the litigious[2] Colonel Dawkins in *Dawkins* v. *Antrobus*,[3] and it was felt that, at least as far as social clubs are concerned, the law should be wary of intervening too readily. This view is no doubt based on the fact that social clubs are voluntary associations and that members should be left to sort out their own difficulties. In theory trade unions are also voluntary associations and yet in recent years the law has shown a greater willingness to intervene. This is so because whatever the legal structure might be, the judges feel that there is a significant difference between social clubs and trade unions, since the latter are able to wield considerable power over an individual and even deprive him of his livelihood.[4]

Even if this is so,[5] the essential question is still whether unions should be treated as purely voluntary organisations; and to some extent this depends on whether they can claim their function to be the effective pursuit of an objective agreed on by the members to the exclusion of the wishes of any dissenting minority.[6] If the effective pursuit of that objective requires a degree of solidarity and loyalty from all members'[7], then the union can claim that it should only accept into membership a person who agrees with its objective, and thus can demand to be regarded as a voluntary organisation and as such to be left to its own devices. On the other hand, from the point of view of the employee union membership may in some cases be compulsory if he is to keep

---

[1] The classic, and still best, article on this subject is Chafee, "The internal affairs of associations not for profit" (1930) 43 Harv. L.R. 993.

[2] He appears to have been involved in a number of other suits: *Dawkins* v. *Lord Rokeby* (1866) 4 F. & F. 806, 176 E.R. 800; *Dawkins* v. *Lord Paulet* (1869) L.R. 5 Q.B. 94; *Dawkins* v. *Lord Rokeby* (1875) L.R. 7 H.L. 744; *Dawkins* v. *Prince Edward of Saxe Weimar* (1876) 1 Q.B.D. 499.

[3] (1881) 17 Ch. D. 615. The plaintiff had been expelled from the Traveller's Club for writing a pamphlet critical of Lieutenant-General Stephenson, another member of the club, and sending a copy of it through the post in a wrapper on which was printed "Dishonourable Conduct of Colonel (now Lieutenant-General) Stephenson." The court declined to interfere.

[4] *Lee* v. *Showmen's Guild* [1952] 2 Q.B. 329 at 343 *per* Denning L.J.; *Mitchell* v. *International Association of Machinists* 196 Cal. App. 2d 796 (1961) where it was said that unions are not like "Republicans, Democrats, Elks and church groups."

[5] And it may also be true in some cases of purely social clubs. Membership of a London club or a local golf club may be of considerable economic significance.

[6] This raises the issue of democracy in a union which is fully discussed in Wellington, *Labour and the legal process*, Chap. 5. See also Kahn-Freund, *Labour and the Law* (2nd ed.), pp. 209–224.

[7] It is this factor which renders a union a corporatist institution.

his job, or at least may be socially or economically desirable, and to this extent a union is not voluntary. If it is not a voluntary organisation it is claimed that it must be responsible to the law for the standard of its internal behaviour towards its members.[8]

In discussing the problem of intervention, Chafee[9] identified four policies relevant to the issue. The first, the "Strangle-hold Policy" is one in favour of intervention, being based on the serious consequences that expulsion from an organisation may have; the second, the "Dismal Swamp Policy" is against interference, on the grounds that courts are often unable to understand and cope with the sub-culture expressed by obscure rules and doctrines; the third, the "Hot Potato Policy" deals with the problem that intervention may do more harm that good in the friction it causes, and the fourth, the "Living Tree Policy" is based on the autonomy necessary for an institution to be able to change to suit its needs.

Application of these ideas to the problem cannot lead one directly to a solution, but it suggested that if on the one hand the need is to protect the interest of the individual, it is, on the other hand, equally necessary to concede the collective interest of the trade union. Whether legal machinery is capable of doing this is not clear, but the balancing of the two interests may be a necessary feature of any reform.[10]

The remainder of this chapter will deal with constitutional issues of trade union government. The problems of individuals in relation to their union, including control of union disciplinary procedure, will be dealt with in Chapter 5.

THE BASIS OF JUDICIAL INTERVENTION

There are three ways in which a court could in theory intervene on behalf of an individual in the internal affairs of a trade union. The first is on the basis of his property interest in the union, the second is based on his contract of membership and the third on his status as a member.

In the early days the courts only recognised the protection of the property interest of an individual as a justification for interference,[11] but today this ground is of very little significance. Indeed it may not be possible at all, for it is difficult to see what property interest a member has in his union's assests. In most cases the property of an unincorporated association is held by trustees on trust for the members, but section 2(1)(*b*) of the Trade Union and Labour Relations Act 1974 makes it clear that so far as trade unions are concerned the trustees hold the property on trust for the *union*, and therefore any interest the members may have is given to them by the contract of membership (*i.e.* the rule book). It could perhaps be argued that the members have a property interest in so far as they will obtain the property if the union is dissolved, but even this is not clear, for on dissolution the property will be dealt with according to the relevant rule, if any, which could order the funds to be transferred to somebody other than the members.

---

[8] See Kahn-Freund, *Labour and the Law* (2nd ed.) p. 181.

[9] Chafee, "The internal affairs of associations not for profit" (1930) 43 Harv. L.R. 993 esp. pp. 1020–1029.

[10] See generally Kahn-Freund, "Trade Unions, the Law and Society" (1970) 33 M.L.R. 241 and Kidner, "The Individual and the Collective Interest in Trade Union Law" (1976) 5 I.L.J. 90.

[11] "I have no doublt whatever that the foundation of the jurisdiction is the right of property vested in the member of the society . . ." *per* Jessel M.R. in *Rigby* v. *Connol* (1880) 14 Ch. D. 482 at 487. See also *Yorkshire Miners Assoc.* v. *Howden* [1905] A.C. 256.

The contract of membership

In practice the only ground on which a court will intervene today is to enforce the contract of membership as contained in the rule book. It is assumed that a person, on joining, makes a contract which may be enforced in the courts, although there is some theoretical doubt as to the other party to the contract. It is normally assumed that such a contract is made with all the other members of the association,[12] but it has been suggested that since the union is in itself capable of making contracts and is of a sufficiently corporate nature the contract of membership is with the union itself. This seems the common sense view.

In the past the enforcement of the rule book has been a matter of considerable complexity owing to the vagueness of the partial relief from the common law doctrine of restraint of trade offered by section 4 of the Trade Union Act 1871. Fortunately this problem no longer exists and no term of the rule book is invalid because of restraint of trade.[13] But it cannot be said that all rules will be enforced, for there are cases where the courts have made it clear that they can refuse to enforce rules on grounds of public policy.[14]

The contract fiction was devised at a time when not only was there a desire (derived from the social club cases) to remain aloof, but also, in cases where intervention was necessary, a desire to appear neutral. But once the desire to abstain had waned and the court intervened on grounds of natural justice or held rules to be unenforceable due to public policy, some new legal theory was needed. It was this that led Lord Denning in *Bonsor* v. *Musicians Union*[15] to declare that union rules are "more like by-laws than a contract," and in *Lee* v. *Showmen's Guild*[16] he specifically rejected the idea that the social club cases were relevant to trade union affairs, abandoning the freedom of contract fiction and voluntarism, for intervention on the basis of "the right to work."[17]

The object of Lord Denning's statements in these cases was to be able to declare a rule void if it was unreasonable.

> "In these circumstances the rules are not only to be construed against the makers of them, but, further, if it should be found that any of the rules are contrary to natural justice, or what comes to the same thing, contrary to what is fair and reasonable, the court would hold them to be invalid."[18]

These views were, however, severely attacked in *Faramus* v. *Film Artistes Associations* both in the Court of Appeal,[19] and in the House of Lords,[20] and in *British Equity* v. *Goring*[21] Lord Denning has himself recanted saying, "I went

---

[12] On the basis of *The Satanita (Clarke* v. *Dunraven* [1895] P. 248, where an entrant in a yacht race was held bound by the rules of the race on the basis of a contract made with all other entrants.

[13] T.U.L.R.A. 1974, s. 2 (5). It is assumed that this section effectively reverses the view of Sachs L.J. in *Edwards* v. *SOGAT* [1971] Ch. 354 at 382 that certain rules may be void as being in restraint of trade.

[14] *e.g.* rules attempting to oust the jurisdiction of the court; rules requiring the exhaustion of internal remedies in disciplinary cases and rules which conflict with natural justice. These are dealt with in Chapter 5.

[15] [1954] Ch. 479. Reversed on appeal: [1956] A.C. 104.

[16] [1952] 2 Q.B. 329 at 343.

[17] This was further developed in *Edwards* v. *SOGAT* [1971] Ch. 354, which is dealt with in Chapter 5.

[18] *Bonsor* v. *Musician's Union* [1954] Ch. 479 at 487.

[19] [1963] 2 Q.B. 527 at 554 *per* Diplock L.J.

[20] [1964] A.C. 925 at 943 *per* Lord Evershed.

[21] [1977] I.C.R. 393 at 396 (C.A.); [1978] I.C.R. 791 (H.L.).

too far when I suggested that the court might hold a rule to be invalid if it was unreasonable."

The fictitious nature of the contract of association has led some to suggest that the proper ground for intervention is the relationship of the individual to the union, *i.e.* status not contract.[22] Only in *Abbott* v. *Sullivan*[23] has a view of this kind been judicially expressed, when in a dissenting judgment Lord Denning referred to a claim by a corn porter that a disciplinary committee were acting *ultra vires* as being "a claim in an uncharted area on the borderland of contract and tort."

However attractive such a view might appear and however desirable it is to establish a proper basis for the common law's intervention in a union's internal affairs, the fiction of the contract of association as the basis for the court's powers is still adhered to, except in cases where it will not suffice, as for example in cases of natural justice and "public policy."[24]

One small issue raised by the adoption of the contract principle, is whether those who are "infants" in law (*i.e.* under the age of 18) may be union members. By *implication* persons of 16 and over may be members since paragraph 31 of schedule 1 to the Trade Union and Labour Relations Act allows "members of trade unions who are not under sixteen" to nominate recipients of provident benefits on their death, but nowhere is it explicitly stated that such persons may be members.[25] In *Doyle* v. *White City Stadium*[26] the issue of the effect of the common law of contract was raised in relation to whether Doyle was, as an infant, bound by a rule of the British Boxing Board of Control. The court held that the contract being analogous to a contract of employment was one that could bind an infant and that this contract taken as a whole was for Doyle's benefit and he was bound by it; but this decision may have been influenced by the fact that he could not box at all unless he signed that contract.[27] It has been suggested[28] that a contract of membership binds an infant if there is a closed shop and membership is necessary to retain the job, but such a distinction may be fortunate.[29]

Judicial interpretation of the rules

Enforcement of the rule book as a contract clearly gives rise to problems of interpretation for it is not only the constitution of the union but it is also a guide to the members. In addition, although there has been a concerted effort in recent years to improve the contents of rule books, there still exists a number of badly drafted rules which are either ambiguous or quite meaning-

[22] Chafee, "The internal affairs of associations not for profit" (1930) 43 Har. L.R. 993, esp. 1007–1010. Selznick, *Law, Society and Industrial Justice* (1969), p. 273.

[23] [1952] 1 K.B. 189 at 206.

[24] Such as the reluctance of the courts to enforce a rule requiring exhaustion of internal remedies in a disciplinary procedure. *Leigh* v. *N.U.R.* [1970] Ch. 326.

[25] The Trade Union Act Amendment Act 1876, s. 9 did explicitly state this, but that was repealed by the Industrial Relations Act 1971.

[26] [1935] 1 K.B. 110.

[27] The view taken of *Doyle's* case by Danckwerts L.J. in *Chaplin* v. *Frewin* [1966] Ch. 71 at 95 was that the "contract was held binding on the infant because it enabled him to earn his living and so was for his benefit."

[28] Grunfeld, *Modern Trade Union Law* (1966), p. 16.

[29] Some strength is lent to such a distinction by the views of Slesser and Romer L.JJ. in *Doyle's* case. Slesser L.J. was "not prepared to say that there is any general principle that all agreements for the benefit of an infant will necessarily bind him."

less. In this situation it would be a mistake to adopt a strict code of interpretation, to treat rule books as statutes, for the rules were not designed for that kind of analysis and it is therefore necessary to adopt a liberal approach. This point was made by Lord Wilberforce in *Heaton's Transport* v. *T.G.W.U.*[30]

> "Trade union rule books are not drafted by parliamentary draftsmen. Courts of law must resist the temptation to construe them as if they were; for that is not how they would be understood by the members who are the parties to the agreement of which the terms, or some of them, are set out in the rule book, or how they would be, and in fact were, understood by the experienced members of the court."

It is perhaps a not uncommon irony that this was said in a case decided against the interests of the union, but it does indicate a willingness to be less strict[31] in interpreting rule books and to take account of social realities.

However, it is not entirely clear if Lord Wilberforce believes that the interpretation of the rule should be guided only by the understanding of trade unionists as to what the rule was designed for and likely to mean, but presumably the proper method is for evidence of custom and practice to be submitted by experienced members of the union and then assessed by the judge. In *Brown* v. *A.U.E.W.*[32] the question arose whether a rule covered a particular procedure and in order to elucidate the rule one side put in an affidavit from the president of the union stating his experience as to past practice. Walton J. said:

> "Where you have such a rule . . . which is amply wide enough on its face to permit the bringing of the kind of appeal which is here in question, and you find that as a matter of practice over many years . . . such kinds of appeals have consistently been brought, then it appears to me that the court is fully justified in reading the rule as comprehending that kind of appeal. *Per contra*, in another union with precisely the same rule, it might be established as a matter of fact that such types of appeal had never been entertained; and this fact would then be at least the beginning of a tenable argument that precisely the same wording should be read in a precisely opposite sense *quoad* this kind of appeal."

That there is an element of choice in the interpretation of an equivocal rule is obvious, and if a non-literal method of interpretation is adopted the question is what criteria are to be applied. Is it the judge's understanding of the purpose of the rule as seen by the members or is it to be the judge's view of what is fair? Lord Denning in *British Equity* v. *Goring*[33] while admitting that he had abandoned the view that rules could be held void for unreasonableness, went on to say:

> "When it comes to construing the rules, it seems to me that they should be construed, not literally according to the very letter, but according to the spirit, the purpose, the intendment, which lies behind them, so as to

---

[30] [1972] I.C.R. 308 at 393.

[31] A more liberal scheme of interpretation might cure the kind of problem that arose in *O'Neill* v. *T.G.W.U.* [1934] I.R. 633 where it was held that the union had no power to dismiss an honorary official despite a rule which empowered them to "suspend and/or dismiss any officer." As this was found in the section headed "Dismissal of all Paid and Permanent Officers" it was held inapplicable.

[32] [1976] I.C.R. 147.

[33] [1977] I.C.R. 393 at 396. See also *per* Roskill L.J. at 401. Reversed in part on appeal: [1978] I.C.R. 791 (H.L.).

ensure—especially in a matter affecting the constitution—that they should be interpreted fairly, having regard to the many interests which its constitutional code is designed to serve . . . The courts when called upon to construe the rules, must do all they can to construe them reasonably, fairly, broadly and liberally in the interests of all concerned in the association."[34]

Going beyond the rule book

A further point is that the terms of the constitution are not to be found in the rule book alone, so it should not be regarded as an exclusive constitutional code. The point arose in *Heaton's Transport Ltd.* v. *T.G.W.U.*[35] where the problem was to define the scope of authority of shop stewards. Unfortunately, the rule book was silent on the question but the House decided that custom and practice may act to supplement the rules. Lord Wilberforce said:[36]

> "It is not to be assumed, as in the case of a commercial contract which has been reduced into writing, that all the terms of the agreement are to be found in the rule book alone: particularly as respects the discretion conferred by the members upon committees or officials of the union as to the way in which they may act on the union's behalf."

It is suggested, however, that this statement must be used with great caution for it has always been understood that a union official only has the powers provided for in the rules, and if there is no rule there is no power. Lord Wilberforce is not of course denying that principle, for he is only saying that custom and practice may amount to a "rule" and thus provide that authority. But, if this is to be so, it is suggested in the evidence that the custom and practice have the same status as the rule needs, to be strong.[37] However the importance of the judgement lies in the fact that the rule book can no longer be regarded as an exclusive constitutional code,[38] but can be supplemented by evidence of custom and practice and of the common understanding of the members. For example, in *Weakley* v. *A.U.E.W.*[39] although, the rule book stated that the members of a committee alone may vote, it was argued that by custom the chairman had a casting vote. As this had been done only three times in 40 years it was held that there was insufficient evidence for the practice to be enforced by the court.

Restrictions on the Contents of the Rule Book

While unions are free to frame their rule books as they wish, there are a

---

[34] Would Lord Denning have approved *Maclelland* v. *N.U.J.* [1975] I.C.R. 116 where a rule that "A chapel may instruct all its members to attend a mandatory meeting. . . ." was construed as meaning that a person having once "attended" need not remain, *i.e.* that he need only "sign on?" Is that the usual meaning of "attend?" If the descision had been otherwise there would have been the problem of the conflict between the contract in the rule book and the contract of employment: *British Homophone* v. *Kunz* (1935) 152 L.T. 859.

[35] [1972] I.C.R. 308.

[36] *Ibid.* at 393.

[37] See Hepple, "Union Responsibility for Shop Stewards" (1972) 1 I.L.J. 197.

[38] See Kahn-Freund, "The Industrial Relations Act 1971—Some retrospective reflections" (1974) 3 I.L.J. 186 esp. pp. 186–191.

[39] *The Times,* June 12, 1975. See also *Chappell* v. *Times Newspapers Ltd.* [1975] 1 W.L.R. 482, where it was argued that the union had authority to give strike notice on behalf of its members.

number of statutory constraints which, while not strictly compulsory rules, need to be taken into account.[40]

The right to resign

It is now provided[41] that each contract of membership contains an implied right to resign on giving reasonable notice and complying with any reasonable conditions. The problem of "reasonable notice" and "reasonable conditions" was discussed in *Ashford* v. *A.S.T.M.S.*,[42] where it was stated that a summary resignation could not be reasonable notice, nor on the facts of the case was seven days notice reasonable.[43] The court laid down no rule but did suggest that where subscriptions were collected monthly, at least one month's notice should be given.[44]

As to "reasonable conditions" the court agreed that resignation could be postponed until the completion of any disciplinary action that was pending, and that a member can be required to make up any arrears. On the matter of reasons for the resignation it was felt that whereas the union could ask for reasons to be given, it could not make it a condition of resignation for the right exists whether the reason is good or bad.

Control of disciplinary procedure

The courts impose a number of restrictions upon unions as to how they should conduct their disciplinary procedure. These provisions, including the rules of natural justice, and the provisions avoiding rules which oust the jurisdiction, together with the reluctance of the courts to uphold rules requiring a member to exhaust his internal remedies before appealing to the courts will be dealt with in Chapter 5.

Discrimination

Rules about discrimination affect unions in a number of ways, including having an effect on discriminatory rules. It is convenient to deal with the subject here.

1. *Racial discrimination*

That trade union members have on some occasions in the past engaged in racial discrimination cannot be denied[45] but in recent years there have been substantial attempts to improve the situation.[46] In relation to membership the Race Relations Act 1976, section 11(2), makes it unlawful[47] for a trade union

[40] There were a number of compulsory rules required by the Trade Union Acts 1871 and 1876, and by the Industrial Relations Act 1971. These have now been repealed, as have ss. 5 & 6 of the Trade Union and Labour Relations Act, 1974.

[41] T.U.L.R.A. 1974, s. 7 as substituted by T.U.L.R. (Amendment) 1976. The remedy is now a contractual one for breach of the rules.

[42] [1973] I.C.R. 296, decided under the comparable provisions of the Industrial Relations Act 1971.

[43] See also *Badger* v. *T.G.W.U.* [1974] I.R.L.R. 57. The N.I.R.C. did not reverse the view of a tribunal that reasonable notice would be 13 weeks. (The tribunal had based their view on the arrears rule.)

[44] Presumably in the case of a union which collects an annual subscription a member may resign on reasonable notice of less than a year but cannot recover any part of his subscription.

[45] Hepple, *Race, jobs and the law in Britain* (2nd ed.), p. 53.

[46] Macdonald, *Race Relations, the new law*, p. 5. See also his Chap. 5 for a thorough description of trade unions and the Race Relations Act 1976.

[47] The remedy is application to an industrial tribunal under s. 54.

to discriminate against a person either by the terms of its rule book or by refusing to accept his application for membership. As to rule books it is clear that any provision which indirectly discriminates is also unlawful and also that the rule book can be the subject of a complaint to the Commission for Racial Equality, even if no particular applicant has been discriminated against. So far as actual applicants for membership are concerned, only the union itself, its employees and agents can be made liable and the question has arisen whether shop stewards or other recruiting stewards can be made liable. Not only does it appear that section 11 was deliberately made narrower than the equivalent provision of the 1968 Act (which it replaced), so as to exclude such liability, but also it seems unlikely that the stewards would have authority to discriminate to bring them within the principle of *Heaton's Transport* v. *T.G.W.U.*[48] in order to render the union liable.

Section 11 of the Race Relations Act 1976 also prohibits discrimination against a person who has become a member either in relation to his access to any benefits, or by the terms of his membership or by subjecting him to any other detriment. It is thought that access to union posts comes within this provision.[49]

It should be noted that there will be no liability where a union makes special training facilities available for a racial group in order to assist them to hold union office, or to make provision to encourage them to hold office.[50]

2. *Sex Discrimination*

The provisions of section 12 of the Sex Discrimination Act 1975 are very similar,[51] *mutatis mutandis*, to those of the Race Relations Act 1976 and similar comments apply.[52] There is, however, an additional provision[53] which legalises provisions which reserve positions on elected bodies for the members of one sex in cases where the organisation believes that a minimum number of members of that sex is necessary, but the provision does not permit discrimination in arrangements for voting or membership of the organisation.

3. *Workers from the EEC*

Article 8 of EEC regulation 1612/68[54] states:

> "A worker who is a national of a Member State and who is employed in the territory of another Member State shall enjoy equality of treatment as regards membership of trade unions and the exercise of rights attaching thereto, including the right to vote and to be eligible for the administration and management posts of a trade union. . . ."

It therefore appears that a rule which restricts membership to British subjects will be regarded as discriminatory, at least so far as EEC nationals are concerned. An interesting question is whether qualifications of residence or

---

[48] [1972] I.C.R. 285. See Macdonald, *Race Relations, the new law*, Chap. 5.

[49] Macdonald, *op.cit.* where the view is put that this is so because union office is either a benefit within s. 11 (3) (*a*), or denial of access is a detriment within s. 11 (3) (*c*).

[50] Race Relations Act 1976, s. 38 (3), but this is subject to the conditions in s. 38 (4) that there are none or a very small proportion of that racial group holding office.

[51] Thus a provision limiting membership to one sex would be unlawful, and may be so even if membership was limited to those who have a "Genuine occupational qualification."

[52] But it should be noted that the Sex Discrimination Act does not apply to any provision made in relation to the death or retirement from work of a member, s. 12 (4).

[53] s. 49.

[54] As amended by 312/76.

membership attached to eligibility for posts would be discriminatory. It is thought that rules about residence would be, but not rules about length of membership.

4. *Non-contributors to the political fund*
The Trade Union Act 1913 lays down provisions to prevent discrimination against those who have contracted out of the political fund. This subject is dealt with in Chapter 17.

Administrative provisions
Every trade union must, in its rules, make provision for the appointment and removal of auditors. This matter is dealt with in Chapter 6.

The Rule Book and Trade Union Government

The most important function of the rule book is to act as the constitution of the union and to determine the rights and duties of the members, and as the rule book has contractual effect a member may sue for breach of it.[55] It is important to note that there is no control by government over the internal affairs of the association[56] and no-one but a member may intervene, so that breaches of the constitution may go uncorrected if no member is willing to take action.

The rule book deals with two kinds of issue. One type covers the enforcement by an individual of his "public" rights in the sense of his rights that the union shall be governed according to the rule book,[57] and the other deals with his private rights, that is that the union officials shall treat him correctly in his capacity as an individual member.[58]

Private rights
A simple example of protection of "private" rights is *Monksfield* v. *NATSOPA*[59] where the union rule imposed a restriction on the freedom of members of the London branch to seek work in Fleet Street, unless they had "more than 20 years membership of the Society." The plaintiff had been a member of the union for 20 years but not of that branch. The union interpreted the phrase as applying to membership of the branch rather than of the union as a whole, but the court thought otherwise, and held that the plaintiff was not subject to the restriction.

The duties owed by the officials to members depend on the rule book and no duty will be imposed without a rule,[60] and where a duty does exist the

[55] Other obligations may be imported by custom and practice: *Heaton's Transport* v. *T.G.W.U.* [1972] I.C.R. 308. It is assumed that such custom is sufficient to found an action, but it is not clear on what basis. Perhaps it could be regarded as an "implied rule," although fictions should be avoided where possible.

[56] The Industrial Relations Act 1971 did permit the Registrar of Trade Unions to intervene of his own accord if there were serious or persistant breaches of the rules (s. 83).These powers were wisely never used.

[57] This also includes the matter of elections which is dealt with separately in the next chapter.

[58] This also includes the subject of control of disciplinary procedure which is dealt with in Chap. 5.

[59] [1972] I.C.R. 469. The case would now be heard in the High Court and the difficulty over the award of damages would not now arise.

[60] See *Oddy* v. *T.S.S.A.* [1973] I.C.R. 524 where the plaintiff, who wished the union to take up with his employer his complaints about his lack of promotion, based himself on one of the objects clauses in the rule book that one function of the union was "to improve the conditions and protect the interests of its members." The court held that this was not a "rule" which would found an action.

content of that duty is determined by the rule book. Thus in two cases[61] which raised the question of the duty owed by union officials to members in relation to the provision of legal assistance, the matter was decided by reference to the content of the rules authorising such assistance.

Public rights

Of greater importance is the protection of a member's "public" right that the union shall be governed constitutionally and according to the rule book. One problem is that the rules themselves may not be adequate for the task of providing a constitutional structure for the union and may be sufficiently vague to allow excessive choice to the executive or the possibility of "creative interpretation" to the courts. Many organisations operate in defiance of their rules, but trade unions are particularly likely to be sued by the dissatisfied member, and it is, therefore, necessary that the rule books should be adequate for their purpose.

Most rule books lay down not only specific rules about the powers of officials but also rules about the functions of various bodies and the proper procedure for taking action. So far as procedure is concerned the terms of the rule book must be followed if the act is to be valid. Thus in *Bisset* v. *National Society of Operative House and Ship Painters and Decorators*[62] it was held that a rule intended to prevent communists from being officers of the union was invalid, as when it was passed the incorrect procedure had been followed. Indeed rules about changing rules have always given rise to difficulty, as a rule change is often the point of crisis in a dispute between different factions within the union.[63]

As to the constitutional function of various bodies the courts will interfere to see that one body does not usurp the function of another. Thus in *Hodgson* v. *NALGO*[64] the annual conference of the union passed a resolution against the entry of Britain into the EEC. Later the National Executive Council, after referring the matter to a sub-committee, adopted the view that it was in favour of entry and instructed the NALGO delegates to the T.U.C. to vote accordingly. The plaintiffs succeeded in their action for a declaration that the instructions were invalid and for injunctions requiring the council to instruct the delegates to vote against. This was so because the council had arrogated to itself a power to determine the policy of the union instead of merely managing its affairs, and also acted in a manner inconsistent with the general policy of the union as laid down by conference. In other words the National Executive Council had acted in breach of the constitution as laid down by the rule book.

Most union rule books have constitutional structures similar to that of NALGO and it has been thought that an analogy could be drawn between the roles of the conference of delegates and Parliament, and between the executive council and the Cabinet. But this idea has been disturbed by the views of the Court of Appeal in *N.U.M. (Kent)* v. *Gormley*,[65] for Lord Denning said that the parliamentary analogy was completely false and he thought that the union executive was if anything more like a board of directors and the

---

[61] *Buckley* v. *N.U.G.M.W.* [1967] 3 All E.R. 767; *Cross* v. *BISAKTA* [1968] 1 All E.R. 250.

[62] *The Times*, April 20 and 21, 1951.

[63] See for example *Dawson* v. *E.T.U. The Times*, May 3, 1962; *Chapple* v. *E.T.U. The Times*, March 30, 1965; *British Actors' Equity Association* v. *Goring* [1978] I.C.R. 791 (H.L.).

[64] [1972] 1 All E.R. 15.

[65] *The Times*, Oct. 20, 1977.

conference like the shareholders.[66] The case is of some importance because it takes a new view of the legal structure of a trade union. The case arose because the executive proposed to hold a ballot to decide whether a national incentive scheme was acceptable to the members. Unfortunately, the union's Conference had defeated a resolution demanding a national scheme and it was alleged by the plaintiffs[67] that the executive had no power under the rules to call a ballot,[68] and that they were acting contrary to a rule which, while giving the executive power to administer the affairs of the union, also stated that "it shall not at any time act contrary to, or in defiance of, any resolution of conference." Geoffrey Lane L.J. rejected the idea that there was a distinction between administering business and performing acts of policy[69] and Lord Denning said that the real authority between conferences lay with the executive and that its authority to hold a ballot was not limited.[70]

The decision appears to involve the view that the executive has considerably more authority than was previously thought and that the power of the conference to circumscribe the activities of the executive is limited. It is unfortunate that the judgments contain expressions of opinion preferring the decision of the executive and suggesting that a conference may not be truly representative of the membership.[71] The issue was not what was desirable[72] but what was lawful, and it is suggested that in this case the court forced a new constitutional structure upon the union without justification, causing considerable doubt about the power of delegate conferences to control their executives.

It is not only the action for breach of the rules that can be used to control trade union government, for of course unions are subject to the usual constraints of the law. Thus the tort of conspiracy was used in the E.T.U. case.[73] In the more recent case of *Drake* v. *Morgan*[74] a member of the N.U.J. sought an injunction to prevent his union paying the fines of those who had been convicted of unlawful picketing. It was held that the resolution authorising the payment of the fines should if possible be construed as not covering illegal acts, and that as the resolution referred to past acts of picketing it was retrospective only and was not illegal.[75] It was, however, clearly stated that any resolution to indemnify members against future crimes would clearly be contrary to public policy and void, as might a series of retrospective resolutions which create an expectation that members would be indemnified.

---

[66] But he did not think even that to be a very close analogy, for unions are a "kind of thing on their own."

[67] The Kent area of the N.U.M.

[68] The rules gave power to the executive to call a ballot in specific instances and it was argued unsuccessfully, that impliedly there was no power to call a ballot at other times. But see Roskill L.J. in the Court of Appeal in *British Equity* v. *Goring* [1977] I.C.R. 393 at 401: "I approach with caution any argument which involves reading or writing into a contract between an association and its members provisions which would perfectly easily have been but were not expressed had anyone thought about the problem."

[69] *The Times,* Oct. 20, 1977.

[70] *Ibid.*

[71] In the event the membership rejected the proposed scheme.

[72] This case was followed in *N.U.M. (Yorkshire)* v. *Gormley, The Times*, Dec. 21, 1977, which is easier to justify as there the proposal was to set up local rather than national incentive schemes, on which no opinion had been expressed by conference.

[73] *Byrne and Chapple* v. *Foulkes and Haxell*, unreported. But see Rolph, *All those in favour?*, and *The Times*, June 29, July 4, 1961, Feb. 1, 1962.

[74] [1978] I.C.R. 56 (H.L.).

[75] Citing *R.* v. *Porter* [1910] 1 K.B. 369.

Amendment of the Rules

Methods of altering the rules vary a great deal, but in all cases an attempt is made to strike a balance between the need to protect the rules against an ill-considered change and the need for flexibility. Most require a special majority or a special meeting, or both, and some unions only permit the change to be made by a rules conference which meets infrequently.[76] Others submit the matter to a ballot of members,[77] and at least one informs the members of the proposed change which is deemed to be passed if no objection is taken within 28 days.[78] The inflexibility of some rules has sometimes led to the need for statute to empower the union to make a change despite its rules. Thus section 3 of the Trade Unions (Amalgamations, etc.) Act 1964 permits an executive committee to make such changes as are necessary to permit the transfer of engagements by another union.[79]

It is clear that there is no power to alter the rules unless such a power is provided by the rule book itself,[80] nor can there be an implied change in the rules by conduct,[81] although the view in *Heaton's Transport Ltd.* v. *T.G.W.U.*[82] that the rule book is not the only source of authority may be thought to affect these well established propositions.[83]

Even if there is a power to alter the rules there is a slight doubt as to the efficacy of this power in two areas. First, does such a power entitle the union to alter its *objects* as distinct from its rules? The matter was discussed briefly in *Osborne* v. *A.S.R.S.*[84] where it was said that there was considerable force in the argument that the power to alter the rules does not confer a power to alter the objects, but no concluded opinion was expressed. The second doubt is whether a union may change its rules so as to exclude existing members from the associaition. In *Tierney* v. *Derbyshire Miners and Bye-Product Workers Union*[85] the association in 1916 decided to limit its members to those who worked in Derbyshire and later purported to exclude the plaintiff because he worked in a pit that had shafts in both Derbyshire and Yorkshire. Sargant J. *obiter*, thought that such a rule change was possible at least "where there were no pecuniary benefits of a permanent character attached to membership."[86]

---

76 *e.g.* T.G.W.U. rules 5 and 26. The conference meets every six years, but the executive may call a special conference in an emergency.

77 E.E.T.P.U. r. 31, as one alternative.

78 N.U.F.L.A.T. r. 138. If there is an objection the matter is put to a ballot.

79 Other examples (of a temporary nature) are The Industrial Relations Act 1971 s. 94, T.U.L.R.A. 1974, s. 20. Both provisions are now spent.

80 *Dawkins* v. *Antrobus* (1881) 17 Ch. D. 615 at 620. *Re Tobacco Trade Benevolent Association* [1958] 3 All E.R. 353.

81 *Faramus* v. *Film Artistes Association* [1963] 2 Q.B. 527 at 552 *per* Diplock L.J.; *Martin* v. *Scottish T.G.W.U.* [1952] S.C. (H.L.) 1 at 7 *per* Lord Normand.

82 [1972] I.C.R. 308.

83 Perhaps a distinction might be drawn between adding to the authority of the officers and changing the rules, so that no authority drawn from custom and practice could be inconsistent with the express rules.

84 [1909] 1 Ch. 163 at 177 *per* Cozens-Hardy M.R. and at 199 *per* Fletcher Moulton L.J. There was no discussion of the distinction between rules and objects, although the power to maintain parliamentary representation was regarded as an object. But see *Janson* v. *Typographical Association, The Times*, July 31, 1948.

85 *The Times*, Feb. 8, 1923.

86 See also *Kimberley* v. *Showmen's Guild, The Times*, Nov. 25, 1953, where the guild admitted that Kimberley was a member by virtue of his ownership of "Dodge-ems" and a Noah's Ark, but wished to establish that his ownership of fish and chip vans did not entitle him to membership. The original rule referred only to stall holders, but the rule had been amended to exclude "chippers." Danckwerts J. held that the purported alteration was invalid as the correct procedure was not followed, and thus the substantive issue never arose.

It only remains to consider a few miscellaneous points about the amendment of rules. First, the fact that a rule is registered with the Certification Officer is no evidence of its validity since his function in relation to the rules is minsterial only.[87] Secondly, a valid alteration in the rules binds all members, both present and future, even if they suffer from incapacity at the time of the amendment.[88] Thirdly, where the rule book provides a number of methods of change without stating who is to make the choice, the selection can be made by the Executive Council, at least if there is a rule empowering the committee to take any action it believes to be in the interests of the union.[89] Finally judicial intervention in this area is limited by the principle that there should be no action for minor infringements of procedure,[90] but the ambit of this principle is extremely uncertain.

THE RULE IN FOSS V. HARBOTTLE

The rule in *Foss* v. *Harbottle*[91] is a rule of company law[92] which has been somewhat unsuccessfully transplanted into trade union law. Its purpose is to restrict intervention by the courts for minor infringements of the rules and stands for the proposition that a formal irregularity will be excused if it could be cured by an ordinary vote at a general meeting of the members. In the past it has been held that the principle only applies to registered trade unions[93] but this may have been due to the degree of corporate personality attributable to such a union and especially to its ability to sue and be sued.[94] Now that all trade unions have this status, it is suggested that the rule applies whether a union is "listed" or not.

The rule is of little practical importance in trade union law,[95] and the exception to the rule together with the present willingness of the judiciary to intervene in internal affairs make it likely that it will continue to be little used. The rule will be applied (that is the irregularity will be excused) first, only if the power which was purported to be exercised was *intra vires* the objects of the association,[96] secondly, if the irregularity could be cured by an ordinary vote of the members and did not need a special majority,[97] and thirdly if the irregularity did not interfere with the personal rights of members. It is this last factor which makes the rule so rare in trade union law. The theory of the rule is that the wrong is done to the association and therefore the association should be

---

[87] *Osborne* v. *A.S.R.S.* [1909] 1 Ch. 163 at 178.

[88] *Burke* v. *Amalgamated Society of Dyers* [1906] 2 K.B. 583. The union altered the rule as to sick benefits to the prejudice of the plaintiff. He was held bound by the amendment even though he was insane at the time.

[89] *Courtney* v. *E.T.U.*, *The Times*, March 30 1965.

[90] *Chapple* v. *E.T.U.*, *The Times*, Nov. 22, 1961. The principle is discussed in the next section. See also *Amalgamated Society of Engineers* v. *Jones* (1913) 29 T.L.R. 484, where it was held that there had been no breach of the rules in the first place. (The need to give notice of a proposed alteration in the rules was held not to mean notice of the resolution ultimately adopted after debate.)

[91] (1843) 2 Hare 461; 67 E.R. 189.

[92] For its application in company law see Gower, *Modern Company Law* (3rd ed.), p. 581 *et seq.*; Pennington, *Company Law*, (3rd ed.), p. 559 *et seq.*

[93] *Hodgson* v. *NALGO* [1972] 1 All E.R. 15.

[94] See *Cotter* v. *N.U.S.* [1929] 2 Ch. 58 at 71 *per* Romer J.

[95] It has been successfully relied upon in only one case—*Cotter* v. *N.U.S.* [1929] 2 Ch. 58. *Steele* v. *South Wales Miners' Federation* [1907] 1 K.B. 361 is thought by some to be an application of the principle, although *Foss* v. *Harbottle* was never cited.

[96] *Edwards* v. *Halliwell* [1950] 2 All E.R. 1064 at 1067 *per* Jenkins L.J.

[97] *Ibid*; *Cotter* v. *N.U.S.* [1929] 2 Ch. 58 at 69 *per* Romer J.

the person to sue; and if the association can put the matter right itself there is no need to sue. However, if the wrong is to an individual, or to put it another way if the individual is suing not as representing the union but as claiming on his own behalf, then the rule has no application. In *Edwards* v. *Halliwell*[98] the plaintiffs complained that the subscription had been increased without the correct procedure being followed. Jenkins L.J. said:

> "The gist of the case is that the personal and individual rights of membership . . . have been invaded by a purported, but invalid, alteration of the tables of contribution. In those circumstances, it seems to me the rule in *Foss* v. *Harbottle* has no application at all, for the individual members who are suing, sue, not in the right of the union, but in their own right to protect from invasion their own individual rights as members."

A further exception to the rule has now been added by *Hodgson* v. *NALGO*.[99] The action was to force the executive committee to withdraw instructions to the union's delegates to the T.U.C. to vote in favour of a motion in defiance of the views of the national conference. It was clear that if the rule were applied and the court declined to intervene the matter could not be corrected by a general meeting (*i.e.* a special conference) before the meeting of the T.U.C. Goulding J. therefore, declared that the rule does not apply if the "constitutional machinery of the body cannot operate in time to be of practical effect"[1] for otherwise the rule could become an instrument of injustice to the majority which could not afterwards be corrected.[2]

It is suggested that in trade union affairs the case will usually either involve the personal rights of a member or will be sufficiently urgent so as to exclude the rule and thus permit an action for breach of the rule book by an individual member.

In addition to the rule in *Foss* v. *Harbottle* there is a general principle inhibiting interference in the internal affairs of associations over minor matters,[3] but given the present climate this reluctance is less widespread than it was. However, one application of this principle is to be seen in *Chapple* v. *E.T.U.*[4] where the plaintiffs alleged that the representatives of 4 out of 50 divisions at a rules revision conference had not been properly elected. The court held that the irregularity in 4 out of 50 cases should not render the proceedings invalid, although the four were advised not to participate.

THE CONDUCT OF MEETINGS

In order to be effective a meeting must be duly summoned and convened according to the rules.[5] It is clear that a notice of meeting must be sent to all members and this is so even if a member of the committee or meeting has

---

[98] [1950] 2 All E.R. 1064 at 1067.

[99] [1972] 1 All E.R. 15.

[1] *Ibid.* at 24.

[2] The alternative ground that the rule did not apply to unregistered unions is, it is suggested, no longer valid.

[3] See for example the dictum of Phillimore J. in *Steele* v. *South Wales Miners' Federation* [1907] 1 K.B. 361 at 370.

[4] *The Times*, Nov. 22, 1961. But see *Weakley* v. *A.U.E.W.*, *The Times*, June 12, 1975 where the court intervened even though the defect was excusable, but the union intended to take drastic action to remedy it. Walton J. intervened because "the court would interfere if the remedy proposed was out of all proportion to the disease which was found to be present in the body politic."

[5] On the subject of meetings generally see Shaw and Smith, *The law of meetings* (4th ed.), esp. Chap. 6; Shackleton, *The Law and Practice of Meetings* (6th ed.).

indicated that he would not attend.[6] The only exception appears to be if it is impossible for the person to attend either through illness or distance.[7]

There appears to be no direct authority on the position where notice is sent but not received, although in *Leary* v. *National Union of Vehicle Builders*,[8] Megarry J. indicated a preliminary view that he would prefer to say that the meeting would be invalidated. The consequences of such a strict rule could be modified by a provision in the rule book.

The meeting must be properly called according to the rules and if there are any special conditions applicable to the calling of the meeting these must be complied with,[9] and in addition it may be that in some cases the law will imply that reasonable notice must be given. Thus in *Maclelland* v. *N.U.J.*[10] Whitford J. held that a mandatory meeting would be invalid unless reasonable notice were given, although he gave no indication what would amount to such notice.[11]

It is also necessary for the items to be discussed to be adequately specified on the agenda. In *Young* v. *Ladies' Imperial Club*[12] the meeting was to discuss the expulsion of a member but the agenda merely noted an item "to report on and discuss the matters concerning Mrs. Young. . . ." It was held that this was insufficient notice to enable the committee to expel the plaintiff.[13]

As to the conduct of the meeting itself it is clear that the meeting will be invalid if a non-member participates in the decision. In *Lane* v. *Norman*[14] North J. said:

> "When persons who do not belong to the committee are summoned to attend the committee, to take part in the discussions which ensue, and to use their influence as to what the committee should do, and to vote upon the point, then in my opinion the body which is acting is not a committee duly appointed, but a committee with an unauthorised addition or additions made to it."

Thus in *Leary* v. *National Union of Vehicle Builders*[15] the committee's decision was invalidated by the fact that a non-member not only participated but even appears to have put the relevant motion.

The chairman of the meeting cannot claim for himself more power than is provided by the rules, so that he cannot introduce an item not on the agenda,[16] except perhaps of an informal nature, nor can of his own accord bring the meeting to an end, although he may adjourn it for a short period to restore order.[17] Nor can he exercise a casting vote unless he is given this power by the rules.[18]

---

[6] *Young* v. *Ladies' Imperial Club* [1920] 2 K.B. 523.

[7] *Ibid.* at 528.

[8] [1971] Ch. 34 at 53.

[9] *Maclelland* v. *N.U.J.* [1975] I.C.R. 116.

[10] *Ibid.*

[11] In the case itself not more than 40 minutes notice was given of the mandatory meeting.

[12] [1920] 2 K.B. 523.

[13] But see *Richardson-Gardner* v. *Fremantle* (1871) 24 L.T. 81 at 86 where on similar facts it was held that a notice stating "Mr. Gardner's case" was sufficient.

[14] (1891) 66 L.T. 83 This view was adopted by Megarry J. in *Leary* v. *National Union of Vehicle Builders* [1971] Ch. 34 at 54, where it was also noted that the headnote in the *Law Times* reported is misleading.

[15] [1971] Ch. 34.

[16] *John* v. *Rees* [1970] Ch. 345 at 377.

[17] *Ibid.* at 379.

[18] *Weakley* v. *A.U.E.W., The Times*, June 12, 1975.

The right to attend meetings

It cannot be said with certainty that the common law provides a member with a right to attend general meetings of his union, although it would be very strange if this were not so. The only time the issue of a right to attend has arisen was in *Goad* v. *A.U.E.W.*[19] which dealt with the statutory right provided by the Industrial Relations Act 1971.

[19] No. 1 [1972] I.C.R. 429. See also No. 2 [1973] I.C.R. 42; No. 3 [1973] I.C.R. 108; *Eckman* v. *Midland Bank* [1973] I.C.R. 71. According to *The Times*, August 2, 1973 Mr. Goad finally left his previous job and became a farm worker.

CHAPTER 4

UNION OFFICIALS

ALTHOUGH there are few special rules of law applicable to trade union officers it is necessary to consider how the law applies to a number of matters, including candidacy, election, confirmation, status, dismissal, and vicarious liability.

ELECTIONS AND EMPLOYMENT

Candidacy

In recent years there has been a number of cases where the courts have been asked to intervene in internal union affairs in order to protect a member's right to stand for office in his union.[1] To some extent this has been due to greater willingness on the part of the judiciary to intervene, but also due to the fact that the rule book is sometimes used as a weapon in internal union struggles. This is one of the areas where an adequate rule book is essential, but the fact that the law has intervened only on procedural rather than substantive issues has meant that there is no external pressures to see that rule books are adequate for the job, although the T.U.C. has itself been urging unions to examine their own rule books.[2]

Breach of the rules

The rule book must be strictly adhered to[3] and cases usually come before the courts by way of an action for breach of the rules alleging that the incumbent officers have either misinterpreted the rules or exceeded their powers in disallowing the plaintiff's nomination. An example of the interpretative function is *Watson* v. *Smith*[4] where a somewhat ungrammatical rule stated that:

> "candidates for the office of executive councilman shall be nominated by and from the division in which he has worked at the industry or signed a

---

[1] See Kidner, "The right to be a candidate for union office," (1973) 2 I.L.J. 65.

[2] Statutory protection was provided by the Industrial Relations Act 1971, s. 65, which stated that "no member of the organisation or of any branch or section of the organisation shall by way of any arbitrary or unreasonable discrimination be excluded (a) from being a candidate for holding office in the organisation. . . ." For an application of this section see *Carling* v. *G.M.W.U.* (1973) 8 I.T.R. 307. See also Rideout, "Responsible self government in British trade unions" (1967) 5 B.J.I.R. 74.

[3] See, for example, *Nelson* v. *National Union of Seamen* (1978) 128 N.L.J. (xxiv) where due to postal delays the plaintiff's nomination form arrived too late. The Court rejected the argument that at common law time is not of the essence of a contract and that, therefore, failure to meet the date in the rule book could not be fatal. It was held that departure from the due date would be a breach of the rule book contract.

[4] [1941] 2 All E.R. 725. See also *Mackay* v. *Constructional Engineering Union*, *The Times*, January 23, 1963, which involved a similar rule.

vacant book and resided for the twelve months immediately preceding the nomination."

The plaintiff had been off sick for eight of the 12 months but was, nevertheless, held to have fulfilled this condition and an injunction was granted preventing the election being held without the plaintiff's name being included in the ballot paper.

An example where officials exceeded their powers in *Leigh* v. *N.U.R.*[5] where the general secretary mistakenly thought that a rule which stated that "no circular will be authorised for distribution until the nomination has been received and approved" gave him the power to reject the nomination on substantive grounds, but the court held that the rule confined the general secretary to purely administrative tasks.[6]

Some candidates have managed to restore their nomination by showing that the rule under which it was rejected was invalid. Thus in *Bissett* v. *National Amalgamated Society of Operative Ship Painters and Decorators*[7] the plaintiff was able to avoid a rule excluding communists from office on the ground that the rule had been passed by an incorrect procedure.

Statute

In one situation the right to be a candidate for union office is protected by statute, and that is where a nomination is held invalid because the candidate is not a contributor to the union's political fund. In *Birch* v. *N.U.R.*[8] the plaintiff, a non-contributor, had been elected chairman of the branch but the election had been disallowed by the union in pursuance of a rule which stated that a non-contributor could not hold an office involving control or management of the political fund. As it happened, the branch chairman had control of both the general and the political funds, but Danckwerts J. held the rule to be invalid as it contravened s.3 of the Trade Union Act 1913[9] which requires that a non-contributor shall not be placed "in any respect either directly or indirectly under any disability or at any disadvantage as compared with other members of the union (except in relation to the control or management of the political fund). . . ." As a result of this case it is now necessary to keep the control of the political fund separate from that of the general fund and the general administration of the union.

Natural Justice

If a person is prevented from being a candidate because of disciplinary action taken against him, the decision to take such action must have complied with the principles of natural justice.[10]

---

[5] [1970] Ch. 326. See also *Chapple* v. *E.T.U.., The Times*, May 26, 1960.

[6] The rules also required the successful candidate to attend the Labour Party Conference. The defendants therefore claimed that the candidate must be a member of the Labour Party at the time of the nomination, which the plaintiff was not. But the court held that this was not so as he could acquire membership between nomination and election. But what if he did not?

[7] *The Times*, April 21, 1951.

[8] [1950] Ch. 602. See further Chap. 17.

[9] The fact that the rule had been approved by the Registrar did not render it immune from challenge.

[10] *Burn* v. *National Amalgamated Labourers' Union* [1920] 2 Ch. 364; *Simms* v. *P.T.U., The Times*, April 5, 1967; *Cohen* v. *National Union of Tailors and Garment Workers, The Times*, January 13, 1962. The principles of natural justice are discussed in Chap. 5.

Elections

Although, from time to time, concern is expressed about whether the results of trade union elections adequately represent the views of the membership it cannot be the function of the law to prescribe constitutions for unions, but only to ensure that the elections are carried out honestly and substantially according to the rules.

As to honesty, many unions now pre-empt criticism by having the elections carried out be an external body such as the Electoral Reform Society, but only in one case has substantial fraud in the conduct of an election been shown to exist and this should be regarded as an isolated but instructive example. *Byrne and Chapple* v. *Foulkes, Haxell and others*[11] involved an action for conspiracy against the defendants for securing the election of Haxell by fraudulent means. It was alleged that the defendants had ordered 26,000 extra ballot papers and that a number of valid votes had been declared invalid on the grounds that they were out of time, by the simple device of having an envelope posted out of time in the relevant town and then claiming that that was the envelope in which the votes had been sent by the branch. It is also significant that the fraud took three years to redress and the legal costs amounted to some £80,000.

As to procedure, it is clear that an election will not be declared invalid simply because there has been some minor irregularity. In *Brown* v. *A.U.E.W.*,[12] for various reasons a number of individuals did not receive ballot papers, and in addition, due to a mistake by the branch secretary, one branch received none at all. In all, about 600 out of 29,000 members were disenfranchised. Walton J. said:

> ". . . (save perhaps in relation to wholly exceptional facts) the crucial question which falls to be asked in this regard is whether the election was conducted substantially in accordance with the procedure laid down in the rules and otherwise in accordance with the directions of the executive council, and is not simply to be answered by pointing to the fact that a considerable number of members did not receive ballot papers, or did not receive ballot papers in time. Any postal ballot must, of its nature be subject to the vagaries of the postal service. Similarly the fact that no members whatsoever of one of the branches received a ballot paper is due, not to any fault in the conduct of the election but to a mistake . . . The fact that that mistake was made had nothing directly to do with the conduct of the election, and hence of its overall validity."

Presumably, however, such a mistake can only be excused if it affects a small proportion of the electorate, otherwise the process ceases to be an election at all.

A further point that arose was whether the executive had the power to extend the deadline for receipt of votes, and whether the fact that they did not announce that they had done so affected the election.[13] It was said that it had been the practice of the executive council to decide all issues relating to late votes in pursuance of the rule stating that elections shall be subject to the general control of the executive council, and that, therefore, the automatic

---

[11] *The Times*, June 29, 1961, July 4, 1961, February 1, 1962. See Rolph, *All those in favour? The E.T.U. Trial*, and Grunfeld, *Modern Trade Union Law*, pp. 154–157.

[12] [1976] I.C.R. 147. See also *Chapple* v. *E.T.U.*, *The Times*, November 22, 1961, *Goode* v. *N.U.M.*, *The Times*, January 29, 1959.

[13] Presumably some members might have voted if they had known of the extension.

extension was not a breach of the rules, or at least of custom and practice. The fact that the extension had not been announced was regarded as "a mere irregularity, highly regretable but not going, as it were, to the root of the election."

A further problem was whether the committee had the power to order a new ballot after it had announced the result of the first ballot. Here Walton J. felt that it was important to "stick to the rule book" and held that there was no rule book power and no implied power.[14] He pointed out that if any difficulties became apparent during the conduct of an election the proper course would be to delay announcing the result, and he gave as the reason that even if some candidates could not be called to account for irregular behaviour, this was preferable to leaving minor irregularities hanging over the candidates head for an indefinite period. It should be remembered, however, that this is not a rule of law: all that is being said is that in the absence of a rule book power, there is no implied power to declare an election void. This may even be so both before[15] as well as after the result has been announced, but normally the rule book will give an executive control of the election and this will include the power to hold a fresh ballot.[16] This power will normally lapse when the result is declared[17] for the election process is then completed.

The remaining facts of *Brown* v. *A.U.E.W.* are too complicated to summarise here but the appalling chaos that resulted from appeals and counter appeals was finally sorted out by declaring that certain of the appeals were *ultra vires.* It is also significant that the original election was held in October 1972 and judgment on the verdict of an internal appeal court of March 1975 was given in July 1976.

Now that the plaintiff had won there remained the problem of his period of office. The rules were silent as to the date from which the period of office of a successful candidate runs, but at one point during the saga the plaintiff had been reinstated and the executive council had then declared that his period of office should run from January 1974. Walton J. said that this was a valid administrative decision of the executive council which it was fully entitled to take, and therefore the plaintiff's three year period of office ran from that date.[18] One might wonder, however, if the executive council should be entirely free to select the starting date of the period of office, at least if there are no special circumstances such as existed here.

Confirmation of appointment

In some cases a union official, once elected, must be confirmed in office by a committee of the union,[19] and one question that has arisen is whether the rules of natural justice apply to this process of confirmation.[20] In *Breen* v. *A.E.U.*[21] the plaintiff had been elected shop steward at the Esso oil refinery at Fawley

[14] But see *Salts* v. *N.G.A., The Times*, May 16, 1978, where a contrary view was taken.

[15] See *Sillars* v. *A.U.E.W., The Times*, March 21, 1951, where it was held that there was no power to declare an election void even before the result was declared. See also *Scanlon* v. *Carron*, *The Times*, July 25, 1962.

[16] *Scanlon* v. *Carron*, *The Times*, July 25, 1962.

[17] *Brown* v. *A.U.E.W.* [1976] I.C.R. 147 at 159.

[18] This was based on the executive's power rather than on an estoppel. [1976] I.C.R. 147 at 168.

[19] See for example T.G.W.U. rule 11 (4).

[20] The doctrine of natural justice is fully considered in the next chapter, but for present purposes it may be said to require that a person be given a chance to state his case and that the hearing should be fair.

[21] [1971] 2 Q.B. 175.

for a number of years, but in 1965 his election was disallowed under a rule that the appointment of shop stewards was subject to approval by the district committee. The case turned on whether the committee had taken into consideration a false allegation that in 1958 Breen had misappropriated union funds to the extent of 19s. 6d.[22]

The legal interest of the case lies in the question whether Breen was entitled to be heard by the committee when they were considering his confirmation. In the event the court reluctantly[23] decided that it could not interfere, but a number of comments were made suggesting that the courts had the power to intervene in such cases if necessary. The widest view was that of Lord Denning who said in his dissenting judgment that "if he is a man who has some right or interest, or some legitimate expectation, of which it would not be fair to deprive him without a hearing. . . ." then he ought to be heard, and the fact that he had been elected and approved for so many years before gave him the necessary "legitimate expectation."

Neither of the other two members of the court were prepared to go so far, but both indicated that there could be circumstances where an official-elect ought to be heard. Edmund Davies L.J. thought that the discretion, though wide, was not untrammelled and had to be fairly exercised, but that there could be no intervention if the decision, though mistaken, was honest.[24] Megaw L.J. thought there were circumstances where fairness would require the committee to allow a hearing.[25] It is therefore not entirely clear when the process of confirmation will require a hearing, but it may be so where an allegation of fact prejudicial to the applicant is to be made, as against a case where prejudicial opinions are expressed about his general ability to hold the post.[26]

Employment of officials

While a large number of people working for trade unions may easily be categorised as "employees" legal difficulties arise in relation to those officials who may fall into one or more of several categories.[27] An official may be an employee, and independent contractor, an office-holder, a worker, or several of these at the same time, and the problem is complicated by the fact that ultimately the determination of the issue will depend on the official's relationship with the union as expressed the rule book.

Employee

The word "employee" is used for a wide variety of purposes, but it will be important for the official mainly because it provides protection against unfair

---

[22] The trial judge held that this had not been taken into account, and the Court of Appeal was unable to disturb this finding, even though Edmund Davies L.J. was unable to understand how the judge arrived at his vital conclusion. [1971] 2 Q.B. 175 at 199.

[23] Lord Denning M.R. dissented and Edmund Davies L.J. entertained "substantial doubts that the judgment I am about to deliver will serve the ends of justice." Part of the problem was that the plaintiff had been given leave to appeal out of time on condition that findings of fact remained undisturbed.

[24] [1971] 2 Q.B. 175 at 195. If the decision was honestly arrived at there is no obligation to give reasons for the rejection: *McInnes* v. *Onslow-Fane*, [1978] 3 All E.R. 211.

[25] *Ibid.* at 200.

[26] See examples given by Edmund Davies L.J. *ibid. at 195* and *Shotton* v. *Hammond, The Times,* October 26, 1976.

[27] For a thorough survey of the role of trade union officers see Clegg, Killick & Adams, *Trade Union Officers* (1961).

dismissal.[28] The common law uses either the "control" test or the "organisation" test, or both, to determine whether a person is an employee and the degree of control or the extent to which an official is integral to the organisation[29] will often depend on the terms of the rule book. In *Wilson* v. *Minister of Pensions and National Insurance*[30] it was held that a member of the executive council of the Constructional Engineering Union was not an employee[31] on the ground that it was the council "who controlled others, not others who controlled them," but the decision is probably inconsistant with another case.[32] There seems no reason why a union official, even a senior one, should not be regarded as an employee,[33] if the rule book either specifies his duties[34] or states that he is responsible to and subject to the control of the union. It is suggested that all those officials who are "administrators" within the union should be regarded as employees.

Independent Contractor

The law reports provide no examples of a union official being held to be an independent contractor,[35] although such a characterisation is possible. For example a union, or a branch, may employ a person to keep the membership records for a relatively small annual payment. Such a person may be an independent contractor.

Office-holder

This is the most difficult of the classifications for there have been few cases defining what an office holder is. The consequence of being declared an office holder is that the rules of natural justice apply on dismissal, so that in the past there may have been a tendency to increase the scope of this category to provide broader protection against dismissal. Nowadays, however, greater protection is provided for the employee by the legislation on unfair dismissal, so there may now be a tendency the other way.[36]

Unfortunately, it is not clear whether a person may be both an office holder and an employee, for sometimes a person is treated as both[37] and sometimes

[28] His status for the purposes of the social security system does not depend on his being an employee at common law for the Social Security Act 1975, s. 2 (1) (*a*) defines an "employed earner" as "a person who is gainfully employed in Great Britain under a contract of service, or in an office (including an elective office) with emoluments chargeable to income tax under Schedule E."

[29] For a discussion of who is an employee see Hepple and O'Higgins, *Employment Law* (2nd ed.) Chap. 3.

[30] *The Times*, February 10, 1955.

[31] Wilson had been killed while on union business and the question was whether he was in insurable employment. The decision for this purpose would now be different. Social Security Act 1975, s. 2 (2) (*a*).

[32] *Balfour* v. *Tillet* (1913) 29 T.L.R. 332. On a procedural point it was held that the defendant, general secretary of the union, could not, as an employee, be required to disclose the contents of documents in the possession of his employer.

[33] In *Stevenson* v. *United Road Transport Union* [1977] I.C.R. 893 at 903 a regional officer was said to be employed by the union, but the issue was not whether he was an employee but whether he was not also an office holder.

[34] See *A.E.U.* v. *Minister of Pensions and National Insurance* [1963] 1 W.L.R. 441 where a sick steward was held to be an employee because of the way in which his duties were specified in the rule book.

[35] The issue was discussed in *A.E.U.* v. *Minister of Pensions and National Insurance* [1963] 1 W.L.R. 441.

[36] See *102 Social Club* v. *Bickerton* [1977] I.C.R. 911 at 917 *per* Phillips J.

[37] As in *Stevenson* v. *United Road Transport Union* [1977] I.C.R. 893.

the terms are regarded as being mutually exclusive.[38] It is tentatively suggested that the position may be explained by saying that there are not two categories, but three. First, there is the pure office holder who cannot be an employee, and this category will include all those who hold office at pleasure,[39] those who hold an office on terms that are fixed by a statute, and those whose position is such that it would be awkward to regard them as employees.[40]

The second group consists of those employees whose particular position either as public office holder or as an officer of a private institution demands that they be given greater protection than that available to the simple employee[41] The regional officer in *Stevenson* v. *United Road Transport Union*[42] was in this category. The third group consists of employees.

The difficulty of distinguishing between these groups is illustrated by *102 Social Club* v. *Bickerton*[43] which seems to have assumed that one cannot be both an officer and an employee. The question was whether the secretary of a social club was an employee,[44] and Phillips J. laid down the following criteria for distinguishing an employee from an office holder.[45]

(a) Whether the payment was an honorarium[46] or a salary.

(b) Whether the payment was fixed in advance or voted at the end of the year in token of the member's work.

(c) Whether there is a right to payment.

(d) The size of the payment.

(e) Whether it is an independent office or whether the person is subject to the orders of the club.

(f) The extent of the duties performed (the less they are the less likely he is to be an employee).

(g) The description given to the payment for tax and national insurance purposes.

These criteria, which were designed to define "employee," are wide in their scope and seem applicable to those who are commonly regarded as office holders. Whether the law will recognise that one can in fact be both an employee and an office holder, or at least an employee who has the same protection as an office holder, remains to be seen.

Worker

It seems likely that most trade union officials would be regarded as "workers,"

[38] *Ibid.* 902.

[39] This group would not be protected by natural justice. *Ridge* v. *Baldwin* [1964] A.C. 40 at 65 *per* Lord Reid. In the classification set out in this passage Lord Reid was only concerned to distinguish between those who did and those who did not benefit from natural justice. The issue of who was an employee did not arise.

[40] Such as the chief constable in *Ridge* v. *Baldwin* [1964] A.C. 40, or very senior officers of an institution or trade union. See also the criteria in *102 Social Club* v. *Bickerton* [1977] I.C.R. 911.

[41] The group might also be defined as those office holders who need the additional protection of being an employee.

[42] [1977] I.C.R. 893. See also *Taylor* v. *N.U.S* [1967] 1 W.L.R. 532 at 550.

[43] [1977] I.C.R. 911.

[44] The issue arose in a curious way. The club steward complained that he was unfairly dismissed and the club resisted on the ground that the complaint was excluded in that the club employed less than four people. If the club secretary was an employee there were four, if not there were less than four. The case was remitted to the tribunal.

[45] It was said that the control and organisation tests are not really suitable for distinguishing between an office holder and an employee.

[46] *i.e.* whether the services were rendered in return for the payment, or whether it was a mere grant or solatium.

as defined by section 30 of the Trade Union and Labour Relations Act 1974, either as working under a contract of employment or as performing personally any work or services under a contract.

Dismissal of a union official

If a union official is an "employee" he will usually be protected by the law of unfair dismissal.[47] There will be no difficulty if the official is appointed, but there could be problems if he is an elected official, for could he sue the union for unfair dismissal if he is not re-elected? In some cases liability for unfair dismissal may be excluded in the contract of employment,[48] but in other cases it would be necessary to decide whether there has been a dismissal and whether it was fair. If the contract is regarded as being for a fixed term and if the contract is made with the union itself rather than with the member, the union may be able to justify non-renewal of the contract on the ground the applicant did not fulfill a qualification for the post, that is election by the members.

If the official is an office holder, whether paid or not,[49] he is entitled to be heard in his own defence at a fairly conducted hearing.[50] This also applies in the case of a specially protected employee, and it is suggested that this is what happened in *Stevenson* v. *United Road Transport Union.*[51] In that case officials were employed "so long as they give satisfaction to the Executive Committee" and these words elevated them above ordinary employees and gave them special protection in that the committee was required to reach a conclusion that the official's performance was unsatisfactory and that this was a judicial activity which imported the rules of natural justice.

Liability for the Acts of Officials

Subject to the statutory immunities which provide that in certain circumstances a trade union cannot be sued,[52] the rules of agency and vicarious liability for the acts of others apply. But the relationship between a union and its various officials, including shop stewards, and the situation in which the problems arise, mean that it is often difficult to apply the rules to such specialised circumstances.

Liability in contract

The rules of agency apply to make a union liable for the authorised act of its official acting on its behalf, but it should be noted that a union may also be liable if it is held to have ratified the unauthorised act of its official even if that act is a breach of the rules.[53]

---

[47] E.P.C.A. 1978, ss. 54–57. See Hepple and O'Higgins, *Employment Law* (2nd ed.) Chap. 17.

[48] If the contract is for a fixed term of two years or more. E.P.C.A. 1978, s. 142 (1).

[49] *Burn* v. *National Amalgamated Labourers' Union* [1920] 2 Ch. 364; See also *O'Neill* v. *T.G.W.U.* [1934] I.R. 633 where it was held that a rule providing a power to dismiss officials which was contained in a section headed "Dismissal of all Paid Officers and Permanent Officials" did not apply to honorary officials.

[50] *Ridge* v. *Baldwin* [1964] A.C. 40.

[51] [1977] I.C.R. 893.

[52] These immunities are discussed in Chaps. 2 and 12.

[53] *Bonsor* v. *Musicians' Union* [1956] A.C. 104 esp. at 147–148 *per* Lord MacDermott. "It has made the act of the branch secretary its act and cannot now say that because the expulsion was unauthorised by the rules it has no responsibility for it." *Denaby and Cadeby Main Collieries* v. *Yorkshire Miners' Association* [1906] A.C. 384 is distinguishable because the payment of strike pay did not on the facts amount to ratification, because by the time it was decided to pay it the strike had become a lock out.

According to *Heaton's Transport Ltd.* v. *T.G.W.U.*[54] the source of authority of an official who is not an employee (in this case a shop steward) depends partly on the rule book and partly on the custom and practice of the union.[55] The case itself concerned an unfair industrial practice under the Industrial Relations Act and therefore may not be direct authority in relation to agency. Lord Wilberforce said[56]: "If authority to take a particular type of action is not excluded by the rules and if such authority is reasonably to be implied from custom and practice, such authority will continue to exist until unequivocably withdrawn.[57]" The evidence and assumptions which formed the basis of the implied authority have been subjected to considerable criticism[58] and it may be that where authority to enter into contracts is concerned more substantial evidence would be necessary. Although in the eyes of the House of Lords[59] the members may have assumed that shop stewards have authority and represent the union in industrial relations, such an assumption may not be so easy as regards authority to make a contract.

It should be noted that officials may act as agents not only for the union but also for the members. It has sometimes been suggested that collective agreements may become incorporated into the contracts of employment of individuals by a process of agency whereby the union official is negotiating and making contracts on behalf of the employees, but this method suffers from a number of difficulties (in particular how terms are incorporated into the contracts of non-members) and has not found favour.[60]

It has also been suggested that union officials act as agents for the members in giving strike notice. In *Chappell* v. *Times Newspapers Ltd.*[61] Lord Denning thought it was clear that this was so, but Stephenson L.J. and Geoffrey Lane L.J. both thought that further evidence would be needed to fill out the terms of the rule book before a conclusion could be reached with certainty.

Liability in tort

A trade union has considerable immunity from liability in tort,[62] but in those areas where liability is possible the usual rules of vicarious liability will apply. Thus in *Giblan* v. *National Amalganated Labourers' Union*[63] the union was held liable both because the officials concerned were "servants and agents" of the union,[64] even though the act done was *ultra vires* and could have been

---

[54] [1972] I.C.R. 308.

[55] The importance of this case for the legal view of the nature of the rule book is discussed in Chap. 3.

[56] [1972] I.C.R. 308 at 394.

[57] The T.G.W.U. did in fact later issue shop stewards with credentials which limited their authority in relation to industrial action.

[58] See Hepple, "Union Responsibility for Shop Stewards" (1972) 1 I.L.J. 197; Kahn Freund, "The Industrial Relations Act" (1974) 3 I.L.J. 186; see also (1973) 36 M.L.R. 78 (P.L. Davies).

[59] It was argued that shop stewards play a dual role, for some purposes representing the union and for others representing the members. Lord Wilberforce firmly stated that "this concept of duality of roles is not one which would be likely to occur to trade unionists." [1972] I.C.R. 308 at 396.

[60] See *Holland* v. *London Society of Compositors* (1924) 40 T.L.R. 440; *Edwards* v. *Skyways* [1964] 1 W.L.R. 349. See Chap. 18.

[61] [1975] 1 W.L.R. 482.

[62] See Chap. 2 and Chap. 12.

[63] [1903] 2 K.B. 600.

[64] *Ibid.* at 624 *per* Stirling L.J.

prevented by an injunction,[65] and because the union had "adopted" the act of the officials at a general meeting.[66]

As to the issue of ratification it is suggested that the decision of the House of Lords in *Denaby and Cadeby Main Collieries Ltd.* v. *Yorkshire Miners' Association*[67] can be explained in a number of ways. In that case the men went on strike in breach of their contracts at the instance on union officials. Later the men were prepared to return but to do so had to sign new contracts which contained different terms. This they refused to do, and the association, which had disapproved of the strike as it was in breach of contract, then began to pay strike pay.[68] It is suggested that the decision that the union was not liable for the tort of its officers in inducing the strike[69] can be based on the fact that the union could not be held legally responsible simply because it furnished financial assistance,[70] nor, even if that was an act of ratification, was it ratification of an illegal act because the strike had become a lock out for which the union was not responsible,[71] and finally because the act of the officials in calling a strike without holding a ballot was outside the scope of their authority altogether.[72]

The problem of *Heaton's Transport* v. *T.G.W.U.*[73] also arises in relation to vicarious liability, but again it is suggested that the actual decision may not be very influential.[74] This is so because it may be possible to infer from the custom and practice authority to engage in trade disputes, but unions are now protected from liability in such cases.[75] It may not be easy to infer authority to engage in other activities causing liability in tort, except those which are connected with everyday activities for which it is suggested there would be liability.

---

[65] *Ibid.* at 625.

[66] *Ibid.* at 617 *per* Vaughan Williams L.J.

[67] [1906] A.C. 384.

[68] The dispute was the same as that which gave rise to *Yorkshire Miners* v. *Howden* [1905] A.C. 256, which held this payment to be a breach of the rules.

[69] The events took place before immunity was conferred by the Trade Disputes Act 1906.

[70] [1906] A.C. 384 at 392 *per* Lord Loreburn L.C.

[71] *Ibid.* at 398 *per* Lord Davey.

[72] *i.e.* it was not just a wrongful mode of doing what they were authorised to do, they were not authorised to do it at all.

[73] [1972] I.C.R. 308.

[74] Lord Wilberforce pointed out that "Liability for tortious acts is outside the scope of this appeal: it may be a closely connected subject, but what is said here does not necessarily apply to it, because it is not under consideration." [1972] I.C.R. 308 at 393. See also *General Aviation Services* v. *T.G.W.U.* [1976] I.R.L.R. 224 (H.L.).

[75] And see *Bird* v. *O'Neal* [1960] A.C. 907 where the Privy Council held that a union could not be liable for the torts of pickets, because even if they were "agents" they were not "servants."

CHAPTER 5

THE CONTROL OF ADMISSION AND DISCIPLINARY PROCEDURE

ONE of the most difficult problems for trade union law today is the extent to which a person may be protected in relation to admission to and expulsion from a union.

Part of the reason why the issue of membership is seen as significant[1] is that it is a point of confrontation between the collective interests of a union and the interests of the individual,[2] but it may be that this is more of a problem of principle than a practical issue.[3] When the Industrial Relations Act did protect membership and other such rights there were not many applications,[4] and it has been suggested that some cases which appear as simple membership problems may be based on factional conflict within the union[5] which are difficult to resolve in the courts. The fact is that this is a complex issue containing many variables and cannot be solved by dogmatic adherence either to individualist or collectivist philosophies, but in which there is room for compromise, not perhaps based on resolution by traditional courts of law but on entrusting the problem to a body with sufficient authority to consider the complex range of competing interests involved.[6]

The Common Law bases its control of unincorporated associations firmly on the law of contract, for not only could that justify abstention on substantive issues but also it sanctioned the freedom of the individual to create relationships for himself; but "the premises of contract run counter to the reality of association,"[7] so that it has been necessary on occasion to depart from the principles of contract when they prove inadequate, and impose controls on the

---

[1] See Kahn-Freund, *Labour and the Law* (2nd ed.), pp. 180–193; Elias, *Trade Union Democracy: Member's Rights and the Law* (forthcoming).

[2] See Kidner, "The individual and the collective interest in trade union law" (1976) 5 I.L.J. 90.

[3] See the Donovan Commission Cmnd 3623, para. 619. The fact that it is a point of principle indicates its difficulty, not that it should not be dealt with.

[4] s. 65. See the report of the Registrar of Trade Unions for the year 1973, where it was noted that between February 28, 1972 and April 30, 1974, 37 applications were received under s. 81 which empowered the Registrar to investigate a breach of the rules or a breach of the principles of s. 65.

[5] Kay, "The settlement of membership disputes in trade unions" in Carby-Hall, *Studies in Labour Law*, p. 161; Kahn-Freund, "Trade Unions, the Law and Society" (1970) 33 M.L.R. 241 at 266 ("The trauma of the Trojan horse").

[6] Kahn-Freund, *Labour and the Law* (2nd ed.), p. 193; Kahn-Freund, "Trade Unions, Law and Society" (1970) 33 M.L.R. 241 at 265; Kidner, "The individual and the collective interest in trade union law" (1976) 5 I.L.J. 90 at 104–106; Rideout, "Responsible Self Government in British Trade Unions" (1967) 5 B.J.I.R. 74; Wellington, *Labour and the Legal Process* (1968), Chap. 5.

[7] Selznick, *Law, Society and Industrial Justice* (1969), p. 70. See also Chafee, "The internal affairs of associaitions not for profit" (1930) 43 Harv.L.R. 993.

ground of "public policy."[8] The relationship is moving from contract to status,[9] and the question for the law is to what extent and by what means that status may be protected.

CONTROL OF ADMISSION PROCEDURE

There is no right to join a trade union, even if the applicant fulfills all the qualifications laid down by the rule book.[10] It has been suggested, however, that both admission and expulsion could be controlled by an embryonic principle called "the right to work," which will be dealt with in this section. It will also be necessary to cover a very different kind of problem, that is the control by the Bridlington Principles over trade unions.

The right to work

The so-called "right to work" began its career in *Nagle* v. *Feilden*[11] where the plaintiff complained that the Jockey Club had acted unlawfully in refusing her a trainer's licence simply because she was a woman,[12] and the Court of Appeal agreed that she had an arguable[13] case. Lord Denning said:[14]

> "When an association, who have the governance of a trade take it upon themselves to licence persons to take part in it, then it is at least arguable that they are not at liberty to withdraw a man's licence—and thus put him out of business—without hearing him. Nor can they refuse a man a licence—and thus prevent him from carrying on his business—in their uncontrolled discretion. If they reject him arbitrarily or capriciously, there is ground for thinking that the courts can intervene."

Lord Denning was thus suggesting that at least in cases where the organisation can prevent the applicant working at his trade at all, the courts may intervene, but it was not clear whether or not this right depended on the restraint of trade doctrine, for if it did there would be difficulty in applying it to trade unions.[15] The issue arose in *Edwards* v. *SOGAT*[16] where Lord Denning

[8] *e.g.* the requirements of natural justice; the refusal to implement a rule requiring exhaustion of internal remedies.

[9] Selznick, *op. cit.* p. 273 "Membership becomes a form of status when the group loses the option, informally or formally, to expel an individual arbitrarily, when membership carries with it the right to some security of tenure."

[10] *R.* v. *Benchers of Lincoln's Inn* (1825) 4 B. & C. 855; 107 E.R. 1277. *Weinberger* v. *Inglis* [1919] A.C. 606. See also *Tierney* v. *Amalgamated Society of Woodworkers* [1959] I.R. 254. The Industrial Relations Act 1971, s. 65 (1) provided a right for qualified applicants not to be excluded from membership by arbitrary or unreasonable discrimination. But see now *Central Council for Education and Training in Social Work* v. *Edwards, The Times*, May 5, 1978, where it was said that if a person is considered for admission to a polytechnic, the polytechnic has a duty to act "fairly" but not "judicially."

[11] [1966] 2 Q.B. 633. For a discussion of this case and admission in general see Rideout, "Admission to non-statutory associations controlling employment" (1967) 30 M.L.R. 389. *C.f. Forbes* v. *N.S.W. Trotting Club* [1977] 2 N.S.W.L.R. 515 (professional punter has no right of admission to a race course).

[12] The case was brought on the grounds of the right to work because it was not clear that training horses was a "vocation" within the Sex Disqualification (Removal) Act 1919.

[13] It is important to note that the appeal was against the decision of the master to strike out the statement of claim as it disclosed no cause of action.

[14] [1966] 2 Q.B. 633 at 646–647.

[15] Because the Trade Union Act 1871 relieved the purposes of trade unions from any disabilities imposed by the doctrine.

[16] [1971] Ch. 354: strictly speaking it may be doubted whether the argument was necessary: the case concerned the admittedly wrongful expulsion of a temporary member. The union claimed it was only liable for nominal damages for it could have expelled the plaintiff at any time. The court held the plaintiff was entitled to his whole actual loss.

seemed to take the view that his "right to work" was independent of restraint of trade. He said[17] that in the case of a closed shop the courts will not allow the power to deprive a person of his livelihood to be exercised arbitrarily or capriciously or with unfair discrimination.

> "A trade union exists to protect the right of each one of its members to earn his living and to take advantage of all that goes with it. It is the very purpose of its being. If the union should assume to make a rule which destroys that right or puts it in jeopardy or is a gratuitous and oppressive interference with it—then the union exceeds its powers. The rule is *ultra vires* and invalid."

It should be noted that Lord Denning is speaking here of expulsion from a union and the avoiding of a rule,[18] and it may be difficult to apply the same reasoning to a refusal to admit a person into membership. But in any event it may be doubted whether the reasoning is sufficient to create an entirely new common law right, and one might in particular question the basic premise that a union exists to protect each individual. Its purpose is rather to protect the interests of its members as a whole and this may require the sacrifice of the interests of a particular member. In addition the application of the *ultra vires* principle to such vaguely expressed objects may be doubted.

In the same case Sachs L.J. based himself entirely on the restraint of trade doctrine and sought to evade the effect of the Trade Union Act 1871 by saying that is was not the purpose of the union which attracted the doctrine but the rule itself. This way out has now been blocked,[19] and thus the only remedy that could be used to protect the right to admission is Lord Denning's "right to work,"[20] but it may be doubted whether it would be successful.

The power to admit

A union has no power to admit a person who is not qualified,[21] nor can it admit an otherwise qualified applicant to a grade of membership that does not exist. The first point is illustrated by *Faramus* v. *Film Artistes Association*[22] where the union had a rule that no person who had committed a criminal offence was eligible for membership and it was held that the plaintiff who had been convicted of offences in Jersey in 1938 and 1940,[23] was not and never had been a member of the union even though he had been treated as such for eight years.

The second point is illustrated by *Martin* v. *Scottish T.G.W.U.*[24] where the applicant had been admitted to the union as a "temporary" member, and the

---

[17] *Ibid.* at 376.

[18] As to a rule providing for automatic forfeiture of membership, Lord Denning was supported by Plowman J. in *Radford* v. *NATSOPA* [1972] I.C.R. 484 at 496.

[19] By T.U.L.R.A. 1974, s. 2 (5). The saving in s. 5 (5) has been repealed by the Trade Union and Labour Relations (Amendment) Act 1976.

[20] For the "right to work" in another context see *Langstone* v. *A.U.E.W.* [1974] I.C.R. 180 (C.A.) and *ibid.* (No. 2) [1974] I.C.R. 510, where the issue was the employer's duty to supply the employee with work (the right to sweat).

[21] A person may obtain a declaration that he is or is not qualified: *Boulting* v. *ACTAT* [1963] 2 Q.B. 606.

[22] [1964] A.C. 925.

[23] The plaintiff had been convicted in 1939 of taking and driving away a motor vehicle and in 1940 of falsely claiming money by stating that his wife was unemployed. Such matters may now be protected by the Rehabilitation of Offenders Act 1974. The plaintiff had also been convicted of possessing propagandist literature and had spent some time in a German concentration camp.

[24] [1952] S.C.1.; [1952] 1 All E.R. 691.

House of Lords held that as the rules of the union did not allow for such a grade of membership the whole transaction was *ultra vires* and void, so that again the plaintiff had never been a member. It should be noted that if the union has no power to admit an applicant it cannot be held to be estopped by its subsequent behaviour in treating him as a member, although such a principle might apply if the defect is procedural only and not an infringement of the rule book.

Acceptance of the application

There is some doubt about the point at which a person becomes a member if the rules are silent on the point, but it is suggested that the decision in *Woodford* v. *Smith*[25] that a qualified person may become a member of an organisation by handing in a completed application form should not be applied to trade unions,[26] for it is usually supposed that applications are subject to approval by the relevant branch,[27] and such a view may be effective on the grounds of "custom and practice."

Whether a person may become a member by conduct alone is now a matter of some uncertainty. It had always been thought that the conclusion to be drawn from *Faramus* v. *Film Artistes Association*[28] and *Martin* v. *Scottish T.GW.U.*[29] was that conduct was not sufficient[30] but these cases have now been distinguished by Foster J. in *Rothwell* v. *APEX*[31] on the ground that in both instances a member had to fulfil certain qualifications, or at least be free of a certain disqualification, but that if the union in question imposes no such qualification then a person may become a member by conduct. It is suggested, however, that such a principle should be used with extreme caution and may be of doubtful validity.

The effect of the Bridlington Agreement

The "Bridlington Agreement"[32] was drawn up in 1939[33] because, in the words of the T.U.C.:

> "trade unionists recognised that, in situations where more than one union was capable of representing a particular grade of worker, it was necessary to prevent the indiscriminate proliferation of unions if stable and rational trade union structures and collective bargaining machinery were to be developed. Their existence has also prevented the instability that would occur if breakaway unions were formed, or if groups of workers were able to move on a whim from one union to another."

---

[25] [1970] 1 W.L.R. 806.

[26] The case concerned the Fulham and Hammersmith Ratepayers' and Residents' Association.

[27] But see *Goad* v. *A.U.E.W.* [1972] I.C.R. 429 where the plaintiff was given a membership card and paid his subscription, but this was later returned to him on the ground that he was not acceptable to the branch. The case proceeded on the assumption that he was a member, partly on the basis that the rules gave a power of veto to the executive committee and not to the branch and was therefore wrongly exercised. The point was never argued.

[28] [1964] A.C. 925. This case makes it clear that a person who is not eligible cannot become a member by conduct.

[29] [1952] S.C.1.; [1952] 1 All E.R. 691.

[30] It is sometimes suggested that *Davis* v. *Carew Pole* [1956] 1 W.L.R. 833 might be extended to cover this issue, but it is suggested that it is inapplicable.

[31] [1976] I.C.R. 211 at 221.

[32] The text is to be found in the T.U.C. pamphlet "T.U.C. Disputes Principles and Procedures" (1976).

[33] The 1939 principles were supplemented by a special congress at Croydon in 1969 and have been amended since.

The agreement thus deals with two kinds of dispute: first, disputes between unions about the transfer of individual members, and secondly "organisational" disputes, that is disputes about which union should organise the workers in a particular unit. If there is no agreement between the unions on these issues the matter is referred to the T.U.C. Disputes Committee under rule 12 of the T.U.C.[34] and although the awards are not legally binding, a union may ultimately be suspended from the T.U.C. for refusal to comply with a decision.[35]

The agreement is relevant to admission because not only may a union be prevented from recruiting members, but also it may not be allowed to accept into membership a person who applies. In relation to organisational activities Principle 5 states that: "no union shall commence organising activities at any establishment or undertaking in respect of any grade or grades of workers in which another union has the majority of workers employed and negotiates wages and conditions, unless by arrangement with that union."

In *Rothwell* v. *APEX*[36] a strict interpretation was placed on this principle so that it was held to apply only to cases where one union has more than 50 per cent. of the relevant employees in membership and in addition it was said that it only applied to commencing "organisational" activities and that this did not include an outside union offering to merge with a union that had a number of members amongst the workforce.[37] The decision of the Disputes Committee was accordingly held to be *ultra vires* and void as it had misapplied the principle.

In relation to disputes over individuals Principle 2 states that: "no one who is or has recently been a member of any affiliated union should be accepted into membership in another without enquiry of his present or former union," and the enquiry form asks if the applicant has resigned, is in arrears, is under discipline or penalty or if there is any other reason why he should not be accepted. If the former union objects he cannot be accepted into membership, but if the accepting union regards the objections as unreasonable it may take the matter to the T.U.C. Disputes Committee. Once again the provision of the principle must be strictly adhered to, and in particular the enquiries must be made before the applicant is admitted, for once admitted it may be difficult to expel him.

Trade union procedures

If a person has been admitted to membership in breach of the Bridlington Agreement the union may wish to undo what it has done and it is clear that any expulsion must be made in accordance with the rule book. Until recently many unions did not have a special rule permitting expulsion on the grounds of compliance with the Bridlington Agreement, and it was due to the lack of such

---

[34] The decisions of the committee are reported in the T.U.C.'s annual report. For a thorough analysis of these decisions see Kalis, "The Adjudication of Inter-union Membership Disputes: the T.U.C. Disputes Committee Revisited." (1977) 6 I.L.J. 19. See also S. Lerner, *Breakaway Unions and the Small Trade Union* (1961); Kalis, "The effectiveness and utility of the Disputes Committee of the T.U.C." (1978) 16 B.J.I.R. 41.

[35] T.U.C. r. 13 (*c*).

[36] [1976] I.C.R. 211 at 223.

[37] A.S.T.M.S. complained that APEX had offered to accept a transfer of engagements from SAGA which had some 3,000 members in General Accident. A.S.T.M.S. had about 1,200, and the total number of relevant employees was 8,300. The Commission on Industrial Relations had earlier recommended a merger between A.S.T.M.S. and SAGA but negotiations had been unsuccessful.

a rule that an expulsion was held void in *Spring* v. *N.A.S.D.S.*[38] Since that time most unions have adopted the T.U.C. model rule to cover such a case, and this rule states that: "Notwithstanding anything in these rules the executive council may, by giving six weeks' notice in writing, terminate the membership of any member, if necessary, in order to comply with a decision of a Disputes Committee of the Trades Union Congress."[39]

In *Rothwell* v. *APEX*[40] it was held that such a rule may only be used in pursuance of a *valid* decision of the committee and thus an expulsion in pursuance of an *ultra vires* decision was ineffective. It was also argued that the rule would not cover a case where the decision was made in bad faith, was perverse or was in breach of natural justice, but no decision was taken on these issues.[41]

One major problem with the model rule is that it may not apply unless there has actually been a decision of the Disputes Committee. In many cases the dispute does not get that far and the matter is settled between the unions concerned, and it is suggested that the rule would be interpreted strictly so as to be inapplicable to an expulsion based on a settlement between unions in pursuance of the Bridlington Agreement. In *Walsh* v. *A.U.E.W.*[42] the union was unable to rely on such a rule because it had not given the requisite notice and also because there had never been an actual decision of the Disputes Committee.[43]

The T.U.C.'s procedure

Apart from the fact that the Disputes' Committee must follow the wording of the relevant principle,[44] it is also essential that it complies with the terms of reference,[44] It has also been held that a decision of the committee would be *ultra vires* if it attempted to undo what had been lawfully done by statute, so that it was unable to require a union to undo a merger.[45] The Disputes Committee is required to apply the principles of natural justice,[46] although it is uncertain how far these principles apply to those who are only indirectly involved in the dispute.[47]

The procedural rules of the T.U.C. were subjected to criticism in *Rothwell* v. *APEX* and they have since been amended.[49]

---

[38] [1956] 1 W.L.R. 585. Attempts to imply a term permitting expulsion were not successful, the court using, in a rather bizarre way, the test of the "officious bystander." See also *Andrews* v. *NUPE*, *The Times*, July 9, 1955.

[39] This version incorporates suggested minor amendments to this rule; see the T.U.C. Annual Report, 1976, para. 92.

[40] [1976] I.C.R. 211.

[41] It was also argued that the rule was void as being against public policy, and fortunately this too was not discussed. For a judicial view that the principles are beneficial see *Phillips* v. *NALGO* [1973] I.R.L.R. 19 at 22 and *Remington* v. *NUPE* [1973] I.R.L.R. 273 at 275

[42] *The Times*, July 15, 1977. The case concerned a dispute between the A.U.E.W. and APEX as to who should organise the A.U.E.W. headquarters staff. A compromise was reached whereby each union represented some of the employees, although it seems odd that a person should be represented by a union that is also his employer.

[43] It was also decided that the union could not rely on a rule permitting the executive to take action which is "necessary or expedient for the welfare or good government of the union."

[44] *Rothwell* v. *APEX* [1976] I.C.R. 211 at 223.

[45] *Ibid.* at 224.

[46] The obligation is contained in r. 11 (*c*) of the T.U.C.

[47] In *Rothwell* v. *APEX* [1976] I.C.R. 211 at 223 it was stated that the failure to hear the plaintiff did not vitiate the hearing. He was not a party to the dispute but was affected by its outcome.

[48] See T.U.C. Annual Report 1976 para. 91 and Annex 2.

The Control of Diciplinary Procedure

All unions provide themselves by their rules books with disciplinary powers to deal with action by members which is considered to be against the interests of the union.[49] Not only is there usually a wide range of offences but also a sophisticated disciplinary structure for dealing with them. The degree to which the law should control these procedures has always been a matter of acute controversy, but it may be said that in general the courts are now more willing to intervene than they once were.[50]

One preliminary issue that needs to be dealt with is what is a disciplinary procedure? The issue arose in *Losinska* v. *C.P.S.A.*[51] where the plaintiff, who was president of the defendant union, had written an article denouncing some of her members as Marxists and extremists whose object was to paralyse local and central government. A number of motions were passed by the National Executive Council deploring her action and in addition some motions of censure were to be put forward at the annual conference. The Court of Appeal granted injunctions preventing the circulation of the motion passed by the executive and forestalling the discussion at conference of the censure motions, on the grounds that they amounted to disciplinary action which should have been dealt with under the appropriate rule. The distinction is a fine one, perhaps too fine, although the problem could no doubt be avoided if what was condemned was not the person expressing the views, but the views themselves.

Breach of the rules

If a union is to discipline one of its members it must have the power to do so and must act in accordance with the rule book.[52] Any breach of the rules will provide an opportunity for the court to intervene either by declaring the disciplinary act to be void or by awarding damages.[53]

The breach may be caused by the union following the incorrect procedure for disciplinary action,[54] or, more commonly, it may be that the committee has misapplied the rules and that in fact no breach had been committed by the member. This latter kind of breach takes two forms: it may be a simple matter of misinterpretation of the meaning of the words in the rules, or it may be that the rule is very widely phrased and the question is whether the conduct of the member could amount to a breach. An example of the first case is *Mclelland* v. *N.U.J.*[55] where the plaintiff was disciplined for having failed to "attend" a mandatory meeting, but Whitford J. held, rather surprisingly, that "attend" only meant "sign on" and that the plaintiff once having attended need not remain in attendance. The disciplinary action was therefore declared void. An example of the second kind of case is *Kelly* v. *NATSOPA*[56] where the court

[49] See Rideout, "The Content of Trade Union Disciplinary Rules" (1965) 3 B.J.I.R. 153.

[50] For a complete survey of the common law see Rideout, *The right to membership of a trade union* (1963). See also Kay, "The settlement of membership disputes in trade unions," in *Studies in Labour Law* (1975) Carby-Hall. Kahn-Freund, *Labour and the Law* (2nd ed.), pp. 180–193.

[51] [1976] I.C.R. 473.

[52] *Lee* v. *Showmen's Guild* [1952] 2 Q.B. 329.

[53] *Bonsor* v. *Musicians' Union* [1956] A.C. 104, overruling *Kelly* v. *NATSOPA* (1915) 31 T.L.R. 632 on this point. See also *Santer* v. *N.G.A.* [1973] I.C.R. 60 where the plaintiff was awarded damages of £1,330 for improper expulsion because of his difficulty in finding another job.

[54] As in *Santer* v. *N.G.A.* [1973] I.C.R. 60.

[55] [1975] I.C.R. 116.

[56] [1915] 31 T.L.R. 632.

held that taking a part time job could not amount to conduct prejudicial to the interests of the union.[57]

This second class of case creates some difficulty for it raises the problem of how far the courts will intervene to determine the facts or the interpretation placed upon them. In *Lee* v. *Showmen's Guild*[58] Lord Denning said that the rules may make the domestic tribunal final arbiters of fact but not of law, but he went on to point out that the court can inquire into the application of the law to the facts. He said:[59]

> "The construction of the rules is so bound up with the application of the rules to the facts that no one can tell one from the other . . . If, however, the facts were not reasonably capable of being held to be a breach, and yet the committee held them to be a breach, then the only inference is that the committee have misconstrued the rules and exceeded their jurisdiction. The proposition is sometimes stated in the form that the court can interfere if there was no evidence to support the finding of the committee; but that only means that the facts were not reasonably capable of supporting the finding."

By this means the courts have given themselves considerable power, especially in cases where the rule in question is one which forbids in general terms action which is contrary to the interests of the union, for then the courts may in effect determine what the union's interests are. A case of this kind arose in *Esterman* v. *NALGO*[60] where the plaintiff was threatened with disciplinary action for refusing to obey an instruction to withold assistance as a returning officer during an election. The case was heard before the union's disciplinary committee even met, so the question was whether as a matter of law the plaintiff's conduct could amount to conduct rendering her unfit to be a member of the union, or as Templeman J. put it[61] whether a prima facia case had been made out that "no committee, applying itself correctly as to the law" could come to that conclusion. In the event it was held that the order to withdraw assistance was one "to which the national executive council had no right to demand his obedience and it was an order which, as a person—a loyal member of NALGO—acting in its best interests, he felt bound to disobey." By this means individual freedom of action was protected at the expense of the union's interest in collective security and the court gave itself extensive powers. It is suggested, however, that they should only be used with the greatest care.

Natural justice

It has been established since *Lee* v. *Showmen's Guild*[62] that internal trade union disciplinary bodies must apply the principles of natural justice for:

> "although the jurisdiction of a domestic tribunal is founded on contract, express or implied, nevertheless the parties are not free to make any contract they like. There are important limitations imposed by public policy. The tribunal must, for instance, observe the principles of natural

[57] See also *Radford* v. *NATSOPA* [1972] I.C.R. 484; *Silvester* v. *N.U.P.B.P.W.* (1966) 1 K.I.R. 679. On the other hand a more permissive attitude was displayed in *Evans* v. *N.U.P.B.P.W.* [1938] 4 All E.R. 51.

[58] [1952] 2 Q.B. 329 at 342.

[59] *Ibid.* at 345.

[60] [1974] I.C.R. 626. See Davies (1975) 4 I.L.J. 112.

[61] *Ibid.* at 632.

[62] [1952] 2 Q.B. 329.

justice. They must give the man notice of the charge and a reasonable opportunity to meet it. Any stipulation to the contrary would be void."[63]

The principles apply to any disciplinary decision,[64] and it is no longer necessary that the body be regarded as acting in a quasi-judicial capacity, although all disciplinary bodies would be acting in such a way. The need to make a decision cannot be avoided by a rule providing for automatic forfeiture of membership, for such a rule may be void.[65]

Notice of the charge

It is clear that a person must not only be given notice[66] in general terms of the facts which are alleged against him, but also of the rule of which a breach is alleged and the potential penalties which may be applied. A person may not be "convicted" of, or sentenced for a breach of a rule of which he has no notice. Thus in *Annamunthodo* v. *Oilfield Workers Union*[67] the plaintiff, who had publicly alleged that certain of the union officers were corrupt, was charged with a number of offences against the rules, but he was finally expelled under a different rule of which he had had no notice. The expulsion was therefore void.

The opportunity to be heard

This is the central provision of the principles of natural justice and the obligation is universal in disciplinary[68] cases, however clear the result may seem to be at the start. In *Johns* v. *Rees*[69] Megarry J. stated the justification for this view by saying:

"As everybody who has anything to do with the law well knows, the path of the law is strewn with examples of open and shut cases which, somehow, were not; of unanswerable charges which, in the event, were completely answered; of inexplicable conduct which was fully explained; of fixed and unalterable determination that by discussion, suffered a change. Nor are those with any knowledge of human nature who presume to think for a moment likely to underestimate the feelings of resentment of those who find that a decision against them has been made without their being afforded any opportunity to influence the course of events."

If, therefore, the member has not been given an opportunity to present his case the decision is invalid,[70] but if a member chooses not to avail himself of an opportunity which is in all respects reasonable the decision may be taken in his

---

[63] *Ibid.* at 342 *per* Denning L.J. It is suggested that this is the view that would be generally accepted today, but see *Lawlor* v. *U.P.W.* [1965] Ch. 712 at 728.

[64] See for example *Hiles* v. *Amalgamated Society of Woodworkers* [1968] Chap. 440; *Annamunthodo* v. *Oilfield Workers Union* [1961] A.C. 945; *Lawlor* v. *U.P.W.* [1965] Chap. 712; *Leary* v. *N.U.V.B.* [1971] Chap. 34; *Roebuck* v. *N.U.M.* [1977] I.C.R. 573. The rule also applies to the confirmation of an official in office in certain circumstances: *Breen* v. *A.E.U.* [1971] 2 Q.B. 175; *Shotton* v. *Hammond*, *The Times*, October 26, 1976.

[65] *Edwards* v. *SOGAT* [1971] Chap. 354; *Radford* v. *NATSOPA* [1972] I.C.R. 484.

[66] *Santer* v. *N.G.A.* [1973] I.C.R. 60 at 67; in construing the provision of a rule that notice must be given, it was said that it is desirable that it should be in writing.

[67] [1961] A.C. 945. See also *Abbott* v. *Sullivan* [1952] 1 K.B. 189.

[68] Expulsion for arrears is not a disciplinary case.

[69] [1970] Ch. 345 at 402.

[70] For examples see *Lawlor* v. *U.P.W.* [1965] Ch. 712; Leary v. *N.U.V.B.* [1971] Ch. 34; *Hiles* v. *Amalgamated Society of Woodworkers* [1968] Ch. 440.

absence, so long as the member has had proper notice of the charges and potential penalties.[71]

Allied to this point is the view that the proposed time and place of the hearing should be such as to give the member a reasonable chance of attending.

Notice of the hearing

It is suggested that the period of notice must be such as to provide the member with an adequate opportunity to prepare his defence to the allegation.

Conduct of the hearing: fairness

It seems that not only should the procedure be fair in the sense of providing an opportunity to be heard but a domestic tribunal must exercise its discretion fairly. In *Breen* v. *A.E.U.*[72] the court claimed that it could intervene on this ground and declare a decision invalid, but it is not clear how far this principle extends. Edmund Davies L.J. said:[73]

> "Discretion up to a point was certainly theirs, but, though wide, it was not untrammelled—it had to be fairly exercised. Nevertheless, their decision was not, in my view, bound to be based on reasons which would convince all right-thinking people. Even though mistaken, they might still arrive at an honest conclusion and, provided they adopted no improper methods in reaching it, the decision itself could not be attacked."[74]

Such a passage could perhaps be used to extend the concept of natural justice beyond procedural fairness to include some elements of substantive fairness, that is that although the disciplinary tribunal could be wrong it could not come to a conclusion that no reasonable tribunal would come to.[75] Furthermore, it is not clear whether the court would intervene if a wholly irrelevant matter was taken into consideration, for in the case itself the court was bound by the condition of the appeal that no finding of fact could be challenged, and one of these facts was that a false accusation was not taken into account.[76]

Conduct of the hearing: bias

It is generally accepted that so far as possible in a judicial enquiry a person should not be judge in his own cause and should not appear to have pre-judged the issue. In relation to trade union disciplinary proceedings such principles need to be amended, since the disciplinary committee may by the constitution of the union be both complainant and judge. It is sometimes inevitable that the persons taking the decision will, as union officials, feel strongly about the member's conduct and may have openly voiced criticism of

---

[71] *Annamunthodo* v. *Oilfield Workers Union* [1961] A.C. 945 where the member did not attend because he was judging a mock trial sponsored by a girls' group. See also *Glynn* v. *Keele University* [1971] 1 W.L.R. 487.

[72] [1971] 2 Q.B. 175.

[73] *Ibid.* at 195.

[74] See also Lord Denning M.R. *ibid.* at 190. Reasons for the decision need not be given: *McInnes* v. *Onslow-Fane* [1978] 3 All E.R. 211.

[75] See for example, *per* Maugham J. in *Maclean* v. *Workers Union* [1929] 1 Ch. 602 at 621; "It is well settled that the decision of such a tribunal cannot be attacked on the ground that it is against the weight of the evidence ... There is perhaps a question whether the decision can be attacked on the ground that there is no evidence ... upon which the tribunal could possibly come to such a conclusion."

[76] [1971] 2 Q.B. 175 at 199.

it. In such a case the traditional view of the common law is summed up by the speech of Viscount Simon in *White* v. *Kuzych*[77] where he said:

> "What those who considered the charges against the respondent and decided whether he was guilty ought to bring to their task was a will to reach an honest conclusion after hearing what was urged on the other side, and a resolve not to make up their minds beforehand on his personal guilt, however firmly they held their conviction as to union policy and however strongly they had shared in previous adverse criticism of the respondent's conduct."[78]

An example of the application of this principle is *Maclean* v. *Workers Union*[79] where the plaintiff was disciplined by the executive committee of his union for refusing to alter his electoral address in accordance with the wishes of the committee. That body had to act in two capacities, and although the matter complained of was action taken against it by the plaintiff, it could still lawfully carry out its disciplinary functions so long as it acted honestly.[80]

However, it may be that the committee and its members are under a duty to do the best they can not only to avoid bias but also to avoid the appearance of bias, so that for example the chairman should not also act as prosecutor.[81] In such a case the complaint is not that the chairman is biased as such, but that the roles of judge and prosecutor should not be combined, at least if the rules do not require it.[81]

Another example of the principle that members must do what they can to avoid the appearance of bias is that a person who is clearly committed should not be a member of the disciplinary committee if this can be avoided under the rules. In *Roebuck* v. *N.U.M. (Yorkshire Area)*[82] the plaintiff was disciplined for allegedly misleading the union's solicitors over a case involving the area president, Mr. Arthur Scargill. Mr. Scargill chaired the disciplinary proceedings, and the court held that as the rules did not require him to be chairman there had been a breach of natural justice because Mr. Scargill had initiated the proceedings and had earlier expressed a view about the culpability of the plaintiffs. This is so even if the chairman does not have a vote, but is merely present when the committee retires to reach its decision. Justice was not seen to be done.[83]

Conduct of the hearing: legal representation

There are no recent cases directly on the question whether a person has the right to be legally represented before a union disciplinary body,[84] but the matter has arisen in relation to other groups. In *Pett* v. *Greyhound Racing Association (No. 1)*[85] Lord Denning thought that at least where a serious

---

[77] [1951] A.C. 585 at 596.

[78] In other words it is not necessary to have the "icy impartiality of Rhadamanthus," *ibid.* at 595 *per* Viscount Simon.

[79] [1929] 1 Ch. 602.

[80] The actual decision was based on wider grounds which will no longer be applied: see *Hiles* v. *Amalgamated Society of Woodworkers* [1968] Ch. 440.

[81] *Taylor* v. *N.U.S.* [1967] 1 W.L.R. 532 at 548.

[82] [1977] I.C.R. 573 (interlocutory); *Roebuck* v. *N.U.M. (No. 2)* [1978] I.C.R. 676 (full trial).

[83] The decision was based on the judgment of Dixon J. in *Australian Workers' Union* v. *Bowen (No. 2)* (1948) 77 C.L.R. 601. See also *Dickason* v. *Edwards* (1910) 10 C.L.R. 243 and *Hall* v. *N.S.W. Trotting Club* [1971] 1 N.S.W.L.R. 378.

[84] But see the view of Maugham J. in *Maclean* v. *Workers Union* [1929] 1 Ch. 602 at 621 that there is no right of representation.

[85] [1968] 1 Q.B. 125 at 132. The case was an interlocutory one.

charge was involved or where a person's reputation or livelihood is at stake he has such a right, but Lyell J. at the full hearing of the case[86] decided that there was no such right.[87]

Lord Denning returned with a slightly different point in *Enderby Town Football Club* v. *Football Association*[88] when he doubted whether a domestic tribunal could pass a rule that a person would never be permitted legal representation, for it should always retain the discretion.[89] His lordship thought that public policy, in the guise of natural justice, could strike down a rule forbidding representation.

The law is therefore confused on this issue, but it is suggested that disciplinary proceedings in trade unions are not so formally organised that legal representation would be useful.[90]

A fair appeal

One question is whether if the initial hearing is defective through breach of the principles of natural justice, can this be cured by a fair appeal? In *Leary* v. *National Union of Vehicle Builders*[91] Megarry J. emphatically said no.

> "If one accepts the contention that a defect of natural justice in the trial body can be cured by the presence of natural justice in the appellate body, this has the result of depriving the member of his right of appeal from the expelling body. If the rules and the law combine to give the member the right to a fair trial and the right of appeal, why should he be told that he ought to be satisfied with an unjust trial and a fair appeal."

Ousting the jurisdiction of the courts

Any attempt to prevent the member from seeking a remedy from the courts at all will be void. In *Lee* v. *Showmen's Guild*[92] Denning L.J. said: "If the parties should seek by agreement, to take the law out of the hands of the courts and put it into the hands of a private tribunal, without any recourse at all to the courts in case of error of law, then the agreement is to that extent contrary to public policy and void."

Thus in *Leigh* v. *N.U.R.*[93] the court held that the rules of the the union purported to oust the jurisdiction of the courts and were to that extent invalid.[94]

The duty to exhaust internal remedies

While a union cannot prevent the member seeking redress from the courts at all, it may wish to postpone such an action until the union's internal disciplinary procedure has been completed. At one time the courts seemed willing to

---

[86] *Pett* v. *Greyhound Racing Association (No. 2)* [1970] 1 Q.B. 46.

[87] But there may be in "a society which has reached some degree of sophistication in its affairs." *Ibid.* at 66.

[88] [1971] 1 Q.B. 591.

[89] See also *Maynard* v. *Osmond* [1977] 1 Q.B. 240 at 252 where these views were repeated.

[90] And see the view of Lord Denning in *Enderby Town Football Club* v. *F.A.* [1971] 1 Ch. 591 at 607 that legal representation should not be ordered before the F.A. because the club wished to press legal points which could be presented to the courts, but if they chose first to go to a lay tribunal they must accept that with all its imperfection, including the lack of legal representation. But such a view ignores the duty to exhaust internal remedies before resort to the courts.

[91] [1971] Ch. 34 at 49.

[92] [1952] 2 Q.B. 329 at 342.

[93] [1970] Ch. 326 at 334.

[94] See also *Lawlor* v. *U.P.W.* [1965] Ch. 712 at 733, *per* Ungoed-Thomas J.

accede to such rules and in *White* v. *Kuzych*[95] the Privy Council refused to consider the plaintiff's case as the respondent was "bound by his contract" to pursue his internal appeal before he could issue his writ.

Since then, however, there has been a clear willingness to circumvent such exhaustion rules and in *Leigh* v. *N.U.R.*[96] Goff J. summarised the effect of previous cases[97] as follows:

> "Where there is an express provision in the rules that the plaintiff must first exhaust his domestic remedies, the court is not absolutely bound by that because its jurisdiction cannot be ousted, but the plaintiff will have to show cause why it should interfere with the contractual position. . . . The second proposition is largely the converse of the first, namely, that in the absence of such a provision the court can readily, or at all events more readily, grant relief without prior recourse to the domestic remedies, but may require the plaintiff to resort first to these remedies."

If, therefore, a rule preventing access to the courts altogether is void, and if the court will exercise its discretion over rules requiring exhaustion of internal remedies, it would be advisable to frame the rule in such a way that the discretion will be exercised in favour of the union's internal structure. But so far as is known there has been no such case[98] recently.

If in the future unions wish to argue that their internal appeal structure should be recognised, it may be relevant that the exhaustion rule provides adequate protection for the member and is able to provide suitable relief. Thus in *Leigh* v. *N.U.R.*[99] it was noted that the appeal structure was such that the plaintiff would be unlikely to obtain relief before the election was held for which he sought to be a candidate, and that although this did not entirely prevent the plaintiff seeking legal redress (for the matter could have been dealt with after the election), the inconvenience of this was so manifest as to permit the court to ignore the internal procedure.

Again, it may be relevant whether the internal procedure preserves the status quo pending the appeal, for in *Hiles* v. *Amalgamated Society of Woodworkers*[1] the court distinguished *White* v. *Kuzych*[2] on the ground that in that case the rules protected the plaintiff until he had exhausted his internal appeal procedure. Such a rule is strongly recommended.

Interlocutory injunctions

A recent procedural innovation has meant that it will be very much easier for union members to get injunctions against their union for breach of the rules or failure to obey the principles of natural justice. This is so because in *American Cyanamid Co.* v. *Ethicon*[3] the House of Lords announced new principles to

---

[95] [1951] A.C. 585 at 601.

[96] [1970] Ch. 326 at 334. See also *Shotton* v. *Hammond, The Times,* October 26, 1976, where Oliver J. thought it was not a factor of great weight.

[97] Including *Lawlor* v. *U.P.W.* [1965] Ch. 712.

[98] See for example *Radford* v. *NATSOPA* [1972] I.C.R. 484 at 499 where it was pointed out that as the case involved interpretation of the rules, it was particularly suitable for hearing directly by the courts. See also the unfortunate case of *Esterman* v. *NALGO* [1974] I.C.R. 625 where the court intervened even before any disciplinary hearings had been held at all.

[99] [1970] Ch. 326 at 335.

[1] [1968] Ch. 440 at 453.

[2] [1951] A.C. 585.

[3] [1975] A.C. 396.

apply in cases of interlocutory injunctions[4] which may be summarised as follows:

1. An applicant for an interlocutory injunction need no longer show that he has a prima facie case, but rather the court should consider the balance of convenience unless the material before the court fails to disclose that the plaintiff has any real prospect of succeeding at the full trial or that there is a serious issue to be tried.

2. In deciding the balance of convenience the court should consider (a) whether if no injunction were awarded and the plaintiff succeeded at the full trial, would damages adequately compensate him for loss suffered in the meantime and (b) whether if the injunctions were granted would the plaintiff's undertakings as to damages be sufficient to compensate the defendant for loss suffered in the meantime if the defendant finally won.

As a result of this decision a member may no longer have to show a prima facie breach of the rules or of natural justice, and in addition it may have weakened such protection as there was under the duty to exhaust internal union remedies. The problem is exacerbated by the probability that in discussing the balance of convenience the courts will prefer the individual interest of the plaintiff to the collective interest of the trade union.[5] The problem would not be so bad if cases in fact went to full trial but it is well known that very few of the cases discussed in this chapter went to full trial after an interlocutory hearing,[6] so that in effect the case can be decided without event a prima facie case being made out that the conduct complained of is illegal. For example in *Losinska* v. *C.P.S.A.*[5] Geoffrey Lane L.J. thought the decision in the case had been simplified by the new procedure, and did not discuss the difficult question of whether the rule dealing with disciplinary procedure applied to what the defendants proposed to do.

It is to be hoped that the *American Cyanamid* principle will be held inapplicable to domestic proceedings. In *Lewis* v. *Heffer*[7] Geoffrey Lane L.J. said that the principles of *American Cyanamid* were practically impossible to apply to a case involving the internal affairs of a constituency Labour Party as they were designed to cover a commercial and not a political situation. However, his reason was that everything was in a state of flux and that *American Cyanamid* was best suited to a case where it was possible to "freeze the situation that existed before the dispute between the parties arose."

"Freezing" may be possible in a trade union case, but it only makes sense if the matter is to be fully considered later. In most cases of internal union affairs it is not and cases are effectively settled at the interlocutory stage.[8]

Mandatory remedies

One of the more disturbing developments is the linking of the *American Cyanamid* principle with the granting of mandatory remedies, because a person can obtain an order for positive action without the illegality or otherwise of the

[4] The effect of the case is ameliorated in relation to trade disputes, T.U.L.R.A. 1974, s. 17 (2).

[5] See for example *Losinska* v. *C.P.S.A.* [1976] I.C.R. 473 and *Hubbard* v. *Pitt* [1975] I.C.R. 308.

[6] By the time the full trial comes on the remedy may be hardly worth having due to the delay, but the action may still be maintained: *Gibson* v. *USDAW* [1968] 1 W.L.R. 1189.

[7] [1978] 1 W.L.R. 1061 at 1078; [1978] 3 All E.R. 354.

[8] See for example *Drake* v. *Morgan* [1978] I.C.R. 56 where at the request of counsel Forbes J. dealt with the substantive issues, rather than decide it on the balance of convenience, even though it was an interlocutory case.

defendant's action being established even on a prima facie basis.[9]

In *Shotton* v. *Hammond*[10] the court, after finding that the refusal to confirm a shop steward in office was in breach of natural justice,[11] ordered the union to convene a meeting of the relevant committee and confirm the plaintiff in his post. As Oliver J. pointed out, the making of a mandatory order against a domestic tribunal based on the court's exercise of discretion was without precedent, but it is difficult to see why the application of *American Cyanamid* principles should make the granting of such an order any easier. First the courts should be wary of making such an order principally on the balance of convenience and without full argument on the legality or otherwise of the defendants conduct, and secondly one wonders if after such a procedure there is any incentive for the plaintiff to go to full trial. Once he has been confirmed in office has he not achieved all he wants?

Damages

It was established by the House of Lords in *Bonsor* v. *Musicians' Union*[12] that a union member who is wrongfully expelled from his union may sue for damages.[13] In that case the plaintiff had been improperly expelled and since the musicians operated a closed shop he was unable to pursue his profession again.[14] In such circumstances the measure of damages will be similar to that which will follow wrongful dismissal from employment at common law,[15] since the general rule is that person is liable for breach of contract to the extent that was reasonably forseeable between the parties at the time of the contract.

In *Edwards* v. *SOGAT*[16] Lord Denning said:

> "[The damages] are to be ascertained by putting the plaintiff in as good a position, so far as money can do it, as if he had never been excluded from the union, taking into account, of course, all the contingencies which might have led to him leaving his employment anyway: and remembering, too, that it was his duty to do what was reasonable to mitigate the damage."

The damages will, therefore, consist of his actual loss up to the date of the trial and his projected future loss. If the plaintiff has been dismissed from his job as a result of his expulsion the damages under the first head will be the wages he would have been paid had he not been expelled from the union, subject to deductions for wages he has actually received for any other job he has taken since, and also deducting unemployment benefit[17] and any tax that

---

[9] It is for this reason that the decision of the House of Lords in *Gouriet* v. *U.P.W.* [1977] 3 All E.R. 70, is so necessary for had the view of the Court of Appeal prevailed a private person who has not suffered any particular damage over and above that of the public generally could have obtained, without establishing a prima facie case, a mandatory remedy to enfore a statutory duty, breach of which would have been a crime, even if the Attorney-General had refused to intervene.

[10] *The Times*, October 26, 1976.

[11] See also *Breen* v. *A.U.E.W.* [1971] 2 Q.B. 195.

[12] [1956] A.C. 104.

[13] The House overruled *Kelly* v. *NATSOPA* (1915) 31 T.L.R. 632 on this point.

[14] The plaintiff died the day before the judgment of the Court of Appeal was delivered and his widow continued with the case. The amount of damages was settled between the parties.

[15] See McGregor, *Damages* (13th ed.), Chap. 27.

[16] [1970] Ch. 354 at 377. The case rejected the argument that as the plaintiff was only a temporary member and could thus be lawfully expelled at any time, he should only receive nominal damages.

[17] *Parsons* v. *B.N.M. Laboratories* [1964] 1 Q.B. 95. But see also *Parry* v. *Cleaver* [1970] A.C. 1. It is submitted that supplementary benefits should not be deducted.

he would have paid on his wages in so far as the damages do not exceed £5,000.[18]

As to projected future loss it has been said[19] that "it would not be right to seek to give an aura of scientific respectibility to the assessment of future damage . . . One must try to assess. One cannot calculate."[20] Thus the assessment must be made "somewhat broadly" and Lord Denning has suggested, in a case involving expulsion where a closed shop operated, that as a base figure one could take losses that might be expected to arise up to two years from his expulsion.[21]

Mitigation of loss

These principles are subject to the all important proviso that a plaintiff is under a duty to mitigate his loss by seeking other work. In cases where the union operates a closed[22] shop on an industry wide scale it may be easy to see complete unemployment flowing from the expulsion for some considerable time. In such cases the question will depend on the extent to which the court thinks it is reasonable for the plaintiff to undertake work other than that at which he is skilled.[23]

Where the union operates a closed shop on the basis of individual establishments the opportunity to mitigate the loss will be greater, and more so of course where no closed shop exists at all.[24]

Mental distress

It has been thought that damages could not be given for the vexation caused by wrongful dismissal but in *Cox* v. *Phillips Industries*[25] Lawson J. did award such damages saying that:

> "I can see no reason in principle why, if a situation arises which within the contemplation of the parties would have given rise to vexation, distress and general disappointment and frustration, the person who is injured by a contractual breach should not be compensated in damages for that breach."

No case has specifically applied this principle to a trade union case but in *Santer* v. *N.G.A.*[26] Melford Stevenson J. had noted that the agreed damages of £1,330 were for the fact that the plaintiff "suffered great tribulation and difficulty in securing employment. It is that tribulation which is reflected in the agreed damages."

---

[18] *B.T.C.* v. *Gourley* [1956] A.C. 185; *Parsons* v. *B.N.M. Laboratories* [1964] 1 Q.B. 95. By the Income and Corporation Taxes Act 1970, ss. 187 and 188, damages over £5,000 are taxable in the hands of the recipient, in so far as they represent lost wages. For a full discussion see Wylie and McGlyne, "Taxation, Damages and Compensation for Unfair Dismisal (1978) 128 N.L.J. 550.

[19] *Edwards* v. *SOGAT* [1970] Ch. 354 at 387, *per* Megaw L.J.

[20] *Ibid. per* Lord Denning M.R. at 378.

[21] *Ibid.* This view was based on para. 661 of the Donovan Commission Report, Cmnd. 3623.

[22] If there is a union membership agreement the plaintiff will not be able to sue his employer for unfair dismissal. E.P.C.A. 1978, s. 58 (3).

[23] *Edwards* v. *SOGAT* [1970] Ch. 354. The issue also arose there of whether the plaintiff had acted reasonably in losing a skilled job he had acquired in a non-union shop in the meantime. The court took the view that he was justified in acting as he did and ironically that if it had been a union shop he probably would not have been dismissed.

[24] In the latter case the plaintiff may well be able to sue his employer for unfair dismissal, in which case the employer will not be allowed to plead that the reason for the dismissal was union pressure. E.P.C.A. 1978, s. 63.

[25] [1976] I.C.R. 138.

[26] [1973] I.C.R. 60 at 68.

Aggravated damages

While it is very unlikely that an award of exemplary damages could be made against a union,[27] the head of aggravated damage has been recognised, so that the judge may take into account "the motives and conduct of the defendant where they aggravate the injury done to the plaintiff. There may be malevolence or spite or the manner of committing the wrong may be such as to injure the plaintiff's proper feelings of dignity and pride."[28] It has been suggested by Lord Denning that such damages are not limited to actions in tort but may also be available in contract,[29] so that an award may be made for loss of reputation and standing and for injury to feelings of pride and dignity, but no other case has commented on this view.

A related matter is the suggestion that the damages can take into account the future attitude of the union to the plaintiff. It was said by Megaw L.J. in *Edwards* v. *SOGAT*[30] that one factor which might enhance the damages "is the relationship existing between the plaintiff and the defendant union. That is relevant so far as the plaintiff may have to rely, for future employment, not on the legal obligations of the defendants towards him (for if they should not be fulfilled there is a remedy) but on the defendant's co-operation outside strict legal obligations." In other words the union must truly repent.

THE T.U.C. "INDEPENDENT REVIEW COMMITTEE"

There has in recent years been considerable disquiet about control of union disciplinary powers and the Industrial Relations Act 1971, s. 65, provided a considerable degree of statutory protection for members. When that Act was repealed similar provisions were inserted in section 5 of the Trade Union and Labour Relations Act 1974. These provisions were in turn repealed,[31] but the T.U.C. gave an undertaking that it would establish its own machinery to cover this problem.

Accordingly in April 1976 the "Independent Review Committee" was established having the task of considering appeals from individuals "who have been dismissed or given notice of dismissal from their jobs as a result of being expelled from, or having been refused admission to, a union in a situation where trade union membership is a condition of employment."[32] Whether this body will be seen by the applicants as independent and as an adequate substitute for statutory arrangements remains to be seen.

As to procedure the committee has stated[32] that it will only consider cases where the applicant has exhausted all internal remedies and will in the first instance try to resolve the issue by agreement between the parties. If the committee proceeds to make a recommendation there are no sanctions levied upon the union for failing to observe it, although "there is a clear responsibility on the part of the union concerned to act upon such a recommendation."[32]

In the first case before the committee,[33] the applicant resigned from the N.U.G.M.W., was accepted into the E.E.T.P.U. in breach of the Bridlington

---

[27] The categories in which such damages can be awarded are limited: *Rookes* v. *Barnard* [1964] A.C. 1129 at 1226 *per* Lord Devlin.

[28] *Ibid.* at 1221.

[29] *Breen* v. *A.E.U.* [1971] 2 Q.B. 175 at 193. Lord Denning was dissenting.

[30] [1970] Ch. 354 at 387.

[31] By the Trade Union and Labour Relations (Amendment) Act 1976.

[32] The terms of reference and a statement of the committee's procedure are contained in the T.U.C. annual report for 1976, para. 89.

[33] *Dennis and the E.E.T.P.U. and the N.U.G.M.W.* T.U.C. Report for 1976, p. 396.

principles, and then expelled. The committee found that as a matter of law the applicant had validly resigned from his old union and was properly a member of E.E.T.P.U. and should be treated as such. However, the committee went on to suggest that despite this legal position there should be a negotiated settlement whereby the applicant would re-join N.U.G.M.W. without penalty and the E.E.T.P.U. would not bring pressure on his employer for his dismissal.

At the first hearing the chairman had said that the committee would "endeavour to reach conclusions which strike a just balance between the interests of the individual complaints and the interests of trade unions seen in the context of the whole trade union movement." In subsequent cases this has led the committee to abjure legal analysis and rely instead on a conception of what is just within the context of trade union principles. Thus in *Walmsley and SOGAT*[34] the Committee felt that a union was justified in expelling a person who attempted to persuade members to join another union, but suggested that the union consider sympathetically the question of re-admitting him as he had been treated more severely than another member.[35] The Committee has also taken cognisance of the principles of natural justice, but does not feel that a breach of the rules should necessarily lead to re-instatement in the union, for other measures (or none at all) may be more appropriate.[36] Thus the committee seems to be concentrating on the collective interests of the trade union and the attitude which the applicant ought to display as a trade unionist, rather than his interests as an individual, and for this reason the individualism of a purely legal approach has been rejected. A recommendation of the committee does not of course preclude an applicant from pursuing any remedy he may have before the courts.

The Right to Resign

Section 7 of the Trade Union and Labour Relations Act 1974[37] provides that each contract of membership shall contain an implied right to resign on giving reasonable notice and complying with any reasonable conditions. A remedy for a breach of this right must be sought from the ordinary courts and not from an industrial tribunal, and is further dealt with in Chapter 3.

[34] T.U.C. Report for 1977, p. 340.

[35] It was also held that a union was justified in expelling a person who had often been in arrears and who had on five occasions failed to comply with union rules on the filling of vacancies for employment. *Carroll and SOGAT*, T.U.C. Report for 1977, p. 339.

[36] *Buxton and T.G.W.U.*, T.U.C. Report for 1977, p. 341. The committee recommended that it should try to conciliate between the parties but the attempt failed.

[37] As amended by the T.U.L.R.A. (Amendment) Act 1976. See *Ashford* v. *A.S.T.M.S.* [1973] I.C.R. 296.

CHAPTER 6

UNION FUNDS AND ACCOUNTS

TRUSTEES

SINCE the Trade Union and Labour Relations Act 1974 prevents a union from being a corporate entity,[1] the property of a union must be vested in trustees.[2] Normally the trustees of an unincorporated association hold the funds on trust for the members of the association, but in the case of trade unions the Act explicitly states that the trustees shall hold the property on trust for the union.[2] It might seem a curious concept to hold the property on trust for a body that in law does not strictly exist as a separate entity, but whatever the logical problems it is, as Farwell J. said in the *Taff Vale*[3] case: "beside the mark to say of such an association that it is unknown to the common law. The Legislature has legalised it and it must be dealt with by the Courts according to the intention of the Legislature." This view was approved by Lord Hanworth M.R. in *Cotter* v. *National Union of Seamen*[4] and he also approved the dictum of Lord Lindley[5] that "The property so held is, however, the property of the union: the union is the beneficial owner." It thus appears that a union member has no proprietary interest in the funds of his union by virtue of the fact that it is an unincorporated association, but he does of course have rights which stem from the rule book and if the funds are used for purposes not permitted by the rules, the *ultra vires* doctrine will protect his interests.

The trustees are best regarded as receptacles of the legal title with little or no power within the union, and indeed most rule books require the trustees to act under the directions of the executive of the union.[6] Although it is usual for trustees to be members of the union[7] there is no legal requirement that they should be[8] and it is in theory possible to appoint a trust corporation instead of individuals[9] There is no provision in trade union legislation limiting the number of trustees, but it is useful for the purposes of conveyancing to appoint

---

[1] s. 2 (2).

[2] T.U.L.R.A. 1974, s. 2 (1) (*b*).

[3] [1901] A.C. 426 at 429.

[4] [1929] 2 Ch. 58 at 103.

[5] *Taff Vale* v. *Amalgamated Society of Railway Servants* [1901] A.C. 426 at 444.

[6] See for example rule 18 (2) of the T.G.W.U. "The funds and property of the Union shall be invested in the joint names of the trustees and dealt with by them as the General Executive Council shall direct."

[7] See for example T.G.W.U. rule 18 (1) which requires trustees to have been members for at least two years.

[8] *Yorkshire Miners Association* v. *Howden* [1905] A.C. 256 at 271.

[9] The argument in *Re National Union of Railwaymen's Rules* [1968] 1 All E.R. 5 that a union's funds could not be transferred to a company limited by guarantee was based on the terms of the Trade Union Act 1871, s. 8 and is no longer applicable.

not less than two and not more than four.[10]

Transfer of property

One of the problems associated with the lack of corporate status is that when for any reason the trustees change, the property must be vested in the new trustees. If one of the trustees dies the property will be vested automatically in the surviving trustees since they hold the property as joint tenants, but where it is desired either to appoint a new trustee because one of the existing trustees has resigned or become ineligible under the rules or to replace a trustee who has died, the Trade Union and Labour Relations Act 1974,[11] relieves some of the burdens imposed by the general law. For example, a trustee of a listed[12] trade union or unincorporated employers' association may be appointed or discharged by a written document rather than by a deed, and the written document may simply consist of a minute of a resolution of the association. Where securities of various kinds need to be registered it is only necessary to produce the document or resolution, together with a list of the securities signed by the president and general secretary, for the necessary entries to be made.

Investment

The trustees of a trade union have the same statutory powers of investment as any other trustees as contained in the Trustee Investments Act 1961.[13] In addition to such powers the rule book will usually provide the trustees with much wider powers of investment than the statute.[14]

Liability of trustees

A trade union trustee owes the same duty to his union as any other trustee to his beneficiary and he may be personally liable for any breach of trust he commits. It should be noted, however, that the liability is personal and not vicarious and that a trustee will not be liable for breaches by other trustees unless he himself is at fault.[15] While a trustee is under a fiduciary duty not to make a secret profit out of his position, he may be paid for his services if the rules of the union permit it.

The trustees of a union may find themselves in a difficult position if under the terms of their appointment they are obliged to carry out the instructions of the executive body of the union, for those instructions might involve action which is *ultra vires* and accordingly a breach of trust for which they may be personally liable. Thus in *Bennett* v. *National Amalgamated Society of Operative House and Ship Painters*[16] the executive council instructed the trustees to invest in a newspaper called the *Daily Citizen*, but the court held that this investment was beyond the power of the union[17] and that the trustees were

[10] The problems concern dealing with land under a trust. See Trustee Act 1925, s. 34 (1); Law of Property Act 1925, s. 27 (2); Settled Land Act 1925, s. 18 (1).

[11] s. 4.

[12] The benefit is confined to listed organisations in order that it should be clear who is entitled to this concession.

[13] See for example Snell, *Principles of Equity* (27th ed.), pp. 206–217.

[14] See for example T.G.W.U. Rule 6 (14).

[15] See Trustee Act 1925 s. 30 (1); *Re City Equitable Fire Insurance Co.* [1925] Ch. 407; *Re Vickery* [1931] 1 Ch. 572; *Re Lucking* [1967] 3 All E.R. 726.

[16] (1915) 113 L.T. 808.

[17] See also *Carter* v. *United Society of Boilermakers* (1915) 32 T.L.R. 40.

liable to make good the money wrongfully applied. It seems, therefore, that in such cases the trustees should resist the directives of the union's executive or seek a declaration as to the legality of the proposed action.

Accounts and Returns

The Trade Union and Labour Relations Act 1974, sections 10–12 and schedule 2, lay down rules for the preparation of accounts and the appointment of auditors. These sections contain some of the few burdens imposed on trade unions by law and are necessary to apply a minimum standard of accounting and reporting for the protection of union assets. The individual member will have an action for breach of the rules in cases of mis-application of funds and the periodical audit will also be an additional safeguard. Although a member has no statutory right to see the accounts, he has the same right as any other member of the public to inspect the union's annual return to the Certification Officer,[18] and in addition he may be given further rights by the rule book. For example rule 23 of the T.G.W.U. states that "every person having an interest[19] in the funds of the union may, on giving due notice, inspect all the books of the union and the names of the members at any place where the same are kept." In such cases the right to inspect the accounts is not limited to the member himself but may be exercised by an accountant acting on his behalf,[20] although the court is prepared to exercise control to prevent abuse of this privilege.[21] For example it would be reasonable to require the accountant to give an undertaking that the information obtained will be used only for assisting his client, and the union may be entitled to resist the inspection if the accountant is personally objectionable to the union, or if too many members apply at the same time or if the union can show that the member is acting in bad faith.[21]

The accounts and annual return

Every trade union and employer's association[22] (whether listed or not) is required to keep proper accounting records which give a true and fair view of the state of affairs of the organisation[23] and also to maintain a satisfactory system of control of such records.[24] In addition, each such organisation must make an annual return to the Certification Officer for each calendar year;[25] this must consist of revenue accounts, a balance sheet, a copy of the rules and a note indicating any change of officers or change of address.[26] These provisions are enforced by the criminal law so that the officer delegated to make the return or keep the accounts is guilty of an offence if he refuses or wilfully neglects to discharge the duty.[27] Furthermore, any person who wilfully alters a

---

[18] T.U.L.R.A. 1974, ss. (11) (4) & (5). This is either free or on payment of a reasonable charge.

[19] It is thought that this word is not limited to those who have an interest in the funds under the rules, but should be interpreted more broadly. Thus those entitled to the property on dissolution may be said to have an interest.

[20] *Norey* v. *Keep* [1909] 1 Ch. 561.

[21] *Dodd* v. *Amalgamated Marine Workers Union* [1924] 1 Ch. 117.

[22] Except those which consist wholly or mainly of constituent or affiliated organisations.

[23] Advice on the accounting requirements of trade unions is being prepared by the Consultative Committee of Accountancy bodies.

[24] T.U.L.R.A. 1974, s. 10.

[25] The return must be submitted by June 1, for the preceding year ending December 31, but this requirement may be waived by the Certification Officer.

[26] T.U.L.R.A. 1974, Sched. 2.

[27] T.U.L.R.A. 1974, s. 12.

document required for these purposes is also guilty of an offence if his object was to falsify the document or enable the organisation to evade its duties under these provisions.

The auditors

Schedule 2 to the 1974 Act also lays down that a union may only employ professionally qualified auditors except where an unqualified auditor has acted continuously since 1971 for a union then registered under the Trade Union Act 1871, or where neither the union's receipts and payments nor its assets exceed £5,000 and it has less than 500 members; in these cases two unqualified persons may act. An officer or employee of the union may not act as auditor.

The rules of a union or employers' association must make provision for the appointment and removal of auditors, but notwithstanding the rules an auditor can only be removed by a resolution passed at a general meeting. Regulations may make provision for the procedure to be followed at such a meeting. The auditor has the right of access to all accounting records and may attend any general meeting and speak on any topic that concerns him as auditor.

Superannuation schemes

Schedule 2 to the 1974 Act also requires that members' superannuation schemes[28] must be examined by a qualified actuary every five years (or such shorter period as the Certification Officer shall direct) except where it is unnecessary for the scheme to be examined because of the small number of members or for any other special reason.[29] In addition the organisation must maintain a fund separate from the general funds for the payment of benefit to members under the scheme.[30]

TAXATION

In general a trade union is subject to the same rules of taxation as other associations, except that special provision is made for sums applied to provident purposes. It is stated[31] that a listed[32] trade union which is precluded by statute or by its rules from assuring a capital sum exceeding £1,000 or £208[33] a year by way of annuity is exempt from income tax, corporation tax and capital gains tax in respect of income which is not trading income and which is applicable and applied for the purpose of provident benefits. This exemption is also available to the Police Federations[34] and to listed employers' associations which were registered as trade unions on September 30, 1971.[35]

---

[28] The scheme must be for members rather than for employees to be included in these provisions.

[29] Of the 41 schemes identified by the Certification Officer in 1976, 16 have been exempted from the need for actuarial examination.

[30] Although these provisions apply equally to employers' associations, no such body is known to have a superannuation scheme for its members.

[31] Income and Corporation Taxes Act 1970, s. 338 as amended by Finance Act 1974, s. 28 (1) and Finance (No. 2) Act 1975, s. 51.

[32] Finance Act 1974, s. 28 (1) (*a*) applies the exemption to listed trade unions. The list is maintained by the Certification Officer.

[33] The amounts were increased to these sums by Finance (No. 2) Act 1975, s. 51.

[34] Finance Act 1977, s. 47.

[35] Finance (No. 2) Act 1975, s. 53.

For the purposes of calculating the limits which may be assured before the exemption is lost there shall be disregarded[36] any "approved annuities," which are defined as annuities approved by the Board which are wholly paid for by the premiums of a person who is liable to tax.[37]

"Provident benefits"

The statute states[38] that the phrase "provident benefits":

> "includes any payment, expressly authorised by the rules of the trade union, which is made to a member during sickness or incapacity from personal injury or while out of work, or to an aged member by way of superannuation, or to a member who has met with an accident, or has lost his tools by fire or theft, and includes a payment in discharge or aid of funeral expenses on the death of a member or the wife of a member or as provision for the children of a deceased member."

This definition was discussed by the Divisional Court in *R.* v. *Special Commissioners of Income Tax, ex parte National Union of Railwaymen*[39] where the union had claimed exemption on the following payments:

(a) Legal costs in claiming compensation for personal injuries on behalf of a member.

(b) Costs in connection with arbitrations and enquiries.

(c) Costs of the union's legal department, including staff salaries pensions and rules.

In the result the court refused the claim and the following points may be made:

(i) The court did not finally decide whether the statutory definition of "provident benefits" was exhaustive or whether in the light of the words "includes" it gave only examples. Lord Parker C.J. regarded it as a "very difficult question" having regard to the legislative history of the provision.[40]

(ii) Nor did the court finally decide whether the payments claimed were applied to provident benefits or not, but Lord Parker C.J. saw considerable practical difficulties in the claim and approved *obiter* the view of the Special Commissioners that such sums could not be included as provident benefits even if the statutory definition was not exhaustive.[40a]

(iii) The court decided the issue on the grounds that as by the statute the sums must not only be applied to provident benefits but must also be *applicable* to them, this meant that the sums must come from a separate provident fund.[41] Therefore, as by the rules of the union the sums claimed had to come from the general fund they were not "applicable" to provident purposes. Exemption can therefore only be claimed for payments which are expressly authorised by the rules and which are made out of a special provident fund.

---

[36] Income and Corporation Taxes Act 1970, s. 338 (3).

[37] *Ibid.* s. 226 (13).

[38] *Ibid.* s. 338 (2) as amended by Finance Act 1974, s. 28 (1) (*b*).

[39] (1966) 43 T.C. 445; [1966] 2 All E.R. 759.

[40] The Trade Union (Provident Funds) Act 1893 used the phrase "means and includes." This provision was consolidated by the Income Tax Act 1918, s. 39 but the word "means" was dropped. It is therefore necessary to avoid the presumption that a consolidating Act did not change the law.

[40a] The Inland Revenue has, however, now conceded that a payment of legal expenses incurred in connection with a member's claim in respect of an accident or injury will now qualify as a provident benefit. I.R. Statement of Practice 6/78.

[41] The court rejected the argument that as the general fund could be used to "top up" a special fund, therefore the general fund was also "applicable" to the purposes of the special fund.

Value Added Tax
Members subscriptions are not liable to VAT[42] but any goods or services that are supplied to members for a fee or charge separate from the subscription are taxable.

Life assurance relief
By virtue of an extra-statutory concession[43] the portion of a member's subscription which is allocated to superannuation benefits, as well as any portion allocated to funeral benefits or life assurance, qualifies for tax relief in the same way as life assurance.

SUBSCRIPTIONS

While a union may sue a member who is in arrears with his subscription for breach of contract such a remedy is extremely cumbersome and never resorted to, but rather union rule books always contain clauses permitting disciplinary action against the recalcitrant member. The sanctions are given extra strength by the provisions of the Bridlington Agreement which prohibit a union from taking into membership a person who is in arrears with another union.[44]

Subscriptions, however, are often collected not directly from the individual but rather are deducted by the employer from the employee's wages and handed over to the union. The authority for the deduction comes from the contract of employment which may either have an express term permitting it or may include a term incorporated from a collective agreement or even implied from custom and practice.

It now seems clear that the "check-off" system is not invalidated by the Truck Act 1831 in relation to those covered by the Act.[45] *Hewlett* v. *Allen*[46] rendered lawful those deductions from wages which had been agreed to by the employee in cases where the money was not kept by the employer but handed on to a third party[47] and a later case has noted that the recipient should be independent of the employer.[48] Recently in *Williams* v. *Butlers Ltd.*[49] the Divisional Court affirmed the view that *Hewlett* v. *Allen* authorised the "check off" system, but they added the controversial point that imposing a condition on withdrawal of consent is also lawful. In that case the employee permitted deduction of his subscription from his wages but after a time he informed his employers that he no longer wished this to be done. The employer, however, continued to make the deduction on the ground that under its collective agreement with the union a deduction could only be terminated by a written instruction from the union office. The court accepted the view propounded in the case stated that this collective agreement was incorporated into the individual contract of employment and that, therefore, the employee was bound to submit his withdrawal of permission through the union. Michael Davies J. stated[50] that there was "nothing in the Truck Act 1831 nor the

---

[42] VAT Notice No. 701 para. 35.

[43] No. A2, 1976.

[44] Matters relating to internal union discipline are dealt with in Chap. 5.

[45] Truck Act 1831, s. 4, covering generally those engaged in manual labour.

[46] [1894] A.C. 383.

[47] The payment was to a sick and accident club.

[48] *Penman* v. *Fife Coal Co. Ltd.* [1936] A.C. 45.

[49] [1975] I.C.R. 208 (Q.B.D.), but see also the earlier hearing [1974] I.R.L.R. 253 and the comment by Freedland (1975) 4 I.L.J. 241.

[50] [1975] I.C.R. 208 at 218.

general law of contract which prohibits or renders illegal, null or void the agreement of the employee to notify the withdrawal of his consent in the same manner as he gave it, that is, through the union."

While it is important to maintain the validity of the check off system[51] it is suggested that this decision may place the employee in a difficult position if the union is reluctant to pass on the cancellation of consent to the employer. The union's administrative arrangements could equally well be protected by a clause in the collective agreement requiring the employer to notify the union of any cancellation and by the clause in the rule book requiring a member to give reasonable notice to the union of his resignation.

Nominations and Payments on Death

Legislation[52] permits any union member over the age of 16 to nominate in writing any person to receive up to £1,500 payable on the death of the member out of union funds. The nomination must be registered at the head office of the union and can be revoked either expressly, or by subsequent marriage (but the payment is valid if the union makes it in ignorance of a subsequent marriage). A nomination may not be made in favour of an officer or employee of the union or their families.

Similarly a trade union may pay up to £1,500 out of union funds to a person entitled to receive it on the death of the member, without letters of administration or probate of any will.

[51] See the Donovan Commission Cmnd. 3623 (1968) paras. 718–722.

[52] T.U.L.R.A. 1974, Sched. 1 para. 31; Trade Union (Nominations) Regulations 1977 (S.I. 1977 No. 789).

CHAPTER 7

AMALGAMATION, SECESSION AND DISSOLUTION

AMALGAMATION

THIS century has witnessed not only a growth of union membership from 2 million members in 1900 to over 12 million at the end of 1976, but at the same time a remarkable reduction in the number of unions catering for these increased numbers. In 1900 there were 1,323 unions, but by the end of 1976 this had been reduced to 462,[1] partly by dissolution but also by merger, and it seems likely that this trend will continue for there are a number of applications for merger each year. While an increase in the size of a union is believed to be beneficial this may not necessarily be so[2] and it may be that some unions could give rise to concern, not because of their size but because of the disparate characteristics of the various sections of the union. A small union might amalgamate with other small unions in order to gain greater security or bargaining power, but if it merges with one of the large unions it is likely to prefer one with a trade group structure since the trade group can provide a forum for its interests and enable it to preserve something of its special character. But a union which increases in this way is in danger of becoming a federation of differing interests which it may be unable to reconcile.[3]

However, throughout this century it has been government policy to facilitate the merger of unions, and the Trade Union (Amalgamations, etc.) Act 1964[4] lays down a relatively straightforward procedure for merger of trade unions (and also for unincorporated employers' associations) which may take one of two forms—amalgamation and transfer of engagements.

Amalgamation

Two or more trade unions[5] may amalgamate to form one union so long as each of the unions involved approves by a simple majority of those voting a notice

---

[1] (1977) 85. Dept. of Employment Gazette, 1204. There are, however, still 68 unions with less than 100 members. Eleven unions, each with a membership of over 250,000 cater for 62.9 per cent. of members.

[2] For a discussion of this point and amalgamation in general see Elias, "Trade Union Amalgamations: Patterns and Procedures" (1973) 2 I.L.J. 125.

[3] Disputes between the different sections of the T.G.W.U. are not unknown.

[4] As amended by the Trade Union and Labour Relations Act 1974 and by the Employment Protection Act 1975.

[5] An amalgamation must be between two *unions*. In *Weeks* v. *National Amalgamated Stevedores and Dockers Union* (1940) 67 Ll.L.Rep. 282, 6000 dockers left the T.G.W.U. and joined the National Amalgamated Stevedores Labour Protection League who changed their name to become the defendant union. The plaintiff sought to vitiate this course of action on the ground that the amalgamation rules had not been complied with, but it was held that the 6000 dockers were not a union, even a temporary one, at the time they joined and so there had been no "amalgamation."

of the instrument of amalgamation which has previously been approved by the Certification Officer.[6] It should be noted that the ballot of members is a minimum requirement and a union may, if it so wishes, provide for an additional requirement in its rule book. For example, in 1967 an amalgamation between two unions was only to be effective if it was subsequently ratified by the conferences of each association, and the Registrar pointed out that "there appears to be nothing to preclude the unions from making the amalgamation conditional on the happening of other events in addition to compliance with the statutory conditions."[7] But where the statutory conditions themselves are concerned, a provision of the rule book may in some cases be disregarded and the procedure of the statute adopted instead. This is so, for example, where the rule book requires a higher majority than the simple majority provided for by the 1964 Act, unless that provision has been specifically excluded by the rules.

Merger by amalgamation suffers from the difficulty that there must be a ballot of the members of *all* the unions involved and merger by transfer of engagements is often found to be more convenient, for then it is only necessary to have a ballot of the members of the transfering union. This will be useful either where a small union is joining a larger one (in order to save the trouble of having a ballot of the larger union), or where more than two unions are merging, for the whole exercise would come to nothing if one of the unions decided against amalgamation. In such a case it may be easier to set up an entirely new union and then have each of the existing unions transfer its engagements to it, for then an adverse vote by one union would not prevent the others carrying on with the scheme.[8]

A further point to note is that it is not sufficient simply to draw up a rule book for the new amalgamated union, for there may be cases where transitional provisions are necessary. The point arose in *Braithwaite* v. *E.T.U.*[9] where the initial expulsion of the plaintiff took place under the old rules, but before his appeal could be heard the union was amalgamated. Whereas the rule book contained rules dealing with disciplinary action against members of the amalgamated union it was held inappropriate to cover pending appeals and therefore the expulsion was invalid. The problem can only be avoided by a transitional rule specifically covering pending appeals.

Transfer of engagements

Again the Certification Officer must approve the notice of the instrument of transfer and the notice must be approved by a simple majority of those voting. The instrument need only be submitted to the transferring union and need not be considered by the members of the receiving union. However, it may be necessary for the receiving union to change its rules in order to accommodate the transfer and section 3 of the 1964 Act permits the executive committee to

[6] The Certification Officer has taken over the role of the Registrar of Friendly Societies in this respect.

[7] Report of the Chief Registrar of Friendly Societies for the year 1967, Pt.4, p. 2. These reports are hereafter referred to as "Registrars' Reports." During the era of the Industrial Relations Act 1971 the duties were undertaken by the Registrar of Trade Unions, but in 1974 the work was returned to the Registrar of Friendly Societies. In 1975 the duties were transferred to the Certification Officer.

[8] See the case of the creation of NUFLAT cited in Elias, "Trade Union Amalgamation: Patterns and Procedures" (1973) 2 I.L.J. 125.

[9] [1969] 2 All E.R. 859.

change the rules so far as necessary, except in cases where the rule book specifically excludes the application of the section.[10]

Requirements of the ballot

In the case of both amalgamation and transfer of engagements section 1 (2) of the 1964 Act lays down conditions for the ballot of members. The relevant union must submit to its members for their approval a notice[11] of the instrument of transfer or amalgamation as the case may be, which must either set out the instrument in full or give an account of it sufficient to enable the members to form a reasonable judgment of the main effects of the proposal.[12] This notice must be approved by the Certification Officer before submission to the members.[13]

In relation to the ballot itself the following conditions must be met:

(1) *Every member of the union must be entitled to vote*

The only difficulty likely to arise here is the meaning of "member,"[14] but the Registrar has held that it should be literally construed so that every person with an interest in the union has the right to cast his vote.[15] Thus apprentices and superannuated members have been held to be entitled to vote,[15] as have members in arrears.[16]

(2) *A fair opportunity of voting*

Section 1 (2) (*b*) of the 1964 Act requires that: "Every member of the union must be allowed to vote without interference or constraint and must, so far as is reasonably possible, be given a fair opportunity of voting." The principal grounds for complaints based on this subsection have been that certain members have not received ballot papers, but the Act only requires that the opportunity be provided so far as is reasonably possible. Thus the Registrar has held that it is reasonable to rely on the Post Office for distribution of the ballot papers,[17] and in other cases it seems to be thought that the statute is complied with if only very few members do not receive ballot papers so long as

---

[10] This requirement is a strict one and it is not sufficient simply to have a rule inconsistent with section 3.

[11] In one case the union submitted not only the notice of the instrument for approval but also the rules of the new union. The complainant alleged that he was being asked to decide two issues with one vote, but this procedure was held valid by the Registrar. *In the matter of Johnston and Sabino, and the E.T.U.,* Registrar's Report for the year 1968.

[12] T.U.A.E.A. 1964, s. 1 (3). If the instrument is not set out in full the notice must state where it may be inspected. The contents of the instrument itself are laid down by the Trade Unions and Employers' Association (Amalgamation Etc.) Regulations 1975, Sched. 1 (Amalgamations) and Sched. 2 (Transfers of Engagement). (S.I. 1975 No. 536).

[13] T.U.A.E.A. 1964, s. 1 (4). See *In the matter of Marshall and the Kodak Senior Staff Association,* Registrar's Report for the year 1974, where the notice was sent before it was approved by the Registrar, but no order was made.

[14] See Grunfeld, (1964) 27 M.L.R. 693.

[15] *In the matter of Crook and the Amalgamated Society of Lithographic Printers*, Registrar's Report for the year 1969, p. 29.

[16] *In the matter of Johnston and Sabino and the E.T.U.*, Registrar's Report for the year 1968. This is so even if the union rules state that a member in arrears is not eligible, for the statute takes precedence over the rules.

[17] *In the matter of Hopper and the Amalgamated Society of Lithographic Printers,* Registrar's Report for the year 1969.

they could by their own efforts have obtained them.[18]

(3) *Marking a voting paper*

Section 1 (2) (*c*) requires that "the methods of voting must involve the marking of a voting paper by the person voting." It has been noted that the statute does not require secrecy, but this may be due to the difficulty of maintaining secrecy on a postal vote at the same time as ensuring that the voter is the person entitled to vote.[19]

(4) *The seven day rule*

Section 1 (2) (*d*) of the Act requires that "all reasonable steps shall have been taken by the union to secure that, not less than seven days before voting on the resolution begins, every member of the union is supplied with a notice in writing approved for the purpose by the Certification Officer."

This well meaning provision has caused considerable difficulty because in so far as it requires the union to see that the notice arrives more than seven days before the voting begins, it might be thought to invalidate any vote cast within seven days of receipt of the notice, but in fact the section relates only to the duty of the union and not to the validity of individual votes. Thus in one case[20] it was clear that at least one member had voted as soon as he received the notice and before seven days had elapsed. As the union had not warned the member to delay voting for seven days and had not told officials to refuse votes cast in that time, there had been a breach of the section, but no order was made.

The fact that the validity of the individual vote is not affected is illustrated by a case[21] where the union had sent out the ballot papers in August with the notice that "voting will commence on September 20, and the papers should not be returned before that date." The union had thus complied with the section, but the question arose whether to count the 4,699 votes sent in before the relevant date. The registrar pointed out that the section only requires the union to take steps to see that seven days elapse between receipt of the notice and voting, and says nothing of the validity of such votes. He, therefore, ruled that such votes should be regarded as valid.

Manner of voting

Section 2 of the 1964 Act provides that the "committee of management" of the union may arrange for the vote to be taken in any manner it thinks fit, notwithstanding anything in the rules. In addition a simple majority of votes recorded[22] is sufficient to approve the merger, even if the rules provide for a greater majority. Thus in one case[23] the rules provided that the amalgamation had to be approved by 75 per cent. of those voting, but this rule was disre-

---

[18] *In the matter of Collins and the Plumbing Trade Unions*, Registrar's Report for the year 1968. *In the matter of Marshall and the Kodak Senior Staff Association*, Registrar's Report for the year 1974.

[19] Grunfeld (1964) 27 M.L.R. 693. For example the voter may be required to sign the envelope containing the ballot paper.

[20] *In the matter of Stevens and the National Society of Electrotypers and Stereotypers*, Registrar's Report for the year 1967, Appendix B.

[21] *In the matter of Massey and the Amalgamated Society of Painters and Decorators*, Registrar's Report for the year 1969.

[22] In *Latham* v. *The Corporation and City of Glasgow* [1921] S.C. 694 it was held that "votes recorded" means all ballot papers put into the ballot boxes and includes spoilt papers.

[23] *In the matter of Marshall and the Kodak Senior Staff Association*, Registrar's Report for the year 1974, Appendix 3.

garded and a simple majority held sufficient. However, these provisions may be ousted by a rule specifically excluding the provisions of sections 2 (2) and 2 (3) of the 1964 Act.

Complaint to the Certification Officer

A member may present a complaint to the Certification Officer if any of the conditions of section 1 (2) of the 1964 Act have not been met or if the arrangements approved under section 2 have not been complied with, or (where the vote is taken in accordance with the rules of the union) if these rules have not been observed, and finally if the votes did not in fact have the effect of approving the merger.

The claim must be presented within six weeks of the application to register the merger being sent to the Certification Officer, who is the only person entitled to hear the complaint. No other legal proceedings will be entertained if the matter is properly within the Officer's jurisdiction. If the complaint is found to be justified, the Certification Officer may either make no order, or may require certain steps to be taken before he will register the instrument of amalgamation or transfer.[24] The Certification Officer has considerable powers to require the attendance of witnesses and the production of documents, and even has power to award costs.[25]

Registration and transfer of property

It is provided[26] that the merger shall not take effect until it has been registered by the Certification Officer and that that shall not be done until six weeks have elapsed from the date when the instrument was sent to him. Two points need to be noted about this provision. The first is that although the instrument may be registered after six weeks, its coming into effect may be delayed by the terms of the instrument itself.[27] The second point is that this provision is "directory" rather than "mandatory" so that if the instrument is inadvertently registered before the six weeks have elapsed it is not void. In *Rothwell* v. *A.P.E.X.*[28] it was suggested that such a registration is valid rather than voidable,[29] but even if this is so it is suggested that such a registration should not affect the right of a member to present a complaint to the Registrar under section 4.

When the instrument of amalgamation[30] or transfer takes effect, property[31]

---

[24] Appeals, on matters of law only, may be taken to the Employment Appeal Tribunal: T.U.A.E.A. 1964, s. 4 (8) as amended by the Employment Protection Act 1975, Sched. 16.

[25] T.U.A.E.A. 1964, Sched. 1. The power to award costs is surprising, especially in view of the fact that legal aid is not available. A rule of no costs and no legal aid may be preferable.

[26] T.U.A.E.A. 1964, s. 1 (5).

[27] See the Registrar's Report for the year 1967, p. 2, noting a case where the instrument of amalgamation itself stated that it should take effect on a date to be determined "by a meeting constituted in the same manner as the proposed National Executive Council of the amalgamated union." The instrument was registered after six weeks but did not become effective until later.

[28] [1976] I.C.R. 211 at 221.

[29] If such a registration were held to be voidable it would be open to challenge in the Divisional Court by an aggrieved party. It appears that once the instrument is registered the Certification Officer has no power under the Act to de-register it.

[30] It should be noted that in the case of amalgamation it is not necessary for the funds to be merged, but rather this is a matter for negotiation between the unions. T.U.A.E.A. 1964, s. 1 (I) *(a)*.

[31] Except stocks and securities in the public funds of the U.K. or Northern Ireland, and property exempted by the instrument of transfer; T.U.A.E.A. 1964, s. 5 (2).

is automatically vested in the new trustees without the need for any conveyance or assignment.

Political funds

Some difficulty is created by the need for special treatment of political funds under the Trade Union Act 1913. Section 5 (4) of the 1964 Act states that when two or more trade unions are amalgamating (but not where they are transferring engagements), and all of them before the amalgamation had political funds, then they shall be treated as having passed a resolution for the purpose of authorising the establishment of a political fund, so long as the political fund rules have been included in the new rule book. The rules must be approved by the Certification Officer, but if they are the levy can be made, subject to the right of members of the new union to give notice within one month of their intention to contract out. But where these conditions do not apply, because one union did not have a political fund, then the full procedure of the Trade Union Act 1913 must be followed by the new amalgamated union.[32]

The case of a transfer of engagements is more difficult, but it may be supposed that where the receiving union has a political fund, the members of the transferring union will automatically belong to it unless they contract out, although it is not unusual to make special provision for this problem in the instrument of transfer.

But where it is the other way about and the transferring union has a political fund but the receiving union does not, the transferring union cannot impose an obligation to contribute to the political fund on the members of the receiving union. It would of course be open to the receiving union to change its rules in accordance with the Trade Union Act 1913 and adopt a political fund. Alternatively, the fund may be dissolved before the transfer takes place and this will be most easily achieved if the political fund rules make provision for the winding up of the fund. If that situation does not exist the proper way of dealing with the fund is a matter of some difficulty.

On the one hand it may be argued that if the political fund rules permit the use of the fund for general purposes, then the fund may be transferred to the general fund of either the transferring or receiving union. If there is no such rule the question turns on whether a political fund may be used for general purposes even in the absence of such a rule, and it is arguable that it may not. The reason is that the levy has been paid by individual members to trustees for the purposes of the fund, which purposes are determined by the rules. The moneys are bound by the trust and the trustees may not apply the fund for purposes other than those for which it was donated. In such a case, therefore, the fund cannot be merged with the general fund of either union. If that happens it is suggested that as the transferring union will have ceased to exist there will be a resulting trust for the subscribers.[33]

---

[32] See for example the Registrar's Report for the year 1967, p. 2 concerning the amalgamation of the Heating and Domestic Engineers' Union and the National Union of Sheet Metal Workers and Coppersmiths. The latter had a political fund but the former did not and a ballot of the new union was necessary under the Trade Union Act 1913. In the event the proposal for a political fund was rejected by the members.

[33] Whether this would be for the benefit of subscribers past and present or for present subscribers only is a matter of some difficulty. See the discussion below on dissolution of union funds. *Re West Sussex Constabulary's Benevolent Fund Trusts* [1971] Ch. 1; *Re Sick and Funeral Society* [1973] 1 Ch. 51; *Re Gillingham Bus Disaster Fund* [1958] Ch. 300.

On the other hand it may be argued that the effect of adopting political fund rules is merely to enlarge the range of purposes for which the union may spend its funds and the levy is paid not for the purposes of the fund alone but for the purposes of the union as a whole. This is so because the effect of the Trade Union Act 1913 and the rules made under it is not that the political fund *must* be used for political purposes but that no other fund may be so used. If this view is adopted the levy is not impressed with a trust (except one to use it for the purposes of the union as a whole) and therefore the political fund could be paid into the general fund of the transferring union. This view at least has the merit of simplicity but the other gives effect to the (perhaps unfounded) view of the subscribers that their contribution must be used for the purposes of the political fund.

Change of Name

Whether it is merging or not a union may wish to change its name. The matter is covered by section 6 of the Trade Union (Amalgamations Etc.) Act 1964, but that section gives little additional power to the union, for it merely provides that a union may change its name if it has an express rule enabling it to do so or by adopting in accordance with its rules an alteration in the rule which contains the union's name.[34] It is also provided by the same section[35] that in the case of listed unions the new name must be approved by the Certification Officer[36] who must be satisfied that the name is not the same as one entered on the list, or so nearly resembling such a name as to be likely to deceive the public.

Secession

Whereas each individual has the right to resign from his union,[37] difficult problems arise when a group of members not only wishes to leave the union but also intends to take its share of the union's assets. The problem will usually arise where members of a branch either wish to join another union or distribute the branch's assets. Secession may be distinguished from the dissolution by noting that in secession only a part of the union is involved.

There are in fact two separate, but often confused, problems in relation to secession. The first is whether a branch has the power to secede so as to bind all members of the branch, and the second is whether seceding members have any rights to the property of the union.

The power to secede

It has been argued that a branch must have an inherent power to secede from a union on an analogy with the power of an individual to resign but in *John* v. *Rees*[38] this analogy was rejected by Megarry J. who said:

"Where the question is one of a club disaffiliating itself from some other

---

[34] Presumably therefore this can only be done by the special procedure, if any, needed to change the rules.

[35] As amended by T.U.L.R.A. 1974 Sched. 3. See *R.* v. *Registrar of Friendly Societies* (1872) 7 L.R.Q.B. 741.

[36] In 1977 the Certification Officer approved changes of name for 10 trade unions and 1 employer's association.

[37] T.U.L.R.A. 1974, s. 7 as amended by Trade Union and Labour Relations (Amendment) Act 1976.

[38] [1969] 2 All E.R. 274 at 300. The case dealt with the attempted secession of the Pembrokeshire Labour Party.

organisation, there is a preliminary question to be resolved, namely, whether the act of disaffiliation was validly done according to the rules of the club as a body. The question 'Has there been a valid decision to resign or disaffiliate?' arises in the case of the club but not in the case of the individual. The analogy between the two categories thus breaks down."

The question will, therefore, have to be dealt with according to the rules of the union, [39] and it has been assumed that if there are no rules dealing with secession by the branches, then any decision to that effect would be *ultra vires*. In *Cope* v. *Crossingham*[40] the members of a branch of the Municipal Employers' Association voted to secede and distribute the branch funds between the members, and although much of the case was concerned with the rights over the union property, it was agreed that the resolution to secede was *ultra vires*.[41] However, it has recently been held in *Keys* v. *Boulter* (No. 2)[42] that the court has an inherent power to wind up an unincorporated association, but that was a case of dissolution of an entire union rather than secession of a part of it. If the power were to be available to permit secession even where there is no rule it could be of some significance, but it is thought that it would be a considerable departure from established theory to allow a branch to secede and take its assets in contravention of, or without the authority of a rule of the union.

Secession and union assets

The second issue has already been touched upon, and that is whether a group of members who are leaving the union can take with them any of the union assets. It is generally assumed that each member is unable to claim his individual share of the unions assets, on the basis that there is an implied contract that members will not sever their interest, if any, in the funds; but where a branch wishes to secede problems arise as to the ownership of the branch's assets, for if every member of the branch agreed to the secession it would be open to them to resign, but they could only take with them assets which belong to the branch as a separate organisation rather than as a constituent of a larger unit. In *Cope* v. *Crossingham*[43] it was noted that the matter is entirely dependent on the rules of the association, and it may be said that generally the central organisation will be thought to have sufficient interest in the branch funds to prevent their dissipation. However, the result may perhaps be different either in cases where the central organisation is simply a federation of local trade unions, or where the union collects two subscriptions, one for headquarters and one for the local branch.

DISSOLUTION

As with the case of secession, there are two separate issues which arise in relation to dissolution of a trade union. First, can the union be dissolved, and,

---

[39] As does the opposite of secession—the compulsory winding up of a branch by the central organisation. See *Maddock* v. *E.T.U.* [1972] S.L.T. 54 (Sheriff Ct.), where the winding up was held to be *ultra vires*. See also *Lewis* v. *Heffer* [1978] 1 W.L.R. 1061, concerning the suspension of a Labour Party branch.

[40] [1909] 2 Ch. 148. One problem was that "its rules are so obscure and so inartistically framed that it is by no means easy to interpret them."

[41] *Ibid.* at 164 *per* Buckley L.J.

[42] [1972] 2 All E.R. 303.

[43] [1909] 2 Ch. 148. Other examples are *Brentall* v. *Hetrick* [1928] N.Z.L.R. 788; *Raymond* v. *Doherty* (1965) 49 D.L.R. 2d 99.

if so, how? Secondly, there is the crucial problem of distribution of the union's assets.

THE POWER TO DISSOLVE

It is usual for trade union rule books to contain a provision relating to dissolution,[44] and in such cases the union may dissolve itself providing the rules are strictly adhered to. If there is no rule it would of course be open to a union to adopt a rule[45] by the proper process, and then dissolve itself, but it may be worth while exploring other methods.

One such method involves the apparent jurisdiction of the High Court to dissolve some kinds of unincorporated associations. The first instance of this power occurred in 1904[46] when it was held that the court could wind up an unregistered friendly society. Since it was clear that until then there was no authority either for or against such a jurisdiction, it is unfortunate that the court did not outline the nature of its powers in this area, but it appears to have been significant, first that there was property belonging to a number of individuals, the use of which was regulated by rules of the association, and secondly, that the society could not continue to perform its proper function under the rules.

This decision was followed by Megarry J. in *Keys* v. *Boulter (No. 2)*[47] which arose out of the need to undo the amalgamation of a number of unions to form SOGAT and it is notable that the power was exercised despite a dissolution rule in the union's constitution. Again, the limits of this jurisdiction were not defined but were thought at least to include what was in effect an unregistered trade union. Whatever these limits may be, it is suggested that this procedure should apply to all trade unions[48] and should be exercised at least in cases where the union cannot carry out its proper functions.[49] Whether it could be extended to cases where winding up would be "just and equitable" may be doubted.

However, another method of winding up may be available to a trade union, for it has been suggested that a trade union may now be wound up as an "unregistered company" under section 399 of the Companies Act 1948.[50] The section applies to "any association,"[51] but it has been suggested that the provision is limited to trading associations[52] since another part of the section refers to its "place of business." However, it would not be difficult to regard a trade union's headquarters as its "place of business," nor to regard it as indulging in a business, at least for the purpose of establishing where its

---

[44] The Trade Union Act (Amendment) Act 1876, s. 14, made a dissolution rule compulsory for all registered unions, but this has been repealed.

[45] Providing it has the power to change its own rules.

[46] *Re Lead Company's Workmen's Fund Society, Lowes* v. *Governor and Company for Smelting Down Lead with Pit and Sea Coal* [1904] 2 Ch. 196.

[47] [1972] 2 All E.R. 303.

[48] Except special register bodies, which are incorporated. The jurisdiction should also include unincorporated employers' associations.

[49] This was true in both the *Lead Company* case [1904] 2 Chap. 196 and *Keys* v. *Boulter No. 2* [1972] 2 All E.R. 303.

[50] This issue did not arise before, since the Trade Union Act 1871, s. 5 stated that the Companies Acts were not to apply to trade unions. The Industrial Relations Act s. 156 specifically applied the Companies Act to trade unions where registration had been cancelled under that Act.

[51] Companies Act 1948, s. 198.

[52] See Buckley, *Companies Acts* (13th ed.), p. 733 and the cases there cited, especially *Re Bristol Athenaeum* (1889) 43 Ch. D. 236, but the procedure has been applied to a friendly society: *Re Victoria Society, Knottingly* [1913] 1 Ch. 167; *Re Sick and Funeral Society* [1973] 1 Ch. 51.

activities are carried on.[53] If the section does apply,[54] an unregistered company may be wound up if it is dissolved or has ceased to carry on business, or if it is unable to pay its debts, or if the court is of the opinion that it would be just and equitable to do so.

The distribution of assets

In the absence of a rule covering distribution of assets upon dissolution, the general law must be applied, but this is no easy task, for as Megarry V.-C. has pointed out "the authorities are in a curious state."[55] There are two lines of authority which might be applied to a trade union.[56] The first, based on *Re Printers and Transferrers Amalgamated Trades Protection Society,*[57] would reimburse members, after the payment of all debts, on the basis of the amount of their contribution to the funds, so that a long serving member or one who has paid at a higher rate would receive more. This view is based on the idea of the resulting trust, but a resulting trust of a peculiar nature since past members were excluded. In *Tierney* v. *Tough*[58] the principle of payment in proportion to contributions was accepted but the reasoning in the *Printers and Transferrers* case was doubted, since the fund to be distributed consisted partly of existing and partly of past members' contributions, and it was difficult to see how existing members acquired an interest in the past members' contributions.

This criticism led to a second line of cases where the funds are distributed between the members existing at the date of winding up[59] on the basis of membership of the society rather than resulting trust. In *Re Sick and Funeral Society*[60] Megarry J. said:

> "Much of the difficulty arises from confusing property with contract. A resulting trust is essentially a property concept. Any property that a man does not effectually dispose of remains his own . . . On the other hand, membership of a club or association is primarily a matter of contract. The members make their payments, and in return they become entitled to the benefits of membership in accordance with the rules. The sums they pay cease to be their individual property, and so cease to be subject to any concept of resulting trust. Instead, they become the property, through the trustees of the club or association, of all the members for the time being, including themselves. A member who, by death or otherwise, ceases to be a member thereby ceases to be part owner of the club's property: those who remain continue owners. If then, dissolution ensues, there must be a division of the property of the club or association among those alone who

---

[53] s. 399 (3) only requires the place of business to be established for the purpose of determining whether jurisdiction belongs to England or Scotland.

[54] But note that the Industrial Relations Act 1971, s. 156 (repealed) found it necessary to amend this section in its application to trade unions.

[55] In *Re Sick and Funeral Society* [1973] 1 Ch. 51 at 58.

[56] It is suggested that a third line based on *Cunnack* v. *Edwards* [1896] 2 Ch. 679 and *Re West Sussex Constabulary's Trusts* [1971] Ch. 1, is not applicable for it depends on the society being for the benefit not of contributors but of third parties. See now *Re Bucks Constabulary Widows and Orphans Fund (No. 2), The Times,* July 13, 1978.

[57] [1899] 2 Ch. 184. This case was followed in *Re Lead Company's Workmens' Fund* [1904] 2 Ch. 196.

[58] [1914] I.R. 142.

[59] *Re St Andrew's Allotment Association Trusts* [1969] 1 All E.R. 167. *Re Sick and Funeral Society* [1973] 1 Ch. 51; *Re Bucks Constabulary Widows and Orphans Fund (No. 2), The Times,* July 13, 1978.

[60] [1973] 1 Ch. 51 at 59.

are owners of that property, to the exclusion of all former members. In that division, I cannot see what relevance there can be in the respective amounts of the contributions."

The fact that the distribution is based on membership rather than property rights does not necessarily mean that the distribution should be based on equality, for the rules themselves may establish different classes of membership who may have different rights on distribution.[61] But it is suggested that in relation to trade unions equality is the basis that would be adopted if the "membership" rather than the "resulting trust" principle were applied. It seems that there are both technical and other reasons to prefer the "membership" cases and equality. First, the resulting trust cannot satisfactorily explain the exclusion of past members, and secondly, there seems no reason why a person who has been a member for 30 years, and has had the benefits of membership for that time, should receive 30 times as much on dissolution as the new member.

It might be thought that where the rule book provides for dissolution and also for the method of distribution of the assets, the courts would apply such rules, but in one case they were ignored. In *Keys* v. *Boulter (No. 2)*[62] it seems that the rule book provided for division of the assets amongst the members of the association, but in fact the funds of SOGAT were distributed between the amalgamating unions which had to a large extent retained their separate identity within the federal structure of SOGAT. Whilst it is clearly a different case from that usually envisaged in the area of dissolution, it is difficult to see how the fund was distributed in opposition to the rule book. Could the court have resisted the claim of an individual member to his share of the assets if such a claim had been presented? The result of the case clearly makes a great deal of sense but it is difficult to see on what legal principle it is based. No doubt in future amalgamations unions would be advised to include in the new rule book a transitional dissolution clause to be operated if the amalgamation fails.

---

[61] As in *Re Sick and Funeral Society* itself where children under 12 contributed and benefited at half the rate of those over 12. "Where the rules have written into them the basis of inequality among different classes of members in relation to the principal contractual burdens and benefits of memberships, it seems to me to follow that this inequality ought also to be applied to the surplus property of the society." *per* Megarry J. [1973] 1 Ch. 51 at 60.

[62] [1972] 2 All E.R. 303.

Part Two

THE UNION MEMBER AND HIS EMPLOYER

CHAPTER 8

INDIVIDUAL RIGHTS OF A UNION MEMBER AGAINST HIS EMPLOYER

WHILE every employee has rights against his employer giving him a measure of security, the law has provided certain additional protection for union members and officials. This takes three forms: first the general rules of unfair dismissal are altered so that it is deemed to be unfair to dismiss a person for becoming a member of an independent union or taking part in its activities (these are called "inadmissible reasons"); secondly, a new right is created to protect a union member against discrimination by his employer, and thirdly, union members are given the right to take time off for various purposes.

These provisions are for the protection of the member as an individual and are not intended to be used to secure collective rights for trade unions. The Industrial Relations Act 1971 provided a number of similar remedies[1] protecting union members, but unfortunately these were drafted in such a way as to allow them to be used for collective purposes, thus to some extent subverting the collective provisions of the Act.[2] For example in *Post Office* v. *U.P.W.*[3] members of one union succeeded in obtaining privileges similar to those of recognised unions on the basis of the right of an individual not to be discriminated against, even though the union had had considerable difficulty in claiming such collective rights under the proper procedure.[4] The present provisions are, therefore, framed in such a way as to limit the remedy to infringement of individual rights and exclude their use for collective purposes.

DISMISSAL FOR TRADE UNION ACTIVITIES

Joining an independent union

Section 58 of the Employment Protection (Consolidation) Act 1978 provides that it shall be deemed unfair to dismiss a person[5] if the reason (or the principal reason) is that he was, or proposed to become, a member of an independent trade union.[6] The limitation of this remedy to members of independent unions is not likely to be significant, but even in the case of a dismissal for belonging to a union that is not "independent" it is still open to

[1] s. 5.

[2] See Kidner, "The Individual and the Collective Interest in Trade Union Law" (1976) 5 I.L.J. 90 at 101–104.

[3] [1974] I.C.R. 378.

[4] *T.S.A.* v. *Post Office* [1974] I.C.R. 658.

[5] These rights do not apply in the case of those who ordinarily work outside Great Britain (E.P.C.A. 1978 s. 141), share fishermen (s. 144), persons in the police service (s. 146 (2)) or to actions between husband and wife (s. 146 (1)).

[6] As defined by T.U.L.R.A. 1974. s. 30.

the applicant to use the normal unfair dismissal procedure and the employer will have to show that he acted reasonably.[7] Where the applicant was a union member before he was employed, the employer may be able to show that the applicant was not dismissed because of his union membership if he can prove that he knew of this fact before taking him on.[8] But where people who are already employed propose to join a union and are dismissed or selected for redundancy and non members are not, the obvious inference may be drawn.[9]

The provision only applies in the case of a person who is employed and then dismissed, and cannot apply to a person who is refused a job on the grounds of his trade union membership. This point was made in *City of Birmingham* v. *Beyer*[10] where the Employment Appeal Tribunal pointed out that a person cannot compel an employer to give him a job and that "there is nothing in the legislation which we have to administer which lays down that an employer may not refuse to employ a man unless he has reasonable grounds for refusing."

Refusing to join a non independent union

It is also provided that it shall be an "inadmissible reason," (and hence the dismissal will be deemed unfair) if the reason is the applicant's refusal to join a union that is not independent.[11]

This provision is of course a far cry from a right not to join a union at all for that right can only be truly said to exist today in the case of a person who objects on grounds of religious belief to joining any trade union at all.[12] It has, however, been argued that Article 11 of the European Convention on Human Rights could be interpreted to provide a general right not to join a trade union,[13] on the grounds that the freedom to associate with others implies the choice as to whom one will associate with, if anybody. Two such cases, involving the closed shop, are pending before the European Commission.[14]

The right to engage in the activities of a trade union

It is also deemed to be unfair to dismiss a person who "had taken, or proposed to take, part at any appropriate time in the activities of an independent trade union,"[15] and it is for the employee to prove that this was the reason.[16] It is clear that this right only applies to activities that take place after the applicant has been employed and does not apply to a case where the applicant alleges that he has been dismissed because of his reputation as a militant trade unionist and his activities before he became employed.[17]

---

[7] E.P.C.A. 1978 s. 57 (3).

[8] *Brown* v. *Percy Trentham* [1976] I.R.L.R. 279. (I.T.—interim application).

[9] *Boorman* v. *Beale* [1973] I.R.L.R. 135. (I.T.).

[10] [1977] I.R.L.R. 211. (E.A.T.).

[11] E.P.C.A. 1978, s. 58 (1) (*c*). There are no examples reported.

[12] This being an exemption from the provisions concerning the closed shop: E.P.C.A. 1978, s. 58 (3).

[13] Article 11 states "Everyone has the right to freedom of peaceful assembly and to freedom of association with others, including the right to form and to join trade unions for the protection of his interests."

[14] *Young and James* v. *U.K.*, Application No. 7601/76; *Webster* v. *U.K.* Application No. 7806/77.

[15] E.P.C.A. 1978, s. 58 (1) (*b*).

[16] *Goodwin* v. *Fitzmaurice* [1977] I.R.L.R. 393 (E.A.T.).

[17] *City of Birmingham* v. *Beyer* [1977] I.R.L.R. 211 (E.A.T.).

"... activities of a trade union"

If the activity is being engaged in by an authorised trade union representative and is the kind of thing such as recruiting members, that is commonly carried out by a union, then there is no difficulty in declaring it to be the activity of a trade union. But it would be quite wrong to limit the phrase to the activities of a union official,[18] for it clearly encompasses acts by an ordinary member, so that recruiting fellow members is a union activity whoever is doing it. Thus it has been established that it is a trade union activity to attempt to form a branch[19] or to seek recognition.[20]

The case is, however, more difficult where the employee takes it upon himself to do something not for the union nor on behalf of the union but rather as an individual, but the activity is the kind of thing one would associate with a trade union. For example in *Chant* v. *Aquaboats*[21] the applicant had organised a "round robin" signed by himself and six others complaining about safety standards. The Employment Appeal Tribunal held that this was not an activity[22] of the trade union, and it made no difference that the document had been vetted by a trade union official.

As it would no doubt be held that a non-member could not "take part in the activities of an independent trade union" the protection is only available to union members, and so the difficulty arises whether an activity should become a trade union activity simply because it is indulged in by a union member, when a non-member who did the same thing would not be protected. In other words, must the activity be one which a non-member would not be able to engage in (such as seeking union recognition or collecting subscriptions) or can it include the ordinary activities of an employee, if engaged in by a trade union member? Although, it is not fatal that a person is in some degree acting for his own benefit,[23] it is suggested that the union must somehow be involved. No precise guide is possible but Phillips J. has indicated [23] that:

> "It is necessary in every case to summarise carefully all the acts and facts relied upon as constituting 'activities', including as an element (but not the only element) whether he is a representative, and then to decide as a matter of common sense whether such acts taken together constitute the activities of an independent union."

Thus it has been suggested that if a member contacts his union concerning his conditions of work and the union then takes action, the member can be said to be participating in the activities of a union.[24]

While it is clear that a strike or industrial action cannot be regarded as a trade union activity,[25] it may be that an individual employee would be protected if he were to stop work in order to consult his union official, so long as the employer has given his consent to such a procedure so as to make it within an "appropriate time."

Even if an activity is objectively covered it may nevertheless be held to be unprotected because of the way in which it is done. Thus in *Lyon* v. *St. James*

---

[18] *Brennan* v. *Ellward* [1976] I.R.L.R. 378 (E.A.T.).

[19] *Lyon* v. *St. James Press* [1976] I.C.R. 413.

[20] *Taylor* v. *Butler Machine Tool* [1976] I.R.L.R. 113 (I.T.).

[21] [1978] I.C.R. 643.

[22] See also *Gardner* v. *Peaks Retail* [1975] I.R.L.R. 244. (I.T.) (Complaint that no "Shops and Offices Act" poster was displayed).

[23] *Brennan* v. *Ellward* [1976] I.R.L.R. 378 *per* Phillips J.

[24] *Dixon and Shaw* v. *West Ella Developments Ltd.* [1978]. I.C.R. 856.

[25] See for example *McQuade* v. *Scotbeef Ltd.* [1975] I.R.L.R. 332 (I.T.).

Press[26] the applicants had been recruiting members and had attempted to form a union branch. While such acts are *prima facie* activities of a trade union it was argued that the secrecy with which it was done had upset otherwise harmonious relationships within the firm and that the dismissals were therefore justified. On the facts this was held not to be so, but Phillips J. accepted the legal point and said,[27]

> "The special protection provided by [section 58] to trade union activities must not be allowed to operate as a cloak or an excuse for conduct which ordinarily would justify dismissal; equally the right to take part in the affairs of a trade union must not be obstructed too easily by finding acts done for that purpose to be a justification for dismissal. The marks are easy to describe, but the channel between them is difficult to navigate."

"... appropriate time"

A dismissal will only be deemed unfair if the union activity is engaged in at "the appropriate time" which is defined[28] as;

> "time which either—
> (a) is outside his working hours, or
> (b) is a time within his working hours at which, in accordance with arrangements agreed or consent given by his employer, it is permissible for him to take part in the activities.

"... outside working hours." The phrase "working hours" is defined by the same sub-section as meaning "any time when in accordance with his contract of employment, he is required to be at work" but this definition is itself ambiguous, since it is not clear whether "at work" means at the place of work or actually working. In *Post Office* v. *U.P.W.*[29] Lord Reid said that it means "while actually working," so that an employee is protected if he engages in the activities of his union on his employer's premises during the lunch break or before work has started; it does not matter if there is no formal contractual right to such breaks for the phrase "in accordance with his contract" should be interpreted as covering what the employer recognises to be customary. It is thus clear that the Act envisages activities of the union taking place on the employer's premises at times when the relevant employees are not required to be working, and that to some extent the right of the employer to control what happens on his premises is abrogated. It is not clear, however, how far this principle extends; Lord Reid has said that the incursion of these rights on the employer's property rights must be reasonable. He said[30]:

> "It is one thing to ask an employer to incur expense or submit to substantial inconvenience. That the worker may not do. But it is a different matter to use facilities which are normally available to the employer's workers or to ask him to submit to some trifling inconvenience. Men carrying on activities of their union on their employer's premises must do so in a manner which does not cause substantial inconvenience either to their employer or to fellow workers who are not members of their trade union—and employers must tolerate minor infringements of their strict legal rights which do them no real harm."

[26] [1976] I.C.R. 413.
[27] *Ibid.* at 418.
[28] E.P.C.A. 1978, s. 58 (2).
[29] [1974] I.C.R. 378.
[30] *Ibid.* at 400.

A number of difficulties could arise out of this clash of property and industrial rights, and in particular it may be asked whether protection is provided in cases where the employee engages in the activities of his union without the consent of his employer at a time when that employee would not normally be permitted on the premises. In whatever way the conflict is resolved it must be borne in mind that the Act does not give a right to engage in union activities as such, but rather it merely provides a remedy for a person who is dismissed for such activity or who has "action short of dismissal" taken against him.[31]

"*. . . arrangements and consent.*" If it is a term of the employee's contract of employment that he will be entitled to engage in union activities at certain times, these times will be "appropriate," and the employer cannot unilaterally withdraw that permission.[32] In most cases the permission will not be a contractual term, but will nevertheless be effective, for the provision covers not only "consent," which implies permission granted to the member directly, but also an "arrangement" which would include an agreement with the union from which the members can benefit. If there is no consent and no "arrangement" the time will not be "appropriate" and the dismissal will be subject to the usual rules.[33]

It is now clear that the arrangement need not be express, and custom and practice will suffice. In *Marley Tile Co.* v. *Shaw*[34] the applicant had taken up the grievance of a member and called a meeting with management. When they queried his authority as a shop steward he called a meeting of the other maintenance men. Even though these things were done without the express consent of the employers the Employment Appeal Tribunal nevertheless held that the time was "appropriate" since the legislation had to be construed in the light of actual industrial practice. The point was made that if express arrangements were necessary such arrangements would only be made with recognised unions; unrecognised unions would be unlikely to be able to make an agreement and would not be able to benefit from the provision. Therefore, the arrangement need not be express and in view of the fact that satisfactory informal relationships had been established between the employer and the unrecognised union, it was thought that a tacit arrangement could be said to exist.

Whatever the legal position about recognition may be, this solution to the problem of the wariness of employers in entering into agreements with unrecognised unions is appropriate so long as there is some evidence of tolerance and acceptance by the employer, but it would be wrong to ignore evidence of the actual views of the employer at the time and base the decision on what is reasonable or usual in the industry, for such an approach would open the way for the use of these individual rights for collective purposes. If that danger is to be avoided an employer must not be deemed to have made an arrangement or be made to consent.

Remedies

When an employee is dismissed for an "inadmissible" reason,[35] the usual

---

[31] E.P.C.A. 1978, s. 23.

[32] *Miller* v. *Rafique* [1975] I.R.L.R. 70 (I.T.).

[33] *Robb* v. *Leon* [1978] I.C.R. 506 (E.A.T.).

[34] [1978] I.C.R. 828. (E.A.T.). See also *Zucker* v. *Astrid Jewels Ltd.* [1978 I.R.L.R. 384 (E.A.T.).

[35] That is for one of the three "trade union" reasons within E.P.C.A. 1978, s. 58 (1).

remedies for unfair dismissal apply. The primary remedy[36] is an order for re-instatement (or alternatively for re-engagement) and in deciding whether to make such an order the tribunal must consider not only the wishes of the employee but also whether it is "practicable" for the employer to comply with such an order.[37] If an order is made and the employer fails to comply with it, and cannot show that it was not practicable for him to do so, the tribunal may order the employer to pay an "additional" award which in the case of an inadmissible reason will be between 26 and 52 weeks pay.[38] This payment is in addition to any other compensation that may be awarded.

If no order for re-instatement or re-engagement is made, or if the employer has refused to comply with such an order, the applicant will also be entitled to a "basic award"[39] and a "compensatory award."[40]

"Interim award"

There is one remedy, of an interlocutory nature, which is peculiar to dismissals for joining an independent union or taking part in its activities.[41] The object is to allow a tribunal to make an interim order of re-instatement or re-engagement or an order continuing the applicant's contract of employment pending the full hearing before the tribunal. The reasoning is that as members are very quick to protect their rights as trade unionists they are more likely to strike to protect these rights and it is hoped that the emergency procedure provided here will allow the case to be resolved without industrial action. But it must be said not only that the interim hearing is unlikely to take place until two or three weeks after the dismissal, but also that some members may feel that industrial action is a more effective and speedy method of protecting a person dismissed for trade union activity.

The employee concerned must apply to the tribunal within seven days of the "effective date of termination"[42] of his contract for an interim order, and within the same period he must present a certificate signed by an authorised trade union official.

The certificate. It has been said that with regard to the certificate "technicalities should be avoided as far as possible and ... a detailed compliance with provisions is not necessary, provided there is a substantial compliance with them."[43] Nevertheless the certificate has caused problems[44] and the following points may be noted.[45]

(a) It should be in the form of a document and should be signed.

(b) It should state that at the date of the dismissal the applicant was or proposed to become a member of the union (this is so whatever the alleged

---

[36] There is no minimum period of employment required to seek a remedy in the case of an "inadmissible" reason. E.P.C.A. 1978, s. 64 (3). But if the applicant has been employed for less than 26 weeks the burden is on him to show that the reason for dismissal was an inadmissible reason; *Smith* v. *Hayle Town Council* [1978] I.R.L.R. 413 (C.A.).

[37] E.P.C.A. 1978, s. 69.

[38] The maximum weeks pay to be used in the calculation is £110. E.P.C.A. 1978, Sched. 14 para. 8 (1). Employment Protection (Variation of Limits) Order 1978. (S.I. 1978 No. 1777).

[39] E.P.C.A. 1978, s. 73.

[40] *Ibid.* s. 74.

[41] *Ibid.* s. 77. It should be noted that this remedy does not apply to dismissal for refusing to join a non-independent union.

[42] As defined by E.P.C.A. 1978, s. 55 (4).

[43] *Stone* v. *Charrington* [1977] I.C.R. 248 at 250 *per* Phillips J.

[44] See for example *Farmeary* v. *Veterinary Drug Co.* [1976] I.R.L.R. 322 (I.T.).

[45] *Stone* v. *Charrington* [1977] I.C.R. 248.

reason for the dismissal, and is not confined to cases where dismissal is alleged to be for union membership).

(c) It should state that it appears to the official that there are reasonable grounds for supposing that the reason (or the principal reason) was the one alleged by the applicant.

If the certificate does not substantially comply with these requirements it is fatal to a claim for interim relief. If a certificate is in proper form it may not later be withdrawn or revoked by the official concerned if a mistake has been made, but in such a case the matter can be put right at the hearing.[46]

"... *authorised official.*" It is clear that an official of the union may not rely on his general authority to provide the necessary certificate, for it is provided that he must be authorised for the purposes of the relevant section.[47] This could be achieved either by a clause in the rule book conferring authority on officials holding certain posts or may be individually provided by a competent authority within the union. In view of the emergency nature of the remedy it is obviously advantageous for each union to establish a network of duly authorised officials.[48]

It would be wise for an official who has granted a certificate to be able to produce his authority to do so, and such a document shall be taken to be proper authorisation unless the contrary can be proved.[49] As a tribunal has to satisfy itself that the reason alleged is likely to be the actual reason it has been suggested[50] that where a certificate is provided by a relatively senior official less enquiry may be necessary than where the certificate comes, for example, from a shop steward.

The tribunal hearing. The tribunal must hear the case as soon as practicable, but must provide the employer with a copy of the application and the union certificate at least seven days before the hearing. The tribunal may be as normally constituted, but may consist of the chairman sitting alone.[51] The tribunal must determine whether "it is likely that"[52] at the full hearing it will find for the applicant.

Remedies. If the employer agrees, the tribunal may make an order of reinstatement, or if both the employer and the employee agree an order of re-engagement may be made. But if neither order is made, or if the employer fails to attend the interim hearing, the tribunal may make an order for the continuation of the applicant's contract of employment pending the full hearing. The effect of such an order is that the contract is deemed to continue in existence for the purposes of protecting the applicant's right to be paid (and protecting other benefits) but it does not continue for the employer's benefit, so that the applicant is entitled to his pay but is not required to work.

The amount he must be paid while the order is in force is the amount he could reasonably have been expected to earn[53] and these payments are

---

[46] *Ibid.* at 251. This ruling does not apply to cases of fraud or forgery.

[47] E.P.C.A. 1978, s. 77 (10).

[48] For an example of an inadequate certificate and inadequate authorisation see *Farmeary* v. *Veterinary Drug Co.* [1976] I.R.L.R. 322. (I.T.).

[49] E.P.C.A. 1978, s. 77 (11).

[50] *Farmeary* v. *Veterinary Drug Co.* [1976] I.R.L.R. 322.

[51] E.P.C.A. 1978, Sched. 9 para. 8. A President of Tribunals, or a chairman elected from a panel of chairmen may also constitute a tribunal.

[52] The applicant must establish that he has "a pretty good chance" of succeeding, *Taplin* v. *Shippam* [1978] I.R.L.R. 450 (E.A.T.).

[53] See for example *Forsyth* v. *Fry's Metals Ltd.* [1977] I.R.L.R. 243.

regarded as earnings for the purposes of social security legislation.[54] The amount of weekly pay must be declared by the tribunal which can take into account any lump sum, either part or all of which was paid in lieu of wages. If the employer fails to comply with the order the tribunal may order him to pay such compensation as it considers just and equitable having regard to the loss flowing from the lack of compliance, but where the full hearing takes place at the same time as the complaint for breach of the interim order the tribunal must quantify separately the amount payable for the breach.[55] What is not entirely clear is the extent to which this amount may be taken into account in determining the amount of the compensatory award, if any, at the full hearing, for if it is fully set off there would be no incentive for the employer to obey the interim award. It is, therefore, suggested that the fact that the employer has been in breach of an interim order is relevant to the determination of the total amount of the compensatory award and to the award for breach of the order.

DISCRIMINATION FOR TRADE UNION ACTIVITIES

It is not sufficient only to protect a union member against dismissal for engaging in trade union activities, for it would then be open to the employer to discriminate against such a member without actually dismissing him. But if such a remedy is provided it may be difficult to reconcile protection of the individual with encouragement of stable collective bargaining by preference for a certain union, since it might be said that providing privileges for a recognised union amounts to discrimination against members of unrecognised unions. It was this dilemma that caused such difficulty under the Industrial Relations Act. Although the N.I.R.C. had seen the problem of reconciling collective and individual rights and had recognised that the individual procedures should not be used for collective purposes,[56] the House of Lords in *Post Office* v. *U.P.W.*[57] held that the Post Office by providing privileges for the recognised union, the U.P.W., had discriminated against a member of the unrecognised T.S.A., for discrimination against a person's union amounted to discrimination against him personally.

As a result of this experience the present provisions have been drafted in such a way as to prevent their use for collective purposes, even though in so doing the extent of protection for the individual has been slightly limited.

Section 23 of The Employment Protection (Consolidation) Act 1978 states:

"every employee shall have the right not to have action (short of dismissal) taken against him as an individual by his employer for the purpose of—

(a) preventing or deterring him from being or seeking to become a member of an independent trade union, or penalising him for doing so; or

(b) preventing or deterring him from taking part in the activities of an independent trade union at any appropriate time, or penalising him for doing so; or

(c) compelling him to be or become a member of a trade union which is not

---

[54] Social Security (Miscellaneous Provisions) Act 1977, s. 18. The ruling applies to amounts "payable" under the order, even if they are not actually paid.

[55] E.P.C.A. 1978, s. 79 (3).

[56] *C.E.G.B.* v. *Coleman* [1973] I.C.R. 230. See also *E.S.U.* v. *C.E.G.B.* [1972] I.C.R. 418 and *Sarvent* v. *C.E.G.B.* [1976] I.R.C.R. 66. (I.T.).

[57] [1974] I.C.R. 378.

independent."[58]

Action short of dismissal

The statute does not require discrimination against the applicant in the sense of making him worse off than his colleagues, but it is not clear that action means detrimental action in the sense that the applicant is worse off than he was before. Would it for example be "action short of dismissal" for the employer to offer a bonus to non union members? In such a case the issue might also be whether it is action taken *against* a member.

A further problem concerns potential changes of circumstances. Is it for example "action short of dismissal" to threaten a sanction or promise a benefit? In *Brassington* v. *Cauldon*[59] the applicant had joined a union which was seeking recognition rights[60] and the employer threatened to close down the business, dismiss the work force and restart it under a different corporate name if the union succeeded in obtaining negotiating rights. Although the issue was not properly before the Employment Appeal Tribunal, it was said that there were technical arguments against regarding a threat as action short of dismissal.[61]

Does it matter whether the applicant is indifferent to or even benefits from the change of circumstances? For example in *Robb* v. *Leon Motor Services*[62] the applicant was moved from long distance coach driving to stage carriage bus driving. In fact he preferred the former, but could he still have succeeded if he was indifferent to the change, or preferred it, and the employer's motive was a prohibited one within the section? It is suggested that in such a case it would be correct to hold the employer liable and make a declaration of the applicant's rights.[63] Again it may be asked whether "action" requires something positive or whether failure to act is sufficient. The most obvious example is the failure to promote a person for an inadmissible reason, and it is suggested that in such a case the decision not to promote can be regarded as an act.[64]

The action must be taken against the applicant as an individual, but it may in some cases still be difficult to distinguish between the applicant's interest as an individual and his interest as part of a collective whole. For example this may be so in the case of a refusal by management to allow a member to be represented in a disciplinary matter by a union official.

The practical problem in all these cases is to prove that the action was in fact discriminatory, and in order to do this the complainant must be compared with his colleagues. In many cases information will be readily available about the situation of these colleagues, but in some cases, such as discrimination over promotion, problems of confidentiality will arise. Thus in *Nasse* v. *Science Research Council*[64] (a race relations case) the plaintiff alleged he had been

---

[58] These rights do not apply in the case of those who ordinarily work outside Great Britain (E.P.C.A. 1973, s. 141), share fishermen (s. 144), those engaged in the police service (s. 146 (2)) nor to actions between husband and wife (s. 146 (1)).

[59] [1978] I.C.R. 405.

[60] In the event the application for recognition was unsuccessful. ACAS report on recognition, No. 105. Of the nine employees canvassed only three wished to have the union represent them. The effect of the threats was not discussed in the report.

[61] These were based on the fact that action and threats of action are distinguished in other sections of the Act.

[62] [1978] I.C.R. 506.

[63] There could also be compensation for any loss flowing from his non-membership or from his inability to engage in his union's activities.

[64] *Nasse* v. *Science Research Council* [1978] I.R.L.R. 352.

discriminated against and asked for discovery of information about the other candidates for promotion. The Court of Appeal refused the application on the grounds that the public interest required that confidentiality should be respected, and Lord Denning said that tribunals should not order or permit the disclosure of reports or references that had been given and received in confidence except in the very rare cases where, after inspection of a particular document, the chairman decided that it was essential in the interests of justice that the confidence should be overridden: and then only subject to such conditions as he thought fit to impose, such as limiting sight of the documents to solicitors and counsel. Such a principle should not, however, be taken too far, and in particular the question may arise whether refusal to order discovery does not in effect defeat the cause of action altogether.

A member's rights

The area of protection is similar to that provided in the case of dismissal, so that for example the "appropriate time" for engaging in the activities of a trade union is defined in the same way. There is, however, one major difference necessitated by the conflict between individual and collective rights, for it is provided that where there is a closed shop a member only has the right to engage in the activities of a union on the employer's premises if that union is the closed shop union or a union specified in the union membership agreement.[65] If one of the purposes of the closed shop is to achieve stable collective bargaining it might have seemed inelegant to provide a right to upset that stability, but one consequence of this provision is that it will be difficult for members who are dissatisfied with their closed shop union to have the union membership agreement terminated if they cannot engage on the employer's premises in the activities of any trade union except the one that has the closed shop.

This limitation on trade union activities applies not only to those individuals actually included in the closed shop but also to exempted members. As statute exempts religious objectors[66] and as the union membership agreement may itself exclude any group of workers, it is provided[67] that the limitation applies to anybody in the same class or grade as employees who are required to be members of the specified union. Thus if the agreement excludes all existing non-members they are still not free to engage in the activities of a non specified union.

Religious objectors

It is also provided that a person should not have action short of dismissal taken against him for the purpose of compelling him to join a trade union if he genuinely objects on grounds of religious belief to being a member of any trade union at all.[68] This provision is similar to the protection available where a closed shop has been established[69] and it is clear that the exemption is based

---

[65] "Specified" is defined for these purposes by E.P.C.A. 1978, s. 23 (5) and includes the case where ACAS has recommended that a union be recognised or where the union has made an application to ACAS for recognition.

[66] E.P.C.A. 1978, s. 58 (3).

[67] *Ibid.* s. 23 (3).

[68] *Ibid.* s. 23 (6).

[69] *Ibid.* s. 58 (3).

on the belief of the individual concerned rather than on the religious organisation to which he belongs.[70]

Remedies

A complaint must be submitted to an industrial tribunal within three months[71] and it is for the employer to show what was the purpose of the action taken and that it was not for one of the prohibited reasons. In doing so the employer is not allowed to allege as a reason that a union applied pressure against him to take action, so that in such a case as he will be unable to allege the true reason (the union pressure) he will be liable.[72]

If the complaint is upheld the tribunal may issue a declaration and award compensation. The damages that can be awarded include the loss to the applicant such as expenses reasonably incurred because of the action complained of[73] and the value of any benefit which the applicant might reasonably have expected but for the action of the employer.[74]

But in addition to compensating for the strict pecuniary loss the statute also requires that the compensation should be such as the tribunal considers just and equitable "in all the circumstances having regard to the infringement of the complainant's right."[75] This does not allow a tribunal to exact a penalty from the employer and "compensation for the employee, not a fine on the employer, however tactfully wrapped up, is the basis of the discretionary monetary award."[76] But this does not mean that the award is limited to pecuniary loss, for compensation may be awarded for other kinds of injury, such as injury to health caused by the victimisation or the frustration of a "deep and sincere wish to join a union, with all the benefits of help and advice which that might entail."[76] But it is not really clear how that situation differs from the one where the only loss alleged is the infringement of the right alone, in which case it is said that a declaration is the only remedy.

TIME OFF WORK

Trade union officials

Trade union officials may ask for time off *with pay* if the person concerned is an official of an independent trade union that is recognised by the employer, in which case the employer must allow him reasonable time off to carry out duties related to industrial relations or to undergo training. If the employer refuses to grant time off the official may present a complaint to an industrial tribunal for a declaration and compensation.[77]

"Officials" of an "independent" "recognised" union

An "official" is defined[78] so as to include any officer of the union or branch

---

[70] *Saggers* v. *B.R.B.* [1977] I.C.R. 809. See Chap. 9.

[71] E.P.C.A. 1978 s. 24 (2): or within such further period as the tribunal permits if it was not reasonably practicable to comply with the 3 month limit.

[72] E.P.C.A. 1978, s. 25 (2). For an analagous case relating to dismissals see *Hazell's Offset Ltd.* v. *Luckett* (1977) 12 I.T.R. 298 (E.A.T.).

[73] Including expenses in attending the tribunal hearing and any loss of wages: *Brassington* v. *Cauldon Wholesale* [1978] I.C.R. 405.

[74] E.P.C.A. 1978, s. 26: The damages are subject to mitigation of damages by the applicant and to his contributory fault; but are not always reduced because of union pressure to take the action.

[75] *Ibid.* s. 26 (1).

[76] *Brassington* v. *Cauldon Wholesale* [1978] I.C.R. 405 per Bristow J.

[77] E.P.C.A. 1978, s. 27.

[78] T.U.L.R.A. 1974, s. 30 (1).

and any other person elected under the union rules to represent the members, and so includes a shop steward. A union is "independent"[79] if it is not under the domination or control of an employer nor liable to interference by him. A union is "recognised" for the purposes of allowing officials time off if it is recognised by the employer to any extent for the purposes of collective bargaining and includes the case where ACAS has made an operative recommendation for recognition.[80]

The purposes of time off

Reasonable time off must be granted if the purpose is "to carry out those duties of his as such an official which are concerned with industrial relations between his employer and any associated employer and their employees."[81] ACAS has drawn up a Code of Practice[82] to provide practical guidance as to what should be covered by these provisions and in relation to the "industrial relations" provision suggests that "an official should be permitted to take reasonable paid time off for such purposes as[83]

(a) collective bargaining with the appropriate level of management;
(b) informing constituents about negotiations or consultations with management;
(c) meetings with other lay officials or with full-time union officers on matters which are concerned with industrial relations between his or her employer and any associated employer and their employees;
(d) interviews with and on behalf of constituents on grievance and discipline matters concerning them and their employer;
(e) appearing on behalf of constituents before an outside official body, such as an industrial tribunal, which is dealing with an industrial relations matter concerning the employer; and
(f) explanations to new employees whom he or she will represent of the role of the union in the workplace industrial structure."

A difficult question is whether there should be added to this list duties relating to the internal management of the union on the grounds that the stability and efficient organisation of the union is a matter "concerned with industrial relations between his employer and any associated employer, and their employees." No doubt this point has been considered by ACAS in drawing up the Code but its omission does not preclude a wider interpretation by the courts.

Reasonable time off must also be given for training which is relevant to such industrial relations duties and which is approved by the T.U.C. or by the union itself.[84] There appears to be no guidance as to the level at which union approval must be given.

Reasonable purposes and reasonable time

Within these guidelines the purpose for which the time off is taken must be reasonable and hence the employer retains some degree of control. This is

[79] *Ibid.* see further Chap. 2.

[80] E.P.C.A. 1978, s. 32; E.P.A. 1975, s. 15. See Chap. 21 below.

[81] E.P.C.A. 1978, s. 57 (1). *Duncan* v. *Weir Pacific Valves* [1978] I.R.L.R. 523.

[82] Code of Practice on "Time off for Trade Union duties and activities" (hereafter Code of Practice 3) prepared by ACAS and approved by Parliament. Employment Protection Code of Practice (Time Off) Order 1977, (S.I. 1977 No. 2076).

[83] Code of Practice 3, para. 13.

[84] See Code of Practice 3, paras. 14–20. *Vine* v. *DRG Ltd.* [1978] I.R.L.R. 475 (I.T.).

bound to cause difficulties for it makes a right to time off look more like a privilege. For example, the Code suggests that if requested the union should provide the employer with a copy of the proposed syllabus for training for which time off is being sought.[85] What, unfortunately, the Code does not do is explain the extent to which the employer can control the contents of that syllabus by arguing that time off for such a course is not reasonable. Tribunals may find themselves undertaking a difficult new task when in effect they are asked to arbitrate on such matters; although they are not required to say what purposes would be reasonable they do have to decide whether the refusal to allow time off for the purposes claimed was unreasonable.

The time taken off must also be reasonable both in terms of the amount taken and the circumstances in which it is taken. As to the amount of time asked for, the task of the tribunal is not to declare what would be reasonable nor to impose conditions as to when and how it may be taken[86] for in theory their only task is to declare whether the amount of time asked for was reasonable or not. But in practice the temptation of acting as arbitrator is going to be difficult to resist.

As to circumstances, the union official will, according to the Code, need to remember that management is responsible for maintaining production and service to customers, and for making the operational arrangements for taking time off[87] and that time off may need to be deferred for reasons such as problems of safety or maintenance of production.

The function of the Act, however, is not to lay down rules about when time off is or is not unreasonable, but rather to encourage parties to make their own agreements with the assistance of the Code of Practice, and to that extent the provisions of the Act offer a "long-stop" against the unreasonable employer. The purpose of the Code is to improve industrial relations by improving communication and that can be done by allowing time off for the official to do his job effectively.

Trade union members

A trade union member is to be allowed reasonable time off during working hours *without pay* to take part in the activities of an independent union recognised by the employer[88] for the purposes of collective bargaining.[89]

The activities

A member is allowed to engage in any activity of the union, including acting as a representative of it, but excluding activities which themselves constitute industrial action. Two different kinds of activity are envisaged here: first a member is permitted time off without pay to act as representative for his union[90] not only within the union, for example as a member of the national executive or as a delegate to conference, but also outside the union, for

---

[85] Code of Practice 3, para. 18.

[86] *Corner* v. *Buckinghamshire C.C.* [1978] I.C.R. 836 (E.A.T.); *Emerson* v. *Commissioners of Inland Revenue* [1977] I.R.L.R. 458 (I.T.).

[87] Code of Practice 3, para. 25.

[88] For the meaning of "independent" and "recognised" see the preceding section on union officials.

[89] E.P.C.A. 1978, s. 58.

[90] In this context union includes a branch: cf. T.U.L.R.A. 1974, s. 30 (1), definition of "union membership agreement."

example as a delegate to the T.U.C.[91] Secondly, a member is allowed time off to take part in the internal activities of his branch and this covers such purposes as voting and attending certain meetings. It is assumed that it is implicit in the provision that the activities and meetings may take place on the employer's premises.

It is explicitly stated that the permissible activities do not include industrial action, whether it is taken in contemplation of a trade dispute or not.[92] "Industrial action" is not defined and it is unfortunate that a euphemistic phrase chosen for its appearance of neutrality has been used in the statute. To explain the phrase it is not enough to say that the action must be detrimental to the employer, for in assessing detriment we must leave out of account the issue we are discussing, that is the time taken off to engage in the action. For example, the problem would arise if a request was made to take time off to protest at the high rate of unemployment or at the government's proposed labour legislation. Such protest may be a union activity, but it can't be described as industrial action just because time off is necessary to do it, for that is what is in issue.

Reasonable purposes and reasonable time

Once again the right is subject to the limitation in purpose and time and the section is phrased in the same terms as are applied in the case of trade union officials. So far as members are concerned the most difficult point will concern union meetings and the extent to which it would be unreasonable for an employer to allow them to take place during working hours. The Code suggests that it may be reasonable to ask for permission to attend meetings that are urgent or "where to do so would not adversely affect production or services," and that such permission may be in the employer's interests if it assists meetings to be representative.[93] Such permission would not allow the meetings to be used as a form of industrial action, but the borderline between permitted purposes and industrial action may be difficult to draw.

Health and safety representatives

A person who is duly appointed by his union as a safety representative is entitled to take time off both for performing his functions in that capacity and for such training as may be reasonable in the circumstances.[94] A Code of Practice issued by the Health and Safety Commission is to deal with the question of reasonableness. The representative is entitled to be paid during such time.[95]

Public Duties

An employer must allow an employee to take time off to perform public duties; this right extends to a person who is a Justice of the Peace and to members of a local authority, a statutory tribunal, a Regional or Area Health Authority, a governing body of a publicly financed educational establishment or a water authority.[96]

---

[91] Code of Practice 3, para. 21.

[92] E.P.C.A. 1978, s. 28 (1).

[93] *Ibid.* para. 22.

[94] The Safety Representatives and Safety Committee Regulations 1977 (S.I. 1977 No. 500). See Chap. 23.

[95] The method of calculation is contained in the schedule to the regulations and is the same as in E.P.A. 1975, s. 57 (4) and (5).

[96] E.P.C.A. 1978, s. 29 (1).

The permissible activities for which time off may be requested include attendance at a meeting of the relevant body and the doing of something approved by the body for the purpose of the discharge of its functions.[97] The right, therefore, only covers duties connected with the proper purposes of the organisation, and these may be difficult to define. Much depends on how narrowly the functions of the relevant body are defined and whether a distinction is taken between matters incidental to and matters pursuant to its obligations.

The amount of time taken must again be reasonable but as there is in this case no Code of Practice some guidance is given by the statute itself.[98] Accordingly the employer (and the tribunal) must consider how much time is required for the performance of the public duties, how much time off, if any, the employee has received for engaging in trade union activities and the effect the employee's absence would have on the employer's business.[99] In making the assessment it is not unreasonable to expect the employee to use at least some of his own free time for his public duties.[1]

Remedies

An employee who is refused permission to take time off is not entitled to take it regardless. If he does he will be subject to the usual rules of discipline, but no doubt if the employer's refusal is considered unreasonable this may affect a tribunal's view of the fairness of the action taken. The proper remedy is an application to an industrial tribunal within 3 months of the refusal for a declaration and compensation. There is no qualifying period of continuous employment needed to claim these remedies. As to compensation where the complaint is that the employer has allowed a union official leave under section 27 of the Act but has not paid him as he was required to do, the tribunal may order the due amount to be paid. In other cases where the entitlement is only to unpaid leave the problem of compensation without apparent pecuniary loss arises. As in the case of the right not to be victimised for trade union activity[2] it is likely to be held that although the section[3] refers to compensation "having regard to the employer's default in failing to permit time off" this does not permit a court to levy a fine. Rather the damages must be compensatory, but are not restricted to pecuniary loss and it may be that the damages could include an item for loss of the right itself even if the benefits which would have been gained from time off are not easily quantifiable.[4]

Exclusions

The rights detailed above are not available to all employees for some are excluded in the following cases:

---

[97] *Ibid.* s. 29 (2).

[98] *Ibid.* s. 29 (4).

[99] For an example of this exercise see *Emmerson* v. *Commissioners of Inland Revenue* [1977] I.R.L.R. 458 where it was decided that it was unreasonable to allow the leader of the opposition of Portsmouth City Council only 18 days off. The tribunal suggested that 30 days might be more appropriate. See also *Corner* v. *Buckinghamshire C.C.* [1978] I.C.R. 836 (E.A.T.).

[1] *Ibid.* See also *Ratcliffe* v. *Dorset C.C.* [1978] I.R.L.R. 191.

[2] E.P.C.A. 1978, s. 23: *Brassington* v. *Cauldon Wholesale* [1978] I.C.R. 405.

[3] E.P.C.A. 1978, s. 30 (2).

[4] Although not the theoretical basis of the award in *Brassington* v. *Cauldon* [1978] I.C.R. 405, this is the practical effect of that award.

(1) *All "time off" rights*
None of the rights dealt with may be claimed where the employer is the husband or wife of the employee, nor are they available to those engaged in the police service or to share fishermen.[5] Equally those who ordinarily work outside Great Britain[6] are excluded.

In addition some part time workers are excluded.[7] The exclusion applies to those who normally work for less than 16 hours weekly except in two cases. First an employee is eligible if he normally works for eight hours or more (but for less than 16 hours) and has been continuously employed for five years, and secondly, he will be eligible for a temporary period of 26 weeks after his normal amount of work goes down below 16 hours per week but is more than 8 hours per week.

(2) *Public Duties*
The right to take time off for public duties does not apply to merchant seamen.[8] In addition where a person employed by the Crown is restricted by the terms of his employment from participating in certain political activities[9] or in activities which conflict with his official functions, he shall not have the right to ask for time off for public duties connected with such activities.[10]

---

[5] E.P.C.A. 1978, s. 146. Police service is defined in s. 146 (3) to mean a person who is a constable or who has the power and privileges of a constable.

[6] *Ibid.* s. 141. For the interpretation of this phrase see *Wilson* v. *Maynard* [1978] I.C.R. 376 where the matter was said to depend not on practice but on the terms of the contract of employment. For merchant seamen see E.P.C.A. 1978, s. 141 (5).

[7] E.P.C.A. 1978, s. 146. But part time workers are eligible for time off to seek work when given notice of redundancy. E.P.C.A. 1978, s. 31.

[8] E.P.C.A. 1978, s. 144 (3). Merchant seaman is defined by s. 144 (5) so as to exclude from the definition those employed in the fishing industry and those employed on a ship by persons other than the owner or charterer (except radio officers who are merchant seamen).

[9] See Hepple, *Public Employee Trade Unions in the U.K.* (1970) p. 30.

[10] E.P.C.A. 1978, s. 138 (8).

CHAPTER 9

THE CLOSED SHOP

"THE closed shop"[1] is not a legal term but for general purposes it has been defined as "a situation in which employees come to realise that a particular job is only to be obtained and retained if they become and remain members of one of a specified number of trade unions."[2] It is not enough to become a member of any union, for where a closed shop exists a person must join either the only available union or one of a number of specified unions so that the practice affects not only non-unionists but also members of the "non-specified" unions.

For this reason the term 100 per cent. trade unionism is not satisfactory as a synonym for "closed shop."[3] It is a euphemism that is sometimes used because it is thought less objectionable to require everybody to join a union than to demand that they join a particular union or unions, but in fact the purpose of a "union membership agreement" establishing a closed shop is to specify which unions must be joined.[4]

Although the practice varies a great deal[5] an important distinction can be made between the pre-entry and the post-entry shop.[6] The former (which is the rarer) applies where the person must be a union member *before* he can obtain a job (or a promotion) and the latter requires a person to become a union member after he has been appointed.

The justification for the closed shop has been a matter of acute controversy[7] but the principal arguments have concerned collective security and opposition to the "free-rider" on the one hand, and freedom of the individual on the other.[8] The problem cannot be solved by saying that if there is a right to be a member of a trade union there must be an equivalent right not to be a

---

[1] The leading work on the closed shop is McCarthy, *The Closed Shop in Britain* (1964).

[2] *Ibid.* p. 3.

[3] The T.U.C. Annual Report for 1946 stated that the distinction between the two terms was fundamental and that "the 'closed shop' in the sense of an establishment in which only members of a particular union can be employed, to the exclusion of members of other unions, is alien to British trade union practice and theory."

[4] It is argued that this deters multi-unionism.

[5] McCarthy, *The Closed Shop in Britain* (1964) Chap. 2.

[6] *Ibid.*

[7] *Ibid.* Part 2; see also the Donovan Commission, Cmnd. 3623 paras. 587–618; Kahn-Freund, *Labour and the Law* (2nd ed.), pp. 198–201.

[8] One interesting example of a way of dealing with the free rider is the agreement entered into by Brighton Corporation Transport Department that non-members will not receive locally negotiated benefits (but do still receive nationally negotiated benefits) *The Guardian*, October, 19, 1977.

member, for the policy of the law is to promote collective bargaining and this is achieved by the former but not by the latter.

This is but one example in trade union law of the tension created by the conflict between individual and collective interests which it is suggested cannot be satisfactorily solved either by the dogma of collective security or of individual freedom. The law has made a number of attempts to resolve the problem in relation to the closed shop, but so far without the success which would be indicated by the acquiescence of both sides of the argument to a solution, and the controversy is likely to continue.[9]

The common law

The common law tolerated but did not encourage the closed shop, so that in most cases in which by chance the closed shop was involved no issue was made of the point.[10] However, in *Reynolds* v. *Shipping Federation*[11] the closed shop was challenged on the grounds of conspiracy, but Sargant J. held that there was no liability because the motive was not malicious but to "advance the business interests of employers and employed alike by securing and maintaining [the] advantages of collective bargaining and control."[12]

The neutrality of the law permitted the adoption of the closed shop by agreement between the union and employer (by whatever means that agreement was reached) and it was enforced by industrial not legal sanctions. In fact of course there was rarely a formal agreement but rather it was usual for the employer simply to acquiesce in the practice of the closed shop, thus indicating his consent.

The Industrial Relations Act 1971

It was the element of informality which made the provisions of the Industrial Relations Act controlling the closed shop difficult to enforce, so that it had little effect on the incidence of the closed shop.[13] The attempt to ban most pre-entry closed shops and to permit a form of post-entry closed shop (called the agency shop) failed and is unlikely to be repeated.[14]

The repeal of the Act did not mean that the law could simply return to the abstentionist attitude of the common law, for the Industrial Relations Act had introduced the right of an employee not to be unfairly dismissed, and it is to cope with the relationship between that right and the closed shop that the present legislation exists.

The Present Law Relating to the Closed Shop

At no time has the law made union membership compulsory but rather the sanctions involved in the closed shop are economic and social. This means that a person may be persuaded to join a specified union because of a threat of

---

[9] For an interesting polemic against the closed shop see Paul Johnson, "Towards the Parasite State" *New Statesman*, September 3, 1976. For a more cautious discussion see "Understanding closed shops" (Church Information Office 1977). Each political party as well as the T.U.C. and the C.B.I. also has published its own view.

[10] *White* v. *Riley* [1921] 1 Ch. 1; *Faramus* v. *Film Artistes Assoc.* [1964] A.C. 925.

[11] [1924] 1 Ch. 28.

[12] Adopting the principle in *Mogul Steamship Co.* v. *McGregor Gow* [1892] A.C. 25, and later confirmed in *Crofter Harris Tweed* v. *Veitch* [1942] A.C. 435.

[13] See generally Weekes, Mellish, Dickens and Lloyd, *Industrial Relations and the Limits of Law* (1975) Chap. 2.

[14] Industrial Relations Act 1971, ss. 7–16.

dismissal by his employer if he does not do so, and the employer makes that threat because he has agreed to do so or because he would be threatened by industrial action if he did not. But an employer cannot be obliged by law to enter into a closed shop agreement,[15] even though by virtue of collective bargaining procedure he may be obliged to discuss the subject. It is, therefore, true to say that there is today no more legal compulsion to institute a closed shop than there was before the Industrial Relations Act, but not only has industrial pressure grown but also individuals who are dismissed are deprived of the benefit of a remedy for unfair dismissal which, although it did not exist in 1970, has been instituted since then for other dismissed employees.

The question, therefore, for the law to answer in a situation where an employee has been dismissed because of the closed shop is in what circumstances, if any, should he be compensated and by whom? The answer is that except in cases of religious objection to trade union membership an individual may be dismissed by his employer where a "union membership agreement" (a closed shop) exists, and he will receive no compensation either from his employer or from the union. Thus, with that one exception, the protection of the unfair dismissal legislation does not apply to a person who is dismissed for his refusal to join the relevant union.

"Union membership agreement"

Whether a "union membership agreement" exists is of considerable significance for not only does it establish the status of the union within the firm, but it also serves to protect the employer against a claim for unfair dismissal in the case of a dismissal in pursuance of a closed shop. It should be noted that the case is between the individual and the employer and it is for the employer to establish the existence of a union membership agreement. He can only do this if he can show that a practical effect of the agreement is membership of the union by his employees, and to this extent the burden of policing the agreement is placed on his shoulders. This legislative provision thus re-inforces the stake that employers have in the closed shop.[16]

A union membership agreement[17] is defined[18] as follows:

"union membership agreement" means an agreement or arrangement which:

(a) is made by or on behalf of, or otherwise exists between, one or more independent trade unions and one or more employers or employers' associations; and
(b) relates to employees of an identifiable class; and
(c) has the effect in practice of requiring the employees for the time being of the class to which it relates (whether or not there is a condition to that effect in their contract of employment) to be or become a member of the union or one of the unions which is or are parties to the agreement or arrangement or of another specified independent trade union...."

---

[15] Nor can it be prevented. In particular the Local Government Act 1972, s. 111 does not prevent a local authority from entering into a union membership agreement. *R.* v. *Greater London Council ex parte Burgess* [1978] I.R.L.R. 261 (Div. Ct.).

[16] For a brief discussion of the role of management and the closed shop see Weekes, "Law and practice of the closed shop" (1976) 5 I.L.J. 211 at 214.

[17] The definition has been considerably amended since its inception and in analysing cases care should be taken to determine the form of the definition in force at the time.

[18] T.U.L.R.A. 1974, s. 30 as amended by the Trade Union and Labour Relations (Amendment) Act 1976.

"... agreement or arrangement"

A union membership agreement need not be formalised but is equally effective if it consists of an "arrangement." An arrangement must be bilateral so there is no question of unilateral imposition of a closed shop but it may be tacit rather than express. The curious legal status of the closed shop is indicated by the ways in which it becomes an issue before a tribunal. If the employer wishes to defend himself against the unfair dismissal claim he must accept the closed shop and prove that the arrangement existed, and in such a situation it may be difficult for the employee who has been dismissed to prove that there is no such understanding. On the other hand if the employer does not wish to concede the closed shop he will not defend the claim and the "arrangement" will not become an issue. The union is not involved and has no opportunity to claim that an "arrangement" exists, although it may give evidence on behalf of the employer if he wishes to resist the claim for unfair dismissal.

"... has the effect in practice"

As it is no longer the rule that the contract of employment of each individual must require him to become a member of the specified union,[19] the source of the obligation to join is clearly not intended to be a legal one. Unfortunately, it is not at all clear what "require in practice" means, for the "obligation" to join could be based on moral, social or economic sanctions exercised by the union, the employer or colleagues. But could these sanctions "require" the employee to be a union member? "Require" might be thought to connote a legal obligation, but to reintroduce the need for such an obligation would defeat the purpose of the amendments which added the words "in practice" and would nullify the effect of the clause which states that the obligation need not be a term of the contract of employment. "Require" must therefore be interpreted as meaning "demand" rather than "legally oblige."[20]

It is clear, therefore, that a degree of compulsion of some kind is required and that it is not sufficient for an employer merely to encourage membership of a particular union.[21] One question is whether the compulsory nature of union membership must be explained to each individual, and it is suggested that it is sufficient if there is evidence that each individual is aware that union membership is necessary. The view expressed in *Gayle* v. *Wilkinson*[22] that knowledge on the part of the employees is not necessary is no longer valid as the statute then in force required the contract of employment to contain the relevant term, and a person need not be aware of the terms of his contract in order to make it binding; but now that the compulsion is social rather than legal a person must be aware of the pressure being applied.

"Independent"

The agreement can only be made or exist between an employer and a union

[19] Before it was amended the definition required the agreement to have the effect of requiring the terms of employment of every employee of the relevant class to include a condition that he must become a member of the union. This more stringent requirement gave rise to some difficulty and was amended by the Trade Union and Labour Relations (Amendment) Act 1976.

[20] It is thought that the addition of the words "in practice" in the definition may be held to reverse the view expressed in *Sarvent* v. *C.E.G.B.* [1976] I.R.L.R. 66 at 69 (I.T.) that what matters is the terms of the agreement rather than its consequences. But the matter is not entirely free from difficulty.

[21] *Dunbar* v. *Ford Motor Co.* [1975] I.R.L.R. 178 (I.T.).

[22] [1978] I.C.R. 154.

that is "independent." In order for a union to be "independent" it must be established that it is not under the domination or control of the employer, nor likely to be so.[23] The purpose of this provision is to prevent an employer establishing or encouraging a union or staff association and then entering into a closed shop agreement with it in an attempt to prevent organisation by a "bona fide" union. Such a situation could also result in too "cosy" a relationship between the union and the employer to the detriment of the interests of the members, but even the requirement of independence cannot guarantee that the two parties do not come to depend too much on each other, although the democratic tradition usually sees that the members' interests are not disregarded because of apathy induced by the security of a closed shop agreement.

It should be noted that even a non-independent union may enter into a closed shop agreement, but only in the case of a "union membership agreement" concluded with an independent union will an employer be protected from an action for unfair dismissal by a person who has been dismissed for non membership of the closed shop union. In other cases the closed shop will exist, but the employer will have to compensate those dismissed in pursuance of it.

"... an identifiable class"

The agreement may relate to employees of *any* identifiable class. It is therefore open to the parties to exclude any group they wish to, and it is not uncommon for exclusion to be agreed for a variety of categories, including existing employees or existing members of other unions, for those who object on a variety of grounds and are willing to pay a sum equivalent to the union subscription to charity, or casual or probationary workers. The law in no way restricts the exclusions that can be written into the agreement, although each agreement is subject to the statutory exclusion in favour of those with a religious objection to joining any trade union.

It is also possible for an agreement to refer to people who are not employees of the employer making the arrangement. For example in *Ashby and Bridges* v. *Coleman*[24] it was held that the employees of a sub-contractor were covered by an agreement entered into by the main site employers and the relevant union, so that the contractor's men could not enter the site without being union members.[25]

"... or another specified union"

The agreement or arrangement need not be for exclusive membership of one union but may provide that the employee could join one of two unions. For example, the British Rail agreement concluded in 1975 requires all employees to join either ASLEF, N.U.R. or T.S.S.A. and as the areas of organisation overlap an employee may have a choice: for example a driver may join either ASLEF or the N.U.R.

In addition the agreement may provide that a person may join another union which is specified in the agreement but is not party to it. This provision is intended to deal for example with the case of a small craft union which exists alongside a larger general union. One question of interpretation that arises is

---

[23] T.U.L.R.A. 1974, s. 30. For a discussion of "independent" see Chap. 2.

[24] [1978] I.R.L.R. 51 (Ashford I.T.).

[25] There was no written agreement produced but it was not disputed that the arrangement applied even to employees of contractors.

whether the agreement *must* provide such a choice or whether the provision is simply permissive. In *Sarvent* v. *C.E.G.B.*[26] the tribunal took the view that it is permissive and therefore it is not fatal to the existence of a union membership agreement if the employee is given no choice of unions. This view was affirmed by the Employment Appeal[27] Tribunal in *Home Counties Dairies* v. *Woods.*[27] It is also provided[28] that a union is to be regarded as a specified union even if it is not so treated by the agreement or arrangement, if ACAS has made a recommendation that it should be recognised for negotiating purposes on behalf of the relevant employee.[29] The provision also covers the case where a recognition issue has been presented to ACAS, but no recommendation has yet been made. It is thus not possible for a closed shop agreement to stifle a recognition claim that has been made to ACAS.

The power to dismiss

If a union membership agreement is in existence, the dismissal of an employee who refuses to join the relevant union and has no religious objection to doing so (or is not exempted by the agreement) is deemed to be fair and the employee gets no compensation from his employer. He will not be able to sue the union.[30]

Section 58 (3) of the Employment Protection (Consolidation) Act 1978 provides:

> Dismissal of an employee by an employer shall be regarded as fair for the purposes of this Part if:
>
> (a) it is the practice, in accordance with a union membership agreement, for employees for the time being of the same class as the dismissed employee to belong to a specified independent trade union, or to one of a number of specified independent trade unions; and
>
> (b) the reason for the dismissal was that the employee was not a member of the specified union or one of the specified unions, or had refused or proposed to refuse to become or remain a member of that union or one of those unions;
>
> unless the employee genuinely objects on grounds of religious belief to being a member of any trade union whatsoever, in which case the dismissal shall be regarded as unfair.

". . . it is the practice. . . ."

It is not necessary for every single employee to belong to the specified union[31] for by definition the applicant himself is not a member. The sub-section is, however, difficult to construe because the word "employees" remains unqualified. The answer is that the employer does not have to prove that any particular number of employees are members but rather that he has a system to enforce the closed shop and that that system is substantially effective in that

---

[26] [1976] I.R.L.R. 66 (I.T.).

[27] [1977] I.C.R. 463 at 467.

[28] E.P.C.A. 1978, s. 58 (4), for the purposes of s. 58 (3) which provides the power to dismiss fairly for failure to belong to a specified union.

[29] *i.e.* has made a recommendation under E.P.A. 1975, s. 12 which is operative under s. 15.

[30] Except in cases where he has been wrongfully expelled from his union: see Chap. 5.

[31] This was so even when the statute required that it be the practice for all employees. "All" has now been omitted. See *Strover* v. *Chrysler* [1975] I.R.L.R. 66; *Home Counties Dairies* v. *Woods* [1977] I.C.R. 463.

almost all the employees are members of the relevant union.[32] The employer will have to show that when it is discovered that a person is not a member of the specified union he takes steps either to see that he becomes a member or to dismiss him.[33]

It is, however, not entirely clear whose duty it is to check that all employees are members of the relevant union, although a system of some kind is necessary. It may be that it is not enough for an employer to take action in cases reported to him by the shop stewards in the union, for he may be required to make a check himself. In *Sarvent* v. *C.E.G.B.*[34] the tribunal found that a "practice" had not been established and therefore that the dismissals in pursuance of a closed shop were not deemed to be fair. It appears that evidence was given that a check was made by shop stewards, but not by the union or the employer. The tribunal found this state of affairs unsatisfactory as no evidence was given of the efficacy of the check by the shop stewards, and the tribunal chairman suggested that a procedure which would satisfy the test would be for the union to supply a list of union members to the employer and for the employer to check this list against the names of employees and to investigate any discrepancies. Objections were made to such a proposal on the grounds that such a procedure would interfere with the independence of unions. It cannot be stated definitely the extent to which the employer must involve himself in searching out non-members especially where the union is wary of co-operation with the employer. The union can rely on industrial sanctions, but the employer needs the protection of the law if he is to avoid paying compensation for unfair dismissal, and in this the assistance of the union may be important.

It is clear, however, that whatever degree of responsibility is placed on the employer, the burden of maintaining the closed shop is to some extent placed with him if he wishes to avoid liability, In other words employers must become active participants in the closed shop.

Non-members

It appears from *Gayle* v. *Wilkinson*[35] that an employer is not required to prove that the applicant actually was a non-member at the time of his dismissal, but only that he honestly believed him to be a non member. No doubt such honest belief can only be established if the employer has sought a definitive statement from the relevant union official and he is not to be held responsible if that official has "perhaps unwittingly, perhaps negligently,[36] even perhaps cynically ... misled the employer."[37] In that case the union admitted that the applicant had been wrongfully expelled from the union and therefore was legally a member at the relevant time, but he was nevertheless excluded from compensation for unfair dismissal.[38] It is important to note that the statute only applies to non-members and this group must be carefully distinguished

---

[32] *Himpfen* v. *Allied Records Ltd.* [1978] I.C.R. 684.

[33] *Strover* v. *Chrysler* [1975] I.R.L.R. 66 (I.T.).

[34] [1976[I.R.L.R. 66.

[35] [1978] I.C.R. 154. See also *Lakhani* v. *Hoover* [1978] I.C.R. 1063.

[36] If a statement is made negligently by an official to the employer, the employee may be able to sue the official for the tort of negligent mis-statement on the basis of a statement by A to B whereby B does an act detrimental to C. *Minister of Housing* v. *Sharp* [1970] 2 Q.B. 233.

[37] [1978] I.C.R. 154 at 159.

[38] In such circumstances a member may have an action against the union for wrongful expulsion: see Chap. 5. The T.U.C. has set up an Independent Review Committee to deal with such cases.

from those who are merely in arrears with their dues. It may be that a person in arrears is deemed by the rules no longer to be a member, but in a number of cases the penalty of expulsion does not automatically follow. Thus if a person in arrears merely loses benefit and not membership, he cannot be fairly dismissed for not complying with the closed shop, and it makes no difference that the union membership agreement requires all members to be paid up.[39]

Non-employees

It has been held that a dismissal is deemed to be fair even where the applicant was not an employee of the employer who made the union membership agreement. In *Ashby and Bridges* v. *Coleman*[40] the applicants worked for a builder and contractor who *inter alia* was engaged to do maintenance work, including painting, at a B.P. refinery. It was established that it was the practice at the refinery for all employees, including employees of contractors, to be union members. The tribunal held that the applicants were deemed to be fairly dismissed even though their employer was not a party to that agreement. The chairman said that there was nothing in the wording of the Act to require the employer to be a party and that:

> "It would be contrary to the practical and pragmatic assessment of the situation which we are required to make to find that a contractor who employs labour on the site is not protected by [section 58 (3)] in respect of a claim for unfair dismissal simply because he is not a party to the union membership agreement. In a case such as the present, 100 per cent. union membership is enforced against contractors and Parliament could not have intended to expose such contractors to lesser protection than that afforded to the employer who is a party to the union membership agreement."

It is suggested, however, that it may be preferable for such a contractor to gain protection by agreement with his own workers for a closed shop, or by refraining from sending non-members to a closed shop site if he has a choice. But the principle contains a further difficulty: if the view of the tribunal is to be accepted, what happens where the contractor does have a closed shop agreement, but with a different union from that on the main site? Can a person still be dismissed? Again what happens where the contractor operates on several sites, each with its own closed shop and each with a different union? In such a situation it is suggested that if the closed shop is enforced on the site against the contractor, he must take the responsibility for selecting the appropriate employees and cannot demand dual or multiple union membership (which anyway is not likely to be obtainable).

Procedure

If an employer is to claim the protection of a union membership agreement he must adhere to the procedure laid down in that agreement. The source of this obligation is not clear and it might be argued that any benefit that is provided by the agreement accrues to the individual if at all by way of his contract of employment (for breach of which he cannot sue in an industrial tribunal) rather than as an element in the unfair dismissal provisions. On the other hand, it could be said that, although not within the strict terms of section 58 (3), the dismissal must be in pursuance of the agreement and that the agree-

[39] *Scott* v. *Kaye* [1978] I.R.L.R. 193 (I.T.).
[40] [1978] I.R.L.R. 51 (Ashford I.T.).

ment compliments the statute so that the employer cannot rely on the bare words of the statute alone. The latter view was taken in *Jeffrey* v. *Laurence Scott*[41] where the union membership agreement incorporated a three stage procedure for dismissal, and it was held that the employers lost the protection of the agreement when they omitted the third stage, even though according to their evidence this would have been a mere formality.[42] Where the closed shop agreement has only just been concluded the employer must give reasonable notice of its existence and reasonable time for his employees to comply with it. It is not sufficient to put up a notice without explanation, but rather the employer must do what a thoughtful employer would do to communicate a change of management's policy.[43]

Unprotected dismissals

If the employer is unable to prove the existence of a union membership agreement or for some other reason fails to establish that he is protected by one, the case falls to be considered by the ordinary principles of unfair dismissal.[44] One particular point to note is that in such a case the employer cannot escape liability on the ground that union pressure forced him to dismiss the applicant.[45] Because the burden is on the employer to prove the reason for the dismissal and since the real reason (union pressure) cannot be put forward, the dismissal will be held to be unfair.[46] In such circumstances the tribunal may take the view that reinstatement is not practicable[47] but the employee will still be awarded damages.

Exemptions from the closed shop

As we have seen it is open to the parties to a union membership agreement to decide who shall be exempted from the closed shop, for the agreement can relate to employees identified by any criterion whatsoever. In the past few years legislation has also provided for a number of statutory exemptions,[48] but the only one applicable now covers those who genuinely object on grounds of religious belief to being a member of any trade union whatsoever, in which case the dismissal shall be treated as unfair.[49]

A number of cases have arisen from dismissals by British Rail,[50] and it appears that the internal tribunal set up under the union membership agreement had taken the view that the applicant must establish that the creed to

---

[41] [1977] I.R.L.R. 466 (I.T.).

[42] The third stage was a meeting between management, a full time employers' association official, the local union committee and a full time union official. It never took place because the inflexibility of the union attitude had been made clear at the second stage.

[43] *Himpfen* v. *Allied Records Ltd.* [1978] I.C.R. 684.

[44] E.P.C.A. 1978, ss. 54–57.

[45] E.P.C.A. 1978, s. 63.

[46] *Hazell's Offset Ltd.* v. *Luckett* (1977) 12 I.T.R. 298 (E.A.T.); *Trend* v. *Chiltern Hunt Ltd.* [1977] I.C.R. 612; *Ford Motor Co.* v. *Hudson* [1978] I.C.R. 482.

[47] E.P.C.A. 1978, s. 69 (5) (*b*); *Sarvent* v. *C.E.G.B.* [1976] I.R.L.R. 66 (I.T.).

[48] Industrial Relations Act 1971, s. 9 permitted in some cases those who objected "on grounds of conscience" to pay the equivalent of a subscription to charity: *Drury* v. *Bakers Union* [1973] I.R.L.R. 171 (I.T.); *Westhead* v. *N.U.S.* [1973] I.R.L.R. 275 (I.T.); *Hynds* v. *Spillers-French Baking* (1974) 9 I.T.R. 261 (N.I.R.C.). T.U.L.R.A. 1974 as originally enacted excluded from the closed shop provisions those who objected "on any reasonable grounds to being a member of a particular trade union." *McColm* v. *Agnew* [1976] I.R.L.R. 13 (I.T.).

[49] E.P.C.A. 1978, s. 58 (3).

[50] The number of employees dismissed up to November 1977 was 40. H.C. Debs. vol. 939, col. 272 (November 15, 1977).

which he adheres prohibits trade union membership. The Employment Appeal Tribunal rejected this view in *Saggers* v. *B.R.B.*[51] saying that what was in issue was the personal belief of the applicant.[52]

> "The word 'belief,' first of all, seems to us to suggest that which is believed by the person whose belief is under consideration; and for that reason it seems to us that the word more naturally describes the content of intellectual acceptance by the person under consideration than an established body of creed or dogma appertaining to himself as well as a number of other persons."

It would of course be usual for the belief of the individual to coincide with the creed of the organisation to which he belongs, and no doubt if his beliefs are too divergent he could not be said to be a member at all. Although the problem is not specifically mentioned in the statute it may have been intended that the exemption should only apply to a person who is a member of some kind of organisation consisting of people holding similar religious beliefs, and could not be applied to the case of a "religion" with only one adherent. But as a matter of interpretation "religious" in section 58 (3) qualifies "belief" and would normally be regarded as applying to a belief in a deity of some kind so that a belief held only by one individual may be "religious" even though nobody else agrees with him.

A number of churches may be equivocal on the subject and admit that a member could reject trade unionism for religious reasons, without it being a tenet of that faith.[53] Exemption has so far been successfully claimed by a Jehovah's Witness,[54] a member of the "Brethren,"[55] a Christadelphian,[56] a member of the "Plymouth Brethren,"[57] a Seventh Day Adventist[58] and a member of the Ecclesia of Christ.[59] But it must be stressed that the test is based on the personal beliefs of the individual and not exclusively on the creed of the organisation.

The Press: special provisions

During the passage through the House of Lords of the Trade Union and Labour Relations (Amendment) Act 1976 considerable concern was expressed about the effect of a closed shop for journalists on the freedom of the press. In particular it was thought that editors might be required to join the National Union of Journalists and therefore be subject to the union's disciplinary procedure; secondly, that the union might attempt to influence the content of the press, and thirdly that expert freelance contributors might be denied access to the press.

---

[51] [1977] I.C.R. 809. The applicant was a Jehovah's Witness; trade union membership is not proscribed. See also *Saggers* v. *B.R.B. (No. 2)* [1978] I.R.L.R. 435 (E.A.T.).

[52] For a similar view in Canada see *Re Funk and the Manitoba Labour Board* (1976) 66 D.L.R. 3rd 35.

[53] For a discussion of the views of the Church of England see *Understanding Closed Shops* (Church Information Office).

[54] *Saggers* v. *B.R.B.* [1977] I.C.R. 809; *ibid.* No. 2 [1978] I.R.L.R. 435 (E.A.T.).

[55] *Goodbody* v. *B.R.B.* [1977] I.R.L.R. 84 (I.T.). This sect was not a strict as the Exclusive Brothers, but more strict than the Open Brothers.

[56] *Cave* v. *B.R.B.* [1976] I.R.L.R. 400 (I.T.).

[57] *The Times*, April 28, 1977, p. 4.

[58] *Roberts* v. *B.R.B.*; I.D.S. Brief No. 110.

[59] *Cotter* v. *Vauxhall Motors*, *ibid.* No. 101.

Whatever the merits of these points,[60] after much debate Parliament agreed[61] that a charter on the freedom of the press should be drawn up, and that although it would not have legislative effect it would, like other codes, be relevant in legal proceedings.

It was hoped that the charter could be drawn up by agreement between the parties, but this proved impossible and it is now the task of the Secretary of State to prepare a draft charter on those issues which have not so far been agreed.

The function of the charter is to give "practical guidance for employers, trade unions and editors and other journalists on matters relating to the freedom of the press"[62] and it is intended that the charter should set up a body to hear complaints by "a person aggrieved by a failure on the part of any person to observe any provision of the charter."[63] The extent of *locus standi* implied by the words "a person aggrieved" could be wide. It is not clear what practical sanctions this body will have, although it will issue a declaration and publish its decision.

In addition to the proposed remedy before the charter tribunal it is provided[64] that although a breach of the charter shall not of itself give rise to legal proceedings, it may be used in evidence and may be relevant in legal proceedings. Such proceedings would include both unfair dismissal and actions for wrongful expulsion from the union. The content of the charter is not yet known but the matter has been discussed by the Royal Commission on the Press,[65] which recommended that the Press Council should take on the task of being the tribunal under the charter and that the charter should be based on the following principles:

1. Freedom of a journalist to act, write, and speak in accordance with conscience without being inhibited by the threat of expulsion or other disciplinary action by his union or his employer.

2. Freedom for an editor of a newspaper, news agency or periodical to accept or reject any contribution whether or not the contributor is a professional journalist or a member of a union, so long as this freedom is not abused.

3. Freedom for an editor to join or not to join any union and, if a member of a union, to take part or not to take part in any industrial action called for by the union.

4. Protection of an editor's right to accept or reject any contribution notwithstanding the views of his proprietor, the management of his company, union chapel or any advertiser or potential advertiser.

5. Proper appeal procedures for complaints of unfair or arbitrary expulsion or exclusion from trade union membership.

6. Assurance that the practices of publishers and of the N.U.J. and I.O.J. in matters affecting the freedom of journalists will conform with the spirit and provisions of the charter.

In pursuance of these principles the Commission recommends that the N.U.J. should adopt rules preventing discrimination within the union on the

---

[60] For a discussion see England and Rees, "A Journalists closed shop in the newspaper industry" (1977) 127 N.L.J. 256, and the Royal Commission on the Press, Cmnd. 6810 paras. 17.1 to 17.10.

[61] T.U.L.R.A. 1974, s. 1A, as inserted by T.U.L.R. (Amendment) Act 1976.

[62] *Ibid.* s. 1A (1).

[63] *Ibid.* 1A (5).

[64] *Ibid.* 1A (10).

[65] Cmnd. 6810.

grounds of the journalist's opinions or because he has commissioned work from a non-member. It was also suggested that editors and three nominated senior journalists should be free not to join the union. The scheme that is envisaged is a voluntary one, but the Commission regards the freedom of the press as such an important principle that, with one dissent, it suggested that after three years the system should be reviewed and if it is found to be unsatisfactory legislation should be introduced to provide sanctions.

Wrongful dismissal at common law

The fact that an employer may be protected by section 58 from a claim for unfair dismissal does not make him immune for an action for wrongful dismissal at common law. Such an action is possible because under the Industrial Relations Act 1971 a number of employees had incorporated into their contracts the right not to be a member of a union[66] and these clauses may have survived. But even in such a case it will usually be possible to terminate the contract by giving due notice

Membership procedures

Where a closed shop exists, becoming or remaining a union member is of special significance, and accordingly many unions have adopted special membership procedures. For example, it is not uncommon for a union membership agreement to state that membership will not be withheld unreasonably from any applicant covered by the closed shop agreement,[67] and it is sometimes provided that an applicant who is rejected may appeal to a specially constituted review tribunal consisting of an independent chairman and representatives of the union and management.[68] Similar arrangements are also made in the case of expulsion from the union.[69]

In addition, the T.U.C. has set up its own Independent Review Committee to consider appeals from individuals who have been dismissed by their employer because they have been expelled from or refused admission to a union which they have been required to join under a union membership agreement. This procedure only applies after internal procedures have been exhausted, including any special procedure laid down in the agreement, and can only be invoked where the union concerned is affiliated to the T.U.C.[70]

Social security

It has been decided[71] that a person who is dismissed because of his refusal to join a union where a closed shop exists cannot be disqualified from social security benefits either on the ground that he voluntarily left employment without just cause or that he lost his employment through misconduct; nor can he be disqualified for having neglected to avail himself of a reasonable opportunity of suitable employment.[72]

---

[66] See for example *Home Counties Dairies* v. *Woods* [1977] I.C.R. 463; *Beaumont* v. *Libby McNeil*, *The Times*, October, 10, 1978.

[67] For example the British Rail agreement, July 1975.

[68] For example the Post Office agreement, May 1976.

[69] The British Steel agreement of June 1977 provides for a special procedure after that provided for in the union rules. This involves consideration by management and union jointly, to be followed if necessary by reference to ACAS whose decision is binding.

[70] See further Chap. 5 above.

[71] R(U) 2/77.

[72] Social Security Act 1975, s. 20: see further Chap. 16.

European Convention on Human Rights

It is open to an individual to petition the European Commission on Human Rights at Strasbourg for an alleged breach of the convention, and if the matter cannot be settled it is referred to the European Court of Human Rights for decision.[73]

Although a number of articles of the convention have been cited against the government by applicants who have been dismissed because of a closed shop,[74] it seems that argument is likely to centre around the effect of article 11. This article states: "Everyone has the right to freedom of peaceful assembly and to freedom of association with others, including the right to form and to join trade unions for the protection of his interests."

The article further provides that restrictions may be placed on this freedom if necessary for the protection of the rights and freedom of others.

In relation to the closed shop the Commission see the main issue as being whether this article protects the right not to join a trade union.[75] The argument is that the freedom to associate necessarily involves a freedom of choice as to whom one will associate with (if anybody), so that compulsion to join A restricts the freedom to join B (or to join nobody at all). There has so far been no ruling on this point, nor on the question whether the closed shop interferes with the freedom of thought, conscience or religion as protected by Article 9.

The Commission has ruled admissible a claim by a British Rail employee who was dismissed in pursuance of the union membership agreement, but it is not entirely clear why the United Kingdom government has been held potentially responsible. The Commission states:[76]

> "Whatever the division of rights and duties between the Board and the respective Minister may be, in the Commission's opinion, there can be no doubt that the Government of the United Kingdom is responsible for their public authorities and thus for the acts of the British Railways Board. As the British Railways Board employed and dismissed both applicants, these acts must be considered as acts by the 'State as employer'."

Traditionally, at least by internal law, public corporations have been regarded as independent of the state, even if they are on some matters subject to direction by the relevant Minister, and it is difficult to see how by United Kingdom law the employees of British Rail could be regarded as being employed by the state[77] or how the government could be responsible for the dismissals.

---

[73] It has been held in a case concerning the closed shop that Article 9 of the Convention is not part of English law and cannot invalidate a closed shop agreement: *R.* v. *Greater London Council ex parte Burgess* [1978] I.R.L.R. 261. (Div. Ct.).

[74] In particular Article 9 (freedom of thought, conscience and religion); article 10 (freedom of expression); Article 13 (failure to provide adequate remedies to protect the freedoms in the Convention).

[75] *Young and James* v. *United Kingdom*, Application No. 7601/76.

[76] *Ibid.* A similar claim in *Webster* v. *United Kingdom* has also been ruled admissible. Application No. 7806/77.

[77] If they are regarded as being employed by the government it is not open to the government to argue that the Convention only applies to it in its capacity as a state: In the *Swedish Engine Drivers Union Case*, European Court of Human Rights, Series A, No. 20, para. 37 the Court stated "The Convention nowhere makes an express distinction between the functions of a contracting state as holder of public power and its responsibilities as employer."

Furthermore, unlike common practice in Europe, the law in this country makes no significant distinction between public and private employees. Such a distinction could come about if it were held that the dismissals cause a breach of the convention.[78]

[78] But not if it were held that the legislation is itself a breach of Article 11; but the case is not being argued on this basis.

CHAPTER 10

INDUSTRIAL ACTION AND THE EMPLOYMENT RELATIONSHIP

THE "right to strike" is not a legal term and indeed it cannot even be said that striking is generally a lawful activity: what can be said is that a strike[1] may or may not be lawful as between employer and employee depending on the kind and length of notice that is given.

The "right to strike" is sometimes used in a collective sense, that is the rights of the employees or union members or the union itself to call for a strike; and sometimes it is used in an individual sense, that is the right of the individual to withdraw his labour.[2] As will be seen,[3] the legality of collective strike action may depend on whether the act is lawful as between employer and employee.

This chapter will deal not only with that problem, that is the effect of a strike on the individual contract of employment at common law, but also with its effect on compensation for unfair dismissal and redundancy.

THE STRIKE AND THE CONTRACT OF EMPLOYMENT AT COMMON LAW

The effect of a strike on a person's contract of employment is important for a variety of reasons. It is of little *direct* significance, for although in cases where such action is held to be a breach of contract the employer may be entitled at common law to dismiss the worker summarily[4] or even to sue him for damages, such action is fairly rare. Of much greater significance for industrial relations is the *indirect* effect of a finding of unlawfulness for this may affect the legality of collective action and whether the leaders may be sued in tort for conspiracy, inducing breach of contract or intimidation.[5] A finding that the strike was unlawful may also affect compensation for redundancy.[6]

Whether strike action is lawful as between employer and employee at common law depends entirely on contractual principles and particularly on the type and length of notice given of the impending action.

---

[1] There is no legal definition of a strike for the purposes of the general law but in *Tramp Shipping* v. *Greenwich Marine* [1975] I.C.R. 261 at 266 Lord Denning said: "a strike is a concerted stoppage of work by men done with a view to improving their wages or conditions, or giving vent to a grievance or making a protest about something or other, or supporting or sympathising with other workmen in such endeavour." For a statutory definition for a limited purpose see E.P.C.A. 1978, Sched. 13 para. 24.

[2] The statutory limitations on members of the armed forces, policemen, merchant seamen and post office workers are discussed in Chap. 2.

[3] Chaps. 11 and 12.

[4] Even if this is so an employee may be able to sue for unfair dismissal.

[5] These torts are discussed in Chap. 12 together with the immunity for acts in contemplation or furtherance of a trade dispute.

[6] *Simmons* v. *Hoover* [1977] I.C.R. 68

"Due" notice

Strike action may be lawful if notice is of the correct length and type. As to length, whether due notice has been given depends on the terms of each individual contract of employment and may vary considerably not only within each work force but also within each grade. Due notice is the minimum notice a person is required to give to terminate his contract. Although there is a statutory minimum of one week[7] this provides little guide to the periods actually contained in individual contracts. There seems little merit today in the suggestion[8] that notice should be given in such general terms as that the contracts will be terminated at the expiry of the due period of notice required by the contracts of employment of the workers concerned, for the due period must still be ascertained and it would be a breach of contract to go on strike before it has expired. One advantage, however, of giving notice in such a form would be to prevent pre-emptive action by the employer if the notice is of the right type for an employer could not treat such notice as anticipatory breach and dismiss the men, whereas he could if the actual period specified was too short.[9] In effect due notice means the longest period of notice to terminate the contract to be found in the contracts of those one wishes to call out on strike.

Types of notice

Notices[10] can be placed into one of three categories in order to determine their effect on the contract of employment.

Categories of strike notice[11]

(a) Those which are expressed clearly as a notice of termination and which are of sufficient length to be in accordance with the contractual requirement as to notice.

(b) Those which are not actually expressed as a notice of termination but which are of a length equivalent to, or greater than, the notice which would be needed to terminate the contract of employment.

(c) Those which are less than the notice contractually required for termination, including the situation where no notice is given at all.

1. Due notice to terminate

If a notice is clearly expressed as a notice to terminate the contract and is of sufficient length it will bring the contract to an end and the consequent strike will be lawful as between the employer and employee, for in effect the employee has resigned.

There is, however, one grave disadvantage to giving strike notice in this form and that is that the worker will not be protected by the unfair dismissal

---

[7] In the case of a person employed for four weeks or more: E.P.C.A. 1978, s. 49 (2).

[8] See *Horizon Holidays Ltd.* v. *A.S.T.M.S.* [1973] I.R.L.R. 22.

[9] But on balance there is little advantage for although the strikers might gain time they would lose the protection of the unfair dismissal legislation.

[10] For a fact based approach see O'Higgins, "Strike Notices: another approach" (1973) 2 I.L.J. 152, commenting on an earlier article by Foster on s. 147 of the Industrial Relations Act, "Strike Notice: section 147" (1973) 2 I.L.J. 28. The fact based approach is also adopted by Hepple and O'Higgins, *Employment Law* (2nd ed.), p. 180. For a comparative study see Blanc-Jouvan, "The effect of industrial action on the status of the individual employee" in Aaron & Wedderburn, *Industrial Conflict, a comparative legal survey* (1972); and see England "Loss of Jobs in strikes: the position in England and Canada compared" (1976) 25 I.C.L.Q. 583.

[11] These classifications are taken from Foster, "Strikes and employment contracts" (1971) 34 M.L.R. 275.

legislation. As will be seen a person who is dismissed while he is on strike may claim compensation for unfair dismissal either if others who went on strike have not been dismissed or where, having been dismissed, some strikers have been re-engaged and the applicant has not.[12] But such provisions cannot apply in cases where the employee has resigned, unless he can claim constructive dismissal on the part of the employer,[13] in which case he must show that the employer himself has broken the contract.[14]

2. Ambiguous notice of due length

Strike notice in practice takes a number of forms, and rarely, if ever, are legal terms used[15] and it will often be difficult to determine the appropriate effect of the notice. The possible legal categories which could be applied are notice to terminate, notice to break the contract and possibly notice to suspend the contract. In some cases the language used may make it clear which category is applicable, but notices to "withdraw labour," "to strike" or "to engage in industrial action" leave open any of the possibilities. As labour law has developed over the last century, so has the court's view of the appropriate interpretation of such notices.

(1) *Notice to terminate the contract*

A notice to strike or withdraw labour could be regarded as a notice to terminate the contract after due notice,[16] in other words to resign. As we have seen this is the only lawful method of engaging in a strike and it is often said that the right to strike rests on interpreting a strike notice in this way.[17] This may have been a useful view when there was no disadvantage to it, but the introduction in 1971 of compensation for unfair dismissal has complicated matters. Because of that the curious position arises that if one acts lawfully and terminates the contract the protection of the legislation is lost, but if one interprets a notice to strike as a notice to act unlawfully the protection is retained. It is suggested that it is no longer appropriate to regard strike notices which are ambiguous as notices to terminate the contract.[18]

(2) *Notice to break the contract*

Although interpreting a notice to strike as a notice to terminate the contract was the traditional view, it was suggested in *Rookes* v. *Barnard*[19] and *Stratford* v. *Lindley*[20] that this may not be appropriate as it was out of accord with reality since the strikers did not intend to sever relations with their employer altogether.

In *Rookes* v. *Barnard*[21] Lord Devlin said:

"As Donovan L.J. said in the Court of Appeal, the object of the notice

---

[12] Employment Protection (Consolidation) Act 1978, s. 62.

[13] *Ibid.* s. 55 (2) (*c*).

[14] *Western Excavations Ltd.* v. *Sharp* [1978] I.C.R. 221. See also *Thompson* v. *Eaton* [1976] I.C.R. 336 at 342.

[15] For a small survey see O'Higgins, "Strike notices: another approach" (1973) 2 I.L.J. 152.

[16] If due notice is not given the action is clearly a breach of contract: *Denaby and Cadeby Main Collieries* v. *Yorkshire Miners Association* [1906] A.C. 384.

[17] Grunfeld, *Modern Trade Union Law* (1966), p. 319; Kahn-Freund, *Labour and the Law* (2nd ed.), p. 269.

[18] See *Simmons* v. *Hoover* [1977] I.C.R. 61 at 69.

[19] [1964] A.C. 1129.

[20] [1965] A.C. 269.

[21] [1964] A.C. 1129 at 1204.

> was not to terminate the contract either before or after the expiry of the seven days. The object was to break the contract by withholding labour but keeping the contract alive for as long as the employers would tolerate the breach without exercising their right of recission."

In such circumstances a notice to strike is to be interpreted as a notice to break the contract in the future: the consequence is that the employer then has the power to summarily dismiss the strikers for repudiation of the contract.[22] In most cases of course this power will not be exercised. Lord Denning expressed a similar point, *obiter*, in *Stratford* v. *Lindley:*[23]

> "Suppose that a trade union officer gives a 'strike notice.' He says to an employer: 'We are going to call a strike on Monday week unless you increase the men's wages by £1 a week'— or 'unless you dismiss yonder man who is not a member of the union'—or 'unless you cease to deal with such and such a customer.' Such a notice is not to be construed as if it were a week's notice on behalf of the men to terminate their employment, for that is the last thing any of the men would desire. They do not want to lose their pension rights and so forth by giving up their jobs. The 'strike notice' is nothing more nor less than a notice that the men will not come to work. In short that they will break their contracts...."

One consequence of this view was recognised by Lord Denning himself in *Morgan* v. *Fry*[24] when he pointed out that if he was right "it would do away with the right to strike in the country." This is not quite correct for it would always be open to an individual to expressly terminate rather than break his contract and thus act lawfully, and it may be that Lord Denning has been misled by assuming that there is in fact a legal right to strike; but it is true that the "breach" theory would in a number of cases increase the risk of exposure of union leaders to tort actions for inducing breach of contract.

One particular aspect of this issue is the suggestion that if strike notice is regarded as notice to break the contract a person who organises a strike may be rendered liable for conspiracy to use unlawful means.[25] No such action has yet been brought and it is doubtful that a breach of contract would be regarded as unlawful means for the purposes of the tort of conspiracy.[26]

One further problem with this interpretation of notice to strike, is that there appears to be some doubt whether a person who repudiates his contract in this way can sue for unfair dismissal. This problem is dealt with below, but if it can be solved (and it is suggested that it can) then despite the considerable criticism of these dicta,[27] it is suggested that this mode of interpretation may be more suited to today's conditions than to interpret strike notice as notice to terminate. A person may be able to put up with the theoretical breach of contract involved and the possibility of dismissal by his employer, so long as he is still protected by the unfair dismissals legislation, and that is only possible if strike notice is regarded as notice to break rather than notice to terminate the contract.

---

[22] This point will need developing for it has been suggested that repudiatory conduct itself amounts to dismissal, and there is no need for the employer to accept the repudiation. This problem is discussed later in this chapter.

[23] [1965] A.C. 269 at 285.

[24] [1968] 2 Q.B. 710 at 725.

[25] Grunfeld, *Modern Trade Union Law* (1966), p. 441.

[26] *Rookes* v. *Barnard* [1964] A.C. 1129 at 1210 *per* Lord Devlin.

[27] See for example Freedland, *The contract of employment,* p. 170 where the view is put forward that the intention of the notice giver is not a proper consideration in the law of contract.

(3) *Notice to suspend the contract*

If a collective agreement which is incorporated into the contracts of the individual employees provides that the effect of a strike shall be to suspend the contracts, then that term will be effective and the strike lawful. But where there is no such term it may be difficult to interpret an ambiguous strike notice as suspension of the contract. When Lord Denning realised that his view[28] that strike notice should be regarded as notice to break a contract would render most strikes unlawful, he attempted to escape from the difficulty by suggesting that the appropriate interpretation was that notice acted as suspension of the contract. Thus in *Morgan* v. *Fry*[29] he said:

> "The truth is that neither employer nor workmen wish to take the drastic action of termination if it can be avoided. The men do not wish to leave their work for ever. The employers do not wish to scatter their labour force to the four winds. Each side is, therefore, content to accept a 'strike notice' of proper length as lawful. It is an implication read into the contract by the modern law as to trade disputes. If a strike takes place, the contract of employment is not terminated. It is suspended during the strike and revives again when the strike is over."

This innovatory doctrine has caused considerable controversy but it is suggested that as the authorities stand it is not the present law. However, Lord Denning's view was accepted in Ireland in *Becton* v. *Lee*[30] and was adopted in statutory form in section 147 of the Industrial Relations Act 1971, but that section suffered from a number of difficulties of interpretation.[31]

On the other hand the Donovan Commission[32] recommended against adopting the suspension theory because of the technical difficulties that would be encountered,[33] and recent cases have also tended to reject it. In *Cummings* v. *Charles Connell*[34] the pursuer sued his employer for instituting a lock out and the employers defended on the basis that as in the case of a strike a lock out merely suspended the contract, but the court refused to imply a term in the contract of employment making provision for such suspension. More recently the Employment Appeal Tribunal, which is technically bound by *Morgan* v. *Fry*[35] declined to accept the consequences of Lord Denning's view and held that an employer was entitled to dismiss an employee for striking in breach of contract.[36]

It therefore appears that as the law presently stands it would be difficult to regard a strike notice as suspending the contract, unless such a power is included in the contract of employment of each individual.

---

28 Expressed in *Stratford* v. *Lindley* [1965] A.C. 269 at 285.

29 [1968] 2 Q.B. 710 at 728.

30 [1973] I.R. 1 at 35.

31 Foster, "Strike Notice: section 147" (1973) 2 I.L.J. 28; O'Higgins, "Strike Notices: another approach" (1973) 2 I.L.J. 152; Lewis, "The Solar Plexus" in Carby-Hall, *Studies in Labour Law*, p. 52.

32 Cmnd. 3623 para. 936 *et seq.*

33 These include such problems as which strikes would the doctrine apply to, official, unofficial, or both, strikes with notice only or also strikes without notice? Would the employer retain the power of dismissal? Could the employee get a job elsewhere during the strike? If conciliation failed when would the contract of employment come to an end?

34 [1969] S.L.T. 25.

35 [1968] 2 Q.B. 710.

36 *Simmons* v. *Hoover* [1977] I.C.R. 61.

3. Notice which is not of the proper length

There is no doubt that a strike which is called without due notice amounts to a breach of contract on the part of each person who engages in the strike.[37]

Summary

(1) A strike is lawful as between employer and employee if the notice is of the proper length and amounts to notice to terminate the contract. In such a case a striker who is discriminatorily dismissed could not sue for unfair dismissal.

(2) A strike is unlawful and amounts to a breach of contract if the notice given is too short or no notice at all is given. A claim for unfair dismissal may be available in such a case.

(3) A strike in pursuance of an ambiguous notice such as "to strike" or "to withdraw labour" or "to engage in industrial action" or is not a breach of contract according to the interpretation of the notice. It is suggested that it is unlikely that the courts would be willing to construe such a notice as a notice to suspend the contract; traditionally the courts have been willing to interpret such notices as notices to terminate, but this would deprive the men of compensation for unfair dismissal; alternatively the notice may be treated as a notice to break the contract, and although it is not certain that in all such cases the unfair dismissal provisions would be available, they probably would be.

Remedies

A decision that a strike is in breach of contract and therefore unlawful has repercussions in a number of areas, notably as providing the element of unlawful means in the torts of intimidation, conspiracy and intimidation.[38] We are, however, here concerned only with its effect as between the parties and the common law remedies available to the employer against the employee.

Dismissal

The traditional view[39] has always been that notice of an intention to strike in breach of contract is an anticipatory breach and that the strike itself amounts to repudiation of the contract which entitles the employer to dismiss the striker. This view has recently been re-enforced by the Employment Appeal Tribunal in *Simmons* v. *Hoover*[40] where it was said:

> "We do not accept [the] submission that if the contract of employment was not suspended, nonetheless the employee's action in going on strike was not repudiatory of the contract. It seems to us to be plain that it was, for here there was a settled, confirmed and continued intention on the part of the employee not to do any of the work which under his contract he had engaged to do; which was the whole purpose of his contract. Judged by the usual standards, such conduct by the employee appears to us to be repudiatory of the contract of employment. We should not be taken to be saying that all strikes are necessarily repudiatory, though usually they will be. For example, it could hardly be said that a strike of

[37] *Denaby and Cadeby Main Collieries* v. *Yorkshire Miners Association* [1906] A.C. 384 at 387 *per* Lord Loreburn L.C.

[38] These torts are discussed in Chap. 12.

[39] See for example *Parkin* v. *South Hetton Coal Co.* (1907) 97 L.T. 98 at 101 *per* Darling J., affirmed on other grounds (1908) 98 L.T. 163.

[40] [1977] I.C.R. 61 at 76.

employees in opposition to demands by an employer in breach of contract by him would be repudiatory. But what may be called a 'real' strike in our judgment always will be."

The usual view[41] is therefore that where a strike occurs in breach of contract the employer has a choice[42] whether to accept the repudiatory conduct or not; if he does, he dismisses the men; and if he does not the contract continues in existence[43] and he has his remedy in damages if he wishes to use it. It seems likely that if he wishes to exercise his right to accept the strike as a repudiation and dismiss the men, the employer must do so while the strike continues, and it is too late to do so when the men are ready and willing to resume work.[44]

Damages

An employer may if he wishes pursue his remedy for damages against each individual who goes on strike in breach of his contract of employment, but for obvious reasons this is very rarely done, for it is unlikely to be in the interests of the employer to exacerbate relations with his work force once the strike is over.

However, if such a remedy is sought the difficulty is to establish the measure of damages. In *Ebbw Vale Steel, Iron and Coal Co.* v. *Tew*[45] some miners[46] were sued for a stoppage and the Court of Appeal rejected the view that the appropriate measure was the aliquot share of overhead expenses. Roche L.J. declared that the judge should ascertain the workman's probable output during the time of default, find its selling value, deduct the expenses which would have been incurred had the workman performed his contract, and which were not incurred when he failed to produce it, and award that amount to the employers. Overhead expenses incurred whether the workman worked or not should not be deducted.

Such a rule may be difficult to apply where the defendant is not a production worker and where he is acting in concert with others so that the degree of loss is increased. Both these problems arose in *National Coal Board* v. *Galley*[47] where the defendant was a colliery deputy who, together with others, refused to work certain shifts. The Court of Appeal decided that the damages should be determined as if he was acting alone and would be the net value of his work to the plaintiffs.

Pearce L.J. said that: "The measure of damages cannot be different because when he broke his contract in this respect he knew that his fellow deputies intended to commit similar breaches, except in so far as it would then be apparent that any damage likely to flow from the breach could not be avoided or lessened by their presence."

Thus the defendant cannot claim that the employers should have mitigated their loss by using someone else to cover his job if he knows no-one else will be avilable, but on the other hand the employers cannot claim the entire loss from just one of the strikers.

---

[41] But see *Davis Transport* v. *Chattaway* [1972] I.C.R. 267 at 271 *per* Brightman J.

[42] The controversial suggestion that by going on strike workers have "dismissed themselves" is discussed below in relation to unfair dismissal. This theory involves the idea that repudiation of itself ends the contract and need not be "accepted" by the injured party to be effective.

[43] *Cardy* v. *City of London* [1950] 2 All E.R. 475; *Hanley* v. *Pease* [1915] 1 K.B. 698.

[44] *Seed* v. *Crowther Ltd.* (1973) 8 I.T.R. 340 at 345–6.

[45] (1935) 79 Sol.Jo. 593; [1935] 1 L.J.N.C.C.A. 284 at 287.

[46] Who had stopped work following a fatal accident.

[47] [1958] 1 W.L.R. 16.

As to the fact that the defendant was not a production worker the measure of damages would still be the net value of the loss of production due to the absence of the defendant alone. In actual fact the defendant in the case would have been engaged in safety work and therefore the Coal Board's damages were limited to the cost of a substitute.[48]

Procedure for Giving Notice

Using the correct procedure to give strike notice is only important if it is desired to give notice in such a form as to make the strike lawful as between employer and employee, that is by giving notice to terminate the contract; but as we have seen it may not necessarily be in the employees interests to give notice in this form.

There is of course no problem if each individual employee gives notice of his intention to terminate the contract,[49] but legal difficulties could arise where the notice is given by the union. If we assume that notice is given only on behalf of members of the union the question arises whether the union can be regarded as agents of its members both to give effective notice to the employer and to bind the members.

In *Ideal Casements* v. *Shamsi*[50] it was made clear that such an agency must be authorised by the rules and that in the absence of such a rule the official must have the authorisation of each individual employee. This point has been developed by the doctrine in *Heatons Transport Ltd.* v. *T.G.W.U.*[51] whereby custom and practice established by sufficient evidence can provide authority in the same way as the rules. It is suggested that authority to negotiate with the employer does not by itself authorise officials to give notice of industrial action and that specific evidence of a custom permitting the giving of such notice must be put forward.[52] Once this has been done a member is bound by the acts of the union officials, although it has been suggested that he may specifically disavow their action.[53]

Industrial Action Short of a Strike

In many cases industrial action does not take the form of a complete withdrawal of labour, but involves some less serious act. If the employees decide that they will do the major part of their work but will refuse to do one particular thing,[54] there is clearly a breach of contract; but depending on the circumstances it may not be so serious a breach as to amount to repudiation of the contract[55] so as to justify summary dismissal and the only remedy available may be damages. If the employee is dismissed he would be protected by the unfair dismissal legislation[56] which prevents an employer discriminating between those who take part in the industrial action. Similar arguments apply in

[48] Estimated at £3 18s. 2d.: but if the Coal Board did not pay Galley for the shift he did not work then surely their net loss was nil for his pay could have been given to the substitute.

[49] This method is sometimes used: see the examples in O'Higgins, "Stike notices: another approach" (1973) 2 I.L.J. 152.

[50] [1972] I.C,R. 408.

[51] [1972] I.C.R. 308.

[52] *Chappell* v. *Times Newspapers* [1975] I.C.R. 145 at 176 *per* Stephenson L.J.

[53] *Ibid.* at 173 *per* Lord Denning.

[54] This would happen where the union has "blacked" a customer of the employer.

[55] But it may do so. In *Bowes* v. *Press* [1894] 1 Q.B. where miners refused to go down in the pit cage with a non unionist, the court seemed to think the act repudiatory although only damages were claimed.

[56] E.P.C.A. 1978, s. 62 which applies to a strike "or other industrial action."

the case of the "go slow"[57] and the kind of action where the employees decide to do their jobs carelessly, both of which amount to a breach of contract.

Work to rule

The work to rule is a tactic that is especially effective in highly organised industries and has been used with considerable effect on the railways. While it is generally considered that such a work to rule does amount to a breach of contract there is considerable concern that this conclusion should be arrived at for the right reason.[58]

The problem is caused by dicta in the Court of Appeal judgments in *Secretary of State for Employment* v. *ASLEF (No. 2)*[59] where the court held that a work to rule by railwaymen amounted to a breach of contract. At its narrowest the case decides that although the rule book was not itself part of the contract of employment,[60] there is a general contractual obligation to obey the rules,[61] and the men had broken the employer's rule that they "must make every effort to facilitate the working of trains and prevent any avoidable delay." However, because of the wider dicta in the judgments it cannot be said for certain that, in the absence of a general rule requiring the reasonable observance of the other rules, a work to rule is not a breach of contract.

The duty not to obstruct

Lord Denning suggested that the employees were in breach of an implied duty not to obstruct their employer wilfully.[62] He pointed out that a person is not bound to do more than his contract requires and thus he may withdraw his "good will,"[63] but: "if he, with the others, takes steps wilfully to disrupt the undertaking, to produce chaos so that it will not run as it should, then each one who is a party to these steps is guilty of a breach of his contract . . . what makes it wrong is the object with which it is done."

What has disturbed some commentators is that in general motive is not relevant in the law of contract and that the question whether a work to rule is a breach of contract should not turn on the reason why the men were "obeying" the rules.

The duty to serve the employer faithfully

The reason given by Buckley L.J. for the breach was that:[64]

> "These are . . . breaches of an implied term to serve the employer faithfully within the requirements of the contract. It does not mean that the employer could require a man to do anything which lay outside his obligations under the contract, such as to work excess hours of work or to

---

[57] "It is an implied undertaking of the worker that, in so far as he is capable of doing so, he should work at a reasonable speed. If he deliberately slows down his work, he breaks his contract." Kahn-Freund, *Labour and the Law* (2nd ed.), p. 265.

[58] See generally on this topic Kahn-Freund, *Labour and the Law* (2nd ed.), p. 265; Kahn-Freund, "The Industrial Relations Act 1971—some retrospective reflections" (1974) 3 I.L.J. 186; Napier, "Working to rule—a breach of the contract of employment?" (1972) 1 I.L.J. 125.

[59] [1972] I.C.R. 19.

[60] *Ibid.* at 54, *per* Lord Denning M.R. Kahn-Freund disagrees: *Labour and the Law* (2nd ed.), p. 266.

[61] *Ibid. per* Roskill L.J. at 71.

[62] *Ibid.* at 55.

[63] That is he may refuse to volunteer: if for example overtime is voluntary it cannot be a breach of contract not to volunteer.

[64] *Secretary of State for Employment* v. *ASLEF (No. 2)* [1972] I.C.R. 19 at 62.

> work an unsafe system of work or anything of that kind, but it does mean that within the terms of the contract the employee must serve the employer faithfully with a view to promoting those commercial interests for which he is employed."

It has been suggested[65] that this amounts to making an employee undertake "the duty of a partner without a partner's rights." Indeed it may be imposing too great a burden to interpret the duty serve faithfully as the duty to *promote* the employee's interests, if the same result could be obtained by positing the duty not to frustrate those interests.

Reasonable interpretation of the rules

Roskill L.J. preferred to decide the case on somewhat narrower grounds, saying that:[66] "I have no hesitation in implying a term into the contract of service that each employee will not, in obeying his lawful instruction, seek to obey them in a wholly unreasonable way which has the effect of disrupting the system. . . ."

As it happened British Rail had a rule specifically to incorporate such a duty, so that its formulation in general terms was strictly unnecessary. But it is suggested that in the absence of such a rule a work to rule will nevertheless be regarded as a breach of contract.

Finally it should be noted that action short of a strike cannot be made lawful by notice. A strike can only be lawful if notice is given to terminate the contract altogether. Notice to do anything less must be construed as notice to break the contract.[67]

The sit-in

Those engaging in a sit-in or a work-in will presumably be in breach of their contracts of employment for they will not be ready to work at the appropriate time under the direction of their employer. But the more important point is that such action will amount to the tort of trespass and may also be a crime.

A sit-in or work-in will be a trespass against the occupier of the premises. While this gives rise to an action for damages, the employer may be more interested in regaining possession under Order 113 of the Rules of the Supreme Court[68] which provides for summary proceedings for the recovery of possession, even in a case where the identity of the occupants is unknown. It is a criminal offence to resist or obstruct an officer of a court who is enforcing such an order.[69]

A number of criminal sanctions could be applied in certain circumstances to a sit-in; in particular it is an offence to use violence to secure entry if some person on the premises is opposing that entry,[70] and also to be on premises as a trespasser (having entered as such), while having any weapon of offence.[71]

---

[65] Kahn-Freund, *Labour and the Law* (2nd ed.), p. 267.

[66] *Secretary of State for Employment* v. *ASLEF (No. 2)* [1972] I.C.R. 19 at 72.

[67] *Seaboard Airlines* v. *T.G.W.U.* [1973] I.C.R. 458 at 461 *per* Sir John Donaldson.

[68] A similar provision is the County Court Rules, Order 26.

[69] Criminal Law Act 1977, s. 10. The maximum sentence is 6 months imprisonment or a fine of £1,000, or both.

[70] *Ibid.* s. 6.

[71] *Ibid.* s. 8. A thing is a weapon of offence if it is made or adapted for causing injury, or if, being an ordinary article, it is intended by the handler for such use: see *Ohlson* v. *Hylton* [1975] 2 All E.R. 490.

Refusal to work overtime

A ban on voluntary overtime is not a breach of contract, but it may sometimes be difficult to determine whether in fact the overtime is legally voluntary or compulsory. Such a matter cannot be determined by practice but will be decided by reference to the individual contract or to a collective agreement which is properly incorporated into that contract.[72]

THE LOCK-OUT

In general the same rules apply to lock-outs as apply to strikes. Thus a lock-out[73] will be a breach of contract by the employer if he does not give due notice to the employee to terminate the contract, and the damages could be substantial, for the proper measure would be the net loss of wages of those locked-out[74]; and it may be that employees would be more willing to sue for a lock-out than are employers for a strike.

In addition, whereas both employer and employee must give the period of notice stipulated in the contract if that is longer than the statutory minimum, that minimum period is longer where the notice is to be given by the employer.[75]

UNFAIR DISMISSAL

Whatever might be the theoretical effect at common law of a strike on the contract of employment, in practice the important issue is the extent to which legislation protects a striker from dismissal. While the common law power of summary dismissal for striking is preserved the policy of the legislation has been to see that this power can only be exercised in relation to the work force as a whole, and any discrimination between strikers could lead to a case of unfair dismissal being brought.

This objective is achieved by saying that where *all* the strikers are dismissed the tribunal shall not have jurisdiction to hear a case of unfair dismissal, but where some strikers are taken back and others not, the claim may be entertained and judged on ordinary principles. It should be noted that discrimination between strikers is not automatically unfair.

Section 62 of the Employment Protection (Consolidation) Act 1978 states that where the employee is at the time of the dismissal taking part in a strike or other industrial action:[76]

> "an industrial tribunal shall not determine whether the dismissal was fair or unfair unless it is shown:
> (a) that one or more relevant employees of the same employer have not been dismissed, or;
> (b) that one or more such employees have been offered re-engagement, and that the employee concerned has not been offered re-engagement."[77]

---

[72] See for example *Horrigan* v. *Lewisham Borough Council* [1978] I.C.R. 15.

[73] A lock-out is not defined for general purposes, but for a statutory definition for a limited purpose see E.P.C.A. 1978, Sched. 13 para. 24.

[74] *Cummings* v. *Connell* [1969] S.L.T. 25.

[75] The statutory minimum is one week on the employee's side. The periods for the employer are; for up to two years employment, one week; up to 12 years, one week's notice for each year; over 12 years, 12 weeks. E.P.C.A. 1978, s. 49.

[76] The same principles apply in the case of a lock-out.

[77] The provisions dealing with strikers have taken a number of different forms and in analysing a case it is important to note which version was in force at the time: Industrial Relations Act 1971, s. 26; T.U.L.R.A. 1974, Sched. 1, paras. 7 and 8; *ibid.* as amended by the Employment Protection Act 1975, Sched. 16 (as now consolidated in the above section).

These provisions give effect to the normal expectation of both sides of industry, for while the employer's power to dismiss strikers is preserved he is not permitted to discriminate by, for example, dismissing the ringleaders and retaining the remainder. While the section gives employees considerable protection it has also been said that it enables an employer "to dismiss the labour force on strike; to take on another labour force without the stigma of its being on unfair dismissal."[78] Furthermore, if the section did not exist the employer would have less bargaining power, for he would have to either submit to the demands of the strikers or go out of business or pay compensation for unfair dismissal.[79]

Jurisdiction: dismissing all strikers

A tribunal has no jurisdiction to hear a complaint where all those engaging in a strike or industrial action have been dismissed. It is unclear what amounts to a strike or industrial action as there is no statutory definition of either term for the purposes of unfair dismissal.[80] In particular it is unclear whether "other industrial action" must necessarily involve a breach of contract or whether lawful action, such as a refusal to work voluntary overtime, could also preclude jurisdiction. The definition of a similar phrase in the Industrial Relations Act 1971 did require the action to be unlawful, but the matter is now technically open. It is suggested, however, that on principle if the action is to preclude a claim for unfair dismissal it should involve a breach of contract. An example of such a case is *Thompson* v. *Eaton*[81] where the employees objected to the way in which the management wished to test some new machines and accordingly on the day in question stopped work and crowded round the machine to prevent it being tested. The court held that the men were at the very least engaged in "industrial action." Even if there is a breach of contract it may not be sufficient to justify summary dismissal at common law so that a remedy for wrongful dismissal may survive even if the remedy for unfair dismissal does not.

Thompson v. *Eaton*,[81] however, also highlights one of the difficulties in the present legislation. The tribunal pointed out that the employer's approach to the problem had been "obtuse" and this led to the argument on behalf of the men that they were not engaged in industrial action at all but were resisting unreasonable coercive action by management. But as the Employment Appeal Tribunal pointed out,[82] if this argument were to be accepted it would mean that the provisions excluding jurisdiction would not apply where the dispute was due to fault on the part of management. Such a view was not warranted by the statute, and furthermore it is a fundamental principle that the courts should not become involved in the merits of a dispute, for the consequences would be compulsory arbitration of disputes by the courts.

But if the view of the court is to be accepted, the question arises whether a person is to be deprived of his remedy if the employer has deliberately brought about the strike. This problem was acknowledged by the court and it was suggested that it could be avoided by saying that if an employer brings about a strike deliberately he has repudiated the contract, and if it can be argued that a

[78] *Heath* v. *Longman Ltd.* [1973] I.C.R. 407 *per* Sir Hugh Griffiths.

[79] *Thompson* v. *Eaton* [1976] I.C.R. 336 at 341.

[80] A strike is defined for the purpose of defining continuous employment: E.P.C.A. 1978, Sched. 13 para. 24 (1).

[81] [1976] I.C.R. 336.

[82] *Ibid.* at 342.

repudiation need not be accepted by the injured party but amounts to automatic dismissal,[83] then the strike occurs *after* the dismissal, and the provisions of section 62 excluding jurisdiction do not apply. However, it is not clear that motive should be relevant to the question whether an act is repudiatory or not, and it is suggested that this way out of the difficulty should be treated with extreme caution because of the consequences elsewhere of adopting the view that repudiation does not need acceptance.[84]

Timing of the dismissal

The employer is only protected if "at the date of dismissal" the employee is on strike, and it is clear that "at the date of" must be interpreted to mean "at the time of" so that if a strike is called off in the early part of a day the employer is not still free to dismiss the men later that day.[85] For the purposes of this provision the date of dismissal is taken to be the date when notice of termination was given, or if there was no notice "the effective date" of termination.[86]

Motive for dismissal

Although the previous legislation required the *reason* for the dismissal to be that the employee in question was on strike,[87] the present section only requires the dismissal to be while the strike is going on, and makes no mention of the reason for the dismissal. It is therefore suggested that the tribunal does not have jurisdiction to hear a case of unfair dismissal where, for example, the employer decides to select all those on strike for redundancy.[88]

Jurisdiction: discrimination between strikers

A tribunal will have jurisdiction to hear a complaint of unfair dismissal where there has been discrimination between the strikers.[89] This will cover the case either where some strikers have not been dismissed, or where all have been dismissed but some have been offered re-engagement,[90] and in considering that question the relevant group to be looked at is all those who took part in the strike or industrial action.[91]

Jurisdiction exists wherever a person who took part in the strike has been taken back *at any time*, even if that person went back before the dismissal of the others. Thus if an employer issues an ultimatum to those on strike that if they do not return to work by a certain date they will be dismissed, and if any one worker returns to work in response to that ultimatum then the remainder

[83] This highly controversial matter is discussed later in this chapter.

[84] The other way of avoiding the problem (that the reason for the dismissal was not the strike but the reasons which led the employer to engineer the strike) is no longer available as under the legislation as it now stands the reason for the dismissal is irrelevant so long as the employee is on strike at the time of dismissal.

[85] *Heath* v. *Longman Ltd.*[1973] I.C.R. 407 at 410.

[86] E.P.C.A. 1978, s. 62 (4). The "effective date" is defined by E.P.C.A. 1978, s. 55 (4) (*b*).

[87] See footnote 77: cases decided on this basis but no longer relevant on this issue are *Lomax* v. *Ladbrooke Ltd.* [1975] I.R.L.R. 363 and *Thompson* v. *Eaton* [1976] I.C.R. 336.

[88] The effect of a strike on redundancy payments is discussed below.

[89] So long as the applicant has been employed for 26 weeks: E.P.C.A. 1978, s. 64 (2); *Winnett* v. *Seamarks Brothers* [1978] I.R.L.R. 387.

[90] In this latter case when it comes to deciding whether the dismissal was fair or unfair, the decision is to be taken on the basis of whether the refusal to re-engage was fair or unfair. E.P.C.A. 1978, s. 62 (3) and 62 (4) (*c*).

[91] In the case of a lock-out (where the same rules apply) the relevant group is all those who are "directly interested" in the dispute in contemplation or furtherance of which the lock-out occurred. E.P.C.A. 1978, s. 62 (4) (*b*).

could make a claim for unfair dismissal. This point is illustrated by *Stock* v. *Frank James (Tipton) Ltd.*[92] where two strikers decided to return to work and the others were dismissed. The House of Lords held that the phrase "took part in the strike"[93] applied to those who took part at any time and could not be limited to those taking part at the date of the dismissal.[94] This provision places the employer in a difficult position for having made an offer to the strikers he cannot safely take back those who accept it and dismiss those who do not, but on the other hand it does mean that he cannot select those whom he wishes to take back, make them individual offers, and then dismiss the remainder.

On the other hand, it also appears that an employer may be liable for unfair dismissal if he re-engages one and fails to re-engage other strikers even some considerable time after the strike is over. This is so because although the claim must be presented to a tribunal within 3 months of the re-engagement there is no time limit on how soon after the strike that re-engagement should take place in order to qualify as discrimination.[95] The lesson, therefore, is never to re-engage a person who has been dismissed for going on strike.

Repudiation: dismissal or self-dismissal?

If the tribunal has jurisdiction to hear the case, the next question is whether there has been a dismissal. One of the fundamental difficulties for labour law which affects not only unfair dismissal but also redundancy and the common law is whether a person who goes on strike has been dismissed by his employer or whether in law he has dismissed himself. It has become increasingly common, especially in Fleet Street, for employers to issue their striking employees with notices to the effect that they have dismissed themselves, but whether this is so as a matter of legal theory depends on the common law of contract and the doctrine of repudiation.

The consequences of a decision in this area are serious, for if a person has "dismissed himself" he cannot sue either for wrongful dismissal at common law or for unfair dismissal under the statute: on the other hand, there may be some cases where an employee could benefit from the concept of self dismissal, especially in redundancy cases,[96] because in reverse it means that a repudiatory act by an employer can automatically amount to dismissal, without the employee having to take any action.[97]

Repudiation at common law

In technical terms the issue is whether it is necessary for a repudiatory act to be "accepted" by the injured party in order to bring the contract to an end or whether the repudiatory act itself does that. The generally accepted view[98] is that expressed by Lord Denning in *Harbutt's Plasticine Ltd.* v. *Wayne Tank and Pump Co.*[99] that a repudiated contract is only brought to an end by

---

[92] [1978] I.C.R. 347. The requirement in the case that the dismissal should be for an "inadmissible reason" no longer exists.

[93] See now E.P.C.A. 1978, s. 62 (4) (*b*).

[94] [1978] I.C.R. 347 at 351 *per* Viscount Dilhorne.

[95] See *Sealey* v. *Avon Aluminium* [1978] I.R.L.R. 285 (I.T.) where disciminatory re-engagement took place four months after the strike.

[96] For example *Marriott* v. *Oxford Co-operative Society (No. 2)* [1970] 1 Q.B. 186.

[97] Note also the suggestion in *Thompson* v. *Eaton* [1976] I.C.R. 336 at 342, that this theory could be adopted to provide a remedy for the victims of a strike engineered by the employer.

[98] Chitty, *Contracts* (24th ed.), para. 3630, but Chitty also accepts that employment may be an exception.

[99] [1970] 1 Q.B. 447 at 464.

acceptance of the repudiation by the injured party, except in cases where the repudiatory act has rendered performance impossible.[1]

In relation to employment contracts it has been suggested that where there has been a repudiation performance has been rendered legally impossible because the courts will not grant an order for specific performance of an employment contract,[2] but this argument ignores the fact that repudiated contracts can in effect be enforced by the re-instatement provisions of the unfair dismissal legislation and that in the vast majority of cases the contracts are performed when the strike is ended. Furthermore, if the "self dismissal" view is adopted and it is assumed that the employer has the power to waive the breach and "revive" the contract, at what point is the contract terminated? When the strike begins or when a reasonable time has elapsed and there has been no waiver?

Traditionally the view has been taken that a strike gives the employer a choice whether to discharge the strikers or not and it has been assumed that the acceptance of the repudiatory act of striking amounts to a dismissal. Thus in *Seed* v. *Crowther (Dyers) Ltd.*[3] the applicants went on strike but returned to work the next day when they were dismissed. The tribunal held that although the strike was a repudiatory act it had to be "accepted" while the strike was continuing and they could not dismiss the men after it had ended. If the "self dismissal" theory was applied to such a case the contract would have been terminated when the strike started (or when the employers decided not to waive the breach).[4]

In *Rookes* v. *Barnard*[5] Lord Devlin pointed out that the object of the strikers was to "break the contract by withholding labour but keeping the contract alive for as long as the employers would tolerate the breach without exercising their right of rescission." It is suggested that this view should continue to be accepted since statutes have consistently proceeded on the basis that termination of a contract for striking involves a dismissal, and it would be inappropriate for an exception to be made to the usual common law view of repudiation in order to give the law extra disciplinary force.

Although a number of cases have concerned repudiatory conduct by the employer[6] the principle has also been applied to such conduct by the employee.[7] The view that a striker has dismissed himself was regarded as "arguable" in *Chappell* v. *Times Newspapers*[8] and has frequently been referred to by employers since. But the doctrine has been rejected by Megarry V.-C. in

---

[1] For a contrary view see Thomson, "The effect of a repudiatory breach" (1978) 41 M.L.R. 137 where it is argued that there is substantial authority for the view that the contract terminates automatically unless the breach is waived by the injured party.

[2] Except in the unlikely event that *Hill* v. *Parsons* [1972] 1 Ch. 305 is applicable.

[3] (1973) 8 I.T.R. 340.

[4] See *Gannon* v. *Firth* [1976] I.R.L.R. 415.

[5] [1964] A.C. 1129 at 1204. See also *Trust Houses Forte Ltd.* v. *Murphy* [1977] I.R.L.R. 186. The self dismissal argument was also rejected on the facts in *Heath* v. *Longman Ltd.* [1973] I.C.R. 407 at 412. *Jeffrey* v. *Laurence Scott* [1977] I.R.L.R. 467 (E.A.T.).

[6] See for example *Marriott* v. *Oxford Co-operative Society (No. 2)* [1970] 1 Q.B. 186. *Sanders* v. *Earnest Neale* [1974] I.C.R. 565. *G.K.N. Cwmbran* v. *Lloyd* [1972] I.C.R. 214.

[7] *Hare* v. *Murphy Bros.* [1974] I.C.R. 603, where a sentence of 12 month's imprisonment terminated the contract; but such an event may be seen to make performance impossible. See also the judgment of Donaldson J. at [1973] I.C.R. 331. See also *Forgings & Presswork Ltd.* v. *McDougall* [1974] I.C.R. 532.

[8] [1975] I.C.R. 145 at 176 *per* Stephenson L.J.

Thomas Marshall v. *Guinle*[9] and it is suggested that the view that acceptance of repudiation is not necessary in an employment contract should be rejected[10] The reason is that adoption of the "self dismissal" view would render quite impotent the unfair dismissal legislation protecting strikers.

But even if the acceptance is necessary it has been suggested by the Employment Appeal Tribunal that acceptance of repudiation should not be regarded as a dismissal. In *Gannon* v. *Firth*[11] some employees went on strike leaving a high pressure steam system switched on. This was held to be a repudiatory act but Bristow J. said that although it was one which had to be accepted by the employer, nevertheless the men had dismissed themselves as acceptance of the repudiation did not amount to dismissal. It is suggested that this view should also be rejected since the act of termination (the acceptance of repudiation) is the act of the employer and therefore amounts to termination by him.[12]

Is the dismissal "unfair"?

Even if the tribunal has got jurisdiction to hear the case, and if the termination of the contract is held to be a dismissal, it must still be decided whether the dismissal was "unfair." In this situation the burden is on the employer to show that the dismissal (or the refusal to re-engage) was fair and he can do this by showing that he acted reasonably in treating the action of the applicant (in contrast to the action of those who were not dismissed or who were re-engaged) as a sufficient reason for dismissal.[13]

It is suggested that as part of the policy of section 62 is to deter employers from discriminating between those who go on strike,[14] tribunals should be wary of undermining that policy by holding such dismissals to be reasonable, and this is all the more so in cases where the applicant is a person the employer regards as a "trouble maker." The strike alone is unlikely to justify dismissal.

One interesting question is the extent to which it might be permissible to select those who had been on strike for redundancy. In *Cruickshank* v. *Hobbs*[15] the defendant dismissed for redundancy five out of six strikers after the strike had ended,[16] and the five claimed compensation for unfair dismissal on the grounds that they had been unreasonably selected for redundancy. Although it was indicated that if the strike had not taken place others would have been selected, the applications were dismissed.

The court believed that a strike could be relevant to selection for redundancy for three reasons; (a) If the strike has caused or aggravated the

---

[9] [1978] I.C.R. 905, see also *Sealey* v. *Avon Aluminium* [1978] I.R.L.R. 285 (I.T.) to the same effect, and where the chairman deplored attempts to delegate to employees the burden of dismissal. Such an attempt should be regarded as an ultimatum, and the dismissal that of the employer.

[10] See the important article by Elias, "Unravelling the concept of dismissal" (1978) 7 I.L.J. 16 and 100. *Wilkins* v. *Cantrell* [1978] I.R.L.R. 483 (E.A.T.).

[11] [1976] I.R.L.R. 415 (E.A.T.).

[12] For the definition of dismissal see E.P.C.A. 1978, s. 55.

[13] E.P.C.A. 1978, s. 57 (3) and 62 (3). See *Sealey* v. *Avon Aluminium* [1978] I.R.L.R. 285 (I.T.) where a failure to re-engage was held to be unfair even though the reason was that the applicants had never applied to be re-engaged and anyway there was no vacancy.

[14] The intention was "to prevent victimisation by an employer of persons who took part in a strike" *Stock* v. *Frank Jones (Tipton) Ltd.* [1978] I.C.R. 347 at 351 *per* Viscount Dilhorne.

[15] [1977] I.C.R. 725.

[16] The tribunal thus had jurisdiction both because the dismissals took place after the strike was over and because there had been discrimination between the strikers. The case arose out of the Newmarket stable lads' strike of 1975.

redundancy, (b) if the strike is long enough so that the re-introduction of the strikers gives rise to practical difficulties arising from administrative or technical changes during their absence, (c) where to sack men who stayed on at work and replace them with strikers would cause such friction between opposing groups that the morale and efficiency of the undertaking is significantly impaired.[17]

It is suggested that the fact that the dismissals were held to be fair in *Cruickshank* v. *Hobbs*[18] does not detract from the general principle that dismissal for striking should not itself be regarded as fair. The case concerned selection for redundancy, so allegedly somebody had to be dismissed and the choice was between those who had been on strike and those who had stayed at work. If *someone* has to be dismissed it may not be unreasonable to select the strikers over those who remained, but that is no argument for suggesting that it is reasonable to dismiss a person who has been on strike when there is no need to dismiss anyone at all.

Redundancy

The provisions dealing with the effect of strike action and other industrial misconduct on the right to receive a redundancy payment are complicated and have given rise to considerable difficulty.[19] Although a number of interpretations are possible[19] the purpose of the legislation is that where a person is made redundant[20] and at the same time is committing, or later commits an act of industrial misconduct which could justify summary dismissal, he loses his redundancy payment,[21] but a limited exception is made to this principle in the case of a person who goes on strike after receiving notice of redundancy.

If the dismissal is wholly due to the misconduct and contains no element of redundancy, then there can be no claim[22] but the following provisions apply where misconduct and redundancy are inter-related, and it has been held that[23] they apply in cases of both single and a double dismissal: that is first, selection for redundancy because of misconduct and secondly dismissal for redundancy (with notice) followed by dismissal for misconduct.

Section 82 (2) of the Employment Protection Consolidation Act 1978 states:

> Except as provided by section 92, an employee shall not be entitled to a redundancy payment by reason of dismissal where his employer, being entitled to terminate his contract of employment without notice by reason of the employee's conduct, terminates it either:
> (a) without notice, or
> (b) by giving shorter notice than that which, in the absence of such conduct, the employer would be required to give to terminate the contract, or
> (c) by giving notice (not being such shorter notice as is mentioned in

---

[17] [1977] I.C.R. 725 at 732.

[18] *Ibid.* The case was decided by a majority.

[19] See generally Grunfeld, *The Law of Redundancy* (1970) p. 121; Hepple and O'Higgins, *Employment law* (2nd ed.), p. 235; *Essen* v. *Vanden Plas* (1966) 1 I.T.R. 186 *per* Sir Diarmaid Conroy.

[20] The provisions cannot create an entitlement to a redundancy payment where none exists before: *Statham* v. *Hadlow's Garage* (1967) 2 I.T.R. 656.

[21] The difficult problem of misconduct that takes place before dismissal for redundancy but is discovered only afterwards is unlikely to arise in relation to strikes: but see *X* v. *Y Ltd.* (1969) 4 I.T.R. 204.

[22] *X* v. *Y Ltd.* (1969) 4 I.T.R. 204.

paragraph (b)) which includes, or is accompanied by, a statement in writing that the employer would, by reason of the employee's conduct, be entitled to terminate the contract without notice.

In relation to strike action three situations may arise:

1. Where the employee (X) goes on strike *after* receiving notice of redundancy.

2. Where X is already on strike at the time when he receives notice of redundancy.

3. Where X is selected for redundancy because he has previously been on strike.

1. Redundancy followed by a strike

If the strike is in breach of contract it is likely that it will be a breach that is sufficiently serious to entitle the employer to terminate the contract.[23] In such a case he may (subject to the effect of section 92) dismiss the striker by giving notice in one of the ways mentioned in section 82 (2) which presumably are designed to indicate to the employee that he is being dismissed for a special reason.[24] If notice is not given in one of the specified ways but the employee is allowed to work out his full redundancy notice without explanation, then the employee retains his right to a redundancy payment.[25]

The exemption for strikes

The effect of section 92 is to provide an exception to the exclusion provisions of section 82 (2). It provides that where a person on strike[26] prima facie loses his redundancy payment because of section 82(2), he may retain his entitlement to it if, and only if, the strike takes place during the *obligatory* period of the employer's notice.[27] The notice which the employer is obliged to give is that which is necessary to terminate the contract of employment, and where the actual notice given is longer than the minimum, the obligatory part of that notice is that which expires together with the actual notice.[28] In other words the obligatory period is the period at the *end* of the notice, so that, for example, where X is dismissed on January 1, with six months notice and the obligatory period is say one month, if X goes on strike immediately he loses his redundancy payment since he is only protected by section 92 during the *last* month of the actual notice, *i.e.* during June.

If the purpose of the section is to protect the employee who goes on strike in response to the notice of redundancy, then the provision fails in that aim and provides a trap for the unwary.

Making up time lost by the strike

It is provided by section 110 of the Employment Protection (Consolidation) Act 1978 that where a person has gone on strike after notice of redundancy, the employer may require that he still work the full number of days provided

---

[23] *Simmons* v. *Hoover* [1977] I.C.R. 61 at 80.

[24] *Essen* v. *Vanden Plas* 1966 I.T.R. 186; *Sanders* v. *Neale* [1974] I.C.R. 565 at 575; *Simmons* v. *Hoover* [1977] I.C.R. 61 at 79.

[25] *Sanders* v. *Neale* [1974] I.C.R. 565 at 575 *per* Sir John Donaldson.

[26] For the purposes of ss. 82 and 92 "strike" is defined by Sched. 13, para. 24 of the Act.

[27] The section also makes provision for the case where the employee has himself given notice to the employer that he intends to claim a redundancy payment because of lay offs within s. 88 E.P.C.A. 1978.

[28] E.P.C.A. 1978, s. 85 (5).

by the original notice. To this end the employer may serve a notice requesting the employee to agree to extend the notice period by the number of days the strike lasted. If the employee does not comply he loses his right to a redundancy payment unless he can show that he was unable to comply or that it was reasonable for him not to comply.

2. Redundancy during a strike

Where the employee is on strike at the time he receives notice of redundancy, whether he receives a redundancy payment again depends on the combined effect of sections 82 and 92.[29] Assuming that the strike amounts to a repudiation of the contract that entitles the employer to dismiss the striker it was held in *Simmons* v. *Hoover*[30] that the strike does fall within section 82[31] and is not saved by section 92, so that no redundancy payment is due. The court thought it clear that section 92 was only intended to apply to cases where the strike followed the redundancy notice.

3. Redundancy following a strike

In some cases a person is selected for redundancy because of his previous misconduct. In such a case the cause of his dismissal is nevertheless redundancy whatever the motive for his selection, and the employee should be entitled to a redundancy payment. Section 82 is not relevant because the employer is not entitled to dismiss the employee after the strike has ended.

A person dismissed in such circumstances may also be able to sue for unfair dismissal on the basis that he has been unfairly selected for redundancy. However, in *Cruickshank* v. *Hobbs*[32] the Employment Appeal Tribunal held that in some cases it may be justifiable to select for redundancy those who have been on strike over those who stayed at work.

Summary

(1) A strike after redundancy notice: the payment will be lost unless the strike takes place during the "obligatory" period of notice given by the employer.

(2) Redundancy during the strike: the payment is lost.

(3) Redundancy following a strike: the payment is retained.

Examples[33]

X is the redundant employee of Y and is entitled to three months notice.

	Section 82	Section 92	Redundancy payment
1. X is dismissed on January 1, with 3 months notice. X goes on strike immediately afterwards. Y[34] terminates the contract forthwith on February 1, by reason of strike.	Yes	Yes	Yes

[29] The question whether in such circumstances he can sue for unfair dismissal is discussed above.

[30] [1977] I.C.R. 61.

[31] The strike falls within the term "employee's conduct" in s. 82: [1977] I.C.R. 61 at 79.

[32] [1977] I.C.R. 725.

[33] The first two examples are taken from the approved appendix to *Simmons* v. *Hoover* [1977] I.C.R. 61 at 82.

[34] The report uses X here, but presumably Y is intended. [1977] I.C.R. 61 at 82.

	Section 82	Section 92	Redundancy payment
2. X is dismissed on January 1, with six months notice. X goes on strike immediately afterwards. Y terminates the contract forthwith on Febraury 1.	Yes	No	No
3. X goes on strike on January 1,[35] and is dismissed on February 1, while the strike is still continuing.	Yes	No	No
4. X goes on strike on January 1,[36] and returns on January 10. He is dismissed on February 1.	No	No	Yes

Continuity of Employment

There is a wide variety of reasons why it might be necessary to establish continuous employment: in some instances statutory rights such as redundancy, unfair dismissal or maternity pay may depend on it, and in others there may be contractual rights such as the right to a pension or to a bonus which depend on whether continuous employment can be established even though a strike has intervened.

Common law

Where contractual rights to some benefit such as a pension or a bonus are in question two issues arise: first do the rights depend on continuous service or continuity of the contract of employment? Secondly, if upon the latter what is the effect of a strike?

It is suggested that only in the very clearest of cases should the right be deemed to depend on continuity of actual work. In one case[37] the plaintiff was entitled to a benefit if he had "served continuously under the Corporation" and Sellers J. dismissed the suggestion that this meant continuity of service and held that it referred to continuity of the contract.[38]

Once it had been established that what is in issue is continuity of the contract it can be said that a strike of which notice has been given in the form of notice to terminate the contract will break continuity, as will a strike where an ambiguous notice is interpreted in that way. Where the strike is a breach of the contract and is a repudiation of it, it will only affect continuity if the repudiation is accepted.[39] Thus in *Cardy* v. *City of London*[40] the plaintiff had gone on strike but the defendants had not accepted this repudiation and therefore the contract continued in existence.[41]

---

[35] This example and the next are not taken from the appendix to *Simmons* v. *Hoover*. This one is intended to illustrate the case itself.

[36] This example depends on the view that an employer is not entitled to dismiss an employee after the strike has ended.

[37] *Cardy* v. *City of London* [1950] 2 All E.R. 475.

[38] The section of the City of London (Various Powers) Act 1944 did not require continuous work, and the judges thought it difficult to distinguish between an interruption of work due to a strike or a holiday or some other blameless cause.

[39] This would not be so if the dubious theory of "self-dismissal" were accepted.

[40] [1950] 2 All E.R. 475.

[41] See also *Hanley* v. *Pease* [1915] 1 K.B. 698.

By Statute

In statutes where continuity of employment is in issue the question will be determined in accordance with the provisions of schedule 13 to the Employment Protection (Consolidation) Act 1978, para. 15 of which provides[42] that continuity of employment shall not be broken by a strike,[43] but nor shall a week in which a strike occurred be counted in cases where a certain number of continuous weeks are required.

This provision clearly covers cases where the strike is in breach of contract, so that continuity is preserved,[44] but there may be a difficulty in cases where the strike notice takes the form of notice to terminate the contract. Logically there should be no difference between such a case and a simple resignation, so that continuity would be lost but it seems unfortunate to discriminate against the person who opts to go on strike lawfully.

If a person is actually dismissed while on strike, continuity is nevertheless preserved if he is re-engaged at the end of the strike.[44] In *Bloomfield* v. *Springfield Hosiery Finishing Co.*[45] the plaintiff went on strike and was dismissed, but was later re-engaged when the strike was over. The court held that even after dismissal the applicants were to be regarded as "persons employed"[46] because in the context of a strike the definition could include those who but for the strike would be employed. Sir John Donaldson continued:

> "The fact that the employer terminates their contracts of employment does not take them outside this category, unless and until he engages other persons on a permanent basis to do the work which the strikers had been doing or he permanently discontinues the activity in which they were employed. Similarly the fact that the striker takes other temporary employment pending the settlement of the dispute does not prevent him claiming that he is taking part in a strike."

As the issue only arises if the striker is re-engaged, this particular problem of determining when there is no continuity will only occur where a person is re-engaged in a different position and his old job has been taken by someone else, and also where the striker has taken on a job during the strike and has then returned to his old employer.

A similar issue arises when the striker is taken on not immediately the strike ends but after a few weeks. In *Clarke Chapman* v. *Walters*[47] this problem was solved by saying that the continuity was preserved while the strike was on, and for the period after the strike but before the re-engagement another paragraph[48] applies which covers cases of temporary cessation of work. It is thus possible to deal with cases of a gradual return to work.

---

[42] The paragraph makes similar provision in the case of a lock-out. For an example see *Bunt* v. *Fishlow Products* (1970) 5 I.T.R. 127.

[43] "Strike" is defined by para. 24 (1) of Sched. 13 to E.P.C.A. 1978.

[44] *McGorry* v. *Earls Court Stand Ltd.* [1973] I.C.R. 100.

[45] [1972] I.C.R. 91.

[46] As used in the definition of a strike. E.P.C.A. 1978 Sched. 13, para. 24.

[47] [1972] I.C.R. 83.

[48] E.P.C.A. 1978 Sched. 13, para. 9 (*b*).

Part Three

THE EXTERNAL ACTIVITIES OF A UNION

CHAPTER 11

THE FREEDOM TO STRIKE AND THE MEANING OF TRADE DISPUTE

IT is a common fallacy that Britain suffers from strikes more than any other industrialised country[1] but perhaps because lawyers, like politicians, tend to concentrate on points of crisis, the way in which the law attempts to control strikes has always been a matter of controversy. It is sometimes forgotten that collective labour law is not principally about industrial action but rather about promoting collective bargaining, although this includes as one element the protection of the freedom to strike. "Freedom to strike" is an emotive phrase but few would doubt that such a freedom must exist if tyranny is to be avoided, for as Professor Kahn-Freund has said,[2] "What legislatures and courts can do to change the habits of people in industrial relations must in democratic societies always and everywhere be limited. To curb strikes by law may be possible in narrow limits. Those who exceed these limits place themselves outside the democratic tradition."

This statement raises the two fundamental questions that must be asked in relation to the law: first to what extent is it desirable to limit the freedom to strike, and the second how effective can the law be? The purpose of the second question is not to suggest that the rule of law be abandoned but only to note that coercive sanctions imposed by law may not be the best method of limiting the damage done by strike action, but rather that measures taken to promote collective bargaining may well be much more effective. Indeed in this country at least the rules of law about to be discussed have never been seen as a "cure" for the incidence of strikes but rather have been designed to lay down the limits of action that may be indulged in when a strike occurs. It is fundamental to the law that with a few exceptions the *reasons* for calling a strike are not in issue: the only matter that is relevant is whether the action pursued consists of the kind of act that is permitted.

As to the justification for the freedom to strike Professor Kahn-Freund has given as the principal reason[3] the "theory of countervailing power which was needed to overcome the mechanical individualism permeating the legal systems . . . of the United Kingdom . . .", citing in his support the view of Holmes J. that:

---

[1] For the 10 years 1967–1976 Britain was eighth in the international league of working days lost through strikes. Canada, the United States and Australia all had a worse record (1977) 85 Department of Employment Gazette, 1343.

[2] Kahn-Freund and Hepple, *Laws against strikes* Fabian research series No. 305 at p. 6. This pamphlet is one of the most perceptive works on the law relating to industrial action.

[3] *Ibid.* at p. 6. Other reasons include the principle of autonomous sanctions whereby failure of collective bargaining provides its own sanctions through strike action rather than through reliance upon state tribunals to determine the merits of the case. This point is again fundamental to understanding the principles of our law.

> "Combination on the one side is patent and powerful. Combination on the other is the necessary and desirable counterpart, if the battle is to be carried on in a fair and equal way. . . . If it be true that working men may combine with a view, among other things, to getting as much as they can for their labour, just as capital may combine with a view to getting the greatest possible return, it must be true that when combined they have the same liberty that combined capital has to support their interests by argument, persuasion, and the bestowal or refusal of these advantages which they otherwise lawfully control."[4]

In this country industrial action may expose a union member to a number of torts, particularly inducing breach of contract, intimidation and conspiracy, but this risk is considerably reduced in cases where the action is, in the words of the "Golden Formula", "in contemplation or furtherance of a trade dispute." Indeed it may generally be said that in such cases it is highly unlikely that union members would be liable,[5] so it becomes clear that the extent of the freedom to strike is determined by the definition of "trade dispute". Thus the considerable argument that has gone on since the Trade Disputes Act 1906[6] about the meaning of that phrase is essentially an argument about the freedom to strike.

THE MEANING OF "TRADE DISPUTE"

The concept of "trade dispute" is absolutely crucial in trade union law, for although it is used for a number of purposes,[7] its main function is to define the freedom to strike, and if we may assume that such a freedom is a necessary concomitant of the freedom to organise and the freedom to bargain, it is clear that such a freedom must be circumscribed. The principal legal limitations on strike action are contained in the torts discussed in the next chapter, but those engaged in industrial action will be to a certain extent be protected from such liability where they act "in contemplation or furtherance of a trade dispute."[8] This "Golden Formula" was first introduced by the Conspiracy and Protection of Property Act 1875, but it was not defined until the Trade Disputes Act 1906, and since then it has been narrowed not only by the Trade Disputes Act 1927 but also by the Industrial Relations Act 1971. However, a more liberal definition has now been provided by the Trade Union and Labour Relations Act 1974 (as amended by the Trade Union and Labour Relations Act (Amendment) Act 1976). As will be seen this active parliamentary history is mirrored by its career in the courts where in general the judges have taken a narrow view of its meaning. But the width of the present statutory definition may be seen as indicating that Parliament believes that strike action may be legitimate in a wide range of cases and perhaps also that even where such action is not legitimate the law should not be involved, but rather that other

---

[4] *Vegelahn* v. *Guntner* 44 N.E. 1077 (1896) at 1081.

[5] The immunity is not a general one, but is granted in specific terms by T.U.L.R.A. 1974 s. 13. The particular provisions of that section will be dealt with under the headings of the various torts. The union itself is protected by T.U.L.R.A. 1974 s. 14.

[6] Strictly speaking the phrase has been with us since the Conspiracy and Protection of Property Act 1875, but it only came into real prominence in 1906.

[7] See for example the Employment Protection Act 1975 ss. 2 and 3 (jurisdiction for conciliation and arbitration); Criminal Law Act 1977, s. 1 (3) (Conspiracy). It should be noted that for the purposes of the Supplementary Benefits Act 1976 s. 8 and the Social Security Act 1975, s. 19 (restriction of benefit for those involved in a stoppage of work due to a trade dispute) the definition is different and is contained in s. 19 (2) of the latter Act.

[8] T.U.L.R.A. 1974 s. 13.

agencies, such as the Advisory Conciliation and Arbitration Service, should be used to resolve the dispute.

As the following discussion will rely heavily on the text of the definition it will be useful to set out here the definition as it now stands.[9]

29 (1) In this Act "trade dispute" means a dispute between employers and workers, or between workers and workers, which is connected with one or more of the following, that is to say:

(a) terms and conditions of employment, or the physical conditions in which any workers are required to work;

(b) engagement or non-engagement, or termination or suspension of employment or the duties of employment, of one or more workers;

(c) allocation of work or the duties of employment as between workers or groups of workers;

(d) matters of discipline;

(e) the membership or non-membership of a trade union on the part of a worker;

(f) facilities for officials of trade unions; and

(g) machinery for negotiation or consultation, and other procedures, relating to any of the foregoing matters, including the recognition by employers or employers' associations of the right of a trade union to represent workers in any such negotiation or consultation or in the carrying out of such procedures.

(2) A dispute between a Minister of the Crown and any workers shall, notwithstanding that he is not the employer of those workers, be treated for the purposes of this Act as a dispute between employer and those workers if the dispute relates:

(a) to matters which have been referred for consideration by a joint body on which, by virtue of any provision made by or under any enactment, that Minister is represented; or

(b) to matters which cannot be settled without that Minister exercising a power conferred on him by or under an enactment.

(3) There is a trade dispute for the purposes of this Act even though it relates to matters occurring outside Great Britain.

(4) A dispute to which a trade union or employers' association is a party shall be treated for the purposes of this Act as a dispute to which workers or, as the case may be, employers are parties.

(5) An act, threat or demand done or made by one person or organisation against another which, if resisted, would have led to a trade dispute with that other, shall, notwithstanding that because that other submits to the act or threat or accedes to the demand no dispute arises, be treated for the purposes of the Act as being done or made in contemplation of a trade dispute with that other.

(6) In this section:

"employment" includes any relationship whereby one person personally does work or performs services for another;

"worker", in relation to a dispute to which an employer is a party, includes any worker even if not employed by that employer.

The definition consists of four distinct elements. The industrial action must (a) be between the correct parties and (b) consist of a dispute which is (c)

[9] T.U.L.R.A. 1974 s. 29 as amended by the Trade Union and Labour Relations (Amendment) Act 1976 s. 1 and by the Criminal Law Act 1977, Sched. 13.

about "trade" matters and (d) the action must be in contemplation or furtherance of that dispute.

The parties

The statute requires that the dispute should be between employers and workers or between workers and workers. Undoubtedly the majority of disputes will be between an employer on the one side and workers on the other,[10] but a few points need to be made about the application of these terms to this area of the law.

First it is clear from section 30 of the 1974 Act that "workers" includes not only those actually employed but also those who seek to work, so that a dispute by workers who have been dismissed but wish to be re-instated will be included. Secondly section 29 (6) states that "worker" includes any worker even if he is not employed by the employer with whom the dispute is being carried on. This point can be illustrated by *Midland Cold Storage* v. *Turner*[11] where the plaintiffs carried on business outside the docks and the London Dock Labour Board had decided that this was not work reserved by law for registered dockers. There was no dispute between the plaintiffs and their own workers (who were represented by USDAW), but the dockers led by a "Joint Shop Stewards Committee" decided to "black" all consignments to the plaintiffs in order to persuade them to employ only registered dockers. Although the dockers were not employed by the plaintiffs there was nevertheless held to be an "industrial" dispute between them.[12]

Thirdly, by virtue of section 29 (4) a dispute initiated by a union is to be treated as one to which workers are deemed to be parties.[13] The point was originally made by Lord Wright in *NALGO* v. *Bolton Corporation*[14] where he said that, "it would be strangely out of date to hold, as was argued, that a trade union cannot act on behalf of its members in a trade dispute, or that a difference between a trade union acting for its members and their employer cannot be a trade dispute."[15] But it is suggested that the effect of the present law is wider than that envisaged by Lord Wright. In *Camellia Tanker* v. *I.T.F.*[16] the defendants procured the blacking of the plaintiff's tanker because they refused to sign an agreement with the Federation. It was argued that there was no trade dispute, first because there had been no dispute until the union arrived on the scene and secondly because at the time the union raised a dispute it had no members amongst the crew. On the first point Templeman J. at first instance[17] said that, "it would be ludicrous if trade unions could not raise a dispute with an employer until a dispute had actually arisen. Trade unions may wish to raise a dispute with an employer not only to protect labour aboard a vessel but also to protect unionists who form the crews of other

---

[10] The two terms are defined by s. 30 of the Act.

[11] [1972] I.C.R. 230. See also *Midland Cold Storage* v. *Steer* [1972] 2 Ch. 630; *General Aviation Services* v. *T.G.W.U.* [1976] I.R.L.R. 224 (H.L.).

[12] The case was decided under the Industrial Relations Act 1971. Dicta in *Torquay Hotels* v. *Cousins* [1969] Ch. 106 that such action would not be a trade dispute are it is suggested laid to rest by s. 29 (6).

[13] The same point applies to employers' associations and employers.

[14] [1943] A.C. 166 at 189.

[15] See also *Beetham* v. *Trinidad Cement* [1960] A.C. 132; *Bird* v. *O'Neal* [1960] A.C. 907.

[16] [1976] I.C.R. 274.

[17] The decision not to grant the injunction was affirmed on appeal on other grounds. The points raised here were not discussed on appeal.

ships." On the second point the judge held that since section 29 (1) (a) covered disputes about the terms and conditions of *any* workers, the union was not limited to raising disputes on behalf of its own members but could have regard to any workers, so that a demand that the crew, even though not yet members, should be paid I.T.F. rates was nevertheless a trade dispute.

As regards the meaning of "employer" a number of issues have been raised which are peculiar to this area of the law. One of the strangest was the point made in the Irish case of *Roundabout Ltd.* v. *Beirne*[18] where the owners of a pub, having closed it (as the defendants thought) to bring pressure on the employees to leave the union, leased it to a company whose directors were the previous owners, an accountant and three barmen; they were paid not a salary but directors fees. In an action by the plaintiffs to restrain picketing the court held that the defendants could not avail themselves of the trade dispute defence since the plaintiffs were not "employers". The Company did not employ anybody but consisted only of working directors.[19] It is suggested that this ingenious method of avoiding the trade dispute legislation should not be permitted to succeed in this country. First the definition of "employer" in section 30 of the 1974 Act should extend to such a case, in so much as it refers to an employer as a person for whom workers seek to work: therefore by picketing the premises in order to be re-instated the defendant had turned the plaintiffs into employers. Secondly it is suggested that the recent Court of Appeal decision in *Examite* v. *Whittaker*[20] shows a willingness to look at the reality of the situation. In that case the A.U.E.W. had called a strike at a company called Baldwins Industrial Services. Later a company called Examite Ltd. was formed to trade under the name Cleveland Crane Hire. Only two shares were issued, one to the company's solicitor and one to the solicitor's secretary, and this company had soon taken over the entire business of Baldwins. Examite Ltd. tried to claim that the dispute was not with them but with Baldwins and that therefore they were not the employer with whom the defendants were in dispute. Lord Denning, however, said[21] that, "in these trade disputes I think we ought to pull aside any curtain over limited companies and see what the real truth is", and he went on to say that the plaintiffs were really the same "employers" as Baldwins.[22] It is suggested that such an approach is wholly to be commended, at least in cases where the change of ownership is done with the object of avoiding the trade dispute legislation.[23]

Section 29 (2) deals with a problem that is becoming increasingly common in an era of pay restraint, where an employer cannot himself resolve the dispute. It is therefore provided that a dispute between a Minister of the Crown and workers shall be a trade dispute where the dispute refers to matters which cannot be settled without the Minister exercising a power conferred on him by statute or which has been referred to a joint body on which the Minister is represented. This does not apply to general protests about pay

[18] [1959] I.R. 423.

[19] The court distinguished *Ferguson* v. *O'Gorman* [1937] I.R. 620 where a similar argument failed, on the ground that in that case the company had taken over a going concern, whereas here the pub was not active when it was leased to the plaintiff.

[20] [1977] I.R.L.R. 312 (C.A.).

[21] [1977] I.R.L.R. 312 at 313.

[22] Roskill and Shaw L.JJ. preferred to decide the case on another ground.

[23] The information available in *Examite* was so scanty that it was not clear that this was the object in that case.

policy[24] nor does it apply in the case of a non statutory pay freeze. In such a case the dispute will still be with the employer and will therefore be a trade dispute on that ground.

The 1974 Act also covers disputes between workers and workers: this matter has always been one of considerable controversy and although the Trade Disputes Act 1906 was in similar terms, the Industrial Relations Act 1971 attempted to exclude such disputes from the definition. This gave rise to a number of difficulties[25] because it was never clear when a dispute that originated between workers and workers escalated into one involving the employer so as to become an industrial dispute. The present legislation, however, clearly covers disputes arising for example out of the refusal of union members to work alongside non-unionists.

The Act does not, however, cover disputes between employers and employers. This point only causes difficulty in cases where workers and employers collaborate in action against another employer and the question is whether such action is essentially between the employers with the assistance on the one side of the union, or whether the dispute is really between the union and an employer. In *Larkin* v. *Long*[26] the plaintiff, a stevedore in the port of Dublin, had refused to join an employers' organisation designed to protect the stevedores against the shipowners. The defendants, who were officials of the Irish T.G.W.U. had conspired with members of the Stevedore's Association to call a strike of their members who worked for the plaintiff, in order to induce the plaintiff to join the association. It was undoubtedly in the interests of the union to have the plaintiff as a member of the association since such an employer would be likely to provide greater security and better conditions of employment, but nevertheless the House of Lords held that this was essentially a dispute between employers and thus not a trade dispute. While the principle may be sound it is suggested that its application to the facts in this case may be open to doubt, for as is indicated by *Barret* v. *Evans*[27] (a case on very similar facts but decided the other way) the distinction can be a very fine one.

Dispute

To a large extent this subject overlaps with the meaning of "in contemplation or furtherance" of a dispute, but two points can be made. The first is to explain the need for section 29 (5) of the Act which deals with the question whether a person who does not resist a threat can be said to be involved in a dispute. In *Cory Lighterage* v. *T.G.W.U.*[28] a Mr. Shute had let his union membership lapse and the workers demanded that he be dismissed. While the employers conceded the demand for 100 per cent. membership they were not given the necessary permission to dismiss Shute by the Dock Labour Board. In the Court of Appeal Buckley L.J. said[29] that there is no dispute where the employer immediately gives in to the threat. "If someone threatens me with physical injury unless I hand over my wallet and I hand it over without demur, no one could, in my opinion, sensibly say that there had been any dispute

[24] But see *Sherard* v. *A.U.E.W.* [1973] I.C.R. 421.

[25] See for example *Cory Literage* v. *T.G.W.U.* [1973] I.C.R. 339; *Coleman* v. *Magnet Joinery* [1975] I.C.R. 46. Also Kahn-Freund, "The legal framework" in Flanders and Clegg, *The system of Industrial Relations in Great Britain.*

[26] [1915] A.C. 814.

[27] (1924) 18 Ll.L.R. 310.

[28] [1973] I.C.R. 339.

[29] [1973] I.C.R. 339 at 362.

about my handing over my wallet." Whatever one's opinion of this view, section 29 (5) now makes it clear that a dispute would exist in such circumstances.

Secondly by virtue of section 29 (3) a trade dispute exists even though it relates to matters occurring outside Great Britain.[30] There has been considerable concern recently about the activities of multi-national companies and many unions have realised that co-operation with unions abroad may be necessary to negotiate effectively with such companies.[31] There must of course be a dispute with the right parties and with the right subject matter in order for an overseas dispute to qualify as a "trade dispute", and indeed such disputes may often be categorised as political disputes, for example those that consist of a boycott of the goods or services of a foreign country.[32]

Thirdly it may be necessary that there should be some "difference" between the parties, so that if they are in fact in agreement over some matter but are being required to act as they do by some other party it has been suggested that there is no "dispute" between them. The reluctant application of government incomes policy may be an example of this phenomenon.[33] On the other hand it could be argued that even if both employer and union wish to implement, for example, a pay rise that is being blocked by the government by non statutory means, there is a dispute if the union intends to take industrial action. The dispute is about pay and exists because of the threat of coercive sanctions.

The subject matter

A trade dispute must be "connected with" one of the seven items listed in section 29, such as terms and conditions of employment. The degree of proximity indicated by the words "connected with" has been a matter of considerable controversy.[34] In *Valentine* v. *Hyde*[35] Astbury J. said[36] that the dispute must be "connected directly with employment or non-employment, and not a dispute about some entirely different subject matter, the non-settlement of which may result in employment or non-employment."

This view was distinguished in *Hodges* v. *Webb*[37] and disapproved in *White* v. *Riley*[38] where it was held on similar facts to *Valentine* v. *Hyde* that a dispute between union men and non-union men was a dispute "connected with" the employment of the non-union men.[39] Warrington L.J. said that,[40] "the dispute is whether while he is not a member of the union to which the other men belong he should be employed by the employers. It is really a dispute as to the terms upon which he should continue in the employment." This rejection of the reasoning of Astbury J. in *Valentine* v. *Hyde* did not, however, effectively solve one of the difficulties. Suppose for example that workers demanded the dismissal of a colleague because he was a Roman Catholic or because he was a member of the Liberal Party or had red hair? Could it still be said that the issue

[30] Although the meaning of trade dispute was not raised, the facts of *Hanseatic Ltd.* v. *I.T.F.* [1974] I.C.R. 112 provide an illustration.
[31] Wedderburn, "Multi-national enterprise and national labour law" (1972) 1 I.L.J. 12.
[32] *Gouriet* v. *Union of Post Office Workers* [1978] A.C. 435.
[33] *Holiday Hall* v. *Chapple, The Times,* February 4, 1978.
[34] The Industrial Relations Act 1971 s. 167 (1) used the phrase "relates wholly or mainly to".
[35] [1919] 2 Ch. 129.
[36] *Ibid.* at 151.
[37] [1920] 2 Ch. 70.
[38] [1921] 1 Ch. 1.
[39] Such a dispute would now be covered by 29 (1) (*e*) of T.U.L.R.A. 1974.
[40] [1921] 1 Ch. 1 at 27.

was "connected with" his engagement or non-engagement? Lord Denning has considered this point in *B.B.C.* v. *Hearn*[41] where the B.B.C. sought an injunction to prevent the defendants from threatening to induce breaches of contracts of employment designed to stop the broadcast of the Cup Final to South Africa via a satellite in the Indian Ocean. The defendants claimed that the proposed action was "connected with" their terms and conditions of employment. Lord Denning rejected this argument citing the dictum of Lord Shaw in *Conway* v. *Wade*[42] that the phrase does not cover "the case of coercive interference in which the intervener may have in his own mind that if he does not get his own way he will thereupon take ways and means to bring a trade dispute into existence." Lord Denning therefore argued that if, for example, printers demanded that an article in a newspaper be withdrawn or else they would go on strike, this does not become a trade dispute simply because the men threaten to break their contracts of employment. He argued that in such a case the dispute would be about publication of the article and not connected with the terms and conditions of employment. So too in this case the dispute was, he alleged, about broadcasting to South Africa. He went on to point out that the only way such a dispute could be considered to be connected with conditions of employment would be if the men had asked for a new clause in their contracts whereby they would not be required to broadcast to South Africa.

The controversy is clearly of considerable significance, for the interpretation put forward by the defendants would permit almost any action to be a trade dispute if the act threatened in case of non compliance with the demand (whatever that demand is about) would be "connected with" the contract of employment. But against the plaintiff's and Lord Denning's interpretation it could be argued that the question is not what the dispute is *about*, but what it is connected with, and that, as a matter of liberal interpretation, may assume a much looser connection.

As to the substance of the dispute the first matter covered by the statute is "terms and conditions of employment".[43] Lord Denning has expressed the view that this phrase "may include not only the contractual terms and conditions but those terms which are understood and applied by the parties in practice, or habitually, or by common consent, without ever being incorporated into the contract."[44]

The other phrase in paragraph (a) of section 29 (1) covers "physical conditions in which any workers are required to work". One problem is whether or not this would be sufficient to cover "psychological" conditions such as occurred in *Scala Ballroom* v. *Ratcliffe*[45] where musicians refused to work at a ballroom which operated a colour bar. Similar problems might arise

[41] [1977] I.C.R. 685; Wedderburn, Note (1978) 41 M.L.R. 80.

[42] [1909] A.C. 506 at 522.

[43] For an interesting distinction see *Esplanade Pharmacy* v. *Larkin* [1957] I.R. 285 where the plaintiffs, owners of a chemist shop at Bray, wished to stay open all day Sunday, although this would not increase the hours worked by their shop assistant. It was held that this related to the conditions of employment of the employers not the employees, or rather to the opening hours not the working hours. The fact that other shop assistants in the area might have their hours extended by their employers' attempt to compete was not considered sufficiently imminent.

[44] *B.B.C.* v. *Hearn* [1977] I.C.R. 685. See also *Brendan Dunne* v. *Fitzpatrick* [1958] I.R. 29. Lord Denning had in fact expressed a contrary view in the earlier case of *Cory Lighterage* v. *T.G.W.U.* [1973] I.C.R. 339.

[45] [1958] 1 W.L.R. 1957.

if workers objected to the bad language of a foreman, unless that could be regarded as a matter of discipline under paragraph (d).

Another phrase which has given rise to difficulty is the inclusion of "termination or suspension of employment or the duties of employment". In *Cory Lighterage* v. *T.G.W.U.*[46] Lord Denning had thought that the phrase "suspension of employment" in the Industrial Relations Act 1971 was applicable only to cases where a person was suspended from both work and pay, and therefore would not cover the case of Mr. Shute who was sent home on full pay. There can be no doubt that the phrase "or the duties of employment" was added to avoid this result. Whether it succeeds in doing so remains to be seen.[47]

Even though a dispute might appear to be connected with the correct subject matter, there is nevertheless a requirement that it be pursued with a proper motive. The general point was put by Lord Loreburn in *Conway* v. *Wade*[48] when he said that,

> "if, however, some meddler sought to use the trade dispute as a cloak beneath which to interfere with impunity in other people's work or business, a jury would be entirely justified in saying that what he did was done in contemplation or furtherance, not of the trade dispute, but of his own designs, sectarian, political, or purely mischievous as the case might be."[49]

This statement has its effect in two particular areas. The first concerns the distinction between a trade dispute and a political dispute, the second the problem of the dispute motivated by malice. An example of a political dispute is to be found in *Associated Newspapers* v. *Flynn*[50] where an injunction was granted to prohibit the calling of a one day strike to protest against the Industrial Relations Bill. In *Gouriet* v. *Union of Post Office Workers*[51] the question was whether the courts below should have thought it likely that the defendants would claim that they acted in contemplation of a trade dispute,[52] and Viscount Dilhorne believed that action in response to a call for international solidarity in the hope of influencing policy on apartheid would not lead the judges to think that the trade dispute defence might be claimed.[53] The question of whether the general strike of 1926 was illegal has been a matter of controversy, but although Astbury J. in *National Sailors and Firemen's Union* v. *Reed*[54] thought it was, the argument was not convincing[55] and academic

---

[46] [1973] I.C.R. 339.

[47] See the doubt cast by Simpson, "Trade Dispute and Industrial Dispute in British Labour Law" (1977) 40 M.L.R. 16 at 19.

[48] [1909] A.C. 506 at 512. See also *The Camilla M, Star Sea Transport Corp.* v. *Slater* [1978] I.R.L.R. 507 (C.A.).

[49] But see the dictum of Cozens-Hardy M.R. in *Dallimore* v. *Williams* (1912) 29 T.L.R. 67 that a case is not taken out of the protection of the Trade Disputes Act if, though the act complained of was done in furtherance of a trade dispute, the defendant was also influenced by malice. The defendant in this case had a hard time for his case first came on before Ridley J. and a jury where he lost. He successfully appealed for a new trial (1912) 29 T.L.R. 67, only to find his new action coming on before Darling J. Having lost again he appealed against the decision and was finally given the verdict by the Court of Appeal. (1914) 30 T.L.R. 432.

[50] (1970) 10 K.I.R. 17.

[51] [1978] A.C. 435.

[52] The issue related to T.U.L.R.A. 1974, s. 17 (1).

[53] [1978] A.C. 435 at 487. Lord Fraser agreed (at 524) but Lord Wilberforce (at 484) was more doubtful.

[54] [1926] 1 Ch. 536.

[55] Although it was approved by Lord Denning in *Sherard* v. *A.U.E.W.* [1973] I.C.R. 421 at 433.

opinion at least supports the view of Professor A. L. Goodhart that it was not illegal.[56]

Although section 29 (2) of the 1974 Act covers cases where a matter can only be resolved by the exercise of a power by a Minister of the Crown, this deals only with individual disputes and not protests against government policy generally. In *Sherard* v. *A.U.E.W.*[57] some union members attempted to prevent their union calling a strike to protest against the Counter-Inflation (Temporary Provisions) Act 1972. At first instance Phillips J. thought it might be too simple to say that the object of the protest was government legislation and that therefore it was a political strike, for underneath the protest there may have been a number of frozen pay claims. In the Court of Appeal, however, Lord Denning thought that a dispute between the government and the T.U.C. was not an industrial dispute.[58] Although the intervention of the government in the economy has become extensive it is suggested that a dispute such as that which occurred in *Sherard* is not a trade dispute unless the object is to press a particular claim against the government as employer.

The remaining issue in this section concerns disputes which appear to be about "trade" matters but which are in fact being pressed for other reasons. Thus action taken for purely personal motives will not be a trade dispute. For example in *Huntley* v. *Thornton*[59] the plaintiff had been called upon to answer a disciplinary charge for refusing to join a one day strike called by his union. The minutes of the meeting declared that, "as Bro. Hugill rose to speak Bro. Huntley jumped to his feet and with arms waving hurled his rule book and his summons letter on the table and walked out of the room shouting we were only a 'shower'." The Executive Council of the union refused to allow his expulsion but nevertheless the defendants hounded the plaintiff out of several jobs. It was held that the plaintiff succeeded in his claim for damages, at least against those[60] defendants who had thought only of their "ruffled dignity", for this took the matter outside the scope of a trade dispute.[61]

"In contemplation or furtherance"

The effect of this phrase is to limit the range of activity in point of time, and the

---

[56] Goodhart "The legality of the general strike in England" (1926–27) 36 Yale L.J. 364. But see the decisions of the Umpire for the purposes of the National Insurance Act 1911 in U.D. 1845/26 and U.D. 1342/26, cited in Hickling, *Labour Disputes and Unemployment Insurance Benefits in England and Canada*: "The General Strike was connected with and arose out of the miners' dispute, and may have been called in furtherance of that dispute, but its immediate cause was a dispute between H.M. Government and the General Council."

[57] [1973] I.C.R. 421.

[58] Lord Denning, however, did think it was arguable that there was an industrial dispute here because there was a dispute between government employees (or some of them) and the government as employers. *Sed Quaere.*

[59] [1957] 1 All E.R. 234.

[60] Two of the defendants were not liable because it was not shown that their motive was to injure the plaintiff rather than forward the interests of the union.

[61] See also *Torquay Hotels* v. *Cousins* [1969] 2 Ch. 106 where Winn L.J. thought the action against the Imperial Hotel was only to punish the manager for the expression of views unpalatable to the union. However, the support of the manager of the Imperial for the Torbay Hotel (which was the subject of the initial dispute) may make it possible to see the case in a different way, although Lord Denning thought that sympathy for one side does not make one a party to the dispute. See also *Stratford* v. *Lindley* [1965] A.C. 269 per Lord Donovan at 341 (ruffled feelings are not a trade dispute) and Lord Pearce at 335 (advancement of unions' prestige not trade dispute).

classic statement interpreting it is again that of Lord Loreburn in *Conway* v. *Wade.*[62]

> "I think [the words] mean that either a dispute is imminent and the act is done in expectation of and with a view to it, or that the dispute is already existing and the act is done in support of one side to it. In either case the act must be genuinely done as described, and the dispute must be a real thing imminent or existing."

These words assumed importance in *Bents Brewery* v. *Hogan*[63] where a union representing public house managers had circulated a questionnaire to its members to determine whether terms and conditions of employment were satisfactory. Answers to some of the questions would have involved some of the managers in breach of their contracts of employment and Lynsky J. granted an injunction to prevent the disclosure of such information as "there was a possibility of a dispute at some future time, but no certainty that such a dispute would arise."[64] This view seems to give preference to the blunt approach which hits first and asks questions later.

It is also necessary for the action to be "in furtherance of" a dispute, so that where industrial action is taken at one place of work because of a dispute at another place of work, it must be action which supports that dispute.[65] In *Beaverbrooke Newspapers* v. *Keys*[66] there was a trade dispute at the Daily Mirror which caused that paper to stop publication. The defendant, who was the general secretary of SOGAT, instructed his members at the Daily Express not to allow the publication of extra copies of the Express to take up the demand resulting from the loss of the Daily Mirror. This instruction was an inducement to the workers at the Daily Express to break their contracts of employment and it was argued that this was protected as it was in furtherance of the dispute at the Daily Mirror.[67] Lord Denning said that the action at the Express was done in consequence of a consequence of a trade dispute but was not in furtherance of it. It was argued that the action did support the strike at the Daily Mirror because by restricting extra copies the defendant was depriving the Daily Mirror of the argument that it would lose its market and unemployment would result, but the court decided that such a defence would be unlikely to succeed. Thus the action was taken because of the initial dispute, but was not in furtherance or in support of it.

In addition some action comes too late to be in furtherance of the dispute. Thus in *Stewart* v. *A.U.E.W.*[68] the plaintiff haulage contracter had defied pickets on strike at a shipyard and after the strike had been settled he was "blacked." It was held that this action may have been in consequence of the dispute but it was not in furtherance of it.[69]

---

[62] [1909] A.C. 506 at 512. [63] [1945] 2 All E.R. 570.

[64] See also *Milligan* v. *Ayr Harbour Trustees* [1965] S.C. 937 where it was said that mere fear of a strike did not make it a trade dispute if there was no proof that the workers contemplated one.

[65] In *United Biscuits* v. *Fall, The Guardian,* January 27, 1979, it was held in an interlocutory application that secondary activity was too remote and not in furtherance of the original dispute. But the matter is not yet finally settled.

[66] [1978] I.C.R. 582. Simpson, *Express Newspapers* v. *N.U.J. The Guardian*, December 22, 1978.

[67] The action at the Daily Express was not itself a trade dispute as there was no dispute about the contracts of employment there. The court rejected the argument that there was a dispute as to whether the workers were bound to publish extra copies.

[68] [1973] I.C.R. 128.

[69] See also *Hutchinson* v. *Aitchison* (1970) 9 K.I.R. 69 which is a more doubtful decision.

Conclusion

Finally, it should be reiterated that a person may act in furtherance of a trade dispute even if he is not directly involved. But although the law does not ask whether he is justified in taking such sympathetic action, it may ask whether that action is likely to assist the original dispute so as to be in furtherance of it, and mere moral support may not be sufficient.[70] Indeed it is the sympathetic strike that has proved most controversial. Many people argue that the freedom to strike should be limited to those directly involved, but it is suggested that such a view misses two fundamental points. The fact is that if the law is prepared to protect the interest of workers in collective security this interest extends beyond the work force directly involved in the dispute, and secondly experience under the Industrial Relations Act has shown that legal action may not be the most effective method of resolving disputes but may indeed exacerbate them.

STATUTORY RESTRICTIONS ON THE FREEDOM TO STRIKE

While the freedom to strike is in general permitted, there are some cases where such a freedom is disallowed or at least limited in the interest of public security or individual safety.

(1) *The armed forces*

Any member of the armed forces who engages in any disruptive activity in order to redress a grievance is likely to be met by internal military sanctions or charged under the disciplinary provisions of, for example, The Army Act 1955.[71] In addition anyone found to be encouraging such activity, could be faced with a charge under section 1 of the Incitement to Disaffection Act 1934 which applies a maximum sentence of 2 years imprisonment to any person who maliciously and advisedly "endeavours to seduce any member of Her Majesty's forces from his duty or allegiance to Her Majesty . . ."[73]

It appears, however, that the Government has no objection in principle to members of the armed forces being members of trade unions and it has been stated[74] that they are permitted to become members at any time in their careers so long as their union activities do not conflict with the requirements of military discipline. In addition tradesmen in the services are encouraged to join an appropriate craft union when they near the end of their military service in order to assist them on their return to civilian life, and the A.U.E.W. has a number of such members. It has also been said[75] that in general there is no demand for trade unionism from the services, and it may be that while there can be no objection to individuals being members of unions, there would be more difficulty in establishing traditional trade unionism and collective bargaining procedures within the structure of military discipline.

(2) *The police*

Similar considerations of public security apply to the police forces, and

[70] *Express Newspapers* v. *N.U.J., The Guardian*, December 22, 1978.

[71] ss. 31–41. See also Air Force Act 1955, ss. 31–41, and the Naval Discipline Act 1957, ss. 8–18.

[72] This and related Acts are being discussed by the Law Commission.

[73] See *R.* v. *Arrowsmith* [1975] 2 Q.B. 678. See also the Incitement to Mutiny Act 1797, s. 1, as amended as to penalty by the Punishment of Offenders Act 1837, s. 1, and extended to the Air Force by the Air Force (Application of Enactment) (No. 2) Order 1918 (S.R. & O. 1918 No. 548).

[74] H. C. Debs., Vol 939, *col. 84* (November 14, 1977).

[75] H.C. Debs., Vol. 940, *col. 1102* (December 6, 1977).

following strikes by the Metropolitan and City of London police in 1918 action was taken[76] to limit their freedom to strike. The provisions are now contained in the Police Act 1964, s. 47 of which forbids a member of the police to join a trade union, although it does permit a policeman who was a member of a trade union before joining the force to retain that membership with the consent of the chief officer. In addition section 53 establishes the offence of causing disaffection or inducing a policeman to withhold his services or commit breaches of discipline.

Trade unionism of a kind is, however, permitted, for section 44 of the Police Act 1964[77] allows the establishment of police federation to represent the interests of members of police forces. There is a condition that such federations shall be independent of any body or organisation outside the police service, but this may be waived by the Secretary of State subject to such restrictions as he may specify.

(3) *Merchant seamen*

The circumstances in which seamen are employed also lead to a military style of discipline, and because of this, and also perhaps because a strike at sea could not be easily resisted by the employer, the freedom to strike is limited. The Merchant Shipping Act 1970 s. 42 states that where a trade dispute is concerned a seaman may give not less than forty-eight hours notice to the ship's master of his intention to terminate his employment so long as his ship is then safely moored in the United Kingdom. Apart from this provision seamen would be exposed to the risk of disciplinary proceedings. It can therefore be seen how, although the freedom to strike exists in limited form, it would be difficult to organise a concerted stoppage of all seamen, and indeed it was for this reason, and also because of the difficulty of organising seamen, that even under the Industrial Relations Act 1971 the seamen's union was allowed a closed shop.

(4) *The Post Office*

Certain statutes make it an offence wilfully to delay or procure the delay of any postal packet[78] or message[79] so that considerable theoretical limitations are placed on the ability of postal and telecommunications employees to go on strike. It was these sections that gave rise to *Gouriet* v. *Union of Post Office Workers*[80] where the House of Lords on an application for an injunction to prevent threatened breaches of the Post Office Act held that the refusal of the Attorney-General to give his consent to a relator action cannot be reviewed and that a private individual could not be granted an injunction to enforce a public right.

(5) *Aliens*

One of the more curious relics of the statute book is section 3 of the Aliens Restriction (Amendment) Act 1919, which provides that it shall be an offence for an alien[81] either to cause sedition or disaffection amongst any of Her Majesty's forces (or amongst the civilian population), or to "promote industrial unrest in any industry in which he has not been bona fide engaged for at

---

[76] Police Act 1919.
[77] As amended by the Police Act 1972 s. 1.
[78] Post Office Act 1953, ss. 58 (1) and 68.
[79] Telegraph Act 1863, s. 45.
[80] [1978] A.C. 435. See also *Stephen* v. *Post Office*, [1977] 1 W.L.R. 1172.
[81] As defined by the British Nationality Act 1948, s. 32 (1).

least two years . . .' It is peculiar in that the criminality depends not only on the thing done but on the status of the person doing it, so what is lawful for one person to do may be unlawful for another, depending on his country of origin. It is suggested that such distinctions are not generally adopted by the law and this provision could be repealed without loss.

(6) *Endangering life*

Although the statutes dealing with particular industries have been repealed,[82] there remains the more general offence contained in section 5 of the Conspiracy and Protection of Property Act 1875[83] which provides:

> "Where any person wilfully and maliciously breaks a contract of service or of hiring, knowing or having reasonable cause to believe that the probable consequences of his so doing, either alone or in combination with others, will be to endanger human life, or cause serious bodily injury, or to expose valuable property whether real or personal to destruction or serious injury," he shall be guilty of an offence.[84]

Such a provision could of course be of considerable importance in certain areas, but it should be noted that it will only apply if the strike action involves a breach of the contract of employment, and cannot apply where the contract is lawfully terminated by due notice.

Freedom of Association: the I.L.O.

The United Kingdom has ratified a number of the Conventions of the International Labour Organisation, two of which deal with the issue of freedom of association. The Convention[85] concerning Freedom of Association and Protection of the Right to Organise requires that "workers and employers, without distinction whatsoever, shall have the right to establish and, subject only to the rules of the organisation concerned, to join organisations of their own choosing without previous authorisation."[86] It is doubtful if this principle is yet fully effective in this country. A further article requires national governments to ensure that "workers and employers may exercise freely the right to organise."[87]

A further convention[88] concerns "the Application of the Principles of the Right to Organise and to Bargain Collectively" and deals with discrimination against trade unions and acts designed to promote organisations dominated by the employer.[89] It was under this latter provision that the National Union of Bank Employees presented a case to the I.L.O. Committee on Freedom of Association in 1963[90] complaining of the encouragement of staff associations in the banks, and the Committee recommended the setting up of national inquiry into the allegations,[91] which considered that there had been no breach

---

[82] *e.g.* Conspiracy and Protection of Property Act 1875, s. 4; Electricity (Supply) Act 1919, s. 31.

[83] This section does not apply to merchant seamen; Conspiracy and Protection of Property Act 1875, s. 16, as amended by the Criminal Law Act 1977 sched. 13.

[84] The maximum penalties are a fine of £20 or imprisonment for 3 months.

[85] Convention No. 97.

[86] *Ibid.* Art. 1.

[87] *Ibid.* Art. 11.

[88] Convention No. 98.

[89] *Ibid.* Arts. 1 and 2.

[90] 67th Report of the Committee on Freedom of Association Case No. 292. I.L.O. Official Bulletin, Vol. 46 No. 2, supp. I. (April 1963).

[91] See the Inquiry by Lord Cameron. Cmnd. 2202.

of the Convention but made a number of suggestions for improving industrial relations in banking. The report was "noted" by the I.L.O. Committee,[92] but as experience under the Industrial Relations Act showed, the problems of staff associations in banking persisted.[93]

The procedure for bringing a case to the I.L.O. is for a union or an employers' association (or the government) to make a complaint to the Committee on the Freedom of Association, which is a tripartite body drawn from the Government, Employers and Workers Groups of the Governing Body. The Committee reports to the Governing Body of the I.L.O. and may recommend that the problem be brought to the attention of the national government concerned in order to remedy the situation or that it should be referred to the Fact-Finding and Conciliation Commission of the I.L.O. Between 1951 and 1976 the Committee on Freedom of Association dealt with over 800 cases, and has produced a digest of the principles it has applied.[94]

---

[92] 76th Report of the Committee on Freedom of Association, Case No. 292. I.L.O. Official Bulletin vol. 47, No. 3, supp. 2. (July 1964).

[93] See for example *NUBE* v. *Barclays Bank International.* [1973] I.C.R. 167 (N.I.R.C.), *NUBE* v. *Anglia Building Society* [1973] I.C.R. 597 (N.I.R.C.).

[94] *Digest of Decisions of the Freedom of Association Committee of the Governing Body of the I.L.O.* (1976).

CHAPTER 12

CIVIL LIABILITY FOR INDUSTRIAL ACTIVITIES

IN the absence of the "trade dispute"[1] exemption union officials would in many cases of industrial action be exposed to various torts, which, although not exclusive to trade union cases, have been developed to cover most varieties of strike action. They are of considerable sophistication having been refined by argument between those who wish to see greater intervention by the law in industrial disputes and those who do not. While it may be said that the judges change from periods of abstention[2] to periods of judicial creativity,[3] and that Conservative governments have favoured greater intervention,[4] and Labour governments less,[5] it would be unfortunate if disputes about this subject (whether legal or political) or indeed the length of this chapter, were to give the impression that these torts are central to the purpose of labour law. They need extensive treatment because of the complexity of the law: they need to be covered because of the risk (however slight) of their being applied in cases of industrial action; but they are more relevant to trade union law than to industrial relations.

INDUCING BREACH OF CONTRACT

In very general terms the tort of inducing breach of contract is committed when a person knowingly interferes with a contract between two other people (either directly, or indirectly and wrongfully) without lawful justification. Unfortunately each element of this description will need elucidation,[6] but first it may be useful to set out the three basic ways in which the tort may be committed.

---

[1] If there is a trade dispute protection is provided by T.U.L.R.A. 1974 s. 13.

[2] As for example from the 'twenties to the 'forties. See Wedderburn "Labour Law and Labour Relations in Britain" (1972) 10 B.J.I.R. 270, where he argues that "the traditional framework of British labour law really rested upon middle-class acquiescence in the current balance of industrial power." As the unions began to exercise their power, that acquiescence waned and brought about more restrictive measures both by the judges and by Parliament.

[3] As in the sixties: *e.g. Rookes* v. *Barnard* [1964] A.C. 1129 and *Stratford* v. *Lindley* [1965] A.C. 307.

[4] See for example the Industrial Relations Act 1971 ss. 96–98 which created "unfair industrial practices" similar to the torts described in this chapter, but which applied in trade dispute cases. It is thought that cases decided under these sections have no authority in the law of tort.

[5] See for example the Trade Disputes Act 1965 (repealed) and the Trade Union and Labour Relations Act 1974, s. 13, as amended.

[6] For a most detailed and comprehensive discussion of this and the other torts in this chapter see Clerk and Lindsell, *Torts* (14th ed.) Chap. 11 (K. W. Wedderburn).

The three species of the tort

(1) *Direct inducing*

This is the original form of the tort and occurs when A directly operates on B in order to induce[7] him to break his contract with C. The tort was first established in *Lumley* v. *Gye*[8] which, although not a trade union case, provides a simple illustration. Miss Johanna Wagner, a singer, had made a contract with the plaintiff, the proprietor of the Queen's Theatre, to sing and perform at his theatre and nowhere else for a period of three months, but the defendant persuaded her to break that contract and sing at his theatre instead. The defendant was held liable for maliciously procuring a breach of contract.

There are three basic cases where this principle might be applied against officials or members of a trade union. The first is where a union official persuades his members to break their contracts of employment. It should be remembered of course that the tort will only be committed (in the absence of a trade dispute) if withdrawl of labour actually involves breaches of the employment contract,[9] and for this reason it is important to bear in mind the legal effect of strike notice on the contract of employment,[10] for if the notice amounts to notice to terminate rather than break the contract no tort will have been committed. Legal action is, however, rarely, if ever, taken in this class of case, even if the strike is a breach of the contract of employment, for it would hardly be conducive to a settlement of the dispute. Secondly, the converse case may arise, so that a threat by the workers to the employer that there will be a strike if X is not dismissed amounts to the commission of the tort, for X's contract of employment has been broken by the employer at the behest of the workers.[11] If, however, his employment was terminated lawfully by the employer, this tort at least would not have been committed.[12] Thirdly "direct inducing" can be applied in the case of the secondary boycott, whereby a union, in order to make a strike more effective than it would be simply by a stoppage of work by the employees in dispute, takes action against the suppliers of the employer or against the distributors of his product, thus causing a breach of the commercial contract involved. A simple example would be for the employees on strike at a bakery to persuade the flour miller not to supply the employer with flour. If this is done by a direct approach to the miller, it is direct inducement of the contract to supply flour, but if they achieve their ends by approaching the employees of the miller, thereby preventing him from delivering flour, this will be indirect inducement of the breach, which is discussed below.

An example of the direct form of the tort from the cases is *Torquay Hotel Co.* v. *Cousins*[13] where, in order to take action against the Imperial Hotel, the defendants telephoned Esso (who supplied the hotel with fuel) telling them that there was a dispute and that any supplies of fuel oil would be stopped, and

---

[7] The term "procure" is often used instead of induce. It is suggested they are interchangeable. The meaning of "induce" is discussed below.

[8] (1853) 2 E. & B. 216, 118 E.R. 749.

[9] *Allen* v. *Flood* [1898] A.C.1.

[10] Chap. 10 above.

[11] See for example the facts of *Read* v. *Friendly Society of Operative Stonemasons* [1902] 2 K.B. 732. That action would now be protected by T.U.L.R.A. 1974 s. 13.

[12] There has been no suggestion yet that a person who induces an employer to terminate a contract without breaking it is liable if the dismissal is unfair.

[13] [1969] 2 Ch. 106.

it was held that the failure of Esso to deliver fuel was due to direct inducement by the defendants.

One question which arises only in cases of directly inducing a breach of contract is whether the person who is induced may sue, as well as the other party to the contract. Thus in the example of the bakery, could the flour miller sue for loss of profit he could have made had he performed the contract? In *Boulting* v. *ACTAT*[14] Upjohn L.J. thought there should be no action by the party induced: "If A procures B to break his contract with C . . . B has no right at law to restrain A from attempting to suborn him from his duty to C. He must resist A's efforts by strength of will." While it may be useful to encourage potential "inducees" to resist the blandishment of inducers, such approaches may take the form of irresistible threats and it may be premature to state that such a person cannot sue.

(2) *Indirect inducing*

This form of the tort is committed when a person induces another to do an unlawful act which leads as a necessary consequence to the breach of a contract to which the plaintiff is a party. Thus if in our example the employees of the bakery approach not the flour miller himself, but rather persuade the miller's drivers in breach of their contracts to refuse to deliver to the baker, the baker may sue (in the absence of a trade dispute) if the refusal to drive the lorries leads as a necessary consequence to the breach of contract. It is of considerable significance that for this form of the tort to be committed illegal means must be employed by the defendant in his attack on the plaintiff. Although in *Daily Mirror Newspapers Ltd.* v. *Gardner*[15] Lord Denning expressed the view that unlawful means were unnecessary in the indirect form of the tort, he has now recanted this view in *Torquay Hotels Ltd.* v. *Cousins*[16] where he re-affirmed that there is a distinction between direct persuasion to break a contract (which is unlawful in itself), and the intentional bringing about of a breach by indirect methods involving wrongdoing. "This distinction", said Lord Denning, "must be maintained, else we should take away the right to strike altogether."

The first case to discuss this form of the tort, although in the end the defendants were held not liable, was *Thomson* v. *Deakin*.[17] Cases of secondary boycott involving indirect inducement of breach of contract are somewhat complicated, and the facts of that case may be illustrated by the following diagram.

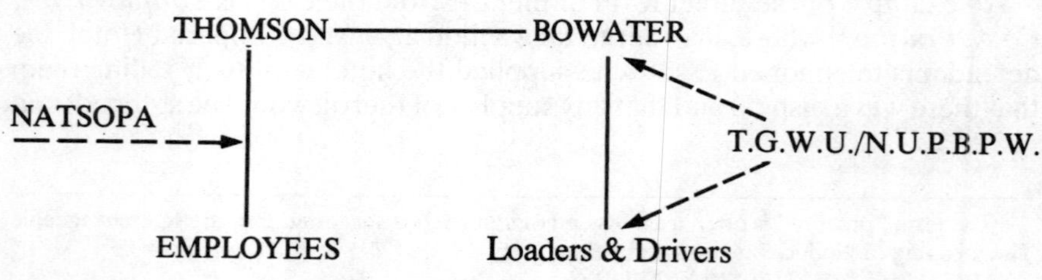

[14] [1963] 2 Q.B. 606 at 640. See also *Camden Exhibition Supply* v. *Lynott* [1966] 1 Q.B. 555 at 569. But see *Hersees of Woodstock* v. *Goldstein* (1963) 38 D.L.R. 2d 449, which it is suggested is no authority to the contrary.

[15] [1968] 2 Q.B. 762.

[16] [1969] 2 Ch. 106 at 138.

[17] [1952] Ch. 646.

Since 1926 D. C. Thompson had a policy of employing only non-union labour and every person on becoming an employee was required to sign a contract whereby he promised not to become a member of any union. However, in 1939 one McKay had become a member of NATSOPA and in 1952 he left the Company.[18] Richard Briginshaw, general secretary of the union, decided to make an issue of it and called out the secret union members at Thomsons and in addition called for help from other unions. Bowaters supplied Thomsons with paper, and officials and members of the T.G.W.U., in support of the NATSOPA men at Thomsons, took action at Bowaters, first by adivising Bowaters not to deliver paper[19] and secondly the drivers indicated they would not deliver paper there if called upon to do so. In addition members of the National Union of Printers, Bookbinders and Paperworkers agreed that they would not load paper bound for Bowaters. In the event Bowaters yielded to the pressure and never did ask the loaders or drivers to deal with the paper: the employees were therefore not in breach of their contracts, and accordingly the necessary unlawful means were not present.

The importance of the case lies in the fact that the Court established that the tort may be committed by indirect means, but in doing so strict limits were placed upon it; limits that have been relaxed in recent years.[20] Jenkins L.J. said,[21]

> "I would hold it strictly confined to cases where it is clearly shown, first, that the person charged with actionable interference knew of the existence of the contract and intended to procure its breach; secondly, that the person so charged did definitely and unequivocally persuade, induce or procure the employees to break their contracts of employment with the intent I have mentioned; thirdly that the employees so persuaded, induced or procured did in fact break their contracts of employment, and, fourthly that the breach of the contract forming the alleged subject of interference ensued as a necessary consequence of the breach of the employees concerned of their contracts of employment."

The most important case where the tort in this form has been applied is *Stratford* v. *Lindley*,[22] which may be illustrated as follows:

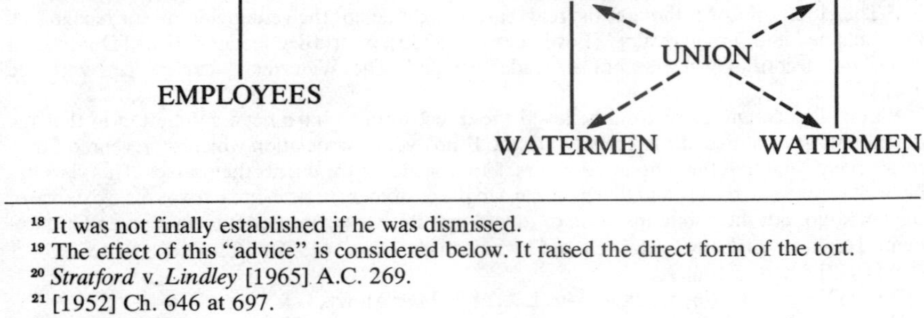

---

[18] It was not finally established if he was dismissed.

[19] The effect of this "advice" is considered below. It raised the direct form of the tort.

[20] *Stratford* v. *Lindley* [1965] A.C. 269.

[21] [1952] Ch. 646 at 697.

[22] [1965] A.C. 269.

Jack Stratford was the chairman and effective controller of two companies: J. T. Stratford Ltd. and Bowker and King Ltd. Bowker and King operated motor barges and of their employees 3 were members of the Watermen, Lightermen, Tugmen and Bargemen's Union and 45 were members of the T.G.W.U. Approaches for recognition had been made by both unions before, but in 1963 Bowker and King recognised the T.G.W.U. The Watermen also wanted recognition,[23] but realising their position at Bowker and King was weak, took action against Stratford's. Stratford's did not employ any members of the Watermen's Union, but it engaged in the business of repairing barges and letting barges out on hire, and their customers did employ members of that union. Accordingly the union called out the employees of Stratford's customers so that no barges were sent for repair and the hired barges were not returned. The majority of the House of Lords considered that what happened amounted to the indirect form of the tort,[24] in that the union had attacked the commercial contracts between Stratfords and their customers and in doing so had used unlawful means by calling out the watermen in breach of their contracts of employment. The case is of interest because the rules on such matters as knowledge and causation laid down by Jenkins L.J. in *Thompson* v. *Deakin*[25] were relaxed against the union's interests so as to produce a somewhat stricter tort. These individual points are dealt with below.

(3) *Direct and wrongful obstruction of the contract*

The third way in which the tort may be committed is to interfere with the contract so as to prevent performance. The tort is only committed if the mode of interference is itself wrongful. This form was referred to in *Thomson* v. *Deakin*[26] where the example was given of removing essential tools or kidnapping an essential employee. The best example of the application of this form is *G.W.K.* v. *Dunlop*,[27] where the plaintiffs, manufacturers of G.W.K. cars, made a contract with the A.R.M. Co. whereby all G.W.K. cars for exhibition were to be fitted with "Bal-lon-ette" tyres. For the Glasgow Exhibition of 1924 the plaintiffs supplied a car so fitted, but on the night before the show opened Dunlop Ltd. caused these tyres to be removed and Dunlop tyres fitted instead, which remained on the cars for the first day of the exhibition. Dunlop were held liable to both G.W.K. Ltd. (who received £500 damages) and to A.R.M. Co. (who received £2,000). The point is that Dunlop did not interfere with either party to the contract, but rather did a wrongful act intending to cause a breach of the contract. It has been said that this form is limited to interference with the subject matter of the contract, but it is suggested that this is but an example, for it should cover the cases put earlier of removing

[23] The House of Lords thought the real reason might be not the genuine desire for recognition but could be "inter union rivalry" (Lord Pearson at 335), or "ruffled feelings" (Lord Donovan at 341), and accordingly it was not a "trade dispute." The Watermen later merged with the T.G.W.U.

[24] Lord Pearce and Lord Reid believed the direct form to have been committed in that the defendants gave notice of the embargo to the Employers' Association which represented Stratford's clients and that this amounted to direct approaches to the clients themselves. This view has been challenged on the ground that what caused the customers to be in breach was the existence of the embargo, not the communication of it, and that this view confused information and inducement. Hughes, "Liability for loss caused by industrial action" (1970) 86 L.Q.R. 181 to 185.

[25] [1952] Ch. 646 at 697.

[26] [1952] Ch. 646 at 695, *per* Jenkins L.J., at 702 *per* Morris L.J.

[27] (1926) 42 T.L.R. 376.

essential tools or even of kidnapping one of the parties to the contract.[28]

FURTHER ELEMENTS OF THE TORT

While the basic forms of the tort have now been described, there remain a number of detailed points which need to be discussed in order to complete the picture. These are (i) the need for a breach of contract, (ii) the meaning of inducing, (iii) the requirement of knowledge, (iv) causation, (v) justification, (vi) the effect of section 13 of the Trade Union and Labour Relations Act 1974.

Breach of contract

It has so far been assumed in discussing the basic forms of the tort that a breach of contract has occurred. However, the situation is more complicated than might appear. Thus in *Midland Cold Storage* v. *Steer*[29] a concerted effort was made to establish a tort of inducing a person not to enter into a contract, but such a concept was decisively rejected by Megarry J., who said:[30]

> "As the authorities stand, I am certainly not prepared to hold on motion that, conspiracy or unlawful means apart, there is a tort of wrongfully inducing a person not to enter into a contract. Unless hedged about with many restrictions, such a tort would have an extremely wide ambit that would be likely to work as much injustice as justice."[31]

This view is supported by the Australian case of *McKernan* v. *Fraser*[32] where seamen had been selected by the Adelaide Steamship Co. for employment as greasers, but before they signed articles the defendants objected to their employment. The court held that the selection process did not amount to a contract of employment which only came into being when the articles were signed. Accordingly the defendants had only prevented future contracts from coming into existence, and had not interfered with any subsisting contractual relationship.[33]

---

[28] See also *Einhorn* v. *Westmount Investments* (1969) 6 D.L.R. 3rd 71 where the plaintiff was owed commission as an estate agent for facilitating the sale of the Old City Hall, Regina to Westmount Investments Ltd. Other defendants who were in control of that company transferred all its assets elsewhere, rendering it incapable of paying the money due. "I am unable to think of a more effective method of rendering performance impossible than that of emptying the till by transferring the contracting party's assets to other persons," *per* Disbery J. The examples given in support were of this form of the tort, but it is difficult to see what unlawful means were involved in transferring the assets. It may be better to regard the case as one of directly preventing performance of the contract, along the lines of *Torquay Hotel Ltd.* v. *Cousins* [1969] 2 Ch. 106. But see Wedderburn (1970) 33 M.L.R. 309 who argues that this case represents a dangerous innovation. And see the appeal: (1970) 11 D.L.R. 3d 509 where it was noted that the only question was whether the statement of claim should be struck out. *Torquay Hotel Co.* v. *Cousins* was not mentioned by the court.

[29] [1972] Ch. 630.

[30] *Ibid.* at 645.

[31] This would not only be true in trade union affairs but also in the commercial sphere. See the fundamental case of *Mogul Steamship Co.* v. *McGregor Gow & Co.* [1892] A.C. 25. (H.L.). See also (1889) 23 Q.B.D. 598 (C.A.).

[32] (1931) 46 C.L.R. 343 *per* Rich, Dixon and McTiernan JJ.

[33] But see the dictum of Pennycuick V.-C. in *Brekkes* v. *Cattel* [1972] Ch. 105 at 114 that it had been established by *Torquay Hotel Co.* v. *Cousins* [1969] Ch. 106 that the tort applies "where there is interference with contracts to be made in accordance with a regular course of dealing." See Clerk and Lindsell, *Torts* (14th ed.) p. 395 where K. W. Wedderburn suggests that the dictum is explained by the view that a person will be liable if he intends to procure a breach of *any* contract that will be made.

It must also be noted that there will be no action where the termination of the contract is lawful, whatever the motive of the defendant in bringing about that termination. This is one of the points established by the great case of *Allen Flood*[34] where during a demarcation dispute between boilermakers and shipwrights over the repair of a ship named the "Sam Weller", the defendant, Allen, informed the management that the boilermakers would "knock off work" if the plaintiff shipwrights were not dismissed. As Lord Macnaghten pointed out[35] the men were free to leave at any time and therefore the termination would not have been unlawful. Even if the defendant had intended to injure the plaintiffs, it was established that a bad motive cannot make a lawful act unlawful.

One interesting question is whether an agreement that is merely unenforceable can be the subject of an action. In the Canadian case of *Brown* v. *Spamberger and Bunting*[36] the court refused to allow an action by an estate agent whose contract for the payment of commission was unenforceable because it had not been reduced to writing, against the defendant who had pointed out this fact to the plaintiff's client. Although it has been suggested that there should be liability in such a case,[37] such a view would not affect the fact that no action can be based on interference with a collective agreement that is not in writing and stated to be binding,[38] for such an agreement has no legal effect, not because it lacks the proper form, but because it is deemed not to have been intended to be legally enforceable. However, a collective agreement, even though unenforceable by the parties to it, may be incorporated into the contract of employment of the individual employee,[39] and may in this way form the basis of an action.[40]

It should be noted, however, that the law of tort is not the only weapon which may be used to prevent interference, for equity will act to prevent the breach of an equitable duty, even against third parties. Thus in *Prudential Assurance Co.* v. *Lorenz*[41] a trade union instructed its members who collected insurance premiums to bank the money but to withhold submission of the weekly accounts. It was held that such an agent owes an equitable duty to account to his principal and an injunction was issued to prevent the defendants from inciting a breach of that duty. Such a case cannot be regarded as a case in tort since inducing a breach of the contract of employment was protected by the Trade Disputes Act 1906, whereas the incitement to break an equitable duty was not.[42]

---

[34] [1898] A.C.1. For an account of the attempt by Lord Halsbury to get a different result by reviving the obsolete procedure of summoning the judges for their advice, see Paterson "Judges a political elite?" (1974) 1 Br.Jnl. of Law and Society 118, and Heuston, *Lives of the Lord Chancellors*, 1885–1940, esp. pp. 119–122. Lord Halsbury did, however, succeed in bringing liability (for conspiracy) home to a union in the not dissimilar case of *Quinn* v. *Leathem* [1901] A.C. 495. For a discussion of industrial relations and the judiciary see Griffith, *The Politics of the Judiciary* (1977), Chap. 3.

[35] [1898] A.C.1. at 148.

[36] (1959) 21 D.L.R. 2d 630.

[37] Winfield and Jolowicz, *Tort*, 10th ed. p. 446.

[38] See T.U.L.R.A. 1974 s. 18.

[39] This matter is discussed below Chap. 18.

[40] But note T.U.L.R.A. 1974 s. 18 (4) which states that a no-strike clause shall not be incorporated unless certain conditions are fulfilled. *Rookes* v. *Barnard* [1964] A.C. 1129 (a case of intimidation) was based on such an incorporated clause.

[41] (1971) 11 K.I.R. 78.

[42] *Bents Brewery* v. *Hogan* [1945] 2 All E.R. 570 was a case on similar facts, but decided principally on inducing breach of contract.

However, there are cases where interference is actionable even though there is technically no breach of contract. The most famous of these cases is *Torquay Hotel Co.* v. *Cousins*[43] which may be illustrated as follows:

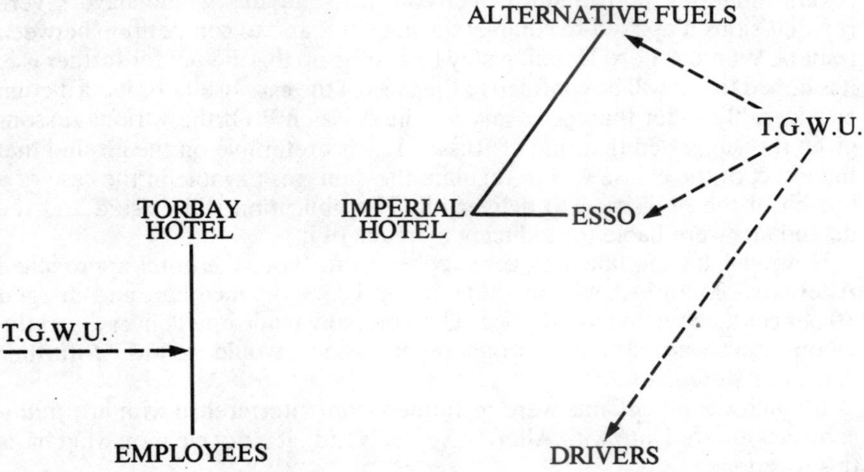

The T.G.W.U. had called a strike at the Torbay Hotel in order to gain recognition, when a Mr. Chapman, manager of the Imperial Hotel, was alleged by the local newspaper to have said that the Hotel Association was determined to stamp out the intervention of the Transport Union into the hotel trade. The T.G.W.U. accordingly took action against the Imperial Hotel.[44] The union picketed the hotel[45] and in addition informed Esso Ltd., who supplied the hotel with fuel oil, that there was an official dispute and that supplies of oil would be stopped.

The facts as related so far give rise to a difficult point, because the contract of supply between Esso and the hotel contained a clause whereby Esso were not to be liable for any failure to fulfill the agreement if they were prevented by labour disputes. Strictly speaking therefore there was no breach of contract by Esso, and thus the case raised the problem adumbrated by Lord Reid in *Stratford* v. *Lindley,*[46] that is whether the tort extends to "deliberate and direct interference with the execution of a contract without that causing any breach." Russell L.J. regarded the clause as "an exception from liability for non-performance rather than an exception from obligation to perform"[47] and Winn L.J. developed this view saying that it was actionable if the course of dealing between the parties had led the parties to expect performance.[48]

Lord Denning preferred the ground that the tort covers a case where there

---

[43] [1969] 2 Ch. 106.

[44] It was held there was no trade dispute at the Imperial Hotel and the acts were not done in furtherance of the dispute at the Torbay Hotel. Although similar cases could not be covered by T.U.L.R.A. 1974 s. 29, this particular case might still be a non trade dispute because of the view that the unions were furthering not a trade dispute but their own fury. [1969] 2 Ch. 106 at 137, *per* Lord Denning.

[45] In so far as this picketing induced tanker drivers to refuse to deliver the oil, in breach of their contracts of employment, it could have brought about an action for indirect inducing by unlawful means.

[46] [1965] A.C. 269 at 324.

[47] [1969] 2 Ch. 106 at 143.

[48] *Ibid.* at 147.

is direct interference which "prevents or hinders one party from performing his contract, even though it be not a breach."[49] It has been suggested[50] that this principle enunciates a new tort which is very uncertain in its scope in so far as it covers hindering performance of a contract, and this would have severe repercussions if applied to commercial activities and to competition between traders. Whereas Lord Denning may be storing up this dictum for further use, it is hoped that it will be confined to the facts of the case itself, for it is a dictum considerably wider than necessary for the decision.[51] Of the various reasons given it is suggested that that of Russell L.J. is preferable on the ground that the effect of the clause was to regulate the damages payable in the case of a breach of the obligation to deliver oil. The obligation still existed and the defendants were liable for inducing a breach of it.

However, having failed to get supplies from Esso, the hotel approached Alternative Fuels Ltd. who did not employ T.G.W.U. members and charged 50 per cent. above the usual price. This company made one delivery, and the union then warned that serious repercussions would follow if further deliveries were made.[52]

Although the defendants were restrained from interference with any *future* contracts entered into with Alternative Fuels Ltd., it is not clear on what basis this was done.[53]

A further point of interest has been the form of the order made in *Stratford* v. *Lindley*[54] which covered contracts made "now or hereafter'. Despite fears that this heralded a change of some significance, in *Midland Cold Storage* v. *Steer*[55] Megarry J. has explained it in these terms:

> "An injunction restraining a person from causing or procuring any breach of contract is not altered in quality by being framed to apply not merely to contracts already made but also to any contracts to which may be made subsequently. In each case, the act enjoined is an interference with a contract; the only difference lies in the date on which the contract is made. This is completely different from an order not to prevent a contract from being made. A breach of the obligations created by a contract is one thing, the prevention of any such legal obligation from being brought into being is quite another."

The problem of explaining cases which prevent interference with future relationships has also arisen in Canada where in one case[56] the defendants took action against the plaintiff by withdrawing his employer's credit, not only causing the employer to terminate his contract of employment but also with the result that the plaintiff was unable to go through with his plan to purchase shares in the company that employed him. In awarding damages for interfer-

[49] *Ibid.* at 138. "There must be interference in the execution of a contract. The interference is not confined to the procurement of a breach of contract."

[50] Clerk and Lindsell, *Torts* (14th ed.) p. 403.

[51] See *Einhorn* v. *Westmount Investments* (1969) 6 D.L.R. 3d 71. This case looks like a mis-application of the third species of the tort but it may also be viewed as an application of Lord Denning's new principle. See Wedderburn (1970) 33 M.L.R. 309. On appeal, the Saskatchewan Court of Appeal refused to strike out the statement of claim on the ground that it disclosed no reasonable cause of action, and noted that this was all that had been decided at first instance. *Torquay Hotel Co.* v. *Cousins* was not referred to in the appeal. (1970) 11 D.L.R. 3d 509.

[52] In fact no further supplies were needed.

[53] [1969] 2 Ch. 106 at 140, *per* Lord Denning.

[54] [1965] A.C. 269 at 339.

[55] [1972] Ch. 630 at 644.

[56] *Gershman* v. *Manitoba Vegetable Producers Marketing Board* (1977) 69 D.L.R. 3d 114.

ence with this prospective advantage O'Sullivan J.A. said "What the plaintiff lost by the defendant's wrongful interference was not the opportunity for the formation of a contract but rather the opportunity to extend his already existing contractual relationship of employment into one that would include acquisition of shares."

It is, however, difficult to see why an opportunity to change a contract should be regarded as protected by the law of tort whereas an opportunity to create a contract is not. Clearly the problem of prospective advantage will be a difficult one to settle now that protection has gone beyond actual breach of contract.

The meaning of "induce"

The degree of pressure which must be applied for a person to be said to "induce" or "procure" an act has been the subject of some dispute, but there can be no doubt that over the years this hurdle has been lowered for the plaintiff. In *Allen* v. *Flood*[57] it was thought that Allen had not induced the dismissal of the plaintiffs when he had merely been the means of communicating the views of the boilermakers. In *Thomson* v. *Deakin*[58] there was a direct approach by officials of the T.G.W.U. to Bowaters but it was said[59] that this was not an inducement since the defendants merely stated the facts as they knew them to be. Furthermore, in relation to the indirect form of the tort it was said[60] that general exhortations would not be an inducement if the object could be achieved by lawful means, since the person advocating the object is not to be taken, without more, to be advocating unlawful means.

But by the time *Stratford* v. *Lindley*[61] and *Torquay Hotel Ltd.* v. *Cousins*[62] came to be decided a stricter attitude prevailed, for in the former case Lord Pearce in referring to the statement made to the employers' association said, "the fact that an inducement to break a contract is couched as an irresistible embargo rather than in terms of seduction does not make it any the less an inducement."[63] In the latter case Winn L.J.[64] said that mere advice could amount to an inducement, giving as examples a father telling his daughter that her fiancé had been convicted of indecent exposure thus causing the engagement to be broken off, and a man telling his mother-in-law that his central heating had broken down, thus causing her to postpone her visit. But if these are to be examples of inducing, a trade union leader may be in some difficulty. If for example he puts to a mass meeting the terms of the employer's offer, without any recommendation, and in response a motion to call a strike is passed, has he induced the strike? Fortunately there is now some authority that providing information is not "inducing", for in *Camellia Tanker Ltd.* v. *I.T.F.*[65] it was said that there was insufficient evidence[66] that the second defendant by informing the tugboat men of the negotiations between the union and the plaintiffs had thereby induced them to break their contracts in

---

[57] [1898] A.C. 1. See especially the speech of Lord Macnaghten at 149–151

[58] [1952] Ch. 646.

[59] *Ibid.* at 685, *per* Lord Evershed M.R.

[60] *Ibid.* at 697–698, *per* Jenkins L.J.

[61] [1965] A.C. 269.

[62] [1969] 2 Ch. 106.

[63] [1965] A.C. 269 at 333.

[64] [1969] 2 Ch. 106 at 147.

[65] [1976] I.C.R. 274.

[66] The proceedings were interlocutory.

support of the union. It is therefore to be hoped that "inducing" may in future be thought to mean more than simply stating a fact, and will only cover cases where the defendant has himself provided the reason for the breach of contract.[67]

The requirement of knowledge

The requirement that the defendant should know of the existence of the contract which has been broken is of considerable importance since it is one of the ways in which the range of potential liability may be limited. In any strike it is foreseeable that a large number of unspecified contracts will be broken or delayed in their performance, and yet it is clear that a defendant should not be liable for remote contracts, but only for those which are in a sense "proximate", and the degree of proximity is established by the defendant's knowledge. Unfortunately this is also a test that has been whittled away over the years to expose potential defendants to a greater risk of liability.[68]

The initial view expressed in *Thomson* v. *Deakin*[69] was that the plaintiff must prove that the defendants had actual knowledge of the contract, and indeed one of the grounds for dismissing the claim for direct inducement of the breach of contract was that the plaintiff had not shown that the defendants knew of the contract with Bowater's, or that even if they thought there might have been some contract, that they knew of its terms.[70] However, by the time *Stratford* v. *Lindley*[71] was decided elements of an objective approach to this question had begun to appear, so that Lord Pearce was able to say[72] that whereas the relevant question was whether the defendants had sufficient knowledge of the terms to know that they were inducing a breach of contract, "it seems unlikely that they would be ignorant of the simple commonplace obligation of the hirers . . .' Lord Radcliffe[73] felt that on the evidence the defendants "must be treated" as having sufficient knowledge. The objective approach has been taken further by Lord Denning who has said that "even if [the defendant] did not know of the actual terms of the contract, but had the means of knowledge—which they deliberately disregarded—that would be enough."[74] It is suggested, however, that there may be dangers in taking the objective approach too far, for the range of potential plaintiffs must be carefully circumscribed.

---

[67] The other case where a problem arises is where the contract breaker is willing to break his contract. See *B.M.T.A.* v. *Salvadori* [1949] Ch. 556 and *Thomson* v. *Deakin* [1952] Ch. 646 at 694, *per* Jenkins L.J., where the view is expressed that there would be actionable interference if there have been dealings inconsistent with the contract. See also *Batts Combe Quarry* v. *Ford* [1942] 2 All E.R. 639.

[68] In this section it is only necessary to discuss intervention which has ceased, for if the industrial action is continuing the plaintiff may serve on the defendant a copy of the contract in question, thus providing him with knowledge for the future. See for example *Torquay Hotel Ltd.* v. *Cousins* [1969] 2 Ch. 106.

[69] [1952] Ch. 646.

[70] *Ibid.* at 686, *per* Evershed M.R., who went on to say that "if all else were satisfactorily proved, it might well be (having regard to common knowledge about the way business is conducted) that absence of such strict proof would not suffice to prevent the grant of relief."

[71] [1965] A.C. 269.

[72] *Ibid.* at 332.

[73] *Ibid.* at 328.

[74] *Emerald Construction* v. *Lowthian* [1966] All E.R. 1013 at 1016. In *Torquay Hotel Ltd.* v. *Cousins* [1969] 2 Ch. 106 at 138 where he said "The person must know of the contract or, at any rate, turn a blind eye to it and intend to interfere with it." See also *Greig* v. *Insole* [1978] 1 W.L.R. 302.

An example of a case which it is submitted went too far is *McMahon* v. *Dunne*,[75] where the plaintiffs imported timber through the port of Dublin and one of their consignments was stranded in the docks due to an embargo placed on all building materials by the defendants. The defendants were not aiming at and did not know of the plaintiffs and the only reason they had to suggest any breach of contract was the presence of the timber in the docks.[76] On the question of knowledge Budd J. said:[77]

> "If we have moved to the stage where constructive knowledge is sufficient is there any reason for confining the ingredient of knowledge to knowledge of a specific contract between specific parties or actual knowledge of any particular contract? In many instances in modern life it must be obvious to the ordinary onlooker that some transaction is taking place on foot of some contract."

It is suggested that if such remarks were adopted the range of potential liability would be too wide, and that such a view fails to take into account the purpose of the requirement of knowledge, which is to do for this tort what duty and remoteness of damage do for the tort of negligence.[78]

The requirement of knowledge is often coupled with the need to prove intention, and in most cases it is assumed that if the defendant knew of the contract in question and deliberately did acts which caused its breach, then he can be said to have intended to cause the breach. There is, however, one case where such an assumption would be false, for it may be that, although all the other ingredients were present, his intention was not that the contract should be broken but that it should be terminated lawfully. In *White* v. *Riley*[79] the defendants had informed their employer that they refused to work with the plaintiff who could have been dismissed lawfully with one week's notice or wages in lieu. The defendants even offered to pay the wages in lieu themselves, but the employer did not accept this offer and dismissed the plaintiff unlawfully. The court held that the defendants had not induced the breach of the contract, but on the contrary had intended to avoid any breach by the employer.

Unfortunately the logic of this proposition did not succeed in *Emerald Construction* v. *Lowthian*[80] where the defendants wanted a labour only sub contract to be terminated. The defendants claimed that they assumed that it could be terminated lawfully[81] and therefore they lacked the necessary intent, but Diplock L.J. replied[82] that ignorance of the terms of the contract was not enough to show absence of intent, and he went on to say that the defendant is liable if he intends to have the contract ended by breach if it cannot be ended lawfully. Thus the defendants were liable because whether the contract was terminated lawfully or not was a matter of indifference to them. In other words defendants are not to be given the benefit of the doubt. It is suggested,

---

[75] (1964) 99 I.L.T.R. 45.

[76] If the plaintiffs had served the defendants with notice of the contract there would have been no problem.

[77] (1964) 99 I.L.T.R. 45 at 54.

[78] It should also be noted that these were interlocutory proceedings, as are most cases in this area, so that the issue was whether there was a fair question to be tried.

[79] [1921] 1 Ch. 1 at 26 *per* Warrington L.J.

[80] [1966] 1 All E.R. 1013.

[81] The contract could only have been terminated lawfully if the contractors did not maintain reasonable progress.

[82] [1966] 1 All E.R. 1013 at 1019.

however, that it would be unfortunate if a defendant is held liable for inducing a breach of contract if that contract would have been terminated lawfully, for in effect what is being done is to protect not legal rights but prospective advantage, and so far English law has not accepted that prospective advantage should be protected.

Causation

The issue here is the degree of causal connection necessary between the act of the defendant and the breach. In *Thomson* v. *Deakin*[83] Jenkins L.J. made it clear that, at least so far as the indirect form was concerned, the breach must be a necessary consequence of the act. He said:[84]

> "it must be shown that, by reason of the withdrawal of the service of the employees concerned, the contract breaker was unable, as a matter of practical possibility, to perform his contract; in other words, I think the continuance of the services of the particular employees concerned must be so vital to the performance of the contract alleged to have been interfered with as to make the effect of their withdrawal comparable, for practical purposes, to a direct invasion of the contractual rights of the party aggrieved. . . ."

While this view was approved by Lord Pearce in *Stratford* v. *Lindley*,[85] in relation to indirect inducement of breach of contract, he did suggest that so far as the direct form is concerned it need only be proved that the breach was a reasonable consequence and that it would be no defence to show that the hirers of the barges could somehow have avoided the breaches.[85]

Justification

According to the English authorities the defence of justification[86] is very narrow in its scope, for in a number of cases in the early part of this century[87] the courts, while admitting the existence of the defence,[88] refused to apply it. In *South Wales Miners' Federation* v. *Glamorgan Coal Co.*[89] the union, fearing a fall in the price of coal,[90] decided to take action in order to restrict the supply and thus maintain the price. Accordingly the union advised its members to engage in one-day strikes on four separate occasions. The House of Lords held that the defendants could not plead self-interest as justification. Unfortunately in none of the cases decided at this time was any statement made as to what would constitute justification, although in the Court of Appeal in the *South Wales Miners* case Romer L.J. did say[91] that in analysing the circumstances: "regard might be had to the nature of the contract broken; the position

[83] [1952] Ch. 646.

[84] *Ibid.* at 697.

[85] [1965] A.C. 269 at 333.

[86] For a full survey of this defence see Heydon, "The defence of justification in cases of intentionally caused economic loss," (1970) 20 Univ. Toronto L.J. 139 and Heydon, *Economic Torts* (2nd ed.) pp. 38–47.

[87] *South Wales Miners Federation* v. *Glamorgan Coal Co.* [1905] A.C. 239; *Read* v. *Friendly Society of Operative Stonemasons of England, Ireland and Wales* [1902] 2 K.B. 732; *Smithies* v. *National Association of Operative Plasterers* [1909] 1 K.B. 310. The defence also failed in *Greig* v. *Insole* [1978] 1 W.L.R. 302.

[88] *South Wales Miners Federation* v. *Glamorgan Coal Co.* [1905] A.C. 239 at 246, *per* Lord Macnaghten.

[89] [1905] A.C. 239.

[90] The miners' wages were fixed in relation to the price of coal.

[91] [1903] 2 K.B. 545 at 574.

of the parties to the contract; the grounds for the breach; the means employed to procure the breach; the relation of the person procuring the breach to the person who breaks the contract; and I think also to the object of the person in procuring the breach."

The defence did succeed in the Canadian case of *Posluns* v. *Toronto Stock Exchange*[92] where the defendants were held to be justified in withdrawing their permission for the plaintiff to be a member of a firm on the stock exchange, thereby causing his dismissal, on the ground that by becoming employed by a member firm he had submitted himself to control by the exchange.[93] The defence has only once succeeded in England, but the case is regarded as of little value as an authority because of its bizarre facts.[94] In *Brimelow* v. *Casson*[95] the defendants induced theatre managers to refuse to book the plaintiff who was a theatre manager and employed a group of chorus girls. It was alleged that they were so badly paid that they were having to lead lives of immorality.[96] If the reason for allowing the defence of justification was that the defendants wished to prevent hardship amongst the chorus girls, then it must be inconsistent with the *South Wales Miners* case,[97] but if it is explicable on the ground that the defendants were protecting public morality, one might wonder whether the law should be involved in this area at all.[98]

While bearing in mind the warning that cases in the Commonwealth "may be no safe guide to English law in so far as they depend upon the relationship of the common law to special legislation,"[99] it is nevertheless suggested that the New Zealand case of *Pete's Towing Services Ltd.* v. *Northern Industrial Chain of Workers*[1] is of considerable interest. In that case the plaintiff owned a barge and due to the inexperience of his crane driver, an alternative method of loading sand had to be found, and the barge was beached so that it could be loaded by a front-end loader. An official of the Watersiders' Union noticed that no member of his union had been asked to do the work, and approached the defendant Arvidson, an official of the union which organised the drivers of the loaders. Arvidson informed his members that the barge had been blacked by the Watersiders' Union. Both union officials told the plaintiff that loading could re-start if the company agreed to enter into negotiations, but this offer was turned down, and in consequence the contract for the load of sand involved was broken.

Speight J. whilst recognising that advancement of one's own interests, even with the highest and most altruistic motives, would not suffice, nevertheless held that the defendant was justified in his action. He did so on the ground that "the inducement was not being used as a sword to procure financial betterment but as a shield to avoid involvement in industrial discord," and that the defendant had a duty to intervene since if he had not "he was entitled to apprehend that his individual members might encounter scorn and reprisals

[92] (1965) 46 D.L.R. 2d 210, affirmed (1968) 67 D.L.R. 2d 165.

[93] See also *Roman Corporation* v. *Hudson's Bay Oil and Gas Co.* (1973) 36 D.L.R. 3d 413 where the Prime Minister's statement that the Government intended to prevent a sale of shares which prevented the transaction from being completed was held not to be tortious.

[94] Heydon, *Economic Torts,* (2nd ed.) p. 43.

[95] [1924] 1 Ch. 302.

[96] It was claimed that one of the girls was living with another member of the company, a deformed dwarf. The show was called the "King Wu Tut Tut Revue."

[97] [1905] A.C. 239.

[98] See Heydon, *Economic Torts,* (2nd ed.) p. 43.

[99] Clerk and Lindsell, *Torts* (14th ed.) p. 414 (K. W. Wedderburn).

[1] [1970] N.Z.L.R. 32.

and his Union in general be exposed to a real possibility of financial detriment which industrial disharmony and breakdown often entails."[2] Whether such a liberal view of justification would prevail in this country remains to be seen,[3] but it seems clear that the tone of the authorities would be against such a change.

The following points may be made on this provision:

(1) The section applies to any person and is not limited to trade union members, but may apply to any individual, including an employer or an employers' association.[8]

(2) The statute only absolves the inducing of a breach of contract and not the breach itself, so that the contracting party remains liable. Thus if A induces B to break his contract with C, A may be absolved if he is acting in furtherance of a trade dispute, but B will be liable to C for breach of the contract.

(3) The immunity applies whoever brings the action.[9]

(4) The immunity does not apply where the act is actionable for a reason other than inducing breach of contract. Thus in *Prudential Assurance Co.* v. *Lorenz*[10] the defendants had induced insurance agents to withhold submission of their accounts, and the court held that this was not only a breach of their contracts of employment (which was protected) but also a breach of their equitable obligation to account (which was not).[11]

Statutory protection from liability

In addition to the general immunity given to trade unions,[4] section 13 of the Trade Union and Labour Relations Act 1974 provides an immunity for individual officials and members in the following terms:[5]

> "An act done by a person in contemplation or furtherance of a trade dispute[6] shall not be actionable in tort on the ground only:
> (a) that it induces another person to break a contract or interferes or induces any other person to interfere with its performance . . ."[7]

---

[2] [1970] N.Z.L.R. 32 at 51.

[3] But see the view of Lord Denning in *Cory Lighterage* v. *T.G.W.U.* [1973] I.C.R. 339 at 356 that if Shute (the man whose resignation from the union caused the trouble) had improper motives, then the union would have been justified in the action they took. It was not stated what principle was being applied.

[4] T.U.L.R.A. 1974 s. 14.

[5] T.U.L.R.A. 1974 s. 13 (1) as amended by the Trade Union and Labour Relations (Amendment) Act 1976.

[6] For the meaning of "in contemplation or furtherance of a trade dispute" see Chap. 11 above.

[7] This section provides a wider immunity than previous legislation, which covered only inducing breaches of contracts of employment. Trade Disputes Act 1906, s. 3; Industrial Relations Act 1971 s. 132.

[8] At least if the association is a corporation. Unincorporated employers' associations and trade unions do not need this section as they are fully protected by s. 14. But s. 14 only protects an incorporated association if the act is done in connection with the regulation of relations between employers and workers. Could an act fall outside that definition and yet be in contemplation or furtherance of a trade dispute? If it could s. 13 would apply and s. 14 would not.

[9] *Camellia Tanker* v. *I.T.F.* [1976] I.C.R. 274. At that time only inducements of breaches of contracts of employment were protected and an attempt was made to say that the section only provided an immunity against the employer and not against others. This view was rejected. See also *Stratford* v. *Lindley* [1965] A.C. 269, at 336, *per* Lord Pearce, and *Morgan* v. *Fry* [1968] 2 Q.B. 710 at 728, *per* Lord Denning.

[10] (1971) 11 K.I.R. 78.

[11] See also *Royal Mutual Insurance Society* v. *Williamson* (1921) 37 T.L.R. 742 where premiums collected were withheld. Russell J. thought the inducement to do so by the defendant "appeared to be an act of piracy," but presumably the collectors only committed the tort of conversion.

(5) A further point is whether the immunity is lost if the act is, apart from inducing breach of contract, not *actionable* in the civil courts, but rather unlawful in some other way. Thus should we say the immunity is lost if the act is otherwise *unlawful* or only if it is otherwise *actionable*?

In *Cunard Steam Ship Co.* v. *Stacey*[12] the plaintiffs sought an interlocutory injunction to prevent the defendants inducing their crews to break their contracts. Such action was also unlawful by virtue of the Merchant Shipping Act 1894. Neither Lord Evershed nor Jenkins L.J.[13] expressed a final view on the matter, although both considered it to be one of great difficulty. Lord Evershed did, however, say, "it equally seems to me that the ground assigned in addition to that of procuration must be a ground that is actionable in the civil Courts. That, at any rate, is my own prima facie view."[14] It is suggested that the addition of the words "in tort" after "shall not be actionable" confirms this view, so that a criminal statute will only destroy the immunity if it is capable of founding an action for breach of statutory duty.

It should also be noted that the effect of section 13 (3) of the 1974 Act is to exclude the possibility that an act which is rendered immune from action by virtue of section 13 (1) could be used to provide the element of unlawful means in another tort. The section states:

"For the avoidance of doubt it is hereby declared that:

(a) an act which by reason of subsection (1) or (2) above is itself not actionable;

(b) a breach of contract in contemplation or furtherance of a trade dispute;

shall not be regarded as the doing of an unlawful act or as the use of unlawful means for the purpose of establishing liability in tort."[15]

This section is of importance not only in relation to inducing breach of contract, but also in relation to intimidation and conspiracy.

As we saw earlier, *Midland Cold Storage* v. *Steer*[16] has temporarily halted attempts to create a tort of interference with prospective advantage; at least so far as cases involving industrial disputes are concerned,[17] for Megarry J. declared:[18]

> "I am certainly not prepared to hold on motion that, conspiracy or unlawful means apart, there is a tort of wrongfully inducing a person not to enter into a contract. Unless hedged about with many restrictions, such a tort would have an extremely wide ambit that would be likely to work as much injustice as justice."

The matter cannot, however, be considered to be beyond doubt, and hence the usefulness of section 13 (2) of the 1974 Act which states:

> "For the avoidance of doubt it is hereby declared that an act done in contemplation or furtherance of a trade dispute is not actionable in tort

---

[12] [1955] 2 Lloyd's Rep. 247.

[13] *Ibid.* at 256.

[14] The case did provide a complication in that one provision of the Merchant Shipping Act 1894 gave the master of a ship the right to claim via the *criminal* process the cost of a substitute for an absent seaman. For Lord Evershed the question was whether this was a civil right so as to take the act of the defendants outside the protection of the Act. See also *Fowler* v. *Kibble* [1922] 1 Ch. 487.

[15] s. 13 (1) (*a*) is set out above; s. 13 (1) (*b*) deals with threats and is set out below. s. 13 (2) follows immediately.

[16] [1972] Ch. 630.

[17] Attempts to develop such a tort in the commercial sphere out of the tort of passing off have been more successful.

[18] [1972] Ch. 630 at 645.

on the ground only that it is an interference with the trade, business or employment of another person, or with the right of another person to dispose of his capital or his labour as he wills."

This section was originally contained in the Trade Disputes Act 1906 when it was not clear whether such a tort existed or would be created,[19] and was inserted "for the avoidance of doubt." One question is whether the section must be limited to "the leading heresy" as it existed then or whether it can refer to subsequent creations, and in particular whether it covers the dicta of Lord Denning in *Torquay Hotel Ltd.* v. *Cousins*[20] concerning potential liability for direct interference with a contract, even if there is no breach and no unlawful means are used. It is suggested that even if such dicta were to be used in the future, section 13 (2) of the Act should not be limited to the purposes for which it was introduced, but may be apt to prevent this attempt to avoid the statutory immunity.

INTIMIDATION

Although a number of early cases can be analysed in terms of intimidation,[21] the tort was made prominent by the famous case of *Rookes* v. *Barnard*[22] in 1964 where it was established that A will be liable if, by threatening to commit an unlawful act in relation to B, he thereby persuades B to act to the detriment of C. C may sue A. In that case Douglas Rookes was a draughtsman employed by B.O.A.C. who, in 1955, had resigned his membership of the Association of Engineering and Shipbuilding Draughtsmen. B.O.A.C. had agreed that where 100 per cent. union membership existed, they would not recruit a non-member, but it was agreed that a member could resign from the union without losing his employment. Despite this agreement the union members in the design office passed the following resolution on January 10, 1956. "We the members of the A.E.S.D. inform B.O.A.C. that if the non-unionist, Mr. D. E. Rookes, is not removed from the design office by 4 p.m., Friday, January 13, 1956, a withdrawal of labour of all A.E.S.D. membership will take place."

Rookes was suspended on January 13 and finally he was lawfully dismissed on March 16, 1956.

It was alleged that the threat to call a strike was a breach of contract by the employees since in 1949 the union and B.O.A.C. had entered into a collective agreement to the effect that no strike or lock out would take place, and that this agreement had been incorporated into the individual contracts of employment of the workers.[23] Two of the defendants, Barnard and Fistal, were

---

[19] Such a tort, described by Lord Devlin in *Rookes* v. *Barnard* [1964] A.C. 1129 at 1216 as "*Quinn* v. *Leathem* without the conspiracy," was regarded by Lord Dunedin in *Sorrell* v. *Smith* [1925] A.C. 700 at 719 as "the leading heresy."

[20] [1969] 2 Ch. 106.

[21] *Tarleton* v. *M'Gawley* (1793) Peake 270; 170 E.R. 153, where the defendant was liable for shooting at natives in order to prevent them trading with the plaintiff. *Garret* v. *Taylor* (1620) Cro.Jac. 567; 79 E.R. 485, where the defendant threatened the plaintiff's workmen and customers.

[22] [1964] A.C. 1129. At the trial the plaintiff was awarded damages of £7,500, but the House of Lords, rejecting exemplary damages, ordered a new trial on the issue of damages only. The case was finally settled for £4,000, but it is not certain how much, if any, of this was kept by him since the Legal Aid Fund had a charge on the damages. *Rookes* v. *Barnard (No. 2)* [1966] 1 Q.B. 176.

[23] This was conceded by counsel for the defendants, but it has often been questioned since whether this concession was necessary. The Trade Union and Labour Relations Act 1974 s. 18 (4) does not permit the incorporation of "no-strike" clauses unless certain conditions are fulfilled.

employed by B.O.A.C. and so would have been in breach of this term, but the third, Silverthorne, was not.[24] In the event the House of Lords held that all three were liable for conspiracy to commit the tort of intimidation,[25] by threatening B.O.A.C. with an unlawful act in order to induce them to dismiss Rookes.

Unlawful means

There is no doubt[26] that A must threaten to use unlawful means against B in his attack on C.[27] As Lord Reid pointed out in *Rookes*,[28] just as *Allen* v. *Flood*[29] had established that there is a fundamental distinction between doing what you have a legal right to do and doing what you have no legal right to do, so equally there must be a distinction between threatening a lawful and an unlawful act. It had been accepted that threats of physical violence against B to induce him to harm C were actionable, and it was assumed that this extended to threats to commit any tort, whether one of violence or not.[30] The essential question in *Rookes* v. *Barnard*[31] was therefore whether a breach of contract constituted unlawful means for the purposes of this tort, and the House of Lords unanimously held that it did. Lord Reid pointed out[32] that "threatening a breach of contract may be a much more coercive weapon than threatening a tort, particularly when the threat is directed against a company," and Lord Devlin said:[33]

> "I find therefore nothing to differentiate a threat of a breach of contract from a threat of physical violence or any other illegal threat ... All that matters to the plaintiff is that, metaphorically speaking, a club has been used. It does not matter to the plaintiff what the club is made of—whether it is a physical club or an economic club, a tortious club or an otherwise illegal club. If an intermediate party is improperly coerced, it does not matter to the plaintiff how he is coerced."

It might, however, be argued that this dictum is too wide and that not every illegal act amounts to unlawful means for the purposes of this tort,[34] and in

---

[24] This gives rise to the question of how Silverthorne was held liable if he did not threaten to use unlawful means for he could not threaten to break his own contract of employment as he was not employed. In *Morgan* v. *Fry* [1968] 2 Q.B. 710 at 729 Lord Denning suggested that Silverthorne not only threatened to induce breaches of contracts of employment but also was party to the conspiracy of the others to break contracts. This explanation is not entirely satisfactory as he would not have been directly liable for conspiracy to injure by unlawful means, but could only be liable for conspiring with others to use the unlawful means of the others.

[25] See Wedderburn, (1964) 27 M.L.R. 257; Hoffman, (1965) 81 L.Q.R. 116; Weir, [1964] C.L.J. 225.

[26] *Morgan* v. *Fry* [1968] 2 Q.B. 710 at 724, *per* Lord Denning.

[27] In *Chaplin* v. *Young* (1911) 31 N.Z.L.R. 214 a ship's fireman tried to have the cook dismissed because he refused to supply him with tinned fish and cocoa, by threatening to advise firemen not to join the ship. The court held him liable, citing dicta of Romer L.J. in *Giblan* v. *National Amalgamated Labourers' Union* [1903] 2 K.B. 600. These views have, however, now been discredited, and as the threat was to do a lawful act there would not now be liability.

[28] [1964] A.C. 1129 at 1169.

[29] [1898] A.C.1.

[30] There is a parallel with the meaning of "intimidation" for the purposes of the Conspiracy and Protection of Property Act 1875, for which see Chap. 13 below. But it is suggested that cases on the meaning of intimidation for the one purpose are no authority for its meaning for the other purpose. See the fears expressed by Judge Chapman in *Tynan* v. *Chief Constable of Liverpool* [1965] 3 All E.R. 99 at 105.

[31] [1964] A.C. 1129.

[32] *Ibid.* at 1169.

[33] *Ibid.* at 1209.

[34] Clerk and Lindsell, *Torts* (14th ed.) pp. 418–419.

particular it may be doubted whether an act that is not otherwise actionable by the party threatened should be regarded as unlawful means. If A threatens B with an unlawful but non-actionable act, and B gives way and harms C, it would be strange if C could sue when, if B resisted and suffered the act, B could not.

There has, however, been considerable criticism of even the narrow view of the case that breach of contract amounts to unlawful means, on the ground that it interferes with fundamental principles of contract: notably the doctrine of privity.[35] This point was raised before the House and dealt with by Lord Devlin who pointed out that:[36] "In no circumstances does C sue on B's contract. The cause of action arises not because B's contract is broken but because it is not broken; it arises because of the action which B has taken to avoid a breach."

Whatever the merits of this or other answers,[37] the fact remains that breach of contract does amount to unlawful means; and in relation to trade unions the danger arises from the fact that traditionally a strike is regarded as a breach of contract unless due notice to terminate the contract has been given.[38] However, as will be seen, section 13 of the Trade Union and Labour Relations Act 1974 confers considerable statutory immunity upon those acting in furtherance of a trade dispute.[39]

"Two party" intimidation

It has been established that where A threatens to commit an unlawful act in relation to B, whereby B does an act to the detriment of C, C may sue A. The question that arises here is whether B may also sue A. If B resists the threat and A does commit the unlawful act then B may of course sue for that,[40] but if B gives way and harms C, B may also suffer loss. For example if in *Rookes* v. *Barnard*[41] Rookes had irreplaceable skills, could B.O.A.C. sue for the losses due to their inability to carry out the scheme that Rookes was engaged in? If A threatens B with an unlawful act so that B refuses to enter into contracts with C, can both B and C sue for the profit they would have made on these contracts?

In *Stratford* v. *Lindley* Lord Reid said:[42]

> "A case where a defendant presents to the plaintiff the alternative of doing what the defendant wants him to do or suffering loss which the defendant can cause him to incur is not necessarily in pari casu and may involve questions which cannot arise where there is intimidation of a third person."

However, in *D & C Builders Ltd.* v. *Rees*[43] Lord Denning indicated, obiter, that an action for two-party intimidation would lie on behalf of a party who

---

[35] Hoffman, (1965) 81 L.Q.R. 116; Wedderburn, (1964) 27 M.L.R. 257.

[36] [1964] A.C. 1129 at 1208.

[37] See also Lord Reid, *ibid.* at 1168.

[38] This matter is fully discussed above, Chap. 10. It should be noted that in *Morgan* v. *Fry* [1968] 2 Q.B. 710 the defendants avoided liability for intimidation on Lord Denning's view that strike notice was not notice to break a contract but only notice to suspend it, and therefore did not amount to unlawful means. This view is not generally accepted.

[39] This legislation was first enacted in the Trade Disputes Act 1965.

[40] Assuming the threat was of an act that was actionable: difficulties would arise if the tort of intimidation applied to threats of acts not actionable.

[41] [1964] A.C. 1129.

[42] [1965] A.C. 269.

[43] [1966] 2 Q.B. 617 at 625.

had given way to the threat and then claimed his loss.[44] The point was more fully discussed by the court of first instance in *Central Canada Potash Co.* v. *A.-G. for Saskatchewan*[45] where it was argued that where the threat is to break a contract the victim of the threat should be left to his remedies either for anticipatory breach or if the threat is carried out for the breach itself. Disbery J. rejected that argument but on appeal[46] the Court preferred the dictum of Lord Reid and rejected the view that the tort ought to be extended to cases of "two-party" intimidation.

Although these various dicta carry considerable weight, it is suggested that the matter cannot yet be regarded as finally resolved.[47]

The threat

The usual definition of "threat" is that of Peterson J. in *Hodges* v. *Webb*:[48]

> "A threat is only an intimation by one to another that unless the latter does or does not do something, the former will do something which the latter will not like."

Just as it is necessary in the tort of inducing breach of contract to distinguish "inducement" and "information" or "advice", so it is necessary to distinguish here between "intimidation" and "warning", but the difficulties of doing so are the same. When does the factual statement that "if X is not dismissed there will be a strike" become a threat? Does it depend on the state of mind of the person who makes the statement, or indeed is the state of mind of the person to whom it is addressed relevant? Since coercion is the essence of the tort it is suggested that a statement only becomes a threat when it is made with a coercive purpose.

The dictum of Peterson J. also points out a further essential factor, that is that a threatened action must be expressed to be conditional on action or lack of it by the victim. Thus if A threatens to hit B unless B pays him £5, that is intimidation, but if A hits B and in order to avoid a repetition of the blow B offers him £5, that is not intimidation.[49] It might be said that B was induced by A's behaviour to act as he did, but he was not intimidated as no demand was made.[50]

Intention

The question here is the extent to which the act of the defendant must be "aimed at" the plaintiff. In *Rookes* v. *Barnard*[51] the defendants were clearly acting with the intention of causing harm to Rookes; but suppose Rookes had an assistant who could not be employed except with Rookes, so that when he was dismissed the assistant had to go too. Could the assistant sue? Clearly the tort cannot be objective in nature, so that the fact that the defendants ought to have realised what would happen would be irrelevant, but the question arises whether they could be liable if they were reckless in relation to the assistant. It

---

[44] See also *Huljich* v. *Hall* [1973] 2 N.Z.L.R. 279 at 285, *per* McCarthy J.
[45] [1976] 57 D.L.R. 3d 7 at 116–123.
[46] (1978) 79 D.L.R. 3d 203 at 229.
[47] For the arguments against the tort see Hoffman (1965) 81 L.Q.R. 116 at 128.
[48] [1920] 2 Ch. 70 at 89.
[49] *Huljich* v. *Hall* [1973] 2 N.Z.L.R. 279 at 286.
[50] "A bare threat without a demand does not to my mind amount to the tort of intimidation," *Stratford* v. *Lindley* [1965] A.C. 269 at 284, *per* Lord Denning.
[51] [1964] A.C. 1129.

is suggested that the tort should be limited to cases where the defendants have the plaintiff directly in mind.

Causation

In *Morgan* v. *Fry*[52] Lord Denning pointed out that the tort applies so long as the threat is "of sufficient consequence to induce the other to submit." The phrase does not, however, adequately cover the question whether it must be the unlawful means alone which must induce the victim to submit or whether the tort can be committed by a powerful person or body who threatens a technical illegality, but whose social or economic power to harm the victim lawfully is the reason for the submission. In *Rookes* v. *Barnard*[53] it is arguable that the defendants could not have acted lawfully,[54] but suppose the "no-strike" clause is disregarded, then the only illegality might have been the giving of three days notice rather than seven. Could they have avoided liability on the ground that what induced B.O.A.C. to act as they did was the threat of a strike and not the threat of an unlawful strike? Clearly there should in principle be some causal link between the illegality and the response of the victim,[55] but it has not been settled how close that link should be. "Incidental" or "collateral" illegality should not of course be sufficient, but in practice it may be that the illegality need not be the sole reason for the other party to give way.

Justification

There is very little authority on the question whether a defendant to an action for intimidation may plead that he was justified,[56] but the clearest statements come from Lord Denning. In *Morgan* v. *Fry*[57] he thought that the defendants might be justified in refusing to work with the plaintiff if he were really a troublemaker who fomented discord in the docks without lawful cause or excuse, and the same point was made in a later case.[58] Whether such a defence will succeed in any case remains to be seen.

Statutory immunity from liability

Section 13 (1) of the Trade Union and Labour Relations Act 1974 states:

"An act done by a person in contemplation or furtherance of a trade dispute shall not be actionable in tort on the ground only:

(a) ....[59]

(b) that it consists in his threatening that a contract (whether one to which he is a party or not) will be broken or its performance interfered with, or that he will induce another person to break a contract or to interfere with its performance."

This provision, first introduced by the Trade Disputes Act 1965 reverses the effect of *Rookes* v. *Barnard*,[60] and makes it almost impossible to sue for

[52] [1968] 2 Q.B. 710 at 724.

[53] [1964] A.C. 1129.

[54] Because of the "no-strike" clause.

[55] Presumably a threat to give lawful notice of a strike written on paper stolen from the employer would not give rise to liability, except in conversion.

[56] The matter was referred to by Lord Devlin but thought not to be in issue; *Rookes* v. *Barnard* [1964] A.C. 1129 at 1209.

[57] [1968] 2 Q.B. 710 at 729.

[58] *Cory Lighterage* v. *T.G.W.U.* [1973] I.C.R. 339 at 357.

[59] For s. 13 (1) (*a*) see above.

[60] [1964] A.C. 1129.

intimidation founded on a breach of contract where a trade dispute exists.[61] In addition section 13 (3) of the Act states that certain acts cannot be treated as unlawful means in order to create the tort; but threats of torts, except inducing breach of contract and conspiracy, would still be sufficient, as may be threats to commit a crime. Thus a threat to "sit-in" would be actionable.

Causing Loss by Unlawful Means

It has been suggested that the tort of intimidation may be but an example of a wider tort of intentionally causing loss by unlawful means.[62] Although *Allen* v. *Flood*[63] has probably settled for good that there is no tort of causing loss by lawful means, there has been some interest in recent years in reviving the notion of a tort of unlawful interference[64] with the trade or business of another, that is to place the individual torts on a higher level of abstraction.[65]

In *Stratford* v. *Lindley*[66] Lord Reid thought that such a tort might exist, but again the clearest statements have come from Lord Denning. In *Daily Mirror* v. *Gardner*[67] he said that "if one person interferes with the trade or business of another, and does so by unlawful means, then he is acting unlawfully . . .," and he substantially repeated this view in *Acrow Ltd.* v. *Rex Chain Belt Inc.*[68] In neither case, however, was this view necessary to the decision and it cannot yet be said with any certainty[69] that such a tort exists.[70]

Statutory immunity

If the tort were to exist section 13 of the Trade Union and Labour Relations Act 1974 would provide immunity for inducing breach of contract and for intimidation. In addition section 13 (3) would have the effect of not permitting a breach of contract committed in contemplation or furtherance of a trade dispute to be counted as unlawful means.

Conspiracy

The essence of trade union power is combination and organisation in sufficient degree to combat the inherent power of the employer, and it is therefore not surprising that one of the weapons used to inhibit the growth of this power

---

[61] Readers should note that some words are applicable to both ss. 13 (1) (*a*) and 13 (1) (*b*) (such as "on the ground only").

[62] Hoffman, (1965) 81 L.Q.R. 116 at 140; Weir [1964] C.L.J. 225.

[63] [1898] A.C.1.

[64] See Heydon, "The future of the economic torts," (1975) 12 U.W.A.L.R. 1 esp. pp. 6–17.

[65] Weir, "Abstraction in the law of torts—economic loss" [1974] City of London Law Review 15. See also Christie, *The liability of strikers in the law of tort*, esp. Chap. 5; Thomson, "Protection of the right to work in the law of torts" (1963) 43 Can.Bar Rev. 167 at 188–198.

[66] [1965] A.C. 269 at 338.

[67] [1968] 2 Q.B. 762 at 783. See also *International Brotherhood of Teamsters* v. *Therien* [1960] S.C.R. 265.

[68] [1971] 1 W.L.R. 1676 at 1683.

[69] The tort has been accepted in Canada. *Mintuck* v. *Valley River Band No. 63A* (1977) 75 D.L.R. 3d 589. The defendant band of indians harassed the plaintiff so that he had to give up farming. It was also a case of intimidation.

[70] It is unlikely that the courts in this country would follow the view of the High Court of Australia in *Beaudesert Shire Council* v. *Smith* (1966) 40 A.L.J.R. 211 that "by an action for damages upon the case, a person who suffers harm or loss as the inevitable consequence of the unlawful, intentional and positive acts of another is entitled to recover damages from that other." See Dworkin and Harari "The Beaudesert Decision—Raising the ghost of the action upon the case," (1966) 40 A.L.J. 296 and 347.

was the doctrine of conspiracy, both in its criminal and its civil form.[71] As has been said:

> "Inherent in the philosophy of laissez-faire economics, which underlay the judicial antipathy to the trade unions, there was a contradiction with which the judges inevitably had to wrestle. Men must be free to compete, and by combining they could compete more effectively; but the extension of freedom of competition to include the right to combine could defeat the economic system.... One answer that 19th century judges gave was that combinations of workers were to be treated differently than other trade combinations."[72]

Fortunately the climate has changed and so far as conspiracy is concerned the days of judicial creativity are over and the law now provides similar privileges to protect one's interests by combination to both traders and union members,[73] and thus the tort of conspiracy is no longer the threat to union activity it once was.

The tort takes two forms:

1. It is a tort to combine with another to injure a third party by taking action which is unlawful in itself.

2. It is a tort to combine with another in order to injure a third party without just cause or excuse, even though the means used are lawful.

Conspiracy to injure by unlawful means

Apart from the requirements of combination and purpose,[74] the essential requirement for this form of the tort is that unlawful means must be used in the attack on the plaintiff, but there is considerable doubt about which kinds of unlawful means are sufficient to constitute the tort. A conspiracy which involves the commission of a separate tort is actionable,[75] and it seems likely that most criminal offences would be sufficient.[76] In *Crofter Hand Woven Harris Tweed Co.* v. *Veitch*[77] Lord Wright thought that an offence under the Conspiracy and Protection of Property Act 1875 would be sufficient, and in the Canadian case of *McKinnon* v. *Woolworth*[78] it has been declared that the commission of a crime is sufficient even if it would not give rise to a cause of action.

Some difficulty arises, however, as to whether breaches of regulatory statutes would be sufficient even though attended by a criminal penalty. In the Australian case of *Williams* v. *Hursey*[79] the Stevedoring Industry Act 1956

---

[71] See Hedges and Winterbottom, *Legal History of Trade Unionism* (1930).

[72] Christie, *The Liability of Strikers in the Law of Tort*, Chap. 3.

[73] But this may be illogical unless the law recognises that the interests which need protection are different. See Stone, *Social Dimensions of Law and Justice*, p. 396. "The proposition that relentless pursuit by the plaintiff of his own interests is always just cause or excuse . . . frustrated the directive to adjust all the interests involved implied in the notion of fairness and reasonableness."

[74] Which although common to both forms of the tort will be discussed in relation to the lawful means form.

[75] *Rookes* v. *Barnard* [1964] A.C. 1129. Note the liability of Silverthorne who did not commit any illegal act as he was not an employee of B.O.A.C.

[76] It should be noted that by virtue of s. 1 (3) of the Criminal Law Act 1977 a summary offence which is not punishable with imprisonment cannot found a charge of criminal conspiracy if it is committed in contemplation or furtherance of a trade dispute. But such an act would be protected from civil liability by s. 13 (4) of the Trade Union and Labour Relations Act 1974.

[77] [1942] A.C. 435 at 462.

[78] [1968] 70 D.L.R. 2d 280 at 287.

[79] (1959) 103 C.L.R. 30 at 79, *per* Fullager J., at 109, *per* Taylor J. and at 127, *per* Menzies J.

made it an offence to interfere by various means with the right of a registered waterside worker to obtain or keep a job, and although it was agreed that the statute did not create a right of action, it was nevertheless sufficient unlawful means to found the action of conspiracy. Such a view naturally raises the question whether the plaintiff should recover on the basis of a statute which gives him no rights, simply because the defendants acted in combination.[80]

It has also been suggested by Lord Denning that an act contrary to the Restrictive Practices Act 1956 amounts to unlawful means,[81] but although conspiracy was pleaded in the case, the remarks were made for the purposes of the proposed tort of causing loss by unlawful means, and thus such an act may not necessarily be sufficient for the purposes of conspiracy.[82] Indeed the view appears misplaced in the light of authorities to the effect that restraint of trade does not amount to unlawful means.[83]

Whether a breach of contract might amount to unlawful means for the purposes of this tort may also be doubted, although it might seem logical that if it is to be sufficient to support an action for intimidation, it should also support conspiracy. But in *Rookes* v. *Barnard*[84] Lord Devlin said:

> "I am not saying that a conspiracy to commit a breach of contract amounts to the tort of conspiracy; that point remains to be decided. I am saying that in the tort of intimidation a threat to break a contract would be a threat of an illegal act. It follows from that that a combination to intimidate by means of a threat of a breach of contract would be an unlawful conspiracy; but it does not necessarily follow that a combination to commit a breach of contract simpliciter would be an unlawful conspiracy."

Whatever the nature of the unlawful means it is suggested that the illegality must not be merely incidental or peripheral to the cause of the damage but must be part and parcel of the method of attack. A mere technical irregularity or an unlawful act unconnected with the purpose of the defendant, such as engaging in pickpocketing while in a picket line, should not be sufficient. In this connection it might also be noted that by virtue of section 1 (2) of the Criminal Law Act 1977 an act will not found a charge of *criminal* conspiracy if the offence is one of absolute liability and the defendant was unaware of the facts which rendered his activity criminal.[85] There seems no reason why such a principle should not extend to civil conspiracy.

Finally it should be noted that although in the wider form of the tort it is easy to establish justification, it may be that there is no defence of justification in

---

[80] See also *Gagnon* v. *Foundation Maritime Ltd.* (1961) 28 D.L.R. 2d 174; but note the powerful dissenting judgment of Judson J.

[81] *Daily Mirror Newspapers* v. *Gardner* [1968] 2 Q.B. 762. The case arose out of a recommendation by the Retail Newsagents Federation to their members to refrain from ordering the Daily Mirror for one week. For subsequent proceedings see *National Federation of Retail Newsagents* v. *Registrar of Restrictive Trading Agreements (Nos. 3 & 4)* (1972) L.R. 7 R.P. 425; and *ibid.* (No. 5) [1973] I.C.R. 649 where the restriction was finally held to be contrary to the public interest.

[82] But see the dictum of Pennycuick J. in *Brekkes* v. *Cattel* [1972] 1 Ch. 105 at 115, where he accepts the view of Clerk and Lindsell, *Torts* that such means are sufficient for conspiracy, although he thought that the distinction between such acts and restraint of trade (which does not amount to unlawful means), might need further elaboration in a higher tribunal.

[83] *Davies* v. *Thomas* [1920] 2 Ch. 189, *per* Warrington L.J.; *Eastham* v. *Newcastle United* [1964] Ch. 413.

[84] [1964] A.C. 1129 at 1210.

[85] See also *Churchill* v. *Walton* [1967] 2 A.C. 224.

the unlawful means version. This view has been taken because it has been thought that the use of unlawful means could never be justified, but now that Lord Denning has suggested it may be applicable in the tort of intimidation,[86] it could also be imported here as a similar basis.

An interesting application of this form of the tort occurred in the Irish case of *Meskell* v. *C.I.E.*[87] where the employer agreed with the trade union to dismiss all the workers and to offer them re-employment on contracts which would include a closed shop provision. The plaintiff refused to accept this condition and the court held the defendants liable for conspiracy on the basis that their action was a breach of the constitutional right to "dissociation" and therefore unlawful means. The court also held that the constitution gave an individual a right of legal action and the case is therefore not authority for the proposition that an act that is not actionable can found liability in conspiracy.It was also held that it was not possible to plead justification in a case of unlawful means even though the defendants took their action to defend their legitimate interest, and that it would be no defence that the defendant's purpose was not unlawful since unlawful means had been achieved to obtain that purpose.

Statutory Protection

Whether an action similar to *Meskell* v. *C.I.E.*[87] would succeed in Britain depends on the effect of section 13 (4) of the Trade Union and Labour Relations Act 1974 which states:

> "An agreement or combination by two or more persons to do or procure the doing of any act in contemplation or furtherance of a trade dispute shall not be actionable in tort if the act is one which, if done without any such agreement or combination, would not be actionable in tort."

The Trade Disputes Act 1906 did not include the words "in tort" at the end of the section and under that legislation it was thought that the unlawful means version of conspiracy was not protected at all. But it is suggested that the addition of the words make a fundamental difference, for now a person will only be exposed to actions for conspiracy by unlawful means if, assuming the act is in contemplation or furtherance of a trade dispute, the unlawful means are tortious in themselves. It is suggested that the words "actionable in tort" cover any case where an individual can recover damages other than under other well defined heads such as for breach of contract. They would not cover acts that are crimes only, but would cover breaches of statutory duty where damages could be awarded, and would probably not be sufficient to cover *Meskell* v. *C.I.E.*[87] where damages could have been awarded for a breach of the Irish constitution. It would be an interesting question whether an action for unfair dismissal would be held to be an action in tort, but on balance, although the circumstances are very similar to tort, it is thought that the classification is distinct, and that accordingly the exemption would apply.

If therefore the words "actionable in tort" are strictly construed, the exemption would apply in trade dispute cases to all cases other than those which are tortious in themselves, and therefore the action for conspiracy by unlawful means is of little advantage to litigants.It should also be noted that by virtue of other provisions of section 13 of the 1974 Act certain acts such as intimidation, inducing breach of contract, or breach of contract itself cannot amount to unlawful means in trade dispute cases.

---

[86] *Cory Lighterage* v. *T.G.W.U.* [1973] I.C.R. 339.
[87] [1973] I.R. 121.

Conspiracy to injure by lawful means

The other form of conspiracy applies where a person combines with another for the purpose of injuring a third party without just cause or excuse, even though the means used are lawful.Such a doctrine was brought to prominence in *Quinn* v. *Leathem*[88] in 1901 where Lord Halsbury achieved his ambition[89] of severely curtailing the effect of *Allen* v. *Flood*,[90] by arguing that a case cannot "be quoted for a proposition that may seem to flow logically from it. Such a mode of reasoning assumes that the law is necessarily a logical code, whereas every lawyer must acknowledge that the law is not always logical at all." Whatever may have been the reasoning behind Lord Halsbury's judgment the doctrine was a severe blow to trade unions until they were relieved of liability by the Trade Disputes Act 1906.

Today not only does the "trade dispute" exemption provide significant protection, but also, as will be seen, the common law itself has developed a "defence" of justification so broad as to include within it all cases where trade unions are acting in their legitimate interests. Fortunately therefore this tort is of little significance in labour relations.

The combination

It is very difficult to justify the fact that an act which is lawful when done by one individual becomes illegal when done by two or more.[91] As Viscount Simon pointed out in the *Crofter* case:[92]

> "The view that the explanation is to be found in the increasing power of numbers to do damage beyond what one individual can do is open to the obvious answer that this depends on the personality and influence of the individual. . . . The action of a simple tyrant may be more potent to inflict suffering on the continent of Europe than a combination of less powerful persons."

Clearly then even if historical arguments can be mustered for the existence of conspiracy in this form,[93] we must accept the view of Lord Halsbury that the tort is illogical.[94]

The existence of a combination is a matter of fact and the plaintiff must prove an agreement between the parties, although action need only be taken against one conspirator alone. As will be seen conspirators may have different motives, but a person who has a justifiable motive will not be liable.[95] To some extent an anomaly exists in that a person who acts lawfully can be held liable for the unlawful means version of the tort if his conspirators act illegally. This is the conclusion from the fact that Silverthorne (who was not an employee of B.O.A.C.) was held liable in *Rookes* v. *Barnard*,[96] although he did not commit

---

[88] [1901] A.C. 495.

[89] See Paterson, "Judges: a political 'elite'?" (1974) 1 Br.Jnl. of Law and Society 118. Opponents of Lord Halsbury in *Allen* v. *Flood* did not sit in *Quinn* v. *Leathem*. "Lord Herschell had died . . . and Lords Davey and James were the only available Law Lords who were not invited by Halsbury to sit on the case."

[90] [1898] A.C. 1.

[91] See Kahn-Freund, "The legal framework," in Flanders and Clegg *The System of Industrial Relations in Great Britain* (1954) p. 115 where he points out that the common law is based on the fiction of equality of individuals.

[92] [1942] A.C. 435 at 443.

[93] Christie, *The liability of strikers in the law of tort*, Chap. 3.

[94] *Quinn* v. *Leathem* [1901] A.C. 495 at 506.

[95] *Huntley* v. *Thornton* [1957] 1 W.L.R. 321; [1957] 1 All E.R. 234.

[96] [1964] A.C. 1129.

or threaten to commit an unlawful act himself, but it is suggested that this will only be so where he knows that the acts of the others are unlawful.

As to parties, company directors may conspire together and with the company since it is a legal entity; so also union officials may conspire but it is doubtful if the union itself is a sufficient legal entity to be a conspirator.[97]

The purpose

It is clear that the action of the defendants must be aimed at the plaintiffs: it must be their purpose to cause injury. In *Crofter Hand Woven Harris Tweed* v. *Veitch*[98] Viscount Simon L.C. said:

> "The test is not what is the natural result to the plaintiffs of such combined action, or what is the resulting damage which the defendants realize or should realize will follow, but what is in truth the object in the minds of the combiners when they acted as they did. It is not consequence that matters, but purposes; the relevant conjunction is not . . . 'so that' but . . . 'in order that'."

This makes it clear that the tort is strictly one of intention, and neither recklessness nor negligence will suffice.

Just cause or excuse

It is apparent that the doctrine of conspiracy could easily inhibit competition between traders by forbidding them to combine in order to compete. The problem arose in *Mogul Steamship Co.* v. *McGregor Gow & Co.*[99] where the defendants combined together to exclude the plaintiff from the China sea trade and thus establish a monopoly. In the days of laissez-faire the courts decided that they should not intervene to determine what were and what were not fair methods of trade, and thus held that as the defendants were acting to advance their own legitimate interests they were not liable. While the courts wisely held they could not regulate competition, the same view was not held on the subject of industrial relations and it was not until 30 years later that the same doctrine was applied to a case involving a trade union.[1]

The leading case in *Crofter Hand Woven Harris Tweed* v. *Veitch*[2] where yarn obtained from the mainland was cheaper than that made in the mills on the island of Lewis. The plaintiffs imported this yarn into the island where it was woven by the crofters. The defendants were officials of the T.G.W.U. to which the workers in the island mills and the dockers at Stornoway belonged, and they combined with the owners of the island mills to establish an embargo on yarn coming from the mainland.The House of Lords held that the predominant purpose of the combiners was the promotion of their own legitimate interests and therefore they were not liable

No definition has been given of what is to be regarded as within a union's legitimate interest. Self interest is clearly sufficient but in the case of altruism it may be more difficult to establish a legitimate interest. However in *Scala Ballroom (Wolverhampton)* v. *Radcliffe*[3] the defendants were held not liable

---

[97] The matter is largely irrelevant since in nearly all cases the union would be protected by T.U.L.R.A. 1974 s. 14.

[98] [1942] A.C. 435 at 445.

[99] [1892] A.C. 25 (H.L.). See also (1889) 23 Q.B.D. 598 (C.A.).

[1] *Reynolds* v. *Shipping Federation* [1924] 1 Ch. 28. The case involved a pre-entry closed shop agreement.

[2] [1942] A.C. 435.

[3] [1958] 1 W.L.R. 1057; [1958] 3 All E.R. 220.

for conspiring to force the plaintiff to lift a colour-bar in his ballroom. Hodson L.J. was not prepared to say that the "interests which can lawfully be protected are confined to the material interests, in the sense of interests which can be exchanged for cash," and he went on to say that the defendants may have been justified in "looking after their members' interests and, taking the long view, in looking after their livelihood as well."[4]

So far as a trade union is concerned "legitimate interests" would certainly cover matters which could form the subject matter of a trade dispute and cases have mentioned the closed shop,[5] more secure collective bargaining, better wage prospects,[6] and "the advantage of the union as a whole."[7] That the phrase is wider than that envisaged by the definition of trade dispute is indicated by the view of Lord Reid in *Stratford* v. *Lindley*[8] that "the respondents acted ... to forward what they believed to be the interests of the union and fundamental trade union principles." An honest belief that these were the objects of the activity was sufficient to exclude liability, even though it was held that there was no trade dispute.

In some cases, however, there is sufficient evidence of ulterior motive to make what appears to be a legitimate activity unjustified. In *Huntley* v. *Thortnton*[9] the plaintiff, having called the members of the district committee of his union "a shower," was expelled from the union and hounded out of a number of jobs. Some defendants were held to have done this for personal reasons, thinking only of their ruffled dignity, and were therefore liable in conspiracy; but two of the defendants were held not liable because their objective was not to injure the plaintiff, but only to pursue what they believed to be valid trade union objectives.

Whether if only one of the defendants had improper motives he could be made liable if the other members had lawful motives is an open question, although a dictum in the High Court of Australia[10] suggests that on the logic of the principle in *Allen* v. *Flood*[11] there should be no liability.

Another problem occurs where the parties to the conspiracy clearly have different interests to protect. In the *Crofter*[12] case itself the unions and the employers had different immediate interests, although it could also be said that they had the common long term interest of a prosperous industry. Lord Wright said:[13]

> "I do not accept, as a general proposition, that there must be a complete identity of interest between parties to a combination. There must, however, be sufficient identity of object, though the advantage to be derived from that object may not be the same."

---

[4] *Ibid.* at 1063. Morris L.J. supported the result on the ground that as "they honestly believe that it is the wish of their members that such policy should prevail, and that there should be no colour bar discrimination, it can be said that the welfare of the members is being advanced, even though it cannot be entirely translated into or shown to be reflected in detailed financial terms."

[5] *Reynolds* v. *Shipping Federation* [1924] 1 Ch. 28.

[6] The *Crofter* case [1942] A.C. 435 at 447, *per* Viscount Simon L.C.

[7] *Ibid.* at 480, *per* Lord Wright.

[8] [1965] A.C. 269 at 323.

[9] [1957] 1 W.L.R. 321. See also *Evaskow* v. *International Brotherhood of Boilermakers* (1969) 4 D.L.R. 3d 684. (Man.Q.B.); (1970) 9 D.L.R. 3d 715 (Man. C.A.).

[10] *McKernan* v. *Frazer* (1931) 46 C.L.R. 343 at 409, *per* Evatt J.

[11] [1898] A.C. 1.

[12] [1942] A.C. 435.

[13] *Ibid.* at 479, *per* Lord Wright.

The opposite of that kind of problem is where the conspirators have in mind different objectives, that is where the combiners feel they are killing two birds with one stone.[14] Viscount Simon said that the matter is to be determined by discovering the "predominant" purpose of the conspiracy.

Statutory protection

Nobody can be made liable for this form of the tort if he is acting in contemplation or furtherance of a trade dispute.[15]

REMEDIES

It is a characteristic of the torts discussed in this chapter that the remedy usually sought by the plaintiff is an interlocutory injunction.[16] Indeed very few such cases ever go to full trial since the plaintiff will usually have obtained what he wants from the interlocutory injunction and the case is then dropped.[17]

The interlocutory injunction has been severely critised in its application to trade dispute cases.[18] First it was permissible to grant the injunction in the absence of the defendants in cases of urgency. This was objectionable if in reality the case was only likely to be heard at the interlocutory stage and in view of the fact that the grant of such an injunction often meant not the delay of the dispute pending the full trial but rather the defeat of the union.[19] Accordingly the Trade Union and Labour Relations Act 1974 section 17 (1) now provides that where the defendant claims, or the court thinks it likely that he will claim, that he acted in contemplation or furtherance of a trade dispute, the court shall not grant the injunction unless it is satisfied that all steps which in the circumstances were reasonable have been taken to secure the defendants an opportunity to be heard.[20]

Secondly the nature of the proceedings is such that the individual interests of an employer-plaintiff are more likely to be protected by the court than the collective interests of the union-defendant. This is so because the interests of the individual are more likely to be quantifiable than those of the union, since the latter may simply consist of the freedom to strike or protest in order to induce action. Whatever may have been the case before 1975, it can now be said that after the decision in *American Cyanamid* v. *Ethicon*[21] the situation is likely to be even less satisfactory, although to some extent it has been remedied by statute.

For present purposes *American Cyanamid* may be said to stand for the following propositions:

(1) An applicant for an interlocutory injunction need no longer show that he

---

[14] *Ibid.* at 445, *per* Viscount Simon.

[15] T.U.L.R.A. 1974 s. 13 (4).

[16] Under R.S.C., Ord. 29 r.1.

[17] See for example *Stratford* v. *Lindley* (No. 2) [1969] 1 W.L.R. 1547, which was concerned only with costs.

[18] See generally Anderman and Davies, "Injunction Procedure in Labour Disputes" (1973) 2 I.L.J. 213 and (1974) 3 I.L.J. 30.

[19] This is so because the union is denied its principal weapon and the employer is not required to resolve the dispute. Even if the employer is required to engage in bargaining, such a process is only enforceable by the sanction of the strike—which has been denied to the union.

[20] But see the application of this provision in *Gouriet* v. *U.P.W.* [1978] A.C. 435, where although the union ultimately claimed that there was a trade dispute the House of Lords held that there was no reason for the court to think they would do so. See *per* Viscount Dilhorne at 487 and *per* Lord Fraser at 524.

[21] [1975] A.C. 396.

has a prima facia case, but rather the court should consider the balance of convenience unless the material before the court fails to disclose that the plaintiff has any real propect of succeeding at the full trial,[22] or that there is a serious issue to be tried.

(2) That in deciding the balance of convenience the court should consider (a) whether if no injunction were awarded and the plaintiff succeeded at the full trial, would damages adequately compensate him for loss suffered in the meantime, and (b) whether if the injunction were granted would the plaintiffs' undertakings as to damages be sufficient to compensate the defendant for loss suffered in the meantime if the defendant finally won.

This formulation of the test to be applied suffers from two principal defects in relation to labour law. First the plaintiff does not have to put up a prima facie case that the defendant's action is illegal, but only that there is a serious question to be tried on the issue. Secondly the formulation of the balance of convenience destroys any real chance of the defendant's collective interest to be protected.[23]

It therefore became obvious that the principles of *American Cyanamid*[24] could quickly subvert the right to strike, not only because the torts in this area are of dubious extent and it could be argued that an attempt to extend the law could be a serious issue to be tried, but also because potential damage to an employer's business was likely to be preferred to the unions' interest in the freedom to strike. Accordingly the Trade Union and Labour Relations Act 1974 section 17 (2)[25] now provides (except in Scotland) that where the defendant claims that he was acting in contemplation or furtherance of a trade dispute the court must, in exercising its discretion, have regard to the likelihood of the defendant establishing at the full trial a defence under section 13, 14 (2) or 15 of the 1974 Act (which broadly deal with statutory protection from the torts in this chapter and from liability for picketing).[26]

The effect of this provision is therefore to reverse the effect of *American Cyanamid*, but only in trade dispute cases and only in so far as the statutory defences are concerned. If the matter in issue relates to the question of whether the actions of the defendant come within the tort at all, then the full rigour of *American Cyanamid* applies to that issue. Unfortunately it appears that the courts are avoiding the need to decide the substantive issues by adopting a procedural approach, and thus appear willing to issue injunctions even in cases where no prima facie case of illegality has been established,[27] and

---

[22] This negative formulation (put forward by Lord Diplock), shows how light the burden is. But see *Camellia Tanker* v. *I.T.F.* [1976] I.C.R. 274 at 300 where it was noted that counsel had "helpfully and realistically conceded that in order to succeed on the motion the plaintiffs had at some stage to show that they had a good arguable case." The use of the heavier burden can only be commended.

[23] See the unfortunate case of *Hubbard* v. *Pitt* [1975] I.C.R. 308 (which did not involve a trade dispute) where the plaintiff's interest in preventing potential partial loss of custom was preferred to the defendant's interest in freedom of speech and demonstration. The legal issues in the case were discussed only by Lord Denning, the other judges preferring to avoid the issues and rely on the procedural solution.

[24] [1975] A.C. 396.

[25] As inserted by E.P.A. 1975 Sched. 16.

[26] See *B.B.C.* v. *Hearn* [1977] I.C.R. 685 where the defendants failed to establish that they would be likely to succeed at the full trial in establishing that there was a trade dispute, and on the balance of convenience an interlocutory injunction was issued. See also *The Camilla M, Star Sea Transport Corp.* v. *Slater* [1978] I.R.L.R. 507 (C.A.).

[27] *Hubbard* v. *Pitt* [1975] I.C.R. 308 and *Losinska* v. *C.P.S.A.* [1976] I.C.R. 473 are examples.

indeed are even prepared to issue mandatory injunctions on such a basis.[28] However, it must be admitted that in the majority of trade dispute cases the issue will be resolved on the basis of the defences available, where the plaintiff's chances of success are now relevant. But it is sincerely to be hoped that the principles of *American Cyanamid*[29] will in time be held to be inapplicable to trade union cases at all.

[28] *Shotton* v. *Hammond, The Times*, October 26, 1976.
[29] [1975] A.C. 396.

CHAPTER 13

PICKETING

CRIMINAL LIABILITY UNDER THE GENERAL LAW

THE criminal law now provides few restraints on the activities of trade unionists; the principal area of interest concerns picketing and the extent to which an immunity is conferred on pickets by statute.

Picketing practice has changed a great deal during the course of this century, for while it used to be directed primarily at preventing the use of blackleg labour and to persuading colleagues to join the strike, attention is now being turned to secondary activity—that is picketing not the picket's own place of work but rather someone else's place of work. For example the miners' strikes of 1972 and 1974 made it clear that a very effective form of picketing is to prevent the use of alternatives to one's own product—in this case preventing the delivery of oil to power stations in order to make the strike more effective more quickly.[1] Some viewed the extension of picketing practice with alarm.[2] At the time a number of promises to review the law of picketing were made, and there are still calls for reform both from those who want to see more stringent laws and from those who want the rules to be made more liberal. In practice, as will be seen, the police possess a more than adequate battery of powers to control activity which goes beyond usual picketing practice; furthermore it can be argued that the present restrictions on picketing severely curtail the freedom of expression whether by speech or by demonstration that was thought to exist.[3] *Hubbard* v. *Pitt*[4] showed just how fragile these freedoms are.

Picketing is also one of those areas where there is widespread misunderstanding of the substance of the applicable rules (or rather of the restrictive interpretation put upon them by the judges) and this has meant a gulf between the expectations of trade unionists and the usual practice on the one hand, and the law itself and its occasional application on the other. Such a misunderstanding makes it difficult to enforce the law.

The control of picketing activity is achieved by applying the general crimi-

---

[1] See Trice "Methods of and attitudes to picketing" (1975) Crim.L.R. 271. During the 1972 strike Mr. Daly said that picketing had been "the one way of shortening this dispute and moving from government dictation to a just settlement". *The Guardian*, January 14, 1972.

[2] It has been held on an interlocutory application that secondary picketing is illegal as it is not in furtherance of the original dispute. *United Biscuits* v. *Fall*, The Guardian, January 27, 1979. But the matter is not yet finally settled.

[3] See the important article by Bercusson, "One hundred years of conspiracy and protection of property: time for a change" (1977) 40 M.L.R. 268, which cogently argues that lawyers and the legal system have persistently adopted a perspective which "attempts to establish an equilibrium based on the maintenance of capitalist interests as owners and employers and sees the picket line as disrupting this equilibrium and thus illegal."

[4] [1975] I.C.R. 77 and 308. The case has been heavily criticised and is discussed below.

nal law, subject to the immunities conferred by statute on those who are acting in contemplation or furtherance of a trade dispute.[5] The offences which are often related to picketing are obstruction of the highway, obstructing a constable in the execution of his duty and engaging in threatening, abusive or insulting behaviour.[6] These will be dealt with in more detail after discussion of the statutory immunity.

The statutory immunity

Section 15 of the Trade Union and Labour Relations Act 1974 states:

"It shall be lawful for one or more persons in contemplation or furtherance of a trade dispute to attend at or near:

(a) a place where another person works or carries on business; or
(b) any other place where another person happens to be, not being a place where he resides,

for the purpose only of peacefully obtaining or communicating information or peacefully persuading any person to work or abstain from working.[7]

Such a section could provide a wide immunity to those engaged in picketing, but in fact it has been very narrowly interpreted by the courts.[8] This has been achieved by saying that the only function of the precursor of this section in the Trade Disputes Act 1906 was to cure the problems created by *Lyons* v. *Wilkins.*[9] That case was mainly concerned with the Conspiracy and Protection of Property Act 1875, but it has been held to be authority for the view that the mere presence of pickets is illegal at common law. Lord Lindley M.R. said[10]:

> "The truth is that to watch or beset a man's house with a view to compel him to do or not do what is lawful for him not to do or to do is wrongful and without lawful authority unless some reasonable justification for it is consistent with the evidence. Such conduct seriously interferes with the ordinary comfort of human existence and ordinary enjoyment of the

---

[5] For general articles on the law relating to picketing see Drake, "The right to picket peacefully" (1972) 1 I.L.J. 212; Wallington "The case of the Longannet Miners and the criminal liability of pickets" (1972) 1 I.L.J. 219; Kidner, "Picketing and the criminal law," [1975] Crim.L.R. 256.

[6] Between June 13, 1977 and January 1978, 500 people were arrested on the (occasionally militant) picket line at Grunwick Laboratories Ltd. The offences for which they were charged were:

Obstructing a police officer in the execution of his duty	208
Threatening, abusive or insulting behaviour	114
Obstruction of the highway	106
Assaulting a police officer	104
Criminal damage	6
Possession of an offensive weapon	4
Assault occasioning grievous bodily harm	1
Assault occasioning actual bodily harm	1

H.C.Debs., Vol. 941, *col. 136*, (January 17, 1978).

[7] The origin of this exemption lies in the proviso to s. 7 of the Conspiracy and Protection of Property Act, 1875. The immunity was extended by the Trade Disputes Act 1906, s. 2. The Industrial Relations Act 1971, s. 134 removed the exemption for picketing a person's house and completely re-drafted the section, but that did not affect the substantive interpretation: *per* Viscount Dilhorne in *Broome* v. *D.P.P.* [1974] I.C.R. 84 at 93. The present statute reverts to the form of the 1906 Act.

[8] See for example *R.* v. *Wall* (1907) 21 Cox 401 where Palles C.B. thought that the right to attend did not cover "watching" on the ground that "attending" is more temporary than "watching". This would not be followed today. See *Ferguson* v. *O'Gorman* [1937] I.R. 620.

[9] [1896] 1 Ch. 811 and [1899] 1 Ch. 255.

[10] [1899] 1 Ch. 255 at 267.

house beset, and such conduct would support an action on the case for nuisance at common law."

The authority for such a statement is extremely doubtful,[11] and it may be that picketing is perfectly lawful at common law.[12] At least this was the view emphatically taken by Lord Denning in his dissenting judgment in *Hubbard* v. *Pitt*[13] when he said that picketing which is not protected by the trade dispute legislation is nevertheless lawful. He said[14]: "Picketing is lawful so long as it is done merely to obtain or communicate information, or peacefully to persuade: and is not such as to submit any other person to any kind of restraint or restriction of his personal freedom."[15]

It is therefore suggested that the substantive decision of *Lyons* v. *Wilkins*[16] is no longer authoritative and that it serves only as an explanation of why the section has been so narrowly interpreted by the judges, despite its potential scope. The point is that in 1906 it was thought necessary to pass legislation to reverse the effect of the case,[17] (if in fact it did declare picketing to be *per se* illegal), and therefore the legislation has been interpreted as being limited to doing that and nothing else.

The mischief at which the statute was aimed was the possibility that picketing amounted to a trespass to the highway and also a nuisance, not because of the obstruction to the highway, but because of the inconvenience caused to the persons being picketed. In *Tynan* v. *Balmer*[18] Widgery J. said:

> "As [Counsel] has suggested, it would seem that the genesis of that section is the decision in the Court of Appeal in *J.Lyons & Sons* v. *Wilkins*[19] . . . It is of great interest to see that in that case it was accepted as possible at common law that watching and besetting a man's house would be a nuisance and a wrongful act, quite apart from any obstruction to the highway thereby caused. One should not, in my judgment therefore regard [the section] as primarily a highway section because there may be many other wrongs which could be committed by citizens which are now authorized by that section."

It is clear therefore that despite the words "it shall be lawful . . ." in the section the effect is not to confer a right to picket as such but to provide an immunity from those offences which a person might by the very nature of his activity commit, and this immunity applies only as long as he has the purpose of

---

[11] See Citrine, *Trade Union Law,* (3rd ed.) pp. 558–562.

[12] *Lyons* v. *Wilkins* was cited with approval in *Thompson-Schwab* v. *Costaki* [1956] 1 W.L.R. 335, but in *Hubbard* v. *Pitt* [1973] I.C.R. 308 at 317 Lord Denning said that the statement quoted "had not stood the test of time". See also *Ward Lock* v. *Operative Printers' Assistants Society* (1906) 22 T.L.R. 327.

[13] [1975] I.C.R. 308.

[14] *Ibid.* at 319.

[15] At first instance Forbes J. followed the traditional view of *Lyons* v. *Wilkins* [1975] I.C.R. 77. Of the majority in the Court of Appeal Orr L.J. confined himself to saying that there was a serious issue to be tried on the *Lyons* v. *Wilkins* issue, and Stamp L.J. said that he could not regard the conclusion of Forbes J. as a satisfactory application of the law to the facts. It is to be sincerely regretted that the majority refused to decide the issue, relying instead on *American Cyanamid* v. *Ethicon* [1975] A.C. 396 and principles relating to interlocutory injunctions. See also *Broome* v. *D.P.P.* [1974] I.C.R. 84 at 96 *per* Lord Salmon where it is assumed that picketing amounts *per se* to a nuisance at common law.

[16] [1899] 1 Ch. 255.

[17] Although it has been argued that this objective may have been achieved by *Ward Lock* v. *Operative Printers' Assistants* (1906) 22 T.L.R. 327.

[18] [1967] 1 Q.B. 91 at 106.

[19] [1899] 1 Ch. 255.

"peacefully[20] communicating information[21] or persuading any person to work or abstain from working." If his purpose changes, he loses the benefit of the section.The courts therefore ask themselves whether anything unlawful was done other than that which was reasonably necessary for the communication of information and in answering this have taken as a paradigm a small number of pickets standing quietly outside factory gates holding placards and requesting passers by to stop and listen to them.The section legitimises such activity: it justifies a trespass to the highway,[22] (but not to private property)[23] and excuses a technical nuisance at common law, but no more.

Bearing in mind the limited nature of the immunity, it remains to be seen how it is applied to certain offences commonly used in relation to picketing.

Obstruction of the highway

One of the most common offences charged is obstruction of the highway contrary to section 121 of the Highways Act 1959 which states:

> "If a person, without lawful authority or excuse, in any way wilfully obstructs the free passage along a highway he shall be guilty of an offence and shall be liable in respect thereof to a fine not exceeding [fifty] pounds."[24]

The leading authority on the interpretation of this section is *Nagy* v. *Weston*[25] where Lord Parker C.J. said :

> "It is undoubtedly true . . . that there must be proof that the use in question was an unreasonable use. Whether or not the user amounting to an obstruction is or is not an unreasonable use of the highway is a question of fact. It depends upon all the circumstances, including the length of time the obstruction continues, the place where it occurs, the purpose for which it is done, and of course whether it does in fact cause an actual obstruction as opposed to a potential obstruction."[26]

In view of the last few words it is clearly not an absolute defence to show that nobody was actually obstructed, but on the other hand neither can there be a conviction on the ground of potential obstruction alone, for that potential obstruction must be shown to be unreasonable.[27] It may be that the effect of section 15 of the Trade Union and Labour Relations Act is to say that reasonable picketing for the relevant purposes is not an unreasonable use of the highway, but that as soon as one leaves the limited protection of that

---

[20] It has been, somewhat bizarrely, suggested that a person is not acting peacefully if the information he is communicating is untrue: *Ryan* v. *Cooke* [1937] I.R. 512 at 522.

[21] It has also been suggested that the right to communicate information does not include the right to suggest that customers of the picketed firm should take their business elsewhere. *Brendan Dunne* v. *Fitzpatrick* [1958] I.R. 29 at 46. It is suggested that this is too narrow an interpretation.

[22] *Fergusson* v. *O'Gorman* [1937] I.R. 620. The prevalence of Irish cases in this topic is to be regretted, as the Irish Courts have consistently taken a stringent approach to the law of picketing.

[23] *Larkin* v. *Belfast Harbour Commissioners* [1908] 2 I.R. 214; *McCusker* v. *Smith* [1918] I.R. 432.

[24] A constable may arrest a person without a warrant for this offence. The maximum fine is laid down by the Criminal Justice Act 1967, s. 92 and Sched. 3.

[25] [1965] 1 W.L.R. 280 at 284.

[26] This quotation was approved by Lord Denning in *Hubbard* v. *Pitt* [1975] I.C.R. 308 at 316 in relation to picketing.

[27] For this reason it is suggested that dicta in *Wolverton U.D.C.* v. *Willis* [1962] 1 All E.R. 243 that any encroachment on the freedom of the public to use the whole of the highway (*i.e.* if the highway is rendered less commodious) should be limited to either the common law or to the particular statute in question in that case, the Town Police Clauses Act 1847, s. 28, dealing with projection into the highway.

statute, the law of obstruction applies.Thus if the purpose is to communicate information or peacefully persuade a person not to work and the pickets are doing no more than is reasonably necessary for that purpose, it is suggested that section 121 of the Highways Act 1959 does not apply.

If the picketing is an obstruction it is no defence to argue that the defendant thought that he had lawful authority to act as he did. Many pickets believe wrongly that there is a "right to picket", but such a belief cannot excuse the act, for *Arrowsmith* v. *Jenkins*[28] makes it clear that *mens rea* is no part of this offence. If anybody by an exercise of free will does something which causes an obstruction, then an offence is committed.[29]

Furthermore it is also apparent that a local authority cannot licence an unlawful use of the highway,[30] so that the offence is committed even if one has the permission of the highway authority. Such permission may however affect the decision whether or not to prosecute.

Obstructing motor vehicles

Information may be communicated to a pedestrian by walking alongside him, but as this is not possible in relation to motor vehicles trade unionists have for some years been claiming the right to stop vehicles in order to attempt to persuade their drivers not to proceed. As a matter of law no such right exists for the claim would be based on the fallacy that there is an enforceable right to communicate information, whereas in fact there is only an immunity from prosecution in certain instances. In *Broome* v. *D.P.P.*[31] the House of Lords made it clear that the stopping of a motor vehicle is an obstruction not permitted by the protective legislation.[32] The House held that the defendant who had stood in front of a lorry trying to enter a factory, was properly convicted under section 121 of the Highways Act 1959. Lord Reid said[33]:

> "Attendance for [the relevant] purpose must I think include the right to try to persude anyone who chooses to stop and listen, at least in so far as this is done in a reasonable way with due consideration for the rights of others.[34] . . . But I see no ground for implying any right to require the person whom it is sought to persuade to submit to any kind of constraint or restriction of his personal freedom. One is familiar with persons at the side of the road signalling to a driver requesting him to stop. It is then for the driver to decide whether he will stop or not. That, in my view, a picket is entitled to do. If the driver stops, the picket can talk to him but only for so long as the driver is willing to listen."

It is, however, not even clear that a picket is legally entitled to signal to a driver to stop, for in *Kavanagh* v. *Hiscock*[35] the police powers to prevent an apprehended breach of the peace and to control the highway were used to prevent pickets even approaching vehicles. This was a case in which there had been an unofficial agreement between the police and the 20–30 pickets that

---

[28] [1963] 2 Q.B. 561.

[29] *Ibid.* at 567 *per* Lord Parker C.J.

[30] *Redbridge London Borough Council* v. *Jacques* [1970] 1 W.L.R. 1604. See also *Hubbard* v. *Pitt* [1975] I.C.R. 77 at 91 *per* Forbes J.

[31] [1974] I.C.R. 84.

[32] See also *Tynan* v. *Balmer* [1967] 1 Q.B. 91 at 107 *per* Lord Parker C.J.

[33] [1974] I.C.R. 84 at 89.

[34] This part of the dictum was explained in *Kavanagh* v. *Hiscock* [1974] I.C.R. 282 at 290 as conferring an immunity, not providing a right.

[35] [1974] I.C.R. 282.

four of their number should be allowed to remain within the police cordon, while the remainder were kept back by the police, as a coach of "blacklegs" was expected. Later the appellant saw these four pickets being cleared from within the cordon and he objected, thinking the rights of the pickets had been infringed. He tried to push through the cordon and in doing so assaulted a policeman, and he was charged with assaulting a constable in the execution of his duty. The Divisional Court upheld the conviction on the ground that the police officer reasonably apprehended a breach of the peace and that the police had a duty to regulate the use of the highway.

Lord Widgery, in explaining the action of the police, said[36]: "It seems to be perfectly clear that the concern of the superintendent was that if nothing was done, the coach would be stopped at the gates [and] there would then be a shouting match . . ."

In his application to the House of Lords for leave to appeal, [37]counsel for the defendant picked up this point and said:

> "If pickets have become demonstrators as they do in such a case, and seek to make their views known from behind a cordon of police officers at a certain distance, then picketing becomes a shouting match, and in my submission there is nothing more likely to be productive of conflict than if pickets are to be restrained behind cordons when there is no suggestion that they are other than peaceful pickets."

The House, however, though the point was covered by *Broom* v. *D.P.P.*[38] saying that while there was a right to attend there was no right to approach, and refused leave to appeal.

Reform picketing of motor vehicles

The particular point that arose in *Kavanagh* v. *Hiscock*[39] was of considerable concern and the then government proposed to deal with it in what became the Employment Protection Act 1975, but the relevant clause was dropped from the Bill.[40]

There has been even more difficulty over the more general question of whether pickets should have the right to actually stop vehicles, but despite promises by the Government to look at this issue no legislation has been forthcoming. The Society of Labour Lawyers has argued[41] that "the provision as to picketing should be extended so as to include a limited right to stop vehicles to communicate with the drivers thereof, due regard being had to other users of the highway." Whether it would be possible to draft such a section may be doubted, and there is considerable resistance to any idea that a motorist should be under a positive duty, presumably backed by criminal sanctions, to stop.

---

[36] *Ibid.* at 288.

[37] [1974] I.R.L.R. 125. (H.L.).

[38] [1974] I.C.R. 84. It is suggested there was room for argument.

[39] [1947] I.C.R. 84.

[40] Cl. 99 of the Bill stated "It is hereby declared that a person exercising a right conferred on him by section 15 of the 1974 Act (peaceful picketing) may, at the place where he is attending, seek by peaceful means, falling short of obstruction of the highway, to persuade another person (whether in a vehicle or not) to stop for the purpose of peacefully obtaining or communicating information from or to that other person or peacefully persuading him to work or abstain from working."

[41] See Donovan Commission, Minutes of Evidence 63. Question 10112.

The Donovan Commission decided against such a right[42] saying that "it would be impossible to define such a right in terms which would avoid considerable obstruction to the highway and serious risk of personal injury to the pickets themselves."[43] It seems that this is the view that is likely to be accepted.

Public nuisance

It is an offence at common law to obstruct the public in the exercise or enjoyment of rights common to all, including the liberty of free passage along the highway.[44]

There is some doubt about the nature of obstruction, but it is suggested that the following points may be made: First the obstruction must be actually unreasonable. Although in *Hubbard* v. *Pitt*[45] Forbes J. held that the elements of nuisance were present because picketing was in itself unreasonable, it is suggested that this dictum places undue reliance on *Lyons* v. *Wilkins*.[46] This view is supported by the fact that in the Court of Appeal[47] Lord Denning believed that unreasonable behaviour of some kind was necessary, and in *R* v. *Clark (No. 2)*[48] the Court of Criminal Appeal pointed out that not only was it necessary to prove the obstruction but also that it was unreasonable. It is therefore suggested that at common law peaceful picketing is not of itself and uneasonable activity, and that to be an offence there must be something more than acts necessary for the communication of information.

Secondly there is the question whether it is necessary to establish an actual obstruction or only that the highway was rendered "less commodious". It is suggested that in principle it should be necessary to prove actual inconvenience but again Forbes J. appeared to take the stricter view and Lord Denning the more liberal.[49]

In *Tynam* v. *Balmer*[50] the issue was whether pickets who were walking in a circle in the public highway were guilty of a public nuisance,[51] and the court stated that leaving aside the trade dispute immunity walking in a circle was an improper use of the highway and therefore a nuisance.[52] The next question was the effect, if any, of the trade dispute exemption. It is probable that if the pickets had been standing *beside* the highway they would have committed no

---

[42] Donovan Commission, Cmnd. 3623 para. 874.

[43] Serious confrontation has occurred between lorries and pickets trying to exercise what they believe to be their legal rights. Mr. Freddie Matthews was killed by an articulated lorry while he was picketing at Keadbey power station. (*The Guardian*, February 4, 1972). Another picket was injured by an oil tanker at Agecroft power station. (*The Guardian*, February 5, 1972), and a police inspector was injured by a lorry at Saltley. (*The Guardian*, February 9, 1972).

[44] The crime is not limited to obstruction, but so far as is known it has not been used against any other activities of pickets.

[45] [1975] I.C.R. 77 at 90.

[46] [1899] 1 Ch. 255.

[47] [1975] I.C.R. 308 at 316. Lord Denning was dissenting, but was the only judge to discuss the substantive issues.

[48] [1964] 2 Q.B. 315.

[49] *Hubbard* v. *Pitt* [1975] 77 and 310. The words "less commodious" are those of Forbes J. at 85. For a thorough discussion of this point (and of this area of the law) see the important article by Wallington, "Injunctions and the right to demonstrate" (1976) 35 C.L.J. 82.

[50] [1967] 1 Q.B. 91.

[51] The charge against the defendant was one of obstructing a constable in execution of his duty, but the court found the case to turn on the issues of public nuisance.

[52] A procession that moves from A to B is not illegal as it would be a proper use of the highway. *Lowdens* v. *Keaveny* [1903] 2 I.R. 82; *Hubbard* v. *Pitt* [1975] I.C.R. 77 at 90 *per* Forbes J.

offence, but the Recorder at first instance found that their purpose and objective in circling in the highway was to seal it off. They therefore lost the protection of the section for their purpose was not only to convey information but also to block the highway. The section authorises the former but not the latter.

The case therefore illustrates the point that even though a picket is doing the very thing allowed by the statute, that is peacefully communicating information, nevertheless he will be liable if his purpose is to do something else as well, such as obstruct the road, unless that degree of obstruction is reasonably necessary for conveying information.

Mass picketing

One issue that has been raised recently is whether mass picketing is of itself illegal as being a public nuisance. If the Trade Union and Labour Relations Act 1974 section 15 allows an individual to attend for the specified purposes can this act become illegal simply because a number of others decide to do the same? The question would often be academic as in many such cases the police would be able to use their powers to prevent an apprehended breach of the peace,[53] but it has been suggested that mass picketing is *per se* illegal. In *Broome* v. *D.P.P.*[54] Lord Reid said:

> "There was a suggestion that if a picket does not have a right to stop a driver or pedestrian the same result could be obtained lawfully by a large number of pickets gathering at the same place and doing nothing . . . But if a picket has a purpose beyond those set out in the section, then his presence becomes unlawful and in many cases such as I have supposed it would not be difficult to infer as a matter of fact that pickets who assemble in unreasonably large numbers do have the purpose of preventing free passage."[55]

Lord Salmon[56] was more doubtful about such a principle saying that the purpose of the pickets would be a matter of fact in each case, although the fact that obstruction was taking place would be some evidence that that was the purpose of the pickets on the ground that men must be taken to intend the natural consequences of their acts.[57]

Breach of the peace

It is an offence under section 51 (3) of the Police Act 1964 to obstruct a constable in the execution of his duty and this charge is often brought in cases of refusal to obey an order given by a constable in pursuance of his duty to control the highway or where he reasonably apprehends a breach of the peace.

In respect of a breach of the peace Lord Parker C.J. said in *Piddington* v. *Bates*.[58]

> "First the mere statement by a constable that he did anticipate that there might be a breach of the peace is clearly not enough. There must exist proved facts from which a constable could reasonably have anticipated

---

[53] *Piddington* v. *Bates* [1960] 3 All E.R. 660.

[54] [1974] I.C.R. 84 at 90.

[55] See also the comments of Judge Chapman at 1st instance in *Tynan* v. *Balmer* [1965] 3 All E.R. 99 at 103.

[56] [1974] I.C.R. 84 at 96.

[57] It appears to be the Home Office view that mere numbers are illegal: see the reply by the Home Secretary H.C. Debs. vol. 831 col. 1487. (February 24, 1972.)

[58] [1960] 3 All E.R. 660.

such a breach. Secondly, it is not enough that his contemplation is that there is a remote possibility but there must be a real possibility of a breach of the peace. Accordingly, in every case it becomes a question whether, on the particular facts, there were reasonable grounds on which a constable charged with this duty reasonably anticipated that a breach of the peace might occur."

In that case two pickets were posted at each entrance of a factory in which about 8 members of staff were working. Piddington wished to join the pickets but was told by the constable that two pickets were quite sufficient. Piddington replied, "I'm going there and you can't stop me. I know my rights," whereupon he "pushed gently past the policeman and was gently arrested." It was noted that there was no obstruction, no intimidation and no threats or intimations of violence. The appellant was charged with obstructing a constable in the execution of his duty and the question arose whether the constable was justified in limiting the number of pickets. Lord Parker C.J. in holding that Piddington was rightly convicted took the view that the police were entitled to limit the number of pickets. He took into account the fact that there were only eight people in the factory,[59] that there were 18 pickets "milling about the street, and trying to form pickets at the doors."[60] He continued:

"The police were fully entitled to think as reasonable men that there was a real danger of something more than mere picketing to obtain or communicate information or to peaceably persuade ... The real criticism, I think, is this: 'Well, to say that only two pickets should be allowed is purely arbitrary. Why two? Why not three? Where do you draw the line? For my part, I think that a police officer charged with the duty of preserving the Queen's peace must be left to take such steps as, on the evidence before him, he thinks are proper.'"

As can be seen *Piddington* v. *Bates*[61] provides the police with considerable power to control the activities of pickets, for everything depends on whether the policeman was justified in apprehending a breach of the peace, and in such a case the statutory exemption for picketing can have no place since it cannot legalise a breach of the peace. *Kavanagh* v. *Hiscock*[62] discussed earlier, is another example of the extensive powers provided by this principle. It should be noted that while the police have the power to arrest for the statutory offence of obstruction of the highway under the Highways Act 1959, there is no power of arrest for obstructing a constable in the execution of his duty in so far as that duty relates to control of the highway, except where a breach of the peace is anticipated.[63] In *Wershof* v. *Metropolitan Police Commissioner*[64] May J. made it clear that a constable might only arrest without a warrant anyone who wilfully obstructed him in the execution of his duty if the nature of that obstruction was such that it actually caused or was likely to cause a breach of the peace, or was calculated to prevent the lawful arrest of another person.

---

[59] There was no evidence that Piddington knew how many people were inside the factory.

[60] He also took into account the fact that the police had been summoned by telephone: but he does not say who made the call or why.

[61] [1960] 3 All E.R. 660.

[62] [1974] I.C.R. 282.

[63] See Leigh, *Police Powers in England and Wales* (1975) p. 92. It has, however, been held sufficient if the facts stated disclose an arrestable offence even if the reason given for the arrest is not such an offence. *Gellberg* v. *Miller* [1961] 1 W.L.R. 153. See Zander, "When is an arrest not an arrest?" (1977) 127 N.L.J. 352 and 379.

[64] [1978] 3 All E.R., 540.

Threatening, abusive or insulting behaviour

Section 5 of the Public Order Act 1936,[65] states:

"Any person who in any public place or at any public meeting:
(a) uses threatening abusive or insulting words or behaviour, or
(b) distributes or displays any writing, sign or visible representation which is threatening, abusive or insulting,
with intent to provoke a breach of the peace or whereby a breach of the peace is likely to be occasioned, shall be guilty of an offence."

It might be thought that this is an offence quite outside the realms of normal picketing, but it seems to be one that is often used against pickets, either for action against those trying to run the picket line or because of abuse of the police. The definition of the offence must be vague but Lord Reid said[66] that vigorous, and it may be distasteful or unmannerly speech or behaviour is permitted so long as it does not go beyond any one of the three limits of being threatening, abusive or insulting, each of which are easily recognisable by the ordinary man.

It is unlikely that any defence under section 15 of the Trade Union Labour Relations Act could be relevant to this charge.

Unlawful assembly, affray and riot

As the activities of pickets drift further away from the norm other offences may become relevant. In *R.* v. *Jones*[67] one of the charges was that of unlawful assembly which was said to consist of (1) the assembly (usually stated as being of three or more) and (2) the intention of fulfilling a common purpose in such a manner as to endanger the public peace.[68] Although theoretically appropriate to picketing this is a rare charge.

Affray consists[69] of unlawful fighting by one or more persons in a public place (or a display of force by one or more persons without actual violence) in such a manner that reasonable people might be frightened or intimidated. While this was also one of the charges in *R.* v. *Jones*,[70] it is not commonly used against pickets. So far as is known riot is not a charge that has been used recently.[71]

Conspiracy

Since the passing of the Criminal Law Act 1977 the ambit of the crime of conspiracy has been reduced, but a charge of conspiracy is still theoretically possible.

[65] As substituted by the Race Relations Act 1965, s. 7 and continued by the Race Relations Act 1976, s. 79 (6).

[66] *Brutus* v. *Cozens* [1972] A.C. 854.

[67] [1974] I.C.R. 310. (The Shrewsbury pickets.)

[68] *Ibid.* at 321 *per* James L.J.

[69] See Smith and Hogan, *Criminal Law*, 4th ed. p. 757; *R.* v. *Summers* (1972) 56 Cr. App. R. 604. See also *Taylor* v. *D.P.P.* (1973) 57 Cr. App. R. 915.

[70] [1974] I.C.R. 310. The convictions for affray were quashed on appeal as the count was bad for duplicity. It was said that each fight or show of force itself constituted an affray, and that each affray must be charged separately.

[71] For these three offences see Archbold, *Criminal Pleading, Evidence and Practice* (39th ed.) Chap. 25; and Lustgarten, Common Law Crimes and Trade Union Activities (1976) 27 N.I.L.Q. 216; Birtles, "The Common Law Power of the Police to Control Public Meetings" (1973) 36 M.L.R. 587.

It is no longer possible to be charged with conspiracy to commit a tort,[72] so that conspiracy to trespass is no longer a crime.[73] In addition section 1 (3) of the Act states that if a person is acting in contemplation or furtherance of a trade dispute he cannot be charged with conspiracy to commit a summary offence which is not punishable with imprisonment. This would make it impossible to bring a charge of conspiracy to obstruct the highway under section 121 of the Highways Act 1959, but it seems theoretically possible to be convicted of conspiracy to commit the common law crime of public nuisance by obstructing the highway.

In *R.* v. *Jones*[74] the defendants were charged with conspiracy to intimidate under section 7 of the Conspiracy and Protection of Property Act 1875. Such a charge is still possible, but by virtue of section 3 of the Criminal Law Act 1977 the maximum sentence of imprisonment for conspiracy is now the same as that for the substantive offence.[75]

Civil Liability

The importance of civil liability[76] for picketing lies not so much in the potential award of damages but in the possibility of obtaining an injunction to restrain the picketing. Unfortunately this subject has been considerably affected by the new principles governing the granting of interlocutory injunctions announced by the House of Lords in *American Cyanamid* v. *Ethicon.*[77] As a result of that decision it is no longer necessary for the plaintiff to establish a prima facie case but only that there is a serious issue to be tried. If that can be done the matter is resolved by the balance of convenience which is largely decided by the question whether if the wrong decision is made at the interlocutory stage the person who loses at the full trial could adequately compensate the person who wins, and consideration of which party will suffer the greater injustice if the injunction is either granted or not granted. The main difficulty with the *American Cyanamid* principle is that it allows the court to grant an interlocutory injunction without the plaintiff having to establish that the conduct of the defendant is prima facie illegal.[78]

In relation to trade dispute cases these disadvantages have been partially ameliorated by section 17 (2) of the Trade Union and Labour Relations Act 1974[79] which requires that where the defendant claims that he was acting in contemplation or furtherance of a trade dispute the court must take into account the likelihood of his being able to establish a defence of lawful picketing under section 15 of the Act. The point to note is that this section does not alter the application of *American Cyanamid* principles to the substantive tort, but only in relation to the statutory defence.

---

[72] Except where the act amounts to conspiracy to defraud: see Chap. 14. The act may still amount to the tort of conspiracy.

[73] But see the Criminal Law Act 1977, s. 6 (using violence to secure entry), s. 7 (occupation of residential premises), s. 8 (trespassing with a weapon), s. 9 (trespassing on foreign mission).

[74] [1974] I.C.R. 310.

[75] Three months imprisonment. Some defendants in *R.* v. *Jones* were sentenced to terms from 9 months to 3 years. The substantive offence is discussed later in this chapter.

[76] For a thorough discussion of this crime see Wallington "Injunctions and the right to demonstrate" (1976) 35 C.L.J. 82.

[77] [1975] A.C. 396.

[78] *Hubbard* v. *Pitt* [1975] I.C.R. 308.

[79] As inserted by the E.P.A. 1975, Sched. 16.

In addition section 15 of the Trade Union and Labour Relations Act 1974 extends the same immunity to a civil action as it does to a criminal prosecution.

Trespass to the highway

One of the torts which could give rise to the issue of an injunction against pickets is trespass to the highway, which involves an improper use of a public right of way. The right of the public to use the highway is somewhat limited and has been defined as "a right to use it reasonably for passage and re-passage and for any other purpose reasonably incidental thereto."[80] If therefore the highway is being used for a purpose other than those mentioned, the participants will be committing a trespass,[81] and picketing would not be regarded as an activity reasonably incidental to the right of passage.[82] However, the only person who could sue for the trespass is the owner of the soil and in most cases today the highway is vested in the local authority. It seems unlikely that a local authority would wish to sue, but even if it did it would be unable to show any substantial loss and would thus be limited to nominal damages only, and as such damages would be adequate for the loss suffered, if any, the court should not be willing to grant the secondary remedy of an injunction.[83] The owner of the adjacent land has no right to sue unless the road is a private one and he owns the soil under the highway up to the median line.[84]

Furthermore section 15 of the Trade Union and Labour Relations Act 1974 clearly legalises a trespass to the highway in trade dispute cases,[85] but only where the purpose of the pickets is to peacefully communicate information or persuade any person to work or abstain from working.

As section 15 of the 1974 Act only provides immunities for pickets who "attend *at or near*" premises it has been held that this does not cover being on or in premises and so does not justify a trespass to private property.[86] Thus in *McCusker* v. *Smith*[87] the defendant was not protected when he entered the plaintiff's pub in order to persuade a customer to go elsewhere.

Nuisance

The most likely torts to be used in a civil action against pickets are public and private nuisance.[88] As we have seen public nuisance is a crime, but it can also found a civil action in the case of a person who suffers damage over and above that suffered by members of the public in general.[89] Private nuisance concerns unreasonable interference with the use and enjoyment of land belonging to another.

While it is clear that loss arising out of one's right to use the highway is a

[80] *Hubbard* v. *Pitt* [1975] I.C.R. 77 at 83 per Forbes J.

[81] *Harrison* v. *Duke of Rutland* [1893] 1 Q.B. 142; *Hickman* v. *Maisey* [1900] 1 Q.B. 752.

[82] But a "moving crowd"—*i.e.* a procession, is lawful, provided the use of the highway is reasonable. *Lowdens* v. *Keaveney* [1903] 2 I.R. 82 at 89.

[83] In *Hubbard* v. *Pitt* [1975] I.C.R. 308 at 317 Lord Denning M.R. said that the local authority could not sue at all as "no wrong had been done to them or their interest". Traditionally, however, trespass to land is actionable *per se*, that is without proof of damage, and it is suggested that Lord Denning's view would not be followed.

[84] The adjoining owner does, however, have remedies in the law of nuisance.

[85] *Ferguson* v. *O'Gorman* [1937] I.R. 620.

[86] *Larkin* v. *Belfast Harbour Commissioners* [1908] 2 I.R. 214.

[87] [1918] 2 I.R. 432.

[88] See generally Winfield and Jolowicz, *Tort* (10th ed.) Chap. 15, Salmond, *Torts* (17th ed.) Chap. 4.

[89] *Barker* v. *Penley* [1893] 2 Ch. 447; *Lyons* v. *Gulliver* [1914] 1 Ch. 631.

matter of public nuisance, there is some doubt as to whether activities on a highway which cause loss to the owners of adjoining premises are a matter of public or private nuisance. While the more traditional view would be that public nuisance is more appropriate in such a case,[90] it is unlikely that the extension of private nuisance to this area will make any significant difference,[91] especially as damage must be proved in both cases.

The central case on the civil liability of pickets (at least where there is no trade dispute) is *Hubbard* v. *Pitt.*[92] In that case the defendants, who were members of the Islington Tenants Campaign, objected to the activities of the plaintiff estate agents on the grounds that they believed them to have been assisting developers who had been harassing tenants. Accordingly a picket, consisting of between four and eight people holding placards, was placed on the highway by the plaintiff's offices. The pickets behaved in an orderly and peaceful manner throughout, but in the event an interlocutory injunction was granted restraining them from attending at the plaintiff's offices.[93]

Unfortunately the form of the case is most unsatisfactory for although at first instance Forbes J. delivered a judgment on the substantive issues, the only judge to do so in the Court of Appeal was Lord Denning, and he dissented. The majority of the Court affirmed the injunction granted by Forbes J. by reference to the principles of *American Cyanamid* v. *Ethicon*[94] on interlocutory injunctions and the balance of convenience, and refused to discuss the substantive issues despite the likelihood that the case would never go to full trial.[95] As Lord Denning realised, this made the court appear to prefer the interest of the plaintiff in uninterrupted access to his commercial property to the defendants' interest in freedom of speech, and it is suggested that the views of Lord Denning are very much to be preferred.

Forbes J. said that the presence of the pickets amounted to both a trespass to the highway and a public nuisance. As to the latter he thought that it was not necessary to show that the obstruction was unreasonable but only that it rendered the highway "less commodious."[96] Lord Denning rejected that view, saying that there could be no action as there was no obstruction and no breach of the peace.[97]

As to private nuisance the main issue is the validity or otherwise of the view of Lindley M.R. in *Lyons* v. *Wilkins*[98] that picketing may of itself amount to a nuisance simply because of the attempt to persuade, and regardless of any obstruction caused. It is suggested that this opinion must be firmly rejected, first because even at the time it was offered there was little authority for it and much against it,[99] secondly because it is inconsistant with *Ward Lock* v. *Operative Printers Assistants Society*[1] and thirdly because it has been con-

[90] *Halsey* v. *Esso Petroleum* [1961] 1 W.L.R. 683.
[91] *Hubbard* v. *Pitt* [1975] I.C.R. 308 per Lord Denning M.R.
[92] [1975] I.C.R. 77 and 308.
[93] Although libel was also alleged, no interlocutory injunction was granted as the defendants had pleaded that the words were true. *Bonnard* v. *Perryman* [1891] 2 Ch. 269.
[94] [1975] A.C. 396.
[95] It never did.
[96] [1975] I.C.R. 77 at 90.
[97] *Ibid.* at 316.
[98] [1879] 1 Ch. 255 at 267.
[99] Citrine, *Trade Union Law (3rd ed.) pp. 558—562.*
[1] (1906) 22 T.L.R. 327.

demned by Lord Denning in *Hubbard* v. *Pitt*,[2] where he said that the view of Lord Lindley "has not stood the test of time."

Lord Denning was therefore able to conclude that so far as the tort of private nuisance is concerned:

> "picketing a person's premises is not unlawful unless it is associated with other conduct such as to constitute the whole conduct a nuisance at common law. Picketing is not a nuisance in itself. Nor is it a nuisance for a group of people to attend at or near the plaintiff's premises in order to obtain or to communicate information or in order peacefully to persuade. It does not become a nuisance unless it is associated with obstruction, violence, intimidation, molestation or threats."[3]

The effect of this dictum would, as Lord Denning intended, be to extend to persons generally the same privileges and immunities applied to those engaging in a trade dispute. But this would not be surprising, for it has often been said that the effect of the Trade Disputes Act 1906, was merely to confirm the effect of the *Ward Lock* case.[4] That view is still perfectly acceptable.

In cases concerning a trade dispute the matter is put beyond doubt by the immunity conferred by section 15 of the 1974 Act.

Inducing breach of contract

The act of picketing may induce breaches of various contracts, either directly, such as the employment contracts of the workers who are persuaded not to cross the picket line, or indirectly by thereby causing breach of a commercial contract. *Torquay Hotel Co.* v. *Cousins*[5] provide a factual example of such breaches, although the case also depended on statements made by union officials. The existence of a picket line is sufficient to "induce" another person to break his contract of employment by not crossing it.[6]

The immunity given by section 15 of the 1974 Act is unlikely to provide any protection against this tort, but there is no need to use that section since in trade dispute cases adequate protection is provided by section 13 of the Act,[7] which deals with immunity against this and other torts such as conspiracy.[8]

Vicarious liability

Bird v. *O'Neal*[9] raised the question of liability of the union for the acts of pickets, and concluded that although a union could only act through its agents, that did not create a relationship of master and servant and therefore there was no vicarious liability.[10]

The matter of vicarious liability was specifically excluded from the discussion of the House of Lords in *Heatons Ltd.* v. *T.G.W.U.*[11] and it is thought that the principles announced in that case would be unlikely to affect a union's liability in this area. A union official could be liable for any tort arising out

---

[2] [1975] I.C.R. 308 at 317.

[3] *Ibid.* at 318. For an example of conduct that did amount to a nuisance see *Bird* v. *O'Neal* [1960] A.C. 907.

[4] (1906) 22 T.L.R. 327.

[5] [1969] 2 Ch. 106.

[6] See *Hersees of Woodstock* v. *Goldstein* (1963) 38 D.L.R. 2d 449 at 453 *per* Aylesworth J.A.

[7] See Chap. 11 above.

[8] For a discussion of the application of the tort of conspiracy see *Bird* v. *O'Neal* [1960] A.C. 907.

[9] *Ibid.*

[10] The subject is dealt with generally in Chap 4.

[11] [1972] I.C.R. 308.

of action he has specifically authorised, as for example in the case of tort arising out of the very existence, as opposed to the conduct of, a picket line which he has call for.

Contempt of court

If a person refuses to obey an injunction issued by a court he may be liable for contempt of court and could even find himself in prison. This situation arose under the Industrial Relations Act 1971 because the picketing immunity did not provide protection in the case of an "unfair industrial practice."[12] Today, however, the exemption provides greater protection but contempt remains a theoretical possibility, if for example, an injunction is granted to prevent picketing which is not in contemplation of a trade dispute and is inducing breaches of contract.

CONSPIRACY AND PROTECTION OF PROPERTY ACT 1875

The offences contained in section 7 of the Conspiracy and Protection of Property Act 1875[13] are clearly allied to picketing and are therefore conveniently dealt with in this chapter. Section 7 states:

> "Every person who, with a view to compel any other person to abstain from doing or to do any act which such other person has a legal right to do or abstain from doing, wrongfully and without legal authority:
>
> 1. Uses violence to or intimidates such other person or his wife or children, or injures his property; or,
> 2. Persistently follows such other person about from place to place; or
> 3. Hides any tools, clothes, or other property owned or used by such other person, or deprives him of or hinders him in the use thereof; or
> 4. Watches or besets the house or other place where such other person resides, or works, or carries on business, or happens to be, or the approach to such house or place; or
> 5. Follows such other person with two or more other persons in a disorderly manner in or through any street or road,
>
> shall, on conviction thereof by a court of summary jurisdiction, be liable either to pay a penalty not exceeding twenty pounds, or to be imprisoned for a term not exceeding three months, with or without hard labour."[14]

This section is of relatively little importance today and prosecutions under it are rare. During the miners' strike of 1972 it was stated[15] that 263 arrests were made for various offences arising out of picketing, but that no case was known where a person had been charged under this section. But it was used to provide the basis of a charge of conspiracy in *R* v. *Jones*[16] in 1974, and in the past it was widely used, and gave rise to a number of difficult points of interpretation.[17]

---

[12] See *Churchman* v. *Joint Shop Stewards Committee* [1972] I.C.R. 222. This was the case where the Official Solicitor intervened to appeal against the order of N.I.R.C. committing the pickets to prison for contempt. See also *Midland Cold Storage* v. *Turner* [1972] I.C.R. 230 where the N.I.R.C. distinguished *Churchman* on the law of picketing, in which view they were correct.

[13] As amended by the Criminal Law Act 1977, s. 65 and Sched. 13 (making the charge triable summarily only), and by the Trade Disputes Act 1906, s. 2.

[14] Hard labour was abolished by the Criminal Justice Act 1948, s. 1.

[15] H.C. Debs. vol. 831 *col. 223* (February 21, 1972). Also of the 500 people charged with picketing offences arising out of the activities at Grunwick Laboratories Ltd. in 1977 none were charged under this section. H.C. Deb. vol. 94, ser. 5, *col. 136* (January 17, 1978).

[16] [1974] I.C.R. 310.

[17] For a detailed discussion see Citrine, *Trade Union Law* (3rd ed.), p. 532–542.

With a view to compel . . .

The introduction to the section governs all five sub-headings that follow and it is therefore necessary to prove that not only was there an act of the kind specified but also an intention to compel another person to do or not do something.[18] In *Lyons* v. *Wilkins*[19] the introduction was given a very wide interpretation when it was said that the offence is committed even though the action is taken against A with a view to compel B.[20] The words themselves might be thought to mean that both the act and the intention to compel must be directed against the same person, but Lindley M.R. said,

> "It is said that to beset one person's house with a view to compel someone else is not within the section. Such a construction would render the Act nugatory in a great number of cases clearly within the mischief intended to be remedied. But a more direct answer to the argument is that 'such other' means 'any other'."[21]

It is suggested, however, that this view is to strain the language of the section too far and that considering the general lack of authority of *Lyons* v. *Wilkins*[22] this interpretation should not be followed.[23]

Wrongfully and without legal authority

Once again the Court of Appeal in *Lyons* v. *Wilkins*[24] has been shown to be unduly restrictive, for the interpretation of these words in that case has been decisively rejected. The issue is simply whether "wrongfully" means wrongful *apart from the statute* or whether an act can be "wrongful" simply because it is contrary to section 7 itself. In *Lyons* v. *Wilkins*[24] the court took the latter view but this was rejected by another Court of Appeal in *Ward Lock* v. *Operative Printers Assistants Society*[25] where Vaughan Williams L.J. (who had also sat in *Lyons* v. *Wilkins*) said,[26] "the words 'wrongfully and without lawful authority' were introduced for the very purpose of limiting the remedy by criminal prosecution to cases so tortious as to give a civil remedy," and Fletcher-Moulton L.J. endorsed this view by saying[27] in what has become a classic statement of the function of the Act,

> "It legalises nothing and it renders nothing wrongful that was not so before. Its object is solely to visit certain selected classes of acts which were previously wrongul—*i.e.* were at least civil torts, with penal consequences."

It is therefore necessary to establish that the act not only comes within one of the sub-headings of section 7, but is also unlawful apart from that section.

---

[18] "View does not import motive. It imports purpose" *per* Chitty L.J. in *Lyons* v. *Wilkins* [1899] 1 Ch. 255 at 270.

[19] [1899] 1 Ch. 255 at 268.

[20] *Ibid.* at 268.

[21] It was also argued on the basis of the Interpretation Act 1889 that person must be read as "persons", thus making the argument limiting the compulsion and the act to the same person "untenable," *ibid.*

[22] [1899] 1 Ch. 255.

[23] The arguments are convincingly presented in Citrine, *Trade Union Law,* (3rd ed.) p. 537.

[24] [1899] 1 Ch. 255.

[25] (1906) 22 T.L.R. 327.

[26] *Ibid.* at 329.

[27] *Ibid*. This interpretation was followed in *Fowler* v. *Kibble* [1922] 1 Ch. 487 and in *Ex parte Farrell; Re Fongold* (1936) S.R. (N.S.W.) 386.

1. "Uses violence to or intimidates"

The principal issue relates to the meaning of "intimidate" which is not defined by the Act.[28] In *Gibson* v. *Lawson*[29] Lord Coleridge said in effect that the section should be limited to such intimidation as implies a threat of personal violence, but this view was rejected by the Court of Appeal in *R.* v. *Jones.*[30] In that case James L.J. while not wishing to define the word exhaustively said,

> " 'intimidate' in this section includes putting persons in fear by the exhibition of force or violence or the threat of force or violence, and there is no limitation restricting the meaning to cases of violence or threats of violence to the person."

Thus displays of force and violence against buildings and equipment were sufficient for "intimidation", but it is not clear what else would be included, particularly whether offensive language which does not threaten violence is enough.

In *Judge* v. *Bennett*[31] A. L. Smith J. thought that it was sufficient to use language which may cause the person threatened to fear and be afraid, and that that was different from a threat to use violence. An example of a conviction for "offensive" words is *The State* v. *District Justice O'Flynn*[32] where a picket had shouted to a woman customer "Don't you know there is a strike on here? You should be damned well ashamed of yourself. You are not entitled to go in there while there is a strike on." These cases may, however, be inconsistent with *Gibson* v. *Lawson*,[33] and furthermore it must be shown that the defendants act is unlawful apart from the Statute. It is thus suggested that offensive language should not of itself be sufficient to amount to intimidation.

Another problem is whether threats of economic damage would be enough, such as where a person threatens that he will secure the dismissal of a fellow worker. In *Tynan* v. *Balmer*[34] at first instance Judge Chapman voiced the question whether *Rookes* v. *Barnard*[35] might have some effect on this area and said that the case may be held "in due course to involve some extension of the scope of the criminal offences of intimidation, but I do not think that in the present case I ought to embark upon a discussion of such a complex and recondite topic.'[36]

It is suggested that *Rookes* v. *Barnard*[37] should not be considered to have extended intimidation under section 7 into the realms of economic threats, partly because a decision in the civil law should not necessarily affect the criminal law and partly because *Rookes* v. *Barnard*[37] was not a case of two party intimidation whereby A threatens B but of three party intimidation whereby A threatens B and B acts to the detriment of C. The case is therefore not in itself an authority, even in the civil law, that a threat of economic force

---

[28] The Trade Disputes and Trade Unions Act 1927, did provide a definition applicable to this section which went so far as to include threats or injury to a person's business, occupation or employment. This statute was repealed by the Trade Disputes and Trade Unions Act 1946.

[29] [1891] 2 Q.B. 545; see also *Curran* v. *Treleaven* [1891] 2 Q.B. 545.

[30] [1974] I.C.R. 310.

[31] [1887] 4 L.T. 75.

[32] [1948] I.R. 343.

[33] [1891] 2 Q.B. 545. The matter was not discussed in *R.* v. *Jones* [1974] I.C.R. 310.

[34] [1967] 1 Q.B. 91.

[35] [1964] A.C. 1129.

[36] [1967] 1 Q.B. 91 at 99–100. Intimidation was not discussed on appeal.

[37] [1964] A.C. 1129.

by A against B is illegal.[38] In order to obtain a conviction under section 7 it is necessary to prove that the conduct is otherwise unlawful, and it may be difficult to establish that two party intimidation is tortious.

Finally it is suggested that *Gibson* v. *Lawson*[39] and *Curran* v. *Treleaven*[39] are good authority against any extension of intimidation. In the latter case Lord Coleridge C.J. said,[40]

> "to tell an employer that if he employs workmen of a certain sort, the workmen of another sort in his employ will be told to leave him, and to tell the men, when the employer will not give way, to "leave their work, use no violence, use no immoderate language, but quietly to cease work and go home" . . . is certainly not intimidation within any reasonable construction of the statute."

The last point is that it has been suggested by *Agnew* v. *Munro*[41] that actual fear on the part of the person intimidated is not necessary, but only that the acts of the defendant would "induce serious apprehension of violence in the mind of a man of ordinary courage."[42] This question may, however, still be open.

Conspiracy to intimidate

While the law of criminal conspiracy applies to all the heads of section seven, it has only been used in relation to intimidation.[43] There would, however, be little advantage in such a charge today since by virtue of section 3 of the Criminal Law Act 1977 the maximum sentence of imprisonment for conspiracy is the same as for the substantive offence, in this case three months. A conspiracy charge may, however, be used against those who are not present at the intimidation. The law already covers the case where a number are present but only a few engage in intimidation. In *Young* v. *Peck*[44] it was held that when thirteen people assembled to barrack black-legs and two of them threw eggs, all were properly convicted of intimidation.

The first heading also deals with the case of a person who injures the property of another. In a charge under this part it is necessary to specify the property injured.[45]

2. Persistently follows . . .

An example of a conviction under this head is *Smith* v. *Thomasson*[46] where the defendant, together with a number of others who were on strike, followed the respondent (who had continued working) through the streets until he was rescued by his employer in a dog cart. The court held that the offence could be committed by just one person alone and even if he made no attempt to speak

---

[38] But see dicta by Lord Denning in *D & C Builders* v. *Rees* [1966] 2 Q.B. 617 and Chap. 12 above.

[39] [1891] 2 Q.B. 545.

[40] *Ibid.* at 562.

[41] [1891] 2 White 611; (1891) 28 S.L.R. 335.

[42] (1891) 28 S.L.R. 335 at 336 *per* Lord Wellwood. The defendant had said to one man "if you don't stop work you will wear sore bones for it one of these nights," and to others that he would "get men to throw them into the dock."

[43] *R.* v. *Jones* [1974] I.C.R. 310.

[44] (1912) 29 T.L.R. 31.

[45] *Smith* v. *Moody* [1903] 1 K.B. 56. In a conviction for intimidation it is necessary to specify the acts of intimidation proved: *Metcalfe* v. *Wiseman* (1888) 52 J.P. 439.

[46] (1890) 62 L.T. 68.

to the victim, for the "silent dogging" of his footsteps was sufficient. It would presumably be argued that such an act is a trespass to the highway so as to apply the further illegality which is necessary,[47] although in the case itself the act would also have been a public nuisance as the victim was being pursued by a crowd throwing refuse and shouting "knobsticks."

3. Hides any tools

There is no case directly on this part of the section, but *Fowler* v. *Kibble*[48] provides an analogous example. In that case the defendants in an attempt to persuade the plaintiffs to join one of the two unions affiliated to the Miners Federation[49] told the lampman not to give lamps to the plaintiffs. It was held that not only was there some doubt as to whether the defendant's acts amounted to hiding tools, but also it was said that as there was a trade dispute the acts were not actionable apart from the statute,[50] being protected by the Trade Disputes Act 1906.

4. Watches or Besets

It is unlikely that this heading now adds anything to the general law of nuisance and obstruction already discussed, especially in view of the fact that the prosecution must prove that the acts are unlawful apart from the Statute,[50] as well as the appropriate motive on the part of the defendant. In addition it must be remembered that this section is subject to the immunity for lawful picketing provided in the Trade Union and Labour Relations Act 1974 so that it will have to be established that the defendant was doing more than attend for the purpose of communicating information or persuading a person not to work. Thus it is suggested there would be no conviction today on the facts of *Charnock* v. *Court*[51] where the defendants had picketed Fleetwood landing stage and Halifax railway station in order to persuade workmen being imported from Ireland not to take the strikers' jobs.

Although the pre-1906 cases may be unreliable so far as the results are concerned, a number of points may be based upon them. Thus it has been said that the watching need only be for a short time[52] and can occur at a place (such as a landing stage) where a person is only present for a moment.[53] Also the persons who are beset need not be employees.[54] As a matter of interest it was an application for an injunction based on this clause that gave rise to the famous case of *Taff Vale Rly.* v. *A.S.R.S.*[55] following the activities of pickets at Cardiff station in attempting to "turn round" blacklegs being sent from London to take their places.

---

[47] *Ward Lock* v. *Operative Printers Assistants Society* (1906) 22 T.L.R. 327. See also *R.* v. *Wall* (1907) 21 Cox C.C. 401 (an Irish case).

[48] [1922] 1 Ch. 487.

[49] The plaintiffs were members of the non-affiliated Wednesfield and District Miners' Association.

[50] The court was thus following *Ward Lock* v. *Operative Printers' Assistants Society* (1906) 22 T.L.R. 327.

[51] [1899] 2 Ch. 35.

[52] *Ibid.* But see *R.* v. *Wall* (1907) 21 Cox C.C. 401 (an Irish case) *per* Palles C.B. "Watching involves persistent watching."

[53] *Charnock* v. *Court* [1899] 2 Ch. 35.

[54] *Farmer* v. *Wilson* (1900) 69 L.J.Q.B. 496.

[55] [1901] A.C. 426. For a full description of these activities see Bagwell, *The Railwaymen* pp. 212–222.

5. Follows in a disorderly manner

A person may clearly be convicted of this offence if he is a member of a hostile crowd which follows the victim. In one such case[56] the crowd consisted of about 200 people, including women and children, and in addition to booing and shouting, a band had been provided which struck up when the three victims left their employer's premises. A further example is *Ex parte Wilkins*[57] where the defendants were charged with following "with more than two persons" in a disorderly manner. It is not clear whether a person acting alone could be disorderly in this sense but there seems no reason why such a charge should not be possible. In *R.* v. *McKenzie*[58] a charge under this head failed as the prosecution had not proved that the motive of the defendant in following was to prevent him from doing what he had a legal right to do.

Procedure

A number of cases under section 7 have raised procedural questions. First it should be noted that the offences under the various heads are only committed if the act is both wrongful apart from the Statute and also if the purpose is "to compel any other person to abstain from doing or to do any act which such other person has a legal right to do or abstain from doing." The absence of this element from the charge is fatal,[58] although it is sufficient to state what the victim was doing even though the charge omits the fact that he had a legal right to do it.[59]

Secondly *Young* v. *Peck*[60] establishes that the information may be laid by the police on their own account and need not involve the person against whom the action was taken.

Thirdly there appears to be some disagreement about the impact on this section of the rule against duplicity, that is that no one count should charge the defendant with more than one offence. The general view (in Ireland and Scotland at least) is that section 7 creates only one offence, so that a count which leads a defendant under more than one head (or with two items in the same head) is not bad for duplicity.[61] The reason is that the gist of the offence is the unlawful compelling in the introduction to the section and the various heads only enumerate the various methods of compulsion. On the other hand in *R.* v. *Edmondes* it was held by Lawrence J. that a count that alleged both violence and intimidation was bad for duplicity.[62]

Finally it should be noted that a private individual who suffers damage over and above that of the public generally may obtain an injunction to restrain the criminal activity without needing the consent of the Attorney-General.[63] Such will usually be the case under this section.[64]

---

[56] *Mckinlay* v. *Hart* (1897) 25 R. (Ct. of Sess.) 7.

[57] (1895) 59 J.P. 294.

[58] [1892] 2 Q.B. 519.

[59] *R.* v. *Hulme* (1913) 9 Cr. App. R. 77.

[60] (1912) 29 T.L.R. 31.

[61] *The State* v. *District Justice O'Flynn* [1948] I.R. 343; *A–G* v. *O'Brien* (1936) 70 I.L.T.R. 101; *Clarkson* v. *Stuart* (1894) 22 R. (Ct. of Just.) 5; *Wilson* v. *Renten* (1909) 47 Sc.L.R. 209.

[62] (1895) 59 J.P. 776. This case also concerned the activities of strikers on the Taff Vale Rly.

[63] *Springhead Spinning Co.* v. *Riley* (1868) L.R. 6 Eq. 551 *per* Malins V-C at 568; confirmed in *Gouriet* v. *U.P.W.* [1978] A.C. 435 at 492 *per* Viscount Dilhorne and at 506 *per* Lord Edmund-Davies.

[64] Examples are *Charnock* v. *Court* [1899] 2 Ch. 35; *Walters* v. *Green* [1899] 2 Ch. 696; *Fowler* v. *Kibble* [1922] 1 Ch. 487; *Ward Lock* v. *Operative Printers' Assistants Society* (1906) 22 T.L.R. 327.

CHAPTER 14
CRIMINAL CONSPIRACY

ALTHOUGH the criminal law of conspiracy was of considerable significance in trade union law during the last century,[1] it is in practice of relatively little importance today as a restraint on the ordinary activities of trade unions. The fact that the common law crime has been largely abolished and replaced by a statutory version of narrower limits[2] does not, however, mean that there is no longer any danger at all of conspiracy being used in the context of industrial relations. While much of the previous law on the position of trade unions in relation to criminal conspiracy is no longer relevant,[3] some mention will have to be made of conspiracy to defraud, which has been retained.

Statutory conspiracy

The statutory crime[4] which has largely replaced common law conspiracy[5] is defined by the Criminal Law Act 1977[6] as follows:

> "If a person agrees with any other person or persons that a course of conduct shall be pursued which will necessarily amount to or involve the commission of any offence or offences by one or more of the parties to the agreement if the agreement is carried out in accordance with their intentions, he is guilty of conspiracy to commit the offence or offences in question."

First it should be noted that statutory conspiracy only covers an agreement to commit a *crime*, and apart from the exception of conspiracy to defraud or to corrupt public morals a person can no longer be convicted of conspiracy to commit a tort or a breach of contract. Furthermore, so far as trade unions are concerned, not all crimes can result in a charge of conspiracy, for it is provided[7] that where the acts agreed upon are to be done in contemplation or

---

[1] See generally Hedges and Winterbottom, *The legal history of trade unionism* (1930) and Wedderburn, *The Worker and the Law* (2nd ed.) pp. 219–223, and Chap. 1 above.

[2] Criminal Law Act 1977, ss. 1 and 5. The common law crimes of conspiracy to defraud and conspiracy to corrupt public morals have been retained.

[3] For a thorough discussion of the common law crime see Wallington, "Criminal Conspiracy and Industrial Conflict" (1975) 4 I.L.J. 69; Lustgarten, "Common Law Crimes and Trade Union Activities" (1976) 27 N.I.L.Q. 216.

[4] For a complete commentary on the new offence see Smith "Conspiracy under the Criminal Law Act 1977" [1977] Crim.L.R. 598 and 638; also Griew, Annotations to *Current Law Statutes* (Criminal Law Act 1977).

[5] The new crime is based on the recommendations of the Law Commission Report on Conspiracy and Criminal Law Reform. (Report No. 76), H.C. 176 (1975–76).

[6] s. 1 (1).

[7] Criminal Law Act 1977, s. 1 (3).

furtherance of a trade dispute,[8] any offence that would be committed shall be disregarded so long as it is a summary offence which is not punishable with imprisonment.

The new provision would not have made any difference (except as to penalty) in the only case of conspiracy that has been brought against trade unionists in recent years. In *R.* v. *Jones*[9] one of the charges[10] (on which 3 of the defendants were convicted) was of conspiracy to intimidate contrary to section 7 of the Conspiracy and Protection of Property Act 1875.

However, in view of the fact that the maximum sentence of imprisonment for conspiracy is now the same as for the substantive offence,[11] there is little advantage in a charge of conspiracy, except where those charged have not actually participated in the criminal activities. This would be so for those who organise a strike that is criminal. For example it is a crime maliciously to break a contract of service knowing that the consequence will be to endanger life,[12] and it could therefore be a crime to organise a strike which necessarily involves such breaches.

More likely, however, would be a charge of conspiracy against the organisers of illegal pickets.[13] It should be noted that so long as the act is in contemplation or furtherance of a trade dispute a charge of conspiracy to obstruct the highway contrary to section 121 of the Highways Act 1959 would no longer be possible,[14] but in similar circumstances it would be possible to bring a charge in respect of public nuisance at common law.[15] If the purpose of the pickets is obstruction, and this is intended by the organisers, the picketing would be outside the statutory protection for lawful picketing[16] and a conspiracy charge could be brought.

Although unlikely to be relevant in crimes concerning trade union members, it should be noted that where a crime of strict liability is concerned, a person cannot be convicted of conspiracy to commit that crime unless it is shown that he (and one other) knew of the relevant fact, even though the substantive offence may be committed without such knowledge.[17]

One of the most important elements of conspiracy is the agreement, but the definition of this requirement[18] has given rise to considerable controversy.[19] Thus there must be agreement that a "course of conduct" shall be pursued, and the question is whether this means simply the physical acts involved or

---

[8] As defined by T.U.L.R.A. 1974, s. 29. See Chap. 11.

[9] [1974] I.C.R. 310.

[10] The defendants were also convicted of unlawful assembly and affray. The affray conviction was quashed on appeal.

[11] Criminal Law Act 1977, s. 3. However, a fine may still be unlimited, and a charge of conspiracy may justify a longer sentence within the maximum.

[12] Conspiracy and Protection of Property Act 1875, s. 5. See also the Aliens Restriction (Amendment) Act 1919. Charges of conspiracy in connection with offences under the Post Office Act 1953, s. 58 (delaying postal packets) would be unnecessary as it is a crime to procure or incite such an act under s. 68.

[13] For crimes connected with picketing see Chap. 13.

[14] Criminal Law Act 1977, s. 1 (3).

[15] Because being punishable with imprisonment it is not saved by the trade dispute exemption.

[16] T.U.L.R.A. 1974, s. 15. For the potential width of public nuisance in this context see *Hubbard* v. *Pitt* [1975] I.C.R. 77 (Forbes J.) and 308 (C.A.).

[17] Criminal Law Act 1977, s. 1 (2), being a statutory version of *Churchill* v. *Walton* [1967] 2 A.C. 224.

[18] Criminal Law Act 1977, s. 1.

[19] Orchard, "Agreement in Criminal Conspiracy" [1974] Crim.L.R. 297, 335; Elliot, Lynch and Smith, "Mens Rea in Statutory Conspiracy" [1978] Crim.L.R. 202.

includes the consequences of those acts. The latter view is preferred,[20] so that conspiracy to commit a crime may be based on the consequences of the intended acts.

A further element of the statutory crime is that the intended course of conduct must *necessarily* amount to or involve the commission of an offence. The interaction of the two elements of agreement and causation may be illustrated by considering a case of conspiracy to commit a public nuisance by picketing. By virtue of section 15 of the Trade Union and Labour Relations Act 1974 it is lawful to attend at a place for specified purposes, but if the purpose of the picketing is to obstruct the highway then the immunity is lost. Therefore if two people agree that they or others will indulge in picketing this does not *necessarily* involve an offence since the picketing could be conducted lawfully. But if the purpose of the organisers is to cause obstruction this would necessarily involve an offence, and a charge of conspiracy to organise a picket with the purpose of causing such an obstruction would be possible, so long as the phrase "course of conduct" is held to relate not just to the physical acts but also to the consequences.

It has also been suggested in this context that purpose could include foresight of the natural consequences of one's acts,[21] so that it is the theoretical possible for a person who organises a picket line to be charged with conspiracy to commit a public nuisance even if he did not intend, but did foresee, an obstruction.

Penalties and procedure

One of the major criticisms laid against the crime of conspiracy at common law was that it permitted a longer sentence than could be imposed for the substantive offence. However, so far as the statutory offence is concerned it is now provided that a conviction for conspiracy cannot give rise to a sentence of imprisonment longer than the maximum for the substantive offence,[22] but the following points should be noted. First in many common law crimes, such as public nuisance, punishment is "at large" and so the maximum is life imprisonment. Secondly the element of combination may make the crime more reprehensible so that a higher sentence may be imposed within the maximum than would be the case for the substantive offence. Thirdly the limitation applies only to sentences of imprisonment, and on conviction for conspiracy a fine of any amount may be levied.

Where the substantive crime is a summary offence no proceedings for conspiracy may be brought without the consent of the Director of Public Prosecutions[23] (except where a charge of the substantive crime would require the consent of the Attorney General, in which case his consent is needed instead). If the offence is not a summary one, but the consent of the D.P.P. or some other person would be necessary for bringing a prosecution, such consent is also necessary for a charge of conspiracy.

Conspiracy at common law

It was probably intended by the framers of the new law that no more would

[20] Smith and Hogan *Criminal Law* 4th ed. p. 218 *et seq.*

[21] *Broome* v. *D.P.P.* [1974] I.C.R. 84 at 90 *per* Lord Reid, but see at 96 *per* Lord Salmon.

[22] Criminal Law Act 1977, s. 3.

[23] This would apply to conspiracy to commit a public nuisance, or conspiracy to intimidate under the Conspiracy and Protection of Property Act 1875, s. 7.

need to be said on the subject of criminal conspiracy in relation to trade unions. This is indicated by the fact that the Criminal Law Act 1977 repeals the earlier legislation which stated that a person acting in contemplation or furtherance of a trade dispute could only be convicted of criminal conspiracy if the act would be a crime when done by one person.[24] It was thought that this provision was now unnecessary because it was assumed that conspiracy to commit a crime was under the new statutory provisions the only kind of conspiracy relevant to trade union cases.

But the statute did not abolish all common law conspiracy for it preserved the common law crime of conspiracy to defraud; and as Professor Smith has pointed out[25] this crime is of very wide ambit and could be relevant to trade unionists. The difficulty is that statutory protection against common law conspiracy has been repealed. The problem arises because it is provided[26] that the statutory crime does not apply wherever the facts amount to conspiracy to defraud, so that where the facts give rise to both the statutory conspiracy to commit a crime and the common law conspiracy to defraud, the latter prevails and the charges must be brought at common law. What is more, this is so even if the accused cannot be convicted of the statutory conspiracy because of the immunity provided in trade dispute cases, for that immunity is contained in section 1 of the Criminal Law Act 1977 and section 5 of the same act states that section 1 shall not apply in any case where the agreement amounts to conspiracy to defraud at common law. Thus the trade dispute immunity cannot apply to common law conspiracy.

Conspiracy to defraud is a crime of wide ambit, and in *Scott* v. *Metrolpolitan Police Commissioner*[27] Viscount Dilhorne while disclaiming an exhaustive definition, said,

> " 'to defraud' ordinarily means, in my opinion, to deprive a person dishonestly of something which is his or of something to which he is or would or might but for the perpetration of fraud be entitled ... an agreement by two or more by dishonesty to deprive a person of something which is his or to which he is or would be or might be entitled and an agreement by two or more by dishonesty to injure some proprietary right of his, suffices to constitute the offence of conspiracy to defraud."

The significant point about this definition is that deceit is not necessary, but that it is sufficient to intend to deprive another of an advantage he has a right to receive. It has also been decided that it is not necessary for the accused to seek a financial advantage for himself by inflicting economic loss on the object of the conspiracy, but that it is sufficient if he intends a course of conduct which puts another's economic interests in jeopardy, even though he does not intend that other to suffer loss.[28] The crime seems therefore to be committed where a person agrees to dishonestly deprive another of an expected economic gain, at least if that other has a legal right to that gain. Much turns then on what is meant by dishonesty and it has been said that this is a matter for the jury to decide.[29] In the context of a strike it is unlikely that an act would be held to be dishonest merely because it is unlawful as a tort and it is therefore

[24] Conspiracy and Protection of Property Act 1875, s. 3.
[25] Smith "Conspiracy under the Criminal Law Act" [1977] Crim.L.R. 598 and 638.
[26] Criminal Law Act 1977, s. 5 (2).
[27] [1975] A.C. 819 at 839 and 840.
[28] *R.* v. *Allsop* (1976) 64 Cr.App.R. 29 (C.A.).
[29] *R.* v. *Feely* [1973] Q.B. 530.

suggested that it would not be a crime to conspire to induce a breach of contract otherwise than in furtherance of a trade dispute.[30] This is all the more so if the trade dispute immunity does apply, even though the effect of the immunity is procedural and makes the act "not actionable" rather than "not unlawful."

It is therefore suggested that if the motive is a proper "industrial" one an act is not dishonest merely because it is known to be unlawful as a tort or a breach of contract, and that dishonesty must import personal gain or malice. It would certainly be remarkable if after a century it were to become a criminal offence to organise a strike, and as this consequence cannot have been intended it may be hoped that no prosecution will be attempted for conspiracy at common law in the area of industrial relations.

[30] If it is in contemplation or furtherance of a trade dispute the act is not actionable in tort. T.U.L.R.A. 1974, s. 13.

CHAPTER 15

EMERGENCY POWERS

NATIONAL emergencies of various kinds call for different responses: at one extreme is political disorder leading to physical violence which is now dealt with by the police, but no doubt the government still has the power which it used to exercise in the last century,[1] to call in the troops to suppress a riot and maintain order.[2]

Of more significance, however, to trade unions is the power to control the economic and social effects of a withdrawal of labour which may be done either by the use of emergency measures under the Emergency Powers Act 1920 or calling for the assistance of the armed forces to do the work of those on strike.

Unlike some industrialised countries Britain no longer has special legislation enabling the government to order either a ballot of the strikers to determine their "true" intention, or to order them to return to work for a cooling off period.[3] The Industrial Relations Act 1971 did include such provisions,[4] but they were not successful in achieving their objectives[5] and experience on the only occasion when the provisions were used[6] indicated that the "cooling off" period was not conducive to further negotiation, and that the ballot if anything merely strengthened the position of the union because of the overwhelming support given to the union executive by the members. It seems unlikely that such provisions would be repeated.

EMERGENCY POWERS ACT 1920

Powers under this Act[7] may be used by the government[8] to ameliorate the effects of a serious strike, and the powers have been invoked by proclamations

---

[1] For example the events at Featherstone in 1893 when the troops were called upon to shoot at striking miners. See Clegg, Fox and Thompson *A history of British trade unions* (1964) vol. I, p. 107.

[2] See Wade and Phillips, *Constitutional and Administrative Law* (9th ed.) pp. 506–513, where it is stated at p. 507 that the power rests on "the duty of the armed forces to come to the aid of the civil authorities," citing the *Charge to the Bristol Grand Jury* (1832) 5 C. & P. 261; 172 E.R. 966.

[3] For a thorough comparative study of emergency legislation see Wedderburn "Industrial action, the State and the public interest" in Aaron and Wedderburn *Industrial Conflict* (1972) pp. 342–377.

[4] ss. 138–145.

[5] See Weekes, Mellish and Dickens, *Industrial Relations and the Limits of Law* (1976) p. 216.

[6] See *Secretary of State for Employment* v. *ASLEF (No. 1)* [1972] I.C.R. 7, *ibid. (No. 2)* [1972] I.C.R. 19.

[7] As amended by the Emergency Powers Act 1964, s. 1.

[8] For a study of the attitude of governments to strikes see Wigham *Strikes and the Government* (1976).

in 1921 (a miners' strike), in 1924 (a tramways strike, but the powers do not appear to have been used), 1926 (for the general strike), 1949 (in relation to a strike by dockers, but the powers under this Act were not used), 1955 (during a rail strike), 1966 (the seamen's strike), 1970 (a dock strike), 1972 (the "first" miners' strike), and 1973 (continuing into 1974 in relation to the "second" miners' strike).[9]

Under the Act a proclamation that a state of emergency exists may be issued where:

> "it appears to His Majesty that there have occurred, or are about to occur, events of such a nature as to be calculated, by interfering with the supply and distribution of food, water, fuel, or light, or with the means of locomotion, to deprive the community, or any substantial portion of the community, of the essentials of life . . ."

The regulations

Once the proclamation has been issued the government[10] may make regulations "for securing the essentials of life to the community"[11] and may confer power on Ministers for a wide variety of purposes, but regulations may not provide for any compulsory military service or industrial conscription; nor may they make it an offence to take part in, or peacefully to persuade others to take part in, a strike. Furthermore the regulations may not alter existing criminal procedure or institute any penalty without trial, but the Act does permit summary trial for a breach of the regulations, with maximum penalties of a fine of £100 or imprisonment for 3 months, or both.

The proclamation must be communicated to Parliament immediately,[12] and will last one month. The regulations issued under the proclamation must be laid before Parliament as soon as they are made and will only last 7 days unless continued by Parliament.

Content of the Regulations

It is now the custom for the government to put through very wide ranging regulations of a general kind which provide much greater powers than are strictly necessary for the specific emergency. The latest set was produced for the emergency caused by the miners' strike of 1974,[13] and they provided for the following powers: control of ports; relaxation of regulations relating to vehicles (including safety regulations and insurance provisions); the control of electricity, gas, water and sewage; the power to fix prices for food and to control its distribution; the relaxation of provisions covering medicines; the regulation of transport; the requisitioning of chattels and taking possession of land; the creation of the offences of sabotage, trespassing on or near the premises of essential services and interfering with the police, armed forces or persons performing essential services, and the power to arrest without warrant for an offence against the regulations.

---

[9] The proclamations are not strictly statutory instruments but are printed in the S.I. volumes. See the *Index to Government Orders* under "Emergency powers."

[10] More strictly, His Majesty in Council.

[11] s. 2 (1) of the 1920 Act.

[12] If Parliament is not then sitting, or going to sit within 5 days, it must be called into session.

[13] The Emergency Regulations 1974 (S.I. 1974 No. 33), in the same terms as S.I. 1974 No. 175 and S.I. 1974 No. 350.

The Use of the Armed Forces

In recent years members of the armed forces have been brought in to perform the work of those on strike in cases of emergency, an example being the use of the army during the firemen's strike of 1977. The government may request the assistance of the armed forces,[14] whose leaders have the power to order their men to do civilian work by virtue of the Defence (Armed Forces) Regulations 1939[15] which state:

> "The Admiralty, the Army Council or the Air Council may by order authorise officers and men of His Majesty's naval, military or air forces under their respective control to be temporarily employed in agricultural work or such other work as may be approved in accordance with instructions issued by the Admiralty, the Army Council or the Air Council, as the case may be, as being urgent work of national importance, and thereupon it shall be the duty of every person subject to the Naval Discipline Act, military law or air-force law to obey any command given by his superior officer in relation to such employment, and every such command shall be deemed to be a lawful command within the meaning of the Naval Discipline Act, the Army Act, 1955 or the Air Force Act, 1955, as the case may be."

Endangering Life

Although not strictly an emergency power, it is possible to prosecute a person who "wilfully and maliciously breaks a contract of service or of hiring, knowing or having reasonable cause to believe that the probable consequences of his so doing, either alone or in combination with others, will be to endanger human life, or cause serious bodily injury, or to expose valuable property whether real or personal to destruction or serious injury. . . ."[16]

It is important to note that not only must the act be wilful but also it must involve a breach of contract,[17] and the section does not therefore render illegal all strikes which endanger life.

It has been noted that in its terms the section could apply both to the employer as well as to the employee,[18] and also that there may be no need to restrict the meaning of "contracts of hiring" to employment contracts but that contracts for services and perhaps even for the hire of goods could be included.[19] In addition the section can be applied to action short of a strike which causes a breach of contract, and even to a case where no loss actually ensues but where it is merely probable that it will.[20]

---

[14] But the Home Guard may not be called out to deal with an industrial dispute: Home Guard Act 1951, s. 1 (4).

[15] These regulations were made permanent by the Emergency Powers Act 1964, s. 2.

[16] Conspiracy and Protection of Property Act 1875, s. 5. The maximum penalty is three month's imprisonment. This section is all that is left of those statutes which applied to workers in certain industries such as gas and water (Conspiracy and Protection of Property Act 1875, s. 4) and electricity (Electricity (Supply) Act 1919, s. 31) where it was thought that greater protection for the public was needed.

[17] See Chap. 10 above.

[18] But it does not apply to merchant seamen: Conspiracy and Protection of Property Act 1875, s. 16 as amended by the Merchant Shipping Act 1970 Sched. 3, para. 1.

[19] Donovan Commission Cmnd. 3623 para. 841.

[20] Citrine, *Trade Union Law* (3rd ed.) pp. 529–530.

In practice this provision is not used, and no prosecution under it is known. Nor does it appear to be effective as a deterrent in preventing industrial action which is likely to lead to injury, but nevertheless the Donovan Commission in 1969 recommended that the provision should remain in force unaltered.[21]

[21] Cmnd. 3623 paras. 840–847.

CHAPTER 16

SOCIAL SECURITY AND TRADE UNION LAW

TRADE union law becomes involved with social security law[1] in two principal areas. The first is where a person loses a benefit because his unemployment is due to a strike. The second concerns the question whether a person should be disqualified if the reason for his leaving employment was that he was not a member of a union.

UNEMPLOYMENT BENEFIT AND TRADE DISPUTES

The rule that a person whose unemployment is due to a strike cannot claim benefit is one that has existed since the national insurance scheme was introduced in 1911,[2] but while the general principle seems to be generally accepted, there has always been considerable controversy over how broad the disqualification should be.

As to the general principle the purpose is not to disqualify those on strike because they are responsible for their own lack of employment, for that issue could be dealt with by the provision disqualifying those who voluntarily leave without just cause. But if that provision were used it would involve the tribunal in having to determine whether in fact the men were justified in going on strike, and it is a fundamental principle of collective labour law that the merits of a dispute should not be an issue before any court or tribunal. The use of the voluntary leaving clause would thus involve the courts in compulsory arbitration, whereas our system of industrial relations is based, in theory at least, on the totally different principle of free collective bargaining.

The purpose of the provision is therefore to preserve the neutrality of the law in the sense that the law only becomes concerned with what is done rather than with why it is done. It is suggested that it is not a sufficient objection to this principle to point out[3] that the courts do become involved with motive when discussing the clause disqualifying those who leave voluntarily without just cause, for those cases involve only individual and not collective action. It is perhaps easier, and doctrinally more acceptable, to assess the merits of an individual's act than to decide upon the merits of collective action, the reasons for which are invariably more complicated than appear on the surface.[4]

---

[1] On this subject generally see Calvert, *Social Security Law* (2nd ed.), esp. Chap. 5; Ogus and Barendt, *The Law of Social Security* (1st ed.), p. 122 *et. seq.*; Pollard, *Social Welfare Law*, esp. Part D (Peter Smith); Fulbrook, *Administrative Justice and the Unemployed.*

[2] National Insurance Act 1911.

[3] Calvert, *Social Security Law*, 2nd ed. p. 148.

[4] It is only argued that this is so in the context of a court hearing on a social security issue: it is of course possible to investigate trade disputes by means of an inquiry.

Indeed the point has been well made[5] that the desire of the legislature is to save tribunals and insurance officers from difficult and politically sensitive decisions, and that "to the extent that the law is regarded as unsatisfactory, it may well be solely because it seeks to abandon the quest for justice in order to avoid controversy."

Neutrality also means that the parties should be left to fight it out using only their own resources and without subsidy from the state. Such a principle is not, and cannot be pursued to its logical conclusion,[6] but even so it should not be thought this principle ensures equality of bargaining power, for it is likely that non-intervention favours the employer, at least initially.

The Donovan Commission pointed out that:[7]

> "The problem is how to ensure that the insurance fund, which is financed by contributions from employers, employees and the State, is confined to relieving hardship resulting from unemployment due to causes other than industrial disputes, while at the same time not denying relief to those losing employment because of such a dispute if their connection or interest in the dispute is non-existent, indirect or remote."

Views on how that problem is to be solved tend to divide along political lines and will no doubt continue to be a matter of controversy.

The present provisions as to disqualification from unemployment benefit are contained in section 19 of the Social Security Act 1975:[8]

> 19 (1) A person who has lost employment as an employed earner by reason of a stoppage of work which was due to a trade dispute at his place of employment shall be disqualified for receiving unemployment benefit so long as the stoppage continues, except in a case where, during the stoppage, he has become bona fide employed elsewhere in the occupation which he usually follows or has become regularly engaged in some other occupation; but this subsection does not apply in the case of a person who proves—
>
> (a) that he is not participating in or directly interested in the trade dispute which caused the stoppage of work.

The disqualification will therefore apply in the following circumstances:

1. There must be a stoppage of work.
2. The employment must be lost by reason of the stoppage.
3. The stoppage must be due to a trade dispute.
4. The stoppage must be at the claimant's place of employment.
5. The claimant must be unable to prove he is not participating or directly interested in the dispute.
6. The disqualification lasts so long as the stoppage continues.
7. The claimant has not become bona fide employed elsewhere in the meantime.

"... a stoppage of work"

It is surprising that there is no direct authority on the meaning of this phrase, but a number of problems could arise. The first issue is whether the phrase

---

[5] Calvert, *Social Security Law* (2nd ed.) p. 148.

[6] Supplementary benefits will be available to the striker's family and in extreme cases to the striker himself. It is suggested that the payment of tax rebates is not a subsidy by the state in this sense, but rather a return of the striker's own money.

[7] Cmnd. 3623, para. 968.

[8] As amended by the Employment Protection Act 1975, s. 111.

refers to the fact that certain individuals are no longer working, or to the cessation or reduction in production at the place of work. If one or two people cease work but production continues regardless, is there a "stoppage"? It is suggested that there is only a stoppage if there is a considerable reduction in production.[9] However those individuals who have left may be disqualified if it can be said that they left voluntarily without just cause.

Secondly it may be asked whether a "work to rule" or a "go-slow" amounts to a stoppage. This is most likely to arise where a work to rule at one part of a factory causes workers in another part to be laid off. Although it would be open to a tribunal to hold that the relevant stoppage is that of the men laid off, it seems likely that the relevant "stoppage" is that of the men working to rule and that this would not amount to a stoppage.[10]

However, if one adopts such a view on the grounds that the individuals concerned are still working, albeit slowly, there may be problems of consistency. There will be no difficulty if it is thought that "stoppage" refers to individuals but if the word is held to apply to production instead, it may be that in order to be consistent one would have to say that work to rule is not a stoppage, except in cases where it causes considerable disruption.

"by reason of" a stoppage

Clearly a person should only be disqualified if there is a causal connection between the stoppage and his loss of employment. One issue that has arisen is whether a claimant who decides to leave before the strike begins is disqualified. In R(U) 29/59 the claimant left a few hours before a strike began, but it was nevertheless held that he left "by reason of" a stoppage since he "must have known that . . . the stoppage of work would occur."[11]

Further difficulties arise in cases where the claimant would have been unemployed anyway, even if there had been no stoppage. One example of this issue is the case of the casual labourer who only works intermittently, and the so-called "12-day rule" creates a rebuttable presumption to cover the problem. The rule was stated in R(U) 8/58 as follows:

> "In the case of a worker whose employment is irregular or intermittent it may be difficult to decide, when a stoppage of work due to a trade dispute occurs during one of his workless spells, whether his lack of employment is due to the trade dispute or to normal unemployment. The Umpire therefore ruled that if an employee whose employment was irregular has been out of work for more than 12 days before the stoppage due to the trade dispute begins, his lack of work (after the stoppage has begun) will be presumed to be due to normal unemployment and benefit will be payable. If, however, a stoppage due to a trade dispute occurs at premises, where he normally works, twelve days or less after his last employment his lack of work (after the stoppage has begun) will be presumed to

[9] This may be implicit in 2191/37 cited in R(U) 7/58 but see also R(U) 17/65. This is also the view expressed in Pollard, *Social Welfare Law*, para. D.770 (Peter Smith), and Hickling, *Labour Disputes and Unemployment Insurance Benefits*, p. 95. For a contrary view see Calvert, *Social Security Law* (2nd ed.), p. 150. The reason for the view expressed is that the stoppage continues until production has been substantially resumed, or until a substantial number of workers have been taken back. The fact that a worker is willing to return does not mean that the stoppage has ended so far as he is concerned. The same principle should be used to establish both the beginning and the end of a stoppage.

[10] See Pollard. *op. cit.* para. D.770 and Calvert, *op. cit.* p. 150.

[11] See also R(U) 30/55.

be due to the stoppage and he will thus be disqualified for receiving unemployment benefit. In any case, either presumption can be rebutted by satisfactory evidence."

Casual labour of the kind envisaged here is less common now than it has been, but the question remains whether the 12 days presumption should be retained. In R(U) 6/71 the Commissioner admitted the arbitrary nature of the rule but reserved his opinion as to the validity of the rule in present-day circumstances.

In some cases it is quite clear that the claimant would have become unemployed anyway, and yet he still loses his benefit. Thus in R(U) 12/72 the claimant was a colliery worker who was given notice of dismissal to take effect on January 22, 1972. A strike began on January 9, and ended on February 26. The claimant whilst admitting that he could not claim for the period he was on strike, sought benefit from the date of his dismissal, but it was held that he was disqualified until the end of the strike.[12] The rule therefore is that if the claimant originally lost his employment "by reason of a stoppage" that cause continues and he remains disqualified.

While such a view is a possible but strict interpretation of the Act disqualification might seem unjust in such cases. Thus in R(U) 6/71 the claimant was employed on the understanding that his employment would terminate when an impending strike began, and it was held that his loss of employment was due to the strike rather than the terms of his contract. On the other hand if the original loss of employment does not give rise to disqualification, the claimant retains his benefit until that cause ceases to operate. Thus in R(U) 12/61 the claimant was suspended under short term working arrangements from October 3, to October 10, 1960. A strike occurred from October 6 to October 12 and the question therefore arose whether he was disqualified for only the last two days, or for the whole period of the strike—the argument being that had he been working he would have gone on strike. The Commissioner limited the disqualification to the last two days as it would be wrong to disqualify him, not for what he had done, but for what he might have done in a situation which did not exist, that is had he been at work when the strike started. Thus a person who is off sick when the strike begins will not lose benefit so long as he remains sick, but if he becomes fit for work and stays away, the disqualification will begin to apply.[13]

"Due to a trade dispute"

Most of the issues of causation have been dealt with in the last section, and it is thought that "due to" gives rise to little difficulty.[14] "Trade dispute" is defined by section 19 (2) (*b*) of the Social Security Act 1975, but it should be noted that that definition is not the same as that provided for other areas of trade union law by section 29 of the Trade Union and Labour Relations Act 1974. The two definitions are used for very different purposes and a case which is authoritative for the one purpose may not be so for the other. It is also unclear whether the more detailed provision of the 1974 Act would be used as a guide to difficulties in the Social Security Act.[15]

---

[12] He was held to be directly interested in the dispute as he would have been entitled to back pay.

[13] See R(U) 13/72.

[14] But see R(U) 17/52.

[15] *e.g.* overseas disputes (29 (3)), the meaning of "dispute" (29 (5)), the parties to a dispute (29 (4)).

> s. 19 (2) (*b*) "trade dispute" means any dispute between employers and employees, or between employees and employees, which is connected with the employment or non-employment or the terms of employment or the conditions of employment of any persons, whether employees in the employment of the employer with whom the dispute arises, or not.

The definition has given rise to surprisingly little litigation over such matters as conditions of employment,[16] but there has been difficulty in cases where the claimant has been forced to stop work by pickets. In R(U) 2/53 the claimant stopped work because of the action of pickets who threatened him with violence if he went back. Whatever may have been the status of the claimant with regard to the main dispute, the Commissioner held that there was a trade dispute between the claimant and the pickets connected with the employment of the claimant and that therefore he was disqualified.[17]

In R(U) 3/69 the Commissioner in similar circumstances said:

> "The trade dispute which caused the stoppage was either the original dispute, regarded as extended to the claimant by the ... confrontations with the pickets, or a second dispute arising out of the confrontations, ancillary to the original dispute."

In the event, however, the Commissioner held that the claimant could not be said to be "participating" in either dispute and therefore could claim the benefit of the proviso to section 19 of the Act. Even if that way out is available,[18] it may seem odd to regard such a confrontation as one which could disqualify the claimant.[19] It has been suggested that these cases may be doubted in the light of the fact that the picketing may well have been unlawful, but that was a point specifically adverted to in R(U) 2/53 without comment.[20]

The issue is a difficult one because the claimant is a striker, albeit an unwilling one. It could perhaps be argued that the dispute is not about the employment or non-employment of the claimant (for all parties would still regard him as the employee of the employers), but rather it is about his refusal to suspend himself from his duties, which although within the definition of trade dispute contained in the Trade Union and Labour Relations Act 1974 is not technically within the Social Security Act definition.

Place of employment

The disqualification only applies if the stoppage takes place at the claimant's place of employment as defined by section 19 (2) (*a*) of the Social Security Act 1975.

> s. 19 (2) (*a*) "place of employment" in relation to any person, means the factory, workshop, farm or other premises or place at which he was

---

[16] See for example R(U) 3/71 (Dispute over the safety of a machine is a trade dispute) and R(U) 12/62. (The skipper of the boat on which the claimant was a member of the crew, being a member of the "Close Brethren," insisted that non-believers should eat at a separate table. As he made it a condition of employment it was a trade dispute. R(U) 5/77 (Dispute over whether employees had to pay for protective clothing was a trade dispute).

[17] This view was supported in R(U) 1/74 where building workers were forced to stop work by flying pickets although they had no dispute with their employers. It was held that either a dispute was imported onto the site by the pickets, or else the claimants had a dispute with the pickets.

[18] It involves reading "participate" as "willingly participate" which could give rise to serious problems, or that a positive act is required.

[19] This is perhaps one of the occasions where the interpretation for the purpose of T.U.L.R.A. 1974, s. 29 could differ from the meaning for the purposes of disqualification.

[20] Calvert, *Social Security Law*, 2nd ed. p. 155.

employed, so, however, that, where separate branches of work which are commonly carried on as separate businesses in separate premises or at separate places are in any case carried on in separate departments on the same premises or at the same place, each of those departments shall for the purposes of this paragraph be deemed to be a separate factory or workshop or farm or separate premises or a separate place, as the case may be.

There is little difficulty, at least in the general part of the section which merely refers to premises at which the claimant was employed. Thus a taxi driver has been held to be employed at the garage where the hiring takes place rather than on the streets,[21] and a dock pilot has been held to be employed at the dock rather than at sea.[22] But it cannot be said to be a hard and fast rule that the place of employment of a worker who moves about is his base, for in R(U) 26/57 it was held that an itinerant chipper and scraper was employed on the dock where he was actually working.

The definition adds a proviso to cover cases where there are separate departments which are carried on as separate businesses in order to limit the boundaries of the "place of employment."[23]

"Participating"

The claimant may avoid disqualification if he can show that he is neither participating nor directly interested in the dispute.[24] If a claimant withdraws his labour or willingly refuses to cross a picket line he is clearly participating, but in R(U) 3/69 it was suggested that a person who was prevented by violence and obstruction from getting to his place of work was not participating either in the original dispute or in the ancillary dispute with the pickets. This could involve considerable difficulty if it were thought that "participating" means "willingly participating" since there are various degrees of persuasion and coercion. It could be argued, however, that the decision only amounts to the view that there must be a positive act in order to participate.[25]

Other problems concern the role of individual union members in the decision to call the strike. In R(U) 5/66 the claimants had been laid off as a result of a stoppage. It was pointed out that being members of the same union as those who went on strike they could have attended the union meeting to vote against the stoppage, but it was held that the failure to vote did not amount to participating. This decision gives rise to the interesting question of whether they would have been participating if they had gone to the meeting and voted in favour of the other men going on strike, or even if they had voted against. It is suggested that in neither case would they be participating.

"Directly interested"

Again a claimant may avoid disqualification if he can prove that he was not directly interested in the dispute. It seems that a claimant is directly interested

---

[21] R(U) 6/51.

[22] R(U) 8/71.

[23] But the entire Ford estate at Dagenham was considered to be one place of employment in R(U) 1/70. See also R(U) 5/61 and R(U) 3/61.

[24] The burden is clearly on the claimant; Social Security Act 1975, s. 19 (1).

[25] On the basis of this line of argument one could also question whether there was a dispute. See the dictum of Buckley L.J. in *Cory Lighterage* v. *T.G.W.U.* [1973] I.C.R. 339 at 362, but see T.U.L.R.A. 1974, s. 29 (5).

if he stands to either gain[26] or lose from the settlement of the dispute. Thus in R(U) 4/65, the claimant was a plater's helper in a shipyard. The platers themselves went on strike because they claimed the sheds were too cold and since the platers' helpers would benefit from any extra heating gained by the platers they were held to be directly interested in the dispute, even though their loss of employment was involuntary.

This principle gives rise to awkward problems where differentials are concerned for it may be argued that if group A succeed in getting higher wages, group B may be directly interested in that dispute if the preservation of differentials would cause their wages to increase as well. In R(U) 13/71, during a strike by cranemen the management were in favour of increasing pay by means of a productivity scheme which would also have covered the claimant tool-room fitters if it had been introduced. The Commissioner thought the fitters were not directly interested in the dispute. He said:

> "Without attempting to define precisely what is meant by "direct interest", I think a claimant should not be regarded as having a direct interest in another person's dispute . . . unless there is a close association between the two occupations concerned, and the outcome of the dispute is likely to affect the claimant, not a number of removes, but virtually automatically, without further intervening contingencies."[27]

The general principles of this view were endorsed in R(U) 8/72, but the Commissioner did doubt the requirement that there should be a close association between the two groups concerned, for he thought that the association inherent in the fact that the dispute must be at the claimant's place of employment was sufficiently close.

It should be noted that it is not only those who might gain from the dispute who will be directly interested, but also those who might lose. In R(U) 1/60 shipwrights were held to be directly interested in a strike called by boilermakers to transfer work away from the shipwrights, for if the boilermakers had succeeded the shipwrights would have had less work.

So long as the stoppage continues

There will always be some doubt about the precise date when a stoppage ceases. It should be noted that this does not necessarily occur when the dispute is settled, for it may take some time after the agreement for the business to regain full production: the stoppage may continue even after the dispute is settled. Thus in R(U) 25/57 a strike was settled on April 4, 1957, when a number of workers returned to work. The claimant was willing to work but was not taken back until May 6, and it was held that the stoppage continued after April 4, but was over by April 13 when about 65 per cent. of the usual work force was working.[28] There is, however, nothing special about the 65 per

---

[26] This is so, however small the potential gain. In R(U) 4/62 an unrelated dispute only affected the claimant in so far as his "unpenalised lateness" time would have been reduced from 7 minutes to 5 minutes per week if there had been no settlement, and yet he was still directly interested.

[27] See R(U) 14/71 where the rates of one group were linked by express agreement to the rates of pay of another group to preserve differentials. The Commissioner held them to be directly interested, and pointed out that the question must always depend very much on the particular facts and circumstances of each case.

[28] In Canada a rule of 85 per cent. is applied. See Hickling, *Labour Disputes and Unemployment Insurance*, p. 141. In Canada this rule is fairly rigid and involves an analysis of production and employment figures.

cent. figure for it is only necessary to show a general or substantial return to work.[29]

A different issue arises in cases where the claimant is dismissed during the dispute. This could either be simply a move in the dispute, or it could be an indication by the employer that he intends to sever relations with the claimant permanently. Despite dicta in R(U) 17/52, the Commissioner in R(U) 1/65 decided that even in the latter case the claimant remains disqualified. He said:

> "I can see no ground whatsoever for holding that a stoppage of work which is due to a trade dispute ceases to be due to a trade dispute simply because the employer decides in regard to certain workmen involved in the stoppage that the stoppage between him and them is to be permanent."

In some cases the dispute may continue, but the stoppage may have terminated, in which case the claimant is no longer disqualified. For example if the men go on strike but the employer fills their places and resumes production the stoppage has terminated.[30]

Bona fide employed elsewhere

If a claimant goes on strike and then obtains bona fide employment elsewhere in the occupation which he usually follows, or has become regularly engaged in some other occupation, this will cancel the disqualification so that if he becomes unemployed again in his new job he will be able to claim benefit. This can be illustrated by R(U) 6/74 where a maintenance fitter went on strike and then got a job as a fitter elsewhere but became unemployed again during the currency of the original strike until that stoppage ended. He was held entitled to receive benefit, for the Commissioner said that there was no justification for equiporating bona fide to "permanently" or "with the intention of permanently severing relations with the original employer." He said:

> "There is nothing prima facie dishonest or mischievous in a person who finds himself out of work and under disqualification, seeking and obtaining employment, even if it turns out to be temporary, or even if he knows from the start it is likely to be temporary, so long as he takes it up with a proper motive—*e.g.* to have a job and earn a livelihood. It would no doubt be dishonest, or at least mischievous, if he took up the employment, knowing it was likely to be of short duration, merely thereby to rid himself of the disqualification and requalify immediately for benefit; or if for a similar motive he purported to take up employment which was merely a 'sham'."

Guarantee Payments

By virtue of section 12 of the Employment Protection (Consolidation) Act 1978 an employee who is laid off is entitled to be paid by his employer a "guarantee payment" for a maximum of five days in any defined 3 month period.[31] The relationship of this benefit to social security legislation is a

---

[29] It is not entirely clear whether this means substantial production has been resumed, or a substantial number of employees have returned, although usually the two would coincide.

[30] See R(U) 12/62.

[31] The Minister may authorise exemption from this scheme. E.P.C.A. 1978, s. 18. See for example Guarantee Payments (Exemption) (No. 1) Order 1977 (S. 1. 1977 No. 156) dealing with workers in civil engineering.

matter of considerable concern[32] in that the regulations may cause a number of claimants to be worse off, since for the days they receive a guarantee payment they will lose their entitlement to unemployment benefit.[33] In addition it seems rather a cumbrous benefit if the principal effect is to transfer some of the burden of unemployment from the state to the employer,[34] and accordingly makes such insurance more complicated.

As with unemployment benefit a claimant will be excluded from receiving a guarantee payment "if the failure to provide him with work occurs in consequence of a trade dispute involving any employee of his employer or of an associated employer."[35]

First it should be noted that for the purposes of this benefit the appropriate definition of trade dispute is that contained in section 29 of the Trade Union and Labour Relations Act 1974, which is a wider definition than that applied to unemployment benefit[36] or supplementary benefit[37] and may cause difficulty.

Secondly the circumstances in which disqualification occurs are very much wider than under the two social security schemes. It seems strange that a section of the Employment Protection Act 1975 should have narrowed the disqualification for the purposes of unemployment benefit[38] and yet have introduced for the purposes of guarantee payments a test that is very much wider, extending not only to all employees of the same employer but also to those of an associated employer.[39] In addition an employee is unable to escape disqualification by proving that he is not "participating" or "directly interested" in the dispute.

Whatever one's view of the extent of this disqualification, another major difficulty is the disharmony it causes with the social security legislation, for in a number of cases a person will not be entitled to a guarantee payment from his employer but will be entitled to unemployment benefit. The administrative burden imposed by the need for the Department of Health and Social Security to check whether the employer is or ought to be paying a guarantee payment makes the system extremely cumbersome. The complexity seems unnecessary.[40]

SUPPLEMENTARY BENEFITS

The circumstances in which a claimant for supplementary benefit will be disqualified as the result of a trade dispute are the same as in the case of

---

[32] See Hepple *et al.* (1977) 6 I.L.J. 54.

[33] Social Security (Unemployment, Sickness and Invalidity Benefit) Amendment Regulation 1976 (S.I. 1976 No. 328); Social Security (Unemployment, Sickness and Invalidity Benefit) Amendment No. 2 Regulations 1976 (S.I. 1976 No. 677). See also Employment Protection (Recoupment of Unemployment Benefit and Supplementary Benefit) Regulations 1977 (S.I. 1977 No. 674). Noted (1977) 6 I.L.J. 192.

[34] The principal benefit is that it will provide protection for the first three days of unemployment which is excluded in the social security system.

[35] E.P.C.A. 1978, s. 13 (1). For an example and an interpretation of "in consequence" see *Thompson* v. *Priest* [1978] I.R.L.R. 99.

[36] Social Security Act 1975, s. 19.

[37] *Ibid.* as applied by the Supplementary Benefit Act 1976, ss. 8 and 34.

[38] s. 111 repeals the "grade or class" disqualification.

[39] As defined by T.U.L.R.A. 1974, s. 30 (5).

[40] It should be noted that a number of Exemption Orders have already been granted which contain widely differing benefits and disqualification provisions.

unemployment benefit.[41] Broadly speaking the effect of the provision is that in such a case the requirements of the person affected are ignored, except in so far as he has a duty to provide for another person; but the resources available to him in providing that support are taken into account. This means that so far as a single person is concerned, he is not entitled to receive anything at all, unless he can bring himself within the provision for urgent need which is discussed below.

The disqualified person's family

It is only the requirements of the disqualified person himself that are ignored, and therefore the requirements of his dependants may be considered, unless they are also involved in the dispute. However, this does not mean such dependants are necessarily entitled to benefit, for the *resources* of the disqualified person are taken into account since the duty to maintain his dependants still continues and he must use whatever resources he still has available to him.[42] Of special interest to those who are disqualified are the provisions which state that "resources" includes both strike pay and tax rebates to which the striker is entitled.[43]

The extent to which the supplementary benefits scheme subsidises strikes by payments to a striker's family is a matter of acute political controversy,[44] but there is little evidence that a reduction or withdrawal of such payments would drastically affect the situation. A recent survey[45] indicates that the degree of support given by supplementary benefits varies a great deal, but that the amounts were not large,[46] and the authors conclude that "if one source of income is removed, then strikers may be able to turn to another. Other members of the family may be able to go to work, casual work may be taken and greater debts run up." But the existence of such alternative sources does not supplant the need for supplementary benefits to be available in trade dispute cases.

Urgent need

Section 4 of the Supplementary Benefits Act 1976 permits payment by the Commission in urgent cases, regardless of the trade dispute disqualification. This will usually apply to single people and the Commission has indicated[47] that it will take into account all income received during the dispute and the individual's personal circumstances, including whether he could rely on relatives. A fairly strict subsistence allowance can then be made.[48]

---

[41] Supplementary Benefits Act 1976, s. 8. Section 34 of that Act applies to section 8 the definition of "trade dispute" contained in the Social Security Act 1975, s. 19. See generally Supplementary Benefits Handbook (H.M.S.O.) paras. 160–164 and leaflet S.B.2.

[42] For a statement of what is meant by "resources" see Pollard, *Social Welfare* Law, paras. E.647–E.803 (J.A. Schofield).

[43] It is the amounts to which the person is entitled that are taken into account, not the amounts actually paid. Tax rebates are not taken into account if paid for "periods of unemployment." Supplementary Benefits Act 1976, Sched. 1 para. 26.

[44] See Duncan and McCarthy, "The State Subsidy Theory of Strikes" (1974) 12 B.J.I.R. 26 and the response by Hunter (1974) 12 B.J.I.R. 438. Gennard and Lasko, "Supplementary Benefits and Strikers" (1974) 12 B.J.I.R. 1.

[45] Gennard and Lasko, "The Individual and the Strike" (1975) 13 B.J.I.R. 346.

[46] *Ibid.* In the postmen's strike of 1971 the amounts varied between the grades from 0 to 21.5 per cent. of "in-strike" income (or 14.5 per cent. for all grades). In-strike income represented a drop of 25.4 per cent. of normal income and a drop of 31.8 per cent. of normal purchasing power.

[47] Supplementary Benefits Handbook (H.M.S.O.) para. 162.

[48] Such amounts cannot be recovered by the Commission.

Return to employment

A person who has been engaged in a trade dispute may claim benefit during the first fifteen days of his return to work, but such amounts may later be recovered by the Commission.[49]

Statistics

In order to place the controversial subject of supplementary benefits and trade disputes into its proper perspective it is useful to see the actual amounts and numbers involved.[50]

Year	Total amount paid Strikers	Strikers' families	Number of claims Strikers	Strikers' families	Proportion of entire fund paid in trade disputes
	£	£			
1971	5,434	4,309,149	1,000	125,000	0.7%
1972	181,447	8,380,124	4,700	235,000	1.2%
1973	2,950	729,302	400	35,700	0.1%
1974	46,957	4,994,090	5,800	151,000	0.6%
1975	2,080	776,441	201	26,343	0.06%
1976	—	—	104	9,948	0.02%

VOLUNTARILY LEAVING AND MISCONDUCT

It is a general principle of social security law that a claimant should be penalised if his unemployment was self-induced, and the issue which impinges upon trade union law is whether refusal to join a union comes within the principle. The Social Security Act 1975, s. 20 (1) states:

"A person shall be disqualified for receiving unemployment benefit for such period not exceeding six weeks as may be determined ... if:

(a) he has lost his employment as an employed earner through his misconduct, or has voluntarily left such employment without just cause."

The issue of whether refusal to join a union amounts to misconduct or voluntarily leaving without just cause was fully discussed in R(U) 2/77 where the claimant, a plate-layer employed by British Rail was dismissed for refusing to join the specified union with which British Rail had a "union membership agreement." Consequently, in accordance with the relevant closed shop provisions, his dismissal was fair,[51] and the issue arose whether he was disqualified from benefit.

Misconduct

In R(U) 2/77 the Commissioner defined misconduct as follows:

> " 'Misconduct' in the sense it is used in a social security context, is conduct which is causally but not necessarily directly connected with the employment, and having regard to the relationship of employer and employee and the rights and duties of both, can fairly be described as blameworthy, reprehensible and wrong."

It was alleged by the insurance officer that the claimant had provoked his employer to dismiss him and that he had made himself unsuitable for his job.

---

[49] Supplementary Benefits Act 1976, s. 9 and Sched. 2.

[50] These figures are taken from the Annual Reports of the Supplementary Benefits Commission 1975 (Cmnd. 6615) and 1976 (Cmnd. 6910).

[51] E.P.C.A. 1978, s. 58 (3). In R(U) 2/77 the Commissioner stated that findings of fact by an Industrial Tribunal are cogent evidence but not binding for social security purposes.

In addition it was alleged that his conduct was blameworthy because he caused himself to become a potential charge on the National Insurance Fund. These views were rejected by the Commissioner who held that it would be "wholly inappropriate to describe the claimant's attitude as misconduct."

Prior to this decision there had been cases which suggested that dismissal of an employee for breach of the contract of employment would be dismissal for misconduct, and it may be that the requirement that the claimant must join the union was a condition of his employment.[52] If so it is not clear whether the effect of the decision is that breach of contract does not by itself amount to misconduct, or only that this particular kind of breach does not. However whichever view is taken a dismissal in pursuance of collective industrial relations policy should not give rise to the penalty of disqualification for an individual.

Voluntarily leaving without just cause

(1) *Voluntarily leaving*

In R(U) 16/52 the Commissioner stated as a general principle that "if a person deliberately and knowingly acts in a way which makes it necessary for the employer to dismiss him he may be regarded as leaving his employment voluntarily."[53] Nevertheless in R(U) 2/77 the Commissioner, while agreeing with that statement, went on to say:

> "I see no reason to impute to the claimant the last thing that he had in mind, namely a volition to leave his employment, which he would have been content to pursue as a non-union man ... it would be a misuse of language to describe the claimant as having voluntarily left."

The former case concerned a canteen assistant who, knowing that she had to have a medical examination, refused to undergo an X-ray test; thus in both cases the claimant knew that the stand taken must lead to dismissal. The issue is not whether a person who provokes his dismissal can be said to leave voluntarily (which is very unlikely) but whether a person who does an act which leaves the employer no choice but to dismiss him does so.[54] It may be that "voluntarily" is to be very strictly defined so as to avoid difficulties with the "just cause" portion of the provision, but the effect of R(U) 2/77 is to draw a distinction between a person who refuses to join a union and resign, and one who waits for the inevitable dismissal.

(2) *Just cause*

The two principal cases on the issue of non-membership[55] have thus avoided the need to consider whether a person who refuses to join a union has "just cause" for leaving, but in two earlier cases it had been held that a person would be justified in refusing to join. In R(U) 4/51 it was thought clear in the case of a person who had an objection in principle, but the case of a person who was

---

[52] In the decision it was said that "the claimants situation was clearly affected by the new injected condition of employment." But it need not be such a condition for T.U.L.R.A. 1974, s. 30 as amended by T.U.L.R. (Amendment) Act 1976 states that it is not necessary that the requirement to join the union should be a condition of employment. What other legal source for the requirement exists is not clear.

[53] See R(U) 16/52.

[54] See also R(U) 5/71 where the employer was obliged by law to dismiss the claimant who had refused to register with the General Teaching Council for Scotland as required. He too did not leave voluntarily.

[55] R(U) 5/71 and R(U) 2/77.

merely unwilling to pay his subscription was left open.[56] In R(U) 38/53 the Commissioner relied on the fact that had the claimant remained at work his position would have become intolerable. However, in the light of changed industrial relations it cannot be said that these cases can be relied upon with any certainty. It is suggested that at least in cases where a union membership agreement operates and the claimant must be dismissed, he should not be penalised for the desire of the employer in entering into the agreement or in dismissing the claimant to protect industrial relations. But in cases where the claimant leaves because he is made to feel unwelcome as a non-unionist such considerations may not apply.[57]

Refusal of a Reasonable Opportunity

Section 20 (1) of the Social Security Act 1957 also states that:

> "A person shall be disqualified for receiving unemployment benefit for such period not exceeding six weeks as may be determined ... if:
> (c) he has neglected to avail himself of a reasonable opportunity of suitable employment."

In circumstances similar to that of a claimant refusing to join a union, the Commissioner has permitted this head to be used to justify disqualification. In R(U) 5/71 a teacher refused to register with the General Teaching Council for Scotland and as he could not be employed without registering, he was dismissed, and in the event he was held to be disqualified from benefit on the ground that his objection was neither one of conscience in the true sense nor reasonable.

This decision was, however, distinguished in R(U) 2/77 where a plate-layer was dismissed for refusing to join a union. It is clear that the essential question is whether the claimant was reasonable in his attitude that a particular factor in his employment made the employment unsuitable for him. In R(U) 5/71 it was said that the refusal to register was an intellectual objection rather than a religious or conscientious objection and no doubt this point could be used as a distinguishing mark, but the Commissioner preferred the ground that in the case of the teacher, registration would not affect his employment as a teacher, whereas in the instant case union membership would not only involve financial contributions but would also entail conforming to union practices in industrial relations. Whatever might be meant by that phrase it would appear that this head would not be suitable grounds for disqualification in union membership cases.

Trade disputes

Section 20 (4) of the Social Security Act 1975 makes it clear that a person who is unemployed should not be disqualified under this head if he refuses to take a job which has become vacant "in consequence of a stoppage of work due to a trade dispute." Presumably the point is that the law should not be seen to be encouraging strike breaking by coercing people to take the jobs of those in dispute.

---

[56] But see R(U) 9/59, where the claimant refused to join his firm's superannuation scheme because he thought he could not afford it, and was held not to have left voluntarily. The issue of just cause was not discussed.

[57] See also R(U) 18/52 where the claimant left after he found that during an absence the work he was engaged on had been completed by unskilled labour. This was contrary to the recognised practice of his trade union, but the factory was a non-union shop. The claimant was held to have left without just cause.

ADJUDICATION

Unemployment benefit

The initial application is made to an "insurance officer" of the Department of Health and Social Security.[58] The application must be made on the day in respect of which the claim is made[59] and the officer must make a decision within fourteen days;[60] if that decision is adverse to the claimant he must give reasons and notice of the right of appeal.[61]

The appeal is to a local tribunal (N.I.L.T.) consisting of three members (an independent chairman, one person drawn from a panel of persons representing employed earners, and one from a panel representing employers and other earners).[62] Notice of appeal must be lodged within 21 days of the initial decision.[63] Reasonable notice must be given of the hearing, at which the claimant, the insurance officer and the Secretary of State are entitled to be heard.[64] The claimant (and other parties entitled to be present) may be represented at the hearing by any person of their choice, whether professionally qualified or not.[65] The tribunal must give reasons for its decision.[66]

An appeal lies from the decision of the tribunal to a National Insurance Commissioner by giving notice at the local office within 3 months of the tribunal's decision.[67] The appeal may be lodged either by the insurance officer or by the claimant, but significantly an appeal may also be brought by a trade union where the claimant was a member both at the time when the issue arose and at the time of the appeal.[68]

The Commissioner is not obliged to hold a hearing if he is satisfied that the appeal can be properly determined without one.[69] If there is a hearing, once again reasonable notice must be given[70] and a participant may select any person to represent him.[71] Reasons must be given for the decision,[72] which is final apart from the possibility of obtaining a prerogative remedy of certiorari or mandamus from the High Court.

---

[58] Social Security Act 1975, s. 98 (1).

[59] Social Security (Claims and Payments) Regulations 1975, reg. 13 and Sched. 1. (S.I. 1975 No. 560), but benefit will not be lost if there was good cause for the failure to make it within the prescribed time: *ibid.* reg. 13 (2).

[60] Social Security Act 1975, s. 99 (1). The officer may decide the issue for or against the claimant or may refer it to a local tribunal, (s. 99 (2)). It is also possible for the issue to be reviewed by another insurance officer where there is a mistake of fact or a change in circumstances: *ibid.* s. 104 (1).

[61] *Ibid.* s. 100 (2).

[62] *Ibid.* s. 97 (2).

[63] *Ibid.* s. 100 (4). The time may be extended by the tribunal chairman for good cause.

[64] Social Security (Determination of claims and questions) Regulations 1975 (S.I. 1975 No. 558), regs. 10 and 11).

[65] *Ibid.* reg. 3 (1) (*b*). The tribunal can proceed in the absence of the claimant or his representative; but if a reasonable explanation for absence is given the hearing must first be adjourned for one month. *Ibid.* reg. 10 (2).

[66] *Ibid.* reg. 12 (2) (*b*).

[67] Social Security Act 1975, s. 101.

[68] *Ibid.* s. 101 (2) and (3). This provision also applies to any other association which exists to promote the interests of its members s. 101 (4).

[69] Social Security (Determination of claims and questions) Regulations 1975 (S.I. 1975 No. 558) reg. 13 (1).

[70] *Ibid.* reg. 13 (2).

[71] *Ibid.* reg. 3 (1) (*b*).

[72] *Ibid.* reg. 13 (*b*).

Supplementary benefits
Where a claim for supplementary benefit is made by a person who is unemployed and the issue is the extent of his entitlement because of his involvement in a trade dispute, the procedure differs from that which applies in most cases of supplementary benefit claims.

In the case of a person who is unemployed the appropriate procedure is to complete form B1 obtainable from the local unemployment benefit office[73] and the initial decision is made by an officer of the Supplementary Benefits Commission. The Commission may review its decision if it is satisfied that the initial decision was due to a mistake or if circumstances have changed.[74]

In normal circumstances the appeal from the decision of the Commission would be to a Supplementary Benefits Appeal Tribunal, but it is provided by the Supplementary Benefits Act 1976[75] that where the issue concerns the disregarding of a person's own requirements because of his being involved in a trade dispute it shall be referred (by the S.B.A.T.) to a National Insurance Local Tribunal and dealt with in the same way as an appeal for disqualification from unemployment benefit.[76]

Guarantee payments
The obligation to pay a guarantee payment is on the employer, and if it is not paid the employee may present a complaint to an industrial tribunal within three months.[77] The tribunal may order the payment to be made.

---

[73] Supplementary Benefits (Claims and Payments) Regulations 1977 (S.I. 1977 No. 1142) reg. 3 (2). The usual procedure for a person not required to register for employment is to complete form S.B.1 obtainable from the Social Security officer or the Post Office.

[74] Supplementary Benefits (General) Regulations 1977 (S.I. 1977 No. 1141) reg. 9. This also applies (reg. 10) to a reduction in benefit due to misconduct applied by virtue of the Supplementary Benefits Act 1976 Sched. 1 para 9.

[75] s. 15 (2).

[76] It is assumed that an appeal then lies to the Commissioner: Social Security Act 1975, s. 101 (1).

[77] E.P.C.A. 1978, s. 17. An appeal on a point of law may be presented to the Employment Appeal Tribunal.

CHAPTER 17

CONTROL OF POLITICAL ACTIVITIES

THE POLITICAL FUND

THE existence of financial support by the trade unions is of fundamental importance to the Labour Party, so much so that in 1976 89 per cent. of affiliation fees and contributions came from that source.[1] Such support is not of course the only use of trade unions' political funds, for a number of unions sponsor M.P.'s directly and engage in more general political activity.[2] Not all unions have political funds,[3] but in the case of those that do the Trade Union Act 1913 lays down that expenditure on certain political activities must come from a separate fund, and that members who do not contribute to that fund must not be discriminated against.

The Act of 1913 was passed in order to reverse the effect of the decision of the House of Lords in *Amalgamated Society of Railway Servants* v. *Osborne*[4] that the use of union funds for political purposes was *ultra vires*.[5] It appears that originally Osborne, who was secretary of the Walthamstow branch, had never desired the ending of the political levy but only that it should not be handed over the Labour Party. He alleged that the Walthamstow branch was "overwhelmingly Liberal" and that when a Parliamentary candidate was put up by the union "the branch had been unanimous in opposing the candidate" but "were compelled to pay levies for his financial support and the name of their branch was presented as being by the affiliation with the Labour Party, supporters of the candidature."[6]

---

[1] Report of the National Executive Committee to the 76th Annual Conference of the Labour Party, 1977 p. 59. The number of members affiliated by the 59 affiliated unions was 5,800,069, but this does not represent all the subscribers to the political funds of the relevant unions, as some unions may decide to affiliate only a proportion of their members who subscribe. See generally Harrison, M. *Trade Unions and the Labour Party since 1945* (1960).

[2] The total income of political funds in 1976 was £2,942,000 and expenditure was £2,278,000. The figures for employers' associations were £6,000 and £9,400 respectively. Report of the Certification Officer for 1977.

[3] In 1977 the number was 79. In addition four employers' associations had political funds. Report of the Certification Officer for the year 1977. In 1977 59 unions were affiliated to the Labour Party.

[4] [1910] A.C. 87. For an account of the proceedings see Bagwell, *The Railwaymen* (1963), Chap. 9.

[5] Such payments had been regarded as valid for a number of years, and had been accepted as such in *Steele* v. *South Wales Miners' Federation* [1907] 1 K.B. 361.

[6] See Osborne W. V. "Sane Trade Unionism" (1913) p. 115 *et seq.* For the events leading up to the case and the dispute between Richard Bell and the Labour Representation Committee see the somewhat one sided account in Cox H., "The Story of the Osborne Case" 68 Nineteenth Century 569. Osborne was finally expelled from the union and he sued again. *Osborne* v. *Amalgamated Society of Railway Servants* [1911] 1 Ch. 540. The expulsion was held to be invalid.

Today there is no general restriction on the use of funds by trade unions and funds may be used for any purpose so long as it is authorised by the rules, but where the expenditure is on a political purpose as defined by the Act of 1913 the terms of that Act must be observed.

The Act applies to any trade union or unincorporated employers' association[7] as defined in section 2 of the Act.[8] The definitions are the same as those contained in the Trade Union and Labour Relations Act 1974 (except that the 1913 Act does not apply to incorporated employers' associations).

Use of the political fund

While it would be usual to find that in practice the political fund is devoted entirely to political purposes, one issue that has not yet been finally decided is whether the political fund may also be used for the general purposes of the union. The effect of the Trade Union Act 1913 is not that the fund *must* be used for political purposes but only that the general fund cannot be so used, for the purpose of the Act, in addition to legalising political funds, was to protect the general fund from such use. Therefore if the political fund rules specifically permit it the fund may be used for general purposes, but if there is no such rule the matter is more difficult.

On the one hand it may be argued that the levy is paid by the individual member to trustees to be used for the purposes of the political fund. The moneys are therefore impressed with a trust and the trustees may not apply the fund for purposes other than those for which it was donated.

On the other hand it may be argued that the effect of adopting political fund rules is simply to enlarge the purposes for which union funds may be applied and that the levy is paid not exclusively for the purposes of the fund but for the purposes of the union as a whole, together with authorisation for its use for political purposes. This view is supported by the fact that the Act does not require the money to be used exclusively for political purposes, nor do the rules that are usually adopted for the fund. If this view is accepted it would be possible to apply the political fund for general purposes, even in the absence of a specific rule.

The source of payments for political purposes

The effect of the 1913 Act is that payments for political purposes, as defined by the Act, can only be made from the separate political fund[9] adopted by the union under the Act, and the union is prohibited from using its general fund for such purposes.

Indirect payments

The statute prohibits[9] payments in furtherance of political objects which are made "either directly or in conjunction with any other trade union, association or body, or otherwise indirectly" unless the payment is made out of the political fund. The problem of indirect payments was raised in the leading case before the Registrar of *Foster and the National Amalgamated Union of Shop*

[7] If the association is a company it is subject to s. 19 of the Companies Act 1967, and the directors must include in their report any sum over £50 given to political purposes which are defined as purposes likely to affect public support for a political party, or as donations to a political party.

[8] These sections were substituted by the Trade Union and Labour Relations Act 1974 Sched. 3.

[9] Trade Union Act 1913, s. 3 (1) (a).

Assistants.[10] One of the many issues was whether the payment by the union of its affiliation fee to the T.U.C. was *ultra vires* because the T.U.C. had paid for the printing of a pamphlet entitled "The T.U.C. General Council Appeal to the Officials and Members of British Trade Unions' which was to be sent to voters in every constituency in which no Labour Party candidate was standing for election. The Registrar held that although the pamphlet was a "political" document the union was not in breach of its political fund rules. This was so because the payment of the affiliation fee was not *in furtherance* of a political object because the union was unable to control the use of T.U.C. funds and was not aware that the funds would be used for political purposes.[11] The exact meaning of the Registrar's decision is unclear, but it is suggested that a payment will be a breach of the political fund rules either if the union is aware that the payment is likely to be used for political purposes or if, being unaware of the likely use of the money, it is able to control the use of the funds of the organisation to which the money is paid.

It is inevitable that there will be a slight subsidy of the political fund by the general fund, such as, for example, by the use of union stationery for political fund business, or the use of a room in the union's headquarters for a committee meeting. A union should not be required to go through the costly procedure of accounting separately for such items. It is suggested that the *de minimis* principle alone will not absolve such payments, since small payments have been held to be *ultra vires.*[12] It is suggested however, that there should be no difficulty where the amounts are both insignificant and collateral to the main purpose of a political fund.

The meaning of "political" objects

The restrictions of the Trade Union Act 1913 apply only to political objects as defined by section 3 (3) of the Act, and therefore a union is free, so long as it is authorised to do so by its rules,[13] to use the general fund for political activities outside the statute, such as the promotion of technical legislation in Parliament to enhance the safety of its members.

Section 3 (3) of the Trade Union Act 1913 states:

"The political objects to which this section applies are the expenditure of money—

(a) on the payment of any expenses incurred either directly or indirectly by a candidate or prospective candidate for election to Parliament or to any public office, before, during, or after the election in connection with his candidature or election; or

(b) on the holding of any meeting or the distribution of any literature or documents in support of any such candidate or prospective candidate; or

---

[10] Report of the Registrar of Friendly Societies for the year 1925.

[11] It might be noted that neither the T.U.C. nor Trades Councils make payments directly for political purposes, although of course they are closely allied with the Labour Party. *Foster's* case was therefore exceptional.

[12] In *Newman and BISAKTA*, Reports of Selected Disputes referred to the Registrar of Friendly Societies 1938–49, p. 237, a payment of one guinea was held *ultra vires* but no order was made. But note the comment of the Registrar in *Foster's* case, Reports of the Registrar for the year 1925, that the attributable amount in that case was "infinitesimal".

[13] *Bennett* v. *National Amalgamated Society of Operative House & Ship Painters & Decorators* (1915) 31 T.L.R. 203; *Carter* v. *United Society of Boilermakers and Steel Shipbuilders* (1915) 32 T.L.R. 40.

(c) on the maintenance of any person who is a member of Parliament or who holds a public office; or
(d) in connection with the registration of electors or the selection of a candidate for Parliament or any public office; or
(e) on the holding of political meetings of any kind, or on the distribution of political literature or political documents of any kind, unless the main purpose of the meetings or of the distribution of the literature or documents is the furtherance of statutory objects within the meaning of this Act.

The expression 'public office' in this section means the office of members of any county, county borough, district, or parish council, or board of guardians, or of any public body who have power to raise money, either directly or indirectly, by means of a rate."

Support for candidates for public office

Support for candidates for political office covers not only aspiring Members of Parliament, but also any county, district, parish or community council or any body that has power to raise money by the levy of a rate. The range of officers is defined exhaustively, and as the section stands at the moment it does not cover elections to the European Assembly. In such a case therefore a candidate's expenses may be paid out of the general fund if the rules permit it.[14] The support which must be paid for out of the political fund covers any assistance given to a candidate before, during or after the election and even covers expenses relating to a prospective candidate. The sub-section thus includes all expenses from the moment a union decides to support a candidate, including expenses involved in getting him selected as a prospective candidate, whether the payments are direct or indirect.

Indirect support. Williams v. *Cotter*[15] raised an interesting point concerning an indirect payment. Cotter, who was President of the Amalgamated Marine Workers Union, stood for election in the Aston division of Birmingham. One Matt Tearle, Secretary of the National Sailors and Firemen's Union, North East Coast, sent a telegram to the Conservative candidate stating, "Seamen of Britain wish you success in fight against trade union wreckers. Cotter . . . started a scab union this year." Cotter lost the ensuing libel action and his union agreed to reimburse his legal costs. The plaintiffs were trustees of the union who sought directions as to whether the money should be paid from the general or the political fund. Russell J. held that it could not come from the general fund as it was not covered by the rules[16] and that it would be "grotesque to say that the costs of this libel action were costs incurred directly or indirectly in connection with Cotter's candidature for Parliament." It is suggested however, that the point may not be so obvious, but at least it can be said that such a payment should not be made out of the general fund.

Mixed purposes. Other paragraphs of section 3 (3) cover more specific "political" activities and include expenses involved in the registration of electors and selection of the candidate.[17] In addition "political" includes the "holding of any meeting or the distribution of any literature or documents in

[14] Or out of the political fund, if the rules of that fund permit it. No change is made by the European Assembly Elections Act 1978. The same is also true of members of the proposed assemblies for Scotland and Wales under the Scotland Act 1978 and the Wales Act 1978.
[15] *The Times*, May 8, 1925.
[16] It was held that the costs did not arise "out of the employment or the work of the union."
[17] s. 3 (3) (d) of the Trade Union Act 1913.

support of any such candidate or prospective candidate."[18] It seems that this definition can render "political" those documents and meetings that have a more general purpose, for in *Foster's* case[19] the Registrar said that "Meetings and documents of the purest trade union kind, without any admixture of Labour or other politics, must be paid for out of the political fund if they are to be held or issued in support of a candidate or prospective candidate." Such a ruling could expecially affect trade union newspapers and it seems that if the paper includes any promotion of the cause of a sponsored candidate the costs of the whole issue may fall on the political fund. Whether this result would follow if the "political" matter is in a physically separate supplement is unclear, but it is suggested that in such a case only the expenses of the supplement should be attributed to the political fund. The ruling also affects union meetings which adopt a person as the union candidate.

Broadcasting. This provision was devised before the days of radio and television and would seem inappropriate to cover such expenses, but paragraph (a) might be held applicable, at least in cases of expenses incurred by an individual candidate. It is not so clear that money paid to support the broadcasting expenses of a party generally would be covered under paragraphs (a) or (d) or even paragraph (e), for paragraphs (a) and (d) refer to individuals, and paragraphs (d) and (e) would be difficult to apply to broadcasting.

Sponsored Members of Parliament and holders of other offices

The tradition of sponsorship of Members of Parliament goes back to 1874 when Thomas Bart and Alexander McDonald were elected[20] and has grown to such an extent that in October 1974 there were 126 sponsored Members.[21] In most cases the sponsorship consists of assistance with election[22] or secretarial expenses, but may include payments to the M.P. himself.[23] Many of these payments will come under paragraphs (a) (b) and (d), but some may be dealt with under paragraph (c) which covers payments for the maintenance of any person who is a Member of Parliament or who holds public office. "Maintenance" would include not only a salary but also assistance with such matters as accommodation, travelling expenses or secretarial help.

In some cases a Member will not only be sponsored by the union but will also hold office within it, and in such cases a distinction must be drawn between payments to him as Member of Parliament and as union official. In *McCarthy and the National Association of Theatrical and Kine Employees*[24] Sir Tom O'Brien was both general secretary of the union and an M.P. It was held

---

[18] s. 3 (3) (b).

[19] Report of the Registrar for the year 1925.

[20] For a general history of sponsorship see Muller, *The Kept Men*? (1977).

[21] Butler and Sloman, *British Political Facts* (4th ed.) pp. 137–139. There were in addition 16 Co-operative Party M.P.s so that out of a total of 319 Labour Members, 142 were sponsored in some way.

[22] These payments are made according to the Hastings agreement. This agreement, adopted by the annual conference of the Labour Party in 1933, limits the amount of assistance unions may offer to a constituency Labour party, and in 1976 the maximum was £350 in boroughs and £420 in county constituences, plus up to 80 per cent. of the election expenses. It is thought that less than half the sponsoring unions pay the maximum.

[23] Sponsorship is now declared in the Register of Members Interests. See the 2nd edition as at May 22, 1976, H.C. 284 (1975–76). For a general description see the Report of the Select Committee on Member's Interests (Declaration) esp. Appendix 3. H.C. 57 (1969–70).

[24] Report of the Registrar for the year 1957.

that his salary as an official could be paid out of the general fund even despite the fact that it was money going to support a person who was an M.P. Thus the words "maintenance of any person who is a Member of Parliament" are construed as meaning "maintenance of any person in *his capacity as* . . ." No doubt however the payments must be for genuine work done as an official and not merely as an evasion of the political fund rules.

Payments for political meetings and political literature

The final issue to be discussed concerns political meetings and political literature of any kind that is not within the statutory objects of the union. The "statutory objects" were formerly of great significance in trade union law, but their function is now limited to the point that if the purpose is a statutory object it cannot be a "political" purpose within the Trade Union Act 1913, even though it is an objective taken up by a political party.[25] In view of its limited significance it is thought unlikely that the definition[26] will give rise to any difficulty in the future.[27]

Paragraph (e) could however have had a serious effect on trade union functions, covering as it does political meetings and literature *of any kind*, but fortunately the Registrar has taken the view that "political" here means "party political." He has said,[28]

> "The definition of political objects ought to be viewed in the light of the decision from which, notoriously, it sprang, unless there is something in the definition itself which militates against such a view. In my opinion, therefore, 'political' in this section is not used in the sense in which Hobbes or Locke or Lord Hardwicke L.C. would use it[29] . . . but in a much narrower sense. To put it as shortly as possible, 'political' as it is used in this section, is not the adjectival form of 'polity' but the adjectival form of 'party politics'."

The case concerned the question whether the affiliation fee of the union to the T.U.C. was used by the T.U.C. for "political" purposes, and amongst the items which were held not be political were expenditure on the National Joint Departments which engaged in research and publicity, the payment of the affiliation fee to the Labour and Socialist International and the publication of the Labour Yearbook. The major issue was whether support for the "Daily Herald" was political, but having analysed the contents of an issue selected at random and having found that only four-and-a-half out of 50 columns could be regarded as "political," the Registrar held that there was no breach of the rules as statutory objects clearly prevailed.

"Distribution". A further point raised in *Foster's case*[30] was the meaning of "distribution" for the purposes of paragraph (e) and the Registrar has suggested that this must be limited to free or subsidised distribution and that

---

[25] See *Foster's* case, Report of the Registrar for the year 1925.

[26] Statutory objects are defined by the Trade Union Act 1913, s. 1. as "the regulation of relations between workmen and masters, or between workmen and workmen, or between masters and masters, or the imposing of restrictive conditions on the conduct of any trade or business, and also the provision of benefits to members.

[27] For a complete discussion of the meaning of statutory objects see Citrine, *Trade Union Law* (3rd ed.), pp. 400–408.

[28] *Foster's* case, Report of the Registrar for the year 1925.

[29] See *Earl of Chesterfield* v. *Jansenn* (1750) 2 Ves. Sen. 125 at 156; 28 E.R. 82 at 100 where he said politics "comprehends everything that concerns the government of the country."

[30] Report of the Registrar for the year 1925.

money spent "in a commercial way on the preparation and production of literature or documents, which will subsequently be sold to the public at an adequate price, or at the price at which the public will buy them, is not within the definition." This distinction has not however found favour, since the words of the statute appear to comprehend distribution of any kind.

Remedies

The remedies for an alleged misapplication of funds are complicated by the fact that two separate avenues may be open to a complainant. On the one hand he may complain to the Certification Officer that there has been a breach of the rules adopted by the union in pursuance of the Trade Union Act 1913, and on the other hand it may be possible for him to bring an action before the courts on the grounds that there has been a breach of the statute itself. As most unions have adopted the model political fund rules issued by the Certification Officer and as these rules closely follow the wording of the statute, the same wording may be applicable whichever route is followed.

Breach of the rules

Each union that has a political fund must adopt rules approved by the Certification Officer, and by virtue of the Trade Union Act 1913, s. 3 (2), he is given exclusive jurisdiction to determine whether there has been a breach of these rules. If he finds that there has been a breach of the rules he may make "such order as he thinks just under the circumstances," and such an order may be enforced as if it were an order of the County Court.[31] An appeal lies from the decision of the Certification Officer to the Employment Appeal Tribunal on any question of law.[32]

Normally the application will be made by a person who does not contribute to the political fund to the effect that money which has been taken from the general fund ought to have been taken from the political fund;[33] but the reverse is also possible so that a person who has contributed to the fund may complain that money taken from the political fund ought to have come from the general fund. This is what happened in the case of *Corrigan and USDAW*[34] where the complainant objected to the fact that contribution to the Hungarian Relief Fund had come from the political fund and he argued that as it was a charitable payment it should have been paid out of the general fund.

This case gave rise to an interesting point about the jurisdiction of the Registrar for it was agreed that it was not a "political" payment within the meaning of section 3 of the Trade Union Act 1913, but as we have seen, if the political fund rules allow it the political fund *can* be used for other purposes. USDAW did have such a rule enabling the fund to be used for purposes wider than those envisaged in the Act, and it was this rule that was in issue. However the Act states that the jurisdiction of the Registrar is limited to rules made *in pursuance of* the Act, and as the rule in question was not limited to "political" purposes it was not made in pursuance of the Act and therefore the Registrar had no jurisdiction to hear the complaint once he had decided the payment

---

[31] The order must first be registered with the County Court: the procedure is laid down in Order 44 of the County Court Rules.

[32] Trade Union Act 1913, s. 5A as inserted by E.P.A. 1975 Sched. 16. See also E.P.C.A. 1978, s. 136 (2).

[33] As in *Foster's* case, Report of the Registrar for the year 1925.

[34] Report of the Registrar for the year 1957.

was not "political." In other words the Registrar does not necessarily have jurisdiction over the political fund of a union or over the rules that govern it, but only has jurisdiction over rules that are required to be passed under the Act.

For example in *Coleman and P.O.E.U.*[35] the registrar declined jurisdiction in a case where a member questioned the validity of the affiliation of his branch to the local Labour Party. This was done on the grounds that the rule permitting affiliation was not a rule that itself provided for a payment in furtherance of political objects, but was merely a rule which when operated may have the consequence that such payments may fall to be made. This seems a somewhat narrow interpretation of section 3 (2) of the Trade Union Act 1913 since it would be difficult to affiliate without paying fees, so that a rule permitting affiliation could be said by implication to authorise the consequent fees if powers are exercised under the rule.

Breach of the statute

The statute is phrased in mandatory terms and it might be thought that a person should have a remedy if its terms are broken. The point arose in *Foster and the National Amalgamated Union of Shop Assistants, Warehousemen and Clerks*[36] where the applicant, having failed to obtain a remedy from the Registrar, presented the same case before the Chancery Division on the grounds that the terms of the statute had been infringed. Eve J. stated that in his opinion the intention was to limit the complainant to his remedy before the Registrar for breach of the rules, because it would be wrong to expose the union to further litigation before the Court if the complainant failed at his first attempt. It is suggested that now that an appeal is provided to the Employment Appeal Tribunal[37] from the decision of the Registrar on points of law this view is likely to be accepted today.

Although the point was not argued, Eve J. also raised the question whether the complainant has a choice whether to apply first to the court or to the Registrar. The point was not decided as in the case itself the complainant had already made his election by going first to the Registrar, and so the point remains open.

However, an action based directly on the terms of the statute may be available if the allegation is not that the political fund rules have been broken, but rather that they do not comply with the Act, and in such a case the fact that the rules have been approved by the Registrar does not prevent the court enquiring into their legality.[38] If the case has previously been before the Registrar for the rules to be interpreted, that interpretation will be accepted by the court.

ESTABLISHING THE POLITICAL FUND

The procedure for establishing a political fund is somewhat complicated, but the process is facilitated by the provision of a document of instruction and model rules by the Certification Officer.

---

[35] Report of the Registrar for the year 1974. See (1976) 5 I.L.J. 261.

[36] [1927] 1 Ch. 539. This case is the sequel to *Foster's* case before the Registrar. See also *Birch* v. *N.U.R.* [1950] Ch. 602 at 609.

[37] Trade Union Act 1913 s. 5A, as inserted by the E.P.A. 1975 Sched. 16.

[38] *Birch* v. *N.U.R.* [1950] Ch. 602.

Adoption of ballot rules

Under the Act the union must first adopt rules authorising it to hold a ballot to approve the political fund rules. It is usual to pass a combined resolution[39] which not only adopts the ballot rules but also agrees that the ballot to have a political fund shall be held, and that political fund rules will be adopted if the procedure is successful.

The combined resolution can then be passed according to the union's own procedure for the alteration of rules, but the statute also provides[40] that it may be passed either by a majority of members or by a majority of delegates at a meeting called for the purpose, notwithstanding the union's rules.

Such ballot rules must then be approved by the Certification Officer[41] who must be satisfied that they ensure that "every member has an equal right, and if reasonably possible, a fair opportunity of voting, and that the secrecy of the ballot is properly secured."[42] Once these rules have been adopted the way is clear to approve the political fund rules themselves.

Approval of the political fund rules

These rules must also be approved by the Certification Officer[43] who has again provided model rules. The rules must require (1) that payments for "political" purposes must be made from a separate political fund; (2) that a member may be exempted from the obligation to contribute if he gives due notice; (3) that a member who does not contribute shall not be under any disadvantage compared with other members; (4) that contribution to the political fund shall not be made a condition of admission to the union.[44] These rules must be passed by a majority of those voting.[44]

Once the political fund rules have been adopted the union may begin to levy the contribution, but the union is first obliged[45] to give notice to each member of his right to contract out of the political levy[46] and if a member does indicate within one month in the proper form[47] that he wishes to contract out that

---

[39] A model for the combined resolution has been drawn up by the Certification Officer and provides as follows:
"It is hereby resolved:
1. That the rules of the organisation be altered by the addition of the rules for ballot under the Trade Union Act 1913, to be approved by the Certification Officer; and that a ballot be taken in accordance with such rules on a resolution approving the furtherance of political objects within the meaning of the said Act as an object of the organisation.
2. That, if a majority of the members of the organisation voting on such ballot pass such resolution, the rules of the organisation be further altered by adding the rules for the political fund of the union, to be approved by the Certification Officer."

[40] Trade Union Act 1913, s. 4 (2).

[41] It is usual to obtain preliminary approval before the ballot rules are adopted, for otherwise if they do not comply with the statute, the whole procedure will have to be repeated.

[42] Trade Union Act 1913, s. 4 (1).

[43] The fact that the rules have been approved does not mean that they necessarily comply with the Trade Union Act 1913. They may still be challenged. *Birch* v. *N.U.R.* [1950] Ch. 602.

[44] Trade Union Act 1913, s. 3 (1).

[45] Trade Union Act 1913, s. 5 (1).

[46] The Certificate Officer has provided a model rule for the giving of notice (alternative rule 3) which requires the notice to be published in such manner as notices are usually given by the union (*e.g.* in the newspaper) and also that a copy shall be posted at the office or meeting place of the branch, and that the secretary of each branch shall take steps to see that so far as practicable each member receives a copy of the notice. The statute does not require that the notice be actually given to each member personally. *Burns and the A.E.U.*, Reports of Selected Disputes 1938–49, p. 227.

[47] The proper form is discussed in the next section.

notice is effective from that date.[48] To accommodate this the model rules state that the levy shall not come into force until one month after publication of the notice.[49]

It should be noted that generally the rules only authorise the union to make the levy and do not oblige it to do so, with the result that it is possible to raise the contributions from only a portion of the membership if that is desired. The point can be illustrated by *Edwards and the National Federation of Insurance Workers*[50] where the Registrar ruled that although the union had adopted political fund rules the complaint that it had failed to collect the levy must be dismissed as the rules placed the union under no duty to do so.

Summary

The following is the order of the procedure for adopting political fund rules[51]

(1) Preliminary approval by the Certification Officer of the proposed ballot rules and political fund rules.

(2) Pass the "combined resolution."

(3) Formal approval of the ballot rules by the Certification Officer.

(4) Ballot to approve the political fund rules.

(5) Inform the Certification Officer of the result of the ballot.

(6) Formal approval of the political fund rules by the Certification Officer.

(7) Notice to members of their right to contract out of the political levy.

(8) Begin the levy of members who have not contracted out.

PROTECTING THE NON-CONTRIBUTOR

The Act requires that a person must be able to contract out of the political levy and provides considerable protection for him once he has done so. In practice about 80 per cent. of members of those unions which do have political funds pay the levy.[52]

The choice between contracting out and contracting in has been a matter of considerable political controversy. Between 1927 and 1946[53] the system was altered so that a person was required to contract in to the political levy and this had a substantial effect on the amounts contributed.[54]

Contracting out

Section 5 of the Act provides that: "A member of a trade union may at any time give notice in the form set out in the Schedule to this Act or in a form to the like effect, that he objects to contribute to the political fund of the union

[48] Trade Union Act 1913, s. 5 (2).

[49] Alternative rule 7 of the Model Rules.

[50] Reports of Selected Disputes 1938–49, p. 241.

[51] This follows the helpful "outline of the procedure for establishing a political fund" provided by the Certification Officer.

[52] The figure in 1977 was 81 per cent. There is however a wide variation between unions. Thus the proportion of NUPE members contributing was 99 per cent., whereas the figure for SOGAT 1975 was 18 per cent. Report of the Certification Officer for 1977. It is thought that in 1978 the contribution averaged about 5 pence per month but in some cases it was twice that.

[53] The system was introduced by the Trade Disputes and Trade Unions Act 1927 and repealed by the Trade Disputes and Trade Unions Act 1946. "Contracting in" is still the rule in Northern Ireland.

[54] In 1927 76 per cent. of members of unions with political funds contributed; in 1928 the figure was 58 per cent.

. . ." and that such notice shall take effect from the first day of January next after the notice is given.[55]

The form of the exemption notice

The notice must either be in the statutory form[56] or in a form "to the like effect." The union cannot insist that the exemption notice be given on a form supplied by the union,[57] and the Registrar has held that no objection can be taken to a form supplied by the Conservative Party[58] if it is in due form.[59] A handwritten notice is perfectly valid,[60] and it may be that a purely oral notice may be effective. That issue arose in *Templeman and the A.U.E.W.*[61] but although there was nothing in the Trade Union Act 1913 to require the notice to be in writing the point was left undecided as it was held that since the union had been treating the notice as a valid notice for some 3 years it was estopped from denying its validity.

Time of contracting out

A member may submit the form at any time but in the case of an existing member the notice will only be effective from January 1 next following.[62] One question is whether a member could claim to have his exemption take effect earlier if the delay is due to the refusal of the union to provide an exemption form. For example if the request for a form is made on December 1 but not delivered until January 5, will the exemption be held to take effect from that January or the next? Since forms may be obtained from many sources,[63] or even devised by the member himself it may be that no concession would be made.[64]

Where the political fund has been newly established the union is under a duty to give notice to members of the union[65] of their right to claim exemption, in which case notice given within one month of the receipt of that information is effective immediately.

The Act makes no provision for people who join a union that has an existing

---

[55] The section also makes provision for notice of the right to contract out to be given to all members when political fund rules are newly adopted. In such a case a demand for exemption given within one month takes effect immediately.

[56] The statutory form states "I hereby give notice that I object to contribute to the Political Fund of the [—] union, and am in consequence exempt, in manner provided by the Trade Union Act 1913 from contributing to that fund."

[57] Nor can the rules require that the member must apply for his form personally from the union. *Flexten and the A.E.U.*, Report of the Registrar for the year 1965.

[58] The Conservative Party has in recent years been distributing a number of exemption forms.

[59] *Hewett and the E.T.U.*, Reports of Selected Disputes 1938–49, p. 221.

[60] *Valentine and the E.T.U.*, Report of the Registrar for the year 1957.

[61] Report of the Registrar for the year 1969.

[62] The form may not be antedated. *Nutter and the A.E.U.* , Reports of Selected Disputes, 1938–49, p. 240. The form signed in July 1947 was antedated to January 1, 1947. It was held that it took effect on January 1, 1948.

[63] The union is not required by the statute to make forms available, but this duty is usually contained in the rules. See the Model Rules of the Certification Officer, rule 3.

[64] The issue could have arisen in *Nutter and the A.E.U.*, Reports of Selected Disputes of 1938–49, p. 240, but the Registrar rejected the claimant's allegation that he had applied for a form before the New Year.

[65] See *Burns and the A.E.U.*, Reports of Selected Disputes, 1938–49, p. 227 where it is stated that the notice need not be given to the member personally but that posting it on a notice board would be sufficient.

political fund, but the Model Rules[66] issued by the Certification Officer apply the same principles to new members as are applied to members in the case of new political funds, so that a new member is given one month to contract out after he is given a copy of the political fund rules. In practice this rule is generally adopted by unions.

Although the Act states that a member may give notice at any time[67] it is clear that he must be a member when he does so. In *Wilson and A.E.U.*[68] the complainant filled in an application form to join the union and in reply to the question "will you contribute to the political fund?" wrote "no." It was held that this was not a notice of exemption since at the time he made the reply he was not a member.

Calculating the exemption

The Act[69] states that the relief from the political levy may be achieved for exempted members in one of two ways. The first, and simplest, is where the levy is collected by means of an additional periodical payment from contributing members, in which case the levy cannot be made upon exempt members. The second method is where the political levy is combined in some way with the ordinary subscription. This is done either by stating that a proportion of a periodical contribution forms the political levy (such as 15p. of the first week's subscription in each quarter)[70] or by saying that the whole of one of the subscriptions shall be the levy (such as the first weekly amount in each year).[71] In either case the rules must specify how the levy is calculated so that a member may know the amount of the dues of which he is relieved.

One difficulty that has arisen in recent years with the more common use of the "check-off" system to collect union dues is whether it is lawful to collect the full subscription (including the levy) and then to repay the political levy to exempt members. It is suggested that such a system would be a breach of the statute since the obligation is to "relieve any members who are exempt from the payment of the whole or any part of any periodical contribution."[72] This makes it clear that the exempt member is under no obligation to pay in the first place, and cannot be required to pay and then accept a refund. The point arose in *Robinson and NACODS (Durham Area)*[73] where the weekly dues were 1s 5½d with an additional ½d for the political levy. It appeared that the Coal Board computer could not handle half-pennies and so the complainant was obliged to pay 1s 6d and was promised a refund of the political levy at the end of the year. It was stated that the demands of the computer must not be allowed to defeat the statutory right of members in relation to exemptions and it was held that there had been a breach of the rules.[74]

It is clear that a union cannot avoid the duty to relieve an exempt member of the levy by relieving instead the contributing members of part of the general

[66] See Model Rule 6.
[67] Trade Union Act 1913, s. 5 (1).
[68] Report of the Registrar for the year 1953.
[69] Trade Union Act 1913, s. 6.
[70] For an example see T.G.W.U. Rule 24 (7).
[71] For an example see E.E.T.P.U. Rule 28 (8).
[72] Trade Union Act 1913, s. 6.
[73] Report of the Registrar for the year 1966.
[74] The point also arose in a case in 1972 but no hearing was necessary to resolve the dispute. Report of the Registrar for the year 1972.

dues. The point is illustrated by *Griffiths and N.U.G.M.W.*[75] where the general fund subscription was 1s and the political levy 4d. On the occasion in question the union exacted only 1s from the contributing members (*i.e.* 8d general fund and 4d political levy), but when the complainant paid only 8d he was marked 4d in arrears. In other words the complainant was being asked to pay a higher rate of general levy than contributing members. It was held that this was a breach of a rule that an exempt member must not be placed under a disadvantage as compared with other members of the union.

Remedies

Once again the remedy is by way of complaint to the Certification Officer,[76] and the points made earlier about remedies for mis-application of funds also apply here, but the following points might also be noted. In relation to contracting out the Registrar may make an order that a member is to be treated as an exempt member, and may also order that he should not be treated as being in arrears.[77]

In addition to ordering that a person be treated as exempt the Registrar may order the refund of any political levy improperly demanded, and may also order the union to pay any expenses incurred as a result of a hearing before him.[78]

Preventing discrimination against exempted members

Section 3 of the Trade Union Act 1913 states that the political fund rules must include a provision that,

> "... a member who is exempt from the obligation to contribute to the political fund of the union shall not be excluded from any benefits of the union, or placed in any respect either directly or indirectly under any disability or at any disadvantage as compared with other members of the union (except in relation to the control or management of the political fund) by reason of his being so exempt, and that contribution to the political fund of the union shall not be made a condition for admission to the union."

Exclusion from union office

One of the most important questions concerning discrimination against the exempt member is whether he may be excluded from holding a union office if part of his functions would be to deal with the political fund. The statute is ambiguous on this point but the matter was referred to the courts in *Birch* v. *N.U.R.*[79] The plaintiff was dismissed from the chairmanship of the Woodford Halse branch of the N.U.R. on the grounds that he did not contribute to the political fund. He complained to the Registrar who held that the office did

---

[75] Report of the Registrar for the year 1928.

[76] Between February 1976 and February 1978 there were 15 complaints to the Certification Officer (covering 22 cases) from members who had been unable to stop payment of the levy. H.C., Debs., vol 944 *col. 387* (February 17, 1978).

[77] See *Griffiths and N.U.G.M.W.* Report of the Registrar for the year 1928, where the point is made that the order need not be such as a County Court would make, but only such as a County Court could enforce under Order 44.

[78] See *Gasson and NACODS*, Report of the Registrar for the year 1969, where the complainant recovered loss of wages due to attending the hearing and travelling expenses, and postage expenses.

[79] [1950] Ch. 602.

involve control or management of the political fund and therefore that there was no breach of a rule[80] (which had been approved by the Registrar)[81] that stated that "such a member shall take no part in the control or management of the political fund of the union and shall be ineligible to occupy any office or representative position involving any such control or management."[82]

The plaintiff thereupon applied to the court for a declaration that the rule did not comply with the requirements of the Trade Union Act 1913 and Danchwerts J. agreed, saying that "as the constitution of the union fails to separate the control and management of the political fund from the other functions of the union, there is no limit to the area of the exception and an exempted member might find himself excluded from practically all the activities of his branch.[83]

The effect of *Birch* v. *N.U.R.*[84] is unclear. In particular it may be asked whether the principle is to be so strictly construed that an exempt member may not be excluded from a post which is principally concerned with political matters, but which also involves other functions. It is suggested that such a view would be mistaken as the Trade Union Act 1913 recognised that it was reasonable to exclude non-contributors from management of the fund.

It has also been suggested that the principle in the case should only be applied to the lower offices of a union, and that it should be permissible to exclude non-contributors from high office.[85] But it is suggested that such a view, although pragmatic, is against principle.

Other political functions

Other functions related to the political fund may include representation of the union on some outside body and taking part in a vote to select a parliamentary candidate. It is suggested that a person can never be restricted from representing the union[86] since such representation is not "in relation to the control or management of the political fund," even if it is on an outside body supported by the political fund.[87] As to taking part in a vote to select a person such as a

---

[80] The rule was not the same as the Registrar's Model Rule.

[81] The fact that the rules had been approved did not mean that they did not contravene the statute: *Birch* v. *N.U.R.* [1950] Ch. 602 at 612.

[82] In *Birch* v. *N.U.R. ibid.,* Danckwerts J. followed the view of Eve J. in *Foster* v. *National Amalgamated Union of Shop Assistants* [1927] 1 Ch. 539 that the court was bound by the terms of the Trade Union Act 1913 to accept the interpretation of the rule by the Registrar.

[83] In the similar case of *Vaughan and the National Association of Plasterers*, Report of the Registrar for the year 1932, the complainant had been turned down for the post of Assistant Secretary on the grounds that he was unsuitable as he did not contribute to the political fund. The rules only required that applicants should be considered for the post, and in addition he was unsuitable because he may have had to deputise for the General Secretary in managing the political fund or attending the Labour Party Conference. The Registrar held that there was no breach of the rules, but the validity of the rules was never tested.

[84] [1950] Ch. 602.

[85] See Grunfeld, *Modern Trade Union Law* (1966) p. 305 and Grunfeld "Political Independence in British Trade Unions: some legal aspects" (1963) 1 B.J.I.R. 23. For a contrary view which is preferred, see Citrine, *Trade Union Law* (3rd ed.) p. 426.

[86] A non-contributor would not be eligible to be a delegate to the Labour Party Conference by virtue of the rules of the Labour Party.

[87] The issue might have arisen in *Cleger and the London District of the Amalgamated Union of Operative Bakers, Confectioners and Allied Workers,* Report of the Registrar for the year 1935, but the Registrar held that the reason for the refusal to send the complainant as a delegate to the London Trades Council was due not to his being an exempt member but because he was a "disruptive element."

Parliamentary candidate it is suggested that this would involve management of the political fund and an exempt member could be excluded.[88]

A duty or a power to exclude?

The Act does not say that a person must be excluded from management of the political fund but only that the union may so exclude him. If therefore a non-contributor does take part in a "political" activity his participation is perfectly lawful unless the power to exclude has been exercised.[88]

Discrimination in non-political matters

An exempt member shall not be deprived of any benefits of the union, nor shall he be placed under any disadvantage as compared with other union members; so that when a union attempted in effect to charge exempt members a higher general subscription, there was a breach of the rules.[89]

Discrimination outside the union

The Registrar only has jurisdiction in cases where the complainant has been put under a disadvantage within the union itself and where an effective order could be made. The Registrar could not involve himself with discrimination affecting a person's position outside his union. Thus in *Bond and T.G.W.U.*[90] the complainant alleged that the union had taken steps to force his employer to dismiss him because he was a non-contributor, but the Registrar denied himself jurisdiction. Such an allegation would now give rise to a case of unfair dismissal against the employer.

BREACH OF PRIVILEGE

The common custom of trade unions sponsoring Members of Parliament raises delicate issues relating to parliamentary privilege[91] and the House of Commons has had to consider the relationship between the union and the M.P. on a number of occasions. Although Parliament is extremely sensitive about the freedom of its members,[92] it has been recommended[92] that the penal jurisdiction of the House in cases of contempt should be exercised as sparingly as possible and "only when the House is satisfied that to exercise it is essential in order to provide reasonable protection for the House, its members and officers, from such improper obstruction or attempt at or threat of obstruction as is causing, or is likely to cause, substantial interference with the performance of their respective functions."

Contractual arrangements

One possible cause of breach of privilege is the relationship between the union and the sponsored M.P. The subject was discussed by the Committee of

---

[88] In *Hobbs and the Clerical and Administrative Workers Union*, Report of the Registrar for the year 1956, a complaint was made that exempt members had voted in an election to nominate Aneurin Bevan as Treasurer of the Labour Party. Whether they could have been excluded was not discussed, as the rules only gave a *power* to exclude and this power had not been exercised.

[89] *Griffiths and N.U.G.M.W.*, Report of the Registrar for the year 1928.

[90] Report of the Registrar for the year 1933.

[91] For breach of privilege generally see Wade and Phillips, *Constitutional and Administrative Law* (9th ed.) Chap. 12. Erskine May, *Parliamentary Practice* (19th ed.) Chap. 5.

[92] Parliamentary Privilege is currently under review: see the Report from the Select Committee on Parliamentary Privilege, H.C. 34 (1966–67) and the Third Report from the Committee of Privileges, H.C. 417 (1976–77).

Privileges[93] and by the House[94] itself in the case of Mr. W. J. Brown, and the report of the committee in this case has come to have almost statutory authority having been debated and approved by the House.[95] The Committee recognised that it is not a breach of privilege for a person to be contractually associated with an outside body but it was concerned that a member should not surrender his freedom of action, and accordingly the House passed the following motion:

> "... it is inconsistent with the dignity of the House, with the duty of a Member to his constituents, and with the maintenance of the privilege of freedom of speech, for any Member of this House to enter into any contractual agreement with an outside body, controlling or limiting the Member's complete independence and freedom of action in Parliament or stipulating that he shall act in any way as the representative of such outside body in regard to any matters to be transacted in Parliament..."

It would therefore be inconsistent with this motion for a union to demand that a Member undertake to support or oppose any particular measure, although no doubt a member who consistently opposes union policy should consider whether he ought to continue to accept the sponsorship. A related issue is the extent to which a union may attempt to discover what the views of the sponsored M.P. are and the degree of sympathy he has for the aims of the union. In one case a Member raised the question whether it was a breach of privilege to ask sponsored M.P.'s to write a 1,000 word essay on trade union power, in order to assess their "political fitness."[96] In the event the Speaker refused to give precedence over the Orders of the Day to debate the issue.[97]

Threats and coercive acts against Members

It seems to be established that a union may take action against its sponsored M.P., but may not do so if the action is taken in order to influence or coerce the Member. In the *Brown* case itself[98] the issue was whether a union was guilty of a breach of privilege by withdrawing its sponsorship and the Committee of Privileges took the view[99] that,

> "It is an inevitable corollary that if an outside body may properly enter into contractual relationships with and make payments to a Member as such, it must in general be entitled to terminate that relationship if it lawfully can where it considers it necessary for the protection of its own interests so to do. What, on the other hand, an outside body is certainly not entitled to do is to use the agreement or the payment as an instrument by which it controls or seeks to control the conduct of a Member or to punish him for what he has done as a Member."

---

[93] H.C. 118 (1946–47).

[94] H.C. Debs, vol. 440, cols. 284–365 (15th July 1947).

[95] *Ibid.* at col. 365.

[96] H.C. Debs., vol. 915, col. 54 (12th July 1976).

[97] *Ibid.*, col. 374 (13th July 1976). Such a ruling is given when the alleged facts do not fall clearly within an area in which a breach of privilege has been found to have been committeed on a previous occasion, or where it does not fall sufficiently clearly within an area in which a possible breach of privilege should be considered. See the explanation by the Speaker, H.C. Debs., vol. 888, col. 535 (12th March 1975). In such a case it is still open to a member to put down a motion. Thus a decision not to give precedence does not amount to a decision either way as to whether the action is a breach of privilege, although it can be said to amount to a preliminary view.

[98] H.C. 118 (1946–47).

[99] *Ibid.* para. 14.

The line is obviously a fine one,[1] the distinction being between a threat made in order to induce the M.P. to act in a certain way, and a decision to have nothing to do with him.

A clear case of an attempt to influence sponsored Members was the act of the Yorkshire Area of the National Union of Mineworkers in passing a resolution indicating that the union would not tolerate their sponsored Members opposing union policy.[2] The resolution stated that "(1) No Miner's M.P. shall vote or speak against union policy on any issues which affects the coal mining industry; (2) No Miner's M.P. shall actively campaign or work against the union policy on any other major issue; (3) If any Miner's M.P. refuses to agree to the 'guidelines' or violates these guidelines, the Area Council shall withdraw sponsorship from that M.P."[3] The Committee regarded this resolution as a serious contempt, but recommended that no action should be taken as the National Executive Committee had taken steps to nullify the resolution.

It is also a clear contempt to attempt to discipline a sponsored M.P. in his capacity as a union member for his parliamentary activities. In a case involving the N.U.J.,[4] the Glasgow Freelance Branch of that union wished to discipline a number of Members for allegedly acting contrary to the interests of the union in that they voted against a motion which in the view of one member of the branch would have been to the financial interest of the trade union movement. The Speaker regarded this as a matter which should have precedence over Orders of the Day,[5] but as an apology had been received no further action was taken.[6]

Strikes

In only one case has the question been raised whether a strike would amount to a breach of privilege.[7] It was alleged[8] "the action of certain public servants and those inciting them to frustrate the work of Parliament" was a breach of privilege, but the Speaker ruled[9] that although the strike involved important issues he would not allow the motion to have precedence over the Orders of the Day.[10]

---

[1] In the event the Committee decided there was no breach of privilege. See also the case of *Robinson,* H.C. 85 (1943–44) where action was taken not because of the Member's activity in the House but because of his constituency record.

[2] Second Report from the Committee of Privileges, H.C. 634 (1974–75) (Scargill's case).

[3] For another example of the threat to withdraw sponsorship see the allegation that a union official had threatened to withdraw support from Members who supported entry into the E.E.C. In the event it was held that the union official had been misreported and he had denied any such threat. The First Report from the Committee of Privileges H.C. 50 (1971–72) (*Kitson's* case).

[4] H.C. Debs., vol. 877, col. 466 (July 17, 1974).

[5] Thus indicating that it was the kind of act that had previously been held to be a contempt. For an explanation of the ruling see fn. 97 above.

[6] H.C. Debs., vol. 877, col. 674 (July 18, 1974).

[7] The cause of the failure to print the Order Paper on May 1, 1969 is not known, but the Speaker ruled that a motion that such a failure was a contempt would not be given precedence over the Orders of the Day. H.C. Debs., vol. 782, cols. 1620, 1650 (May 1, 1969), and 1767 (May 2, 1969).

[8] H.C. Debs., vol. 888, col. 284 (March 11, 1975).

[9] *Ibid.* col. 535 (March 12, 1975).

[10] For an explanation of this ruling see fn. 97 above.

Part Four

STATUTORY ASSISTANCE FOR COLLECTIVE BARGAINING

INTRODUCTION

THE system of industrial relations in Britain is based on the principle of free collective bargaining.[1] This means first that management has conceded that certain matters are no longer subject only to managerial prerogative (and there can be bargaining about which matters those are) and secondly that decisions in the relevant area should be based on mutual agreement.[2]

The function of the law is not to set standards against which the collective bargain may be judged, nor in general to control the behaviour of the parties.[3] Its purpose is first to impose limits on the kinds of internal sanction (strikes or lockouts) that may be used by one party against the other;[4] secondly to establish a kind of statutory collective bargain which lays down minimum standards,[5] and thirdly to encourage the strength and growth of the voluntary bargaining system.[6]

This part of the book deals with that final function and explains not only those provisions of the law which attempt to promote agreement in individual disputes, but also the procedures that are made available for promoting collective bargaining in general. Before doing so however it may be useful to explain the jurisdiction of the two principal agencies of the law set up to fulfill these functions.

Advisory, Conciliation and Arbitration Service

For many years the Department of Employment and its predecessors had undertaken a number of functions in the field of industrial relations, such as the provision of conciliation procedures, advice and arbitration. A number of similar functions were exercised by other bodies, notably the Commission on Industrial Relations, and in 1974 all these functions (and also largely the personnel) were transferred to the new Service.[7]

The Service is now subject to the terms of the Employment Protection Act 1975 and is under the general duty "of promoting the improvement of

---

[1] See generally, Clegg *The System of Industrial Relations in Great Britain* (2nd ed.).

[2] See Kahn Freund *Labour and the Law* (2nd ed.) Chap. 3; Rideout, *Principles of Labour Law* (2nd ed.) Chap. 2.

[3] Wages control is rarely done by resort to legal machinery (but see Prices and Incomes Act 1966) but is usually achieved (as is common in a corporatist situation) by alegal means, such as preventing those who break the wages guidelines bidding for Government contracts.

[4] For example by the law of tort: Chaps. 11 and 12.

[5] For example maternity benefits (E.P.C.A. 1978, ss. 33–48).

[6] For example the provision of procedures for recognition claims: E.P.A. 1975, ss. 11–16. See Kahn Freund *Labour and the Law* (2nd ed.) Chap. 4.

[7] For the full background see ACAS Annual Report 1975 Chap. 1.

industrial relations, and in particular of encouraging the extension of collective bargaining and the development and, where necessary, reform of collective bargaining machinery."[8]

It is important to note the claim that ACAS is independent of all interested parties and particularly of the government, for "the functions of the Service and of its officers and servants shall be performed on behalf of the Crown but, ..., the Service shall not be subject to directions of any kind from any Minister of the Crown as to manner in which it is to exercise any of its functions under any enactment."[9]

ACAS is directed by a Council which consists of a full-time Chairman and nine[10] other members appointed by the Secretary of State. As to the nine, three are appointed after consultation with employers' organisations, and three after consulting unions. The function of the Council is to give overall guidance on the running of the Service and it usually meets monthly. The Service is organised on a regional basis[11] and all enquiries should be made to the appropriate regional office.

The powers and functions of ACAS are as follows and will be dealt with in more detail in the succeeding chapters:

(1) At the request of any person the Service may offer its assistance (whether by way of conciliation, mediation or otherwise) to parties engaged in a trade dispute.[12]

(2) It provides facilities for the conciliation of individual cases before industrial tribunals.[13] This includes such matters as unfair dismissals, redundancy payments, rights to guarantee payments, maternity benefits, protective awards in cases of redundancy, and cases under the Equal Pay Act 1970 and the Sex Discimination Act 1975.

(3) With the consent of both parties to a trade dispute it may offer arbitration either by a person selected by ACAS or by the Central Arbitration Committee.[14]

(4) The Service may provide advice on industrial relations matters, either generally or on a particular subject.[15]

(5) The Service may inquire into any aspect of industrial relations, either generally or in a particular industry or undertaking.[16]

(6) As a support to the new industrial legislation the Service may issue Codes of Practice containing practical guidance for promoting the improvement of industrial relations.[17]

(7) At the request of a trade union it may make a recommendation on recognition of the union by the employer.[18]

(8) The Service may attempt to conciliate on the question of providing a

---

[8] E.P.A. 1975, s. 1 (2).

[9] E.P.A. 1975, Sched. 1 para. 11 (1).

[10] The Secretary of State may appoint a further two members if he thinks fit.

[11] The regions are: South Eastern, South Western, Midlands, North Western, Yorkshire and Humberside, Northern, Scotland and Wales.

[12] E.P.A. 1975, s. 2.

[13] E.P.A. 1975, s. 2 (4).

[14] E.P.A. 1975, s. 3.

[15] E.P.A. 1975, s. 4.

[16] E.P.A. 1975, s. 5.

[17] E.P.A. 1975, s. 6.

[18] E.P.A. 1975, ss. 11–16.

union with information for collective bargaining purposes if the case is referred to it by the Central Arbitration Committee.[19]

(9) It may receive and attempt to resolve a claim for the extension of terms and conditions of employment.[20]

(10) It may inquire into the operation of wages councils or statutory joint industrial councils, either in relation to a particular council or generally,[21] and may advise on their establishment or abolition.

(11) The Service is responsible for providing staff and premises for the Certification Officer, and must be consulted on his appointment.[22]

(12) The Service must provide premises and staff for the Central Arbitration Committee and must be consulted on the appointment of the chairman, and must nominate persons representative of both sides of industry for selection as members of the Committee.[23]

The Central Arbitration Committee

The C.A.C. may trace its origins back to the Industrial Court which was set up by the Industrial Courts Act 1919 to provide a forum for arbitration. This body became known as the Industrial Arbitration Board during the brief life of the Industrial Relations Act 1971, and the C.A.C. has now taken over its functions.

The Committee consists of a chairman and an unspecified member of other members. In 1977 due to the pressure of business there were 18 deputy chairmen and 63 other members.

The structure of each sitting of a committee is not laid down but is usual for there to be a tribunal of three, consisting of a chairman (who must be the chairman himself or one of the nominated deputy chairmen) and one member representative of employers and one of workers. Assessors may also attend. If a unanimous decision is impossible the chairman has the full power of an umpire and so may decide the matter himself.

The Committee may sit in public or private and its decisions are published. Once again the Committee shall not be subject to any directions of any kind from a Minister of the Crown. Part I of the Arbitration Act 1950 does not apply.[24]

The Powers and Functions of the Committee

(a) Arbitration. The Committee may arbitrate on matters referred to it by ACAS or where it is incorporated in a collective agreement as arbitrator. A number of statutes covering particular industries also appoint the Committee as arbitrator.

(b) The Committee may also arbitrate on matters referred to it by the Secretary of State under the Fair Wages Resolution.

(c) The Committee also decides a case that is brought by a trade union for extension of terms and conditions of service under Sched. 11 of the Employment Protection Act 1975.

(d) Under the Equal Pay Act 1970 the Committee may make amendments

---

[19] E.P.A. 1975, s. 19 (2).
[20] E.P.A. 1975, Sched. 11.
[21] E.P.A. 1975, s. 96.
[22] E.P.A. 1975, s. 7.
[23] E.P.A. 1975, Sched. 1.
[24] E.P.A. 1975, s. 3.

in a collective agreement (or in a Wages Council order) to make it comply with that Act.[25]

(e) The Committee also has jurisdiction to decide disputes concerning the provision of information for the purposes of collective bargaining.[26]

(f) If an employer has failed to comply with a recommendation of ACAS that it should recognise a union, the Committee may make a declaration as to recognition and award new terms and conditions of service.[27]

(g) Where the two sides of a statutory joint industrial council are unable to agree the matter may be referred to the Committee.[28]

---

[25] Equal Pay Act 1970, ss. 3 and 4.
[26] E.P.A. 1975, ss. 19–21.
[27] E.P.A. 1975, s. 16.
[28] E.P.A. 1975, s. 92.

CHAPTER 18

THE LEGAL STATUS OF A COLLECTIVE AGREEMENT

THERE are two entirely separate questions that need to be asked about the legal effect of a collective agreement. The first is, what is its effect between the parties, that is between the union and the employer or employer's association? The second is, what is its effect as between the employer and the individual employee, that is, when is it incorporated into the individual's contract of employment? It is essential to distinguish between these two issues.

THE LEGAL EFFECT AS BETWEEN THE PARTIES TO THE AGREEMENT

By statute: before 1971 and after 1974

Section 18 of the Trade Union and Labour Relations Act states that a collective agreement as defined by the Act[1] which has been entered into before December 1, 1971, or after September 16, 1974, shall be conclusively presumed not to have been intended by the parties to be a legally enforceable agreement, unless it is both in writing[2] and also includes a provision to the effect that the parties intend it to be legally enforceable. The same principle is also applied to parts of an agreement, so that it is perfectly possible to provide that only certain parts are to be legally binding, in which case the Act provides that the non-binding parts may be used to assist in the interpretation of the remainder.[3] If the proviso does apply (so that the agreement is intended to be binding), it will be effective as a binding contract if it otherwise conforms to the general law of contract.

The provision applies to any agreement made between a union and an employer which relates to the matters specified in section 29 (1) of the Act, and these cover most of the subject matter of collective bargaining. It would however be possible to bargain about a matter not so covered, in which case the agreement will be subject to the common law. Where an agreement includes both statutory matters and others, it is thought that the statutory definition and rules ought to be applied.

By statute: 1971–1974

During the era of the Industrial Relations Act 1971 the presumption was the other way round, so that where the agreement was made in writing it was presumed to be intended to be legally binding unless there was express clause

---

[1] T.U.L.R.A. 1974, s. 30.

[2] For the view that an oral agreement that is later confirmed in writing is "made in writing" (under s. 34 of the Industrial Relations Act 1971) see *Mitsubishi Bank* v. *National Union of Bank Employees* [1973] I.R.L.R. 370 (C.A.).

[3] T.U.L.R.A. 1974, s. 18 (3).

stating that that was not the intention. Nearly all agreements concluded during this period did include such a clause, and it is unlikely that an agreement made under the Industrial Relations Act will come up for enforcement in the courts.[4]

The Common Law

For an agreement to be legally binding at Common Law it is often assumed that at the time of its creation it must be intended by the parties to create a legally binding relationship.[5] It was the view of the Donovan Commission[6] that although it was perfectly possible for an employer and a union to make an agreement that was legally binding, this was not usually the result as almost invariably the parties did not intend the collective agreement to have legal effect.[7]

This view was adopted by Geoffrey Lane J. in *Ford* v. *Amalgamated Union of Engineering and Foundry Workers*[8] in which the plaintiffs sought an interlocutory injunction restraining the defendants from acting in breach of a procedure agreement. In refusing the injunction the judge said,[9]

> "If one applies the subjective test and asks what the intentions of the various parties were, the answer is that so far as they had any express intentions, they were certainly not to make the agreement enforceable at law. If one applies an objective test and asks what intention must be imputed from all the circumstances of the case, the answer is the same. The fact that the agreements prima facie deal with commercial relationships is outweighed by the other considerations, by the wording of the agreements, by the nature of the agreements, and by the climate of opinion voiced and evidenced by the extra-judicial authorities. Agreements such as these, composed largely of optimistic aspirations, presenting grave practical problems of enforcement and reached against a background of opinion adverse to enforceability, are, in my judgment, not contracts in the legal sense and are not enforceable at law. Without clear and express provisions making them amenable to legal action, they remain in the realm of undertakings binding in honour."

This decision has been subjected to considerable and penetrating criticism[10] and it is undoubtedly open to a court in the future to hold collective agreement binding at common law either on the ground that the *Ford* case was incorrectly decided or because the particular agreement in question was of a kind that was suitable for legal enforcement and was intended by the parties to be so. However, the only agreements to which the common law applies today are

---

[4] But if it does regard would have to be had to T.U.L.R.A. 1974, s. 23 (3).

[5] *Balfour* v. *Balfour* [1919] 2 K.B. 571. But such a view is not universally accepted.

[6] Royal Commission on Trade Unions and Employers' Associations, Cmnd. 3623 paras. 465–474. See also Adell, *The legal status of collective agreements in England, the United States and Canada* (1970), esp. Chap. 3.

[7] This was also the view put forward earlier by Prof. Kahn-Freund: see Flanders and Clegg (eds.), *The System of Industrial Relations in Great Britain* (1954). But for an earlier view see Kahn-Freund, "Collective Agreements Under War Legislation" (1942) 6 M.L.R. 112. See now Kahn-Freund *Labour and the Law* (2nd ed.) pp. 125–132.

[8] [1969] 2 Q.B. 303; See also *Stuart* v. *Ministry of Defence* [1973] I.R.L.R. 143 (N.I.R.C.).

[9] *Ibid.* at 330.

[10] See especially Selwyn, "Collective Agreements and the Law" (1969) 32 M.L.R. 377, Hepple "Intention to Create Legal Relations" [1970] C.L.J. 122.

agreements which deal with matters outside the statutory definition,[11] and it is unlikely that such an agreement will be brought before the courts.[12]

INCORPORATION OF THE COLLECTIVE AGREEMENT IN CONTRACTS OF EMPLOYMENT

Although strictly outside the limits of this book it may be useful to deal briefly with the more important aspect of the collective agreement, that is the extent to which it may become part of the contract of employment of the individual worker. It is essential to keep in mind that this subject is entirely different from the one just discussed and it is perfectly possible for an agreement that is not binding between the parties to it (*i.e.* the union and the employer) nevertheless to be effective as between the employer and the employee as part of that employee's contract of employment.

It is, however, quite remarkable that a subject as important as the determination of one of the sources of the terms of the employment contract has not been fully resolved by the law, and although in many instances it is assumed that a collectively agreed term becomes part of the individual's contract, it is often not entirely clear how this comes about.

Incorporation by express agreement

An individual's contract of employment may itself state that it incorporates the terms of a collective agreement[13] either as it presently exists or, more usually, as it stands from time to time.[14] This process of express incorporation has been facilitated by the fact that under section 1 of the Employment Protection (Consolidation) Act 1978 an employer is bound to give notice to the employee of certain terms of the contract[15] and although such a notice need not refer to a collective agreement it will often do so, thus making the evidential burden of proving knowledge of the existence of the collective agreement somewhat easier.[16] Thus in *Tarmac Roadstone Holdings* v. *Peacock*[17] it was held that where the notice simply stated that wages, holidays and other terms were "as for slag industry" this would be sufficient to incorporate the terms of the agreements made by the National Joint Industrial Council for the Slag Industry. Wherever possible, however, the incorporation should be specifically related to a particular agreement and also to specific parts of that agreement so as to incorporate terms on such issues as pay and holidays, but not others which may be less appropriate for incorporation.

Whether a collective agreement is incorporated in no way depends on whether it is binding as between the union and the employer, for it is quite clear that it may be incorporated even if it is not binding between the parties and indeed it may remain part of the individual's contract of employment even

---

[11] T.U.L.R.A. 1974, s. 30, referring to s. 29 (1).

[12] An example of an agreement outside the statutory definition would be an agreement for the use of the canteen outside working hours for social purposes.

[13] *N.C.B.* v. *Galley* [1958] 1 W.L.R. 16; *Camden Exhibition and Display Ltd.* v. *Lynott* [1966] 1 Q.B. 555.

[14] *Callison* v. *Ford* (1969) 4 I.T.R. 24 where the contract stated "I understand that such agreement is subject to the terms of agreements made from time to time between the company and the trade unions and to the company's rules and regulations."

[15] The notice is of course not the contract itself, which must have been entered into previously.

[16] See Freedland *The Contract of Employment* (1976) p. 374.

[17] [1973] I.C.R. 273. See also *Joel* v. *Cammell Laird* [1969] 4 I.T.R. 206.

if it has been revoked as between the parties. Thus in *Morris* v. *Bailey*[18] the employers wrote to the union terminating the agreement, but it was held that despite this the terms of that agreement still formed part of the contracts of employment of individuals.[19]

A further problem occurs where two collective agreements which seem to be applicable are in conflict, for example where a national agreement is supplemented by a local agreement. It is undoubtedly useful if the parties have already considered this point, and it is sometimes declared which agreement is to take precedence.[20] Problems of this kind have arisen in cases of redundancy payments where the question is whether the working week is to be based on the national agreement or the local agreement, and it appears that the courts have tended to favour the national agreement;[21] there is, however, a suspicion that this attitude may be based on the irrelevant assumption that the local agreement is not intended to be binding between the parties but is only a "gentleman's agreement" to "iron out local labour difficulties".[22] The status of the agreement as between the union and employer has no bearing on the question of the terms of the individual's contract of employment.

The union as agent for the members

It has sometimes been suggested that a collective agreement may become part of an individual's contract because the union is acting as agent for the individual. This suggestion has received little approval because of the obvious problem of determining the terms of the contracts of employees who are not members of the union, but nevertheless it is occasionally relied upon.

Thus in *Rookes* v. *Barnard*[23] at first instance it was conceded by counsel and accepted by Sachs J. that the union representatives were authorised to bind the union as a whole and the members individually so that a no-strike clause[24] became part of the contracts of individual members.[25] Lord Denning has suggested that a union member must be taken to authorise the acts of his union in negotiating better terms of employment or in taking industrial action unless he specifically disavows it.[26]

The problem of non-members was mentioned briefly in *Singh* v. *British Steel Corporation*[27] where the plaintiff had resigned from the union and therefore was held not to be bound by an agreement about a new system of working. Nor could it be said that there was an implied term that as a non-member he would be bound by terms agreed between the union and the employer.

The unsatisfactory nature of the agency principle in these cases has been noted by the Employment Appeal Tribunal in *Burton* v. *Smith*[28] where the

---

[18] [1969] 2 Lloyds Rep. 215.

[19] *Ibid.* at 219–220. See also *Burroughes Machines Ltd.* v. *Timmoney* [1977] I.R.L.R. 404. (Ct. of Session).

[20] For an example of such a clause see *Gascol Conversions* v. *Mercer* [1974] I.C.R. 420.

[21] *Ibid.* at 425 per Lord Denning. *Loman* v. *Merseyside Transport Ltd.* (1968) 3 I.T.R. 108 at 112 per Lord Parker C.J. See Wedderburn, (1969) 32 M.L.R. 99.

[22] (1968) 3 I.T.R. 108 at 112.

[23] [1963] 1 Q.B. 623.

[24] For incorporation of no-strike clauses today see later in this chapter.

[25] [1963] 1 Q.B. 623 at 625: see also [1961] 2 All E.R. 825 at 827.

[26] *Chappell* v. *Times Newspaper* [1975] I.C.R. 145 at 173.

[27] [1974] I.R.L.R. 131. (I.T.)

[28] [1977] I.R.L.R. 351. See also *Ideal Casements* v. *Shamsi* [1972] I.C.R. 408.

question arose whether notice of dismissal given to the union could be treated as notice to the individual. Arnold J. said,

> "There is no reason at all why, in a particular case, union representatives should not be the agents of an employee to make a contract, or to receive a notice or otherwise effect a binding transaction on his behalf. But that agency so to do does not stem from the mere fact that they are union representatives and that he is a member of the union; it must be supported in the particular case by the creation of some specific agency, and that can arise only if the evidence supports the conclusion that there was such an agency."

It is suggested that this is the correct approach and the courts should be wary of implying a contract of agency between union and member, and this is all the more so in cases where both members and non-members are employed.[29]

Implied incorporation

It is possible for a court to imply a collective agreement into an individual's contract. In a recent case[30] an industrial tribunal adopted the view of Lord Esher in *Hamlyn* v. *Wood*[31] where he said in relation to a contract of sale,

> "I have for a long time understood that rule to be that the Court has no right to imply in a written contract any such stipulation, unless, on considering the terms of the contract in a reasonable and business manner, an implication necessarily arises that the parties must have intended that the suggested stipulation should exist."[32]

In many cases it may be said that where a person is engaged "on the usual terms" or even "at the going rate" these statements suggest that an agreement is understood by both parties to be applicable to them, of which the relevant terms may be incorporated. But it appears that an agreement cannot be incorporated simply because it is adhered to between the parties. In *Young* v. *Canadian Northern Rly*[33] it had been argued that the terms of the collective agreement had in fact been applied by the employer, but the Privy Council thought that this fact was "equally consistent with the view that it did so, not because it was bound contractually to apply it to [the appellant], but because as a matter of policy it deemed it expedient to apply it to all,"[34] and it was thought that the agreement could only be incorporated if it could be shown that contractual obligation rather than generosity or convenience was the only possible explanation for the employer's actions. Such a view may however be too strict.[35]

But even if it can be shown that incorporation is "obvious" it still has to be shown that the agreement is one that is "adapted for conversion into or incorporation with a service agreement, so as to entitle master and servant

---

[29] *Edwards* v. *Skyways Ltd.* [1964] 1 W.L.R. 349 is sometimes cited as a case which turned on agency, but although it is difficult to explain it any other way there was no discussion of the subject.

[30] *Singh* v. *British Steel Corporation* [1974] I.R.L.R. 131 at 135. (I.T.)

[31] [1891] 2 Q.B. 488 at 491.

[32] See also the test of the officious bystander invented by Mackinnon L.J. in *Shirlaw* v. *Southern Foundries Ltd*. [1939] 2 K.B. 206: but it is suggested that this test is less appropriate for use in contracts of employment. But see *Spring* v. *N.A.S.D.S.* [1956] 2 All E.R. 221 where it was used in relation to a contract of union membership.

[33] *Young* v. *Canadian Northern Rly.* [1931] A.C. 83.

[34] *Ibid.* at 89.

[35] See *Joel* v. *Cammell Laird* (1969) 4 I.T.R. 206 at 211–212 where previous conduct on the part of the employee seems to have been relevant.

to enforce *inter se* the terms thereof."[36] It is not clear what kind of promises are thought to be "appropriate" but clauses of a collective nature concerning the relationship of the union and employer only would not be suitable. Thus it has been suggested that clauses about conciliation machinery may not necessarily be incorporated,[37] and in *British Leyland* v. *McQuilken*[38] it was held that a collective agreement which provided a choice of retraining or redundancy for employees on the closure of a department conferred no contractual rights on the individual.

The Privy Council also seems to have thought that legal sanctions are not appropriate in collective bargaining at all, whether it is the union or the employee who seeks to enforce the contract, for it was suggested that the appropriate remedy was a strike. The case was decided at a time when the courts were clearly adopting an abstentionist policy in relation to trade union law, and it may be that the strictness of *Young* v. *Canadian Northern Rly*[39] would not be followed today.

Incorporation of "no-strike" clauses

In the case of a "no-strike" clause Parliament has made it clear that there should be no unwitting incorporation into the contracts of individual workers.[40] Section 18 of the Trade Union and Labour Relations Act 1974 provides that a clause which prohibits or restricts the right of workers to engage in industrial action shall not be incorporated into the individual contracts unless it is agreed to by a trade union that is "independent"[41] and (a) it is in writing; (b) it states that such a clause shall or may be incorporated; (c) the terms of the clause are reasonably accessible to the workers to whom it applies and (d) the contract of employment expressly or impliedly incorporates the clause.

[36] *Young* v. *Canadian Northern Rly.* [1931] A.C. 83 at 89.

[37] *Joel* v. *Cammell Laird* (1969) 4 I.T.R. 206.

[38] [1978] I.R.L.R. 245. (E.A.T.). The question was whether the employer was in breach of the contract of employment when he refused to implement the agreement.

[39] [1931] A.C. 83.

[40] Such as appears to have been assumed in *Rookes* v. *Barnard* [1964] A.C. 1129. See *per* Sachs J. [1963] 1 Q.B. 623 at 625 and Donovan L.J. *ibid.* at 675.

[41] As defined by T.U.L.R.A. 1974, s. 30.

CHAPTER 19

CONCILIATION AND ARBITRATION

NOW that labour legislation has become more interventionist in the area of industrial relations it is not possible to ascribe to it any one particular function, but rather it may be classified in three ways. First there is the legislation which lays down minimum standards for employment, secondly the law may encourage the parties to a dispute to reach a settlement themselves and may provide assistance for this purpose, and thirdly there are cases where a party may be required to submit a dispute to resolution by a court or arbitrator. This and subsequent chapters will look at the second and third categories.[1]

It should be noted that the vast majority of disputes are settled by voluntary collective bargaining without any assistance from the law or outside agencies, and it is the clear policy of the law to encourage such methods by promoting the extension of collective bargaining. Even when the law does become involved it does so more often by providing assistance to the parties to reach agreement and only rarely does it fulfill its traditional function of adjudication. Thus, although there are some areas (such as maternity benefits or guarantee payments) where the law does concern itself with the content of an agreement by laying down minimum terms, in general the law and its agencies are more concerned with procedure than with substance.

CONCILIATION, MEDIATION AND ADVICE

The speedy and effective resolution of disputes or differences between employers and unions is clearly seen to be in the national interest, but it is also apparent that any attempt to impose a solution could aggravate rather than solve the problem, at least until every effort has been made to bring about a voluntary settlement. To this end the Advisory Conciliation and Arbitration Service is provided with a number of powers to assist the parties to a dispute in coming to an agreement.

Conciliation

Where a trade dispute[2] exists ACAS may "by way of conciliation or by other means ... offer assistance to the parties to the dispute with a view to bringing about a settlement."[3]

---

[1] On the subject matter of this and subsequent chapters see Wedderburn and Davies, *Employment Grievances and Disputes Procedures in Britain* (1969); Kahn-Freund, *Labour and the Law* (2nd ed.) Chaps. 3–6.

[2] Trade dispute is defined by T.U.L.R.A. 1974, s. 29 (1).

[3] E.P.A. 1975, s. 2. The functions were previously performed by the Department of Employment by virtue of the Conciliation Act 1896.

Conciliation is quite distinct from mediation and arbitration, and involves the provision of a forum in which the parties can reach their *own* solution to the dispute.[4] The conciliation officer concerned must be a person experienced in the problems of industrial relations who is able to identify the problems and discuss them with the parties to the dispute. He does not make his own suggestion as to what the solution should be (for that would be mediation) but rather he may put forward ideas to each side for their consideration, and by means of such informal assistance it is hoped the parties will come to an agreement.

It should be noted that in such a case the solution is that of the parties and so the responsibility for any difficulties with a governmental wages policy lies with them and not with the Service. The process is entirely voluntary and the Service will not usually become involved unless both parties agree[5] and unless the internal procedure under any collective agreement has been completed or has been abandoned by both sides.[6] The Service may also offer its assistance of its own initiative, but it would not intervene without the consent of both sides.

The conciliation process is now of considerable importance as a method of resolving disputes, and in 1977 the Service received 3,299 requests for assistance and completed 2,891 cases.[7] It claims that the process assisted in achieving a settlement in 74 per cent. of the cases completed during that year. Disputes over pay and other terms and conditions of employment represented over half the cases, and recognition cases amounted to almost a quarter.[8]

It should be noted that ACAS is also involved in conciliation in a number of other specific situations. For example it offers conciliation on cases of unfair dismissal and as a preliminary to a recognition claim under section 11 of the Employment Protection Act 1975.

Mediation

Mediation differs from conciliation in that the mediator will make recommendations of his own accord as to a possible solution and it is then for the parties to negotiate and decide whether they will adopt vary or reject the recommendation. The mediator can be either a member of the ACAS staff or someone brought in from outside[9] and mediation may be carried on by a single individual or by a board set up for the purpose.[10]

Mediation is useful as a half-way stage between conciliation and arbitration for on the one hand those engaged in conciliation may welcome more positive recommendations if conciliation has failed, and on the other hand mediation may be preferable to arbitration where the parties do not wish to be limited to either acceptance or rejection of the recommendation.

---

[4] For a description see ACAS Annual Report for 1975 Chap. 3.

[5] One of the initial objectives of the workers in a dispute may well be to get the union to bring industrial pressure on the employer to agree to conciliation.

[6] The duty to have regard to agreed procedures is imposed on the Service by E.P.A. 1975, s. 2 (3).

[7] ACAS annual report for 1977, p. 8. In 53.5 per cent. of the cases completed the request for conciliation came from the union. The employer referred 20 per cent., and 23.2 per cent. were joint requests. ACAS acted on its own initiative in 3.3 per cent. of the cases.

[8] These figures (635 cases) are separate from those which proceeded under the recognition procedure contained in E.P.A. 1975, s. 11.

[9] E.P.A. 1975, s. 2.

[10] In 1977 there were 31 cases referred to mediation: 27 to a single mediator and four to a board. ACAS Annual Report for 1977, p. 65.

Advice

The recent spate of legislation on industrial relations matters has caused both employers and unions to pay attention to a much broader range of issues than before, and has called for reconsideration of policies by a number of employers. Accordingly ACAS has devoted considerable attention to advising employers on the effects of the new legislation both in general and in relation to specific issues.

The Service can engage in advisory work in a number of ways. On the one hand it is prepared to offer advice either on a specific problem or on the whole industrial relations structure of a firm, and on the other hand it may offer advice on an aspect of industrial relations in general, such as, for example, job evaluation.[11] Closely allied to this is the duty to issue Codes of Practice in a number of cases; so far Codes have been issued on disciplinary practice, disclosure of information and time off for trade union duties.

Again the advisory function of ACAS is an important addition to the range of services available for not only does it enable advice to be given on general issues, but more importantly it enables an employer or a union to seek advice on a specific issue before a dispute arises. In such a case the information and interpretation offered by ACAS may be the basis of agreement between the parties.

INQUIRIES

The industrial relations system provides for a number of different kinds of inquiry, from the very formal Court of Inquiry which resembles a court of law, to an informal inquiry conducted by ACAS. While an official inquiry delves into the facts and issues in greater detail than in the case of mediation, the theoretical function is not dissimilar for in both cases the recommendations are not binding but are the subject of further discussion between the parties. However in many cases the recommendations are adopted without variation.

Courts of Inquiry

The most formal kind of inquiry is a Court of Inquiry set up under the Industrial Courts Act 1919.[12] The Act provides that where a trade dispute exists[13] the Minister[14] may refer any matter connected with the dispute to a Court of Inquiry, which may consist either of an individual acting alone or of a board.

Since the passing of the Act in 1919 there have been 105 courts of inquiry,[15] but few have been held in recent years. Of those that have perhaps the most well known are the Wilberforce Inquiry[16] during the miners' strike of 1972 and the Scarman Inquiry of 1977[17] into events following the recognition dispute at Grunwick Processing Laboratories. Although it might appear from this that the court of inquiry is only used in politically sensitive cases where the independence of the report is seen to be paramount, it is nevertheless used in

---

[11] ACAS Guide No. 1. "Job evaluation."

[12] As amended by E.P.A. 1975 Sched. 16.

[13] "trade dispute" is defined by T.U.L.R.A. 1974, s. 29 (1).

[14] Now the Secretary of State for Employment.

[15] For a study of the courts from 1919–1965 see McCarthy and Clifford, "The Work of Industrial Courts of Inquiry" (1966) 4 B.J.I.R. 39; Wedderburn and Davies, *op. cit.* Chap. 11.

[16] Cmnd. 4903.

[17] Cmnd. 6922.

other, but equally difficult cases such as the dispute in 1977 concerning helicopter pilots at Aberdeen.[18]

Although the Industrial Courts Act 1919 allows for rules regulating procedure to be made, none have in fact been adopted and procedure is regulated by the Act itself and by the terms of reference of the particular committee. The hearing (which is usually in public) is a formal affair and evidence may be heard on oath. Of more significance is the fact that the court may compel a witness to attend and give evidence.[19] A person may not be represented by counsel or by a solicitor unless this is allowed by the rules contained in the terms of reference, but such representation is usually permitted. The court may ask assessors to attend. In other respects the court is entitled to regulate its own procedure.[20]

Departmental Committees of Inquiry

The departmental committee of inquiry (or investigation) is a much less formal affair than the Court of Inquiry, and may be set up by any minister by virtue of what are described as his general ministerial powers.[21] This power is not limited to cases where a trade dispute exists. As ACAS now has equally wide powers of inquiry, the departmental system may now assume less importance.

Inquiry by ACAS

ACAS may conduct inquiries at a number of levels,[22] whether there is a trade dispute or not. First it may inquire into any aspect of industrial relations generally; secondly it may inquire into industrial relations in a particular industry; and thirdly it may look into the problems of a particular employer. Examples of the second category are investigations into the newspaper industry[23] and into negotiating arrangements in the electricity supply industry.[24] An example of the third group is the report of the Court of Inquiry into a dispute between the National Union of Blastfurnacemen and the British Steel Corporation[25] which dealt with a dispute over the commissioning of a blast furnace.

Arbitration (1)—Voluntary Arbitration

Section 3 of the Employment Protection Act 1975 makes provision for a wide variety of arbitration services to be made available, for where a trade dispute[26] exists or is apprehended a matter may be referred to arbitration by the Service with the consent of all the parties,[27] so long as two conditions are fulfilled. First

---

[18] Report of a Court of Inquiry into a trade dispute at Dyce Airport, Aberdeen. Cmnd. 6951. For a general classification into four groups see McCarthy and Clifford, *op. cit.* p. 43.

[19] Industrial Courts Act 1919, s. 4 (5).

[20] See for example the rules of procedure in Cmnd. 6922 and Cmnd. 6951.

[21] See for example "Report of the Committee of Inquiry into the Pay of Non-University Teachers' (Houghton Report) Cmnd. 5848. This was set up in 1974 by the Secretary of State for Education.

[22] E.P.A. 1975, s. 5.

[23] Royal Commission on the Press, Cmnd. 6810–2.

[24] ACAS report No. 4.

[25] ACAS report No. 3.

[26] "trade dispute" is defined by T.U.L.R.A. 1974, s. 29 (1).

[27] As Bercusson points out (Annotations to *Current Law Statutes* E.P.A. 1975, s. 3) it is not clear who the parties are and he asks whether a compliant trade union could impose arbitration on more militant members.

the Service must be satisfied that the internal procedures have been used and have failed to produce a settlement, but this requirement may be overridden if the Service believes that there is a "special reason"[28] which justifies ignoring internal procedure. Secondly the Service must consider the likelihood of the dispute being settled by conciliation.

The arbitration may be conducted by a single arbitrator or a board appointed by ACAS,[29] or the case may be referred to the Central Arbitration Committee. One point to note is that if the case is referred to a person appointed by ACAS the award may be kept secret, but if the C.A.C. is involved the award is published. During 1977 the Service referred 247 cases to a single arbitrator, 40 to a board of arbitration and 7 to the C.A.C.[30]

One feature of this system is that as the Arbitration Act 1950, part I, does not apply the awards are not legally binding, but as the consent of both parties is necessary to refer the case to arbitration, it is usual for the award to be adhered to.

In a number of cases the reference to ACAS is not made on an ad hoc basis, but rather the machinery is built into a particular procedure agreement. In addition the Service may be responsible for an industry wide tribunal, such as the Post Office Arbitration Tribunal. The Service is also responsible for arbitration under the Remuneration of Teachers Act 1965.[31]

ARBITRATION (2)—EXTENSION OF TERMS AND CONDICTIONS OF SERVICE

A system which has its origins in the emergency legislation of the Second World War[32] lays down that where a person is not being provided with the agreed terms and conditions of employment which cover him or, where there are no such terms, if he is not receiving the general level of terms for the trade in the district, a trade union may present a claim to ACAS and thence to the Central Arbitration Committee.[33] These provisions, which are now contained in schedule 11 to the Employment Protection Act 1975, are a substantial improvement on the previous legislation and now contain two distinct elements: first the right to "recognised terms and conditions" and secondly the right to the "general level."[34] As will be seen the two provisions are mutually

---

[28] No guidance is given as to what might constitute a special reason.

[29] ACAS maintains a list of arbitrators. Staff of ACAS cannot serve.

[30] See for example C.A.C. award No. 39, *Inverclyde District Council and NALGO* concerning a dispute over the opening of a public library on Saturday afternoons; also C.A.C. award No. 275, *Glow-Worm Ltd. and N.U.D.A.G.M.W.*, concerning a dispute about payment for a day when employees were laid off.

[31] s. 3. See also Remuneration of Teachers (Scotland) Act 1967.

[32] The provision has its origin in the Conditions of Employment and National Arbitration Order 1940 (S.R. & O. No. 1305), parts of which became the Industrial Disputes Order 1951 (1951 S.I. No. 1376). This was followed by s. 8 of the Terms and Conditions of Employment Act 1959. The provisions were substantially amended and are now in E.P.A. 1975 Sched. 11. See generally Hepple "Compulsory arbitration in Great Britain" in Lowenberg *et al.*, *Compulsory Arbitration,* 1976.

[33] On this section generally see Wood, "The Central Arbitration Committee's approach to Schedule 11 to the Employment Protection Act 1975 and the Fair Wages Resolution 1946" (1978) 7 I.L.J. 65, and Bercusson "The New Fair Wages Policy: Schedule 11 to the Employment Protection Act" (1976) 5 I.L.J. 129.

[34] The Schedule 11 rights are therefore very similar to the Fair Wages Resolution, but while a number of points are common to both, the latter will be treated separately.

exclusive, for the "general level" cannot be claimed if recognised terms exist.[35]

So far as "recognised terms" are concerned the purpose is that where an agreement lays down general rates a particular employer should not be permitted to refuse to recognise that that agreement sets a rate which is appropriate for him and accordingly the terms of the agreement are extended to him. Where the "general level" is concerned the point is that an employer should not be able to take advantage of the absence of an agreement by paying less than the "going rate."

"Recognised terms and conditions"

The claim under this head is that the employer is observing terms and conditions of employment which are less favourable than the "recognised terms." Schedule 11 provides that "recognised terms and conditions" means,

> "terms and conditions of workers in comparable employment in the trade or industry, or section of a trade or industry, in which the employer in question is engaged, either generally or in the district in which he is so engaged, which have been settled by an agreement or award, to which the parties are employers' associations and independent trade unions which represent (generally or in the district in question, as the case may be) a substantial proportion of the employers and of the workers in the trade industry or section, being workers of the description to which the agreement or award relates."

This complicated provision lays down a number of important conditions. First the comparison is made with an agreement made at national or regional level, and agreements made at plant level cannot be used as comparisons,[35] even if they are used to supplement the national agreement. Thus where a national agreement sets the minimum and this is added to by plant level bargaining, the relevant rate is the national minimum and not the effective rate actually paid.

Secondly the parties to that agreement must be an employers' association and an independent trade union, both of whom must represent a substantial proportion of either employers or workers in the trade, industry or section,[36] and this is calculated by reference to the proportion represented either nationally or in the relevant district.[37]

Thirdly the terms must be "settled by agreement or award," and thus a degree of formality is required.

Fourthly the employer must be engaged in the same trade or industry (or section thereof) as that to which the recognised terms related. This condition is a popular defence for an employer and can give rise to difficulty. On the one hand the employer may claim he is simply not in the same business at all as the comparator, and the distinction can be rather fine: thus in *Dover Motor Boat Co. and T.G.W.U.*[38] it was held that a company providing a boat service for shipping was in different industry from the Dover Harbour Board whose boatmen provided a service for running the harbour.

On the other hand he may claim that only some of his workers are engaged

---

[35] *R.* v. *C.A.C. ex parte Deltaflow* [1978] I.C.R. 534.

[36] "Section" here relations to function and not to geographical situation; *R.* v. *Industrial Disputes Tribunal ex parte Courage & Co.* [1956] 1 W.L.R. 1062 at 1068.

[37] So far as the union is concerned the workers to be included in establishing a substantial proportion are those of a description to which the agreement being used as a comparison relates.

[38] C.A.C. award No. 225.

in a different industry. This may be difficult to substantiate because the question is not what trade are the employees exercising, but rather what trade is the employer engaged in? Thus in *Sutton's Bakeries and T.G.W.U.*[39] the relevant comparison for maintenance workers in a bakery was not the engineering industry but rather other bakeries.

Fifthly the workers with whom comparison is being made must be "in comparable employment." Thus in the instance of the bakery the detailed comparison is to be made with maintenance men in other bakeries where the job content is similar. It is not necessary that the workers should be of the same grade or description.

Finally in seeking to determine whether the terms offered are less favourable than the recognised terms,[40] the duty of the Committee is to look at the terms as a whole,[41] but the Committee has also said that certain basic terms may be directly compared in their own right and that normally it is "only in the case of more peripheral items that we would expect to take into account the whole of a company's terms and conditions to see if a deficiency in one area was compensated for by other areas."[42]

The general level

A claim that workers should be paid the general level can only be made if there are no recognised terms and conditions.[43] This leads to a peculiar problem for as recognised terms may mean the minimum terms, a person who is covered by recognised terms will be limited to these minimum terms and cannot claim the higher "general level"; but a person who is not covered by any terms at all may claim the general level.

The Central Arbitration Committee attempted to avoid some of these consequences in *Deltaflow Ltd. and T.G.W.U.*[44] where the national agreement laid down a minimum rate of £42 per week. It was however assumed that this was not the rate actually being paid but that it had been supplemented by plant agreements and that £42 was a totally unrealistic rate. The Committee therefore held that there was no "effective" recognised rate which could bar a general level claim. This approach was however rejected by the Divisional Court[45] for what was relevant was the "agreement" and the relevant agreement was still the national agreement, for,

> "nothing can destroy or modify the provisions of the written agreement of May 1975, except some new agreement, made by competent people ... The idea of a kind of tacit alteration in the terms of that central agreement derived from the fact that nobody bothered with it much for a year is not a way in which a formal document can be effectively varied."

This decision therefore places a severe limitation on the effectiveness of the "general level" provision, especially in view of the large number of national agreements which are supplemented at plant level.

The general level is defined as,[46]

[39] C.A.C. award No. 226. See also *Scott Kershaw Ltd. and UCATT*, C.A.C. Award No. 78/25 (joiners employed by kitchen design firm, held firm in retail not building trade).

[40] Recognised terms can mean minimum terms. Sched. 11 para. 2.

[41] E.P.A. 1975 Sched. 11, para. 9. See for example *Van den Berghs & Jergens Ltd. and USDAW*, C.A.C. award No. 353.

[42] *T.I. Sunhouse Ltd. and A.S.T.M.S.*, C.A.C. award No. 235.

[43] *R.* v. *C.A.C. ex parte Deltaflow* [1978] I.C.R. 534.

[44] C.A.C. award No. 236.

[45] *R.* v. *C.A.C. ex parte Deltaflow* [1978] I.C.R. 534.

[46] E.P.A. 1975 Sched. 11, para. 2.

"the general level of terms and conditions observed for comparable workers by employers—

(a) in the trade, industry or section in which the employer in question is engaged in the district in which he is so engaged; and

(b) whose circumstances are similar to those of the employer in question."

Once again the employer with whom the comparison is made must be in the same trade or industry and the workers must be "comparable" but here the comparison is made with the general level in the district. The concept of district is usually related to the idea of a labour market, so that what is relevant is the area in which the employer finds his supply of labour. The relevant district may well differ within one company depending on the category of employees at issue, so that for example the "district" for skilled men may be larger than the "district" for unskilled workers.[47]

The relevant district will also vary widely from industry to industry, and may even be defined so as to cover the entire country. For example this was so in the case of the lighthouse "industry" for in *Northern Lighthouse Board and T.G.W.U.*[48] both the Northern Lighthouse Board and Trinity House were held to operate in the same district, that is Great Britain as a whole.

The comparison must also be with employers in "similar circumstances" but it is not clear now flexible this condition is to be. It has been said that "the nub of the issue is the type of operation,"[49] and it may be that economic factors will not be relevant, for the Committee has rejected the view that the financial ability to absorb higher costs due to the greater size of the other company is sufficient to make the comparison invalid.[49]

The comparison must be made with a level that is "general" and it has been held that this can be done even if there is only one other employer of that kind of labour in the district.[50] One problem is the extent to which levels of pay within the same company or group of companies is relevant; the Committee has decided that purely internal pay relationships are not sufficient to establish a general level,[51] but has also said that the terms of employment may be relevant where each establishment within a company negotiates its terms independently.[52]

It should also be noted that the general level is not to be equated with the average level of earninings. This is so because exceptionally high or low rates within the range may distort the average, and it will therefore be more appropriate to look at the narrower range of rates most commonly applied.[53]

This leads to the problem of the limitations of the wages policy, which provide difficulties in relation to both heads of schedule 11 and to the Fair Wages Resolution. The duty of the Committee is to determine the relevant levels of wages that ought to be paid and the awards are therefore not subject to the restraints of pay policy. This has meant that the work of the committee has been enormously increased because this is almost the only way of avoiding the policy, and a number of cases have not been defended by employers because they are willing to pay the increases if they can do so.[53] It has,

[47] *Hoval-Ferrar Boilers Ltd. and A.U.E.W.*, C.A.C. award No. 363.

[48] C.A.C. award No. 377. See also *General Accident and APEX*, C.A.C. award No. 219. *R.H.M. Bakeries and URTU*, C.A.C. award No. 78/126.

[50] *Northern Lighthouse Board and T.G.W.U.*, C.A.C. award No. 377.

[51] *Dowty Group and A.U.E.W. et al.*, C.A.C. awards No. 342–350.

[52] *Hawker Siddeley Aviation Ltd. and A.U.E.W.*, C.A.C. award No. 134.

[53] *Wyeth Bros. Ltd. and T.G.W.U.*, C.A.C. award No. 150.

however, been pointed out that the procedure is not to be used simply as an appeal against pay policy,[54] for the union must still show that a better "general level" exists.

Wages Councils

A special provision applies where a person is covered by a Wages Council order[55] and his union (which must be an independent union) is party to a collective agreement in a significant number of establishments covered by the order. In such a case the union may claim that the member should be paid not less than the lowest current rate in any such agreement, even if the wages council rate is lower. The "general level" procedure would not be available as the wages council order would be an "award" covering the employment.

Procedure and Jurisdiction

The claim must be made to ACAS which "shall take any steps which seem to it expedient"[56] to settle the claim or refer it to other machinery to settle the claim. But if there is no solution the case is referred to the Central Arbitration Committee. Where the claim is based on recognised terms and conditions any independent union or employers' association may make the claim so long as it is one of the parties to the agreement regarded as providing the "recognised terms."

So far as a "general level" claim is concerned the case may be brought by any trade union (whether independent or not) of which any worker concerned is a member, but if the employer recognises an independent union for that description of worker, only that recognised union may claim.[57] It is clear that a union may present a claim when it has any member in the group which is concerned, and there may be argument over how narrowly the group should be defined. The point arose in *Grunwick Processing Laboratories and APEX*[58] where a claim had been made for eight classifications of workers, but the court held that the case could be treated as one claim, for the process and despatch workers were one group.[59] It was therefore only necessary for the union to show that it had members in that group rather than in each of the eight classifications.

The Committee is precluded from considering a claim where the minimum terms are fixed by statute.[60]

So far as the burden of proof is concerned it is for the person making the

---

[54] *Brent Voluntary Service Council and T.G.W.U.*, C.A.C. award No. 325.

[55] Wages Councils are discussed in Chap. 20.

[56] This phrase was discussed in *Grunwick Processing Laboratories and APEX*, C.A.C. award No. 329, where it was said that the Committee would assume that proper steps had been taken, but that if either side thought conciliation might provide a settlement the Committee would adjourn. Failure to conciliate was not a ground for refusing to proceed.

[57] E.P.A. 1975 Sched. 11, para. 5. A claim may also be made by an employers' association which has members engaged in the industry in the relevant district. *ibid.*

[58] C.A.C. award No. 329.

[59] The Committee was less certain about including computer punch card operators within the group, but the point did not need to be decided as the union could establish that it had members within that group.

[60] E.P.A. 1975 Sched. 11, para. 3. But it may consider cases where workers are covered by the Agricultural Wages Act 1948, the Wages Councils Act 1959 or by a statutory joint industrial council. In *R.* v. *C.A.C. ex parte North Western Regional Health Authority*, this provision did prevent the committee hearing a claim relating to the National Health Service where the workers could not be paid more than the amount approved by the Secretary of State [1978] I.C.R. 1228.

claim to show that there are recognised terms and conditions, or as the case may be, what the general level is. But it may be presumed that if the claim is for the general level it is for the employer to show that such a claim is precluded by the existence of recognised terms. It is for the employer to show that he is in fact observing terms no less favourable than the recognised terms or the general level.

If the Committee finds the claim justified it may make an award specifying the terms to be observed, the person to whom they are to apply and the date from which they are to be observed.[61] The award takes effect as a term of the individual contract of employment and may thus be enforced before the ordinary civil courts.

Judicial control

There is no appeal from a decision of the Central Arbitration Committee, and therefore the only control is by an order of certiorari or mandamus by the High Court. In such a case the Court will only intervene where the Committee has exceeded its jurisdiction, has not complied with the principles of natural justice, or where the reasons made public disclose an error of law.[62] A decision may also be set aside if it is one which no reasonable tribunal could have reached.

ARBITRATION (3)—THE FAIR WAGES RESOLUTION

The main provisions of the Fair Wages Resolution, which was adopted by the House of Commons in 1946,[63] are very similar to schedule 11 to the Employment Protection Act 1975. Clause 1 states:

1(a) The contractor shall pay rates of wages, and observe hours and conditions of labour, not less favourable than those established for the trade or industry, in the district where the work is carried out, by machinery of negotiation or arbitration to which the parties are organisations of employers and trade union representatives, respectively, of substantial proportions of the employers and workers engaged in the trade or industry in the district.

(b) In the absence of any rates of wages, hours or conditions of labour so established the contractor shall pay rates of wages, and observe hours and conditions of labour, which are not less favourable than the general level of wages, hours and conditions observed by other employers whose general circumstances in the trade or industry in which the contractor is engaged are similar."[64]

The resolution takes the form of a clause inserted in every government contract[65] and is relevant not just to the workers employed on the contract but

---

[61] Which can pre-date the award, but must not be earlier than the date on which the employer was first informed of the claim by the union.

[62] *R.* v. *C.A.C. ex parte T.I. Tube Division Services Ltd.* [1978] I.R.L.R. 183 (Div. Ct.).

[63] Following earlier resolutions of 1891 and 1909. See Kahn-Freund, "Legislation through adjudication: the legal aspect of Fair Wages clauses and recognised conditions." (1948) 11 M.L.R. 269 and 429. Bercusson, *Fair Wages Resolutions* (1978).

[64] It is also provided (Clause 4) that the contractor shall recognise the freedom of his workpeople to be members of Trade Unions, and that the contractor is responsible for the observance of the resolution by his subcontractors.

[65] The resolution may be incorporated by other bodies: see *Robert Hudson (Raletrux) Ltd. and A.U.E.W.*, C.A.C. award No. 355, where the clause was incorporated in a Coal Board contract and enforced in the usual way. It is also common in local authority contracts.

rather to all employees of the contractor.[66] If a dispute arises the matter is referred by the Minister to the Central Arbitration Committee which sits as an arbitrator,[67] but it has been held that the Arbitration Act 1950 does not apply so as to require the Committee to state a Special Case for consideration by the courts.[68] Indeed it may be that in its capacity under the Resolution the Committee is subject to no form of judicial control at all. The decision is not legally binding, but the penalty is that if the award is not honoured the employer would henceforward be excluded from government contracting.

The resolution does not confer any rights on the individual worker[69] and only the relevant union may refer the claim to the Minister, who will pass it on to the C.A.C.

The principal advantage of the Fair Wages Resolution over the schedule 11 procedure is that where recognised terms exist a union may nevertheless make a claim under "the general level" provision. This was the view taken by the then Industrial Arbitration Board in *Crittall-Hope and the Pay Board*[70] which set out in some detail the Board's understanding of the terms of the Resolution. However, the High Court took a different view in *Racal Communications* v. *The Pay Board*[71] for it was there held that a general level claim was precluded by the existence of established terms. But both the Industrial Arbitration Board and the C.A.C. have chosen not to apply the reasoning in that case,[72] and, at least so far as the C.A.C. is concerned, a general level claim can be made despite the existence of established rates.

Statutory extension of the fair wages clause

Where an activity is largely financed by the government or where it requires a licence it is not uncommon for statute to extend the fair wages principle to that industry. Thus the Independent Broadcasting Authority Act 1973[73] requires programme contractors to observe terms and conditions which are no less favourable than those that would have to be provided if the Fair Wages Resolution applied.[74] A dispute on such an issue goes before the Central Arbitration Committee and the award becomes an implied term in the individual contracts of employment.

Similar provisions are to be found in the following statutes: Road Haulage Wages Act 1938, s. 4 (1); Civil Aviation Act 1949, s. 15; Road Traffic Act 1960, s. 152; Films Act 1960, s. 42.

Arbitration (4)—Equal Pay

Whereas an individual may present a claim to an industrial tribunal under the Equal Pay Act 1970 for a breach of the "equality clause" implied in his or her contract of employment, a trade union[75] may refer to the Central Arbitration

[66] See for example *Worcester Royal Porcelain Co. and A.U.E.W.*, C.A.C. award No. 126, where the government contract amounted to only 0.5 per cent. of the company's business.

[67] *R.* v. *Industrial Court ex parte ASSET* [1965] 1 Q.B. 377.

[68] *I.M.I. (Kynoch) Ltd.* v. *A.U.E.W.* [1978] I. R.L.R. 407 (C.A.).

[69] *Simpson* v. *Kodak* [1948] 2 K.B. 184.

[70] Award No. 3290: (1974) 16 K.I.R. 477.

[71] [1974] I.C.R. 591. The action was against the Pay Board, and the Industrial Arbitration Board was not directly involved.

[72] See I.A.B. award Nos. 3296 and 3300. *Kelvin Hughes and A.U.E.W.*, C.A.C. award No. 78.

[73] s. 16, as amended by E.P.A. 1975 Sched. 16.

[74] Unless otherwise agreed by the relevant trade union.

[75] Strictly any party to the collective agreement, or the Secretary of State.

Committee a collective agreement which offends against the Act.[76] The task of the Committee is to remove from the agreement discrimination between men and women. The award takes effect by amending the collective agreement and hence can alter the terms incorporated in the individual contract.

The Committee must first determine whether there are any terms of the agreement which apply specifically to men only or to women only. This question is decided not only by reference to the formal classifications in the agreement but also by looking at the practical reality, so that it is not sufficient simply to change the name of the discriminatory grade or to admit a few persons of the opposite sex to the grade. Thus in *Thames Valley Eggs Ltd. and T.G.W.U.*[77] it was said that,

> "If a pay structure has been established which overtly discriminates between male and female employees and that pay structure has persisted unchanged in essentials from year to year, then the mere removal of identifying labels and the formal, but not in practice significant, admission of either sex to any grade does not, in the Committee's view, alter the reality of discrimination which it becomes the Committee's duty to remove."

But it should be noted that the discrimination must be because of sex, and if the reason for different treatment can be otherwise explained the Committee will not have jurisdiction. Thus in *Rolls Royce (1971) Ltd. and National Society of Metal Mechanics*[78] because of the introduction of the three shift system the Factories Act 1961 required that women workers had to be given a break of half an hour in each shift. The women were not paid for this break, but it was shown that this was not discriminatory since the company would apply the same terms to any worker who was entitled by law to take a break.

If the case is proved the committee may order that the rate applied to men of the same grade shall also be applied to women, but where there is no equivalent male grade the women must not be paid less than any of the men. In practice the application of such a rigid formula is not necessarily the best solution, and the Committee has found that rather than make an order it may be preferable to offer the parties advice on how to settle the issue, and in particular that a job evaluation study may prove useful. If the agreement is reached this can be embodied in an order.[79]

---

[76] Equal Pay Act 1970, s. 3.

[77] C.A.C. award Nos. 328 and 328A.

[78] C.A.C. award No. 361.

[79] An example of this procedure is *Thames Valley Eggs Ltd. and T.G.W.U.*, C.A.C. award Nos. 328 and 328A.

CHAPTER 20

WAGES COUNCILS

WAGES Councils[1] were instituted on an experimental basis in four industries[2] by the Trade Boards Act 1909[3] and were designed to deal with the problems of low pay in the "sweated" industries. The system was extended in 1918[4] and today there are some 43 wages councils[5] covering just under three million workers,[6] and they are to be found in those areas where union organisation has been poor and low pay common, such as catering and retailing.[7]

Wages Councils represented a significant departure from the dogma of "free collective bargaining" and introduced a mild form of wage regulation in that the minimum rate of wages is fixed by a statutory body and is imposed upon an employer whether he likes it or not. But it also contains elements of the collective bargain, even if that bargain is compulsory, for the wages council consists of representatives of employers and workers, as well as having independent members.

The dogma has however survived, for a wages council is regarded only as a necessary device for those areas where union organisation and collective bargaining are unable to flourish. The view taken is that whenever possible unionisation should be encouraged so that collective bargaining may be established and the wages council abolished. It has been said however that the very existence of a wages council inhibits this process, for wage regulation by a separate authority gives little incentive to employees to join the union, which therefore finds it difficult to establish itself as a bargaining agency. However, important changes were made in 1975 to try and alleviate this problem by permitting the conversion of a wages council to a statutory joint industrial council which consists only of the two sides of industry and has no independent members.

Unfortunately wages councils do little to affect the differentials between the low paid and others[8] for part of the problem is that the effect of a wages council order is not limited to the low paid, for often the rate of increase applied to the statutory minimum is used as the appropriate rate of increase for higher paid

---

[1] See Baylis, F. J., *British Wages Councils* (1962).

[2] They were ready-made and wholesale bespoke tailoring, box making, machine made lace and "hammered and dollied or tommied chain making."

[3] 9 Edw. 7 c. 22. They were known as Trade Boards until the Wages Councils Act 1945.

[4] Trade Boards Act 1918.

[5] This figure includes some separate Scottish councils, so the number of trades covered is somewhat less.

[6] H.C. Debs., vol. 930 *col. 229* (April 25, 1977).

[7] A similar system operates for agriculture under the Agricultural Wages Act 1948.

[8] Donovan Commission 1968, Cmnd. 3623, para. 259.

workers, and indeed the rate specified in the order may bear little relation to the rates actually paid. Thus the problem of relative low pay (which can be very important in times of inflation) remains.

On the other hand the wages councils do set a minimum rate which some individuals would not receive but for the orders of the relevant council and their enforcement by the wages inspectorate. Indeed the fact that so many employers covered by wages councils still (illegally) pay below the statutory minimum indicates how necessary such institutions are. This is not to say that wages councils have been successful in combatting the problems of low pay, but only that the situation might be worse without them. Whether the kinds of trades in which wages councils now operate can be sufficiently organised to permit free collective bargaining and the abolition of regulation remains to be seen.[9]

The Constitution of a Wages Council

A wages council consists of independent members, representatives of employers and representatives of workers.[10] The independent members, of whom there may be not more than three, are appointed by the Secretary of State and may be paid for their services. One of the independent panel is nominated as chairman. The other members (who are unpaid but may be reimbursed for travelling expenses and loss or earnings) are nominated by trade unions and employers' associations selected for that purpose by the Secretary of State. All members hold office for up to five years but may be re-appointed. There must be an equal number of representatives of workers and employers appointed to the Council.

Procedure

In order for there to be a quorum there must be at least one of the independent members and one third of the representative members present.[11] Each member has a vote, but voting may be taken by sides. This may be done at the discretion of the chairman and must be done at the request of more than half of the representatives of either side. In such a case the majority vote of each side is deemed to be the vote of that side, and in cases of disagreement between the two sides the matter is determined by a majority of the independent members.

Advisory Committees

At the request of a wages council the Minister may appoint an advisory committee and the council may refer to it any matter it wishes for investigation.[12] The committee must consist of an independent chairman and equal numbers of persons representing employers and workers. It is not a committee of the wages council itself but is independently appointed.

Powers of a Wages Council

A wages council may make an order which fixes the remuneration of workers

[9] There has, however, been some reorganisation and merger of wages councils recently, and a few were abolished in 1975. There have been a number of investigations recently by ACAS, *e.g.* the Button Manufacturing Wages Council (ACAS Report No. 11).

[10] W.C.A. 1959, s. 1 (4) and Sched. 2 as amended by E.P.A. 1975 Sched. 7.

[11] Wages Councils (Meetings and Procedure) Regulations 1975, (S.I. 1975 No. 2136).

[12] W.C.A. 1959, s. 8 and Sched. 3.

covered by the council, and in addition it may require that holidays be allowed, and determine any other terms and conditions of employment.[13]

Before making an order the Council may make such investigations as it thinks fit and once it has formulated proposals it must give notice of them. This is done by means of the London or Edinburgh Gazette and by sending a notice to every employer who is likely to be affected by the proposal, and allowing at least fourteen days for representations to be made.[14] After considering any submissions (and if necesssary circulating the amended proposals) the Council may make the order. Again notice must be given to the employers, and they are obliged to put up copies of the order in such a way as to bring it to the attention of the workers who are affected by it.[14]

The order is now made by the council itself rather than by the Secretary of State and is a statutory instrument. The order may take effect from a date earlier than that on which it was made, but not earlier than the date on which the proposals were first formulated.[15] The new wage rate must be paid from the beginning of the wages period which follows the date when the order takes effect. A wages council may delegate any of its functions (except that of making orders) to a committee of its members as long as the number of representatives of workers and employers on the committee is equal.

A wages council may be required by the Minister or any government department to submit a report on the industrial conditions prevailing in the area of its concern, or may submit such a report of its own accord.[16] This power is little used.[17]

Equal Pay

Where an order of a wages council contains a discriminatory clause in breach of the Equal Pay Act 1970 the Secretary of State may[18] refer the order to the Central Arbitration Committee who may declare what amendements are necessary in the order to remove the discrimination.[19] The wages council must implement the decision of the C.A.C. by making a further order within five months of the decision.

Enforcement of a Wages Council Order

The effect of a wages council order is that where the contract of employment of any given individual contains terms less favourable than those laid down in the order, the provisions of the order take effect as terms of the contract.[20] Thus if the employer is paying less than the minimum wage the employee may recover the difference by a civil action for a period up to six years.

The Act, however, also provides that in the case of failure to pay the

---

[13] W.C.A. 1959, s. 11 (1) as amended by E.P.A. 1975 Sched. 7. Ss. 11 (2) and 11 (2) (a) make further provision for holidays and holiday pay.

[14] Wages Councils and Statutory Joint Industrial Councils (Notices) Regulations 1975 (S.I. 1975 No. 2138).

[15] W.C.A. 1959, s. 11 (4).

[16] W.C.A. 1959, s. 10.

[17] Note also the power to approve an instrument of apprenticeship which involves the charging of a premium. (W.C.A. 1959, s. 16) and the power to grant a permit allowing an incapacitated or infirm worker to be paid less than the statutory minimum. (W.C.A. 1959, s. 13).

[18] He must make the reference if requested to do so by a relevant employers' association or trade union.

[19] Equal Pay Act 1970, s. 4, as amended by the Sex Discrimination Act 1975.

[20] W.C.A. 1959, s. 12 (1) as amended by E.P.A. 1975 Sched. 7.

statutory minimum or to pay holiday pay or to permit holidays to be taken, a breach of the order shall be a criminal offence[21] punishable on summary conviction by a fine not exceeding £100. In addition, following conviction for such an offence a court may order the employer to make up the difference between actual pay and the statutory minimum for the period of two years before the date of the offence for which he was convicted.[22]

The number of prosecutions for breach of a wages council order is very small.[23] The reason given for this[24] is that only second offenders are considered for potential prosecution and (a) few second inspections are carried out, (b) most employers who are inspected for a second time have put matters right and (c) the time lag between first and second inspections may be such that not only have the orders changed but so have the managers of the employing firm. However, continuing concern with the problems of low pay and the widespread evasion of wages councils orders may result in more prosecutions in the future, especially if second inspections become more common.

The Wages Inspectorate

The main burden of enforcing the orders of wages councils falls on the wages inspectorate. The wages inspector is given power[25] to enter the premises of any employer to whom an order applies and to require the production of wages records.[26] He may also question any employer or worker to whom an order relates and obstruction of an inspector is an offence punishable by a fine of up to £100. In addition the inspector may institute criminal proceedings for breach of an order and may also bring civil proceedings on behalf of an underpaid worker.

However, the task of policing low pay seems intractable, and indeed the rate of underpayment seems to be increasing.[27] In 1975 there were about 130 wages inspectors[28] who were responsible for 457,656 employers covered by wages council orders[29] and although the inspectorate aims to inspect 7.5 per cent. of all such establishments each year this target was not reached in 1975. The chances of an offender escaping detection are quite high, for a firm may be visited once every 13–14 years and even if he is discovered he is likely to have to pay only the amount of underpayment, for criminal prosecution for breach of an order is very rare indeed.

As a supplement to the programme of regular inspection the inspectorate instituted a "blitz" in selected towns in 1976. The advantages were that much

---

[21] A special defence, that the offence was due to the act or default of another is provided by W.C.A. 1959, s. 18.

[22] *Ibid.* s. 12 (2) and 12 (3). If a claim for back pay is to be made notice must be served with the summons.

[23] There were five cases between 1970 and 1976. Wingard, *The Weak Arm of the Law?* 1976 (Low Pay Unit paper No. 13).

[24] (1977) 85 Dept. of Employment Gazette, p. 102 at 109.

[25] W.C.A. 1959, s. 19. See also E.P.A. 1975, s. 95 which gives the Secretary of State the power to demand any information.

[26] It is an offence punishable by up to 3 months imprisonment or a fine up to £400 knowingly to produce false records.

[27] For much of what follows see "The Wages Inspector Cometh," 85 Dept. of Employment Gazette 107; Wingard *Policing Low Pay,* Low Pay Unit Paper No. 4 (1976); Wingard *The Weak Arm of the Law?* Low Pay Unit Paper No. 13 (1976).

[28] The figure for Jan. 1978 was 133. H.C. Debs., vol. 941, *col. 634* (25th January 1978).

[29] The inspectorate is also responsible for the Truck Acts 1831–96.

greater publicity was accorded to the wages councils by a co-ordinated surprise inspection and the higher proportion of inspection within a given area gave a better idea of the degree of evasion. The results were most disturbing, for the number of employers underpaying ranged from 23 per cent. in Wakefield to 45 per cent. in Blackpool. When classed by industry it seems that the worst areas were bookselling (52 per cent.), unlicensed restaurants (43 per cent.), newsagents and tobacconists (41 per cent.), retail bread (40 per cent.) and licensed restaurants (39 per cent.).[30] As a result of the "blitz" nearly £50,000 was recovered for underpaid workers, amounting to an average of £45.50 per person.

It seems, however, that experience during this period has not changed the policy of the wages inspectorate over prosecution of offenders, for of the 54 employers who were found to be in breach of an order for the second time only three were selected for prosecution.[31] However the suggestion that the number of second inspections should increase may lead to more prosecutions, but even so the maximum fine of £100 may not be a great deterrent. It would be wrong however to suppose that all cases of failure to comply with an order are malicious, and many breaches are based on ignorance and misunderstanding, and accordingly greater publicity and simplification of the terms of the orders may also achieve useful results.

Establishing a Wages Council

The Secretary of State may establish a wages council by order in one of three ways:[32]

(1) if he is of the opinion that no adequate machinery exists for the effective regulation of the remuneration of the relevant workers. It is unlikely that this method would now be used as it involves the minister making an order of his own accord and without taking the advice of ACAS.

(2) if he wishes to give effect to a recommendation of ACAS on a case which has been referred to it by the Minister because there is no machinery for wage fixing or because such machinery is inadequate or likely to cease to exist.

(3) if he wishes to give effect to a recommendation of ACAS on a case which was referred to it by the Minister following representation to him by a joint industrial council, a conciliation board or a similar organisation, or jointly by an employers' organisation and a union engaged in the relevant area. (But if there are other unions or employers' associations involved in the same area they must be consulted before the reference to ACAS is made.)

When a question is referred to it ACAS has wide terms of reference[33] for not only can it consider the problem of the area of employment referred to it but also "any other question or matter which in the opinion of the service is relevant," and in particular it may consider whether any other workers should be dealt with at the same time.

As the establishment of a wages council is to some extent considered a solution of last resort, ACAS may, if it finds that machinery for regulating wages and conditions of employment exists but is inadequate, recommend

---

[30] These figures are for employers underpaying: the order is slightly different when judged by employees underpaid.

[31] H.C. Debs., vol. 918, *col. 729* (November 5, 1976). There were two prosecutions in 1975 and two in 1974 but none in the previous two years.

[32] W.C.A. 1959, s. 1.

[33] W.C.A. 1959, s. 3.

improvements in such machinery and the Minister is under a duty to take such steps as are practicable to secure such improvements. Only if negotiating machinery does not exist (or will soon cease to exist) or if such machinery is inadequate and cannot be improved, may the Service recommend the establishment of a wages council.

Before making the order the Minister must publish the draft order and allow 40 days for objections to be submitted.[34] Finally the order comes into effect on the day on which it is published, or such later date as is specified in the order.

Abolition of a Wages Council[35]

The Minister may by order abolish a wages council either of his own accord or after taking the advice of ACAS. In addition an application may be made to the Minister to refer the matter to ACAS by a joint industrial council or some other such body or by the unions and employers jointly. The fact that such applications needed the consent of both sides may have impeded the abolition of some councils and it is now provided[36] that such an application may also be made unilaterally by a union representing a substantial proportion of the relevant workers.[37] The application is made on the ground that the wages council is no longer necessary for maintaining a reasonable standard of remuneration for those covered by it, and this would only occur when some other form of collective bargaining machinery has or is about to replace it.

The Service may either recommend the abolition of the council or it may suggest that certain groups should be excluded from the ambit of the council or transferred to the jurisdiction of a different council. Once again the Minister must publish notice of his proposal and give an opportunity for objections to be made within 40 days and if necessary the matter may be referred again to ACAS to consider the objections.[38]

It seems generally agreed that it is desirable where possible to abolish wages councils, not because of the inadequacy of such bodies but because the fact of their existence indicates lack of organisation amongst the workers concerned or outmoded employment policies by the employers. If collective bargaining can be established then it is encouraged and the wages council abolished. However there have not been many examples of outright abolition in recent years, and it seems likely that in the future the usual route to abolition and the establishment of collective bargaining will be by way of a period of existence as a statutory joint industrial council.[39]

Recent examples of abolition include the Keg and Drum Wages Council[40] where the forerunner of ACAS, the Commission in Industrial Relations had concluded[41] that the Council could safely be abolished as the wage rates it set

---

[34] W.C.A. 1959 Sched. 3.

[35] *Ibid.* s. 4.

[36] *Ibid.* s. 5 (1) (c) as added by the Industrial Relations Act 1971 Sched. 8.

[37] In such a case the Minister must also consult the wages council itself and representatives of the employers' side.

[38] W.C.A. 1959 Sched. 1. See for example Retail Wages Councils, ACAS Report No. 10.

[39] Although this was not so with the most recent example of abolition where the Road Haulage Wages Council was abolished outright rather than converted into a statutory joint industrial council as collective bargaining arrangements were adequate. Road Haulage Wages Council (Abolition) Order 1978 (S.I. 1978 No. 966), following ACAS Report No. 6.

[40] Abolished by the Keg and Drum Wages Council (Great Britain) (Abolition) Order 1975 (S.I. 1975 No. 646).

[41] C.I.R. Report No. 48.

were so low as to be largely irrelevant, and because three quarters of the employers covered by the Council were included in collective bargaining arrangements.[42] On the other hand, after inquiry[43] the Pin, Hook and Eye Snap Fastener Wages Council was retained because otherwise there would be no method of statutory supervision of the wages of home-workers who lacked any form of union organisation and were likely to remain unorganised.

In some cases the abolition process is used to effect a merger. Thus the Retail Bespoke Tailoring Wages Council (Great Britain) was created out of separate councils for England and Wales, and Scotland.[44] Perhaps of more significance was the recent proposal to abolish nine wages councils in the field of retail distribution to create two councils (Food and Non-Food) to cover the whole area.[45]

Variation of a Wages Council Order

Much the same procedure applies to variation as it does to abolition.[46] The matter may be decided by the Minister or may be referred by him to ACAS.

The field of operation of a wages council is usually determined by a definition of the relevant trades, but this sometimes produces too indiscriminate a coverage. Thus a council may be retained covering a large number of workers just for the sake of a few, or it may be abolished leaving the few who need protection to fend for themselves.[47] There is however a new power to deal with this problem, so that upon a variation order workers may be excluded from the jurisdiction of a council not by reference to their trade but by reference to their employer, or more particularly by reference to their employer's employers' association.[48]

The advantage of such a scheme is that the better organised sectors of an industry may be separated off and the wages council order would no longer have the effect of automatically raising their pay and thus preserving differentials, but would be limited to the less well organised and the lower paid sectors of the industry.

However, a variation may also increase the scope of a wages council, perhaps due to the emergence of new technology. Thus the Coffin Furniture and Cerement Making Wages Council increased its jurisdiction by including those engaged in finishing and packing plastic coffin furniture.[49]

STATUTORY JOINT INDUSTRIAL COUNCILS

In order to ameliorate the supposed disadvantages of wages councils that they inhibit trade union growth, and in order to encourage the parties to rely less on

---

[42] The employers were in general against abolition, whereas both unions involved were in favour.

[43] C.I.R. Report No. 49.

[44] Retail Bespoke Tailoring Wages Councils (Abolition and Establishment) Order 1977 (S.I. 1977 No. 1688).

[45] See C.I.R. Report No. 89; ACAS Report No. 10 on Retail Wages Councils.

[46] W.C.A. 1959, ss.4 and 6.

[47] See for example the Paper Box Wages Council (C.I.R. Report No. 83, abolished by S. 1 1975 No. 41) where the Commission recommended that the Minister should seek an assurance from the Unions that they would employ extra resources to recruit employees in small establishments in the trade.

[48] W.C.A. 1959, s. 4 (2A) as inserted by E.P.A. 1975 Sched. 7.

[49] Coffin Furniture and Cerement Making Wages Council (Great Britain) (Variation) Order 1975 (S.I. 1975 No. 758), C.I.R. Report No. 46.

the independent members and to bargain more effectively between themselves, the Employment Protection Act 1975 provided for the conversion of a wages council into a statutory joint industrial council.[50] Such a body has the same powers as a wages council but consists only of representatives of employers and workers and has no independent members. The council must consist of equal numbers of representatives of each side and elects its own chairman and regulates its own procedure. Expenses for travelling and loss of wages are paid by the Secretary of State who also pays for the running of the council.

In such a body there is the obvious risk that the two sides will be unable to agree and it is provided[51] that in such a case the matter should initially be referred to ACAS who must attempt to bring about a settlement. If this fails the case is referred either to one or more arbitrators appointed by ACAS or to the Central Arbitration Committee. The decision of the arbitrator is binding on the council so that an order under section 11 of the Wages Council Act 1959 must be made in pursuance of it.

Establishment and abolition

The conversion from a wages council is achieved by order of the Secretary of State after investigation of the case by ACAS. An application for such a conversion may be made to the Secretary of State either by the nominated employers' association or by the nominated trade union on the wages council. The Secretary of State may abolish a statutory joint industrial council by order either on his own accord after consulting the council or on the application of the council. He may also seek the advice of ACAS.

Central Co-ordinating Committees

The Wages Councils Act 1959 makes provision for the Secretary of State to establish central co-ordinating committees to cover groups of wages councils or statutory joint industrial councils. The function of the committee is to consider whether the field of operation of the councils is properly divided between them, to make recommendation to the councils on the exercise of their statutory powers, and to consider any other question referred to it by the Minister or the relevant councils.

It is thought that there is no such committee currently in existence.

---

[50] E.P.A. 1975, ss 90 to 94 and Sched. 8.
[51] *Ibid.* s. 92.

CHAPTER 21

TRADE UNION RECOGNITION

AS industrial relations policy is based on collective bargaining, the act of recognising a union's right to engage in such bargaining is a matter of crucial importance to both sides of industry; for the employer it means accepting limitations on the managerial prerogative and for the union it provides the ability to fulfill its primary role of negotiating on behalf of its members.

The essence of recognition is that the employer has agreed to bargain with the union, although that fact does not imply anything about the contents of the agreements that will be reached, nor that there will be agreement at all. (Although an obstinate refusal to make an agreement may be construed as a refusal to bargain). Whether the final agreement is legally binding between the parties is of no practical significance,[1] although it may be important to know the extent to which the terms agreed between the union and the employer are incorporated into the contracts of employment of the individual workers.[1]

The practical consequences of the agreement are that industrial rather than legal sanctions may be used by either side if the agreement is unilaterally broken. So far as representation is concerned, as the union has made an agreement on behalf of its members the employer can argue that he need not, and perhaps should not, deal with an individual employee except through the union, and on the other hand it should be noted that the union is not required to bargain on behalf of non members. In practice the terms reached with the union are usually applied to non members, but the union is under no duty to represent the interests of such people.[2]

For the law there are two main issues concerning recognition. First, as an employer owes certain legal obligations to a union which he recognises, it is important to define recognition. Secondly the law has taken steps to encourage the growth of collective bargaining and has therefore instituted a procedure for gaining recognition.

THE DEFINITION OF RECOGNITION

There are three cases where a court may have to decide whether a union has been recognised or not. First an employer is under a duty to provide a recognised union with information which is necessary for collective bargaining;[3] secondly where an employer proposes to make a person redundant he

---

[1] The legal issues are discussed in Chap. 18.

[2] The position is otherwise in the U.S.A. where the union is under a duty of fair representation. *Steele* v. *Louisville & N.R.R.* 323 U.S. 192 (1944).

[3] E.P.A. 1975, s. 17. See Chap. 23.

must consult any recognised trade union which bargains on behalf of that employee,[4] and thirdly an employer must allow reasonable time off for trade union officials and members to engage in the activities of a recognised union.[5]

The statutory definition

Recognition is defined, rather unhelpfully as "recognition of the union by an employer, or two or more associated employers, to any extent, for the purposes of collective bargaining."[6] If for the moment we take it that recognition means willingness to bargain, the definition gives rise to a few points of interpretation.

"Collective bargaining"

The effect of the phrase "collective bargaining" is to define the purposes for which the employer must bargain. In other words if recognition is to be held to exist the two parties must be bargaining about things that are called "collective bargaining," and when a union applies under the proper procedure to ACAS for recognition by a recalcitrant employer, it may be that ACAS can only recommend that the parties should bargain about things within the definition.

The definition of collective bargaining states[7] in effect that bargaining means "negotiations relating to or connected with" such matters as may be the subject of a trade dispute within the Trade Union and Labour Relations Act 1974. It may seem odd that a phrase designed to define the limits of the freedom to strike should be thought appropriate to limit the areas in which an employer may be required to bargain, but the definition of trade dispute has been drawn widely. Briefly[8] it covers the following matters:[9]

(a) terms and conditions of employment, or the physical conditions in which any workers are required to work;
(b) engagement of non-engagement, or termination or suspension of employment or the duties of employment, of one or more workers;
(c) allocation of work or the duties of employment as between workers or groups of workers;
(d) matters of discipline;
(e) the membership or non-membership of a trade union on the part of a worker;
(f) facilities for officials of trade unions; and
(g) machinery for negotiation or consultation, and other procedures, relating to any of the foregoing matters, including the recognition by employers or employers' associations of the right of a trade union to represent workers in any such negotiation or consultation or in the carrying out of such procedures.

It has been argued[10] that this definition should not limit the area of bargaining which may be recommended by ACAS on an application under section 11 of the Employment Protection Act. This view is put forward on the grounds that the definition only applies "except so far as the context otherwise

[4] E.P.A. 1975, s. 99. See Chap. 22.
[5] E.P.C.A. 1978, ss. 27 and 28.
[6] E.P.A. 1975, s. 126 and s. 11 (2).
[7] E.P.A. 1975, s. 126, referring to T.U.L.R.A, 1974, s. 29 (1).
[8] The meaning of "trade dispute" is fully discussed in Chap. 11.
[9] T.U.L.R.A. 1974, s. 29 (1).
[10] Bercusson, annotations to *Current Law Statutes,* Employment Protection Act 1975, s. 11 (2).

requires"[11] and that the enforcement sections[12] envisage no limit on the extent of bargaining. It should be noted that ACAS has taken the view that the right of an individual member to be represented by a union official does not amount to collective bargaining and therefore cannot be the subject of a recognition recommendation.[13]

It is suggested that ACAS is likely to regard itself as bound by the definition for the purposes of limiting the range of matters about which bargaining should take place and certainly the definition has been used to determine whether voluntary recognition has in fact taken place. Thus if a union is to be regarded as "recognised" it must bargain about at least one of the issues listed above.[14]

Finally it should be noted that the definition is in terms of "negotiations" rather than "consultations." This means that the decision is arrived at jointly by the two parties and thus involves a decrease in the area of the managerial prerogative. Consultation preserves the final power of decision in the hands of management and does not amount to recognition. This works both ways, for if consultation rights only are granted the union has none of the rights concerning information or consultation over redundancy, but on the other hand it is not prevented from pursuing a claim for recognition as it would be if its negotiating rights were simply inadequate.

"Associated Employer"

The term "associated employer" is defined[15] so as to cover cases where one employer controls the other and where both are controlled by a third party; the phrase does not include an employers' association and accordingly recognition is only legally relevant when it is with the employer (or the person who controls the employer) and not an association of employers.

"To any extent"

It might have been argued on the basis of the words "recognition to any extent" that there can be qualitative degrees of recognition. Thus in *NUGSAT* v. *Albury*[16] it was argued that as the employers were members of the employers' association, and as they in practice honoured agreements between that association and the union and as the employers were willing to discuss the agreement with the union, therefore the union was recognised to some extent at least. It was held however that recognition is not a matter of degree in that sense but that it postulates some kind of direct contact between the unions and the employers for the purpose of negotiating terms and conditions of employment.[17]

In other words "to any extent" does not apply to the *kind* of recognition but refers to the subject matter concerning which bargaining may take place,[18] or

---

[11] E.P.A. 1975, s. 126 (1).

[12] *Ibid.* ss. 11–16.

[13] ACAS Annual Report 1977, p. 50.

[14] *T.G.W.U.* v. *Dyer* [1977] I.R.L.R. 93 (E.A.T.) where it was said that recognition has the same meaning throughout the Act.

[15] E.P.A. 1975, s. 126; T.U.L.R.A. 1974, s. 30 (5).

[16] [1978] I.R.L.R. 504.

[17] [1978] I.C.R. 62 at 67 *per* Phillips J.

[18] *T.G.W.U.* v. *Dyer* [1977] I.R.L.R. 93, where it was argued that willingness to discuss recognition does not of itself amount to recognition. This point was not conceded by the union at first instance in *NUGSAT* v. *Albury* [1978] I.C.R. 62.

to the groups of employees covered; thus a union is recognised even if the employer has agreed to bargain over only some of the matters contained in the definition, or only for some employees.

One consequence of this approach is that the remedies for defective collective bargaining could be limited. Thus if an employer "recognises" a union, but is consistently unwilling to come to an agreement, it may be argued that recognition nevertheless exists. This would have the effect of blocking a reference to ACAS. Although a claim may be made to ACAS for "further recognition"[19] this applies only to areas of negotiation and groups of employees covered and does not refer to the quality of the bargaining.

On the other hand in a case such as that suggested it could be argued that the employer is not engaging in "negotiations" at all, and as the definition of collective bargaining requires negotiations,[20] recognition has either not been granted or has lapsed, and therefore an approach could be made to ACAS. It is suggested that this is the better view.

Agreement to bargain

The central problem in determining whether recognition has taken place is whether an employer has willingly agreed to bargain. It may seem strange that this can become a contested issue, but in some cases the question is not whether the employer now recognises the union (for he may withdraw recognition at any time), but whether at the relevant date the union *was* recognised.[21]

In most cases of recognition there is no difficulty because the employer and the union will have entered into a procedure agreement which defines the areas suitable for bargaining, the employees covered and the procedure to be followed. Such a formal system is not however necessary for recognition to have taken place, and the difficult issue is the extent to which previous conduct can establish recognition.

It is clear that recognition is a mutual act and cannot be imposed unilaterally. Thus in *N.U.T.G.W.* v. *Ingram*[22] Phillips J. said,

> "Recognition plainly, we think, implies agreement—which, of course, involves consent. That is to say it is a mutual process by which the employers recognise the union, which obviously agrees to be recognised, and it may come about in a number of ways. There may be a written agreement that the union should be recognised. There may be an express agreement not in writing. Or, as we think, it is sufficient if neither of these exists but the established facts are such that it can be said of them that they are clear and unequivocal and give rise to the clear inference that the employers have recognised the union. This will normally involve conduct over a period of time."

The theory therefore is that there must be clear and unequivocal evidence of consent to recognition: this is because of the importance attached by both sides to recognition[23] and because of the danger of holding an employer to

---

[19] E.P.A. 1975, s. 11 (3).

[20] E.P.A. 1975, s. 126 (1).

[21] It is assumed that for the purposes of giving information the relevant date is the date on which the wages or other claim was made, for which the information was required; for redundancy consultation it is assumed that the relevant date is the date on which the proposal to make employees redundant was made.

[22] [1977] I.C.R. 530.

[23] *Wilson* v. *USDAW* [1978] I.C.R. 614 at 617.

have recognised a union without his realising it, or at least being in a situation where he ought to have realised it.

Thus in *T.G.W.U.* v. *Dyer*[24] the fact that an employer unwillingly discussed re-instatement of an employee with the union did not amount to recognition, or if it did it was only to the degree necessary to resolve that particular issue. On the other hand in *Wilson* v. *USDAW*[25] the employer agreed with a union representative to abide by a nationally agreed wages award and allowed him to put up a notice to this effect. This was held to be an act of recognition.[26]

However if recognition is to be held to exist the conduct must be between the proper parties, that is between an employer and a trade union. Thus an employers' association cannot be a party to statutory recognition, and it has been held that evidence that an employer is a member of an employers' association which bargains with a union nationally is not sufficient evidence of recognition at the local level.[27] Furthermore recognition is of a union and therefore the conduct which establishes such recognition must be in relation to a union official rather than a representative of the work force generally.[28] Finally, as recognition is consensual in nature it binds only the parties directly involved. Thus a successor in title to the business of an employer who has recognised the union is not automatically bound by that recognition.[29]

Even if a union is held to be "recognised" by the employer it should be noted that this does not mean that it is necessarily recognised for all purposes, for it may be recognised for some purposes and not for others.

ACAS Recommendation

For a number of purposes a union is deemed to be recognised when ACAS has made an operative recommendation[30] that it should be recognised, even though no agreement to that effect has followed. This is so in cases of consultation over redundancies,[31] time off for officials or members to engage in the activities of a recognised union,[32] and the right to information for the purposes of collective bargaining.[33]

CLAIMS FOR RECOGNITION

One of the most important issues for a system of industrial relations that has no provision for compulsory arbitration is the extent to which the law should encourage or compel parties to engage in collective bargaining. Not only can recognition problems (either with the employer or between unions) be a rich source of industrial disputes but also the extension of collective bargaining is seen by all governments as the proper way forward for industrial relations. It is thought that not only should the number of workers covered be increased, but so should the range of topics which are subject to bargaining rather than managerial prerogative.

---

[24] [1977] I.R.L.R. 93 (E.A.T.).
[25] [1978] I.C.R. 614.
[26] See also *N.U.T.G.W.* v. *Ingram* [1977] I.C.R. 530.
[27] *NUGSAT* v. *Albury* [1978] I.R.L.R. 504.
[28] *A.U.E.W.* v. *Sefton* [1976] I.R.L.R. 318 (I.T.).
[29] *UCATT* v. *Burrage* [1978] I.C.R. 314.
[30] Within E.P.A. 1975 s. 15.
[31] E.P.A. 1975, s. 106 (1).
[32] E.P.C.A. 1978, s. 32 (a).
[33] E.P.A. 1975, s. 17 (2) (b).

A form of statutory encouragement for recognition was advocated by the Donovan Commission,[34] but a much more ambitious system was provided by Industrial Relations Act 1971.[35] The procedures were somewhat legalistic and inflexible,[36] but because they existed and could be called in aid to enforce recognition, many smaller employers who had never considered granting recognition before, now did so, and by this means the range of collective bargaining was considerably extended.

The principle of stimulation for the extension of recognition survived the 1971 Act, but the present procedures are more flexible and have a different emphasis, in so far as the inter union dispute is not seen as the main difficulty.[37] In the large majority of cases a recognition problem is solved by agreement between the parties (even if industrial pressure may have been applied), but that legal measures to encourage recognition are still necessary is indicated by the fact that in 1977 there were 577 references to ACAS for recognition.[38] However the very existence of the legal procedure has brought about recognition by agreement in numerous cases.

The nature of the claim

An independent[39] trade union may present a claim to ACAS asking for a recommendation that it should be recognised by the named employer.[40] A request (and a subsequent recommendation) may be for full recognition over the whole range of matters considered suitable for collective bargaining,[41] or it may be for recognition in order to bargain over a limited range of matters, such as issues not dealt with by a national agreement. A request may be made even though some other union has already been recognised by the employers,[42] but if both unions are affiliated to the T.U.C. such cases may involve difficulty with the Bridlington principles.

Where recognition is already accorded to a limited extent a union may apply for "further recognition"[43] which means not only the subject matter of bargaining but also the groups of employees to be covered.

If a recommendation has been made but there has been no agreement between the parties in pursuance of it, either party (or both together) may apply for a variation of the recommendation.[44] Where the application for variation is from one side only the Service must be satisfied the reconsideration is justified because of changed circumstances or further information, or that a condition of the recommendation is not being complied with. The most

[34] Cmnd. 3623, 1968, paras. 253–256.

[35] ss. 37–60.

[36] For examples of the procedure see *T.S.A.* v. *Post Office* [1974] I.C.R. 658; *E.S.U.* v. *C.E.G.B.* [1972] I.C.R. 418 (a forerunner of the closed shop case, *Sarvent* v. *C.E.G.B.* [1976] I.R.L.R. 66); *N.A.L.H.M.* v. *Allied Breweries* [1972] I.C.R. 257 followed by C.I.R. Report No. 38.

[37] Kahn-Freund *Labour and the Law* (2nd ed.) Chap. 4.

[38] ACAS Annual Report 1977, p. 73.

[39] For the meaning of "independent" see Chap. 2.

[40] The meaning of recognition is discussed above. The claim can only be against a named employer and not against an employers' association.

[41] Collective bargaining is defined by E.P.A. 1975, s. 126 and T.U.L.R.A. 1974, s. 29 (1).

[42] See for example *Tewy and Sons Ltd. and APEX*, ACAS Report on recognition, No. 114 where it was recommended that APEX should be recognised even though the company had recognised its own staff association.

[43] E.P.A. 1975, s. 12 (3).

[44] E.P.A. 1975, s. 13.

common ground for such a request on behalf of the employer is that union membership has fallen after ACAS made its enquiries or that it has not increased as much as expected.

A claim may be withdrawn by the applicant union at any time[45] and ACAS may refuse to proceed with the case if it believes the issue to be substantially the same as one which it has previously dealt with.[46]

The duties and powers of ACAS

The first duty of ACAS when it receives a request for recognition is to attempt to bring about settlement of the dispute by agreement between the parties,[47] and indeed conciliation is kept in mind throughout the handling of the reference.[48] Otherwise the Service must conduct an inquiry and make a report.

If conciliation has failed or looks unlikely to succeed the Service "shall examine the issue, shall consult all parties who it considers will be affected by the outcome of the reference and shall make such inquiries as it thinks fit."[49] Furthermore "in the course of its inquiries into a recognition issue ... the Service shall ascertain the opinions of workers to whom the issue relates by any means it thinks fit..."[50]

It was the duties to inquire and to ascertain opinion as contained in these sections that gave rise to the problems in the famous case of *Grunwick Ltd.* v. *ACAS*.[51] In that case there was a strike over a disciplinary matter at the defendant's film processing factory which culminated in a recognition dispute with the union (APEX) to which the strikers had turned for assistance. A recognition claim was presented to ACAS, but the Service found itself hampered in its inquiries by the fact that the employer refused to provide the names and addresses of the employees who were still working. After some delay ACAS decided to go ahead and send questionnaires only to those who were on strike and had been dismissed. The opinion of those workers who replied was unanimously in favour of the union and recognition was recommended.[52]

The recommendation was successfully challenged in the House of Lords where a number of points were made. First it was argued that ACAS should not have sought the opinion of those workers who had been dismissed, but this argument was rejected on the ground that the statutory definition[53] of "worker" covers not only those who work but also those who seek to work, and the strikers were seeking re-instatement.

---

[45] E.P.A. 1975, s. 12 (3) (b).

[46] E.P.A. 1975, s. 12 (2).

[47] E.P.A. 1975, s. 12 (3) (a).

[48] There were 1038 references between February 1, 1976 and December 31, 1977, of which 408 had been withdrawn. Of the 408 cases, full recognition has been accorded in 178 cases and partial recognition in 35. ACAS Annual Report 1977 Appendix A table 18. ACAS may also conciliate on a recognition issue under its general powers of conciliation: EPA 1975, s. 2. There were 635 such cases in 1977.

[49] E.P.A. 1975, s. 12 (1). There is a discretion, which must be exercised reasonably, to delay action if it is desirable in order to fulfil properly the duties of inquiry and report, *E.M.A.* v. *ACAS* [1978] I.C.R. 875 at 892.

[50] E.P.A. 1975, s. 14 (1).

[51] [1978] I.C.R. 231. See also Rogaly J. *Grunwick* (1977); Ward G. *Fort Grunwick* (1977) and the Scarman Report, Cmnd. 6922.

[52] ACAS report on recognition, No. 19.

[53] T.U.L.R.A. 1974, s. 30 (1).

Secondly the House held that the section which states that the Service "shall ascertain the opinion of workers"[54] is mandatory rather than directory and puts the Service under an obligation to ascertain opinion and the section cannot be qualified by a phrase such as "so far as reasonably practicable."

Thirdly there was the question whether ACAS must canvass the opinion of all the workers or whether it may select only some: the statute simply refers to "the opinion of workers." Lord Diplock considered that "to treat the section as if it said "the workers" or "all the workers" is to place upon ACAS a more meticulous requirement than is warranted in the absence of the definite article,"[55] but this did not mean that the opinions of sections of the work force could be ignored. He said:[56]

> "the words . . . make manifest a statutory intention that . . . ACAS should ascertain and take into consideration the opinions on that issue of the work force as a whole, and, where there is a reasonable possibility that there may be a conflict of opinions, should ascertain and take into consideration those that are held by every group of workers of any significant size that forms part of the work force that would be affected by the recommendation."[57]

The result is that where management is unco-operative the Service must nevertheless try to obtain the opinion of the employees without their assistance.[58] This may be done by obtaining the names from another source or even by calling a meeting of the work force, but if despite such attempts the opinion of any section of the work force has still[59] not been obtained the only course of action for ACAS is to publish a report stating that it is debarred from making any recommendation.[60] In other words the Act does not impose on the Service a duty to make a decision.[61]

Methods of ascertaining opinion

The Service may ascertain the opinion of workers "by any means it thinks fit."[62] This includes questionnaires, the holding of meetings or even sounding opinion through reliable representatives.[63]

However if the Service chooses to ascertain opinion by means of a ballot certain statutory requirements apply, and some doubt has arisen as to when a questionnaire amounts to a ballot, thus bringing these requirements into operation. It has been said that a ballot is "a secret vote directed to discerning the opinions of workers to whom the issue relates upon the issue itself, on the result of which ACAS will be either totally or partly basing its recommenda-

---

[54] E.P.A. 1975, s. 14 (1).

[55] [1978] I.C.R. 231 at 259.

[56] *Ibid.* at 262.

[57] See also per Lord Salmon, *ibid.* at 270 and per Lord Edmund Davies at 273 ("the general state of opinion among the affected workers as a whole").

[58] The Employment Protection Bill (Bill 13, 1978) would have modified the duties of ACAS by declaring that it needs only ascertain the opinion of workers "so far as reasonably practicable." The Bill lapsed.

[59] There is no time limit imposed on ACAS within which it must report.

[60] [1978] I.C.R. 231 at 264 per Lord Diplock.

[61] ACAS abandoned the attempt to resolve the Grunwick dispute in July 1978. *The Times*, July 13, 1978.

[62] E.P.A. 1975, s. 14 (1).

[63] [1978] I.C.R. 231 at 247 per Browne L. J..

tion."[64] Thus it is suggested that almost all forms of questionnaire will amount in law to a ballot. The fact that the statute refers to a "formal" ballot adds nothing to the meaning of ballot, but only indicates that it is being used in a strict sense,[64] and the fact that the form which is distributed not only asked for opinions but also for information does not render the opinion part any the less a ballot.[65]

If the questionnaire is in law a formal ballot[66] the following conditions apply:[67]

(a) ACAS must give notice to every employer and union concerned of the group of workers to be balloted, the questions to be asked, the manner of conducting the ballot, and must consider any representations that are made.

(b) The Service "must have regard to the need" to see that each worker included in the ballot has an equal right and a fair opportunity of voting, and that each individual vote will be kept secret.

(c) After the ballot ACAS must inform each union and employer of the result and the employer must notify his employees.

Who should be balloted?

Although linked to the question of the definition of the bargaining unit which should be recommended for recognition, the issue of the extent of the ballot is slightly different. ACAS has taken the view that it "will consider sympathetically any representations that opinion surveys should be broader rather than narrower in scope."[68] This is so because a wider survey can provide relevant information without prejudice to any decision as to the eventual scope of the bargaining unit.

The question to be asked

The attitude of the courts to the requirement that the opinion of the relevant workers must be ascertained is that it is an important safeguard for the individual and therefore must be scrupulously carried out. In *Powley* v. *ACAS*[69] Browne-Wilkinson J. said,

> "As a result of the statutory machinery an individual can have a substantial measure of control over his own working life compulsorily delegated to an agent, or trade union, which he has not selected and may even have his contract of service varied without his consent . . . it is the courts duty to ensure that the rights of the individual are not to be lost to him except in strict accordance with the statutory procedure laid down."[70]

Accordingly as accurate a view as possible must be obtained of the opinion of the work force, and this involves difficult technical questions concerning the way in which a question may tend to elicit a particular response. The usual

---

[64] *Grunwick Ltd.* v. *ACAS* [1978] I.C.R. 231 at 251 per Geoffrey Lane L. J. The matter was not discussed in the House of Lords.

[65] *Ibid.* See also at 240 *per* Lord Denning M.R. and at 248 *per* Browne L. J.

[66] This is a matter of law and not for ACAS to decide: *Grunwick Ltd.* v. *ACAS* [1978] I.C.R. 231 at 251 *per* Geoffrey Lane L.J.

[67] E.P.A. 1975, s. 14.

[68] ACAS Annual Report, 1977, p. 44.

[69] [1978] I.C.R. 123 at 135.

[70] This view was approved by Lord Denning M.R. in *Grunwick Ltd.* v. *ACAS* [1978] I.C.R. 231, but he disapproved the view that recognition was analogous to the compulsory acquisition of property.

form of the questionnaire, at least where only one union is involved, is as follows:[71]

(a) Do you wish to have your pay and conditions of employment determined by negotiations between the company and a trade union acting on your behalf?

(b) Do you wish the *X* union to represent you in negotiations with the company about pay and conditions of employment?

Where two or more unions are concerned the task of determining opinion is more complicated. ACAS had taken the view that it need only ask whether workers wanted the union which was making the application to be recognised, but this view was rejected by the courts in *Powley* v. *ACAS*.[72] A.S.T.M.S. had made an application to ACAS for recognition by the Legal and General Assurance Society which had a number of employees who were members of the Legal and General Staff Association. The court held that one of the important facts for consideration by ACAS was the degree of support for unions other than that which was making the application, and decided that the staff association's name must appear on the questionnaire. This was so even though, if a majority preferred the staff association, the Service would be unable to recommend that it should be recognised because it was not the applicant.

Accordingly, in such cases the usual form of the second question is "which trade union or other organisation of workers, if any, do you wish to represent you in negotiations with the company about pay and conditions of employment?" This is followed by a list of the possible unions.[73]

Improper pressure

There is no statutory provision governing the conduct of the employer or the union at the time when the opinion of the work force is being sought, but in *Grunwick Ltd.* v. *ACAS* Lord Salmon made it clear[74] that "if ACAS had reasonable grounds for believing that the opinions expressed by the workers were not genuine opinions but opinions improperly induced by pressure from one side or the other, ACAS would have the power to ignore them." In such a case the Service should state in its report the grounds on which it took its decision.

No guidance is given as to what would be improper pressure. Presumably it would be open to either side to provide the work force with a factual statement of its position, but threats would be regarded as illegitimate.[75] It is not yet clear what view should be taken of setting up a staff association in response to a claim for recognition by an independent union.[75]

---

[71] It is also customary to ask if a person is already a member of the union and, if not, whether he would join it if it were recognised.

[72] [1978] I.C.R. 123.

[73] See for example *Howard Doris Ltd. and UCATT,* ACAS Report on recognition s. 12, No. 115.

[74] [1978] I.C.R. 231 at 270.

[75] See for example *Playboy Club and T.G.W.U..,* ACAS Report on recognition, No. 34, where recognition was recommended despite support by only 56 out of 176 employees because of the actions of the management. This report was later withdrawn. The management had stated in a letter that "many of the benefits already obtained would be dismantled, discontinued or not instituted ... if the union comes in all "bets are off." We will in effect go back to square one and negotiate the terms of employment here on the basis of confrontation ..."

The report

If it is able to do so, the Service should produce a report stating whether or not it recommends that a particular union or unions should be recognised by the employer. The report must specify not only the parties to be affected but also the scope of the bargaining unit, the extent of subject matter over which the parties must bargain, and the level at which it must take place.[76] Conditions may be attached to the recommendation.[77]

General Policy

The general policy of the Act is that "the Service shall be charged with the general duty of promoting the improvement of industrial relations, and in particular encouraging the extension of collective bargaining and the development, and, where necessary, reform of collective bargaining machinery."[78] The opinion is sometimes expressed that ACAS is biased in favour of recognition, but the answer is that the Service, while being independent of the government, is nevertheless subject to the broad policy direction stated in the Act and so is required to be "positive in promoting collective bargaining, based on trade union recognition, as the best method of conducting industrial relations."[79]

The bargaining unit

One of the most difficult problems is to determine the scope of the bargaining unit, that is to say the group or groups of workers for whom the trade union should be allowed to bargain. The fact that there is no statutory guidance on this issue indicates that ACAS is intended to have a wide discretion and that the decisions are to be pragmatic.

ACAS itself has indicated that the following factors may be relevant:[80]

(a) practice in the industry concerned, with regard to union recognition for particular categories of employees, trade union policies and any collective agreements which the employer may apply;

(b) collective organisation and wishes of the employees, including their membership of the union, and wishes for collective representation;

(c) the nature of the work being done and associated requirements such as the skills, training, qualifications and experience needed to do it;

(d) the employer's organisational structures and employment policies, including working arrangements, such as hours, shifts, geographical location and interchangeability of employees; payment systems, pay structures and other conditions of employment, promotion patterns and sources of recruitment.

The determination of the appropriate group of employees may be crucial in determining whether recognition should be granted, for in a firm of say 100 employees of whom only 20 want recognition, if it is possible to separate off a group which includes that 20, then recognition is likely to be recommended for that group, but if the firm is looked as a whole, recognition is unlikely.[81]

---

[76] E.P.A. 1975, s. 12 (5).

[77] *Ibid.*, s. 12 (6).

[78] E.P.A. 1975, s. 1 (2).

[79] ACAS Annual Report 1976, p. 51.

[80] ACAS Annual Report 1977, p. 46.

[81] See for example *Autogem and T.G.W.U.,* ACAS report on recognition No. 64, where a group of 26 packers/assemblers were separated out from other workers. The total workforce was 56. See also *Racal Ltd. and A.U.E.W.* ACAS report on recognition No. 73, where production workers were treated separately from toolroom workers.

Degree of employee support necessary

Once again there is no statutory guidance on the degree of support necessary for recognition to be granted, but it is clear that the number of employees supporting the union is not the only factor.

In assessing support the Service usually gathers information on the number of members of the relevant union, the number who would join the union if it were recognised, the number who want collective bargaining and the number who want to be represented by the applicant union.

Where there is a majority of those replying who want to be represented by the relevant union, recognition will normally be recommended, but in exceptional circumstances other factors may be taken into account despite a majority in favour of recognition.[82] If this were not so ACAS would become a mere balloting agency, which was clearly not intended, but rather the recommendation is intended to be based on the judgment of the Service while stressing the wishes of the employees concerned.

ACAS had taken the view that two factors in particular might be important in deciding whether to refuse to accede to the wishes of the majority. The first was that recognition would cause fragmentation of bargaining and that other bargaining arrangements were available, or that local recognition would not fit into the scheme of national bargaining.[83] Such a view would have meant that it would have been very difficult for a change in representation to take place.[84] The second factor was that other unions would oppose recognition.[85] Both these points have however been rejected by the courts for in *UKAPE* v. *ACAS*[86] May J. said that in allowing such matters to outweigh the view of the majority the Service had misinterpreted its duty under the Act, and had not followed its general duty of encouraging collective bargaining, and had taken into account matters and views which it should not have done. In view of this, the opinion of the Service that it is also relevant that the union preferred by the majority is not independent[87] is not likely to survive.

While most cases will be decided on the basis of the degree of support shown by the relevant employees, it is inevitable that other factors must be allowed to enter into the calculation. However the extent to which ACAS is seen as impartial in this area may depend on the degree to which such judgments are seen to be reasonable.

---

[82] "There is nothing in the Act which expressly states that the view of the majority shall prevail, but it is, in my view, implicit that it shall, save perhaps in very exceptional circumstances." *Grunwick Ltd.* v. *ACAS* [1978] I.C.R. 231 at 270 *per* Lord Salmon. See also *UKAPE* v. *ACAS*, [1978] I.R.L.R. 336.

[83] W. H. Allen and UKAPE ACAS report on recognition No. 68. See also *Electro Dynamic Construction Co. and UKAPE*, report No. 112. See also some cases on polytechnics; *Hampshire C.C. and A.P.T.*, ACAS report on recognition, No. 118; *Coventry City Council and A.P.T.*, report on recognition, No. 119. Compare *Polytechnic of North London and A.P.T.*, report on recognition No. 120.

[84] See for example *British Steel and E.E.S.A.*, report on recognition No. 133 where 91 per cent. of a group of 33 electrical engineers voted in favour of representation by E.E.S.A. but recognition was still not recommended on the grounds that recognition would involve fragmentation of bargaining.

[85] The UKAPE Cases, fn. 83 above.

[86] [1978] I.R.L.R. 336; affirmed by the Court of Appeal, (1979) 129 N.L.J. 91 (C.A.).

[87] *Joseph Terry & Sons and APEX*, ACAS report on recognition No. 114.

Inter union disputes

One of the more controversial aspects of recognition where more than one union is involved is the extent to which unions which are affiliated to the T.U.C. should be prevented from referring issues to ACAS before submitting the case to the disputes procedure of the T.U.C. The problem of recognition concerns not only refusals by an employer to recognise a union, but also disputes between unions as to which one, if any, should be recognised. The function of the T.U.C. Disputes Committee is to resolve such disputes by the application of the "Bridlington Principles,"[88] and accordingly the T.U.C. has recommended[89] that,

> "an affiliated union should not invoke the Acts procedure on recognition without consultation and agreement with any other affiliated union with an interest in the matters. Where there is disagreement between affiliated unions about a claim for recognition the matter should be resolved through the T.U.C. disputes procedure."[90]

Some unions have found the T.U.C. procedure unsatisfactory, partly because it allows the other party to delay the issue and partly because of the approach taken by the T.U.C., but nevertheless the procedure offers a useful alternative method of resolution of such disputes. It is not however possible, or desirable, to prevent a union taking its dispute to ACAS.[90]

Judicial Control of ACAS

ACAS has considerable discretion as to how it exercises its wide powers and none of its decisions is subject to appeal. However it is subject to the usual principles of judicial control of administrative action and to that extent is subject to the jurisdiction of the High Court.[91] It is suggested that the following principles apply:[92] First the Service must direct itself correctly as to the law. Secondly in the exercise of its discretion it must consider all the matters it is bound to consider and exclude all matters which are irrelevant. Thirdly it must not reach a decision which no reasonable such body would reach.[93]

These principles in fact provide a very narrow basis for challenging a discretionary decision and it is to be hoped that the courts will not allow such challenges to be used as an appeal procedure, for the decisions of ACAS are not judicial but executive. As the Service is independent of the Government it is subject to no other control.

Refusal to comply with ACAS recommendation

The decision of ACAS is only a recommendation to the parties, but the Act does provide a somewhat cumbersome enforcement procedure if that recommendation is not followed.[94]

---

[88] "T.U.C. Disputes Principles & Procedures," Principle seven requires the union involved in a recognition dispute to notify the T.U.C. so that it can be dealt with by a Disputes Committee.

[89] *Ibid*. Also presented in T.U.C. Annual Report 1976, p. 99.

[90] This recommendation is not legally binding on affiliated unions, not only because it is a recommendation, but also because if it were more it would be avoided by E.P.A. 1975, s. 118 (1).

[91] See De Smith, *Judicial Review of Administrative Action* (3rd ed.) Chap. 6.

[92] *Associated Provincial Picture House* v. *Wednesbury Corporation* [1948] 1 K.B. 223 at 228–229 *per* Lord Greene M.R. Approved in relation to ACAS by *Grunwick Ltd.* v. *ACAS* [1978] I.C.R. 231 at 261 *per* Lord Diplock, at 269 *per* Lord Salmon, at 273 *per* Lord Keith; *Powley* v. *ACAS* [1978] I.C.R. 123.

[93] *UKAPE* v. *ACAS* [1978] I.R.L.R. 336.

[94] E.P.A. 1975, ss. 15 and 16.

A recommendation becomes "operative"[95] 14 days after the ACAS report is received by the employer. It should be noted that although the previous procedures all applied to "workers," the recommendation only becomes operative in relation to "employees."[96] As the definition of worker is wider than that of employee, a number of people, such as "lump" workers, could be excluded from the recommendation. Oddly enough the opinions of these excluded categories are relevant in deciding whether to grant recognition, and could in theory be the deciding factor.

It was expected that a recommendation would normally be followed by an agreement between the parties which would supercede the recommendation. Where that does not happen the union concerned may, after two months have elapsed from the date on which the recommendation became operative, refer the case again to ACAS on the grounds that the employer is "not then taking such action by way of or with a view to carrying on negotiations as might reasonably be expected to be taken by an employer ready and willing to carry on such negotiations as are envisaged by the recommendation."[97] The Service is under a duty to attempt to resolve the problem by conciliation.[98]

The next step is for the union to refer the matter to the Central Arbitration Committee.[99] The C.A.C. may hear the case and if it finds it substantiated may issue a declaration. Such a declaration however has no legal force against a determined employer, and the only method of enforcement of the ACAS recommendation lies in the ability of the C.A.C. to make an award incorporating certain terms and conditions in the contracts of employment of individual employees. If these terms are in turn not obeyed the employee must sue in the ordinary courts for breach of contract.

It should be noted that the terms which may be incorporated do not include the term that the union should be recognised: the C.A.C. "has no power to impose recognition of a particular union as an obligation, on an employer in a contract of employment."[1]

Furthermore it may be difficult for the committee to make any award of a collective nature. This is because the remedy is by way of incorporation in individual contracts of employment, and the committee may be limited by the view that only certain kinds of terms are appropriate for incorporation.[2] This is generally taken to mean that collective rights are not usually appropriate, but it is suggested that this may not always be so; for example the establishment of a grievance procedure may be regarded as both a collective and an individual right. But even if the problem of "appropriateness" could be overcome there would still be the difficulty of privity of contract, that is of how the union could take advantage of the contract between the employer and the individual. It is suggested that in a case of a breach of a collective term by the employer damages would not be an adequate remedy for the individual

[95] The fact that a recommendation is "operative" may be significant in a number of cases: (1) the right to information (E.P.A. 1975, s. 17 (21); (2) redundancy consultation (E.P.A. 1975, s. 106 (1)); time off for officials and members (E.P.C.A. 1978, s. 32); discrimination for trade union activities (E.P.C.A. 1978, s. 23 (5)); the closed shop (E.P.C.A. 1978, s. 58 (4)).

[96] "Worker" and "employee" are defined by T.U.L.R.A. 1974, s. 30.

[97] If the recommendation is conditional the period is 14 days after the employer is informed that all conditions have been complied with.

[98] E.P.A. 1975, s. 15 (2).

[99] Except in relation to Crown Employment. E.P.A. 1975, s. 121 (1).

[1] *Phoenix Timber Co. and T.G.W.U.* C.A.C. award No. 272.

[2] *Young* v. *Canadian Northern Railway* [1931] A.C. 83. See further Chap. 18.

concerned, and that he would be granted specific performance of the contract, which would accrue to the benefit of the union.[3]

In effect therefore the C.A.C. procedure amounts to unilateral arbitration of a claim, such as a wage claim, that would, had the recommendation been followed, have been put through the negotiation procedure. Thus in *Phoenix Timber and T.G.W.U.*[4] the Committee's award was that the terms of an agreement between the union and an employer's association should be applied to the relevant employer. On the other hand in *Avis Rent-a-Car Ltd. and T.G.W.U.*,[5] while a declaration was granted that the ACAS recommendation had not been followed, no award was made as the union's claim was for a matter which was negotiated nationally, whereas the recognition was to have been limited to matters which fell within the discretion of local management.

The award of the Committee may be superceded by a collective agreement between the employer and the union which represents the relevant employee covered by the award; or by an agreement between the employer and the employee himself, but in this latter case only in so far as the agreement improves any terms of the award.[6] It is thought that it would not be sufficient to show that the new agreement is on balance an improvement, but that only those particular terms which themselves are an improvement will supersede the provisions of the award.[7]

Effectiveness of the procedure

The statutory procedures are only necessary where the parties are unable to agree, and the powers of ACAS to make a recommendation are only used if conciliation has failed. Therefore by the time the recommendation is made the parties are in a state of confrontation and it appears that the decisions of ACAS are not on the whole successful in reducing the area of disagreement, for in few cases has a recommendation for recognition been followed by an agreement between the parties. Thus of the 63 recommendations for recognition made up to October 1977, only 10 had resulted in recognition by the following February.[8] It has been suggested[9] that this is due not only to the fact that recommendations are only necessary in the hardest of cases, but also that small groups without industrial power find it difficult to bring about agreement. In addition it has been claimed that delays in producing reports may also be a factor, but whatever the reason it is likely that some unions which cannot reach agreement will nevertheless refrain from pursuing a remedy before the C.A.C. because of the inadequate nature of the remedy.

The duty to consult in nationalised industries

In a number of nationalised industries statute imposes upon the governing

---

[3] *Beswick* v. *Beswick* [1968] A.C. 58. See also *Coulls* v. *Bagots' Executor* (1966) 40 A.L.J.R. 471.

[4] C.A.C. Award No. 272.

[5] C.A.C. Award No. 189.

[6] E.P.A. 1975, s. 16 (7).

[7] It is also provided that an employee may take the better of the terms of the award of the C.A.C. and the terms of any provision for minimum wages in pursuance of any enactment.

[8] Industrial Relations Review and Report No. 169 (February 1978).

[9] *Ibid.* See also Dickens "ACAS and the Union Recognition Procedure" (1978) 7 I.L.J. 160.

body a duty to engage in collective bargaining.[10] The most recent version[11] requires the employer to consult appropriate organisations with a view to setting up machinery for the settlement by negotiation of terms and conditions of employment, for the promotion of measures affecting efficiency and for the encouragement of measures affecting safety.[12]

In *Gallaher* v. *Post Office*[13] it was held that such a statute does not confer any rights on the individual employee so as to enable him to require that his union be recognised.

[10] The relevant statutes are: Coal Industry Nationalisation Act 1946, s. 46; Atomic Energy Authority Act 1954, s. 7; Electricity Act 1957, s. 12; Remuneration of Teachers Act 1965, s. 1; Remuneration of Teachers (Scotland) Act 1967, s. 1; Transport Act 1968, s. 137; Post Office Act 1969, Sched. 1, para. 11; Gas Act 1972, s. 35; Iron and Steel Act 1975, s. 7.

[11] Iron and Steel Act 1975, s. 7.

[12] See Hepple and O'Higgins, *Public Employee Trade Unionism in the United Kingdom* (1971).

[13] [1970] 3 All E.R. 712.

CHAPTER 22

REDUNDANCY PROCEDURES

The Employment Protection Act 1975 provides[1] further support for the collective bargaining process in the particular field of redundancies. An employer is required to consult any recognised union if he proposes to make any employee redundant, and must also notify the Secretary of State for employment if 10 or more redundancies are planned. Once again a collective right is enforced by individual procedures so that the employee is given certain rights if the consultation procedure has not taken place. The provisions follow from a directive of the E.E.C. Council.[2]

THE DUTY TO CONSULT TRADE UNIONS

Section 99 (1) of the Employment Protection Act 1975 states:

"An employer proposing to dismiss as redundant[3] an employee of a description in respect of which an independent trade union is recognised by him shall consult representatives of that trade union about the dismissal . . ."

This provision, and the sections which follow it, have given rise to considerable difficulty and the law is of great complexity.[4]

The content of the duty

The duty is one of consultation when any employee (even just one) is to be made redundant and this is achieved by providing the union with the following specified information in writing.[5]

(1) The reasons for the proposals.
(2) The numbers and descriptions of employees it is proposed to dismiss as redundant.[6]
(3) The total number of employees at the relevant establishment of the same description as those to be made redundant.
(4) The proposed method of selecting the employees who may be dismissed.

---

[1] ss. 99–107.

[2] E.E.C. Directive of February 17 1975, 75/129. (O.J. L48/29).

[3] Redundant is defined by E.P.A. 1975, s. 126 (6). The definition differs from that in E.P.C.A. 1978, s. 81 in only one minor detail. See Grunfeld "The Law of Redundancy" (1971). The burden of showing the dismissal was not due to redundancy is on the employer. E.P.A. 1975 s. 106 (2).

[4] See especially the very useful annotation to E.P.A. 1975, *Current Law Statutes,* by B. Bercusson. See also Kahn-Freund, *Labour and the Law* (2nd ed.) 1977, pp. 91–94.

[5] E.P.A. 1975, s. 99 (5).

[6] As the consultation must take place before the dismissals this information should not include the names of the individuals concerned.

(5) The proposed method of carrying out the dismissals, including the period over which the dismissals are to take effect.

It is clear that the duty to consult the union is expressed in general terms and relates to numbers and descriptions of employees and the methods of selection. The consultation should not be so detailed as to be concerned with the names of individuals for this may be to invite the union to perform the invidious task of deciding which of their members should be dismissed.[7] Although decisions on which category of employees should be dismissed may amount to the same thing in some cases, it is suggested that there is a difference in principle between consultation over categories and consultation over individuals.

The union may make representations on the proposals which must be considered by the employer, and if he rejects any views of the union he must state his reasons. It should be emphasised that the duty is one of consultation only and is not by virtue of the statute one of negotiation. It is possible of course for there to be an agreement with the union providing for negotiation rather than consultation.

Representatives of a recognised union

The union concerned must be an "independent"[8] trade union which is "recognised"[9] by the employer. It is important to note that this is only a condition for the duty to arise and does not in any way limit the extent of the obligation. Thus it is clear that the duty to consult applies even if the only employees to be made redundant are not members of the union, for the section applies when any employee to be made redundant is *of the same description* as that for which the union is recognised. In such a situation the union may not be concerned to protect the individual non-member, but it may be interested in preserving the jobs. This provision may also mean that more than one union must be consulted even though the workers to be dismissed all belong to one union: this is so where two or more unions are recognised for the same description of worker.

The consultation must be with a "representative"[10] of the union and that term is defined[11] as meaning "an official or other person authorised to carry on collective bargaining with the employer in question by that trade union." An "official" is further defined[12] so as to include a shop steward, but the real issue is not the status of the person concerned, but rather whether he is authorised by the union to carry on collective bargaining.[13] Such authority may be expressed or implied.

When the obligation arises

The employer is under a duty to consult the union "at the earliest opportunity."[14] As the provisions only apply to an employer who "proposes" to

[7] *Clyde Pipeworks Ltd.* v. *Foster* [1978] I.R.L.R. 313 (E.A.T. Scotland).
[8] Independent is defined by T.U.L.R.A. 1974, s. 30 (1). See Chap. 2.
[9] Recognised is defined by E.P.A. 1975, ss. 126 (1) and 11. See Chap. 21.
[10] Although the statute speaks of representatives in the plural, consultation with one is sufficient: Interpretation Act 1978, *G.M.W.U.* v. *Wailes Dove Bitumastic* [1977] I.R.L.R. 45 (I.T.).
[11] E.P.A. 1975, s. 99 (2).
[12] T.U.L.R.A. 1974, s. 30 (1).
[13] For example see *G.M.W.U.* v. *Wailes Dove Bitumastic* [1977] I.R.L.R. 45 (I.T.).
[14] E.P.A. 1975, s. 99 (3).

make workers redundant it may be important to determine what is meant by that phrase for it is then that the employer must consult the union.

The proposal need not be a final decision that redundancies are appropriate, although a decision or at least a definite state of affairs of some kind is necessary. A proposal does not exist where redundancy is only a remote possibility,[15] but rather the employer must have formed some view on the subject which he can put to the union.[16]

Particular difficulty has been experienced in the construction industry where the work and the workforce continually fluctuate. Where work is taken on for a fixed term contract it is always likely that men will be made redundant when the contract is completed. Accordingly it has been suggested that discussions should begin almost at the same time as the contract work begins and should continue throughout its existence. A "proposal" comes about when there is something definite known about the future demands for labour. Thus in *UCATT* v. *Ellison Carpentry Contractors*[17] the tribunal rejected the view that a proposal comes into existence only when a definite decision has been taken as to the number and date of the redundancies, and held that a redundancy situation had come about once the work had reached its peak and had begun to run out, or "when no more men are being engaged and it is apparent that the next move shall be a reduction, and not an increase, in the number of men employed."[17] Consultations should then begin.

It is also clear that the consultation must take place before the dismissals. In *N.U.T.* v. *Avon C.C.*[18] the finance committee had made a recommendation on October 21, 1976, that certain teachers should be dismissed and on October 28 this was accepted by the education committee, which immediately sent out notices of dismissal to take effect in December. The union was informed the following day. The Employment Appeal Tribunal held that "dismiss" in the statute refers to the giving of notice rather than to the date when the dismissal takes effect, so that the proposal to dismiss must come before notice is given. This view is made all the clearer by the fact that one of the matters upon which there must be consultation is the method of selection for redundancy, which can only be done before the decision to dismiss particular individuals has been taken. Whether it would be legal (at least in cases where less than 10 employees are to be dismissed[19]) to inform the union the day before the giving of notice was left open, but it might be thought that such action does not amount to consultation at all, especially in view of the fact that the law lays down a minimum protected period of 28 days if the statute is not adhered to.[20]

A further problem arises as to who makes the relevant proposal.[21] For example in *NALGO* v. *National Travel (Midlands) Ltd.*[22] the National Bus Co. (the parent company) decided on or before February 8, 1977, to merge two of its subsidiaries, which would bring about redundancies. The announcement to this effect was made on February 14 by the defendant

[15] *NUPE* v. *General Cleaning Contractor Ltd.* [1976] I.R.L.R. 362 (I.T.).

[16] *Association of Pattern Makers and Allied Craftsmen* v. *Kirvin Ltd.* [1978] I.R.L.R. 318 (E.A.T. Scotland) but see *Bakers' Union* v. *Clarks of Hove* [1978] I.R.L.R. 366 (C.A.).

[17] [1976] I.R.L.R. 398. (I.T.).

[18] [1978] I.C.R. 626.

[19] There are fixed limits of the length of consultation where 10 or more are involved: E.P.A. 1975, s. 99 (3).

[20] E.P.A. 1975, s. 101.

[21] E.P.A. 1975, s. 99 (3).

[22] [1978] I.C.R. 598.

subsidiary and the unions were then consulted. The question of whether consultation took place "at the earliest opportunity" depended on who made the proposal, the parent company or the subsidiary. In rejecting the claim, and in holding that in this case the proposal was that of the subsidiary, the Court noted first that the contract of employment was with the subsidiary and secondly that there was no evidence that the two companies were in all respects one corporate entity or that the subsidiary was "bound hand and foot to the other"[23] and must do what the parent says. Unfortunately the Court gave no guidance on the situation where the parent company has effective control of the subsidiary, but it is suggested that in the absence of evidence of deliberate intention to evade the Act, the contract of employment may prevail, if only for reasons of simplicity.

The period of consultation

Consultation must begin at the earliest opportunity, but where mass redundancies are concerned the law lays down minimum periods of consultation which apply unless there are special circumstances which render it not reasonably practical to comply with the periods laid down.[24]

Accordingly when an employer proposes to dismiss 10 or more employees at any one establishment within a period of 30 days, consultation must begin at least 60 days before the first dismissal takes effect. Where 100 or more are to be dismissed within 90 days the minimum period of consultation is 90 days.[25]

Staggered redundancies

In determining the number of relevant employees to be dismissed no account is to be taken of those employees for whom consultations have already begun. If therefore consultations have begun in relation to a group of say seven employees, a later proposal within 30 days to make a further five redundant does not bring the minimum period of 60 days into operation. But it suggested that this provision cannot be used as a method of evading the Act for if when the first group is made redundant the employer already has it in mind to dismiss the second group then that amounts to a proposal to dismiss more than 10 employees.[26] It would however be possible to avoid the Act by making the proposals in separate 30 or 90 day periods.

"Establishment"

The minimum periods only apply where the proposal relates to the relevant number at one establishment.[27] In dealing with the meaning of "establishment" some reliance has been placed on its interpretation for the purposes of Selective Employment Tax.[28] In *Secretary of State for Employment* v. *Vic Hallam Ltd.*[29] Lord Parker considered the matter to be one of broad common sense, and he thought that the following indications might be relevant; first whether there is exclusive occupation of premises, secondly whether there was

[23] *D.H.N. Food Distributors Ltd.* v. *Tower Hamlets London Borough Council* [1976] 1 W.L.R. 852 at 860 *per* Lord Denning M.R. For a statement of the relevant tests see *Smith, Stone and Knight* v. *Birmingham Corporation* [1939] 4 All E.R. 116 at 121.

[24] E.P.A. 1975, ss. 93 (3) and (8). The special circumstances are discussed below.

[25] E.P.A. 1975, s. 99 (3).

[26] *T.G.W.U.* v. *Nationwide Haulage Ltd.* [1978] I.R.L.R. 143 (I.T.).

[27] E.P.A. 1975, s. 99 (3).

[28] Selective Employment Payments Act 1966, s. 1; Finance Act 1967, s. 26.

[29] (1969) 5 I.T.R. 108.

some degree of permanence and thirdly whether there is "some organisation on the premises, an organisation of the men who are working there."[30]

Thus for the purposes of the redundancy procedure it has been held that 14 housebuilding sites are not each a separate establishment, especially in view of the temporary nature of the "premises."[31] Similarly it has been held that bakery employees were employed at one establishment even though that covered 28 shops a bakery and a factory.[32]

Wages in lieu of notice

A surprising result of the Act is that where an employer does allow for the relevant period of consultation but agrees to let some of the men go with wages in lieu of notice, he is in breach of the Act. This is so because the consultation must be so many days before the dismissal, and in this context dismissal means not the day the notice would have run out had it been given, but the day the employee leaves.[33]

Thus in *A.S.T.M.S.* v. *Hawker Siddeley Aviation*[34] consultations began on August 18, 1976, in time to allow the requisite 90 days before the dismissal, but the company agreed to allow wages in lieu so that the first dismissal in fact took effect only nine days later. The company was held to be in breach of the Act, but no protective award was made.[35]

Special circumstances

If the employer is able to show that there are "special circumstances which render it not reasonably practicable" for him to comply he may be exempted from the duties to consult at the earliest opportunity (or within the minimum periods) or to give the statutory information, or to consider representations by the union.[36] But in such a case he must nevertheless take all such steps towards compliance with those duties as are reasonably practicable in the circumstances.[36] It seems that this phrase is to be interpreted on its own account and little assistance is to be gained from its use elsewhere in the law, such as for the purpose of time limits on application to a tribunal[37] or for the purposes of the Road Traffic Acts.[38]

It seems likely that the courts will hold that to be a special circumstance the difficulty must be out of the ordinary and sudden. Thus in *Bakers' Union* v. *Clarks of Hove*[39] it was held that bankruptcy was not of itself a special

---

[30] *Ibid.* at 110. These dicta were approved by the House of Lords in *Lord Advocate* v. *Babcock and Wilcox (Operations) Ltd.* [1972] 1 All E.R. 1130; see also *Secretary of State* v. *Clark Chapman* [1971] 2 All E.R. 798.

[31] *Barratt Development* v. *UCATT* [1978] I.C.R. 319.

[32] *Bakers Union* v. *Clarks of Hove* [1977] I.R.L.R. 167, not disturbed on appeal [1978] I.R.L.R. 366 (C.A.). On the other hand see *Barley* v. *Amey Roadstone* [1978] I.C.R. 190 where the E.A.T. doubted but did not disturb the view of the tribunal that individual depots are separate establishments.

[33] *Dedman* v. *British Building and Engineering Ltd.* (1974) 9 I.T.R. 100 (C.A.).

[34] [1977] I.R.L.R. 418.

[35] But this may not always be so in such cases: see *E.E.S.A.* v. *Scott* [1976] I.R.L.R. 319 where in similar circumstances an award was made because the intentions of the company would not have satisfied the Act anyway.

[36] E.P.A. 1975, s. 99 (8). *Armour* v. *A.S.T.M.S.* [1979] I.R.L.R. 24 (E.A.T.).

[37] *Dedman* v. *British Building and Engineering Ltd.* [1974] 9 I.T.R. 100 (C.A.); application of analogies not supported, *UCATT* v. *Rooke* [1978] I.R.L.R. 204 (E.A.T.) disapproving a contrary implication in *Wilson* v. *USDAW* [1978] I.R.L.R. 120 (E.A.T.).

[38] *Bakers' Union* v. *Clarks of Hove* [1978] I.R.L.R. 366 (C.A.).

[39] [1978] I.R.L.R. 366 (C.A.). But see *Armour* v. *A.S.T.M.S.* [1979] I.R.L.R. 24 (E.A.T.).

circumstance and that much depended on the surrounding factors. Therefore, as the trouble was due to a gradual run down of the company, consultations should have begun at an earlier stage, even if the directors had hoped that "something might turn up."[40] On the other hand if a fire were to destroy the premises and there is no other work for the employees to do, this would amount to special circumstances.

As is usual, ignorance of the law cannot be a special circumstance, even if the employer is misled by another into thinking the provisions do not apply.[41]

Exclusion from the provisions

The following groups are excluded from the operation of the duty to consult over redundancies:[42]

(1) Share fishermen[43]
(2) Where the employee ordinarily works outside Great Britain[44]
(3) Where the contract is for a fixed term of 12 weeks or less[45]
(4) Merchant seamen[46]
(5) Persons in Crown employment[47]
(6) Registered dock workers[48]

It should be noted that an employee who works for less than 16 hours per week is nevertheless covered by the redundancy provisions.[49]

The Secretary of State may make an order excluding certain employees from the redundancy provisions if he is satisfied that a collective agreement covering them is at least as favourable as the statutory provisions and that it either provides for arbitration or recourse to an industrial tribunal under the Act in the event of a dispute.[50]

REMEDIES (1)—THE PROTECTIVE AWARD

If the employer has failed to fulfill his duty of consultation an appropriate trade union may present a complaint to an industrial tribunal within three months of the date when the dismissal takes effect.[51] If it finds the complaint to be justified the tribunal may make a declaration to that effect and may also make a protective award. The protective award provides that the employees shall be paid,[52] for the specified period, which in the case of the dismissal of between 1 and 9 employees cannot be more than 28 days, between 10 and 99

---

[40] See to the same effect *T.G.W,U,* v. *Nationwide Haulage Ltd.* [1978] I.R.L.R. 143 (I.T.).

[41] *UCATT* v. *Rooke* [1978] I.C.R. 818 (E.A.T.) (misled by Department of Employment, but no award made).

[42] And also from the duty to notify the Secretary of State under E.P.A. 1975, s. 100.

[43] E.P.A. 1975, s. 119 (4).

[44] E.P.A. 1975, s. 119 (5) See *Wilson* v. *Maynard Shipbuilding Consultants* [1978] I.C.R. 376; *Todd* v. *British Midland Airways* [1978] I.R.L.R. 370 (C.A.).

[45] E.P.A. 1975, s. 119 (7).

[46] E.P.A. 1975, s. 119 (12) as elaborated by 119 (13) and (14).

[47] E.P.A. 1975, s. 121 (1).

[48] E.P.A. 1975, s. 119 (3). To be superseded by the Dock Work Regulation Act 1976 s. 14 (6) (which is to the same effect) when Sched. 6 to that Act is brought into force.

[49] E.P.C.A. 1978, s. 146 (4), which excludes such employees from other rights but does not exclude them from consultation over redundancy.

[50] E.P.A. 1975, s. 107.

[51] E.P.A. 1975, s. 101.

[52] But cannot be required to work by virtue of the award, but may still be required to work by virtue of the contract of employment or by virtue of E.P.A. 1975, s. 102 (5) which permits the employer to make an offer, which if unreasonably refused may cause a loss of the compensation: see below.

the maximum period is 60 days and for 100 or over it is 90 days. The award takes effect on the date of the first dismissal or the date of the award, whichever is the earlier.[53]

This is therefore another example of the enforcement of a collective right by individual means, and in this case also the clumsiness of the remedy is apparent, for the claim is by the union but the implementation of it is by the individual employee.

"Appropriate trade union"

It is important to note that only the union can present a claim for a protective award, but the award can only be enforced by an individual. Thus once the union has obtained the declaration and the award, the individual can demand to be paid for the relevant period.

But which union can make the claim? The answer is that any independent union which is recognised for the purposes of that description of employee. It is not that the union must be recognised as being able to bargain for that *employee*, but rather for that *description* of employee. This has curious consequences. Thus it may be that two or more unions are recognised for that description and so each may claim. On the other hand there may be no appropriate union because the employee is not within a recognised bargaining unit. While it may seem unjust that the employee covered by a recognition unit may recover what amounts to damages whereas the person not so covered may not, the difficulty really arises from the peculiarity of the remedy. What is being enforced is not the individual right to damages but the collective right to consultation. Unfortunately the dogmatic rejection of enforcing collective rights (by the employer or the union) and the adherence to the individual contract as the vehicle of enforcement gives rise to the injustice.

But even stranger consequences appear when it is asked whether a union can be forced to make a claim for a protective award. If there has been a delay in consultation, but the union is not prepared in view of later events to make a claim, can an individual member of the relevant union demand that the union should try and obtain an award and thus provide a benefit for the individual? In the absence of a rule in the rulebook requiring the union to obtain benefits for members, it seems unlikely that they will be under an implied duty to do so; but it cannot be denied that the possibility of such an action is there.[54]

A further problem concerns the non-member. Suppose that the only people to be made redundant are non-members and accordingly, even though they are of a description for which the union is recognised, the union decides to take no action to protect them; can the non-members force the union to make a claim? Again the problem arises because the remedy confuses the protection of the collective and individual interests. It may be difficult for a court to impose a statutory duty on the union to sue, for that would be to create a limited duty of fair representaion which so far has found no place in British labour law. On the other hand could the courts allow a union to refuse to collect a benefit for people for whom it is responsible within the statute?

---

[53] E.P.A. 1975, s. 101.

[54] But an objects clause to the effect that the union exists to look after the members interests is not a rule giving rights to an individual member. *Oddy* v. *T.S.S.A.* [1973] I.C.R. 524. But note *Buckley* v. *N.U.G.M.W.* [1967] 3 All E.R. 767 where a power to provide legal assistance imported a duty to act carefully.

REMEDIES (2)—THE ENTITLEMENT OF THE EMPLOYEE

The employee will be entitled to be paid for the period of the protective award, but the detailed provisions are "of the most fearful complexity."[55] The application must be made within three months of the last day of the protective award for which the employee is claiming remuneration, but the tribunal has power to extend the period where it was not reasonably practicable to do so within the limit.[56] This power may need to be exercised where the union has delayed claiming the protective award (which may be back-dated to the date of the dismissal) or where the claimant is a non-member and nobody has informed him that a protective award has been obtained by the union which is applicable to him. Equally there may be difficulties where the union is unwilling to claim an award because of other benefits offered in lieu, or because the only people concerned are non-members.

The length of the protective award

Once again the confusion in the nature of the remedy becomes apparent, because although it might be argued that the collective right of consultation should be protected by a penalty, the remedy is in fact in terms of loss to the employee. This is so because the Employment Appeal Tribunal has taken the view[57] that following experience under the Industrial Relations Act 1971, imposition of penalties would be a retrograde step in the field of industrial relations. Accordingly, by a majority, the court decided to look primarily to compensation and the loss to the employee rather than to the fault of the employer in disregarding the Act. Thus the attitude of the employer is to be relevant in so far as it has affected the employees, but not in so far as it has affected the trade union which should have been consulted.

It is not clear how far the award should reflect not only the number of days over which there should have been consultation but also the chance of averting the the redundancies during that process, but in *Talke Fashions*[57] despite the blatant disregard of the duty to consult, the court appears to have taken the view that the compensation is for the fact that the workers receive less notice (and thus have less time to look for alternative work) than they would have done had the duty to consult the union been carried through.[58]

Even if it were to take the compensatory view it would seem that this should include an element for the chance of improved redundancy terms or deferment of the redundancies altogether. Such a chance may be difficult to assess.

There are however some grounds for thinking that the emphasis of *Talke Fashions*[59] is incorrect, for the statute itself states[60] that the period shall be such as is "just and equitable in all the circumstances having regard to the seriousness of the employers' default ..." Such a phrase is of course ambiguous for it could mean that however high the compensatory loss, the award

---

[55] Kahn Freund, *Labour and the Law* (2nd ed.) p. 94: see also the admirable analysis by Bercusson of ss. 101 and 102, *Current Law Statutes.*

[56] E.P.A. 1975, s. 103.

[57] *Talke Fashions* v. *Amalg. Society of Textile Workers and Kindred Trades* [1977] I.R.L.R. 309; [1978] 2 All E.R. 649 (E.A.T.).

[58] Even if this view were correct it is suggested that the court should not have taken the consultation period plus the notice period as the amount of total notice the employees would have had, as the duty to consult arose 60 days before the dismissal and not before the giving of notice. In other words notice can be given during the consultation period.

[59] [1978] 2 All E.R. 649.

[60] E.P.A. 1975, s. 101 (5).

should be limited by the degree of fault, or it could mean that the compensatory award should be increased because of the degree of fault.

It has also been pointed out[61] that the basis of compensation is to some extent hypothetical since no account is taken of the individual circumstances of those who are to be compensated, but rather they are treated as a group having identical losses. Furthermore, unlike other areas of compensation, there is no deduction for contributory fault nor for damages obtained for unfair dismissal (at least where the unfair dismissal proceedings have taken place before the protective award).

There are therefore fundamental conflicts of principle inherent in the protective award which are due to the attempt to protect a collective right by individual compensation. The choices for the future are either to permit enforceable orders in industrial relations,[62] to regard the award as punitive or to fix a scale of compensation to the individual.

Just and equitable

The length of the protective award is always subject to the view that it must be just and equitable having regard to the employers default.[63] Thus awards have been resisted on the ground that the employer was misled by the Department of Employment,[64] and that the employer was technically in breach because he had allowed workers to leave with wages in lieu, thus shortening the length of the consultation period.[65]

Calculation of the payment

The employee is entitled to a week's pay for each week of the protective period,[66] but this is subject to a set off for any wages he receives (or receives in lieu of notice) during the period.[67] It is also subject to any amount received as damages for breach of contract, but not, it seems, to damages for unfair dismissal.[68] The protective period begins to run either on the date of the award on the claim by the trade union (not the date of the claim by the individual), or on the date the dismissal takes effect, whichever is the earlier.[69]

The effect of these provisions, when combined with statutory or contractual provisions as to length of notice is complicated and may be illustrated as follows,[70] and no doubt further variations could be constructed:

A is the date of notice of redundancy.
B is the last day of the normal consultation period.
C is the date of dismissal with notice.
D is the date of the end of notice (or where no notice is given, the end of the period covered by wages in lieu).

---

[61] *T.G.W.U.* v. *Nationwide Haulage* [1978] I.R.L.R. 143 (I.T.).

[62] Such a view would of course apply equally to trade unions, a point that has been strongly resisted by them.

[63] E.P.A. 1975, s. 101 (5); *T.G.W.U.* v. *Gainsborough Distributors Ltd.* [1978] I.R.L.R. 460 (E.A.T.).

[64] *UCATT* v. *Rooke* [1978] I.C.R. 818 (E.A.T.).

[65] *A.S.T.M.S.* v. *Hawker Siddeley* [1977] I.R.L.R. 418.

[66] But he is not required to work, unless by virtue of his contract or E.P.A. 1975, s. 102 (6) discussed below.

[67] E.P.A. 1975, s. 102 (3).

[68] *T.G.W.U.* v. *Nationwide Haulage* [1978] I.R.L.R. 143 (I.T.). s. 102 (3) speaks only of deducting "damages for breach of that contract."

[69] E.P.A. 1975, s. 101 (5).

[70] See the annotation by B. Bercusson to E.P.A. 1975, s. 101, *Current Law Statutes*.

E is the date of dismissal without notice with wages in lieu.
F (where there are two groups of dismissals) is the date of the first dismissals taking effect.
J is the date of the second group of dismissals taking effect.
K is the date the protective award takes effect (being either the date of the award or the date the dismissal takes effect).
L is the end of the protective award.

(1) Where the dismissal is with notice and the union applies immediately for an award.

```
(A
(C          K          D          B          L
_________________________________________________
```

The period of compensation runs from D–L.

The period K–D is deducted because wages will have been received for that period.

(2) Where the dismissal is with notice and the award is delayed until after the dismissal takes effect.

```
(A                     (D
(C                     (K          B          L
_________________________________________________
```

The period of compensation runs from D/K–L.

No deduction is made and the award and the wages under notice are continuous.

(3) Where the dismissal is without notice with wages in lieu.

```
(A
(E                                (B
(K                     D          (L
_________________________________________________
```

The period of compensation runs from D–B/L.

The wages in lieu are deducted, but the period begins at the date of dismissal.

(4) Where the dismissal is without notice with wages in lieu, but the notional period of notice for which wages are paid exceeds the protective period.

```
(A
(E          (B
(K          (L          D
_________________________________________________
```

No award is paid, for the wages paid in lieu of period E–D are offset.

(5) Where there are two groups of dismissals within the same period.

```
            (F
A           (K          J          B          L
_________________________________________________
```

The periods of compensation run from F/K and J–L.

The award begins to run when the first group of dismissals takes effect.

Refusal of an alternative request to work

Although the protective award does not itself require that the employee work during the period, he may nevertheless lose his right to an award if he unreasonably refuses a request by the employer that he should work.[71] The employer may make an offer at any time to re-new the contract of employment or to re-engage the employee during the protected period: that offer must be on the same terms as the previous employment or must constitute an offer of suitable employment. If the employee unreasonably refuses such an offer he loses his entitlement to an award. If he accepts the offer he is not bound by it until a trial period of four weeks has expired, and if he then rejects the work he again loses his entitlement if the rejection was unreasonable.[72]

Fair dismissal

If during the period when the protective award and the contract of employment overlap, the employee is fairly dismissed or unreasonably terminates his employment he loses his right to payment under the award.[73]

The effect on social security payments

Where a person is in receipt of payments under a protective award the relevant days will not be regarded as days of unemployment and so he will be unable to obtain unemployment benefit until the protective period runs out.[74]

It may however happen that the employee receives unemployment benefit for the period before the award is made, and in such a case provision is made for the recoupment of the benefit.[75] Under this scheme no deduction is made by the tribunal for the benefit[76] received, but deduction is made by the employer when he pays the award.

Within 10 days of the award the employer is required to give to the Secretary of State for Employment the names of those covered by the award and the date of their dismissal; within 21 days of the notice being received the Secretary of State must serve a recoupment notice on the employer who is then obliged to deduct the relevant amount and pay it to the Department, giving the balance to the employee. He cannot pay the award until he has instructions from the Department, but if he does so he still remains liable to pay the deductions demanded. The amount to be deducted shall be the lesser of benefit paid up to the time the Secretary of State receives notice from the employer or the amount (less tax and social security contributions) which fell due to the employee under the protective award up to the same time. If the employee disputes the deduction he must do so with the Department and not with the employer or the tribunal.

Unfair dismissal

It has been established that a dismissal may be rendered unfair due to the employer's failure to consult the appropriate union, for it is "a requirement of the law that in such a situation, unless there are exceptional circumstances,

---

[71] E.P.A. 1975, s. 102 (6)–(11). See also E.P.C.A. 1978, s. 82 (3).

[72] E.P.A. 1975, s. 102 (10) and (11). See on a similar provision *Wragg* v. *Wood* [1976] I.R.L.R. 145 (E.A.T.) *Fowler* v. *Parkin* [1975] I.R.L.R. 89 (Q.B.D.); *Toolan* v. *Beck* [1975] I.R.L.R. 183; *Fuller* v. *Bowman* [1977] I.R.L.R. 87 (I.T.).

[73] E.P.A. 1975, s. 102 (5).

[74] Social Security (Unemployment, Sickness and Invalidity Benefit) Amendment Regulations 1976 (1976 S.I. No. 328).

[75] E.P.C.A. 1978, s. 132; Employment Protection (Recoupment of Unemployment Benefit and Supplementary Benenfit) Regulations 1977 (1977 S.I. No. 674).

[76] The provisions apply to both unemployment benefit and supplementary benefit.

warning and consultation are necessary."[77] It may be however that in such a case the claimant will be unable to show that even if there had been proper consultation he would have benefited thereby, and may thus be unable to show any loss.[78]

If compensation for unfair dismissal is awarded no provision is made for deducting it from a protective award made at a later hearing.[79] However a protective award may be taken into account in assessing damages for unfair dismissal, and so it would be in the interests of the employee if the dismissal proceedings are heard first, but that involves the tribunal in deciding prematurely that there has not been the proper consultations.

The Duty to Notify the Secretary of State

The employer is also under a duty to notify the Secretary of State for Employment when he proposes to make 10 or more employees redundant.[80]

It should be noted that in distinction to the provisions about union consultation this obligation applies even though no union is recognised, but does not apply where less than 10 are to be dismissed.

Penalties

Where no notice has been given to the Secretary of State the penalties are either a reduction in redundancy rebate[81] or prosecution for a criminal offence[82] (but not both). If the employer is entitled to a rebate it may be reduced by a proportion of up to one-tenth.[83] An appeal against reduction may be made to an industrial tribunal. The alternative remedy is prosecution with the consent of the Secretary of State. The maximum fine is £400.

---

[77] *Kelly* v. *Upholstery and Cabinet Works* [1977] I.R.L.R. 91 *per* Phillips J.; see also *North East Midlands Co-op.* v. *Allen* [1977] I.R.L.R. 213 (E.A.T.).

[78] *Barley* v. *Amey Roadstone (No. 2)* [1978] I.C.R. 190.

[79] *T.G.W.U.* v. *Nationwide Haulage* [1978] I.R.L.R. 143 (I.T.).

[80] E.P.A. 1975, s. 100. As in s. 99 the Act applies to dismissal of 10 within 30 days, and 100 within 90 days, and provides notice periods of 60 and 90 days respectively.

[81] E.P.A. 1975. s. 104.

[82] E.P.A. 1975, s. 105.

[83] For present standard proportions see E.P.C.A. 1978 Sched. 6.

CHAPTER 23

THE RIGHT TO INFORMATION

ONE of the primary objectives of the present labour legislation is the improvement of industrial relations by extending and enhancing collective bargaining. But adequate collective bargaining cannot be carried on without proper information, and many employers (and governments) see secrecy and confidentiality as methods by which incursions on the managerial prerogative may be resisted. Accordingly the law has taken steps to encourage the more open management of companies, not only in relation to trade unions but also in relation to shareholders and the government. Although the provisions to be discussed may not in themselves be very effective against a recalcitrant employer, the existence of the obligation to disclose information is in most cases sufficient to improve communication between union and employer, especially in the areas where the union is unable to use industrial sanctions to bring about proper negotiation.

There are four possible sources of information for the union which need to be discussed: first the duty of the employer to disclose information needed for collective bargaining; secondly the duty to disclose to the Government (and thence to the union) under the Industry Act 1975, thirdly the duty to disclose to shareholders under the Companies Acts 1948 and 1967, and fourthly the duty to disclose information concerning health and safety.[1]

THE DUTY TO DISCLOSE INFORMATION FOR COLLECTIVE BARGAINING

Provision for the disclosure of information had been made by the Industrial Relations Act 1971[2] but the relevant section was never brought into force. However, a similar obligation came into existence in 1977 with the introduction of section 17 of the Employment Protection Act 1975.[3]

The parties to disclosure

Information may be sought by an independent[4] trade union which is recognised[5] by the relevant employer. The information requested must be relevant

[1] The provisions concerning information on redundancies are discussed in Chap. 22.

[2] s. 57. See also the Commission on Industrial Relations, Report No. 31 "Disclosure of Information."

[3] Employment Protection Code of Practice (Disclosure of Information) Order 1977 (S.I. 1977 No. 937).

[4] "independent" is defined by T.U.L.R.A. 1974, s. 30: see Chap. 2.

[5] "recognised" is defined by E.P.A. 1975, s. 11, and see Chap. 21. It also includes the case where ACAS has made an operative recommendation for recognition under E.P.A. 1975, s. 15 even though there has been no subsequent agreement on recognition. E.P.A. 1975, s. 17 (2) (*b*).

for the *description* of workers for which the union is recognised, so that if more than one union is recognised for that description of worker the same information may be requested by them all, and so long as a union is recognised for the relevant description of worker it does not matter how many members it has in that area, if any.

The information may only be sought from an employer, but may include information that is in the possession of an associated employer. In this context associated employer means[6] a company which controls the employer or which is a subsidiary of the same holding company. This could give rise to an interesting problem for the statute makes no provision for the case where the information requested is in the hands of the associated employer but that company refuses to hand it over. The obligation to disclose is on the employer, not on the associated company.[7]

As the duty is placed only on the employer it is clear that an employers' association is not under any obligation to disclose information, although it is of course open to the union to request the information from each individual member of the association by whom it is recognised. Such a process would, however, cause considerable delay and frustration.

It should be noted that the function of disclosure is only to assist collective bargaining and is not intended to be for the use or benefit of individual employees,[8] and accordingly the statutory right to obtain information applies only to representatives of the trade union. As "representative" is defined[9] as being an official or other person authorised by the union to carry on collective bargaining the phrase can include a shop steward; and it is thought that "authorised by the union" means authorised by an official of the union who has power under the rules (whether express or implied)[10] to provide such authority, rather than authorisation by the members of the union at the workplace involved.

A further point is whether the employer may require that the information should be limited to the trade union representatives; in other words can he insist that the information remains confidential to those directly involved in the negotiations? It is suggested that so far as information which must be disclosed under the statute is concerned, he may not insist on secrecy, for the negotiators are responsible to their executives and ultimately to the membership as a whole. But in practice the giving of such an undertaking may expedite the provision of the information.

If asked to do so the union must put the request for information into writing, and conversely the union may require that the information be provided in writing.[11]

Information which should be disclosed

The employer is required to disclose for the purposes of all stages of collective bargaining information which is *both:*

(a) information without which the trade union representatives would be to

[6] E.P.A. 1975, s. 126; T.U.L.R.A. 1974, s. 30 (5).

[7] See Bercusson, Annotations to *Current Law Statutes*, E.P.A. 1975, s. 17.

[8] Kahn Freund, *Labour and the Law* (2nd ed.) pp. 85–87. The Industrial Relations Act 1971, s. 57 did require certain limited information to be given to individuals.

[9] E.P.A. 1975, s. 17 (2).

[10] *Heatons Transport* v. *T.G.W.U.* [1972] I.C.R. 308 at 393.

[11] E.P.A. 1975, s. 17 (3) and (5).

a material extent impeded in carrying on with him such collective bargaining, and

(b) information which it would be in accordance with good industrial relations practice that he should disclose to them for the purposes of collective bargaining."[12]

As information need only be provided for the purposes of "collective bargaining" as defined by the Act[13] the kind of information which may be demanded is limited by that definition. Thus information need only be supplied if it is relevant for bargaining about any of the following matters:

(1) terms and conditions of employment, or the physical conditions in which any workers are required to work;

(2) engagement or non-engagement, or termination or suspension of employment or the duties of employment, of one or more workers;

(3) allocation of work or the duties of employment as between workers or groups of workers;

(4) matters of discipline;

(5) the membership or non-membership of a trade union on the part of a worker;

(6) facilities for officials of trade unions; and

(7) machinery for negotiation or consultation, and other procedures, relating to any of the foregoing matters, including the recognition by employers or employers' associations of the right of a trade union to represent workers in any such negotiation or consultation or in the carrying out of such procedures.

Thus it has been pointed out[14] that information could not be demanded on such topics as product costs and marketing policy.[15]

The kind of information to be supplied may also be limited by the degree of recognition accorded to the union, and recognition may be limited either in relation to the description of workers covered or in relation to the kinds of subject matter on which bargaining takes place.[16] Thus information must be relevant to negotiations on behalf of employees for whom the union is recognised and must be relevant to the subject matter of the recognition.

The range of information which may be asked for is also limited by the fact that the information must relate to the employer's undertaking. Thus in *Joint Credit Card Co. and NUBE*[17] the employers subscribed to a survey which analysed and set out salaries over the entire industry, but even though the salaries paid by the employer concerned formed part of this analysis it was held that it did not relate to his undertaking and need not therefore be disclosed.

"impeded to a material extent"

The first requirement is that the information must be such that without it collective bargaining would be impeded to a material extent.[18] Even though

[12] E.P.A. 1975, s. 17 (1).

[13] E.P.A. 1975, s. 126; T.U.L.R.A. 1974, s. 29 (1).

[14] Gospel, "Disclosure of Information to Trade Unions," [1976] 5 I.L.J. 223.

[15] But see "Industrial Democracy," Cmnd. 7231 para. 9 which recommends that companies employing more than 500 employees should discuss with their workforce all major proposals affecting the employees.

[16] See for example *Clydesdale Bank Ltd. and A.S.T.M.S.*, C.A.C. Award No. 78/277.

[17] C.A.C. Award No. 78/212.

[18] An early example of failure on this ground is *Dunlop and A.U.E.W.*, C.A.C. Award No. 78/241 where the union asked for a page containing guidance notes on a job evaluation scheme.

the clear policy of the Act is to encourage the flow of information[19] it has been said that it is not sufficient for the information to be relevant to collective bargaining but it must also be important to it.[20]

"good industrial relations practice"

Even if the first hurdle is overcome it must still be shown that disclosure accords with good industrial relations practice. To assist in determining this question a Code of Practice has been drawn up by ACAS[21] and although the recommendations are not obligatory they may be used in any subsequent proceedings, but it should be noted that good practice may also be established by other means.[22]

Unfortunately the Code makes no positive recommendations as to the items which should be disclosed, but rather provides examples of what *could* be relevant.[23] The list of examples (which follows) is not exhaustive but nor is it intended to be used as a "check list," for what is suitable for disclosure will depend to a great extent on the kind of bargaining which is involved and the level at which it is conducted.

(a) *Pay and benefits* principles and structure of payment systems; job evaluation systems and grading criteria; earnings and hours analysed according to work-group, grade, plant, sex, out-workers and homeworkers, department or division, giving, where appropriate, distributions and make-up of pay showing any additions to basic rate or salary; total pay bill; details of fringe benefits and non-wage labour costs.

(b) *Conditions of service* policies on recruitment, redeployment, redundancy, training, equal opportunity, and promotion; appraisal systems; health, welfare and safety matters.

(c) *Manpower* numbers employed analysed according to grade, department, location, age and sex; labour turnover; absenteeism; overtime and short-time; manning standards; planned changes in work methods, materials, equipment or organisation; available manpower plans; investment plans.

(d) *Performance* productivity and efficiency data; savings from increased productivity and output; return on capital invested; sales and state of order book.

(e) *Financial* cost structures; gross and net profits; sources of earnings; assets; liabilities; allocation of profits; details of government financial assistance; transfer prices; loans to parent or subsidiary companies and interest charged.

A general issue surrounding the degree of disclosure that is required is the extent to which it fulfills the aspirations of those who wish to see a greater degree of industrial democracy. There are those who see this coming about by worker participation in the structure of the company itself, while others feel

---

[19] *Daily Telegraph Ltd. and I.O.J.*, C.A.C. Award No. 78/353.

[20] *Ibid.* The Committee believed that that particular case also required the information to be "closely relevant." The union was seeking information about the pay of other workers.

[21] "Disclosure of information to trade unions for collective bargaining purposes," ACAS Code of Practice No. 2. The Code came into force on August 22, 1977, Employment Protection Code of Practice (Disclosure of information) Order 1977 (S.I. 1977 No. 937).

[22] E.P.A. 1975, s. 17 (4).

[23] See also "Disclosure of information," Commission on Industrial Relations Report No. 31 produced for the purposes of the Industrial Relations Act 1971 but never implemented.

that it may be achieved by developing the collective bargaining process supported by greater disclosure.[24] To the latter group the present provisions on disclosure are seen as inadequate for developing greater industrial democracy, principally because the limits placed on disclosure by the definition of collective bargaining mean that such matters as future company strategy may not be eligible for disclosure.[25] However, a White Paper[26] has suggested that there should be disclosure on such issues in the case of companies employing more than 500 people.

Restrictions on disclosure

There are a number of cases[27] of a substantive nature where the employer is relieved of his obligation to disclose information. The burden of establishing the right to exemption lies with the employer.

(1) *National security*

Disclosure may be resisted where it would be against the interests of national security. A certificate to that effect signed by a Minister is to be regarded as conclusive.[28]

(2) *Copyright*

Where disclosure would contravene a prohibition imposed by statute it need not be disclosed. This heading is wide enough to prevent disclosure which would infringe a copyright held by a third party.[29] Thus even if the information is in the possession of the employer, "publication" of it without the consent of the third party could infringe the Copyright Act 1956.

(3) *Confidentiality*

Information is protected where it has been communicated to the employer in confidence,[30] or where he has obtained it in consequence of the confidence reposed in him by another person.[31] Thus in *Joint Credit Card Co. and NUBE*[32] a survey and analysis of salaries paid in the industry was stated by the firm that produced it to be confidential and the Committee held that this prevented disclosure.[33] It should also be noted that an employee is not permitted to pass on to his trade union information which is confidential to his employer.[34]

(4) *Individuals*

The employer need not disclose information specifically relating to an indi-

[24] See "Report of the Committee of Inquiry on Industrial Democracy" (Bullock report) Cmnd. 6706, and "Industrial Democracy," Cmnd. 7231.

[25] Gospel "Disclosure of information to Trade Unions," (1976) 5 I.L.J. 223.

[26] Industrial Democracy, Cmnd. 7231. Para. 9 mentions investment plans, mergers, takeovers, expansion or contraction of establishments and major organisational changes.

[27] E.P.A. 1975, s. 18.

[28] E.P.A. 1975, s. 19 (7).

[29] *Joint Credit Card Co. and NUBE*, C.A.C. Award No. 78/212.

[30] For protection of confidential information in equity see *Prince Albert* v. *Strange* (1849) 1 Mac. & G. 25, 41 E.R. 1171; *Seager* v. *Copydex* [1967] 2 All E.R. 415; *Fraser* v. *Evans* [1969] 1 Q.B. 349.

[31] For the difficulties in this phrase see Wedderburn "Employment Protection Act 1975" (1976) 39 M.L.R. 169 at 179.

[32] C.A.C. Award No. 78/212.

[33] Disclosure would also have been a breach of copyright.

[34] *Bents Brewery Ltd.* v. *Hogan* [1945] 2 All E.R. 570.

vidual unless that person has consented. The information must relate to an identifiable individual, but what is not entirely clear is whether the employer could claim the exemption when the information is presented in an anonymous form but could by elimination and research be related to individuals—for example a graph showing earnings of individuals related to years of employment or age. It is thought there is an obligation to disclose in such a case as it must be assumed in the absence of evidence to the contrary that the union would put the information to its proper collective bargaining purposes rather than the illegitimate purpose of discovering information about specific individuals.

(5) *Substantial injury*

An employer may claim that disclosure would cause substantial injury to his undertaking.[35] This is potentially the most important of the defences available to the employer and the issue has been discussed in the ACAS Code of Practice.[36] Once again no clear recommendation has been made but rather the Service has indicated areas where substantial injury *may* occur. These include cases where customers would be lost to competitors, or where suppliers would refuse to supply necessary materials or where the ability to raise funds to finance the company would be seriously impaired. The Code specifically places the burden of proving that such consequences *would* follow on the employer, and it is clear that it is not sufficient merely to show that such results *might* occur. Although the exemption does not apply where the injury would be because of the effect on collective bargaining,[37] it is suggested that this does not prevent the employer claiming that disclosure would injure industrial relations, as for example in a case where one group demands information about special rates paid to another group, thus causing friction between the two.[38]

(6) *Legal proceedings*

An employer can refuse to disclose information which he has obtained for the purpose of bringing or defending any legal proceedings.

(7) *Excessive difficulty in compliling information*

An employer may be relieved of his duty to disclose information if "the compilation or assembly would involve an amount of work or expenditure out of all reasonable proportion to the value of the information in the conduct of collective bargaining."[39] The balancing of expense to the employer and value to the union may be a difficult task.

A general question is whether an employer should be permitted to avoid disclosure on the grounds that the information requested is known (or is available to) each individual to whom it relates, and that the union could therefore seek the information from its own members.[40] It is suggested that

---

[35] In relation to the Crown injury to the undertaking means injury to the national interest: E.P.A. 1975, s. 121 (7) (*e*).

[36] ACAS Code No. 2 paras. 14 and 15.

[37] E.P.A. 1975, s. 18 (1) (*e*).

[38] *Daily Telegraph Ltd. and I.O.J.*, C.A.C. Award No. 78/353, where the argument did not succeed.

[39] E.P.A. 1975, s. 18 (2) (*b*).

[40] The point was raised but not answered in *Clydesdale Bank Ltd. and A.S.T.M.S.*, C.A.C. Award No. 78/277.

such a claim should be strenuously resisted because the fact that the information may be available from the members does not absolve the employer of his statutory duty; furthermore it may be doubted whether in such a case the complete information could be obtained from members, and finally the duty of the employer is to provide information relating to workers of a *description* for which the union is recognised, and as not all those workers need be members of the union the employer's duty therefore also relates to non-members from whom by definition the union cannot obtain the information.

Method of disclosure

The union may require that the information be provided in writing,[41] but the employer is not under an obligation to produce or allow inspection of any document (other of course than that which is drafted in order to convey the information). Since neither copies nor original documents need be produced the union is unable to check the information in any way and must take it on trust.

If the information turns out to be incorrect it is not clear that the union or the members would have a legal remedy for any damage suffered thereby, although in so far as the "information" has not been provided the remedies under the Act are available. If the mistake was due to negligence the union may be able to sue if it has suffered damage,[42] but it is unlikely to have done so. If the members wish to sue they face the difficulty that no statement was made to them, but nevertheless it may be actionable if A makes a statement to B and B acts (or fails to act) to the detriment of C;[43] if so the members could sue for benefits they would have received had the information been correct. If the statement is intentionally incorrect it is thought the member is in no stronger position because the tort of deceit is limited to cases where the plaintiff himself relied on the statement.

Remedies

Once again the law is attempting to provide a remedy for a collective right by way of the individual contract of employment and again the result is cumbersome.[44]

The first step is for the union to lodge a complaint with the Central Arbitration Committee[45] who may refer the matter to ACAS for settlement by conciliation. Failing a solution a hearing is held by the C.A.C. at which not only the parties but also anyone else whom the Committee considers to have a proper interest in the matter may be heard.[46] (This would include, for example, an associated employer who has possession of the information which the employer is being asked to divulge.) It appears that the Committee has no power to order that the information be produced in confidence to the tribunal and thus may have to decide without knowing exactly what is in issue, but the

---

[41] E.P.A. 1975, s. 17 (5).

[42] *Hedley Byrne & Co.* v. *Heller & Partners* [1964] A.C. 465; but see the generally disapproved limitations imposed by *Mutual Life and Citizens Assurance Co.* v. *Evatt* [1971] A.C. 793.

[43] *Ministry of Housing* v. *Sharp* [1970] 2 Q.B. 223 may have been such a case.

[44] Compare the similar remedies for refusal to comply with a recommendation of ACAS as to recognition: Chap. 21.

[45] E.P.A. 1975, s. 19.

[46] In *Joint Credit Card Co. and NUBE*, C.A.C. Award No. 78/212 a company which supplied a survey and analysis of salaries in the industry to the employer was entitled to be heard under this provision.

employer may need to show the information to the Committee in order to prove his case. If the complaint is well founded the Committee may make a declaration specifying the information which ought to be disclosed and the date on which this should be done (which must be within one week of the decision).

If the employer still fails to disclose the information the union may bring a further complaint before the Committee who may again issue a declaration.[47] However, at the same time as making its "further complaint" (or later) the union may begin the proceedings which may attach a "sanction"[48] to the failure to disclose information, by putting in a claim for changes to be made in the contracts of employment of individual employees. The employer may avoid an award by the C.A.C. by providing the information at any time before the award is made without suffering any penalty, but he will have achieved considerable delay.

In effect therefore, as in the case of recognition, the remedy amounts to compulsory arbitration of the union's claim by the Central Arbitration Committee, whose decision takes effect by incorporation in the contracts of the relevant employees[49] as from the date specified (which cannot be earlier than the award of the Committee on the first complaint).[50]

The essential difficulty with the procedure is first the extent to which collective terms may be incorporated into individual contracts and secondly the extent, if any, to which the new terms must be causally connected to the information. As to the first issue it is not clear whether the Committee may include a term requiring the employer to disclose the information either to the union or to the employee. Once again, as with the remedies over recognition, the difficulty is that the contract can only be enforced before the ordinary courts. If the term requires disclosure to the union the union will be prevented by the doctrine of privity from enforcing it. If the individual sues he will have suffered no loss and may be unable to get specific performance of the contract and may be limited to the primary remedy of damages; but it is suggested that in such a case, as the courts were prepared in *Beswick* v. *Beswick*[51] to grant specific performance of a contract in order to protect consideration provided by the plaintiff,[52] so should they be prepared to enforce a "contract" imposed by statute.

If the committee orders disclosure to the individual instead similar problems arise because by failing to receive the information the individual will have suffered no loss, for the information is only of any use to the union as a whole in the collective bargaining process.

It is therefore clear that even if the Committee does decide that it has the power to incorporate a collective[53] term in an individual contract, the prob-

[47] E.P.A. 1975, s. 20.

[48] The final award need not be a penalty for the employer could be better off by going for arbitration before the C.A.C. than disclosing the information.

[49] As in the case of recognition the enforcement procedure does not apply to "workers," although their position is relevant at all other stages. Nor does enforcement (nor the further complaint procedure) apply to Crown employment. E.P.A. 1975, s. 121.

[50] The award may be superseded by a collective agreement, or alternatively by agreement with the individual employee to the extent that each particular change is an improvement. E.P.A. 1975, s. 21 (6).

[51] [1968] A.C. 58; *Coulls* v. *Bagot's Executor* (1967) 40 A.L.J.R. 471.

[52] Davies "Trusts" [1967] A.S.C.L. 376 at 387.

[53] For a discussion of whether such a term is "appropriate" for incorporation see Chap. 21 and Chap. 18. *Young* v. *Canadian Northern Rly.* [1931] A.C. 83.

lems of enforcing that award before the ordinary courts could be substantial.

The second question is if the union makes a claim for other terms and conditions of employment (such as wages or hours) to be determined by the Committee, to what extent should the award be related to the terms which might have been achieved by collective bargaining had the information been granted? The Act[54] states that the Committee may award the terms claimed or other terms which the Committee considers appropriate, and it is suggested that there is no causal limitation on the terms which may be incorporated. Thus the Committee is not limited to what might have been achieved by the union, but might nevertheless consider it appropriate for the award to be limited to the area of bargaining in which the information would have been useful.

Disclosure Under the Industry Act 1975

Disclosure under the Industry Act 1975 has a purpose quite distinct from that under the Employment Protection Act for it is designed to assist not collective bargaining within the company but future planning of the economy as a whole. The provisions are contained in the Act[55] which set up the National Enterprise Board, instituted the system of planning agreements to be made between the government and important commercial enterprises, and ordered the government to construct a macro-economic model of the economy for forecasting. In pursuance of these policies the government may demand information from certain companies, and it was thought that as in some circumstances trade unions should also be involved in the discussions, provision should also be made for information to be divulged to them.

Disclosure to the Government

The Minister[56] may ask any company mainly engaged in manufacturing, which makes a significant contribution to a sector of an industry which is important to the economy to provide certain information.[57] He may ask for information needed to form national economic policies, or for consultations between government, employers and workers on the outlook for any sector or company in manufacturing industry. This is done by a "preliminary notice"[58] which asks for the information to be divulged voluntarily to the Minister and also to a representative of the relevant trade union.[59] After receiving the notice the employer is obliged to inform each relevant trade union of the fact that he has the notice and to give the Minister the names of the representatives who have been informed.[60]

If the company does not voluntarily supply the information the Minister may, within 3 months of the original notice, serve an order on the company, after consulting both it and the relevant unions. The order must be laid before Parliament and can be annulled by a resolution of either House.

The order can only require certain kinds of information to be disclosed and

---

[54] E.P.A. 1975, s. 21 (3).
[55] Which followed the White Paper "The Regeneration of British Industry" Cmnd. 5710.
[56] Either the Secretary of State for Industry or the Minister of Agriculture.
[57] Industry Act 1975, s. 28.
[58] The fact that such a notice has been given must be communicated to Parliament. s. 28 (3).
[59] A relevant trade union is one that is "independent" and recognised for collective bargaining. Industry Act 1975, s. 28 (2). "Representative" is defined by s. 29.
[60] Industry Act 1975, s. 28 (2) (*c*).

no other.[61] The list is as follows:

(1) the persons employed in the undertaking, or persons normally so employed (but not specifically as to individuals);
(2) the undertaking's capital expenditure;
(3) fixed capital assets used in the undertaking;
(4) any disposal or intended disposal of such assets;
(5) any acquisition or intended acquisition of fixed capital assets for use in the undertaking;
(6) the productive capacity and capacity utilisation of the undertaking;
(7) the undertaking's output and productivity;
(8) sales of the undertaking's products;
(9) exports of those products by the undertaking;
(10) sales of industrial or intellectual property owned or used in connection with the undertaking, grants of rights in respect of such property, and contracts for any such sales or grants; and
(11) expenditure on any research or development programme.

The important point about this list is that the company may be required to make forecasts about the future, especially about the acquisition or disposal of assets, and it is in this area that the unions will be most interested. The company is not required to divulge any "industrial or intellectual property" or "know-how."[62]

Refusal to obey an order is punishable by a fine of up to £400 and by further fines of £40 per day of non compliance.[63]

Disclosure to trade unions

As we have seen the preliminary notice envisages that the company will voluntarily disclose information both to the government and to the relevant unions, but if it does not do so the Minister may set in motion machinery to enforce disclosure of specified information to the union.[64]

The Minister may order the company to disclose within 28 days all or part of the information provided to him in pursuance of an order under section 30 of the Act, but shall not do so where he considers that it would be undesirable in the national interest or would involve breach of a statutory prohibition.

The Minister must give preliminary notice to both the union and the company, and must consider whether "special reasons" apply. The "special reasons" which can prevent disclosure are that the information was given to the company in confidence, or that disclosure of it would cause substantial injury to the undertaking or would cause substantial injury to a substantial number of employees.[65]

Once the Minister has decided in such a case whether to order or refuse disclosure either the union or the company may require him to refer the matter to an advisory committee whose task it is to give advice on whether the special reasons do or do not apply. The committee consists[66] of a lawyer and 2

---

[61] The penalty for knowingly or recklessly providing false information is a fine of £400. s. 34 (1) (*c*).

[62] Industry Act 1975, s. 30 (5) and (6).

[63] *Ibid.* s. 34 (2). Proceedings may only be begun with the consent of the Attorney-General and may apply to individual officers of the company.

[64] *Ibid.* s. 31.

[65] *Ibid.* s. 31 (4): for the first two heads see above in relation to the provisions on disclosure for collective bargaining.

[66] *Ibid.* Sched. 6.

others, one having experience as an employer and the other as a workers representative.

However, the final decision lies with the Minister and he may reject the recommendation of the advisory committee, but if he does so the order requiring disclosure must be laid before Parliament where it may be annulled by a resolution of either House.[67]

The importance of the disclosure provision of the Industry Act is that it *may* provide unions with forecasts of a company's future activity, but it should be noted that the union can never directly initiate the procedure, for disclosure only comes about at the request of the Minister. Much will therefore depend on the extent to which any particular minister believes that unions should be involved in planning both the future of the relevant companies in co-operation with the government and the future of manufacturing industry as a whole.

Confidentiality

Where the information has been disclosed to the Minister but has not been made available to the trade union representatives, it must not be further disclosed (unless with the consent of the company providing it) except to a government department for its use, to an advisory committee, or to agencies set up under the Employment and Training Act 1973.[68] Breach of such confidentiality is a criminal offence punishable by conviction or indictment by a fine or imprisonment of up to two years.[69]

Disclosure Under the Companies Acts

Although primarily intended for the benefit of shareholders, information made public under the Companies Acts 1948 and 1967 may be of value to trade unions. Every company is required to make an annual return to the Registrar of Companies,[70] and although this in itself provides little useful information it must be accompanied by a copy of the balance sheet and the director's report.[71]

The Companies Act 1948[72] requires that "every balance sheet shall give a true and fair view of the state of affairs of the company as at the end of its financial year, and every profit and loss account of a company shall give a true and fair view of the profit and loss account of the company for the financial year."[73] The "true and fair view" will normally be achieved by adhering to standard accounting practices, but it should be noted that there has been considerable controversy in recent years over the proper way to deal with the problems of inflation and accordingly there has been variation in opinions as to the way in which the profitability of a company should be presented.

The directors are also required to report on "the state of the company's affairs,"[74] and again the requirements are directed towards the protection of the shareholder but the union will nevertheless be interested in a number of items. These include the proposed dividend payable to shareholders and the

---

[67] *Ibid.* s. 32 (13).
[68] *Ibid.* s. 33.
[69] *Ibid.* s. 34 (3).
[70] Companies Act 1948, s. 124.
[71] *Ibid.* Sched. 6.
[72] s. 149 (1).
[73] The detailed requirements are set out in Companies Act 1967 Sched. 2.
[74] Companies Act 1948, s. 157 (1).

amount to be transferred to reserves. In addition if the company has a turnover of £50,000 or more (or is a holding company) and two or more classes of business are carried on there must be a statement indicating the proportion of total turnover made by each class of business and the approximate contribution of each class to the profit or loss of the company.[75]

There must also be a statement[76] indicating the average number of persons employed by it in each week and the aggregate remuneration paid to these persons over the year. The report must also note all contributions to charity or to political purposes where the total exceeds £50.[77] As to Health and Safety, the Secretary of State may make an order requiring directors' reports to state the arrangements in force for securing the health, safety and welfare of the employees.[78]

If the company is listed with the Stock Exchange, the "listing agreement" of that body may require further disclosure, for example whether a different basis of accounting is being used and, if the company operates abroad, a geographical analysis of its turnover in each country.

Health and Safety at Work

One of the most important functions of a trade union is the protection of the safety of its members, and under the Health and Safety at Work Act 1974[79] the employer is under a duty to consult safety representatives "with a view to the making and maintenance of arrangements which will enable him and his employees to co-operate effectively in promoting and developing measures to ensure the health and safety at work of the employees, and in checking the effectiveness of such measures."

The safety representatives[80] are appointed by a union which is recognised[81] by the employer,[82] and in addition to representing the employees in consultation with the employer, have the following specific functions:[83]

1. to investigate potential hazards and dangerous occurrences at the workplace (whether or not they are drawn to his attention by the employees he represents) and to examine the causes of accidents at the workplace;
2. to investigage complaints by any employee he represents relating to that employee's health, safety or welfare at work;
3. to make representations to the employers on the above matters;
4. to make representation to the employer on general matters affecting the health, safety or welfare at work of the employees at the workplace;
5. to carry out inspections of the workplace: this may be done as of right after giving reasonable notice and also if there has been no inspection for three months, or where there has been a substantial change in the

[75] Companies Act 1967, s. 17.

[76] *Ibid.* s. 18: except where the number of employees is less than 100 or where the company is a wholly owned subsidiary, for in such a case the parent company must make the return.

[77] Companies Act 1967, s. 19.

[78] *Ibid.* s. 16 (1) (*g*) as added by Health and Safety at Work Act 1974, s. 79.

[79] s. 2 (4) and 2 (6); for all that follows see Safety Representatives and Safety Committees Regulations 1977 (S.I. 1977 No. 500). See also the Code of Practice issued by the Health and Safety Commission "Safety Representatives and Safety Committees."

[80] The representatives should either have been employed for 2 years by that employer or have had 2 years experience in similar employment.

[81] Recognised is defined by E.P.A. 1975, s. 11: see Chap. 21.

[82] In the case of representatives appointed by British Actors' Equity Association or by the Musicians' Union they need not be employees of the employer.

[83] Regulations 1977 (fn. 79 above) paras. 4–6.

conditions of work (*e.g.* by the introduction of new machinery), or where there has been "a notifiable accident or a dangerous occurrence";

6. to represent the employees he was appointed to represent in consultation at the workplace with inspectors of the Health and Safety Executive and of any other enforcing authority;[84]
7. to receive (from inspectors) information which relates to the premises or which concerns action the inspector has or proposes to take;[85]
8. to attend meetings of Safety Committees where he attends in his capacity as a safety representative in connection with any of the above functions.

The safety representative is entitled to take time off with pay for the above purposes and also for such training as is reasonable in the circumstances.[86] A safety committee must be set up by the employer within three months if he is requested to do so by two safety representatives.

The provision of information

After giving the employer reasonable notice a safety representative is entitled to inspect and take copies of any document relevant to the workplace or to the employees he represents[87] which the employer is required to keep by virtue of certain statutory provisions.[88]

In more general terms the employer must make available information which is within his knowledge and which is necessary for the safety representatives to fulfill their functions. The Health and Safety Commission has recommended in a Code of Practice that information which employers should make available under this provision includes:

(1) information about the plans and performance of their undertaking and any changes proposed insofar as they affect the health and safety at work of their employees;

(2) information of a technical nature about hazards to health and safety and precautions deemed necessary to eliminate or minimise them, in respect of machinery, plant, equipment, processes, systems of work and substances in use at work, including any relevant information provided by consultants or designers or by the manufacturer, importer or supplier of any article or substance used, or proposed to be used, at work by their employees;

(3) information which the employer keeps relating to the occurrence of any accident, dangerous occurrence or notifiable industrial disease and any statistical records relating to such accidents, dangerous occurrences or cases of notifiable industrial disease;

(4) any other information specifically related to matters affecting the health and safety at work of his employees, including the results of any measurements taken by the employer or persons acting on his behalf in

---

[84] An "enforcing authority" may be a local authority: Health and Safety (Enforcing Authority) Regulations 1977 (S.I. 1977 No. 746).

[85] Health and Safety at Work 1974, s. 28 (8).

[86] See the Code of Practice on time off for training safety representatives to be issued by the Health and Safety Executive.

[87] Except information on the health record of an identifiable individual.

[88] The relevant provisions are the Health and Safety at Work Act 1974, ss. 1–54 and the statutes listed in Sched. 1 thereto (of which there are 32) and the regulations made thereunder. See in particular Factories Act 1961, s. 80 (accidents) s. 82 (diseases).

the course of checking the effectiveness of his health and safety arrangements;

(5) information on articles or substances which an employer issues to homeworkers.

An employer may resist a demand under this more general provision on a number of grounds. These are (1) if disclosure would be against the interests of national security; (2) if disclosure would contravene a statutory prohibition; (3) if it relates specifically to an individual (unless he consents to disclosure); (4) if it would cause substantial injury to the employer's undertaking or on the undertaking of another person who supplied the information to the employer; (5) if the information is obtained by the employer for bringing legal proceedings.[89]

A union may also receive information on safety matters from an inspector, for where an inspector feels it is necessary in order to keep the employees adequately informed he may release factual information he has obtained and also information on action he has taken or proposes to take.[90]

---

[89] These defences are similar to those available in the case of disclosure for collective bargaining: see above.

[90] Health and Safety at Work, etc., Act 1974, s. 28 (8).

INDEX